le to attack and
tacker, then the
veryone and fortify
ore and more –
is being lost."

The City between

Contested Public Spaces
in the 21st Century

Birkhäuser Basel

Freedom

Deane Simpson
Vibeke Jensen
Anders Rubing
(eds.)

and

Security

Contents

A — Introduction

7 Foreword: BAS
Cecilie Andersson

9 Foreword: NSM/PST
Jack Fischer Eriksen, Thomas Haneborg, Håvard Walla

11 Introduction: On Urban Indefensibility: Friction Points and Friction Lines in the Production of the Open City
Deane Simpson, Vibeke Jensen, Anders Rubing

15 The City Between Freedom and Security: Project Journal
Deane Simpson, Vibeke Jensen, Anders Rubing

B — Discursive Texts

34 For a Theory of Destituent Power
Giorgio Agamben

35 Protecting Vulnerable Cities from Terrorism: Enhancing the Resilience of Everyday Urban Infrastructure
Jon Coaffee

48 Photo Essay: Melilla, Spain

56 The Fear Factor
Michael Sorkin

65 Defensible Space as a Crime Preventive Measure
Oscar Newman

78 "Fortress Britain": High Security, Insecurity and the Challenge of Preventing Harm
Anna Minton and Jody Aked

84 Photo Essay: Wall Street, New York, NY, USA

99 Situational Crime Prevention: Theoretical Background and Current Practice
Ronald V. Clarke

114 When Life Itself Is War: The Urbanization of Military and Security Doctrine
Stephen Graham

129 Securing the State: National Security and Secret Intelligence
David Omand

153 Designing Peace of Mind: Counterterrorism in Great Britain
CPNI [Compiled by Haakon Rasmussen and Anders Sletten Eide]

156 The Right to the City
David Harvey

172 Photo Essay: Israel/Palestine

C — Contested Sites

- 176 Introduction: Contested Sites
- 178 World Terrorism Index and Events
- 184 Europe

- 186 London, England
- 188 Summer Olympics, 2012
- 192 Ring of Steel
- 196 Canary Wharf

- 202 Melilla Enclave, Spain/Morocco Border
- 204 Border Evolution

- 206 New York
- 208 Schaefer Landing
- 210 Occupy Wall Street, 2011
- 216 Wall Street
- 220 World Trade Center

- 224 Sydney, Australia
  APEC Summit, 2007

- 228 Ramallah, West Bank
  Qalandia Checkpoint

- 232 Gaza, Palestine
  Egypt – Gaza border
- 236 Gaza Flotilla, 2010

- 238 Istanbul, Turkey
  Gezi Park, 2013
- 242 Iftar Meal

- 244 Padua, Italy
  Via Anelli Wall, 2006

- 246 Oslo, Norway
- 248 Tjuvholmen Residential Area
- 249 Blitz and the Blitzhouse
- 250 The American Embassy
- 251 The Norwegian Parliament
- 252 Government Quarter
- 254 Temporary Security Measures
- 256 City Hall Plaza

D — Expert Interviews

- **258 Photo Essay: Oslo, Norway**

- 262 Léopold Lambert

- 268 Ludovica Rogers

- **272 Photo Essay: Occupy Wall Street, New York, NY, USA**

- 278 Sunniva F. Meyer

- 282 Susannah C. Drake

- 284 Yuval Yasky

- 288 Ivor Terret

- **290 Photo Essay: Tahrir Square, Cairo, Egypt**

- 296 Jack Fischer Eriksen

E — Discursive Proposals

- 302 Discursive Design Proposals

- 304 Dystopian Scenario for Extreme Security
  Line Myhre

- 306 Positive – Sum Game
  Anders Sletten Eide

- 308 Mutual Concessions
  Line Myhre

- 310 Grafting the Political to the Processional
  Pavel Waddling

- 312 Participatory Adaptation
  Shreya Nagrath

- 314 In(tro)verted Security
  Mathilde Rønning

- 316 Decentralized Security
  Wenzel Mielke

- 317 Security through Urban Mixtures
  Bjarte Sandal

F — Glossary

- 318 Glossary

G — Notes and References

- 328 Notes and References

- 335 Acknowledgments

Foreword: BAS

One can be afraid of flying because of turbulence or inclement weather. One can read the self-help book *It Is Not Dangerous to Fly* to learn that it is not dangerous to fly, mechanically and statistically. But still one has to explain to oneself the anxiety in the bottom of one's heart. What is statistically to fear the most is not a threat, but one's own fear.

Through this book it is pinpointed how our fear is manifested in physical, spatial interventions. We can see these spatial interpretations of threat in the form of bollards in the streets and fenced-in public places organized to handle violent crowds and lone wolves. The situations studied and presented in this book reveal an architecture of threat prevention that visually and spatially expresses our fear, just as much as it expresses the risk we are exposed to, but to what degree does it also cater to expressions of freedom or enable subjective initiatives in the public domain?

Grounding the freedom of both the subject and the group to position oneself and to find one's place in a broader public discourse is essential in catering for democracy. In this book this is challenged with the focus on security in places and buildings. Through careful readings of means and thoughts constituting this architecture of security, can we start to distinguish our fear from the threat, and through that start a new approach of spatial negotiation of power relations, agencies, and interests premised by expressions of freedom?

At Bergen School of Architecture (BAS) we believe in understanding public space as a generous field for various groups and interests to find and develop their subjective place within the common public space. Through our education we strive to negotiate place and facilitate for the users to take part in shaping their grounding of ambiguous positions in the public. Through courses like City Secure we get to challenge these ideals up against measures of strain. Through this book the theme of security and freedom can be challenged not as biased or conflicting interests, but seen to coexist to encompass a good framework for an inclusive public life for all.

This book would not be a reality if it had not been for the master course "City Secure," arranged at BAS in autumn 2013 in collaboration with the Norwegian Police Security Service (PST), the Norwegian National Security Authority (NSM) and COWI, Center for Risk-Reducing Design. The course was in terms of ambitions and relevance the most far-reaching collaborative course ever arranged at BAS. The teachers and professors engaged in this course provided competence on a leading international, academic, artistic, and military analytical level. The students were met in a way that lifted their professional aspirations and analytical mode, and they responded with inquiring curiosity, engagement, and commitment. The discussions were informed by a broad array of stakeholders who conveyed their sincere attitude, interest, experience, and expertise throughout the entire process. The inquiries done in this course will through this book contribute to the important discussion on the sociospatial mechanism of negotiating democratic aspects of place-making.

The school is very grateful to the teachers, architects, and students who urged to bring the questions and inquiries from the course further into a process leading to this ambitious publication. We are also very grateful to NSM, PST, COWI, KRIPOS and TØI for the initiatives, support, and engaged involvement throughout the master course and in supporting and contributing to the publication. This support and commitment was essential to pursue the ambition level of this book.

All through the course and the process of the publication all interested parties have been clear in the aspiration and attitude toward creating a forum for the many various and conflicting voices in this debate. This angle of approach has been vital for our interest in the project. While the publication withholds closed or rigid judgement, we are grateful for the clear angle of approach every contributor and stakeholder in this publication has taken and grateful for the huge work done by the editors to weave these different voices into a dialogue where differences and nuances are brought forward.

Many of the cases in this book represent high-risk areas with a high level of security measures. It is with unease that we imagine ourselves negotiating our everyday practice within these spaces of manifested threat. We refuse to accept that architecture can be reduced to objects: While urban planning is not dealing solely with sites but with complex situations, threat is still site-specific and not seen as generic; site-specific interventions are carried out in a visual language that can be understood as generic although situated.

But despite this, these places are part of people's everyday lives, they are part of a public life, and they constitute the space we in centuries have negotiated in relation to aspects of safety. These circumstances cannot ease the need for a discussion on how to handle security without compromising freedom. Therefore it is essential that architects, planners, strategists, and politicians engage in the questions of how to cater for both security and freedom when the city and its spatial boundaries and borders are to be negotiated. This promises a book proposing a different set of urgencies, where relations to justice and freedom are spatially situated.

Cecilie Andersson,
Rector, Bergen School of Architecture

Foreword: NSM/PST

Whatever conceptions exist of security, it is in essence a balancing act. Function, budgets, resilience, form – all of these are inputs in considering security. In a public discourse on security, the major balancing act in an open and democratic society is the area between freedom and security.

There are few academic courses internationally, and until recently none in Norway, on the topic of secure design. We believe it is important to create a coherent understanding of the topic on all levels.

Wishing to dispel myths and explore alternative paths in the field of secure design, the National Security Authority (NSM)[1] and the Police Security Service (PST)[2] engage academia in joining at exploring security as a discourse. Though NSM and PST had previously arranged training with various professions, including architects, a full master course came to fruition when PST engaged with the Bergen School of Architecture (BAS).[3] The cooperation resulted in a series of lectures by both government authorities and private stakeholders, along with in-depth assisted study trips to Great Britain, Norway, and the Middle East. Preconditions such as culture and threat level play an intricate part in the design and outlook of security. Physical security measures are as a point of departure relatively easy to plan and implement, but the political and economic consequences may be huge. This is not least the case when democratic principles such as openness and accessibility are concerned.

NSM and PST have partly overlapping tasks in providing advisories to the public on protective security, as well as preventing espionage, terrorism, and sabotage in their respective fields of expertise. A rule of thumb is, if security is a consideration in the early stages of planning, it is a more cost-effective and less intrusive feature than the retrofitting of security measures. No security measure should infringe more than strictly necessary and at the same time it should be robust and functional. Public security may also be multifunctional beyond security, and even contribute to more open urban areas, pedestrian zones, and environmental benefits. The key to achieving this is proper planning and sufficient multidisciplinary knowledge.

Apart from a very successful master course, this publication is a result of an academic exploration. It is intended as a reference for architects, city planners, designers, artists, engineers, and academia as well as security advisors and specialists. A mutual understanding of concepts and common reference on the topic of design and security will increase the output for all professionals involved. We do not intend to serve any absolute truths, but encourage an informed debate of what kind of role a balanced security will play in our society.

It is a prerequisite for us that both the course and this publication should reflect a comprehensive view and bring forward all views of essential questions in security policy. PST and NSM are concerned about security discipline and would like the interaction between security, safety, and openness to become the center of attention. PST and NSM are not responsible for the content of the publication, nor the groundwork and conclusions which the students or BAS reuse or mention.

This publication aims to serve as a basis for further discussions on the topic of secure design. By maintaining focus we will be able to continue to improve and explore better ways of preserving a balance in which freedom and security are not at odds with each other.

The NSM and PST would like to thank and acknowledge the assistance of both public and private contributors to the professional contents of this publication and the master course at BAS, such as Norwegian National Crime Investigation Service (KRIPOS),[4] the Norwegian Government Security and Service Organization (DSS),[5] and COWI.

For our international cooperation a special acknowledgment goes to the UK's National Counter Terrorism Security Office (NaCTSO) and Centre for Protection of National Infrastructure (CPNI), as well as to the Norwegian Embassy in Israel.

Jack Fischer Eriksen
Security Adviser PST

Thomas Haneborg
Senior Security Adviser PST

Håvard Walla
Senior Security Adviser NSM

Introduction

Introduction: On urban Indefensibility: Friction Lines in the Production of the Open City

"In the new military doctrine of asymmetric war [...] the prosaic and everyday sites, circulation and spaces of the city are becoming the main 'battlespace' both at home and abroad."
Stephen Graham, *Cities Under Siege*

"If every space is susceptible to attack and every person a potential attacker, then the only recourse is to watch everyone and fortify everyplace. If every communication is potentially a fragment of conspiracy, then all must be recorded. Walking the streets nowadays, with troops at the subway entrance, barricades around buildings, cameras staring from lampposts [...] it feels – more and more – like the battle for freedom is being lost."
Michael Sorkin, *Indefensible Space*

In recent years, terror events in cities such as New York (2001), Madrid (2004), London (2005), Boston (2013), Paris (2015), and Brussels (2016) have contributed to – and have been used as justification for – a renewed militarization and securitization of cities in the west.[1] This has led to a condition in which contemporary urban settings are, according to Stephen Graham, increasingly "...saturated by intelligent surveillance systems, checkpoints, defensive urban design and planning strategies, and intensifying security."[2] In the United States and Europe in particular, this process has not only had considerable impact on the physical composition of urban public space, but also upon the citizenry's access to it, and the activities and uses legally or practically tolerated within those spaces.

The attacks of July 2011 in Oslo would intensify the debate on terror in the Nordic setting. In the immediate aftermath of these events the rhetorics of then Norwegian Prime Minister, Jens Stoltenberg focused on preserving the ethos and functioning of an open democratic civil society, in the face of a perceived elevated risk of terrorism. This was communicated with the statement: "Our answer is more democracy, more openness, and more humanity, but never naivety."[3] For external commentators these words were welcomed as generous and mature – in contrast to common political statements following other terror events tending to emphasise retribution, and the will to impose a state of exception. Stoltenberg's statement, it has also been argued, more closely reflects the cultural perspective of the Nordic countries – within which the notion of trust plays a central role. It remains to be seen whether these words only represent political rhetoric – or sincere ambitions destined to be undermined by risk-averse state security agencies or the later government. Might such inclinations suggest the potential for an alternative political and cultural starting point, thus enabling an alternative discourse and an alternative set of spatial responses to the perceived threat of terror?

In the context of this evolving situation, and with the necessity to develop security approaches to the rebuilding of the heavily bomb-damaged Government Quarter in Oslo, the Norwegian Police Security Service (PST) and the Norwegian National Security Authority (NSM) approached the Bergen Architecture School (BAS). Their inquiry was directed toward whether the school would be interested in exploring alternative approaches to the challenge of safety and security in the city in the context of a master course on security by design. Their interest was in responses that might avoid limitations such as what they referred to as American "security theatre." These representatives expressed an interest in exploring a possible relationship between security and accessibility (and the associated right to the city) that was not one of mutual exclusivity. They suggested the potential contribution of design toward more aesthetic and less visible approaches to physical security measures, and in exploring how to integrate security thinking in the planning phase of buildings and public spaces rather than relying on expensive retrofits. The proposal appeared positioned between a sincere and humble gesture to engage architectural and urban research and design on the one hand, and a public relations effort on behalf of agencies that had not come out unscathed from investigations into the 2011 events, on the other. This involved the BAS teaching team maintaining academic independence to run a course and control its content, while PST and NSM contributed their knowledge, and those of various experts, as possible inputs among others. Our own reticence toward organizations of this nature was heightened by the increasingly sensational exposure at the time of the expansive and intrusive actions of state security apparatuses[4] – just as we had reservations concerning the behaviorist bent of the "security by design" and "crime prevention through environmental design" discourses that the security experts were interested in.[5]

After further deliberation, those concerns were gradually outweighed by what the editors agreed represented a unique opportunity to gain unprecedented access to the mind-sets and workings of these agencies, to potentially influence those who were most likely to impose security thinking on the future design of the Government Quarter in Oslo, and on public space in Norway in general. The agencies' interest in supporting a publication resulting from the course – which they intended to function as a textbook for security and spatial professionals – suggested further opportunities to contribute to a broader long-term debate beyond an internal discussion with like-minded architects. At the same time, we believed that the collaboration could offer a productive pedagogical experience, exposing the students to an entire gamut of thinking and dynamics behind this issue, allowing them to position themselves critically within it.

Such a starting point would open up a wide range of questions and issues for discussion.

To what extent is the notion of the secure or safe city produced at the cost of the city of freedom, democracy, and the right to the city? This introduces competing histories, and conceptions, as well as aspirations for the city, framing on the one hand, a city understood through the terms of security (evident in the city's intimate coupling with conflict and warfare), and, on the other hand, a city functioning as a site of freedom (and emancipation, as well as social and political dynamism).

The reemergence of the former – the securitized city – is presented by Graham as the culmination of a historical arc following the entwinement of warfare and the city, one that originates with cities and city states, in premodern and early modern times functioning as both "...primary agents, as well as the main targets of war."[6] This connection is evident in historical urban morphology reflecting defensive and offensive logics from various ages. The specific organizing dimensions, geometries, and construction formats of pre-nineteenth-century walled cities – such as Vauban's fortified cities of the late 1600s – are indicative of this, as are their subsequent obsolescence and removal due to advancements in offensive military technology in the middle of the nineteenth century. The subsequent distancing of specific acts of war from the city culminates in the mid-twentieth century in "a long period when Western military thought was preoccupied with planning globe-straddling nuclear exchanges between superpowers or massed tank engagements across rural plains."[7] With the return of the historical arc to the contemporary period of asymmetrical conflict, or "the long war," warfare and "military and security imaginaries" reenter the city.[8]

The opposing historical, conceptual, and aspirational vision, position the city as a site of freedom, emancipation, social and political dynamism, as well as democratic dissent. Evoked in Hegel's formalization of the eleventh-century German proverb "city air makes one free" – the history of this city may be tied to the longer tradition of the spaces of the Greek agora or the Roman forum. In broader contemporary terms, this may be tied to notions of and aspirations toward the open city (Richard Sennett, Kees Christiaanse) / the "inclusive city" (Ash Amin) / the democratic city (Sennett) / and in more specific terms, the right to the city (Henri Lefebvre, David Harvey.) For David Harvey, "The right to the city is far more than the individual liberty to access urban resources: it is a right to change ourselves by changing the city. It is, moreover, a common rather than an individual right since this transformation inevitably depends upon the exercise of a collective power to reshape the processes of urbanization. The freedom to make and remake our cities and ourselves is, I want to argue, one of the most precious yet most neglected of our human rights."[9] It is this right – enabling the city as a site of social and political dynamism, democratic dissent, and even civil disobedience – that many have argued is increasingly under threat from the renewed securitization process taking place in cities, the components of which include: increased physical security measures in our cities, the privatization of public space, the militarization of urban police forces, and increasingly constrained laws addressing public assembly, particularly those related to states of exception responsible for the criminalization of protest, among other aspects.[10]

It is relevant to also mention that these contrasting conceptions of the city do not always neatly function in exclusion of one another – but can from time to time be characterised by a more complex set of relations, and overlaps. Physical security measures, such as hostile vehicle mitigation barriers surrounding a public space like a parliamentary square, can also perform as a driver for the pedestrianization of urban areas. While vibrant, densely inhabited urban areas can be interpreted as sites of possible risk, the presence of many "eyes on the street" may also be understood as supporting a form of passive surveillance and increased safety.

To what extent do the perceived political pressures immediately following a terror event – in which political figures feel an obligation to show strong leadership in implementing security measures – lead to the introduction of a state of exception that potentially endures as a permanent condition? What discrepancies are present between the rhetorics justifying these security measures, and their actual disposition? Critics of various securitization strategies have focused on such discrepancies between these poles. For example, the Israeli-Palestinian separation barrier is presented largely in terms of the rhetorics of terror prevention, while its disposition tends toward an extended state of exception allowing territorial annexation and settlement expansion, and the systematic punishment on an everyday basis of Palestinians. The securitization measures of the 2007 APEC Summit in Sydney were justified according to the rhetorics of the protection of heads of state from potential terror attacks while critique was directed toward the disposition of such extreme measures in intimidating, preventing, and criminalizing demonstrations. The law enforcement reaction to Occupy Wall Street was presented in terms of the rhetorics of maintaining public order and public health in contrast to the disposition of the actions taken to criminalize and shut down social/political movement that was in the process of challenging existing political, social and economic orders.

Is the intensity of political attention and resources attributed to the process of securitization proportional to the threat in terms loss of life, injuries (or property damage) that terror (and crime) produces? To what extent is the economic influence of the security industry supporting the drive to securitize the city? What would be an appropriate balance between securing against terror vs against other forms of crime or other threats? American critics of the disproportional character of securitization compare, for example, the casualties and preventative investments addressing terrorism, to those of other causes of death such as heart disease, cancer, or stroke. In the US, one is over a thousand times more likely to die from gun violence than from a terrorist attack. The probability of death from lightning strike, for example, is three times more likely than by terrorism.[11]

To what extent is the public discourse on terror (and crime) and the everyday lived experience of urban space dominated by purely irrational emotions and thought processes? And to what extent should physical security measures address these psychological states? In the post-July 2011 period, for example, according to a security advisor in the Norwegian government, "...we never receive any calls [when blue or red vans park outside government offices]. But when a white van parks in front of a government building, the department and the police receive dozens of calls from panicked government employees."[12]

Does the classified threat information controlled by intelligence agencies provide an opportunity to elevate or maintain a high threat level, and in so doing be able to promote the urgency and importance of their own work? For example, the low frequency of attacks and the presentation by authorities that an indeterminate number of threats have been neutralized may be presented as the result of the security measures taken to protect us, the details of which have to be maintained as secret.

If our cities are in a state of constant war – and if we see a widening range of vulnerable targets from politically symbolic objects (for example, New York, September 11, 2001) to expanded sites of everyday life (for example, Paris, November 13, 2015) – can the city really be secured against these ever-expanding threats? What determines the stopping points for the introduction of physical security measures? Is it a relevant project to attempt to eliminate risk to the degree that the security-industrial complex proposes? Do we not live with risk on an everyday basis, whether crossing the road, riding a bicycle, or living with the possibility of having a stroke or heart attack? In the case of dynamic and changing threats, is it feasible for physical measures – which are often slow and expensive to implement, and tend to become permanent – to respond appropriately?
A proposed reaction to the 2016 Brussels Airport bombing, for example, which took place in the departure check-in area, involves moving the security screening location to the departure hall entry, just as it has been done at Israeli airports. But does that not lead to the displacement of that threat to the drop-off area and X-ray screening line immediately outside the new security point? Should the screening then take place at the boarding points of trains and buses taking passengers to airports? This highlights the difficulty, and sometimes absurdity, of eliminating risk, and the problem of undefined stopping points.

If trust is one of the key strengths of Nordic societies and built into the logic of its urban spaces, what impact does the securitization of the city have on the experience of the city as a space of trust? How vulnerable are these spaces to physical and nonphysical measures associated with securitization? Do these measures impact on the vitality of urban life and on political and social dynamism?

While the publication does not seek to provide comprehensive or definitive answers to all of the questions above, reflections on them resonate throughout the project in its various sections. To understand how these questions have been addressed in existing contexts, we proposed for the studio members to travel (and take those from PST and NSM with us) to some of what we saw as some of the most problematic and oppressive forms of security thinking applied to urban space outside the United States: the UK, Israel, and Palestine. While PST and NSM offered to arrange meetings for us with representatives from security organizations such as Britain's MI5, and the counterterrorism department of the London Metropolitan Police, we also arranged meetings with representatives of organizations focused on the threat that the security apparatus poses to civil liberties, free speech and the right to the city, such as the Occupy Movement and the Olympic Monitor in London, and academics, civil rights groups, and activists addressing security measures deployed in the UK and in the Israeli occupation of the West Bank. This rich, varied, and at times, extraordinary and disconcerting range of experiences have informed the concept for this publication – one approaching a broad audience in contemporary debates at the intersection of architecture, urbanism, and security.

The publication is comprised of six sections, under the headings: *Introduction, Discursive Texts, Contested Sites, Expert Interviews, Discursive Proposals,* and *Glossary*. The *Introduction* section outlines the context and thematics associated with the project. It includes a *Project Journal* chronicling the experiences and inputs occurring during the duration of the master course. Significant events and important friction lines are highlighted within the running journal text.

The *Discursive Texts* section presents key theoretical works curated from contrasting viewpoints. The section builds upon, on the one hand, an existing body of critical literature such as: Stephen Graham's *Cities Under Siege* (Verso, 2010); Graham's edited volumes *Architectures of Fear* (CCCB, 2008), *Cities, War, and Terrorism* (Blackwell, 2004); Eyal Weizman's *Hollow Land* (Verso, 2007); the Michael Sorkin edited *Indefensible Space* (Routledge, 2007); Tim Reiniets and Philipp Misselwitz's *City of Collision: Jerusalem and the Principles of Conflict Urbanism* (Birkhäuser, 2006); and Gerd De Bruyn, Stephan Trüby, et al's *5 Codes: Architecture, Paranoia and Risk in Times of Terror* (Birkhäuser, 2006). This strain of publications locates security prerogatives as one of the dominant obsessions of our zeitgeist – which at the same time represents one of the most fundamental challenges/threats to the ideals of open, accessible, and democratic cities. On the other hand, the section presents an opposing body of security- and risk-focused literature such as: Ronald V. Clarke and Graeme Newman's *Outsmarting the Terrorists* (Praeger Security, 2008); Jon Coaffee's *Terrorism, Risk and the Global City* (Blackwell, 2009), the US Department of Housing and Urban Development Office of Policy Development and Research's *Creating Defensible Space* (1996); and guides published by the Home Office in UK (for example: *Protecting Crowded Places: Design and Technical Issues*) which are frequently referenced in the security field. These publications are representative of the security by design literature featuring theories and strategies for securing, stratifying, and hardening our cities by tactics of situational terror prevention (partly derived from strategies of situational crime prevention) and resiliency to prevent/minimize the impact of terror attacks. Texts aligned to the two perspectives are juxtaposed on facing sides of each spread, separated by a white interpretive space. Key excerpts from each text protrude into that space, creating a dialogue between the opposing sides. The white space is additionally occupied by key words providing links to explanations in the *Glossary* section at the back of the book.

The *Contested Sites* section documents international instances of security architecture through drawings, maps, analytical diagrams, and timelines. These documents, developed in draft form by the students, unfold the composition, organization, and disposition – as well as the consequences of – the securitization of space in different settings. Collectively the documentation of these sites forms an inventory of spatial instruments and techniques associated with securitization.

The *Expert Interviews* section documents conversations with a range of relevant experts addressing specific aspects of the theme from different perspectives. Both the *Expert Interviews* and the *Discursive Texts* sections are interspersed with annotated *Photo Essays*, providing a candid visual travelogue of the expanded series of sites analyzed.

The *Discursive Design Proposals* section presents student-generated scenarios for the reconstruction of the Oslo Government Quarter affected by the 2011 bombing. These proposals explore a range of responses to the pressures for securitized urban space, from the prioritization of the design of security measures to a negotiated balance between security measures and architectural/urban quality and the right to the city to outright resistance to the securitization of urban space.

The final *Glossary* section unfolds approximately eighty terms that are central to the securitization discussion, from *displacement* and *Foucault's boomerang* to the *onion principle* and *target hardening*. These *Glossary* explanations are linked from the other sections of the book.

The diverse sections of the book – interposing theoretical texts, interviews, photo essays, projects, etc., from a range of perspectives – provide a platform to position the reader in the center of a debate that carries particular urgency for all of us, one which foregrounds the fragility of our urban settings as sites supporting trust, openness, and social and political dynamism in the face of securitization tendencies.

Deane Simpson
Vibeke Jensen
Anders Rubing

The City Between Freedom and Security: Project Journal

Consisting of observations, notes, and reflections, the following entries are selected excerpts from a Project Journal, recording relevant experiences and interactions during the project period.

Bergen School of Architecture (BAS) representatives (in order of appearance):

Anders Rubing (AR)
    diploma student BAS 2012, teacher City-Secure master course 2013, coeditor
Deane Simpson (DS)
    diploma tutor BAS 2012, Professor APP City-Secure master course 2013, coeditor
Vibeke Jensen (VJ)
    diploma tutor BAS 2012, Professor DAV City-Secure master course 2013, coeditor
Sixten Rahlff (SR)
    acting dean BAS 2011–13, partner 3RW
Haakon Rasmussen (HR)
    teacher BAS, partner 3RW, teacher City-Secure master course 2013, advisor
Cecilie Andersson (CA)
    vice dean BAS 2011–13, rector BAS 2013–, advisor

Security representatives (in order of appearance):

Thomas Haneborg (TH)
    PST (Norwegian Police Security Service)
Jack Fischer Eriksen (JFE)
    PST
Håvard Walla (HW)
    NSM (Norwegian National Security Authority)
Audun Vestli (AV)
    COWI

14.03.12 BAS Bergen
BAS diploma project: Site shift to the Norwegian Government Quarter

Inspired by the role of public space during the Arab Spring – in particular Cairo's Tahrir Square – BAS diploma students AR and Erlend Bolstad spend several weeks in Cairo in preparation for a proposal on the square for their graduation project – due to be submitted in August. They get cold feet as a result of their ongoing research and the reaction of locals. As AR mentions in an e-mail from Cairo to their tutor DS: "About half of the Egyptians we have talked to think it is too early to make anything in Tahrir." During a Skype conversation between tutor VJ, AR, and Erlend Bolstad, VJ suggests that they change focus from Tahrir to the Oslo Government

1. Tahrir Square, Cairo

2. Government Quarter, Oslo. Site of attack, postrestoration

3. Government Quarter, Oslo. Site of attack interior, postrestoration

4. Government Quarter, Oslo. Site of attack, cleanup period

Quarter, in order to directly engage in a critical situation at home – in light of what they had experienced in Cairo and learned from other protest space case studies. Upon their return to Norway, they research further the context for the redevelopment of the Government Quarter in Oslo, meeting with a number of the key actors and stakeholders in the discussion of its future. In April they meet representatives of the Norwegian Police Security Service (PST) in Oslo to discuss the challenges of redeveloping the Government Quarter in light of the reaction to the events of July 2011 and the heightened discussion around security. AR and Bolstad's project attempts to transform the fragmented and ill-defined public spaces around the quarter into a larger single identifiable access supporting a "democratic space" of public demonstration and representation – with an attempt to explore how selected security logics could encourage other possibilities. The resulting project presented in August gets caught in an ambiguous space. The decision to suspend the Prime Minister's office in the form of a glass volume over the square above typical safe blast distances argued by its authors according to the intention to make power somehow "transparent," visually accessible, and "accountable" – is interpreted by some critics as an Orwellian demonstration of power.

04.05.12 BAS Bergen
PST/NSM make contact with the acting Dean of BAS, Sixten Rahlff, and teacher at BAS, Haakon Rasmussen.

PST are reportedly impressed by the previous approach from the BAS students and the perceived interest in exploring alternative approaches to security in public space at the Government Quarter by thinking "outside of the box." PST/NSM pose the question to BAS, "would there be an interest in collaborating on a master course on the theme of 'security by design'?"

09.04.13 BAS Bergen
Meeting: Cecilie Andersson, Vice Dean at BAS; Deane Simpson, professor at BAS

DS is asked if he would be interested in leading an exploration into the problem of urban security. VJ and HR are suggested as possible teaching collaborators. There is some hesitancy over agreeing to collaborate with organizations such as PST and NSM, and with the principle of security playing a dominant role in architecture and urban design, and in our cities in general. A number of questions emerge. Is there not a fundamental danger in the premise of designing public space with the intention of making it secure? Does such a mode of conceptualizing the city not result in diminishing its access, openness, and its possibility to support the free expression of its citizens? Does this not result in shutting down the possibility for the city to perform as an open site of democratic expression? Is the twenty-first-century obsession with, and fear of, terrorism and the resulting "protective measures" we see expanding in our cities not out of proportion with all forms of probability for an event occurring? For example, despite the impression gained from the popular media, statistics would suggest that, in Europe or the United States, one is far more likely to die from accidental electrocution or choking on one's own vomit than by terrorism.

25.04.13 BAS Bergen
Meeting: Sixten Rahlff, Haakon Rasmussen, Cecilie Andersson, Vibeke Jensen, Deane Simpson

SR and HR describe a previous meeting with PST representatives regarding a possible collaboration on the studio/course. We discuss if this is something we want to do. There is a mounting sense of the undeniable relevance of the theme – and the threat that security thinking poses to the access to, and the right to the city, and the increasing challenges to protest and demonstration within it. DS and VJ are particularly suspicious of the role of security logics applied to the city based on their experiences in New York in the aftermath of 9/11. We discuss the potential of study tours to some of the most problematic sites of security thinking – for example, London, Israel, the West Bank, as a way of exposing the oppressive nature of these spatial logics, and dangers of "security by design" thinking. Could such visits, and the introduction of voices from the other side of the debate – those who clearly articulate the various threats our cities face as sites of open access, democratic expression, and free speech, be ways to "educate" key members of the Norwegian security apparatus and our students on the fragility of the city and its performance?

We leave the decision of the collaboration open, and agree to take the step to meet with PST/NSM.

Lastly, DS and VJ suggest AR as a member of the teaching team based on his research and general interest in the theme – if the studio/course goes ahead.

22.05.13 PST Offices, Nydalen, Oslo
Meeting between PST: Thomas Haneborg, Jack Fischer Eriksen, Lars Erik Svendsen; NSM: Håvard Walla; and BAS: Haakon Rasmussen, Vibeke Jensen, Anders Rubing, Deane Simpson

5. PST Headquarters, Nydalen, Oslo

We meet at PST headquarters – a relatively anonymous multistory block in an area of Oslo dominated by corporate office complexes built during the past decade. While largely nondescript, the building is bounded by a considerable amount of temporary concrete barriers. After entering the building, we are allowed to enter the first layer of security after surrendering passports and mobile phones. The meeting room is located outside of the main core of the building – which we will be invited into later in the year. Everyone introduces themselves. As we anticipated, the two groups represent entirely different cultures. The PST and NSM representatives' backgrounds are in military intelligence. This is a rather exotic conversation for us. They express their interest in supporting a master course in security by design. The security experts present a general argument for the importance of integrating security by design thinking early in the design process – argued both in terms of cost, performance, and aesthetics.

The cultural dimension of urban security emerges as an interesting aspect of the conversation. There is an apparent appreciation on their part for the "British model" over the "American model" of security design. The American one is described in terms of the notion of "security theater" – with particular reference to the various physical measures applied to "protecting" installations such as American embassies and other federal buildings. We gradually realize, as the weeks pass, that what they are referring to in the British context is not some kind of intrinsic trust and generosity toward the concept of the citizenry as collective subjects in public space; but the intersection of a very high level of surveillance, control and top-down security on the one hand, and the apparent relative invisibility of a range of associated measures on the other. In the specific context of Norway, those we meet with suggest the need for a different, less invasive approach to security in public space and public buildings.

During the meeting, we gain a growing awareness of the highly instrumental set of measures played out in space. We are exposed to another vocabulary, range of knowledge, and standards. Buildings (and most other things) are referred to as "assets." There is an energetic discussion on the part of the security experts on the theme of passive security vs. active security, and on the implications of various formats of risk analysis. Norwegian Risk Assessment standards are introduced: NS5814, for example, takes into account probability – according to them, not relevant in considering terrorism or sabotage, but useful for espionage. NS5832 addresses risk in terms of the cost of an event possibly happening, and so forth. The Norwegian National Security Act is discussed in this context – interestingly, it is described as "cynical toward human life."

In their language, outcomes in architecture or urban design may be categorized under the heading of "physical security measures." Oscar Newman's theories of defensible space are discussed as a founding document in discussions of "security by design." Nassim Nicholas Taleb's *The Black Swan* is introduced as an important reference from the security side, with respect to events that have a large impact and are both hard to predict and rare.

We propose the idea of possible field trips to London, Israel, and the West Bank – insisting that we think it would be important to look at those locations. The security experts are receptive to the idea and offer the possibility of arranging meetings with local experts and members of their networks in each of the suggested locations.

Possible Norwegian sites of study for the course are discussed – other than the most obvious one, the Government Quarter in Oslo. Perceived "vulnerable" sites are discussed such as Oslo S, the Central Railway Station; the royal castle; the Oslo City Hall, large shopping malls, etc.; as well as vulnerable events such as the National Day Celebrations. There is a discussion concerning how the course could run, and how some kind of collaboration or dialogue would work. Tentative concerns emerge from our security experts about the composition of our student body. The question: "Do we have any Iranian, Russian, or Chinese students?" is apparently triggered by previous cases of state spying from "students" of these nationalities from Norwegian higher education institutions.

After the meeting, DS, VJ, HR and AR gather in a nearby café. We are intrigued by the apparent openness – reinforced by statements suggesting they "do not have all the answers," and also by their general astuteness. It is evident that there is an agenda on their part in exploring the potential of design in somehow "improving the security of the city." As there is the discussion on their part of possible media coverage of the course, and their involvement in it, we also sense an additional agenda attached to the proposed project – a strategy to improve their organizations' public images in the fallout of the criticisms in the report on the 2011 attacks.

While we debate whether it makes sense to collaborate with such institutions with such agendas, we are undeniably curious about the possibility of entering into a dialogue with those holding different interests from us. And to somehow have the possibility to influence them – particularly in an interest to avoid the outcomes seen elsewhere in the world, where security-centric logics have dominated. Whether this will actually be possible or not becomes an open question. We finally agree to go ahead with the collaboration.

06.13 Bergen, Copenhagen, New York
Studio/Course Preparations

We move forward with planning the studio. We fix the schedule of the study tours and lectures. AR contacts various groups including representatives of the Occupy London movement, ACRI, the Olympic Monitor, and together we contact academics such as Yuval Yaski, Stephen Graham, and Eyal Weizman. As we think further through the possibilities of the project, we are increasingly certain of its relevance and potential – and its political implications.

At the same time, we have a strange sense, along with the list of students who have just signed up for the studio, that we are in the process of being put through a range of extensive background checks.

25.06.13 BAS Bergen
E-mail Correspondence from BAS Administration

We receive an email from BAS Administration regarding our plans to visit the West Bank, which AR has been organizing: "SR [the acting Dean] is slightly worried about your travel plans for the coming semester, could you please comment on the destination and the safety for the students. As a higher-education institution, we can under no circumstances send students to potentially dangerous areas. So we just want to make sure that this is closely considered. We cancelled a master course to Burkina Faso for this reason because it was too uncertain." We respond with various extracts from travel advisories and emphasize that the Gaza Strip will not be a destination.

06.08.13 BAS Bergen
Meeting: Audun Vestli, COWI; Deane Simpson, BAS; Anders Rubing, BAS

After being approached by Audun Vestli (AV), a security consultant with the engineering firm COWI, we agree to meet. AV is in dialogue with PST and NSM and expresses his interest in being involved in the studio. He has a similar background to the PST and NSM contacts – as a military intelligence officer, with previous postings in locations such as the Balkans and Afghanistan. He is currently responsible for building up COWI's position as a consultant within the security industry. He is involved for example in risk assessment consultancy related to proposals combining the city bus station with the existing Oslo Central Railway Station. As a strong proponent of "security by design," AV describes his background and expertise in risk assessment and situational measures. He is highly enthusiastic about these subjects, and talks for more than an hour practically without stopping. He argues for the relevance of not only considering terror, but also crime in general in relation to "security by design" thinking – in these terms, terror is framed as a subset of crime. In addition to linking a chain of relations in his work – between asset, threat, risk assessment, vulnerability, likelihood, consequences, etc. – he describes three levels of security to be considered. Primary security would involve physical elements such as locks, bolts, bollards, etc. Secondary security involves culture, environment, how people grow up; while tertiary security would include: legislation, the court system, etc. He describes how he believes architecture can play an important part in the secondary level of security in affecting a sense of care, ownership, protection, and as a result, contribute to reducing crime. AV seems knowledgeable and engaged, but we begin to get a sense of the intensity of private-sector interests and agendas in the security industry.

17.08.13 BAS Bergen
Semester Start

The semester proper begins with an introductory lecture addressed to the students. We introduce the hypothesis of two competing histories and conceptions of the city. One is the city defined as a space of security, control, safety, and protection; the other, the city as a site of freedom, democracy, civil liberties, and emancipation. We begin by posing a series of questions around the theme.

– To what extent would it be possible to argue that freedom is based upon a limited level of security?

– How do the pressures of security thinking – defined by terms such as "risk and threat scenarios" – affect urbanism and architecture and impact upon its design and use?

– Is "security by design" viable? If so, at what costs? If not, why is it presented so frequently as a solution to the "problem" of public space? Should it still be an aspiration?

– Is there any possibility that the contemporary pressure to secure the city could be hijacked for the purpose of producing positive and novel qualities, atmospheres, social potentials – and new liberations?

– Could there be any way that the quest for heightened security could support rather than limit tolerance, coexistence, exchange, conflict, negotiation, protest, diversity, transparency, engagement, empowerment, and participation?

We issue the students with the task of studying the spatial regimes of security in various critical locations and in the context of various key events, and issue texts for the reading seminar.

19–29.08.13 BAS Bergen
Theory Seminar

6. BAS Studio, Bergen

Introduced by VJ and AR, the theory seminar involves a range of texts from authors including: Nan Elin, Eyal Weizman, Stephen Graham, Oscar Newman, Setha Low, and David Harvey. After studying and debating the texts, the students are asked to produce maps, timelines, and diagrams that analyze and draw relationships between theories and events.

26.8.13 BAS Bergen
Start-Up Workshop Lecture: Håvard Walla, Norwegian National Security Authority (NSM), "Security Management in the Public Sector – Building a Resilient Society"

After reading literature on the theme, the students are now introduced to the everyday work of a security professional in a Norwegian context. Walla begins the day with a presentation on security management and introduces security thinking from his perspective in Norway. In the Norwegian language *security* and *safety* are the same word (*sikkerhet*), and consequently Walla suggests that important differentiations in the terminology is lacking. He goes on to address a paradigm shift after the terror attack in 2011. "[In Norway] We know the forces of nature, we know the acts of God, and we have prepared for them for probably 2000 years or so [...] but there was a paradigm shift on July twenty-second." He introduces NSM, which was established in 2003 between the Ministry of Defense and the Ministry of Justice to address three areas of concern: (1) espionage; (2) sabotage; and (3) terrorism.

NSM's mission is to protect critical national infrastructure by providing protective security to information and (national) assets against events that are large-impact, hard to predict, and rare (LHR). Characteristics and implications of LHR events include:

1. It is impractical to try to accurately estimate the likelihood of LHR events (Taleb's *Black Swan*, 2007). While nature repeats itself (e.g., floods), history does not always repeat itself.
2. LHR requires diverse risk-assessment approaches (Hole and Netland, 2010).[1]
3. Protective measures, tailored or situational, are based on variable such as risk appetite and residual risk.
4. Cost is likely to vary among stakeholders according to the risk pyramid of: asset (what do you want to protect?), threat (what bad things could happen?), and vulnerability (what weaknesses exist?). In this context, NSM focuses on:

1. Protective security – what can be done before an incident in order to prevent it from occurring in the first place?
2. Contingency – prepared actions that would play out in conjunction with an incident.
3. Crisis management – addressing the situation during and after an event.

As part of this work, asset evaluation is important, whether addressing an information asset or a physical asset. (In the Norwegian law, assets are limited to physical objects and information – the law does not define humans as assets.)

Walla introduces six possible strategy responses to risk: (1) avoid; (2) ignore; (3) reduce; (4) accept; (5) transfer; and (6) exploit.

The workflow of his projects are framed in terms of risk-management cycles – diagrams include:
– planning and organization
– asset evaluation
– security goals
– threat assessment
– vulnerability assessment
– risk assessment
– determining strategy
– reevaluation of goals
– risk analysis and deciding implementation of measures
– implementation of security measures.

26.8.13 BAS Bergen
**Start-Up Workshop Lecture:
Anne-Catherine Gustafson,
Police Superintendent, KRIPOS**

Representing KRIPOS, the department of the national police force focused on combatting organized crime, Gustafson presents a number of videos of organized crime employing various techniques, including: ram-raids with automobiles; roof skylight break-ins, or literally cutting through prefabricated metal sandwich facade panels.

Giving many of us in the audience an uncomfortable feeling, Gustafson presented through various statistics the notion that almost all organized crime perpetrators in Norway originate from foreign crime gangs – with particular national and ethnic groups of Eastern European origin being represented disproportionally. It was indicated that organized criminals conducting crime in Norway tended to be less violent in Norway than in their home countries. This was explained in part due to the fact that Norwegian Police were not typically carrying firearms.

26.8.13 BAS Bergen
Start-Up Workshop Lecture: Jack Fischer Eriksen, Police Superintendent, PST

7. Jack Fischer Eriksen, PST

Eriksen's agenda appears to be in making the terror threat tangible to the audience, claiming that there have been more than twenty thwarted terror attacks in Europe since 9/11 – involving approximately 100 cells. He identifies the sources of major threats to Norway in right-wing extremists, lone terrorists, left-wing groups, and Islamic extremist groups – referring to a YouTube video in which Allah is praised and asked to destroy the enemy and inflict pain. Ericksen also discusses counterintelligence and espionage, including how a local telecom provider experiences more than 10,000 hacking attempts every day.

Several videos of terror blasts from various locations and periods are presented – with a focus on the lethal role flying glass plays in producing casualties. One slow-motion video shows how a curtain wall collapses in a bomb attack during the IRA Docklands bombing in 1996.

26.8.13 BAS Bergen
Start-Up Workshop Lecture: Thomas Haneborg, MSc, Security Advisor, PST

Haneborg addresses the theme of terror and crime prevention. In the context of the framing of terrorism as a criminal act, he begins his lecture with the question: why do people become criminals? He describes different forms of crime prevention: Social crime prevention involves avoiding the crime occurring through efforts to reform criminals, prevent the emergence of ghettos, and integrate ethnic minorities into the wider society. Situational Crime Prevention differs in that it focuses on preventing the potential criminal from committing a crime in the moment at a specific time and place. He attempts to unfold concepts like risk management, asset evaluation, target hardening, displacement, and threat assessment. In these terms he emphasizes a key formula: Probability × Consequence = Risk. Haneborg also discusses the most commonly used weapons, including hunting rifles, AK-47, AG-3, Glock 17, and HK416. He presents their availability, cost, and effects, including their performance against bulletproof glass or metal.

Lastly, he presents various Internet recruitment strategies for terror groups, along with their promotion through online magazines such as Al-Qaeda's *Inspire*, which include guides and manuals describing how to make a bomb or commit other terror activities. With reference to *Inspire* magazine, Haneborg insists, "Never, ever open the site. Do not even do a Google search for it." We understand by implication that we will be flagged, surveilled, and potentially detained if we follow this link. Airport travel is likely to become far more laborious.

27.8.13 BAS Bergen
**Start-Up Workshop Lecture:
Anders Rubing, BAS**

AR presents his research on protest spaces in Cairo and other locations, and walks through his proposal for a civic space for political expression in the Governmental Quarter in Oslo. Our security collaborators appear surprisingly enthusiastic about the presentation, and comment on their support for thinking "outside the box."

27.8.13 BAS Bergen
Start-Up Workshop Lecture: Dag Bjarne Astor, Head of Section, Departementenes Service Senter (DSS)

8. Dag Bjarne Astor, DSS

As the person responsible for technical security within HSE (Health, Safety and Environment) at the Departementenes Service Senter (DSS), Astor addresses how government employees working within the buildings he oversees want security but do not want to be burdened by it. In these terms, he explains the difficulty with the users of the buildings rendering them insecure. "If you open a window – all security measures are gone." "Smokers will seek the shortest way out to an outdoor smoking space. They will often break open emergency exit doors, and despite warnings, continue to do so every day." Continuing discussing the problem of employees' free will overriding the workings of the building's security systems, he believes that people do not prioritize the security of their workplace on an everyday basis. His recommendation for an architectural response to the problem of security in governmental workplaces is to start with a closed concrete box, make openings for windows and doors, and add several physical layers of security measures to delay penetration into the core of the space.

As the result of the 2011 Oslo bomb being delivered in a white van, Astor refers to government workers' deep and irrational fears of white vans in the post–July 2011 period. Whenever a white van is parked in front of any governmental building, several phone calls are made to his office at DSS.

Lastly Astor summarizes his learnings as a result of the relocation of government workers to temporary locations around Oslo after the July 2011 attack. Most notable from his perspective is the necessity to design for security early on in the process of designing a building due to the extraordinary expense of introducing necessary security measures after a building has already been constructed.

27.8.13 BAS Bergen
Start-Up Workshop Lecture: Sunniva Frislid Meier, Ph.D, Transportøkonomisk Institutt

Meier, a social scientist with the Norwegian Transportøkonomisk Institutt, enjoys a prominent role in the national security discussion. She is one of only a few security researchers working at an advanced level before and after the 2011 terror attack. It becomes clear to us that she is highly respected by PST and the other external security lecturers.

Meier outlines her work developing scenarios for terror attacks and analyzing how they can be prevented by spatial and social interventions. Employing theory stemming from the field of "situational crime prevention" she describes how the reduction of the amount of rubbish bins, or passive surveillance executed by cleaning personnel, can reduce the risk of terror attacks.

9. Sunniva Frislid Meier, Transportøkonomisk Institutt

She describes her latest academic work analyzing the July 2011 attack, identifying how the risk of its occurring could have been reduced by situational measures. This analysis involves making "crime scripts," in which the intent and the necessary steps to achieve the result are described. This is connected to a narrative describing the unfolding of the event, and finally the analysis discussed what form of measures could have been employed to disturb either the intent, or the steps required to achieve the intended result.

27.8.13 BAS Bergen
Start-Up Workshop Lecture: Audun Vestli, engineering firm COWI

10. Audun Vestli, COWI

Vestli's presentation is made with a single slide as background image – a proposed bus terminal within the planned renovation of the main train station in Oslo. He describes the challenges of promoting the value of security to the private sector. This is outlined in terms of the common situation in which comfort and functionality are valued ahead of security, which is often given the lowest priority. Vestli explains the related problem of limited time allocated for important work such as risk-assessment reports, in spite of the high-value nature of some targets. He also touches upon a problem he perceives in the security industry of an inflexibility of thinking among security advisors – something he tries to overcome in the approach to his assignments. Vestli closes by advocating the necessity for architects to challenge the conventional low prioritization of security, the importance of analyzing uncertainties, and the importance of designing intelligent security measures into projects early on in the design process.

11–14.9.13 London Study Tour
Participants: PST: Thomas Haneborg and Jack Fischer Ericksen; NSM: Håvard Walla; BAS: DS, VJ, HR, AR and 15 master students

11.9.13 London
Tour of Battersea Park Nine Elms development: Bill Margetts, Design Out Crime Officer, London Metropolitan Police, "Design Out Crime/Secured by Design"

Margetts is a police officer and Design Out Crime Officer (DOCO) in the London borough of Wandsworth – which happens to be the location with the highest number of CCTV cameras per inhabitant in the UK, the country with one of the highest number of CCTV cameras per inhabitant in the world. We meet Margetts in the entry space to the Battersea Park Station in Nine Elms. He leads us along construction barriers toward the Battersea Power Station to present the proposed plans for the development in the visitor center. As he has played an important role as DOCO on the project, he presents the plan proudly. We are struck, and somewhat concerned, with the resemblance of tone of the policeman to that of an urban planner and designer as Margetts explains the new developments around the Battersea Power Station. He talks about the plans for new "burglary-proof" luxury housing within the development, which will generously contain "affordable housing" for "doctors or lawyers not able to afford inner-city real estate." The new American Embassy, a centerpiece of the larger development, is described as a contributor to securing the area from "unwanted elements." We are curious what he exactly means by this, but the discussion has moved on quickly before we have a chance to ask. Thomas Haneborg from PST asks, "Why put a potential terror target in a residential neighborhood?" Margetts responds, "The Americans will be able to take care of themselves." Håvard Walla from NSM asks, "Why not put a mosque next to the site of the US embassy?" We are often surprised by such moments in these kinds of discussions.

The last phase of the tour is intended to be a social housing project in the nearby area built in the 1970s. As we arrive at the area, Margetts looks concerned. After some phone calls, he announces that he cannot vouch for the safety of our group in the area, as the local police officers who were scheduled to protect us have not arrived. While waiting for the local police, the party is required to eat their lunch in front of a nearby supermarket. Margetts finally announces that we have to leave the project unseen, as the local police protection has still not arrived.

As we depart, Margetts gives us his official DOCO business card. It includes the slogan "Total Policing: Every Opportunity, Every Tactic."

11. Bill Margetts, London Metropolitan Police. Nine Elms model presentation, London

12. Study group visiting Tower Hamlets, London

11.9.13 London
Tour of London Olympic Park: Julian Cheyne, Games Monitor

We meet in the now-deserted Olympic Park next to the Olympic Stadium and the Fred Wigg Tower. Cheyne is a community activist and spokesperson for the Games organization that has been campaigning against what he calls "the draconian imposition of power that came with the London Games." He introduces himself just as Julian. His own story, which he touches upon, involves his, and around 450 others', forcible eviction from their homes in the Clays Lane Housing Estate as part of the construction project for the infrastructure and venues of the London Olympics. He openly mentions that this experience has obviously colored his view of the Olympics.

14. Study group visiting London Summer Olympic Games site (PST representatives in back row with sunglasses)

As we stand on-site, Cheyne points to and describes a series of "surreal and exaggerated security measures" that were present during the period of the Games. He mentions the associated budget of £1.6 billion, which he describes as both "extreme and opaque," dedicated to Games security. The elements he points to include 5,000-volt electrified perimeter fences, the positioning of missile launchers on top of the nearby buildings, the use of armed drones (which were not officially confirmed), and the imposition of an extended "Olympic Security Zone," within which demonstration was legally not allowed. Cheyne describes how these extreme measures were linked to a heightened anxiety around social behavior — which included "Dispersal Zones" established by the authorities and organizers to prevent youth from congregating. He refers to an event involving a group of 182 bike riders for example who were kettled and arrested for riding bikes within the zone. Cheyne notes a general systemic problem of the draconian imposition of power and severely heavy-handed policing. It is in this context that he describes "The Olympics' function[ing] as a test bed for new authoritarian measures, such as the use of drones or altered bail laws."

We sense a somewhat awkward and icy atmosphere from the security advisors in response to the statements and concerns Cheyne raises. They stand silently at the back of the group, with sunglasses on and arms folded.

12.9.13 British Colonial Club, London
Lecture: Paul X, Centre for the Protection of National Infrastructure (CPNI)/MI5

Between the secret identity of the speaker, the nature of the video material, the way it is delivered, and the background setting, this is a surreal experience. Our venue is coordinated by Håvard Walla from NSM – a classic English men's club, where our group is brought in through the back entrance. The room is decorated with the animal riches of the former British Empire, including taxidermied heads of rhinoceros, bison, and moose. For security reasons, we are informed that we are not allowed to know the last name of the speaker. He will simply be known to us as Paul.

Paul describes the various security challenges and responses of CPNI to the types of sites it is responsible for. He provides four examples: 1. Parliament Buildings; 2. Canary Wharf; 3. Financial area Data Center (processing £350B of transactions per day) – in this case, the discretion of the building design is an important part of the design strategy; and 4. Difficult long-perimeter sites such as airports.

15. 16. Interior, British Colonial Club, London. Site of CPNI presentation. (Speaker's identity concealed)

He further describes the UK's general approach to counterterrorism: 1. Assess the threat (a function of a. the capability of the terrorist and b. malicious intent); 2. Identify vulnerabilities/criticalities; 3. Calculate risk; and 4. Propose commensurate (proportionate) measures.

Paul places emphasis on the main threat focused on in his work – vehicle-borne threats – of which he describes five styles:
1. Parked (most common) – identification helped by eyes and ears of the general public
2. Encroachment – exploiting gaps in site defenses (without impact); or tailgating through an active barrier system; or preempted by tampering with an electrical control cabinet

13. Julian Cheyne, Games Monitor

3. Penetrative impact (ramming)
4. Entry by deception – human blagging (talk your way in); use of a "Trojan vehicle," for example, delivery/cleaning/pizza/emergency services/postal services vehicles
5. Entry by duress – duress against a guard to provide access; duress against a legitimate driver to act as a "mule"

The discussion then moves on to the role of static vs. active protective measures in relation to these types of threats. For example, Paul describes how expensive passive-security measures can be rendered ineffective by breaches allowed by active measures controlled by "a minimum-wage, low-motivation G4S worker at a point ten hours into a twelve-hour shift." This particular image of the security worker will become a recurring one throughout the project period. These different threats and types of events are illustrated with a sequence of video surveillance clips – resembling a kind of violent highlight compilation of a range of American action films – but in low resolution, without sound. They are described with a rather distant English public-school voiceover.

Paul describes further vehicle-borne threats including "the use of a vehicle as a killing tool" referring to its promotion in Al-Qaeda's online *Inspire* publication documenting a technique to attach knife blades to the front of a car to kill or maim. Paul, just as Thomas Haneborg had emphasized, warns us: "Don't try and download it!" We wonder how many of the students have done so with such tempting warnings.

In a part of the presentation addressing the effect of bomb blasts, Paul describes the condition of a solid becoming gas in an extremely short period of time. This produces both an air shock, a ground shock, and a fire wall. Similarly, after the punch effect of the air shock, there is negative pressure or a sucking effect. In terms of casualties, 95 percent come from flying fragments; and 95 percent of those are from glass. A major countermeasure to this is the application of laminated glazing – a response that is unfortunately considerably more expensive than the installation of nonlaminated glass. It introduces other challenges, notably the challenge of keeping the glass in the frame, as well as the need to keep the frame fixed to the wall in the case of the impact of a blast. It is in this context that the necessity of maximizing standoff distance, or the distancing of the blast from the asset, is emphasized as highly important. According to Paul, "every meter of standoff counts."

Paul goes on to describe the main groups of hostile vehicle mitigation (HVM) strategies:
1. Total traffic exclusion from an entire area (often politically impossible)
2. Traffic inclusion but with screening of all vehicles entering the area
3. Traffic inclusion: free flow within the area but local protection of all critical/vulnerable assets within that area with traffic calming and traffic barriers
4. Temporary/supplementary or preinstalled barriers

Preferred measures are described as follows:
– Traffic calming with horizontal deflections: chicanes
– Vehicle restraint, using gravity: bunds and berms
– Bollards, of which seven types exist: circular hollow section steel tube multiple hollow section steel tube concrete-filled tube (requires deep foundations) rolled steel (solid bar) cast manganese steel (one-third of the thickness for same effect) polycarbonate spring steel

Paul's enthusiasm for bollards continues unabated.

Bollards normally require deep foundations, approximately 750mm deep, which often produces conflicts with existing underground utilities, necessitating their being moved. This translates into considerable time and expense. Alternate types of shallow/no-foundation plated bollard systems have been developed which are surface-mounted and linked together. The high costs of security have been offset in some urban settings with selling advertising, for example, to Marks and Spencer.

Paul ventures deeper into the bollard world describing the testing of new bollard technologies and BSI (British Standards) for crash testing: PAS 68 Impact Testing, PAS 69 Installation Guidance, and the CPNI tested list. Design guides include: Hostile Vehicle Mitigation Guide (2010), Landscape Architecture Guide, and Home Office Guide to Protecting Crowded Spaces. Several videos are presented documenting tests of various vehicle mitigation strategies – this mostly involves slow-motion videos of trucks driving at speed into bollards, trenches, and berms.

Paul introduces the basic design parameters of bollard placement. The maximum air gap should be 1.2 m, which he argues does not slow or impede the flow of pedestrians. Some tips: "Be careful of transitions. Concrete blocks placed directly on a road or pavement surface do not work, as they require a 'key-in.'"

Additional functional objects capable of functioning as vehicle barriers include:
– leaf and pond edging
– seats at the water's edge
– decorative planters
– shallow-mount and narrow planters
– energy-absorbing planters

Paul concludes by introducing the architects who CPNI have collaborated with on the vehicle protection along Whitehall, where different ministries and other important assets are located.

12.9.13 London
Lecture: London Security Architect
Peter Heath, Public Realm Design Director – Atkins

Heath, an older gentlemanly architect, wearing a bow tie and round glasses, seems to have a close collaboration with Paul and CPNI. He informs us of his background as an architect, town planner, and designer integrating security requirements into urban environments such as Whitehall in central London. Heath describes his general ambition in urban design settings is to remove or reduce the presence of urban "clutter" – such as CCTV equipment and a multitude of street furniture. He describes working with historical photographs of the sites he works on, in part to highlight the extent of existing clutter.

He describes the necessity of understanding a range of parameters and issues in his work, from knowledge of off-the-shelf product design ranges, to aesthetic, functional, economic and security parameters. Heath describes the adaptation of bus shelter design, for example, in relation to these parameters. The examples he goes into more detail with involve the design adaptation of a line of bollards into low walls, with the introduction of variety based on ground level changes. The detailed interior steel structure of a circular seating bench in front of one of the most prominent buildings in Whitehall is presented as the pièce de résistance of Paul and Peter's presentation. It embeds the latest bollard research and technology within a neoclassically styled exterior – which he describes in terms of contextual appropriateness. The performance of security and the associated technical and material innovations are intentionally rendered invisible.

12.9.13 London
Tour of Whitehall, British Government Ministry Area, Vehicle Protection Barriers: Paul X, Centre for the Protection of National Infrastructure (CPNI)/MI5; Peter Heath, Public Realm Design Director – Atkins

17. Study group touring Whitehall, London

We tour sites of recently completed security measures in the Whitehall area containing ministries such as the Ministry of Defence, the Foreign Ministry, the Treasury, etc. We are pointed toward the standard bollard employed in the area, of which our hosts are quite proud. We observe low Georgian-style continuous walls at the pedestrian scale (lower than 1 m in height) including the seating bench in front of the foreign ministry.

During our walk, we observe a demonstration taking place on the opposite side of the street and are asked by one of the UK security representatives if they are our "friends." We answer, "Yes."

13.9.13 London
Tour of Ring of Steel: Henriette Williams, photographer and videographer

Henriette Williams is a photographer and videographer whose work addresses the theme of security and surveillance within the UK. Starting from the Barbican Centre, Williams leads us on a walking tour along key sections of the "Ring of Steel," which follows the approximate line of the original Roman wall of London. Developed in response to the 1993 IRA Bishopsgate bombing, the strategy and term itself originates from Northern Ireland, and protective measures installed during the period of "The Troubles" in Belfast. Williams presents this as an example of Foucault's boomerang, where techniques applied to colonial contexts turn back on the original "home" context (see Stephen Graham's "New Military Urbanism," in *Cities Under Siege*). In London, the "Ring of Steel" is not literally a continuous steel wall, but an assemblage of measures, including road-narrowing devices, small sentry boxes, CCTV, etc., that are positioned at entry and exit points into the City of London area – collectively forming a fully surveilled and controlled perimeter.

18. Study group touring Ring of Steel, London with Henrietta Williams

In its current configuration, according to Williams, the CCTV system hardware overlaps with the traffic congestion-pricing hardware and is hardly visible if one does not know it is there. She suggests that this aspect of the system of surveillance is in fact more scary and disturbing because it is less visible.

Distinct from the diversity of eyes and ears on the street of the natural surveillance of Jane Jacobs, Williams describes the problematic of a singular interest and agenda of security controlled from a central control room.

Our guide highlights the coincidence of the phenomena of securitization and privatization within the City of London. In this sense, the Ring not only functions as a surveillance system, but also as the physical closure of roads by bollards, walls, fences, and other measures. These spaces tend toward a form of monocultural "public space" where the suitability/appropriateness of the users in a particular space is often determined by private security guards.

On our walk around the area, we are struck by the coexistence – in the same space – of manicured flowers in flower boxes; wall signs marking private property and the right of the owner to remove those partaking in inappropriate activity; and fences topped with barbed wire or other forms of sharp-edged material.

When asked for successful examples of safe or secure public space, Henriette refers to the Southbank Centre, as a site of many mixed activities, well-planned public spaces, and a site of natural surveillance.

She informs us further about her research into the security industry, in which she attends events such as arms fairs and security industry fairs – enabled by her press card. She speaks of the recurring issue of an immense number of CCTVs in operation, and the extraordinary challenge of the person power necessary to actually monitor them. She describes how their use is not preventative in real time but performs as a partial deterrent, and is predominantly employed as a source of evidence in the period after an event. This has been a recurring theme in the discussions with security experts including the Norwegian security consultants we have been in dialogue with. In an attempt to address this challenge of information overflow, automated systems are being developed to support real-time detection through algorithmic technologies – effectively monitoring programs designed to detect abnormal behaviors through algorithmic scanning/tracking technologies. We imagine flashing sirens and SWAT teams descending upon those with disabilities and associated gait differences; those accompanied by small children walking slowly and erratically; an artist photographing a specific series of objects; or an apparent loiterer looking for a recently lost glove.

13.9.13 Southbank Centre, London
Lecture and discussion on Occupy London: Maria Ludovica Rogers, architect and activist, Occupy London

19. Tense discussions prior to Occupy meeting, London

We experience an awkward moment with our security collaborators. They say that they are not able to join our meeting with Occupy London. They also discourage us from meeting with them. They mention that according to their British associates, members of the organization are on no-fly lists, and for this reason it would be diplomatically insensitive toward their British hosts, as representatives of the Norwegian government, to be involved in the meeting. We are surprised by the hostility that this suggests for the Occupy Movement from the perspective of the intelligence community. We inform the security experts that we will not change our plans. Minus the security experts, we meet with Maria Ludovica Rogers, a London-based, Italian-born architect from the Occupy London movement. She played a central role in the Saint Paul's occupation, being involved in designing and laying out the camp during the protests that ran there from October 2011 to February 2012.

20. Study group meeting with Ludovica Rogers, Occupy London

We meet in the public meeting spaces of the Southbank Centre, as a group of around twenty, seated in a circle at Rogers's suggestion. After we are settled, she begins by asking us, "What makes us feel secure?" and "What makes us feel insecure?" She introduces a set of British legal definitions, which represent the legal frameworks that Occupy's activities are forced to work within. This is based on *The Protest Handbook* – a document written by lawyers for protesters. Rogers frames the definitions for three typologies of *protest* from the book:

– a "public procession" – a body of people moving along a route in public space; – a "public assembly" – an assembly of two or more persons in public space which is wholly or partly open to the air; –an "occupation" – use of physical presence in space for more than one hour. This is not necessarily based on same people but the same space.

While we previously imagined that the Occupy movement operates in relation to the rules and regulations of the occupation of public space, we were surprised by the extent to which the legal context defines the framework for their actions. In the case of their occupation, there were key roles played by lawyers within the organization in laying out the framework for their activities.

Rogers presents the legal definition of *public space* in the UK, which somewhat surprises us. Here, we understand that a highway is the only legally defined public space – with all other spaces considered as private. There are however, many private spaces to which the public has right of access. She describes the different ways the state and the police control public-access space and protests within it. Any protest (except for an assembly) requires 6 days' advanced notice to the police, including the start location, route, and organizers. The naming of "organizers" in the case of Occupy is complicated by its stance of being a leaderless group, but this naming also has implications for those persons who are named – who, Rogers suggested, are often exposed to forms of harassment by police. During the Olympic Games, police enforced a ban on mass protests throughout the whole of North London for "security reasons." This ban saw one event in which 180 persons were "kettled" (kettling is a crowd control tactic in which police surround and contain protesters in a limited area), arrested, and restrained on a bus for six to eight hours without access to food or a toilet. Additionally, during the Olympic Games period, new bail conditions were introduced that suspend the right to be in a designated area of the city. Just as Cheyne had suggested, Rogers argues that events such as the Olympics provide a convenient excuse for the authorities to introduce more oppressive forms of control that limit – ones that tend to stay in place after the event. She summarizes the situation as a highly constraining and challenging landscape to protest within – in which, for example, it is not possible to protest in Parliament Square. This is reinforced by a suite of legislation that includes, the Public Order Act, the Anti-social Behaviour Act, and the Terror Act.

Rogers goes on to outline other police tactics, including having police "stuff cameras in your face" during protests. Another tactic employed involves police liaison officers who follow along on the march "appearing chatty and friendly; they are actually gathering information used in the police's interests." Also described are other forms of police surveillance and data collection applied to the group. According to Rogers: "We are evolving into a period in which the state is wanting complete control over everything to avoid the bad bits. The issue is who uses power and how?"

Rogers outlines some possible countermeasures available to protesters, including: protesters' recording police behavior and directly broadcasting live to Internet; and what is referred to as the "Squatters Shield": a Section 6 (of the Criminal Law Act 1977) legal notice on the front door of a nonresidential building/space which means that the police are not able to forcibly enter.

We ask Rogers to expand on her experiences with Occupy and the Saint Paul's encampment. She describes the organization as a nonviolent leaderless movement that emerged in London with the call to occupy Paternoster Square in front of the London Stock Exchange – a planned protest that was blocked by police after a court injunction revoked the space's license for public use. The protest moved to the space in front of the nearby Saint Paul's Cathedral. She briefly describes the encampment and its organization, including in particular the working groups responsible for specific tasks, such as press, basic needs, tents, etc. She refers to the experience as an amazing one in terms of the specific form of "organic" architecture that emerged from it.

13.9.13 Canary Wharf, London
Occupy London Tours: Canary Wharf

21. 22. Occupy London Tour, Canary Wharf, London

Just as we had been actively discouraged by the security experts from meeting with the Occupy London representative at the Southbank Centre, we were similarly discouraged from taking the Occupy London's Canary Wharf tour. "Do not go" we were told, as if we were about to commit some deeply subversive act or heinous crime. Perhaps this was done out of genuine concern for what database our photographs would end up in, or list our names would be placed on. We had understood that the event would involve a guided narrated tour of the area with commentary from members of the movement.

We prebook our tour and arrive at the designated meeting place near the exit from the Underground. We are met by a man and a woman in their twenties in Victorian-period attire. During the tour, we are followed continuously by one uniformed "policeman" of the Canary Wharf private security force (dressed in uniforms closely resembling those of the London Metropolitan Police), and a plain-clothed security representative, along with our group of around twenty Occupy tour members. We are also tailed by an additional uniformed "policeman" following behind. The choreographed tour performance has been running weekly for some months as part of a rehearsed sequence of stops, and this is clear from the largely one-way banter directed toward the familiar "police detail" by the presenters. The tour moves between the spaces in front of the various building lobbies, where our guides tell us well-crafted narratives of financial misadventure of the various institutions – particularly leading up to the crisis and in its aftermath. Below is an excerpt from the script, at the final stop of the tour, HSBC:

> Welcome to HSBC, the world's second largest bank (and it's most local of course!). The lions are called Stephen [roaring one] and Stitt [quiet one] – after two HSBC managers in Shanghai in the 1920s; and inside the building, you can see a "history wall." Now, we've taken a look, and realized there were a few bits missing from the story. So we thought we'd fill you in.
>
> In fact, HSBC was created in the aftermath of the mid-nineteenth-century Opium Wars to finance the opium trade that the British and allies had declared war on China in order to maintain. "HSBC" actually stands for Hong Kong and Shanghai Banking Corporation, reminding us of its birth from the rubble of an imperial drug war. But if you thought HSBC's drug-money days were over – think again. In July 2012 a US Senate investigation uncovered "astounding complacency" in HSBC's US bank, which was found to have been facilitating the extraction of drug

money. It even helped move 7 billion in physical dollars out of the US and into Mexico.

HSBC agreed to a fine of just under $2 billion in December 2012 for this and other offenses. But US authorities decided not to criminally prosecute the bank, and risk it losing its banking license. Eric Holder, the US Attorney General, said in June 2013 in front of the Senate Judiciary Committee: "I am concerned that the size of . . . these institutions becomes so large that it does become difficult for us to prosecute them, when we are hit with indications that . . . it will have a negative impact on the national economy, perhaps even the world economy." Translation? Banks are still not only too big to fail – but too big to jail.

Despite the established sequence of stops in front of the lobbies of the various company towers – which include HSBC, Moody's, Citigroup, Barclays, KPMG, etc., we are surprised by the intensity, urgency, and hostility that the small, quiet, and well-behaved group receives from the various security details in each of the tower lobbies. The Occupy group stands for between 5 and 10 minutes outside each lobby along the tour. In almost every case, the security guards move quickly to block the doors and windows on the interior of the lobbies in a repeated hostile experience. It is clear that they have been instructed to consider us as a serious security threat.

After the tour, as when we break off into smaller groups of two or three persons, we are tailed by our silent friends from the Canary Wharf "police force." The final phase of our experience involves being barred by other security guards from passing through the underground shopping mall area adjacent to the Underground train station due to our association with the Occupy tour. When we enquire as to why we were not being admitted to the space, the guards were silent – as they let other nontour participants through unimpeded.

14.9.13 Royal Air Force Club, London
Lecture and discussion: Spike Townsend, NaCTSO, London Metropolitan Police

23. (From right) Spike Townsend of NaCTSO, JFE, and AV

24. Interior, Royal Air Force Club, London. Site of NaCTSO presentation

Our venue, the Royal Air Force Club in Mayfair, has a similar atmosphere to that of the site of our meeting with Paul from MI5. In this case, the animal heads and spears are replaced by paintings of Spitfires, Hurricanes, and Lancasters. Håvard Walla has arranged for us to meet with Spike Townsend, who is a National Counter Terrorism Security Officer (part of CPNI). He has parallel roles as family liaison officer and architecture liaison for the London Metropolitan Police. Townsend describes three main objectives in NaCTSO's work: to support the protection of critical infrastructure; to support the protection of radioactive materials and chemical weapons; and to be the national lead in the protection of crowded spaces. Their approach to these objectives is described according to the four Ps of the "Contest" strategy:
 – *P*revent radicalization
 – *P*rotect borders, infrastructure, crowded places (particularly locations where there is the potential for a high number of causalities) – also the protection of people, cultural heritage, economy, etc.
 – *P*repare responses
 – *P*ursue terrorism

NaCTSO's work is carried out by 220 personnel trained in counterterrorism. In working in crime/terror prevention and providing security advice to industry, they utilize approaches such as RAT (Risk Assessment Theory); the onion ring principle; and general crime-prevention concepts.

Townsend outlines how design recommendations they offer are assessed on a risk-based approach starting with the question: What is the risk of terror? A key concept in this, according to Townsend is *proportionality* – "there is no point in designing a fortress if there is not a high likelihood, or a high impact. By contrast, if Canary Wharf, for example was attacked, it would be catastrophic." On vulnerable or critical sites such as this, the main focus of their work is on: firstly, stopping vehicles from entering the area (to protect against car bombs); and secondly, to address the danger of glass (to lower the impact of a backpack bomb). Just as we have been previously informed by the Norwegian experts, 85 to 90 percent of casualties are from injuries associated with flying glass shards (as seen in attacks in Pakistan and Iraq). The reaction to the second challenge involves using laminated and shatterproof glass products. Townsend mentions that requirements to address the danger of glass can offer other benefits. For example, laminated glazing contributes to carbon emission reduction by lowering heat gain; while on the ground floor storefronts with laminated glazing make smash-and-grab or ram-raid attacks more difficult.

Townsend discusses their ongoing work with "Secured by Design," in particular the way that developers have the possibility through the scheme to apply for a security award, based on a set of criteria. He argues that these awards become selling points for the safety and security of the property, while also representing a good way to showcase innovative approaches to security. Part of this discussion involves what he calls "aesthetic design." He mentions the example of Paul X's bollards. Here Spike accidentally utters the full name of the secret figure. He frames the challenge of "how to design to not make it look like a fortress?" He mentions camouflaging tactics in which bollard performance is attributed to other objects such as flagpoles, benches, signage, or cycle racks.

The advantages of different forms of surveillance in relation to "Secured by Design" are presented – in particular, the advantages of CCTV vs. natural surveillance. In this context, Townsend argues for his preference toward natural surveillance, characterized by: clear lines of sight (hedges can hold things); larger open spaces support less fear. He describes an additional advantage to open space – it allows the atmospheric pressure of a blast to return to normal more quickly. It is suggested that passive surveillance should not be the only form of surveillance – but is best in combination with CCTV and private guards.

In the discussion afterwards, some interesting issues came up. One question from a Norwegian security consultant addresses the asymmetry in resource levels applied to this form of security work between the UK (approx. 450 persons) and Norway (approx. 10 persons). The Norwegian insider take describes a situation in which private companies in Norway address the potential impact of terror/sabotage/espionage through large insurance policies.

17.09.13 BAS Bergen,
Lecture and Discussion: Åse Gilje Østensen, University of Bergen, Norwegian Naval Academy, "Private Military and Security Companies" (PMSC's)

A political scientist and associate professor at the Royal Norwegian Naval Academy,

Åse Gilje Østensen speaks about the rise of private military and security companies (PMSC) – her primary research focus – and the extent of the growing security industry. She describes a history of these companies stretching back to the outsourcing coordinated by the American military during the Vietnam War in the 1960s. She identifies the period after the end of the Cold War, and the massive surplus of military equipment and redundant military personnel, as an important trigger of growth in the industry – a moment that coincided with the expansion of many smaller and more widely dispersed conflicts. The period in the aftermath of September 11, 2001, and the new wars the US would enter into, both at home and abroad, saw further explosive growth in the industry.

PMSCs developed since the 1990s from single-service companies to "one-stop shop" solutions, as conventional state armies have become increasingly dependent on the industry. In this sense, she describes how violence, previously monopolized by the state, becomes a service like all other services on the free market, purchased by the state, and awarded to the best bidder. Østensen introduces Executive Outcomes as the mother of all PMSCs. Founded in 1989 by Eeben Barlow, a former member of the South African Defence Forces, the company emerged as the government's military units were being dismantled due to pressure from the ANC. Before it was dissolved in 1998, Executive Outcomes would go on to carry out combat roles in Angola and Sierra Leone, as well as contracts with corporations such as De Beers, Chevron, and Texaco.

Østensen describes four service niches provided by such companies:
– security and risk administration for business and commercial clients
– tasks formerly performed by state armed forces
– security and support provided to civilian actors (such as NGOs and aid organizations) in zones of conflict
– support of state-building activities such as institution building and democracy support (such as training a new police force in Afghanistan).

She speaks of the versatility, adaptability, and responsiveness of the industry particularly since the mid-2000s. This is evident in the capacity of companies to rebrand and rename to reestablish their legitimacy (for example, Blackwater becomes XE Services, and then becomes Academi); to provide flexible service menus to prospective clients; to deploy extremely quickly; to operate within assemblages and networks of security governance within the context of a risk society. Also discussed are concerns over the democratic challenges associated with the industry. For example:

– "the fox guarding the henhouse"
– reduction of transparency
– blurring the division between public and private
– their expertise grants them authority in decision-making related to security, but there is limited accountability and little legitimacy
– there is no comprehensive legal framework internationally (largely fragmented)
– there is a question as to whether self-regulation leads to PMSCs setting their own standards.

Lastly, Østensen emphasizes the theme that PMSCs do not represent a neutral service, in the sense that these companies are not likely to downplay the risk attached to various environments or conditions – but rather that PMSCs are more likely to exaggerate risk as it is in their interest to do so.

23.09.13 Quality Airport Hotel Gardermoen, Oslo
COWI, Secured by Design Conference

COWI invites us to present our work at their Secured by Design Conference in Oslo. A high proportion of the Norwegian Security Advisors we meet are either working with colleagues in the UK or have been educated in the UK, or both. As a result, the Norwegian security standards and discourse are to a large degree influenced by the UK. This comes across in the makeup of the day in several topics addressed by a range of speakers. These include:
– Risk assessment, why and when? (Norwegian PST)
– Designing out crime (BREEAM UK)
– Secured by design, the concept (ACPO UK)
– Threats, security design (Norwegian PST)
– Protection against blast and shock (NDEA)
– Threats and people's need of feeling safe (Henrik Syse)
– Summary (President of COWI Norway)

In one presentation, a representative of BRE (UK Building Research Establishment) – the same company that invented the BREEAM standard – describes the way architectural components are standardized and listed in the UK (by BRE). A speaker describes how security products are tested, with a tester receiving a set of tools – including, for example, a screwdriver, pipe, hammer or crowbar, and an electric drill. They have a time limit to break into, or force entry through a building component like a window or door.

Representatives of the formerly public, now private company that founded, implemented, and standardized Design Out Crime in the UK presents after the BRE. They describe the influence on their work of the theories of Oscar Newman and other early Crime Prevention Through Environmental Design (CPTED) thinking, as well as the relevance of the "broken windows theory." They describe the main concepts they work with:
– Access control
– Natural surveillance
– Territoriality

These presentations begin to repeat much of what we have already been exposed to in the previous months, but perhaps with less nuance. An interesting moment however occurs when these themes are related – in what feels to be a somewhat forced way – to environmental issues when the presenter cites research evaluating the "carbon cost of crime."

The presenter from the Norwegian Defense Estates Agency speaks about protection against blast and shock. This seems to rehash the material the students the students have already been exposed to in London and Bergen. With some of the same videos we have been shown by Paul in London but with a less precise spoken accompaniment. One of the students in the audience puts up his hand and questions some of the details of the presentation, based on their knowledge from London. PST is apparently happy with this display from the students.

We make our presentation, addressing our reservations and concerns with the potential securitization of Nordic cities – to a somewhat muted response. It gradually becomes clear that for the great majority of attendees at this conference, security and securitization represent their economic livelihoods.

30.09.13 BAS Bergen
Lecture: Thomas Hilberth, Associate Professor, Aarhus School of Architecture, "Control Space"

Hilberth's research addresses the intersection of fear/anxiety and architecture. In his presentation, he distinguishes between fear (when we know what we are afraid of) and anxiety (when we do not know what we are afraid of). He attempts to unfold the increasing role of fear and anxiety – as some of the most basic and powerful human emotions – in the production of contemporary spaces and territories. He relates these emotions – common between humans and animals – to the typical reactions of *freeze, flight,* or *fight*. Hilberth expands upon the centrality of these drivers in relation to Abraham Maslow's hierarchy of needs, or what he refers to as *instinctoid needs*, in which security and safety are near the base of the pyramid, sitting immediately above the basic physiological needs such as food, water, warmth and rest. He presents the centrality of the reaction of defending territory and the associated spatial techniques that outline a terminology for the twenty-first century, including: cocooning, wallification, sacrificial facades, CCTV, CPTED, fail-safe dimensions, panic rooms, etc. After he passes through a relatively familiar bibliography, including Foucault, Deleuze and Virilio, Jacobs, Gehl, Blakely and Snyder, Weizman, etc., we ask Hilberth his position on appropriate spatial reactions to fear and anxiety. He argues that there should not be a spatial reaction.

7–13 October 2013 Israel Study Tour
Participants: PST: Thomas Haneborg and Jack Fischer Ericksen; NSM: Håvard Walla; BAS: DS, VJ, HR, AR and 15 master students

7.10.13 Ben Gurion International Airport, Tel Aviv
Group Arrival

HR and AR arrive with the majority of the student group. Soon after disembarking the aircraft, a substantial distance from the passport checkpoint, AR and HR are stopped and questioned by two Israeli officers in civilian clothing waiting on the top of a one-way escalator. HR and AR are asked about their intentions for the visit, and are required to provide the officers with a day-by-day verbal description of their plans. This is somewhat surprising to them as prior to the trip both the Israeli and Norwegian embassies are informed of the visit and the context within which it is being carried out.

8.10.13 Norwegian Embassy, Tel Aviv
Lecture and discussion: Henrik Width, Norwegian Cultural Secretary/Attache, and Svein Sevje, Norwegian Ambassador

25. VJ and AR, Norwegian Embassy, Tel Aviv

The Norwegian Embassy in Tel Aviv is a small temporary office on the thirteenth floor of a nondescript office building. Like most other countries, Norway refuses to recognize Jerusalem as the Israeli capital and maintains its embassy in Tel Aviv. The ambassador, Svein Sevje, welcomes us and informs us of the long relationship between Norway and Israel. He outlines Israel's changing narrative from defensive to offensive military state, and explains Norway's more recent position as one of Israel's most vocal critics – particularly in terms of Israel's settlement policies in the Palestinian territories.

Norway provides 500 million NOK in humanitarian aid to Palestine, and has a representative office in Ramallah functioning effectively as an embassy. Ironically, in a somewhat tragic sense, it is now located on the Israeli side of the wall, reducing the possibility for Palestinians to access it. Sevje goes on to describe the increased hardening of Israeli politics, and that – in spite of the general public's being in favor of it – a two-state solution appears increasingly unlikely. We get a clear sense of the difficult situation for a foreign ambassador in a setting where so many fundamental differences exist with the host country.

9.10.13 Tel Aviv
Lecture and Tour, Yafo Municipality: Yael Enoch Maoz, International Relations, Yafo Municipality, and David Aharony, Director of Emergency and Security Department, Yafo Municipality

26. Study group meeting with Tel Aviv-Yafo Municipality, Tel Aviv

We are invited to the headquarters of the municipality of Yafo, the central municipality of Tel Aviv. Here we pass through metal detectors and our bags are searched before we are escorted to a large meeting room on an upper floor with views over large parts of Tel Aviv. We have made a request to representatives of the municipality to make a presentation addressing how they work with the theme of security. Maoz, the international relations officer first highlights the key characteristics that differentiate the city from the rest of Israel. We hear it from her, as we will hear it from many others – Tel Aviv is a liberal, friendly, secular, and cosmopolitan island within the country, where one of the greatest challenges is, in her opinion, the shortage of affordable housing. In these conversations, crime is presented by one of our hosts as a phenomenon that "comes from the outside" – or more specifically from the quarter of the population consisting of refugees and migrant workers.

27. Study group visiting underground park/bomb-shelter beneath Habima Square, Tel Aviv

Aharony, as director of the Emergency and Security Department introduces the municipality's various forms of threat response. A key concern in Yafo is hostile missile or chemical weapons attack – addressed in a law (introduced in 1991) requiring each apartment building in the municipality to have a shelter, with housing built at that time also being required to have an extra secure room. Today the municipality is focused on building centralized shelters. There are 353 bomb shelters, 93 underground parking garages converted to public shelters totaling 1.2 million m^2, and plans for 71 temporary evacuation centers with space for 25,000 beds. (Tel Aviv's total population is 400,000 residents.) Five-story buildings are at the same time reinforced and made earthquake-proof. During the meeting, we are taken on a tour to the largest of the new bomb shelters under the recently completed Habima Square. It is a huge underground space that doubles as an underground parking area, and – with large bomb-proof and chemical/fallout-proof doors, and lift-up entry stairs on the upper plaza surface – a bomb shelter.

They present wider plans for disaster management addressing earthquakes or tsunamis to possible epidemics such as influenza, smallpox, polio, anthrax, or avian flu. The municipality describes detailed plans as to how to deploy camps and temporary housing in parks and public space. The municipality requires this type of planning when developing new neighborhoods.

9.10.13 Tel Aviv
Tour: Etzel Museum

After having visited the museum on a previous day, HW proposes that our group visit the museum of the Etzel underground military group – an organization that was apparently one of three groups instrumental in establishing the state of Israel in the late 1940s. We arrive at the museum, near the waterfront, which consists of a black-tinted glass box that has landed somewhat awkwardly on top of a ruined stone fortress. An older man,

28. Study group in front of Etzel Museum, Tel Aviv

29. Interior, Etzel Museum, Tel Aviv

probably in his 80s or 90s, who himself apparently played a part in the Etzel battles, functions as our guide, offering details of the militarized struggle that "built the state of Israel." Speaking in proud and somewhat nostalgic terms toward the violence, sorrows, and satisfaction of winning the war – the speaker is less focused on providing the background to the conflict than delivering entertaining and heroic war stories. As our guide relives various battles and military subterfuge, HW jokes: "One man's terrorist is another man's freedom fighter."

10.10.13 Jerusalem
Lecture and Discussion: Yuval Yaski, Chair, Department of Architecture, Bezalel Academy of Arts and Design

30. Scene upon study group's arrival in Jerusalem

We travel to Jerusalem and sense a radically different atmosphere from Tel Aviv.

Chair of the Bezalel Academy of Arts and Design, Yuval Yaski welcomes us at a relatively deserted architecture school, while students are still on vacation. The school is surrounded by walls, and we pass through a security checkpoint to get into the campus. We all sit down in one of the lecture halls. He describes the architecture school as a political setting focused on nurturing critical thinking. The department has both Israeli and Palestinian professors with projects being carried out, for example, in East Jerusalem and in Bedouin communities in the south of the country. He describes the school's interests in educating planners and architects who are active in developing mapping techniques, visual testimonials, and design strategies capable of confronting existing Israeli master plans and master narratives. As with the rest of the tour, we are joined by our Norwegian security experts, who seem to be slightly uncomfortable with the content of Yaski's talk.

In the studio he teaches – which addresses the Bedouin territories – he describes the use of comparative mapping approaches that evaluate differences between official maps and actual conditions. Yaski emphasizes the heavily planned nature of the territory controlled by the Israelis – where the state uses planning for the purpose of realizing its geopolitical ambitions. In that context, infrastructure for example is not a neutral, apolitical intervention, but a measure laid out in many cases to control, oppress, or gain other geopolitical advantages. He speaks of these territorial logics imposed by the state in relation to a notion of the welfare state. He argues that the notion of a welfare state is largely reserved for Zionist settlers; while at the same time, services, education, and rights to housing are being limited or withdrawn from the roughly 350,000 Palestinians in Jerusalem.

We ask Yaski to talk further about his everyday experience of security in a city like Jerusalem. He explains the role of profiling. The police and security personnel make a first screening of a person by listening to their language and dialect. As a member of the Israeli elite he describes his privileged position in which he is not heavily inconvenienced by these checks. He suggests that while the socially conscious are against it, the Israeli elite and middle class generally see security in positive terms. While Tel Aviv is a liberal enclave in a security state, in Jerusalem security is more visible – young soldiers crowd the streets, both male and female, carrying guns, sometimes uniformed and sometimes off duty, sitting around café tables with their weapons on their chairs.

10.10.13 East Jerusalem
Walking Tour of Silwan: Ronit Sela, Public Outreach Director for the Department of Human Rights in the Occupied Palestinian Territories, ACRI (Association of Civil Rights in Israel)

31. Study group on ACRI tour of East Jerusalem

32. Study group on ACRI tour of East Jerusalem. The Separation Barrier

33. Study group on ACRI tour of East Jerusalem. Settler home

34. Study group on ACRI tour of East Jerusalem. Settler home

The Norwegian Embassy arranges a tour for us with the NGO Association of Civil Rights in Israel. ACRI is "Israel's oldest and largest human rights organization" with a mandate "to ensure Israel's accountability and respect for human rights, by addressing violations committed by the Israeli authorities in Israel, the Occupied Territories, or elsewhere." A Norwegian Embassy employee joins us on the trip, along with the Norwegian security experts. We meet in central Jerusalem, where the ACRI team pick us up in a tour bus. We drive to the East Jerusalem neighborhood of Silwan, a valley close to the old city, where we experience a quite different pattern of housing from that of central Jerusalem. On one side of the valley we observe a number of houses adorned with Israeli flags, a high concentration of CCTV cameras, and in some cases, small guardhouses. The other side of the valley is a dense neighborhood consisting of similarly informally built houses that constitute the still intact largely Palestinian area.

Our guides explain the process by which Israeli authorities and Israeli settlers contest Palestinians' rights to homes in this part of East Jerusalem with various methods – one of which involves the withholding of citizenship from Palestinians living in East Jerusalem – which in turn limits those residents' rights. Other related methods include: forced evictions, challenged residency permits, withholding building permits and services, disinvestment in infrastructure and schools, etc. Sela describes how three hundred mostly ultraorthodox Israeli settlers have built their homes in this part of East Jerusalem, in walled-off compounds equipped with CCTV and guarded around the clock by security guards. We are struck by this much smaller scale of infiltrating Israeli settlements, their extremely close proximity to the Palestinian houses, and the obvious heightened tension that this introduces – in relation to the more separated condition of many of the other settlements further into the West Bank.

ACRI attempts to fight for the necessary services for the 55,000 Palestinians in East Jerusalem. Sela explains how those Palestinian residents pay taxes to Israel but get very little in return. There are for example only nine schools in East Jerusalem, none of which have playgrounds. Since 1967 the population of the neighborhood has increased by a factor of more than four, but almost no building permits have been issued in that period. In response to the resulting overcrowding, residents have had to build anyway, making many homes exposed to Israeli demolition. We are informed also about the settlers' claims to Palestinian houses and lands in East Jerusalem by making assertions to the antiquities authorities as to important Jewish archaeological sites.

The bus takes us further into East Jerusalem, where the students have their first close-up experience of the "separation wall" or "security wall." We stop at one of the checkpoints, where Sela describes the effects of the wall not only as a fixed spatial barrier, which separates Palestinians from family members or workplaces, but also as a concerted method to "exhaust, humiliate, and demoralize" the Palestinian people. The unreliable waiting time and treatment when trying to pass through the checkpoints, as well as the complexity involved in moving between walled-off Palestinian neighborhoods discourages the population from passing to the Israeli side of the wall. Sela explains how ACRI organizes ongoing efforts to inform the press about police mistreatment at the Separation Barrier checkpoints.

11.10.13 West Bank
Bus Tour: Abu Hasan (AH), organizer of West Bank tours, formerly PLO

36. Study group on West Bank tour in Ramallah

Our tour guide in the West Bank, Abu Hasan, is an enthusiastic and knowledgeable character. TH and JFE from PST join us – equipped, it appears, with provisions for more than a day, and police-style pants containing knee protection disguised as casual clothing. The first day-trip is focused on East Jerusalem, the separation wall and Ramallah. On our way out of Jerusalem we are driven through Israeli settlements that are particularly suburban and surprisingly banal in character. They appear well tended-to, with schools, playgrounds, stores, and so forth. AH speaks passionately about the decades of illegal Israeli-built settlements in the West Bank – built with disregard for international law and several UN resolutions forbidding them. He describes the economic incentives for settlers provided by the Israeli government, including a five-year tax-free period and reduced rent expenses, equivalent to one-quarter of the cost of a similar living space in Jerusalem. AH addresses the contrasting challenges in the Palestinian areas where, for example, there is a considerable deficit of school places for children.

From the vantage point of the settlements we can see the Palestinian neighborhoods encircled as islands. Wall sections such as these snake through Palestinian territory claiming 780 km^2 more land than that defined by the green line – the demarcation line set out after the 1948 Arab–Israeli War. We are informed that the wall's position is intended to place wells and other resources on the Israeli side while separating Palestinians from one another. The International Court of Justice in The Hague has demanded that Israel take down the wall; instead, the wall is continuously expanded. AH describes the severity of the resulting deficiency of resources and services on the Palestinian side of the wall: half the homes have no water, there is no waste removal or police, and fire and emergency medical services in many cases do not exist.

The main checkpoint between Jerusalem and Ramallah – Qalandia – is the administrative center of the Occupied West Bank, through which 5,000–7,000 people cross daily. As we pass through the separation barrier toward the West Bank there appear to be no difficulties in passing through. To return to Jerusalem from the West Bank, however, will be quite a different situation.

As we drive on the roads of the West Bank, AH describes the division of the territory into zones according to the Oslo Accords. Area A, containing Palestinian cities and their surrounding areas, is under full civil and security control by the Palestinian Authority, constituting approximately 18 percent of the West Bank's total area. Despite being forbidden from this zone, the Israeli Defense Forces regularly enter this area, mostly at night to conduct raids. Area B, containing Palestinian villages, is under Palestinian civil control and joint Israeli-Palestinian security control, and comprises around 22 percent of the West Bank's area. Area C, including Israeli settlements, is under full Israeli civil and security control. It comprises around 63 percent of the West Bank's area. AH explains to us when we are leaving one area and entering another. We are struck by the ubiquity of the Israeli lookout towers – which are a somewhat disturbing presence, and the wreckage sprawled around the landscape.

35. Study group on ACRI tour of East Jerusalem. The Separation Barrier

37. Yasser Arafat's Mausoleum, Palestinian Authority Headquarters, Ramallah

38. Study group at the Separation Barrier

As the day goes on, we ask our AH about his own past. He describes how he has, like many other Palestinian men, spent several years in prison on "terror" charges (eleven years in total in his case, spread over three separate occasions). The first time was for six months at age thirteen, when he was accused of throwing stones. After his brother was killed and he joined the PLO youth organization when he was sixteen years old, he spent five years in prison. One year out of prison, he would return for a six further years. AH was released as a result of the Oslo Agreement. He describes how he is now fortunate to be able to continue to run his tours of the West Bank due to support from the German and Greek embassies. AH says his ongoing political work involves travels to Europe to advocate for Palestine more than a dozen times a year.

We visit the headquarters of the Palestinian Authority in Ramallah, which includes observing Yasser Arafat's tomb. Before going to the memorial, JFE tells us about his time in the Norwegian Police's Close Protection Unit, when he was Arafat's personal bodyguard in Oslo during the Oslo Accord talks in the early 1990s. He speaks of Arafat's enormous charisma and of the respect he held for him. JFE asks to have his picture taken at the tomb. Afterward, the group explores Ramallah. Later, at AH's suggestion, the bus stops and we each buy an ice cream, which we eat together on the main street of Ramallah.

12.10.13 West Bank
Bus Tour: Abu Hasan (AH), organizer of West Bank tours, formerly PLO

During the second day of our West Bank tour, we visit Nablus and the Balata refugee camp.

A city of about around 140,000 inhabitants, Nablus has been described by an Israeli Defense Forces (IDF) spokesperson in the late 2000s as the "capital of terror" in the West Bank, and the center of Palestinian rocket production. During the second intifada the area was blocked off by IDF roadblocks as the city became the site of some of the most aggressive IDF incursions. These roadblocks, according to AH, would reap huge damage on the local industries. Military actions by the Israelis in the early 2000s would lead to the death of 522 and injury of more than 3,000 Palestinians, along with serious damage caused to historical monuments. We walk through the beautiful streets and space of the ancient city, including a bathhouse and soap factory. As we walk through the streets and squares, we come across several shrines to young martyrs as AH explains the various scenarios behind the youths' deaths – including one case of illegal weapons used by the Israelis. We are invited to meet with local representatives of the youth club.

39. Study group at Yafa Cultural Center, Balata Refugee Camp, Nablus

40. Balata refugee camp, Nablus

41. Study group at Balata refugee camp, Nablus

The Balata refugee camp was established as a temporary refugee tent camp for 500 people in 1952. Currently, according to AH, approximately 28,000 people live within the same 1 km^2 with little in the way of jobs, education, or health care. At the time of their original displacement, these refugees had been farmers; there is now little to no hope of returning to their original land. We walk around the camp, which is characterized by an extraordinary dense urban fabric of what looks to be largely self-made concrete. In the narrow streets, we see sim-

42. Balata refugee camp, Nablus

43. Study group meeting in youth club, Nablus

44. Abu Hassan, West Bank Tours

ilar martyr photographs to those we saw in Nablus, with young boys holding machine guns. We visit the Yafa Cultural Center, established in 1995, which runs three schools along with courses including traditional arts and crafts, oral history, and rights awareness. The center runs a computer lab, library, and clinic with one doctor. We are impressed by the dedication and efforts of the volunteers.

On our return trip to Jerusalem our bus is stopped by guards with machine guns and reflective sunglasses. Our driver is double-checked.

13.10.13 Tel Aviv
Group Departure

Before checking in to fly out of the Tel Aviv Airport, DS is singled out in the prechecks by the airport security team. This not only involves several bag searches but a series of particularly aggressive and repeated questioning sessions. We discuss afterwards if this was related to an awareness on the part of Israeli intelligence of the time we spent in the West Bank.

14.10.13 Oslo Study Tour

14.10.13 Oslo
Introduction to Oslo Program, Benedicte Bjørnland, PST Chief, The Norwegian Police Security Service (PST) Headquarters

After arriving in Oslo the previous evening, we meet in the morning at the PST headquarters together with the students. We leave our bags, IDs, and mobile phones in security boxes in the outer "public" area, and are guided into the lobby of the main auditorium of the inner part of the complex. The lobby showcases historical spy equipment. The oddest of all is a display of a camera hidden inside of a baby pram from the 1960s or 1970s, with an accompanying photograph presenting its original use. Once inside the auditorium, Benedicte Bjørneland, the chief of the PST, gives a brief speech describing the collaboration as a "new and good step toward the future" in which architects play a key role "in finding the balance between security and openness." She asks what role architects can play in "reducing vulnerability" and in providing tools in "fighting terrorism in the long term." Bjørnland finishes her speech abruptly and quickly disappears.

14.10.13 Oslo
Lars Erik Svendsen, PST Close Protection Unit, The Norwegian Police Security Service (PST) Headquarters

The next speaker is Lars Erik Svendsen, whose work involves the very direct protection of people – in particular, Norwegian officials who travel abroad, VIPs, or guests. For a short while the discussion is less about bombs, shattered glass, and hostile vehicle mitigation, but rather about multiple points of escape, overview, sight lines, decoy motorcades, and safe rooms. According to Svendsen, 90 percent of his job is about meticulous planning. He describes the necessary training in his job to support reading behavior in crowds, detecting nervousness, and lurking. A series of events are shown and discussed, from the Westgate Mall attack in Nairobi in 2013, to the Marriott Hotel attack in Islamabad, to the Serena Hotel attack in Kabul in 2008 – with a reflection on the conditions and mistakes that allowed these attacks to take place. To additionally read spatial conditions through this lens requires, according to one of the students, another act of mental gymnastics.

14.10.13 Oslo
Tour of Oslo Opera House with Head of Security

45. Study group at Oslo Opera House

The group travels together to the Oslo Opera House. According to our security experts and the head of security of the Opera complex, security had not been a priority in the planning and design of this popular and celebrated public building, other than securing it against fire. This is discussed, for example, in relation to the building's exposure to vehicles on the northern facade to Operagata, and in the potential openness of the roofscape. In smaller groups we discuss whether the integration of more intense security scrutiny during the earlier stages of the design of the project would have compromised the design. Many of us agreed that limited measures might not, such as more stringent HVM measures on the north facade, but we agree that there are dangers that if the building's securitization had been taken further, the strength of the project may never have emerged. Lars Erik Svendsen also discusses the building in more detail through his lens of protecting important persons. We go into the bowels of the building to the surveillance room, where a security worker watches CCTV monitors. The "secret" Justin Bieber concert of 2012, which was described earlier by the head of the opera house's security, is mentioned again by the security worker as one of the greatest tests of the building's security. He describes the panic associated with having between 15,000 and 20,000 Beliebers on the roof of the building, and the ensuing challenges related to that number of persons being squeezed into that area for several hours with a minimal supply of food, lavatories, and water.

14.10.13 Oslo
Brief from DSS (Department Service Center), Government Quarter: Matius Eckel, head of the Department of Security Management; and Marius Orningård Madsen, senior advisor, Department of Security Management

Our traveling group meets with representatives of DSS (Department Service Center) – the governmental department responsible for the everyday life of the government and the security of government buildings. They describe the security situation as a split narrative, addressing what was done before the 2011 attack, and what has happened afterward. Prior to the attack, they refer to the struggle of obtaining approval for security measures – particularly with regards to the "slowness of the Norwegian planning system." The challenge after the attack is described more according to the need to reassure workers that they are safe behind the increased security measures. It is in these terms that Madsen asks: "What is security – Is it a real or conceived condition?" They describe some of the discussions they have been having regarding the definition of the security brief for the future renovated Government Quarter. One of them refers to an interest in new technologies such as a smoke-screen product – already apparently used as a security measure in petrol stations – that is deployed at the time of a potential attack, eliminating visibility for a potential attacker. We have difficulty overcoming our skepticism toward this proposal.

14.10.13 Oslo
Inspection of bomb-damaged Government Quarter

After the meeting, which included the presentation of AR's diploma project to some curious DSS officials, the group is led by the DSS team into the closed-off site of the 2011 attack on the government quarter. On our way we discuss further the temporary security measures – involving an orgy of concrete Jersey barriers that have been distributed around the streets and public spaces of the area. We enter into the H-block and the R4-Block buildings which were the epicenter of the attack. They have been significantly cleaned of debris since the 2011 event, but they are nonetheless sites of considerable damage. We can clearly see the extent of the blown-out windows and the impact of flying glass and debris on various architectural surfaces. While the crater immediately under the location of the vehicle bomb has been repaired, we are mildly surprised at the resilience of the original concrete surfaces in the lobby of the H-building, which was only meters from the bomb.

Observing security advisors from three different departments of government, we begin to recognize differences in their mind-sets. DSS, being responsible for the ongoing day-to-day security for government employees in the Government Quarter, appear to be trying to make the best of a difficult temporary situation. They are tending not only to the security of the employees, but are also attentive to reducing fear among employees through simply taking action. We pass one of the buildings where DSS has increased the original standoff distance between the building facade and the vehicle-accessible street edge by 1.5 m through the deployment of temporary concrete Jersey barriers. It becomes obvious that the other security consultants disagree. The discussion moves from the problematic appearance of the

14.10.13 Oslo
Briefing on Security at Oslo Central Station: Tor Saghaug, ROM Eiendom

50. Study group at ROM Eiendom presentation, Oslo Central Station

ROM Eiendom is a company that owns the buildings within the Norwegian railroad network, including approximately 330 stations. Tor Saghaug, a project director at ROM, makes a presentation of the company, the Oslo S station, and the plans for its future renovation based on an architectural competition awarded in 2008. While the main security concerns on an everyday basis are petty crime such as pickpocketing and unsocial behavior, we are meeting with ROM primarily due to the fact that PST and NSM see Oslo S as a target vulnerable to a potential terror attack. It is evident to us that an attack in such a busy location, relying on the free and rapid movement of many persons would be extremely difficult to prevent.

The station was the site of a previous attack in 1982, in which a suitcase bomb was detonated in the luggage area, killing one and injuring eleven persons. The architecture of the station was adapted after that bombing with the movement of all the luggage storage to a location between two other buildings. The new area was covered with a lightweight roof that would support the dissipation of energy from an explosion upward – with the ambition of leaving the rest of the station undamaged.

We are presented the 2008 proposal for the new central station and it is challenged by some of the students, who identify what they see as its security shortcomings.

The presentation is followed by a walking tour around the station.

18.10.13 E-mail from Haakon Rasmussen
Four days after the Oslo S visit, HR contacts us by e-mail concerning our students' "testing the security" at the Oslo S main station.

Regarding police attention toward two of our students
From: Haakon Rasmussen
Sent: Friday 18 October 2013 10:00
To: Anders Rubing; Deane Alan Simpson; Vibeke Jensen

46. Study group at Høyblokken, Government Quarter, Oslo

47. Study group in secured Government Quarter, Oslo

49. Study group in Høyblokken foyer, Government Quarter, Oslo

48. Study group at Government Quarter, Oslo

barriers to how much, if any, security they provide. The question is posed whether the increased standoff distance is helpful when, in the event of a hostile vehicle bomb attack, concrete debris from the Jersey barriers could be more dangerous than the effect of a reduced standoff distance.

Hi!
The day after our visit to the Oslo Central station, two of our students went on their own past the gates into the goods-delivery area at Oslo S and were apprehended by security guards and taken to the police for registration of their IDs and deletion of the pictures they had taken. When they were apprehended, the students told the police and the guards that they were "testing the security."

I have spoken to the police and to ROM-Eiendom about it, and luckily there will be no legal aftermath to this, but we should talk some sense into the students about it. They had all the opportunities to take contact with the people that we spoke to on Monday, and would then have been let into the area for their individual research. But when they try to pull off a more 007 approach and break into the area like they did, people get slightly annoyed.

Any ideas on how we should deal with this?

I include the security log for the event below.

"Observe two men walking down to the delivery entrance from the barrier at Track 19. Send security guards to check. Before guards get there, the men check car doors and photograph the map of the delivery entrance. They disappear up the stairs by the freight elevator. The guards gain control over them. They claim they were there yesterday with ROM Eiendom [real estate company developing and maintaining property of the Norwegian railway], and would now test the security. They are escorted to the police post for ID-check and expelled/discharged. Photograph of the map of the delivery entrance is deleted."

11.11.13 BAS Bergen
Studio Midterm Review

51. BAS mid-term review

In the weeks leading up to and following the study tours, the students are asked to develop a series of initial design proposals for the sites, based on five different scenarios. This range of scenarios is intended to prompt their experimentation into different registers of response to the site.

The scenario outlines are:
1. Fortress – what if security is the only parameter, without regards to other qualities or other design parameters?
2. Win-Win – Could the project both give enhanced security and enhanced urban qualities?
3. Passivity – What could forms of conscious passivity yield?
4. Ignore and Enhance – What is possible based upon ignoring security concerns and instead focusing on enhancing urban qualities?
5. Exploit logics of security as an excuse for other ends. Could there be the possibility that focused argumentation and design language of securitization can be deployed to enhance urban qualities?

Attending the review is the core team of security experts and the teaching team:
Håvard Walla, NSM
Jack Fischer Eriksen, Police Superintendent, PST Thomas Haneborg, MSc / Security Advisor, PST
Deane Simpson, Professor, BAS
Vibeke Jensen, Visiting Professor BAS
Haakon Rasmussen, 3RW
Anders Rubing, Teacher BAS

The students present a plethora of approaches to the sites. The security experts are clearly impressed with the students' grasp of their tools and the delivery of "outside the box" thinking – but they struggle in some cases to address the spatial aspects of the projects, and to address the projects on the students' terms. Some of the students are enjoying the political nature of the theme, and are exploring the potential to prod and provoke.

During the midterm, one of the surprises on our part is the introduction by the security experts of additional threats to design for, in particular that of espionage. If we are to take this threat seriously as a design parameter, it adds an entirely different rationale to the forming of the quarter. Espionage in this case is defined as largely industrial espionage in relation to recently developed eavesdropping technologies such as the laser microphone that employs a laser directed at a distant window to pick up sound vibrations. If such a threat is to be incorporated into the design brief, it means a building without windows or without visible windows, for example. We challenge this framing of the brief based also on the rapidly changing nature of these technologies. Would it not be highly likely that an entire building complex designed to eliminate visible windows from the street or surrounding buildings, would be made obsolete in a short time by a further technological measure, such as a laser microphone jammer?

05.11.13 BAS Bergen
Post Midterm written comments from PST/NSM

At the suggestion of the security experts, the students are asked to send their projects to JFE and TH from PST and HW from NSM for a more formal evaluation of the security performance of their schemes. The feedback is divided under nine headings which describe an interesting taxonomy for security analysis, providing an insight into their way of approaching the spatial through the lens of security:
– Threats
– Description of concept
– Detection
– Resilience
– Vulnerabilities
– Robustness
– Distance and perimeter
– Surveillance
– Line of sight
– Creativity.

Below is an example of a review for one of the proposals:
Threats:
– terrorism
– crime in general
– sabotage
– hostile reconnaissance

Detection:
The layers and cobweb limits the overview of the area and enhances the need of technical use of surveillance. The different floors could require added use of security guards.

Resilience:
Difficult to see the resilient ability in the layers of transport facilities. A structural collapse will affect nearly all transport systems. A threat against one or more of the different transport types will affect all of them. A plus is the exclusivity of transport and not added functions.

Vulnerabilities:
Concerns regarding emergency response and rescue, because accessibility is unclear. No quick entries for emergency services. [...] A more holistic explanation of this project would be beneficial.

Surveillance:
Good opportunities for natural surveillance on ground level; on the below-ground level, technical measures need to be added.

Line of sight:
Target acquisition (humans) is easy on ground level. Line of sight is heavily reduced on transport system below ground level.

Creativity:
A very unison use of well-known security principles.

A good approach for creating open spaces and separate different functions. The distance of the different functions (shopping center / train station / bus station) will reduce damage effects from serious threats.

Below is an evaluation of a "fortress scenario" proposal:
Threats:
– terrorism
– crime in general
– sabotage
– espionage

Description of concept:
Existing buildings structures are mainly kept in place, with an extensive use of visible security measures. A well-outlined and informal context. A clearly defined perimeter and intention of desired security level.

Detection:
A very heavy emphasis on technical solutions, with a hard outer shell and internal zoning. Unclear if there is visible connection between the watchtowers. A massive scale of monitoring detection systems is required.

Resilience:
Difficult to assess the innovation of resilience in this concept. A penetration of the different zones may cause logistical problems (for example, partial refurnishing after a fire, etc.).

Vulnerabilities:
The vehicle lock is meandering into the perimeter, where there is possibility to exclude it from the very same perimeter.

The concept is vulnerable to insider threat in the security management.

Concerns regarding emergency response and rescue. No quick entries for emergency services.

Choke point at entrance. Delivery services access the area.

VIP entrance a possible target point. Questions arise regarding the logistics and movement within the perimeter. Underground garage under R5 is unnecessary and unwanted in this level of security.

Distance and perimeter:
Very well thought-out. Hostile vehicle mitigation is apparently well-maintained, however vehicle access is not excluded. Public access is nonexistent and therefore not an issue.

Surveillance:
Extreme levels of technical measures needed to conduct surveillance. Natural surveillance is possible to some extent on both sides of perimeter. Not all blind spots seem eliminated.

Line of sight:
Target acquisition is limited; target of opportunity is nearly nonexistent. Hostile reconnaissance is difficult, as nearby buildings are expropriated and demolished.

Creativity:
A very unison [sic] use of well-known security principles. Absolutely no reuse of public space. A dystopian image of security. Few design and innovative security features. Traditional martial approach for securing, excluding the public.

Closing remarks:
A well-explained use of security measures, but with little practical use for democratic governance. High-profile security measures, with obvious security gaps such as deliveries. The concept displaces risk to other targets.

In the second evaluation in particular, there are further security challenges introduced, such as concerns for hostile penetration in one part of the building translating into expanded logistical problems elsewhere, or the requirement that all blind spots must be eliminated. These considerations add to the complexity and difficulty of satisfying security ambitions, a high quality of design, and the continued right and access to the city.

18.12.13 BAS, Bergen
Final Semester Review

Present:
Jack Fischer Eriksen, Police Superintendent, PST
Thomas Haneborg, MSc / Security Advisor, PST
Audun Vestli, COWI
Deane Simpson, Professor, BAS
Vibeke Jensen, Visiting Professor BAS
Anders Rubing, Teacher BAS

We begin the final day of the project with a short introductory presentation. DS attempts to frame the central challenges and dilemmas of the semester. He presents a 3-axis graph showing different spaces that can be occupied within the figure between varying levels of security, design quality, and access/right to the city. After his introduction the students, arranged in pairs grouped by theme, present their final projects. In the last weeks, the students have struggled to find a balance between their responses to the security feedback from the midterm review and the continued feedback from the teachers. In that sense, the final review becomes a somewhat two-layered discussion: one discussion takes place between the security consultants and the student; and the other between students and teachers, despite concerted efforts to bridge what emerges as two competing cultures and agendas.

As the student projects have developed, so have the security concerns from the consultants, and at the same time the teachers and the consultants have further critiqued the same projects based on their design quality and their relation to the notion of the right to the city. One example is a project in which the loading dock is indoors. Although perfectly separated from the rest of the building in security terms, it becomes a concern as to how the building would react to a 20,000 kg bomb, as one theoretically could enter the loading dock with a truck. The discussion moves on to how to design and construct a building system capable of absorbing the hypothetical bomb in a place where only logistical personnel would work. Similar to the discussion about espionage at the midterm review, this concern is entirely new to us. Such feedback also occurs in relation to the Government Quarter projects, where sight lines and the risk of being attacked (with firearms) is being discussed as a reality. We challenge the rationale behind this thinking, in the context of a country largely free from politically motivated assassination, apart from the 2011 attack. This tendency of demanding increasingly secured environments – represented in the escalating feedback by the security consultants, mirrors what we see in realized securitization projects such as the American embassies. From being open to the public, they are hidden by more and more layers of bollards, fences, and surveillance until they have to move out of the city centers in order to comply with security and standoff distance demands, a situation where the regime of fear produces an involuntary abandonment of the city itself.

Theme: Democracy and Security
Author: Giorgio Agamben

For a Theory of Destituent Power
Public Lecture in Athens, November 16, 2013

Theme: Security and Design
Author: Jon Coaffee

Protecting Vulnerable Cities from Terrorism:
Enhancing the Resilience of Everyday Urban Infrastructure

Democracy[F21]

Security[F69]

A reflection on the destiny of democracy today here in Athens is in some way disturbing, because it obliges us to think on the end of democracy in the very place where it was born. As a matter of fact, the hypothesis I would like to suggest is that the prevailing governmental paradigm in Europe today is not only nondemocratic, but that it cannot either be considered as political. I will try therefore to show that the European society today is no more a political society: it is something entirely new, for which we lack a proper terminology and we have therefore to invent a new strategy.

Let me begin with a concept which seems, starting from September 2001, to have replaced any other political notion: security. As you know, the formula "for security reasons" functions today in any domain, from everyday life to international conflicts, as a password in order to impose measures that the people have no reason to accept. I will try to show that the real purpose of the security measures is not, as it is currently assumed, to prevent dangers, troubles, or even catastrophes. I will be consequently obliged to make a short genealogy of the concept of security.

One possible way to sketch such a genealogy would be to inscribe its origin and history in the paradigm of the state of exception. In this perspective, we could trace it back to the Roman principle *Salus publica suprema lex*, "public safety is the highest law," and connect it with Roman dictatorship, with the canonistic principle that necessity does not acknowledge any law, with the Comité de salut publique during the French Revolution and finally with Article 48 of the Weimar Republic, which was the juridical ground for the Nazi regime. Such a genealogy is certainly correct, but I do not think that it could really explain the functioning of the security apparatuses and measures which are familiar to us. While the state of exception was originally conceived as a provisional measure, which was meant to cope with an immediate danger in order to restore the normal situation, the security reasons constitute today a pemanent technology of government. When in 2003 I published a book in which I tried to show precisely how the state of exception was becoming in Western democracies a normal system of government, I could not imagine that my diagnosis would prove so accurate. The only clear precedent was the Nazi regime. When Hitler took power in February 1933, he immediately proclaimed a decree

Agamben

The prominent Italian philosopher Giorgio Agamben (1942–) is best known for his work addressing notions such as the *state of exception* and *Homo sacer*. In this lecture Agamben describes the emergence of the contemporary security state, its facilitation by the *state of exception*, and its undermining influence on democracy and politics in contemporary Europe. In describing an emerging form of *destituent power*, he touches upon relevant concepts and frameworks within the discourses on security and freedom, democracy, and public space, including Michel Foucault's biopower and biopolitics, and Gilles Deleuze's *control state*.

The transcript of the lecture was first published by *Chronos Magazine* in February 2014.

> "The real purpose of the security measures is not, as it is currently assumed, to prevent dangers."

> "The state of exception was originally conceived as a provisional measure."

Target Hardening[F77]

Coaffee
British urban geographer Jon Coaffee (1972-) is most well known for his book *Terrorism, Risk and the City: The Making of a Contemporary Urban Landscape* (2003). His work – addressing the intersection of urbanism and security – has most recently been framed in terms of the notion of urban resilience in the face of a range of vulnerabilities. Focusing on the UK, Coaffee describes in this essay how the perceived threat of terrorism in cities has evolved, and how changing approaches to counterterrorism led by security agencies have influenced the physical urban environment. In particular, he describes a shift, from the perception of a selective number of higher-profile targets to the vulnerability of a wider realm of everyday life.

This is an edited version of a text first published in *International Affairs* 86, no. 4 (2010).

In February 2010, amidst some controversy, proposed architectural plans were unveiled for the design of a new US Embassy building on a currently vacant site in Wandsworth, South West London. Upon planning permission being granted, building work started in November 2013 and is due to be completed by 2017, at a cost of well over £1 billion. The requirement for a new embassy was deemed vital for "security purposes," with the existing embassy site seen as vulnerable, and difficult and costly to protect from terrorist attack, given its constrained location. The current embassy site in Grosvenor Square, central London, has, since the events of September 11, 2001 (henceforth 9/11) become a virtual citadel surrounded by residential and commercial premises, and has seen much public protest regarding the high fences, concrete barriers, crash-rated steel blockers and armed guards that currently encircle the site to protect it from vehicle bombing.[1]

In recent times the existing embassy – dubbed "the fortress in the square" – is said to have offended the "aesthetic sensibilities" of local residents, some of whom have moved away rather than live near a perceived terrorist target.[2] The 2010 design for the new embassy and the rationale for relocation from the current site, incorporated in a singular design a number of the characteristics of contemporary counterterrorist protective design as embodied in the *Protect* strand of the UK counterterrorism strategy (CONTEST). This is a strategy that has received increased prominence since the July 2005 terrorist attacks on the London transport network (henceforth 7/7).

Moreover, it can be argued that in an international context, many states, notably the US and UK, are "visually exaggerating interests of national security through the architectures of overseas embassies" with the aim of transmitting a message of physical defense from attack.[3] Even in the most liberal of cities, embassies are being subjected to acute target hardening with resultant impacts upon the everyday city.[4] As such, the aim of ensuring an impregnable sealed site has become a key modus operandi for designers of many embassies worldwide.

However, in more recent times, the fortress emblem design of many embassies, which was common in the Cold War period and, in many cases, intensified in the immediate post-9/11 era has begun to pay increased attention to the aesthetics of architectural design, and the wider impact such structures can have upon surrounding areas and communities.[5] With this key principle in mind, the current plans for the new US Embassy in South West London has sought to incorporate a number of innovative and largely "stealthy" counterterrorism design features. Many of these features are reminiscent of medieval times, notably the blueprint for a stronghold castle: a protected castle keep surrounded by

"Even in the most liberal of cities, embassies are being subjected to acute target hardening with resultant impacts upon the everyday city."

suspending the articles of the Weimar constitution concerning personal liberties. The decree was never revoked, so that the entire Third Reich can be considered as a state of exception which lasted twelve years.

What is happening today is still different. A formal state of exception is not declared and we see instead that vague nonjuridical notions – like the security reasons – are used to [establish] a stable state of creeping and fictitious emergency without any clearly identifiable danger. An example of such nonjuridical notions which are used as emergency-producing factors is the concept of crisis. Besides the juridical meaning of judgment in a trial, two semantic traditions converge in the history of this term which, as it is evident for you, comes from the Greek verb *crino*: a medical and a theological one. In the medical tradition, *crisis* means the moment in which the doctor has to judge, to decide if the patient will die or survive. The day or the days in which this decision is taken are called *crisimoi*, the decisive days. In theology, *crisis* is the Last Judgment pronounced by Christ in the end of times. As you can see, what is essential in both traditions is the connection with a certain moment in time. In the present usage of the term, it is precisely this connection which is abolished. The crisis, the judgment is split from its temporal index and coincides now with the cronological course of time, so that, not only in economics and politics, but in every aspect of social life, the crisis coincides with normality and becomes, in this way, just a tool of government. Consequently, the capability to decide once [and] for all disappears and the continuous decision-making process decides nothing. To state it in paradoxical terms, we could say that, having to face a continuous state of exception, the government tends to take the form of a perpetual coup d'état. By the way, this paradox would be an accurate description of what happens here in Greece as well as in Italy, where to govern means to make a continuous series of small coups d'état. The present government of Italy is not legitimate.

This is why I think that, in order to understand the peculiar governmentality under which we live, the paradigm of the state of exception is not entirely adequate. I will therefore follow Michel Foucault's suggestion and investigate the origin of the concept of security in the beginning of [the] modern economy, by François Quesnay and the Physiocrats, whose influence on modern governmentality could not be overestimated. Starting with [the Peace of Westphalia], the great absolutist European states begin to introduce in their political discourse the idea that the sovereign has to take care of his subjects' security. But Quesnay is the first to establish security (sûreté) as the central notion in the theory of government – and this in a very peculiar way.

One of the main problems governments had to cope with at the time was the problem of famines. Before Quesnay, the usual methodology was trying to prevent famines by the creation of public granaries and forbidding the exportation of cereals. Both [these] measures had negative effects on the production.

> "We could say that, having to face a continuous state of exception, the government tends to take the form of a perpetual coup d'état."

Moat[F43] Ditch[F25]

Blast Zone[F08]

"Protective security has become an increasingly important part of the UK governments CONTEST strategy in the aftermath of 9/11."

Terrorism[F81]

moats or ditches which could be crossed using ramparts. The lead architect from Pennsylvania firm Kieran Timberlake, noted that his designs had been stimulated by European castle architecture and that, in addition to the use of a blast-proof glass facade, he had also sought to use landscape features imaginatively as security devices. This was to minimize the use of fences and walls to avoid giving a "fortress feel" to the site. Ponds and multilevel gardens were also suggested as security features, in part, to provide a 30-meter protective "blast zone" around the site. Referring to his largely glass-based design, the lead architect further noted in the *Guardian* newspaper that "we hope the message everyone will see is that it is open and welcoming" and that "it is a beacon of democracy – light-filled and light-emitting."[6]

Although widely condemned by some on its architectural merits, the embassy design highlighted a number of key features of contemporary counterterrorism philosophy as applied to the protection of urban areas and their critical infrastructure: the need to integrate effective protective security into the design of at-risk sites; the increased importance of built environment professionals such as planners, architects, and urban designers in security planning; and the need to consider the visible impact of security measures, and where appropriate, make these as unobtrusive as possible. These questions of proportionality, collective responsibility, and visibility of protective counterterrorism security will be addressed as the chapter progresses and their impacts on the everyday city highlighted. Here, what is meant by the everyday city and how this intersects with terrorist risk is therefore important. In the context of this chapter it refers to how the discourse and practice of terrorism in urban areas impacts upon individual and collective experience, and leads to new forms of collaborative decision-making regarding counterterrorism.

As the chapter progresses this analysis of terrorist risk and the everyday city will be explored within a broader narrative that highlights how protective security has become an increasingly important part of the UK government's CONTEST strategy in the aftermath of 9/11, and moreover, 7/7. This will be undertaken in four main sections. First, the historical context for protective physical security prior to 9/11 will be developed arguing that although increasingly important in protecting selective areas against vehicle bombs, such approaches were deemed only partially appropriate after the Twin Towers attacks. The second section will highlight the changing terrorist philosophies deployed against Western cities that were laid bare by 9/11. Here the focus on "soft targets" by dynamic no-warning attacks is seen to present a significantly new security challenge. Third, the policy response to such terrorist tactics is unpacked though an analysis of the *Protect* strand of the UK CONTEST strategy. Here it is argued that key issues such as the need to ensure proportionality, the increased devolution of responsibility to wider stakeholder groups, and the need to consider aesthetic dimensions, characterized the evolving UK response post-7/7. The fourth and final section then questions the limits of protective security and argues that the overall counterterrorist strategy is becoming more integrated and reflexive.

Quesnay's idea was to reverse the process: instead of trying to prevent famines, he decided to let them happen and to be able to govern them once they occurred, liberalizing both internal and foreign exchanges. "To govern" retains here its etymological cybernetical meaning: a good *kybernes*, a good pilot can't avoid tempests, but, if a tempest occurs, he must be able to govern his boat, using the force of waves and winds for the navigation. This is the meaning of the famous motto *Laisser faire, laissez passer*: it is not only the catchword of economic liberalism: it is a paradigm of government, which conceives of security (*sûreté*, in Quesnay's words) not as the prevention of troubles, but rather as the ability to govern and guide them in the good direction once they take place.

> "If government aims to the effects and not to the causes, it will be obliged to extend and multiply controls."

We should not neglect the philosophical implications of this reversal. It means an epoch-making transformation in the very idea of government, which overturns the traditional hierarchical relation between causes and effects. Since governing the causes is difficult and expensive, it is more safe and useful to try to govern the effects. I would suggest that this theorem by Quesnay is the axiom of modern governmentality. The ancien régime aimed to rule the causes; modernity pretends to control the effects. And this axiom applies to every domain, from economy to ecology, from foreign and military politics to the internal measures of police. We must realize that European governments today gave up any attempt to rule the causes; they only want to govern the effects. And Quesnay's theorem makes also understandable a fact which seems otherwise inexplicable: I mean the paradoxical convergence today of an absolutely liberal paradigm in economy with an unprecedented and equally absolute paradigm of state and police control. If government aims to the effects and not to the causes, it will be obliged to extend and multiply controls. Causes demand to be known, while effects can only be checked and controlled.

One important sphere in which the axiom is operative is that of biometrical security apparatuses, which is increasingly pervading every aspect of social life. When biometrical technologies first appeared in the eighteenth century in France with Alphonse Bertillon and in England with Francis Galton, the inventor of [a method for categorizing fingerprints], they were obviously not meant to prevent crimes, but only to recognize recidivist delinquents. Only once a second crime has occurred, you can use the biometrical data to identify the offender.

Biometrical technologies, which had been invented for recividist criminals, remained for [a long time] their exclusive privilege. In 1943 the Congress of the USA still refused the Citizen Identification Act, which was meant to introduce for every citizen an identity card with fingerprints. But according to a sort of fatality or unwritten law of modernity, the technologies which have been invented for animals, for criminals, strangers or Jews, will finally be extended to all human beings. Therefore in the course of twentieth century, biometric technologies have been applied to all citizens, and Bertillon's identifying photograph and

Surveillance[F75]

Defending the Everyday City

Defending vulnerable urban spaces of Western cities against the ever-changing nature of international terrorism has long occupied state security services. That said, although until recently the selective nature of targets under threat meant that this has seldom had major impacts upon everyday life in the city, or upon the practice of built environment professionals (planners, architects, surveyors, etc.) and the police.

Prior to 9/11 threats of urban terrorism were predominantly seen as emanating from vehicle-borne improvised explosive devices (VBIEDs) targeting major financial or political centers. In response, counterterrorist security managers tended to utilize policing tactics, planning regulations and advanced technology in order to construct "security zones" or "rings of steel" where access was restricted and surveillance significantly enhanced.[7] This initially drew on 1970s ideas within spatial planning of "defensible space," whereby the threat from crime, or in this case terrorism, could in part be reduced by utilizing certain space designs whereby territorial control could be achieved. In the 1970s this approach to "designing-out" terrorism was utilized in numerous areas in Northern Ireland where physical defensive cordons were placed around a number of urban centers.[8] In the 1990s, following a spate of car-bomb attacks against financial targets in England, such security zoning began to become more focused upon available technology, particularly in the form of advanced closed-circuit television cameras. At this time the financial zones in central London perhaps provided the primary examples of such territorial approaches to counterterrorist security; with the so-called ring of steel being established in the City of London in 1992 and the self-styled "Iron Collar" being put in place in the London Docklands in 1996 in order to prevent further Provisional IRA attacks.[9]

Further international examples in this era can also be drawn from the US and Israel[10] where military considerations were increasingly embedded within land use decision-making concerning 'at risk' sites. In the US the attack against the World Trade Center in New York in 1993 and the subsequent attack in downtown Oklahoma in 1995, led to legalization being passed in order to make it easier to "bomb proof" federal structures. This process often utilized techniques deployed during the Cold War to build blast-resistant military facilities, such as missile silos or bunkers.[11] As commentators have noted, embedding such counterterrorist features into the urban landscape has implications for those that design, plan, and manage the everyday city:

> In the wake of these incidents, as the American public became increasingly aware of the threat of "home-grown" terrorism and the vulnerability of the built environment, the practical response by statutory agencies was rather reactionary, adopting crude but robust approaches to territorial security and once again pursuing the ideas of defensible space as their key modus operandi. By extension, the potential role that urban built-environment professionals could play in "terror-proofing" cities became more apparent.[12]

"Security zoning began to become more focused upon available technology, particularly in the form of advanced closed-circuit television cameras."

Galton's fingerprints are currently used in every country for ID cards.

But the extreme step has been taken only in our days, and it is still in the process of full realization. The development of new digital technologies, with optical scanners which can easily record not only fingerprints but also the retina or the eye iris structure, biometrical apparatuses tend to move beyond the police stations and immigration offices and spread to everyday life. In many countries, the access to student's restaurants or even to schools is controlled by a biometric apparatus on which the student just puts his hand. The European industries in this field, which are quickly growing, recommend that citizens get used to this kind of controls from their early youth. The phenomenon is really disturbing, because the European Commissions for the development of security (like the ESPR, European Security Research Program) include among their permanent members the representatives of the big industries in the field, which are just armaments producers like Thales, Finmeccanica, EADS [and] BAE Systems, that have converted to the security business.

It is easy to imagine the dangers represented by a power that could have at its disposal the unlimited biometric and genetic information of all its citizens. With such a power at hand, the extermination of the Jews, which was undertaken on the basis of incomparably less efficient documentation, would have been total and incredibly swift. But I will not dwell on this important aspect of the security problem. The reflections I would like to share with you concern rather the transformation of political identity and of political relationships that are involved in security technologies. This transformation is so extreme that we can legitimately ask not only if the society in which we live is still a democratic one, but also if this society can be still considered as political.

Christian Meier has shown how in [the] fifty century [BC] a transformation of the political conceptuality took place in Athens, which was grounded on what he calls a "politicization" (*politisierung*) of citizenship. While till that moment the fact of belonging to the *polis* was defined by a number of conditions and social status of different kind — for instance, belonging to nobility or to a certain cultual community, to be peasant or merchant, member of a certain family, etc. — from now on citizenship became the main criterion of social identity.

"The result was a specifically Greek conception of citizenship, in which the fact that men had to behave as citizens found an institutional form. The belonging to economical or religious communities was removed to a secondary rank. The citizens of a democracy considered themselves as members of the *polis*, only in so far as they devoted themselves to a political life. *Polis* and *politeia*, city and citizenship, constituted and defined one another. Citizenship became in that way a form of life, by means of which the *polis* constituted itself in a domain clearly distinct from the *oikos*, the house. Politics became therefore a free public

> "It is easy to imagine the dangers represented by a power that could have at its disposal the unlimited biometric and genetic information of all its citizens."

Public Space[F60]

Home Office[F33]

"Increasingly with the public spaces of the city being targeted, military planners were also forced to consider not just how robust they could make buildings, but were faced with the added challenge of 'budgetary and aesthetic considerations that were never meant to accommodate blast hardening.'"

However, increasingly with the public spaces of the city being targeted, military planners were also forced to consider not just how robust they could make buildings, but were faced with the added challenge of "budgetary and aesthetic considerations that were never meant to accommodate blast hardening."[13] These are key issues that are only now, in the twenty-first century, being recognized and incorporated into the design and decision-making of the planning and architectural professions as they consider designing in counterterrorism features to the urban landscape.

Changing Terrorist Philosophies and the Strategic Protection of Soft Targets

The events on 9/11 and 7/7 made traditional territorial approaches to counterterrorist security appear largely inadequate.[14] These events saw national security policy being rearticulated in terms of the need to respond proactively, and to develop preemptive solutions in order to embed a greater degree of resilience into both physical design of structures and the associated management systems.[15]

Traditional emergency planning and counterterrorist strategies were rethought given the increased appreciation of the multiple and fluid threats faced from international terrorism. Although this was initially postulated in terms of the fear from chemical, biological, radiological, or nuclear (CBRN) attack, the threat posed by no-warning, and often person-borne explosive devices, in a multitude of crowded public places also began to set significant new challenges for the security agencies.[16] As noted:

> Although debates continue about the relationship between new and traditional threats, the methods and tactics adopted by terror groups are novel, innovative, and increasingly focused on mass-casualty strikes or multiple coordinated attacks. Such attacks [are] often conducted by suicide attackers and tactically aimed at soft targets such as hospitals, schools, shopping promenades, and more generally crowded places....[17]

These targets of choice – crowded areas – have features in common, most notably their easy accessibility that cannot be altered without radically changing citizen experience of such largely public places. In the UK, such crowded places are now defined by the Home Office as "sites [which] are regarded as locations or environments to which members of the public have access that, on the basis of intelligence, credible threat or terrorist methodology, may be considered potentially liable to terrorist attack by virtue of their crowd density,' and include the following sectors: 'bars, pubs and night clubs; restaurants and hotels; shopping centers; sports and entertainment stadia; cinemas and theatres; visitor attractions; major events; commercial centers; the health sector; the education sector; and religious sites/places of worship."[18]

Contesting Terrorism

UK policymakers and the security services increasingly perceive attacks against crowded public places as one of their key priorities

space as such opposed to the private space, which was the reign of necessity." According to Meier, this specifically Greek process of politicization was transmitted to Western politics, where citizenship remained the decisive element.

The hypothesis I would like to propose to you is that this fundamental political factor has entered an irrevocable process that we can only define as a process of increasing depoliticization. What was in the beginning a way of living, an essentially and irreducibly active condition, has now become a purely passive juridical status, in which action and inaction, the private and the public are progressively blurred and become indistinguishable. This process of depoliticization of citizenship is so evident that I will not dwell on it.

I will rather try to show how the paradigm of security and the security apparatuses have played a decisive role in this process. The growing extension to citizens of technologies which were conceived for criminals has inevitably consequences on the political identity of the citizen. For the first time in the history of humanity, identity is no longer a function of the social personality and its recognition by others, but rather a function of biological data, which cannot bear any relation to it, like the arabesques of the fingerprints or the disposition of the genes in the double helix of DNA. The most neutral and private thing becomes the decisive factor of social identity, which loses therefore its public character.

"Every citizen is a potential terrorist."

If my identity is now determined by biological facts that in no way depend on my will and over which I have no control, then the construction of something like a political and ethical identity becomes problematic. What relationship can I establish with my fingerprints or my genetic code? The new identity is an identity without the person, as it were, in which the space of politics and ethics loses its sense and must be thought again from the ground up. While the Greek citizen was defined through the opposition between the private and the public, the *oikos*, which is the place of reproductive life, and the *polis*, place of political action, the modern citizen seems rather to move in a zone of indifference between the private and the public, or, to quote Hobbes's terms, the physical and the political body.

The materialization in space of this zone of indifference is the video surveillance of the streets and the squares of our cities. Here again an apparatus that had been conceived for the prisons has been extended to public places. But it is evident that a video-recorded place is no more an <u>agora</u> and becomes a hybrid of public and private, a zone of indifference between the prison and the forum. This transformation of the political space is certainly a complex phenomenon that involves a multiplicity of causes, and among them the birth of biopower holds a special place. The primacy of the biological identity over the political identity is certainly linked to the politicization of bare life in modern states. But one should never forget that the leveling of social identity on body identity began with the attempt to identify the recidivist criminals. We should not be astonished if today the normal relationship between the state and its citizens

Agora[F01]

in the ongoing "war on terror." Since the early 2000s, the UK has developed a long-term strategy for developing resilience against terrorism – CONTEST. The aim of this strategy is to reduce the risk of terrorism, so that people can go about their daily lives freely and with confidence. CONTEST is divided into four strands: *Prevent*, *Pursue*, *Protect*, and *Prepare*.[19]

Through the *Protect* strand of CONTEST since the mid-2000s, protecting crowded public places against attack has become a priority of the UK government. Such areas are seen as an integral part of the critical national infrastructure seen here as "...those key elements of the national infrastructure which are crucial to the continued delivery of essential services to the UK...without [which] the UK could suffer serious consequences, including severe economic damage, grave social disruption, or large-scale loss of life."[20] For example the Centre for the Protection of National Infrastructure (CPNI)[21] argue that "the *Protect* strand is concerned with reducing the vulnerability of the UK and UK interests overseas to a terrorist attack..."[22] and covers a range of issues including: strengthening border security, protecting key utilities; reducing the risk and impact of terrorist attack against the transport network; and, most importantly from the perspective of attempting to reduce the threat against soft targets, "protecting people going about their daily lives in crowded places."

Initially in the wake of 9/11 the spatial expression of the *Protect* strategy on the cityscape in at-risk locations, most notably but not exclusively in central London, was dominated by a combination of robust physical approaches and technology which utilized barrier methods to delimited access to public spaces. Most visibly this included the "sealing off" of government sites and other potential "target risks"[23] through the use of concrete or reinforced steel barriers and the rolling out of a seemingly ubiquitous supply of reinforced bollards.[24]

The entrance to the London Docklands "Iron Collar."

Protecting critical infrastructure at this time was given the highest priority and was largely reactionary given the fear of imminent attack. The reaction among UK policy communities was not however unique. Many commentators argued that the immediacy of the perceived need to respond, with little time to contemplate the longer-term consequences of action, characterized the initial international post-9/11 reaction. In short, this was seen by some as the "end of reflection," where speed of response was prioritized over deliberative and long-term decision-making.[25] Moreover, whilst the focus on protecting key urban areas can be seen as necessarily reactionary, it also served a political purpose in terms of visibly demonstrating that the state was acting to protect the UK from terrorist outrage.[26] As noted elsewhere there is a political imperative for demonstrable visible protection to reassure the public that the government are in control:

> "UK policymakers and the security services increasingly perceive attacks against crowded public places as one of their key priorities in the ongoing 'war on terror.'"

is defined by suspicion, police filing and control. The unspoken principle which rules our society can be stated like that: Every citizen is a potential terrorist. But what is a state which is ruled by such a principle? Can we still define it as democratic state? Can we even consider it as being something political? In which kind of state do we live today?

You will probably know that Michel Foucault, in his book *Discipline and Punish* and in his courses at the Collège de France sketched a typological classification of modern states. He shows how the state of the ancien régime, that he calls *territorial* or *sovereign state* and whose motto was *Faire mourir et laisser vivre*, evolves progressively in a population state and in a disciplinary state, whose motto reverses now in *Faire vivre et laisser mourir*, as it will take care of the citizen's life in order to produce healthy, well-ordered, and manageable bodies.

"The government did not want that the police maintain order, but that it manage disorder."

The state in which we live now is no more a disciplinary state. Gilles Deleuze suggested to call it *état de contrôle*, control state, because what it wants, is not to order and to impose discipline, but rather to manage and to control. Deleuze's definition is correct, because management and control do not necessarily coincide with order and discipline. No one has told it so clearly as the Italian police officer, who, after the turmoils of Genoa in July 2001, declared that the government did not want that the police maintain order, but that it manage disorder.

American politologists, who have tried to analyze the constitutional transformation involved in the PATRIOT Act and in the other laws which followed September 2001, prefer to speak of a *security state*. But what does *security* here mean? It is during the French Revolution that the notion of security – *sûreté*, as they used to say – is linked to the definition of *police*. The laws of March 16, 1791, and August 11, 1792, introduce thus in the French legislation the notion of *police de sûreté* (security police), which was doomed to have a long history in modernity.
If you read the debates which preceded the votation of these laws, you will see that police and security define one another, but no one among the speakers (Brissot, Hérault de Séchelles, Gensonné) is able to define *police* or *security* by themselves.

The debates focused on the situation of the police with respect to justice and judicial power. Gensonné maintains that they are "two separate and distinct powers"; yet, while the function of the judicial power is clear, it is impossible to define the role of the police. An analysis of the debate shows that the place and function of the police is undecidable and must remain undecidable, because, if it were really absorbed in the judicial power, police could no more exist. This is the discretionary power which still today defines the action of the police officer, who, in a concrete situation of danger for the public security, acts so to speak as a sovereign. But, even when he exerts this discretionary power, he does not really take a decision, nor prepares, as is usually stated, the judge's decision. Every decision concerns the causes, while the police acts on effects, which are by definition undecidable.

USA
PATRIOT Act
of 2001 F82

...the need for the state to illustrate that it is taking the terrorist threat seriously...for instance, [through] the swamping of potential targets by armed police and in some cases military hardware, or the "temporary" manipulation of spaces adjacent to sites through the placement of concrete Jersey (crash) barriers to create an exclusion area for potentially hostile vehicles, can be used to proclaim to the public that a threat is being heeded.[27]

The Policy Response:
Resilient Design for the Inevitable Attack

In the UK after 9/11, there was a sense of fatalism about the likelihood of London, in particular, being targeted by international terrorists utilizing nontraditional methods of attack. The primary aims of counterterrorism therefore centered upon restricting the opportunities for terrorists to strike and in preparing the capital for the *inevitable* attack (which can be argued came on 7/7).[28] This was not a new rhetoric. Sir John Stevens, Commissioner of the Metropolitan Police, speaking in the wake of the 2004 Madrid train attacks[29] noted that a terror attack on London is "inevitable":

> We do know that we have actually stopped terrorist attacks happening in London but...there is an inevitability that some sort of attack will get through; but my job is to make sure that does not happen.[30]

The BBC also cited the then London Mayor who noted it would be "miraculous" if London escaped attack. After 7/7 the rhetoric of inescapable attack was particularly prominent, not only with regard to the transport network, but also London's key business districts where a police report at the time talked of an "inevitable" attack against "the obvious target" – the financial zones of London.[31]

In the UK in the wake of 7/7 countering international terrorism was increasingly focused upon the protection of crowded public places and was driven forward in policy terms by the CPNI and the Home Office alongside a host of partner agencies, private businesses, local government, the police, and academia, who collectively sought to reduce the vulnerability of such locations. In particular, through the UK Research Councils (RCUK), the academic community were increasingly co-opted into counterterrorist research. Flagship research programs focused on "New Security Challenges"[32] and "Global Uncertainties"[33] sought to facilitate new thinking about the fluid nature of the terrorist threat and how policymakers and practitioners might respond. Given the impact of 7/7 and continual stories circulated via the media, that public places were key targets of inevitable attack, specific workshops were convened by the RCUK in 2006 involving CPNI and other parts of the security services. The aim was to develop specific research projects around protecting public places from terrorism. Projects that emerged from this process sought to establish ways by which crowded places could effectively design in counterterrorism measures in ways that didn't detract from the experiences of the everyday city.[34] In other words, "for counterterrorist resilient design to be successful it must not only be effective but must also be acceptable to the

> "A police report at the time talked of an 'inevitable' attack against 'the obvious target' – the financial zones of London."

48　　　Photo Essay

MELILLA, SPAIN
Visited September 30, 2014

Melilla, Spain

01. Checkpoint between the Melilla enclave and Morocco. Due to differentials in tax and customs regulations between the two sides of the border, an informal economy carrying goods to the Moroccan side exists.

02. 2014 border developments, including new moat and fence on the Moroccan side of the border

03. Triple-layered fence system

04. Local citizens in yellow caps supervise border crossings.

05. Temporary steel towers become permanent concrete structures.

Photo Essay

6

06. Unloaded goods to be carried over the border on foot

07. Road used by the Civil Guard to patrol the border area

08. Detail of multiple fencing layers

Melilla, Spain

7

8

The name of this undecidable element is no more today, like it was in the eighteenth century, *raison d'état*, state reason: it is rather security reasons. The security state is a police state: but, again, in the juridical theory, the police is a kind of black hole. All we can say is that when the so-called science of the police first appears in the eighteenth century, *police* is brought back to its etymology from the Greek *politeia* and opposed as such to *politics*. But it is surprising to see that *police* coincides now with the true political function, while the term *politics* is reserved to the foreign policy. Thus Von Justi, in his treatise on *Policey-Wissenschaft*, calls *Politik* the relationship of a state with other states, while he calls *Polizei* the relationship of a state with itself. It is worthwhile to reflect upon this definition: (I quote): "Police is the relationship of a state with itself."

The hypothesis I would like to suggest here is that, placing itself under the sign of security, modern state has left the domain of politics to enter a no-man's-land, whose geography and whose borders are still unknown. The security state, whose name seems to refer to an absence of cares *(securus* from *sine cura)* should, on the contrary, make us worry about the dangers it involves for democracy, because in it, political life has become impossible, while democracy means precisely the possibility of a political life.

But I would like to conclude – or better to simply stop my lecture (in philosophy like in art, no conclusion is possible, you can only abandon your work) with something which, as far as I can see now, is perhaps the most urgent political problem. If the state we have in front of us is the security state I described, we have to think anew the traditional strategies of political conflicts. What shall we do, what strategy shall we follow?

The security paradigm implies that each dissention, each more or less violent attempt to overhrow its order, become an opportunity to govern them in a profitable direction. This is evident in the dialectics which binds tightly together terrorism and state in an endless vicious spiral. Starting with [the] French Revolution, the political tradition of modernity has conceived of radical changes in the form of a revolutionary process that acts as the *pouvoir constituant*, the constituent power of a new institutional order. I think that we have to abandon this paradigm and try to think [of] something as a *puissance destituante,* a purely destituent power that cannot be captured in the spiral of security.

It is a destituent power of this sort that Benjamin has in mind in his essay "On the Critique of Violence" when he tries to define a pure violence which could "break the false dialectics of lawmaking violence and law-preserving violence," an example of which is Sorel's proletarian general strike. "On the breaking of this cycle," he writes in the end of the essay, "maintained by mythic forms of law, on the destitution of law with all the forces on which it depends, finally therefore on the abolition of state power, a new historical epoch is founded." While a constituent power destroys law only to re-create it in a new form, destituent power, insofar as it deposes once [and] for all the law, can open a really new historical epoch.

"The security state is a police state ..."

Border[F10]

owners, inhabitants, and users of particular places [and that]...this acceptability encompasses complex financial, social and aesthetic considerations."[35]

The importance of the crowded places dimension within the *Protect* strand of the UK CONTEST strategy was further ratcheted up by a series of terrorist incidents in London and Glasgow in the summer of 2007[36] two years after the devastating 7/7 attacks. In response in July 2007 the Prime Minister provided a "statement on security" in which he argued that protecting the UK's crowded places from terrorist attack required "constant vigilance."[37] He also noted that in recent weeks the countries' shopping centers, sports stadia and other crowded venues had all been assessed for security vulnerabilities.[38]

He then tasked Lord West (parliamentary under-secretary of state for security and counterterrorism) with undertaking a review of how government could best protect "crowded places, transport infrastructure and critical national infrastructure from terrorist attack."[39]

"Protecting the UK's crowded places from terrorist attack required 'constant vigilance.'"

The review, which was completed in November 2007, highlighted the need to improve the resilience of "strategic national infrastructure (stations, ports, and airports) and other crowded places, and to step up physical protection against possible vehicle bomb attacks."[40] Constructing an argument that protecting such crowded areas was a collective concern, it was also noted that that the government would work with planners, architects, and designers to encourage them to design in protective security measures to new buildings, including safe areas, traffic control measures and the use of blast-resistant materials. In a statement coinciding with the review, the Prime Minister's spokesperson, highlighting the possible impact of such measures on the everyday city noted that "the public...may start to see some changes in the physical layout of buildings where people gather."[41] Here the inference was clear; namely that the crowded places sector was where significant improvements were required in protective security.[42]

Key Design Principles

With regard to this perceived need to reduce the vulnerability of crowded places through the *Protect* strand of CONTEST, a number of general principles were implied in the West Review with regard to the embedding of protective security into the built fabric of cities: proportionality; collective responsibility; and visibility.

First, it was argued that protective security measures deployed should be proportionate to the risk faced. This desire for proportionality has been further outlined in more recent UK government documentation where it was argued that the risk faced within crowded places should be judged in a standard way in accordance with a "risk assessment matrix." This would allow local partners to "prioritize their work to reduce the vulnerability of crowded places to terrorist attack."[43] A proportionate approach was deemed necessary in order to minimize disruption to everyday activities and to "the ability of individuals and businesses to carry out their normal social, economic, and democratic activities."[44]

Second, the November 2007 West Review highlighted that cooperation among a host of associated stakeholders, most notably private businesses and built-environment professionals, was required in

Risk Assessment[F65]

To think such a purely destituent power is not an easy task. Benjamin wrote once that nothing is so anarchical as the bourgeois order. In the same sense, Pasolini in his last movie has one of the four Salò masters saying to their slaves: "true anarchy is the anarchy of power." It is precisely because power constitutes itself through the inclusion and the capture of anarchy and anomie, that it is so difficult to have an immediate access to these dimensions, it is so hard to think today [of] something as a true anarchy or a true anomie. I think that a praxis which would succeed in exposing clearly the anarchy and the anomie captured in the security government technologies could act as a purely destituent power. A really new political dimension becomes possible only when we grasp and depose the anarchy and the anomie of power. But this is not only a theoretical task: it means first of all the rediscovery of a form of life, the access to a new figure of that political life whose memory the security state tries at any price to cancel.

Reinforced bi-steel barrier surrounding UK Parliament

order to make crowded places safer. In particular, the Prime Minister noted that "more is done to protect buildings from terrorism from the design stage onwards" and that this would be conducted with the support of relevant professional bodies to raise the awareness and skills of architects, planners, and police in relation to counterterrorism protective security.[45] Here delivering a noticeable reduction in vulnerability was seen not just in terms of the delivery of guidance to local authorities and business by security specialists, but in the actual implementation of measures to increase the safety of those crowded spaces deemed to be at highest risk of attack. This is in line with broader concerns surrounding the overall resilience of cities against a range of hazards which has necessarily broadened out the range of experts and professions whose input should be coordinated. As has been suggested, a resilient built environment "should be designed, located, built, operated, and maintained in a way that maximizes the ability of built assets, associated support systems (physical and institutional) and the people that reside or work within the built assets, to withstand, recover from, and mitigate for, the impacts of extreme natural and human-induced hazards."[46]

Third, it was noted that the imposition of additional security features should not, where possible, negatively impact upon everyday economic and democratic activities. This realization of the importance of the social acceptability of counterterrorism features led to the West Review announcing that security features should be as unobtrusive as possible, where finding the right balance between "subtlety" and "safety" was seen as vital.[47] As argued at this time, the adoption of counterterrorist principles within designs had traditionally often led to visibly unattractive architecture and the increased control of access to public space. But this need not be so. As one commentator more recently argued, "We might live in dangerous times, but they don't have to be ugly ones too."[48] In response to this challenge we now see security features being increasingly camouflaged and covertly embedded within the urban landscape so that to the general public they do not obviously serve a counterterrorism purpose.[49] Examples of such "stealthy" features include the sorts of ornamental or landscaped measures suggested for the design of the new US embassy (see earlier).

Likewise, recent balustrades erected as part of public-realm "streetscape" improvements in the government security zone in central London have also sought to design in security more attractively and inconspicuously (instead of using bollards). Further along what has been documented as a spectrum of visible security features, we can also see "invisible" types of security emerging within architectural practice such as collapsible pavements (so-called Tiger Traps); although such features come with political challenges in that their very invisibility means they potentially become an uncontested element of political and public policy.[50] This, as one commentator has noted, potentially "represents the future of the hardening of public buildings and public space – soft on the outside, hard within, the iron hand inside the civic velvet glove."[51]

Theme: Democracy and Security
Author: Michael Sorkin

The Fear Factor

"The future of the hardening of public buildings and public space – soft on the outside, hard within, the iron hand inside the civic velvet glove."

Resilience[F62]

In line with these core principles of proportionality, collective responsibility, and visibility, the intention since 2007 in the UK has been to develop a national framework for the rolling out of protective security within crowded places. This is in order to deliver a sustained and noticeable decrease in vulnerability over a number of years. The development of such a framework has a number of constituent elements, including:

1. Drawing on existing expertise in local areas such as crime and disorder reduction partnership and local resilience forums where the police, local government, and other key stakeholders come together and work collectively to reduce vulnerability;

2. Developing a national network of well-trained counterterrorism specialists and security advisors who can provide guidance and advice to local stakeholders with regard to threat levels faced and the proportionate use of protective security interventions;

3. The creation of performance management indicators at the local level to assist local government to focus on the requirement of reducing the vulnerability of crowded spaces against terrorist attack. The use of such performance management tools indicates that a local authority and its partners, in liaison with the local police and specialist counterterrorism security advisors, will have a statutory duty to ensure that the protection of crowded places is "robust."[52]

4. Improving the skills base of built-environment professionals through workshops run by the National Counter Terrorism Security Office (called Project Argus Processional[53]), the issuing of specific planning guidance for designing in counterterrorism features, and through delivering enhanced training schemes for local police involved in urban design guidance.[54]

The Limits of Protective Counterterrorist Security

The focus of this chapter has been upon the *Protect* strand of CONTEST, and in particular how evolving counterterrorism design strategies are attempting to balance the twin aims of effectiveness and acceptability. In the wake of 9/11 and 7/7 *Protect* became perhaps the most high-profile of the four CONTEST strands. Over time the dynamic nature of the terrorist threat, and the occurrence of particular incidents, has meant that modification has been made to the *Protect* strand, alongside attempts made to better integrate all UK counterterrorist activity. This was reflected in the UK government's revised and updated CONTEST II strategy, published in 2009, which aimed to build on the existing CONTEST policy, and in turn provide the basis for coordination across counterterrorism spheres.[55] As noted "...the threat is always changing. New groups emerge and terrorists continue to develop new methods and make use of new technologies. Learning from our experience over the past few years, we have updated all aspects of our strategy to take account of this changing threat."[56]

Across the street from the building where I have my studio is a massive, block-square federal building with separate entrances for the Passport Agency, Veterans Administration, Labor Department centers, and a post office. Although they have no identity on the street, a number of other agencies are also housed in the building and there are rumors of secret facilities, including a branch detention facility for terrorist suspects. Since 9/11, the building has been progressively fortified. Access to the Passport Agency requires an airport-style walk through a metal detector – shoes, belt, briefcase on the X-ray belt, proof of identity, and an appointment, guards everywhere. The building perimeter has been secured by a wall of bollards and massive concrete "planters." Exterior walls are festooned with CCTV cameras and a walk around the neighborhood reveals dozens more, inscrutably – but certainly – networked, and plans have recently been announced by the city to add additional thousands. Uniformed police are ubiquitous: New York City cops sit in a parked cruiser opposite the building, Port Authority officers constantly cruise by, federal police of various stripes man the entrances, and the cars and troopers of the new "Homeland Security" police lurk everywhere.

This scene increasingly repeats itself around the city, around the country, and around the world, part of an accelerating transformation of the built and political environments: for every bomb that falls on Iraq, it seems twenty bollards (generally with little actual defensive value) are added in front of yet another high-value target at home – status symbols. America is in the grips of war fever, a delirium of suspicion and fear. A new Fortress America is being built but its bulwarks are not simply directed – like those bombproof planters – at a threat that can be physically externalized. The barrier turns inward as well, making each of us simultaneously soldier and suspect, enmeshed inextricably in the permanent warfare of all against us.

The number of American dead in Iraq has now passed the number killed on 9/11, with no end in sight. This melancholy marker signals both the militarization of the event for us and its radical civilianization for the people of Iraq, where as many as 100,000 have now died, victims of the chaos unleashed by our invasion or "collateral" damage from our violence. Back home, the "war" on terror, with its opaque objectives and sinister rhetoric,

Sorkin
New York-based American architect and urbanist Michael Sorkin (1948–) is a prolific and outspoken writer and critic on architecture and urbanism. His preoccupation with contested spaces of the contemporary city is evident in edited volumes such as *Variations on a Theme Park: The New American City and the End of Public Space* (1992), *Against the Wall: Israel's Barrier to Peace* (2005), and *Indefensible Space: The Architecture of the National Insecurity State* (2008). The name of the latter publication, from which this introductory essay is excerpted, is a critical reference to Oscar Newman's 1972 book *Defensible Space*. In this piece, Sorkin describes the role of disproportionate insecurity in the development of a post-9/11 "garrison state," and the pivotal role of spatial arrangements such as bollards, barricades, or CCTV as nonneutral tools of social and political control that threaten "the right to the city."

 The text was first published in the book *Indefensible Space* (New York: Routledge, 2008).

CCTV F12

"For every bomb that falls on Iraq, it seems twenty bollards (generally with little actual defensive value) are added in front of yet another high-value target at home – status symbols."

For example the 2008 Mumbai attacks led to a reassessment of threat against crowded places and calls for fresh thinking regarding the trajectory of the *Protect* strand, whilst at the same time accelerating rollout of protective security guidance for hotels, restaurants, airports, and other vulnerable crowded places. But perhaps more importantly, the Mumbai attacks raised a series of questions for the *Protect* strand regarding whether urban areas were prepared for similar fedayeen-style attacks. This was amidst reports of a potentially imminent attack against central London targets. As reported in the *Times*, "Mumbai is coming to London" and organization should be prepared for an attack "involving a small number of gunmen with handguns and improvized explosive devices."[57] As such, post-Mumbai, an urgent review of UK security and intelligence agency assumptions about the likely style of terrorist attack in the UK was launched which had implications for counterterrorism policy. For example, if the assumption is that the types of tactics deployed in Mumbai will migrate to Western cities, what does this tell us about the limited capacity to prevent such attacks against soft targets through planned-in urban fortification techniques that appear almost de rigueur?[58] More recently, similar reviews have ben undertaken as a result of fedayeen-style attacks in Paris in January 2015 where three days of attacks by gunmen brought terror to Paris and its surrounding areas.

With regard to the *Protect* strand, the increased resources that have been given over to counterterrorism since 7/7 has led to the training of tens of thousands of public- and private-sector workers in vigilance for terrorist activity and instruction about what to do in the event of an attack, whilst the CONTEST II strategy reiterated that effort must be made to ensure planners, architects, and designers should be responsible for designing out vulnerabilities.[59]

It is also important to think about the increased hybridizing of the CONTEST strands of *Pursue, Prevent,* and *Prepare* with the *Protect* strand, and in particular how this impacts upon attempts to reduce the vulnerability of crowded places. With regard to the *Prevent* strand, which is concerned with tackling the underlying causes of terrorism particularly those linked to violent extremism, we might ask what impact visible security features have upon individual and group perceptions of public space? Does it make people feel vulnerable, alienated, or excluded? Can these feelings contribute to violent extremism? And more specifically, can a fortress environment mirror "radical" tendencies, or can a sensitively designed built environment help mediate them?

The connection between the *Protect* and *Prepare* strands of CONTEST is also vital to ensuring a more integrated counterterrorism strategy that encompass a range of "hard" engineering and design solutions and "soft" governance and management arrangements. Since the early 2000s in the UK civil contingencies legislation has been blended with CONTEST in order to assist the development of a more resilient urban environment, and to reduce the risk of a wide and unpredictable variety of terrorist threats through a combination of physical and managerial means.[60] As one commentator has noted:

> "We might ask what impact visible security features have upon individual and group perceptions of public space? Does it make people feel vulnerable, alienated, or excluded?"

Paranoia[F54]

has also been transformative and the country takes on more and more aspects of a garrison state, defended by a labyrinth of intrusions that, relying on the constantly stoked paranoia over an invisible, shape-shifting enemy, makes suspicion universal. The bugaboo is no longer "Reds under the beds" but illegal aliens, terrorists, perverts, Muslims, who legitimate the swelling Orwellian apparatus that pervades our national life.

> "9/11 has provided justification for a range of measures that have radically altered the character of daily life."

9/11 was accelerant for processes long under way, a boon for the fear-mongering state and for our own Al-Qaeda, the "network" of global corporations that profits so handsomely from antiterror operations. Constantly evoked as an unanswerable claim on our compliance, 9/11 has provided justification for a range of measures that have radically altered the character of daily life. The intrusion into bank records and phone calls. The biometric screening of international arrivals at airports. The mandatory DNA tests. The call for tamperproof ID cards for aliens or their massive expulsion and the construction of a wall – and the deployment of troops – along the Mexican border to keep them from coming back. The appointment of a general to head the "civilian" CIA. The suspension of the right to trial and the growth of a global gulag for the incarceration of terror suspects, often "rendered" to states with less delicacy in matters of torture.

The reconstruction of the cityscape with blast barriers, checkpoints, and other defensive architectures. The cameras. The sniffer dogs. The random searches. The robot drones circling soundlessly overhead.

And this is just the beginning. Owners have, for years, been able to obtain implants for their pets and livestock, subcutaneous microchips that – via GPS – locate roving dogs and cows within feet anywhere on the planet. Human implants of such radio frequency identity chips are under way, with the nominally benign initial "household" purpose of allowing keyless access to cars, computers, or medical records.

Parents equip their kids with GPS cell phones that allow their movements to be tracked at all times, a response to a general sense of danger, the threat posed by a variety of threatening others that lurk in the shadowland of our anxieties, bombers, kidnappers, molesters, gangs. Schools are guarded against Columbine-style terror attacks, giving children an early introduction to metal detectors and police oversight, to random searches of their bags and lockers, to the care they must take to avoid the telling remark or the foolish hyperbole that might appear to conceal an actual threat.

Following the arrest of an alleged terror "cell" in the spring of 2006, accused of plotting to blow up the Sears Tower in Chicago – America's current tallest building – Attorney General Gonzalez described the motley plan as "more aspirational than operational." The buffoonish group at the heart of the conspiracy had been aggressively manipulated by an FBI informant who organized their slap-stick recitation of an Al-Qaeda "pledge of

A hostile vehicle mitigation (HVM) barrier at the Emirates Stadium in North London

Threats are unpredictable and the full range of threats probably unknowable. Security in this situation needs to be flexible and agile and capable of addressing new threats as they emerge. Protective technologies have a key role to play in making our cities safer but only if supported by organizations and people who can develop pre-attack security strategies, manage the response to an attack, and hasten recovery from it.[61]

With regard to the *Pursue* strand of CONTEST, which aims to monitor and tract terrorist activity and those that support it, much technological innovation has been forthcoming[62] and embedded within the urban landscape. A good deal of this work has been focused upon either "spotting" those engaged in hostile reconnaissance of target sites, or identifying those who are intent upon suicide terrorism. In particular, work in relatively "closed" and controlled environments such as airports[63] is being utilized to consider how security experts can position citizens through technological arrangements oriented to hold and monitor individuals in specifically designed spaces. In other words, can an urban space be designed in such a way as to elicit particular behavioral cues from individuals, which can then be recognized by either technology or trained security staff? As recently published guidance on *Protect* and countering the terrorist threat using advances in social and behavioral science,[64] noted:

> An individual's behavior may contain clues as to their intent. We need to develop techniques that enable identification of terrorist actions and behaviors in a range of contexts: these might include crowded places, key infrastructure locations, or security checkpoints...[65]

More specifically the challenge here was to:

> develop methods and approaches that might facilitate the detection of terrorist research, reconnaissance and attack planning, or help frustrate and deter such activities [and to] improve systems and human processes to automate the detection of these indicators.[66]

Most notably to date, new types of high-tech camera algorithms have been developed which are aimed at pre-event disruption through the identification of suspicious behavior.[67] For example, on parts of the London Underground in 2004, in response to the Madrid train bombings, a high-tech "smart" CCTV surveillance software system was rolled out. This system, in theory, automatically alerts operators to "suspicious" behavior, unattended packages, and potential suicide bombing attempts on the Tube system.[68] In addition many of the security staff at key London locations are receiving training in behavior pattern recognition – related to the body language displayed by suicide bombers before they blow themselves up, or those undertaking hostile reconnaissance.[69]

The Future of Protective Counterterrorism

In the same month (March 2010) as the designs for a new US Embassy in London were unveiled, highlighting how innovative design measures could be incorporated seamlessly into futuristic architectural

allegiance" and took their shoe sizes to purchase the fashionable combat boots required to undertake the mission. Recent arrests of members of a group discussing the possibility of blowing up a tunnel under the Hudson River and flooding lower Manhattan was also preemptive: although this group seemed comprised of marginally more competent individuals than those accused of trying to bring down Sears, they, too, were just at the "talking stage." Like free speech, conspiracy is a usefully elastic concept.

> "Like free speech, conspiracy is a usefully elastic concept."

Freedom of speech – the articulation, hence politicization, of freedom of thought – depends on the protection both of its contents and its sites: speech has no meaning unless it is heard. In the physical environment, democracy expresses itself in freedom of assembly, association, and movement, in what Henri Lefebvre has called "the right to the city." The steady ratcheting-up of constraints on this right marks the insinuation of a militarized network of command and control that constantly tests the limits of its authority. At one scale, the Department of Homeland Security's "National Asset Data Base" is an anticipatory (or aspirational) target list, a compilation of 77,000 sites that might figure in terrorist desires. The list appears ridiculous, including – among the bridges and power plants – the Amish Country Popcorn Factory, the Sweetwater Flea Market, and the Columbia Tennessee Mule Day Parade, and finding twice as many sites at risk in Indiana than in California. However, by publicizing the probabilistic absurdity of these places, a geography of paranoia is extended to embrace the most marginal and remote sites, drafting virtually any assembly into the regime of anxiety. A subsidiary benefit is to portray Homeland Security as Keystone-Copsish, an obvious far cry from anyone's Gestapo or KGB, taking the sting out of the existence of their lists.

Make no mistake, though: there are plenty who wish America ill, plenty ready to try to deliver, plenty angry at unexpected places: who could anticipate anthrax in the mail room of the *Star*, the shootings at Columbine, or the bodies under John Wayne Gacy's floorboards. This volume is not intended to debate our own responsibility in creating this animus – whether in the psychopathology of individuals or in the victimization of groups – rather to investigate what we, and others, are doing in response to it and what those responses mean for us. Although terrorism has a long history and invariably exists in a context of grievance, this book seeks to avoid unanswerable questions of cause and equivalence, weighing superior wrongs, original sin. The doomed outcome of such discussions is nowhere better exhibited than in the clogged conflict between Israel and Palestine in which attempts to assign differential responsibility – historically, ethically, metaphysically – are invariably manipulated to serve the purposes of intransigence. That situation is discussed in this book (which is mainly focused on US examples and models) precisely because it is so exemplary, a field of experiment for advanced strategies of terror and control, filled with revelatory asymmetries. As the pious and arcane discussion of

Right to the City F63

Homeland Security F34

structures, the UK government released a set of guidance documents for built-environment and security professionals concerned with reducing vulnerabilities in urban areas. Here it was reinforced that the threat from terrorist attack against crowded places was real and likely, and that in response the government had developed a strategic framework by which a range of key partners, including local government, the police, businesses, and built-environment professionals can reduce the vulnerability of crowded places to terrorist attack – *Working Together to Protect Crowded Places*.[70] More specifically, for those involved in the protective security of the everyday city, a series of technical and procedural guides were unveiled which aimed to give clarity over how counterterrorism might be appropriately and proportionately designed into the built fabric of cities.[71]

These documents highlighted that following 7/7 a much more proactive and integrated approach to protective counterterrorist security has emerged where instead of reacting at pace, a more reflexive response is now possible which accounts for issue, such as proportionality and aesthetics of design, as well as developing a strategic framework whereby many more stakeholders are given responsibility for delivering the CONTEST agenda. Protective counterterrorism is no longer just a police and security services issue, as many professional and practice communities, and the general public, are being enrolled in the fight against terrorism. In this sense it can be argued that we are all counterterrorists, engaged in the development of a more resilient and robust urban landscape. Although the *Protect* strand of CONTEST has helped reduce the occurrence and impact of terror attack, crowded places are still particularly vulnerable to terrorism as demonstrated on March 29, 2010, in Moscow; who suffered their own 7/7-style attack when two female suicide bombers attacked the underground system with devastating result – killing 39 and seriously injuring over 70. As the *Guardian* newspaper noted in its next-day editorial, "the impact is indiscriminate and lethal, in many cases life-ending, in all others life-changing. For a while chaos reigns in the city. Then comes the call for action and the pledges of revenge. Five years ago the city was London. Yesterday morning it was Moscow."[72]

Ornamental hostile vehicle mitigation (HVM) balustrades in Whitehall, central London

origins twists through its endless involutions, the technologies of repression do their dirty jobs and the web of hatred grows.

Political violence always seeks to justify itself, and the violence produced by the war on terror is no exception. The questions pursued here are primarily about the nature of that violence, the web of institutions and practices it produces, and the striking and coercive transformations in our physical and mental landscapes that are so profoundly coercive. There is a well-cultivated climate of fear in America and it registers at every level of our national life. This fear has its origins in both events and interests and the purpose of this collection is not to delve into this history in detail, rather to unpack some of its effects. These essays examine this mainly from the perspective of space, the kinds of rearrangements of the physical environment that mark an ongoing transition to a new set of conditions and constraints that have deep implications both for our habitat and our freedoms.

> "Political violence always seeks to justify itself, and the violence produced by the war on terror is no exception."

In order to understand these physical shifts, it is also important to understand transformations in the enabling discourse of the environment, structures that march in the streets to produce arrangements observable on the ground. These include, among other things, a new theoretical intercourse between urban and military theory, a shift in seeing that remakes both our own cities and those of our "adversaries" according to the values of war, rather than community, and a growing newspeak lexicon to insulate us from the real meaning of events.

There are a number of classic texts that anticipate the paranoid, militarized, character of this contemporary space. A dystopian literary tradition – from George Orwell's *1984* to Philip K. Dick's *Minority Report* – has portrayed the physical and mental media of totalitarian control with scary prescience. Cinematic science fiction – from *Metropolis* to *Blade Runner* to *Star Wars* to *The Truman Show*, the most telling medium for the projective imagination of city life – has, for years, given us almost nothing but nightmares, irresistible portraits of a creepy future, of pervasive mind control, dangerous and alienating spaces, concentrated power, endless violence, and cultural flatness against which the only recourse is death. The images surely dance in the stunted imaginations of Bush and Bin Laden both, two rich men decked out as warriors – flyboy or jihadist – with the semiotic panache of an Edith Head. In a world of total media, image is prophecy. Michel Foucault has founded what is perhaps the central metaphor for contemporary dystopian space (one that hovers over many of these essays): the Panopticon, Jeremy Bentham's proposal for a model prison built as a ring of cells supervised by an unseen jailor in a guard box at the center of the circle. The Panopticon is both a resonant symbol of the systems of surveillance that leave no corner of the earth unseen and of the mental life that they produce. The genius of the panoptic scheme lay less in its efficient supervisory geometry than in invisibility of the eyes at its center. Once the prisoners had been inculcated with the idea of their perpetual exposure, the prison

Panopticon[F53]

Theme: Security and Design
Author: Oscar Newman

Defensible Space as a Crime Preventive Measure
From: *Architectural Design for Crime Prevention*

could function even when the guard was absent. Persuaded that there was no escape from the gaze of authority, prisoners internalized the means of their own repression and behaved as *if* they were being watched, even without any concrete evidence that they were.

The idea of spatial arrangements as tools of control has a long history. The practices of architecture and urbanism – like that of so many human practices – are an endless dialectic of both physical and representational effects, invariably political in the concreteness with which they diagram social relations. Spaces of freedom – from the Athenian *polis*, to the cities of the Hanseatic League, to the barricaded streets of the Paris Commune, to Woodstock – offer empowered, if contested, images of constructed environments. Modernism, spawn of the Enlightenment, was – and is – suffused with narcissistic rationality and its rhetoric rang with reform. Building was to be a means of radical redistribution, providing access not simply to sunny, safe, and sanitary dwellings in a world in which everyone worked, and happily, but the crucible from which the "New Man" – the universal subject – was to emerge.

The urban project of modernism had, as its stimulating antagonist, the vision of the industrial city of the nineteenth century, with it darkness and filth, its enslavement of the working class to the machinery of production, and the horrible circumstances of daily life under Mammon's foot. Modernism's relationship to the parallel emergence of the bourgeois city was a shade more ambivalent. Here was a place of sumptuary inequality at once entrancing and fraught, simultaneously dedicated to private consumption and filled with spaces of public life. The boulevards and cafés, the department stores and electric light, the crowds and the movement, required new subjects, new behaviors, new analysis, new politics. Captivated and distressed, its great observers – Poe, Dreiser, Simmel, Beaudelaire, Wharton, Benjamin, Marx, Flaubert – understood the rapidity with which new sites for both freedom and constraint were being produced by it. The model citizens of the city – the detective, the flaneur, the clerk, the bohemian, the shopper – peopled a discourse in which space and behavior were both entangled and autonomous.

These complex antinomies of degradation and pleasure, liberation and control, openness and defense, form the imaginative substrate for the formal study of the city and for the emergence of modern urban planning that took place during the nineteenth and twentieth centuries. Successively codified and inflected in the field, these practices assumed both that the city could be understood – demographically, economically, sociologically, ecologically, politically, morphologically – and, by extension, that it could be designed to achieve these effects. Although issues of control of both internal and external disorder and contamination have been part of the history of cities from the

Barricade[F07]

"The practices of architecture and urbanism – like that of so many human practices – are an endless dialectic of both physical and representational effects, invariably political in the concreteness with which they diagram social relations."

A. Origins of Defensible Space

The term *defensible space* was born at Washington University in St. Louis, Mo., in the spring of 1964 when a group involved in the study of ghetto life in the now notorious public housing project Pruitt-Igoe, began an inquiry into the possible effects of the architectural setting on the social malaise of the community, and on the crime and vandalism rampant there.

At roundtable discussions involving two sociologists, Lee Rainwater and Roger Walker; two architects, Oscar Newman and Roger Montgomery; and members of the St. Louis Police Academy, an endeavor was made to isolate those physical features which produced secure residential settings – even in the midst of social disintegration and terror. Plans of isolated, well-functioning groupings of apartments, within the Pruitt-Igoe complex, were examined to determine what those physical ingredients were that made them workable.

At first hesitatingly, and then with increased assurance, it was agreed that something in the positioning of these limited number of units encouraged tenants to adopt a protective attitude toward the shared space outside their apartments, and that this attitude led to the upkeep of the area and to its safe use. Everywhere else in the Pruitt-Igoe project, apartments were so positioned along corridors that tenants and intruders alike unmistakably understood that the space outside apartments was public and under nobody's sphere of influence. Privacy began on the inside of a family's apartment door – everything else was just not defendable.

In our subsequent interviews with tenants it became clear that the terms they were using to distinguish those areas they felt they had rights to were in fact evocative of descriptions of besieged encampments. *Defensible space* became for resident and researcher the term most aptly describing the problem at hand.

Five years later the sickness of Pruitt-Igoe has become a national malaise and inner-city life universally recognized as a risky venture. In response, the President's Safe Streets Act of 1968 created the opportunity for intensive, long-term studies of the problem, among which is this analysis of the influence of the physical environment on the occurrence of crime.

Over the past two years, an interdisciplinary team of architects and social scientists at New York University have been involved in determining the extent to which the physical design of residential complexes and their disposition in the urban setting affects the frequency of crime and vandalism. How, through the choice of building prototypes, the grouping and positioning of apartment units and buildings, the placement of paths, windows, stairwells, doors, and elevators,

---

Newman

Canadian-born American architect Oscar Newman (1935–2004) is credited as a forerunner to theories of Crime Prevention Through Environmental Design (CPTED) with his theory of defensible space. His 1972 book of the same name was based on a study of the relationship between crime and specific spatial configurations in the infamous Pruitt-Igoe houses in St. Louis, Missouri, in the late 1960s and early 1970s carried out in collaboration with a team of architects, sociologists, and criminologists. Informed by a behaviorist reading of spatial environments, (according to the book website defensiblespace.com), the defensible space theory proposes the physical restructuring of housing projects and residential communities to reduce crime and improve stability through an emphasis on individual resident responsibility, private property, and territoriality. Newman's theories, which focus on spatial rather than social causes of crime, would have wide influence in the United States, the UK, and elsewhere, for example, as one of the main inspirations for UK programs Designing Out Crime and Security by Design. Newman's thinking is similarly influential among Norwegian security advisors, who have predominantly been educated in the UK.

This text was first published in Newman's book *Architectural Design for Crime Prevention* (Washington, DC: Government Printing Office, 1973).

first and have registered physically in the form of walls, castles, passages, turnstiles, cathedrals, plazas, aqueducts, coliseums, dungeons, and the rest of the infrastructure of urban construction, the combination of the totalizing style of rationalism, the appearance of a population of modern urban subjects, the dramatic increase in the scale of urbanization, the availability of new technologies of movement, communication, and hygiene, and the rise of bureaucratic systems of urban governance and management, engendered a radical shift in ideas about what the city could be and what it could do.

As many will have recognized, the title of this volume evokes Oscar Newman's *Defensible Space* of 1973. Subtitled *Crime Prevention through Urban Design*, Newman's book was part of a broader critique of the public housing projects of postwar urban renewal, increasingly seen as vertical ghettoes and – like the environments they were meant to "cure" – more and more ravaged by crime. Like Jane Jacobs, who argued in her 1961 *Death and Life of Great American Cities* that a vital neighborhood ecology required the constant presence of the benign "eyes on the street" provided by shopkeepers, pedestrians, and intimate scale, Newman believed that the key to a safe environment lay in a sense of its tractability and control. His prescriptions for "defensible" places were about physical means of establishing a sense of proprietorship for individuals via articulate hierarchies of public and private, careful modulations of visibility, and clarity of intended use.

> "The fallacy lies in the imagined eternity of good intentions, in the notion of technology's neutrality, in the idea that, treated properly, Big Brother can be a helpful guy."

Although Newman's analysis originated in a liberal perspective, and while many of his prescriptions made sense – particularly in their desire to promote architectures that would affirm individual identity and control – the book has a disquietingly behaviorist aura, raises many problematic questions about the relationship of community and privacy (and of medium and message), and – by emphasizing the physical – mislocates larger issues. He praises, for example, the architecture of a middle-class urban renewal scheme on the South Side of Chicago (much reviled by Jacobs) while ignoring the context of the removal of a poor population previously on-site. He proposes a system of "natural surveillance through electronic devices" for a New York City housing project but suggests it be monitored by "tenant patrols." The fallacy lies in the imagined eternity of good intentions, in the notion of technology's neutrality, in the idea that, treated properly, Big Brother can be a helpful guy.

While Newman's work may have been well intended, his project carried on the larger idea of an instrumental architecture, able to conduce forms of good behavior, a project embodied in the founding rationality of the same failed housing projects Newman sought to reform, not to mention the Panopticon itself. Although the line between empowerment and manipulation can be fine, design culture today is again shot through with a sense of the preventive dimension of its practices and – especially

Natural Surveillance[F47]

architects unintentionally produce residential settings which make their inhabitants prone to victimization. By contrast where buildings and ground designs are able to reinforce tenant attitudes, they enable inhabitants to adopt behavior which can lead to safer, more productively functioning living environments. All of which can serve to temper the fear and paranoia presently pervading the urban scene.

Fundamentally, the physical mechanisms we have isolated as contributing to the creation of defensible space have the purpose of enabling inhabitants to themselves assume primary authority for insuring safe, well-maintained residential areas.

Where the research component of our study predominantly involves public housing projects, the results of our findings are applicable to the residential settings of most income groups. The final chapter of this monograph, "Current Practitioners of Defensible Space," presents examples of housing ranging from the inner city to the suburbs – from the East Coast to the West. But in all these instances, the physical mechanisms operating to create safety and improve upkeep fall under the category of "self-help." The designs catalyze the natural productive impulses of residents, rather than lead them to surrender these shared social responsibilities to an area of formal authority: police, management, security guards, or doormen.

> "The designs catalyze the natural productive impulses of residents, rather than lead them to surrender these shared social responsibilities to an area of formal authority."

B. Physical Mechanisms for Achieving Defensible Space

We have isolated four categories of physical design ingredients which, independently and in concert, we see as significantly contributing to the creation of secure environments:

Those which serve to define spheres of territorial influence by dividing the residential environment into subzones within which occupants can easily adopt proprietary attitudes;

Those which improve the natural capability of residents and their agents to visually survey the exterior and interior public areas of their residential environment;

Those which enhance the safety of adjoining areas through the strategic geographic location of intensively used communal facilities;

And finally, those which through judicious use of building materials, the tools of architectural composition and site planning are able to reduce the perception of peculiarity – the vulnerability, isolation, and stigma of housing projects and their residents.

C. Apologies to the Right and Left

There have been many occasions over the past three years to discuss our findings with public housing residents, police, and community leaders. It would be misleading to suggest that our ideas have always been warmly received. More often than not, they have met with initial skepticism. Residents, living with the hour-to-hour terror of public

since 9/11 – virtually every aspect is being reimagined from the perspective of threat, whether of terrorism, criminal intrusion, environmental decay, or giant hurricanes. Articulated as completely comparable to measures to assure fire safety or structural integrity in buildings, this threat resistance is naturalized by association with these unarguable operations, as if there were a universal equivalence in risk between earthquakes and machine gun attacks.

One of the more sinister locutions of the effort to co-opt planning and design for national security purposes is the "deputizing" of ordinary objects to do double duty as barriers. The proliferation of blast-proof planters, bollard phalanxes, and beefed-up street lamps represents the same instrumental mentality that helped inform Newman's work, now dramatically modified by a very different threat and a very different set of objectives. In both practices, though, the presumption of danger becomes the defining criterion for planning: a high level of risk is always assumed and everything that follows is simply tactical. It is part of the astute manipulation by the operatives of the Insecurity State that the discussion of its methods always seems to engage the very risks they pose to our liberties as a way of forestalling any question of their larger necessity. I have just gotten off the phone with a reporter from *USA Today* who has called for my opinion about the design of bollards, about whether their unsightliness might be mitigated by greater use of the more inconspicuous CCTV. I have told her that this is like asking whether the cells at Guantánamo should be wallpapered or carpeted, that the problem with the prison is not the design but the fact. And so we are left answering questions about how the medium of security should present itself, the visible cameras versus the hidden ones, the uniformed cop versus the one in plain clothes, the obvious barrier versus the more behavioral one, how *much* freedom to give up for the sake of "security." Proportionality is an issue that arises only *after* the surrender to fear.

The struggle over the roll-out of the National Insecurity State must engage whether it is really necessary – defensible – and the question of to whom its benefits are actually addressed. Halliburton stock is doing nicely. The Department of Homeland Security is hemorrhaging personnel to the go-go private security sector, to creepy corporations founded on lucrative anxiety like Fortress America, Civitas Group, Roam Secure, Good Harbor Consulting, Shifting Culture, ChoicePoint, Global Secure, Cross Match Technology, as well as to historic defense heavies such as Lockheed Martin, GE, or Unisys. The lacuna in national purpose opened by the end of the Cold War is being filled by a recontoured `military-security-industrial-infotainment complex`, even as Kim Jong Il – as if on signal – lofts his dud missiles to rejuvenate the languishing Star Wars program. The intelligence "community" sees its resources and possibilities expanding exponentially. Hundreds of billions of dollars are pumped down

> "The presumption of danger becomes the defining criterion for planning: a high level of risk is always assumed and everything that follows is simply tactical."

Security-Industrial Complex F70

> "The full impact of what is possible through architectural design is not commonly known. Architecture design does not deal only with style, image, and comfort; it can create and prevent opportunity for encounter within a space, in many instances, simply by not providing that space."

housing, behind steel-plated doors showing the scars of axe blows, have at times expressed incredulous wonder at our naïveté. Police, coping with groups of roving teenagers and with drug addicts, both apparently unconcerned with the risks involved or with the possibility of apprehension, have pointed out the costs of physical modifications when compared with police reinforcements. Ghetto community leaders and social scientists involved in antipoverty programs have challenged our fundamental premise, asking if we believe that the crime born of a poverty of means, of opportunity, of education, of representation, could really be answered by the dictates of architectural form. It may be necessary, therefore, to speak to these questions before going into further detail on our work.

We have found that as universal as the skepticism that greets us is the lack of knowledge that a variety of different residential building prototypes can be employed to do the same job, and usually at the same costs. The 150 families trapped in the isolation of the double-loaded corridors of a high-rise apartment building with a single entry found it hard to understand that the three- to six-story buildings across the street, where two to three families share a hallway and only six to twelve share an entry, was a building alternate which could accommodate equal densities and could be built at the same cost. Where their building suffered the ravages of crime and vandalism, the other building prototype, different from theirs, succeeded in avoiding many of their problems simply by not having created them in the first place. The full impact of what is possible through architectural design is not commonly known. Architecture design does not deal only with style, image, and comfort; it can create and prevent opportunity for encounter within a space, in many instances, simply by not providing that space.

Police were surprised to learn that the attitudes of people toward policemen – people from the same areas of their precincts and sharing identical social characteristics, were radically different in different building types. In comparing the attitudes of tenants in two building prototypes situated adjacent to each other in a high-crime area, we found that residents in one felt positively about police and their capacity to come to their assistance while their neighbors expressed skepticism and what appeared to be a fear of police. Interviewed on both projects, police said they experienced greater difficulty in responding to calls in the latter because of tenant indifference and hostility, coupled with the problems involved in actually locating apartments within the labyrinth of the project. Some police also noted that the means of evasion and egress open to the criminal in the latter building prototype were so numerous, in the profusion of corridors, fire-stairs and exits, that pursuit was impossible – and immediate response was unlikely to lead to arrests.

It is important that we emphasize at the outset that our proposals for the modifications of building form to improve security are not intended as an alternate expenditure to police protection, but rather as an alternate to other building forms notorious for the security problems they inherently create. [...]

this pipeline, diverting attention and resources from other risks – disease, environmental degradation, mass starvation, automobile accidents, killers on a scale that makes the aggregate effects of terrorism microscopic, however focusing they may be for collective anxiety.

Although the threat of "terror" is surely real, this volume questions its location and weighs the relationship between its plausible danger and the nature of our response. The "homeland" has not been attacked since 9/11 but it is not clear whether this is the product of increased vigilance (signaled by periodic announcements of the interception of some unspecified threat or the presentation of "aspirational" conspirators nipped in the bud) or simply *post hoc ergo propter hoc*. In either case, the credibility of the threat barometer depends on persuasive evidence of the imminence of mass destruction. Absent any at home, the administration and the media rely on a pathetic displacement. Images of the horrific carnage in Iraq, of the daily car bombs, IEDs, suicide attacks, and mass murders, are leveraged by a fallacious logic to suggest that if it weren't happening there, it would be here. And what if we were to leave Iraq and bombs failed to go off on Broadway?

Cultures produce the threats they need and the "war on terror" is part of a larger project of fear-fed manipulations that is a profound danger to our rights and possibilities. This book is conceived in alarm and, looking at the spaces around us, it seeks to focus attention on the rapid institutionalization of a series of protocols and arrangements that – in the guise of offering us "comfort" – narrow the terms of our freedom of association, interaction, and choice. We are being trained to be phobic, to be constantly on guard, to stay at home, to be wary of difference. Gated communities and the homogeneities of gentrification provide "safe" communities via radical resegregation. American houses grow exponentially larger, laced with security and communications devices, demanding a protective indolence and estranging us from neighborliness. Architectures of vague nostalgia reassure us of the vitality and relevance of family values and less dangerous times and call other forms of expression – sexual, artistic, political – into question. Surveillance is everywhere.

Scare tactics are nothing new. My own first exposure to the architecture of state-sponsored terror came during the Cold War days. After the repeated duck-and-cover training that began in grammar school, after the school visit to the neighborhood Nike missile site, after an afternoon of frantically trying to dig a fallout shelter in the backyard, I had been thoroughly introduced to a style of paranoia, the well-named dread specific to the day. That complex of fears – much like today's – had enormous consequences for the investment of the national wealth, the definition of a population of irredeemable others who viewed us with pure, unreasoned malevolence, and the deepening suspicion of the presence of an invisible seam of traitors that could only be detected through police-state scrutiny and a

> "Hundreds of billions of dollars are pumped down this pipeline, diverting attention and resources from other risks."

Displace-ment [F24]

We see our work as operating at a different and independent level of crime prevention. It should not be seen as a replacement of antipoverty programs or additional police, but rather as an independently operating mechanism. If we thought that public officials involved in the allocation of scarce resources saw our proposals as an alternate to investment in other programs, then a case could indeed be made that we were detracting from more primary efforts at crime prevention. However, the need for low- and middle-income housing will be with us for a long time to come. In fact it is just beginning to be felt; and as long as we are going to provide it, we might as well learn something about the success and failure of what we have been providing in the past. Our study is directed at developing directives for insuring that funds put into new housing result in secure and productive living environments.

Lee Rainwater in his article, "Fear and the House as Haven," about his study of Pruitt-Igoe, defined security as the most important need to be satisfied in a residence for low-income groups.[1]

He further demonstrates that feelings of insecurity in one's residential environment can lead to the adoption of a negative and defeatist view of oneself, to ambivalence about job-finding and to expressions of general impotence in the capacity to cope with the outside world. The secure residential environment – understood by a resident as haven and read by outsiders as an expression of his ego – may in fact be a most cogent form of social rehabilitation, significant on the level of antipoverty programs.

D. Defensible Space as a Crime Preventive Measure

The prevention of crime covers a wide range of activities: Eliminating social conditions closely associated with crime; improving the ability of the criminal justice system to detect, apprehend, judge, and reintegrate into their communities those who commit crimes; and reducing the situations in which crimes are most likely to be committed.

The Challenge of Crime in a Free Society. Report by the President's Commission on Law Enforcement and Administration of Justice[2]

From the above one can identify three approaches to crime and delinquency prevention: Corrective prevention, punitive prevention, and mechanical prevention.

Programs of corrective prevention begin with the premise that criminal behavior is the result of various social, psychological, and economic factors. Corrective prevention is therefore directed at understanding and eliminating those causes before their effect on the individual channels him into crime. Factors frequently cited as precipitating criminal behavior include economic instability, a history of family problems, lack of opportunity for participation in the accepted lifestyle of society, and a personal susceptibility to narcotics addiction.

Punitive prevention, by contrast, involves efforts by authorities at forestalling crime by making more evident the threat of punishment

> "One can identify three approaches to crime and delinquency prevention: corrective prevention, punitive prevention, and mechanical prevention."

manly disdain for civil liberties, privacy, and freedom from fear of the Big Other. It had also, in part, dictated the pattern of the suburbs where I lived. Encouraged by national subsidy for highways and mortgages, the suburbs were, inter alia, a settlement pattern created to promote a protective dispersion of population, to vitiate the effects of the A-bomb.

Paul Virilio has written about the relationship of warfare and the scopic – the weapon and the eye – the cinematic view from above that has universalized the planet as a target. One is amazed and appalled by assassinations carried out by American and Israeli robot planes, firing missiles through the windows of cars or apartments, but quickly understands that this is the contemporary projection of panoptic power: to be seen is to be dead. In the words of former US Defense Secretary William Perry, "once you can see the target, you can expect to destroy it." The willing surrender of our privacy because of the blandishments of an illusory fear makes us all targets of suspicion, of attack. Because of new technologies of intrusion, architecture is rapidly losing its primal role as a barrier to seeing.

Hellfire missiles are just part of the threat. The symmetries between our networks of consumption and surveillance, between A. J. Nielsen and the NSA, are not simply technological coincidences. A legion of spooks is trying to corner Osama with the same cookies that flood my computer with spam. Bin Laden's star power – the clarity of his brand – makes the whole thing go, works for both sides with equal effect. This is the meaning of "brandscape": the environment is becoming a field of choices controlled from the top, in which the power of the image is everything. As neoliberal economics reorganizes the planet into a unitary field of consumption, our choices become at once limitless and nil. Terrorism usefully inspires acquiescence in the rules and regs, the disciplines that come with living under siege. To escape the bombers, the child molesters, the alien hordes, the pathogenic atmosphere, the implacable misery of a world of inexplicable, raging, irrational, uncivilized others, we rip off our clothes for Panopticon, the price we pay for being safe. The terror and the violence, in its very randomness, also reassures us that accidents can still happen, that Big Brother (how dangerous could that idiot Bush be?) is not really in control, that we still have room.

"The lacuna in national purpose opened by the end of the Cold War is being filled by a recontoured military-security-industrial-infotainment complex, even as Kim Jong II – as if on signal – lofts his dud missiles to rejuvenate the languishing Star Wars program."

The surfeit of physicality of bombing and warfare, directed at the destruction of living flesh, lives in balance with the disembodied world of virtual and conceptual space. This fundamentally new condition informs the so-called revolution in military affairs, a fantasy tenaciously installed by the Rumsfeld Pentagon, in which warfare, conducted by remote control, is to have no effect on our own human "assets," only on the enemy other, still living in his or her own skin. But, because of a disturbing symmetry in asymmetrical warfare, the enemy flashes through

Asset[F03]

Lock^{F41}

and the likelihood of apprehension. Operationally, this includes the enactment of new and tougher laws; the reduction of the time period between arrest and trial; and the streamlining of the indicting process.

Programs of mechanical prevention are concerned with placing obstacles in the paths of criminals. It is a policy which for the moment accepts the existence of criminals, their modus operandi, and their victims, and frames a program for hardening criminal targets by making them more inaccessible. This is accomplished by providing more secure barriers in the form of better hardware and personnel. The operating mechanisms involve the hardening of target, increasing the risk of apprehension, and, finally, increasing the criminal's awareness of these risks.

Current local governmental efforts at crime prevention involve all three of the above categories: corrective, punitive, and mechanical. Mechanical prevention is usually advocated as the most immediate panacea, although programs directed at corrective prevention and at improving the judicial and punitive apparatus are under serious study in many cities.

Typical means for improving mechanical prevention include: manpower increases in the form of police, security guards, doormen, tenant patrols, and dogs; and mechanical and electronic devices in the form of more and better locks, alarms, electronic visual and auditory sensors, and motorized vehicles to improve the mobility and surveillance capacities of personnel.

The form of crime prevention we will be describing at length in this monograph, defensible space, was seen initially as a new form of mechanical prevention. However, as our work in understanding and defining the operating mechanisms of defensible space progressed over the course of two years of study, it became apparent that a good many of our formulations could, when implemented, act as rather cogent forms of *corrective prevention*: mechanisms which could, perhaps, contribute to the alleviation of some of the root causes of criminal behavior.

As an example, our study of housing projects has revealed that children who live in high-rise buildings have a poorly developed perception of individual privacy and little respect for territory. The extent to which a similar lack of awareness of the personal space and property rights of others, in equivalent-aged middle-class children, leads to subsequent criminal behavior remains for later study. What is of immediate importance to us is that there is early evidence that the physical form of the residential environment can in itself play a significant role in shaping the perception of children and in making them cognizant of the existence of zones of influence and therefore of the rights of others.

1. Security in Low- versus
Middle-Income Housing

The report of the President's Commission on Law Enforcement and Administration of Justice, 1968, in attempting to understand the nature of the current crime problem, was able to isolate the prevalence of crime in inner-city areas:

[...] of 2,780,015 offenses known to the police in 1965 - these were index crimes - some two million occurred in cities, more than half

the Web, self-organizing digital agency with an "improvised" explosion at the end. And so we must also police communications and ideas in their ethereal, disembodied, transactions – any one of which might be suspect – justified by the risk they pose to our bodies, ourselves. Are we surprised that the spectral Osama remains "uncaught" while simultaneously appearing everywhere? Because he is loose in hyperspace, we have reason to extend our domination – put our boots on the ground and our ears to the ether – to the ends of the earth and the spectrum. We sanction his free expression (despite occasional tepid cavils about Al Jazeera) in order to more effectively repress our own. Every tape that slips from his cave adds another layer to the form and meaning of the Insecurity State.

A recently passed Florida law forbids sex offenders from living within 1,000 feet of a school bus stop, effectively excluding them from almost every community in the state. It's classic zoning, red-lining the landscape with territories of exclusion. We have long segregated Native Americans, African Americans, Asian Americans, poor Americans with the authoritative rigor of "planning," protecting privilege by the construction of reservations, ghettos, internment camps, prisons, and gated communities. We have segregated female Americans in inviolate homes where many have endured the special terrorism of domestic violence. We have skillfully demonized recognizable groups – Irish, Blacks, Jews, immigrants – for their criminal potential, placing them under discriminatory scrutiny. Our tactics of selective repression are so well developed, they simply appear to be part of the landscape.

What makes the new war on terror more singular – more sinister – is that the convergence of unsettling fear, shadowy demonized foe, hyper-technology of ubiquitous reach, and the communal power of the corporate state, has truly globalized the condition of fear. If every space is susceptible to attack and every person a potential attacker, then the only recourse is to watch everyone and fortify everyplace. If every communication is potentially a fragment of conspiracy, then all must be recorded. Walking the streets nowadays, with troops at the subway entrance, barricades around buildings, cameras staring from lampposts, metal detectors and card-swipes at the office door, cops profuse, newsstands billboarding alerts from every cover, involuntary anxiety at the sight of handbags and kerchiefs, it feels – more and more – like the battle for freedom is being lost. This book seeks to be part of the defense.

> "If every space is susceptible to attack and every person a potential attacker, then the only recourse is to watch everyone and fortify everyplace."

a million occurred in suburbs, and about 170,000 occurred in rural areas.[3]

[...] Crime rates in American cities tend to be highest in the city center and decrease in relationship to the distance from the center. This typical distribution of crime rates is found even in medium-sized cities such as the city of Grand Rapids, Michigan.[4]

Although the President's Commission identifies the consistency with which serious crime occurs in low-income deteriorated areas, it is difficult to properly assign the causes of this increasing concentration of criminal behavior in our core urban residential areas over the past decade. Contributory factors are probably both social and physical in nature, and may involve the increasing concentration of the disadvantaged in our older urban areas; the mix of contrasting income groups in cities not normally present in our economically homogeneous suburbs; and possibly, the peculiar susceptibility of the form of our currently evolving inner urban areas to criminal behavior. A further factor may be concentration of criminal elements in what they have come to recognize as an easy target area; one in which their anonymity is assured and the evasion of pursuit and arrest simplified.

In any case, society's capacity for coping with these problems does not appear to have been able to keep pace with their rate of increase. Those members of the community who are in a position to exercise choice in the housing marketplace are moving their families to suburban areas. Many realize that the problems they are trying to escape may end up following them, but they hope at a much slower pace.

Our concern, within the framework of this study, lies in determining means for improving the livability and security of residential environments within the urban setting, particularly for low- and low-middle-income groups. There are approximately four million people living in public housing across the nation today and a comparable figure living in federally subsidized low-middle-income housing. These are people for whom housing choice in a free-market economy is severely limited. By the nature of their residential location and social associations they tend to be the most continually victimized. Victimization is also a more totally devastating experience to their life structure than it is for upper-income inhabitants. The provision of doormen and security personnel and the maintenance of costly security equipment have been the traditional means employed by upper-income groups for coping with crime problems in housing. These means are not possible within the budget allowance of public housing or federally assisted low-middle-income housing.

We feel that the present response of upper-income residents to the increasing crime problem is one which is introverted and withdrawn, and involves intentional isolation, restricting, and hardening of their private dwelling at the expense of immediately adjacent surroundings. This is coupled with their relegation to others of the traditional responsibilities adopted by citizenry for insuring the continuance of a viable, functioning living environment for their family and surrounding community.

Over the past year and a half we have been exploring the problem of security in low- and middle-income housing where provision of doormen and expensive security hardware is impossible; we have

Theme: Democracy and Security
Authors: Anna Minton and Jody Aked

"Fortress Britain": High Security, Insecurity and the Challenge of Preventing Harm

uncovered residential environments which by the nature of their physical layout are able to provide security and continue to function in even high-crime areas. In some instances we have been able to find these environments in immediate juxtaposition to others of different design which suffer the worst agonies of crime. An illustration will perhaps serve to point up the fundamental differences in security design for low- versus middle- and upper-income housing. The use of a doorman usually requires that entry be restricted to one point in a large complex. To accomplish this it is usually necessary to wall off a two- to ten-acre housing project. This can result in thousands of feet of street being removed from all forms of social and visual contact. A natural mechanism for providing for the safety of streets has therefore been sacrificed to insure the security of the residents only when within the confines of the complex.

> "The present response of upper-income residents to the increasing crime problem is one which is introverted and withdrawn, and involves intentional isolation."

In developments where the use of doormen is not possible due to prohibitive costs, successful designs have been those with as few units as possible sharing a common entry off the street. The designers of these projects have so positioned units, their windows and entries, and so prescribed paths of movement and activity areas, as to provide continuous natural surveillance to the street as well as the building.

While developments embodying both of the above solutions are directed at providing maximum security to their respective inhabitants, there is a fundamental difference in approach and in the beneficial spin-offs which obtain. The first approach is one in which tenants relegate responsibility for security to a hired individual. A doorman guarding one entry to a building complex serving 200 to 500 families is concerned predominantly with restricting entry into the complex. He cannot, by the definition of his job and within the framework of what is physically possible, also be concerned with the bordering streets on which the project sites. The second approach involves tying residential units to their service streets and requires of their occupants that they assume responsibility for the safety of these streets as an extension of their concern for their own domains. Where in the first instance internal security has been achieved by disavowing concern for the surrounding areas, in the second it has been accomplished by insuring that the surrounding streets be made equally secure. For the nonresident user of the street, the second solution is clearly preferable.

2. Nature of Crime and Its Occurrence
in Public Housing Projects
[...]
Perhaps the most revealing of the figures is that 70 percent of all recorded crime taking place in housing projects occurs within the buildings proper. This includes nearly all serious crime: Robbery, burglary, larceny, rape, and felonious assault. It leads us to conclude that the buildings themselves, rather than the grounds, are understood by criminals as being areas where his victim is most vulnerable and where the possibility for his observation or apprehension is most minimal. Much of this may be the result of the policy that public

Secured by Design [F68]

Introduction

Not long ago, Manchester City Council laid on a coach tour for policy experts. As we swept into an estate in a deprived part of the city, the whole coachload gasped and the tour guide exclaimed in shock. The square in the center of the estate was surrounded by thirty-foot-high spiked railings and the council building at one end resembled a militarized fortress.

This is a particularly extreme example, but today all our public buildings, including schools, hospitals and housing, come with high levels of security which are transforming the nature of the environment around us. At the same time fear of crime and concerns about safety and security are at an all-time high. Although crime has been falling steadily since 1995, the vast majority believe it is rising.[1]

High security is a now prerequisite of planning permission for all new developments, through a government-backed design policy called Secured by Design[2] which is aimed at housing, town center development and public buildings, from schools to hospitals. While this includes sensible recommendations, such as the need for adequate locks on doors and windows, the application of Secured by Design standards tends to create very-high-security environments which can appear threatening. For example, a gated development in East London which won a Secured by Design award was commended for its small windows, reinforced steel door with full-size iron gate and gray aluminum military-style roof.

Schools, in particular, have become high-security environments, emphasizing gating, high fences, and CCTV. Because Secured by Design requirements for schools and public buildings are based on an audit of local crime risk, higher-crime areas, which correlate with higher deprivation scores, are now characterized by public buildings, like the council building in Manchester, with a militarized feel to them. At the same time, greater concentrations of social housing, built to Secured by Design standards, tend to cluster in deprived areas. The unintended consequence is that fortress levels of security are now a visual marker for poor parts of Britain and a contemporary feature throughout the landscape.

Rising fear of crime and growing levels of distrust are key issues for policymakers. Supported by the police and the private

---

Minton & Aked

British journalist Anna Minton (1970–), known for her 2009 book *Ground Control: Fear and Happiness in the Twenty-first-Century City*, and psychologist Jody Aked (1981–) address the process by which regimes of high security in everyday urban environments have been normalized in the UK – environments such as public spaces, schools, and housing projects. Recounting the historic development of Secured by Design in the UK and its ties to the interpretation of the environmental determinist theories of Canadian-American architect Oscar Newman in the work of British geographer Alice Coleman, Minton and Aked ask if these approaches represent the solution or part of the problem. The article presents a field study into the effects of Secured by Design in Peabody Avenue, a social housing estate in Pimlico, London – addressing both residents and practitioners. It explores the extent to which the presence of high levels of security support or counter feelings of safety and trust among residents.

This text was first published by the New Economics Foundation in 2012.

"The square in the center of the estate was surrounded by thirty-foot-high spiked railings and the council building at one end resembled a militarized fortress."

housing projects by law and tradition are open to all members of the community. The interior of the buildings suffers, therefore, from being public in nature and yet hidden from public view and consequently unable to benefit from the continual surveillance to which the public areas of our cities are normally subject. [...]

E. The Secluded Adult Middle-Class Environment

In September of 1970, a 50,000-unit housing development, Co-op City, built privately for cooperative ownership, was completed in an outlying area of the Bronx, N.Y. It was occupied almost overnight, predominantly by an older middle-income-class population fleeing their neighborhood in an adjacent area of the Bronx. In a random interview of 50 residents, most found their new environs inferior to the areas they had abandoned:

Their apartments were smaller; the commercial facilities were few and goods more costly; there was little to no entertainment available: they had left many friends and institutions behind – and so on. Where many of these deficiencies may be remedied with the completion of the project in future years, the new residents bemoaned their loss only briefly. They all felt that the deficiencies were a small price to be paying for having been provided with what they most craved: security. They had succeeded in escaping from an environment, once friendly, but which now terrified them. The frequency of muggings, robberies, assaults – on an older generation – by new immigrants to "their neighborhood" had made continued life there impossible. Almost all of those interviewed said that in their old neighborhood they had long since given up any thought of going out at night. All knew of or had experienced burglaries firsthand.

What is fascinating and fearful is the way the population chose to solve its problem: They had fled en masse and isolated themselves in a new lower-middle-class ghetto of their own making. Now in Co-op City they live among their own kind: middle-aged or older, largely Jewish, Italian, or other ethnic backgrounds, with average incomes about $10,000. Normally, a gregarious, culture-seeking involved group, they now make do so that they can breathe more easily.

Interestingly from the viewpoint of this study, the buildings and residential settings they now occupy are much less defensible than what they left behind. If only a small percentage of the criminals that victimized them was transferred to within striking distance, they could wreak a havoc which would have made their abandoned neighborhood look a haven. In understanding what makes Co-op City safe and workable, if only for the present, there is much to be learned about the problems of securing residential environments and of the limitations of defensible space theory.

The New York City RAND Corp., in a study of crime in public housing to be published shortly, estimated that about half of the people responsible for crime lived in the very projects they victimized.

This estimate was difficult to make in that only a small percentage of criminals are apprehended; trial procedures are long, and convictions few. Nevertheless our interviews of hundreds of tenants and

> "The interior of the buildings suffers, therefore, from being public in nature and yet hidden from public view."

security and insurance industries, and meshing with the terrorism agenda, Secured by Design has been a reaction to very visible social problems faced by communities up and down the country, such as antisocial behavior and intergenerational distrust. Yet the focus on technological solutions has corresponded with reduced investment in "eyes on the ground," with efficiency drives leading to the disappearance of guardianship figures such as caretakers, park keepers, and bus conductors.

High security is now institutionalized by means of required security "standards." How and why did this become contemporary orthodoxy? How far does it help to prevent crime and fear of crime? Are current policies part of the solution or part of the problem? We explore these questions here, drawing upon a small field study and other research. We look first at the history of private security and theories of defensible space. Next, we set out the findings from field research in a London housing estate. We then examine the dynamics of high security and conclude by drawing out lessons for the prevention of harm.

The Spread of Private Security

Over the last thirty years, private property has become increasingly prominent in Britain. This has happened because of the growing importance placed on home ownership, and the spread of "mass private property," in the form of shopping malls, finance districts, airports, leisure parks, conference centers, university and hospital campuses and gated communities. The "mass private property thesis"[3] was defined by criminologists [Clifford] Shearing and [Phillip] Stenning in a seminal article in 1981, which pointed out that mass private property inevitably demanded private security.

> "Mass private property inevitably demanded private security."

This increase in private security creates a significantly different environment to that afforded by public policing. While the rule of law and the protection of the public is the goal of public policing, private security gives priority to the protection of property. The principle aim of the latter is to prevent harm to property in order to maximize commercial returns through rental and property values, to the satisfaction of clients and shareholders.

As private security has spread throughout urban environments, efficiency drives have led to the removal of local supervisory workers, such as park keepers, caretakers, and bus conductors. These – usually benign – authority figures were there to do a job which they carried out within the public realm and as a sideline they provided a guardianship role. By contrast, private security guards are there primarily as agents of enforcement, and may have powers to issue fines and sanctions.

Around the same time as the concept of mass private property entered intellectual discourse, the idea of "defensible space" was becoming influential. Coined by Oscar Newman, an American architect and town planner, this powerful design idea took hold on both sides of the Atlantic. It amounted to a new political and intellectual philosophy for crime and its prevention, expounding the virtues of private space, individual responsibility,

Housing Authority police confirm these findings with the following distinctions: That criminals do live a few blocks away but both within projects and surrounding area, and a criminal seldom if ever victimizes his own building except in cases involving interpersonal confrontations.

In this light, if one considers that low income also correlates highly with crime, moving away from an area which was becoming increasingly occupied by low-income families was correctly moving from crime. The question remains how far away is away? How long before the vulnerability of the new development is recognized? How long before the criminal extends his mobility and range of operation?

Distance we recognize is one operating mechanism at Co-op City that insures security – population uniformity is another. So long as all the families in Co-op City are white, middle-class and elderly, any dark-skinned young person, not partial to respectable habit, will stand out and have the police sicced on him. But there is already a small percentage of black and Puerto Rican young families living at Co-op City – equally seeking the good and secure life. This no doubt complicates things and will increasingly do so as the dust of the new development settles.

> "Segregation of income and age group remains the most potent crime preventive mechanism in operation at Co-op City."

Segregation of income and age group remains the most potent crime preventive mechanism in operation at Co-op City. The President's Commission found, as did all previous correlations of crime and age group, that males between the ages of 15 and 24 are the most crime-prone group in the population – and for the last 5 years this age group has been the fastest-growing in the population. Co-op City has fewer than 5 percent of its population between the ages of 15 and 24, while the 1970 census indicates a national average of 11.3 percent. The question is how long can Co-op City remain disproportionately populated? Criminologists suggest that high-density urban residential areas like the abandoned Bronx district provide a high degree of anonymity and social isolation which makes the communal control of the criminal difficult.

Interestingly, Co-op City at 50 dwelling units to the acre (including commercial facilities and roads) rivals this density. Strangely, too, the building prototypes employed, and their relative positioning makes the opportunity for anonymity far greater.

The fundamental premise of our "defensible space" proposals is the subdivision of the residential complex to allow inhabitants to distinguish neighbor from intruder. Where at Co-op City this was achieved by isolating a large, uniform population, it is a tactic not possible in existing, contiguous, diverse urban agglomerations. The scale for creating distinctions must therefore become finer. The very ingredient that prohibits the criminal from hitting his own building – the chance that he may be recognized, is the mechanism we wish to exploit and extend. Through hierarchical subclustering and extension of the areas of territorial domain to the public street, we hypothesize that an equivalent capacity for distinguishing neighbor from intruder can be achieved.

Our work is directed at the reorganization of the existing urban residential fabric to make it effective in today's evolving circumstance. We are committed to working for a low- and middle- income who

84 Photo Essay

WALL STREET, New York, NY, USA
Visited April 2, 2014

01. Active vehicle barriers and patrol booth

02. 03. 04. No-Go bollards deployed in tandem with Jersey barriers, buried mobile vehicle barriers and patrol booths.

Integrated cobble turnpikes have malfunctioned regularly and are now replaced by a buried mobile vehicle barrier.

Wall Street, New York, NY, USA

Photo Essay

Wall Street, New York, NY, USA

05. Fortified street and subway entrance

06. No-Go bollards and integrated cobble turnpikes have malfunctioned regularly and are now replaced by a buried mobile vehicle barrier.

07. To enter through the police barriers visitors must pass through a tent checkpoint.

and territoriality. It chimed with the rise of neoliberalism and moved to center stage with regard to urban policy in both America and Britain.

Well before 9/11 and the "War on Terror," high levels of security were an entrenched part of the environment. The "ring of steel" was a feature of the City of London from the early 1990s; changes in technology enabled John Major's government to roll out CCTV. Britain's preeminence in electronic surveillance can be traced to the adaptation for civilian purposes of military technology deployed in Northern Ireland. As a result, Britain became the world leader in CCTV.

The events of 9/11 and later the 7/7 London bombings widened and intensified the government's approach to security. In 2009 the Home Office issued "Working Together to Protect Crowded Places," signaling a shift in emphasis from "hard" to "soft" targets such as shopping centers, visitor attractions, major events, commercial centers, the health sector, the education sector, and "generally crowded places."[4] A subsequent Home Office review outlined how government should work with planners, architects and designers to "design in" security, with built environment professionals exhorted to work with private sector security businesses to these ends.[5]

The combined impact of the antiterrorism agenda, "defensible space" ideas and Secured by Design policy has been to normalize high security as part of the daily environment. These approaches now form a significant part of the security industry, which is one of Britain's fastest-growing sectors. A notoriously difficult industry to quantify, it encompasses individual operators and medium-sized firms selling security products and providing security services, all the way to vast multinational security conglomerates such as G4S, which has 530,000 employees worldwide. The UK industry body, the British Security Industry Association, estimated in 2006 that the industry employed 75,500 people and had a turnover of £4.3 billion, a figure which is likely to be much higher today. In 2010 it was estimated that the US security industry produced revenue of nearly $60 billion.[6] It is an industry which is subject to minimal scrutiny and debate – the recent G4S scandal over the London Olympics excepted[7] – with the threat of terrorism the justification for ever-increasing security.

Defensible Space

Oscar Newman's ideas originated with research on crime and violence in public housing, carried out in three housing projects in New York, which resulted in his landmark book, *Defensible Space: People and Design in the Violent City*, published in 1972.[8] The context for his work was growing concern over the rise in crime which appeared to be sweeping urban America, fueling fears that the US was experiencing a breakdown in society. In this climate of urgency, with policymakers desperate to find

Territoriality[F79]

"The combined impact of the antiterrorism agenda, 'defensible space' ideas and Secured by Design policy has been to normalize high security as part of the daily environment."

G4S[F31]

cannot buy the alternatives of moving out or personal doormen. Our interviews show rather conclusively that most ghetto and inner urban residents are as terrified and as victimized as the Co-op City escapees. The recently published Justice Department survey[5] reveals that where crime rates in ghetto areas are five times the urban average, most of the victims are ghetto residents. Only a very small percentage of ghetto dwellers are criminals – most are victims. What we are endeavoring is to find a means for strengthening the resistance capacity of the low-income victim.

Subtle difficulties arise in attempting to improve the security of low-income, as compared with middle-income housing; these are mainly a function of the social forces at work on the resident populations. The social characteristics of the middle class greatly facilitate the task of providing them with a secure environment. Middle-class people have developed a refined sense of property and ownership; they have a measure of self-confidence and pride in their personal capabilities. Their everyday experiences reinforce their social competence; they can retain some control over the forces that shape their lives, and they recognize alternatives among which they can choose. These positive social contacts give them a feeling of potency in protecting and enforcing their rights within a defined sphere of influence; for instance, they are well-practiced in their demand for and use of police protection.

In contrast, it is more difficult to improve security for a lower-class population, not because of a higher concentration of people with criminal intent, or because of limited financial resources, but because of attendant social problems. The life of the lower-class is conducted under duress. For the lower-class person, daily social contacts reinforce his feelings of impotence, erode his self-confidence, and make remote any possibility of improving the quality of his life. Having been closed out of the game – financially, politically, educationally, psychologically – he responds by changing the rules. It may indeed be unrealistic to expect an individual to assume positive social attitudes and influence in one sphere of his life when he has been told, clearly and consistently, in the other facets of his existence, that he has no such power.

It may appear, in our defensible space proposals, that we are viewing the world from a middle-class perspective; that we are trying to encourage everyone to assimilate middle-class values, and to assert essentially middle-class proprietary attitudes by providing them with a middle-class environment. Are we not forcing an attitude and lifestyle upon people who in fact do not desire it? To the contrary: our interviews with hundreds of public housing residents have revealed that an overwhelming majority of lower-class people hold the same goals and aspirations as do the middle class. Their formation of a distinct subculture has been their response to the constraints, both actual and psychological, imposed by the larger society. These findings are similar to those documented by Lee Rainwater in his study of Pruitt–Igoe residents, *Behind Ghetto Walls*:

> Lower-class people are amply exposed to both of these cultural ideals. They know that some people make it big by the job they have and the money they are able to accumulate, that others do not make it so big but manage to live comfortably in homes in pleasant

a way of dealing with the crime problem, Newman's research provided a relatively simple solution: rather than engaging with complex social relations as the underlying causes of crime, his work promoted the idea that the design of the environment was the key influence over behavior.

The appeal of Newman's thesis for policymakers was that it put forward a straightforward solution for preventing crime in highly complex situations, championing a "can do" method of changing people's behavior, which Newman claimed worked even in the poorest areas. He wrote: "The time has come to go back to first principles, to reexamine human habitat as it has evolved, to become attuned again to all the subtle devices invented over time and forgotten in our need and haste to house the many. For even within the widespread chaos of our cities, it is still possible to find isolated examples of working living environments which are crime-free, although at times located in the highest-crime precincts of our cities."[9]

From his study of three housing schemes – which were in particularly deprived neighborhoods – Newman's main finding was that "territoriality" created space that could defend itself. By marking out boundaries clearly, residents would feel a sense of ownership over places, encouraging them to look after their patch and discouraging strangers and opportunistic criminals from entering, so creating a safe haven.

Despite skepticism in academic circles, where Newman's ideas were criticized for their particular brand of environmental determinism, his book had such an influence on policymakers that, within two years of its publication, substantial American government funding was made available to study and implement defensible space concepts. Newman was subsequently employed by the US Department for Housing and Urban Development and the New York City Housing Authority, with his research funded by the National Institute of Law Enforcement and the US Department of Justice.[10]

Although the term Crime Prevention through Environmental Design (CPTED) was not originally coined by Newman, it became the umbrella term for a new industry on both sides of the Atlantic. In the US, practitioners in housing and the police were trained to implement the principles of CPTED in public housing. As the idea took hold, CPTED expanded into the design of private housing and public space.

The key figure responsible for importing Newman's ideas to Britain was the controversial geographer Alice Coleman. If Newman's work was received with skepticism among American peers, Coleman's 1985 book *Utopia on Trial: Visions and Reality in Planned Housing* was excoriated by critics who claimed that her dismissal of the influence of poverty was based on "pseudo science." Coleman's method was to map design features – from block size and number of stories to spatial arrangement, with "lapses in civil behavior" – such as litter, vandalism, and excrement. Unlike Newman, she did not have access to crime statistics so she had to rely on "material clues which could be objectively observed."[11]

On her initial encounter with the Department of Environment,

CPTED[F18]

neighborhoods, surrounded by an increasing measure of material comfort. Most lower-class people at some time entertain aspirations in one or both of these directions, and it makes no sense to talk of a lower-class culture so divorced from that of the larger society that the validity of these goals is denied. However, many lower-class people come to the conclusion that neither of these ways of life are possible for them.[6]

1. Territorial Exclusion and Crime Displacement

If the territorial reinforcement we are advocating does in fact empower certain groups to control the semipublic space adjacent to their dwelling units to the exclusion of others, are we not by this exclusion placing a further restriction on the already limited resources of our cities? Our early findings tend to give us hope that the opposite may in fact be true. Studies of the use of grounds of seven housing projects, paralleled with tenant interviews, has shown that the grounds of projects which were intentionally left open for public use – as a contribution by the housing authority to the open-space needs of the city – were unused by either group, public housing residents or members of the surrounding community. Each group, by experience, had found their activities easily disrupted by other groups and found that their laying claim to the right to use the space for play was difficult to enforce. By contrast, such space provided within the interior of a project and clearly defined by boundaries was more intensely used by both groups – by project residents first and most frequently and by surrounding neighborhood children and groups secondarily and casually at the invitation of the local group.

Publicly owned and perceived space in city playgrounds was found to be workable with the provision of a playground director who served as definer of the rules of space use, as settler of disputes, policeman, judge and executioner (. . . Out!). Is this perhaps not also the present role of city police in insuring the safe use of public streets?

In the course of our work we have received expressions of concern from members of communities adjacent to the projects we have been working in. Their concern is that our endeavors will only succeed in displacing crime from one area to another. There is some evidence to support their hypotheses. Arnold Berkman, Housing Authority police captain, who keeps careful tabulations of variations in crime rates in all areas of his jurisdiction, informs us that as a vigorous police effort takes place in one high-crime area, criminals respond by moving into adjacent areas. There is no evidence, however, that this is a 100 percent displacement.

The nature of criminal acts are sometimes distinguished by the intent and motivation of the criminal. Projects which have been made defensible will succeed only in displacing the hardened criminal involved in premeditated crime. Since a sizable percentage of crime is estimated to be crime of opportunity, our work in reducing opportunity may not result in too much displacement.

> "In the course of our work we have received expressions of concern from members of communities adjacent to the projects we have been working in. Their concern is that our endeavors will only succeed in displacing crime from one area to another."

Coleman was dismissed for failing to account for socioeconomic factors, but she nonetheless went on to gain the ear of Margaret Thatcher, whom she met in 1988. The upshot of that meeting was an unprecedented £50 million in government funding for what Thatcher considered "an important social experiment." The result was the Design Improvement Controlled Experiment (DICE), which enabled Coleman to introduce her design improvements into seven estates in London.[12] Thatcher later recalled in her memoirs: "I went further than the DoE in believing that the design of estates was crucial to their success and reducing the amount of crime. I was a great admirer of the works of Professor Alice Coleman and I had made her an advisor to the DoE, to their dismay."[13]

As defensible space ideas filtered into British policy-making circles, Secured by Design, which is the British version of CPTED, came into being under the auspices of the Association of Chief Police Officers (ACPO). Like CPTED, Secured by Design, which started life in 1989, led to police officers' being trained as crime prevention design advisors, known as Architectural Liaison Officers, and has created design standards and an awards scheme. Its influence is considerable: planning permission for all public buildings, housing, and schools is now contingent on meeting Secured by Design standards.

Although it is administered by the Association of Chief Police Officers, Secured by Design is now an independent private company, funded by 480 security companies which sell products which qualify for Secured by Design standards.

> "Planning permission for all public buildings, housing, and schools is now contingent on meeting Secured by Design standards."

Schools

Secured by Design standards for schools were introduced in the UK in 2004, coinciding with the New Labour government's large school-building program. The result has been that schools in the UK have become high-security environments. Growing anxiety around child protection issues and concerns over antisocial behavior among young people have created a culture of acceptance of growing security, among both young people and staff.

The starting point for Secured by Design in schools is a crime risk assessment which is carried out for the local area. While high fences, walls, or other "effective barriers" are a "prerequisite" for any school, the crime risk assessment will indicate where additional security measures are necessary.[14] This means that in higher-crime areas security around schools is much greater, creating schools which have a militarized feel to them. Higher-crime areas tend to be poor or to have pockets of poverty. As a result, deprived neighborhoods are now characterized by schools – and other public buildings such as council offices – which come with fortress levels of security.

Fence F28

> "In higher-crime areas security around schools is much greater, creating schools which have a militarized feel to them."

Our work is primarily concerned with making the residential environment a haven from external crime. The long-term crime prevention implications of a secure home cannot be understated – particularly for low-income groups. In many ways we would be content in achieving only that. But in so doing it may be that through the ensuing displacement of crime we would be making other non-residential functional areas of our cities more unsafe: shopping, institutional and business areas. For the moment we are content to argue that we feel these areas are served better and inherently benefit more from formal police protection.

Perhaps too, having succeeded in securing the residential environment from crime, and accepting for the sake of argument that displacement is total, it may not be an altogether insignificant accomplishment. If one accepts as a proposition that the total amount of crime cannot be diminished, only displaced, the question arises is it then preferable to have a pattern of uniformly distributed crime or one of crime concentrated in particular areas and absent in others? We feel the second proposition to be more desirable: the home and its environs must be felt to be secure or we begin to threaten the very fabric of our society. People will, we believe from our interviewing, accept the fact that certain areas of their city are unsafe and that there is risk involved in their use. This will and does limit people's use of them to special or necessary occasions. And too, people will, if very frightened, find collective means for using these areas to add to their safety. But the home is the area on which no restriction of use can be placed. We spend most of our time there; it is where our future generations are raised – where our most susceptible members live. It is the shelter to which we return from our forays. It must he secured, even at the expense of making other areas more dangerous.

There are, however, serious moral implications to the question of displacement and they are not easily dismissed. In the next few years of our study we will be examining the changing patterns of crime in the areas surrounding the projects we have altered just as closely as the projects themselves. The full extent of the displacement problem must be understood and means for coping with it developed.

2. Conspicuous Absence of Consideration Given to Security by Architects

Another point must be made: This in the form of an apology for the architectural profession. As it becomes evident from our ensuing discussion that different physical environments can, in fact, so affect behavior as to reduce crime and vandalism rates by over 50 percent, the question must occur, "as to why the architectural profession continues to provide those environments which result in high-crime rates, the destruction of property and the terrorization of inhabitants, and which make the residential population particularly prone to criminal action." The explanation probably does little to enhance the view of the profession held by the public, but we hope that the very act of this research will also temper any critical view we may be responsible for creating.

Little work has been done within the profession to scientifically measure the impact of physical design on the psychological attitudes and social behavior of an environment's users. The number of factors requiring synthesis and resolution in the design of a building is so

The Secured by Design Schools Guidance document accepts that this can create a shocking visual marker, but maintains that this is offset by reducing crime risk. "It is accepted that some security-rated fencing systems can be both costly and aesthetically unpleasing. However, the type of fencing that is required in order to gain SBD recognition must ultimately be determined by local crime risks," the document states. In high-crime locations "antiram" bollards are recommended to protect entrances.[15]

The Secured by Design guidance document includes 31 specific recommendations for all schools. These range from fencing, gates, and security bollards to roller shutters and grilles, electronic locking systems, metal detectors, and, of course, CCTV. The 31 product categories link directly to the "members and products" section of the Secured by Design website, where the security products can be purchased.

The group Big Brother Watch estimates that there are now more than 100,000 CCTV cameras in secondary schools and academies in England, Scotland, and Wales, despite the lack of any compelling evidence that CCTV improves safety or reduces fear of crime. At Saint Mary's CE high school, for example, in Cheshunt, in Hertfordshire, 162 cameras have been introduced, including 18 in the toilets. The number of cameras installed complies with the guidance received when this secondary school building was completed in 2010.[16]

It is important to note that increased security measures are not a matter for debate but are now "standards" which must be met. Indeed, the granting of a Secured by Design certificate depends not only on creating a secure teaching environment but also on reducing the school's carbon footprint.[17] Secured by Design is now institutionalized, as much a part of conventional orthodoxy as carbon reduction.

Reflecting the level of demand for these types of security measures, the director of a company providing security fencing said: "We started off doing things like prisons, airports… high-security environments, and now we're increasingly doing more schools and multiuse games areas [playgrounds]."

Consequences: The Impact of
Growing Security in the Environment

How far do the ideas and policies of "defensible space" and Secured by Design prevent crime or fear of crime, or help to create strong, stable communities? There are clearly many sensible recommendations associated with Secured by Design products, such as adequate locks on doors and windows and the need for open spaces to be overlooked. However, there is scant evidence that the spread of gating, CCTV, and defensible space strategies create safe, cohesive, and trusting communities. Of the few existing studies, an investigation into CCTV by the Scottish Office found that, while people often believed CCTV would make them feel safer, the opposite was true: both crime and the fear of crime rose in the area investigated. The author concluded the introduction of CCTV had undermined people's personal and collective responsibility for each other's safety.[18] Research on defensible space, which discourages the presence of strangers,

Bollard[F09]

large, and at times so conflicting, that unsubstantiated insights into the relationship of architecture to behavior often go by the board. In justice, we have encountered many architects who intuitively shared our findings. Many have incorporated them as directives in some building designs, but have excluded them in others, in what may appear as facile inconsistency. Their justification for this apparent ambivalence is their uncertainty as to the real effectiveness of these design considerations. Another set of important pressures are the building and fire codes of each community and the economic restraints on the developer which together conspire to make secondary any consideration of insights into the security implications of design.

Restrictions on the Planning Freedom of Architects

For the most part the planning directives which result from our hypotheses can be incorporated in the design of residential groupings without restricting either the compositional imagination of the architect-planner or restricting his more professional role of providing for the functional needs of residents. The rules governing design for defensibility are not of the nature that they replace other design heuristics, or prevent inclusion of other functions. On the contrary, as should be made plain later, they can ensure that those amenities provided will actually be used.

Our preliminary work has already indicated that some of our design directives will run afoul of building codes and fire regulations in some cities. Other of our innovations indicate the need for revising accepted high-rise housing design practices, presently dictated by and strongly reflecting frugal economic practice. These issues will have to be dealt with in detail and at length in a future component of the study dealing with effectuation. Until we can address ourselves fully to these questions, we have selected for inclusion in this monograph only those examples and proposals which are immediately applicable.

Limitations in Causal Capacities

Fundamental to this monograph is the proposition that through manipulation of the building and spatial configurations we can create areas for which people will adopt a territorial concern. This may suggest that if our data and design were sophisticated enough, it would be possible to predict and control a wide range of behavior and social relationships through provision of particular architectural settings. Ours is a much smaller thesis: That it is possible through the provision of facilities in certain juxtapositions to allow the release of behavioral attitudes and social relationships which are latent. As an example: The provision of play facilities for infants at each floor level of an apartment building, defined by the doors of the apartments facing it, may bring mothers out to use it and may further result in the development of limited friendships and the cognizance of neighbors; a desire to keep up the facility and make it secure for the children; and a recognition and screening of strangers.

These relationships are understood to be those of mutual assistance to support commonly desired situations. Mutual assistance may in some instances lead to further friendships and the sharing of responsibilities in the care of children, etc., but these are unimportant to the operation of our hypotheses. The recorded instances of a few

suggests that this approach can in fact increase fear of strangers: an "unintended consequence" of extra security can be to raise concerns over safety and "symbols of security can remind us of our insecurities."[19]

Professor Jon Coaffee questions the impact of visible security measures on individual and group perceptions, examining whether they can make people feel vulnerable, alienated, or excluded. His research is focused on terrorism and extremism, and his findings suggest that a fortress environment mirrors "radical" tendencies while a sensitively built environment might help mediate them.[20] This may apply similarly to high-security architecture in deprived areas, which correlate with higher-crime areas.

Research into the causes of social stress, which has been associated with urban environments, has found that an important determinant is the degree of control that people feel they have over their immediate environment.[21] American planner Kevin Lynch emphasizes the importance of open, flexible spaces that enable individuals to "demonstrate mastery" over the environment.[22] Research into uncertainty, powerlessness, and change in the workplace offer further insights: "We tend to withdraw, become more self-serving, and more defensive. We focus on smaller and smaller details, those things we can control. It becomes more difficult to work together, and nearly impossible to focus on the bigger picture," writes Margaret Wheatley.[23]

To add to this rather slim body of research, our field study examines the effects of Secured by Design in a social housing estate in south-west London.

> "While people often believed CCTV would make them feel safer, the opposite was true: both crime and the fear of crime rose in the area investigated."

Peabody Avenue, Pimlico

To determine attitudes and perceptions to security, fear, trust, and cohesion among communities living in a Secured by Design environment, focus groups and interviews were carried out with residents and practitioners working on Peabody Avenue, a Peabody Trust estate in Pimlico in London. The practitioners worked in neighborhood management, estate services, community safety, youth services, and outdoor spaces. Fifty-five new homes were recently completed at Peabody Avenue, so that architects and housing managers were bound to become closely acquainted with Secured by Design guidelines. Housing standards for Secured by Design are based on the advice of the local Architectural Liaison Officer, the police design advisor tasked with ensuring Secured by Design standards are met in new developments.

At the beginning of the sessions we began by defining what high security meant for the groups. Their definition included gating, fencing, removing permeable spaces, gating off entrances and exits, CCTV across the whole site, security guards wearing high-visibility uniforms, alarm systems, and electronic systems. This covered some elements of Secured by Design and missed out others; it should not be seen as directly interchangeable with Secured by Design policies.

welfare-supported mothers cooperatively sharing a house is not we feel a byproduct of a shared architectural setting, but of a social and possibly cultural need. No building groupings or architectural setting is likely to find its reflection in the creation of a particularly structured society, regardless of how preciously this notion may have been held. Isomorphism remains a happy delusion of architects.

We are concerned that some might read in our hypotheses and proposals the implication that architecture can have a direct causal effect on social interactions; ours, rather, is a concern with psychological attitudes and behavior. It is our contention that in instances when architecture appears to affect social relationships, it is in fact only providing opportunity for latent social tendencies to come to the fore. The psychological implications of physical form appear, by contrast, to be much more significant and universal.

Some might conclude that, if for whatever reason it were found desirable, it might be possible to apply our findings in reverse: for authorities to develop environments which would intentionally isolate people and elicit their antagonisms, fears, and paranoia. The rules developed for one end, if valid, could after all be employed to achieve another. Where this might be partially true, our research indicates that even the most disadvantaged of people will not tolerate extreme negativism in their living environment. Pruitt-Igoe, an accidental architectural and administrative atrocity, did, for a while, succeed in creating a subculture of antisocial human beings, victimized by criminals and the deranged and by residents preying on each other. Most residents rebelled by simply moving out; others got together to insist on administrative and physical changes. With a 70 percent vacancy rate, in circumstances where housing for welfare recipients is in very short supply, Pruitt-Igoe suggests there is little to fear in the advent of intentional negative planning to achieve negative results.

> "We are concerned that some might read in our hypotheses and proposals the implication that architecture can have a direct causal effect on social interactions; ours, rather, is a concern with psychological attitudes and behavior."

Antisocial Behavior

Incidents of actual crime were rarely mentioned in discussions with residents or practitioners. Instead, a raft of problematic behaviors among young people, which fall under the ill-defined umbrella of "antisocial behavior," emerged as the key concern.

By far the biggest problem was young people hanging around late into the night around the play area in the courtyard of Peabody Avenue, which is surrounded by housing. On a number of occasions the play area had been vandalized. Two views emerged among practitioners and residents. The first was that security innovations to try to keep young people out were the solution and were viewed by many as a power struggle, with young people playing "a game" to outsmart authority. The other view was that that, while disruption to residents into the early hours was unacceptable, there were too few alternative activities and places to go for young people in the wider area.

"We've got young people from nine, eight-o-clock onwards that are going on into the early hours of the morning, they're vandalizing the area when it's dark and the CCTV can't capture it. And in addition to that you've got this entire block of leaseholders that are saying all they can hear over their TVs is the noise of young people shouting and so forth. And now because we've given them an area I think that actually spirals and creates more antisocial behavior. They've got a place they can sit and they get bored with just sitting, or it gets cold so they decide they're going to go and vandalize a door and kick their way into seven stairwells." (Practitioner)

"It's like the local open air youth club, open until two in the morning for the whole of this part of Pimlico." (Resident)

"For the young people, they just thought, okay, they've blocked off that bit because they obviously don't want us to go to that bit, but what we might try and do is try and find another way.' So, it almost becomes a bit of a game for some of them. Because they have to find other ways…so they can actually try and infiltrate or penetrate the wall."

"You've got to have somewhere to go. We're securing everything but there's nowhere for them to go. One thing that's lacking is a youth club. You have to have the money to pay for qualified youth workers." (Resident)

Because the young people in question were either Peabody residents or friends of Peabody residents, barring access to the estate through the use of gates did not seem sensible: residents – who could bring in friends – would in any case be allowed access. CCTV was already in place and not deterring the antisocial behavior. Our study suggested that high security was offered as a technical response to a complex social problem, which would require a different kind of solution.

Wall F28

Theme: Security and Design
Author: Ronald V. Clarke

Situational Crime Prevention: Theoretical Background and Current Practice

Responses to Gates, CCTV, and Defensible Space

Our respondents echoed the findings from other research that efforts to create defensible space could increase fear of strangers. They worried about gates restricting access for elderly and disabled people. There was also concern that high security gave a message to those outside that "something is wrong with that estate."

"I have difficulty with more locking up and more security in the sense, my wife's disabled, we depend on getting a taxi right to the door, so she can move quickly. As soon as you start locking off areas that the taxi needs to come in, it creates a very big difficulty." (Resident)

"I think the other thing I've noticed is the fear of not being able to get out, gated can be lovely because you've got a secured area but then you're in that secured area if you do have to encounter any issues so you're stuck there." (Practitioner)

"The more you secure a block or an estate the more it gives a message to anybody outsider there something is wrong with that estate." (Practitioner)

"Because of the doors, if you see someone you don't know, there is an element of 'who is this?'" (Resident)

Some practitioners were certain that security and design had deterred crime in their area of concern, only to move the problem to another location. One practitioner described the outcome of a landscaping project on another Peabody estate. The aim had been to remove trees and shrubs, which had provided cover for sex workers:

> "Fear of crime does not correlate with actual crime – which was barely discussed by the groups – but it does correlate directly with trust. In turn, high levels of trust correlate with well-being."

"We think we just moved them. What's happened is we haven't got rid of the problem, we've just moved them away...I did actually inadvertently move the problem from where they were working but kept it in the estate because they found the bin stores quite an attractive option...I must admit with what I'm doing I don't necessarily deal with the problem. I move it on."

CCTV was very popular with residents, although it did not necessarily add to feelings of safety, with residents reporting the presence of CCTV could in fact increase feelings of anxiety. Practitioners, who were skeptical about blanket CCTV coverage as a solution to rising fear of crime, reported that they felt pressured by residents' demands for more security, which they often gave in to. The high cost of repair and maintenance of CCTV, internal doors, and gates was also a concern for practitioners.

SCP[F71]

Situational crime prevention is quite different from most other criminological approaches to crime control. Proceeding from an analysis of the settings giving rise to specific kinds of crime or disorder, it seeks to introduce discrete managerial and environmental changes that will reduce the opportunities or incentives for crime. Thus, it is focused on the settings in which crimes occur, rather than on those committing criminal acts. It does not try to eliminate criminal tendencies by arresting and sanctioning offenders or by improving society or its institutions. Rather, it seeks to make crime less attractive and it operates, not through the criminal justice system, but through a host of public and private organizations and agencies – schools, hospitals, transit systems, shops and malls, manufacturing businesses and phone companies, local parks and entertainment facilities, pubs and parking lots – whose products, services, and operations spawn opportunities and incentives for a vast range of different crimes. Marcus Felson (2002) describes the main sources of these opportunities and incentives under the five categories of criminogenic products, poor management, poorly designed buildings and places, "leaky systems," and criminogenic laws.

Researchers in the Home Office Research Unit, the British government's criminological research department, formulated situational prevention nearly thirty years ago (Clarke 1980). It was originally thought to be applicable only to "opportunistic" property offenses, such as car theft vandalism and burglary. Quite soon, however, it was applied successfully to assaults, robberies, drug dealing, and prostitution and, more recently, to a much wider variety of crime including fraud and identity theft (for example, Blais and Bacher 2007; McNally and Newman 2008; Newman and Clarke 2003), child sexual abuse (Wortley and Smallbone 2006), crime and misbehavior in prisons (Wortley 2002), organized crime (van de Bunt and van der Schoot 2003), and terrorism (Clarke and Newman 2006). It has accumulated a considerable record of success, with many dozens of evaluated case studies (listed on www.popcenter.org) and it is now clear that it can be used to reduce every form of crime. This account of situational prevention begins with its theoretical background.

Clarke
American-based British criminologist Ronald V. Clarke (1941–) is credited as one of the founders of situational crime prevention for his work with the British Home Office in the late 1970s and early 1980s. He would go on to develop the related framework for situational terror prevention in the mid-2000s. Informed in part by C. Ray Jeffrey's 1971 work *Crime Prevention through Environmental Design* and Oscar Newman's 1972 work *Defensible Space*, situational crime prevention focuses on reducing the opportunity for crime, and is informed by three complementary theories: rational choice perspective, routine activity theory, and crime pattern theory. Codified according to twenty-five techniques, situational crime prevention has been highly influential in a range of countries including the UK, US, and Norway, despite drawing criticism concerning the geographical and socioeconomic displacement of crime, and what is referred to as criminal adaptation.

This text was first published in *Handbook on Crime and Deviance*, ed. Marvin D. Krohn, Alan J. Lizotte, and Gina Penly Hall (Dordrecht: Springer, 2009).

Theoretical Background

When it was originally proposed, situational prevention was criticized as a superficial response to crime without a theoretical base. In fact, it was informed by social learning theory (Bandura 1976; Mischel 1968) and had grown out of an extensive Home Office research program conducted in the 1960s and early 1970s on the effectiveness of residential treatments for delinquency (Sinclair and Clarke 1982). Initially, this program sought to identify the characteristics of delin-

"I'm mixed when I see the CCTV, I still don't feel safe, in fact sometimes it makes me feel even more anxious." (Resident)

"It's the first thing they say about trouble on the estate and [about] security problems the comment is normally, 'we need some CCTV, that would be the end of our problems.'" (Practitioner)

"On one of our challenging estates…we've increased, like tripled the CCTV over the last three years but they still want more CCTV, they want it monitored 24 hours a day because the perception is where there's CCTV things don't happen. And also I think it's a question of, 'We need CCTV.' 'You've got CCTV.' 'Well, we need more. It needs to be located in a different place.' But CCTV's not the answer." (Practitioner)

"When I see the CCTV, I still don't feel safe, in fact sometimes it makes me feel more anxious. Because I think I'm in a bad area, I get into a panic sometimes because, for one, you're not sure the cameras are working. You see them and you see a lot of them highly visible and it just makes me feel scared. It doesn't have the effect of making me feel safe, it raises emotions of feeling frightened and intimidated and you're not sure what's lurking round the corner." (Resident)

Fear, Trust and "Knowing People"

Fear of crime does not correlate with actual crime – which was barely discussed by the groups – but it does correlate directly with trust.[24] In turn, high levels of trust correlate with well-being.[25]

The residents interviewed felt that "knowing people," whether it be caretakers, youth workers, or each other, was the key to creating trust. Acknowledging the complexity of the issue, many residents also reflected that feelings of safety or fear were not due to the design and security of the surrounding environment but were rooted in past, personal experience.

"When I say I feel unsafe, my unsafety is not just based in Pimlico, it's based along from childhood experiences to adult experiences…cause a lot's happened to me." (Resident)

"I say I feel safe, because I've never been mugged, I've never been threatened with a knife…That is pure luck, I could be walking down the street tomorrow and get mugged, and my opinion then would be different from what it is today. But I think you're realistically safe." (Resident)

The vital importance of knowing people gave rise to a discussion on the role of caretakers, who lived on the estate until 2005. Caretakers, or "supers" as they were known, were badly missed by practitioners and residents alike, who commented that technological solutions had replaced "people on the ground." The unintended consequence of this change particularly affected elderly and isolated people, who

quents who were likely to be reconvicted after treatment and paid limited attention to the treatment process itself. Later, the program sought to relate particular aspects of treatment both to the chances of reconviction and to institutional misbehavior. The main findings of the research can be summarized as follows:

1. The best (but nonetheless weak) predictors of reconviction were pretreatment delinquency, current family environment and, to a lesser extent, delinquency during treatment.

2. The various forms of treatment differed little in their long-term effectiveness in preventing reconviction.

3. There were large differences in misbehavior during treatment (as measured by offending or absconding) that were related to differences in institutional regimes and environments.

The first two findings contributed to the "nothing works" (Martinson 1974) doctrine of the era, but the three findings together were interpreted by the Home Office team to argue that delinquency is mainly a response to a current living situation (for example, the family or an institution), which provides the stimuli and opportunities for offending as well as the reinforcements. Insofar as the situation remains unchanged, delinquency itself is likely to persist. Some transfer of learning is possible from one environment to another, but the general unpredictability of delinquency is a function of changing environmental pressures which make a delinquent response more or less likely. The influence of the environment also helps to account for the ineffectiveness of treatment: though willing conformity or compliance may be found among those under treatment, the contemporary environment reasserts its power on release.

This formulation of the determinants of delinquency influenced the direction of a subsequent program of Home Office research, begun in the mid-1970s, to find a more effective means of reducing delinquency (Clarke and Cornish 1982). Instead of seeking to alter delinquent "dispositions," this new program of research explored the potential for altering situations to reduce the opportunities for delinquency and crime. Additional support for the program aims was provided by recently published studies in the United States on "crime prevention through environmental design" by C. Ray Jeffery (1971) and on "defensible space" design by Oscar Newman (1972), both of which were premised on opportunity reduction. The results of the research were pulled together in a Home Office Research Unit publication, "Crime as Opportunity" (Mayhew, Clarke, Sturman, and Hough 1976), which, as the title suggests, argued that opportunity has a powerful role in crime. By the time the policy implications of these results had been translated into the concept of situational prevention (Clarke 1980), the social learning theory underlying the research had been abandoned, partly influenced by deviance theory, in favor of a simple "choice" model of crime. The model required information about:

> "Instead of seeking to alter delinquent 'dispositions,' this new program of research explored the potential for altering situations to reduce the opportunities for delinquency and crime."

found great reassurance from the presence of known individuals with friendly faces, who would also notice if certain residents hadn't been seen for a few days.

"I think the physical security measures have increased such as gating, intercom systems, CCTV, and the eyes on the ground have been removed. I just wonder whether one method has been replaced by another. That we've become more technological. There's more CCTV, there's less manpower." (Practitioner)

"It's the unintended consequences – no one is asking where's Mrs. So and So...she hasn't been seen for a few days. The rent collector used to be like a social worker. Suddenly there are a lot more lonely people, they're more vulnerable. The milk man's gone. We might be saving money on not having caretakers living in but we have to have the CCTV, the clamper. We're losing the human touch across the board and that's what brings communities together." (Practitioner)

> "Caretakers, or 'supers' as they were known, were badly missed by practitioners and residents alike, who commented that technological solutions had replaced 'people on the ground.'"

"I think they're great. They're the social glue. They chat to everyone. They know what's going on with the old ladies. Are they dead or not – seriously." (Practitioner)

"I think the caretakers knowing the parents makes a real difference." (Resident)

"A lot of elderly people prefer people on-site [rather than a call center]. For example an old lady who's being called all the time and told it's because she's vulnerable. She doesn't want to be called – it's not personal. It's systems." (Resident)

"Knowing people" also raised the question of housing allocation policies on the estate and how they had changed, breaking up families and communities of people who had known each other for generations. While there was a feeling that "that time has gone," residents continually highlighted how difficult it was to create strong communities when grown-up children invariably had to move far away, so that intergenerational relationships, where parents would know each other's children, broke down.

"Where people know each other they trust each other. It's when you don't know the people that you can't, well you can't trust somebody that you don't know." (Resident)

"One of the main differences is, I can easily explain it, my granddad was born in Peabody, his friends and people lived in Peabody, his children lived in Peabody. Now, that's my

(1) the offender's motives; (2) his mood; (3) his moral judgments regarding the act in question and the "techniques of neutralization" open to him (see Sykes & Matza 1957, his capacity to "neutralize" guilt); (4) the extent of his crime knowledge and perception of criminal opportunities; (5) his assessment of the risks of being caught as well as the likely consequences; and finally, as well as of a different order, (6) whether he has been drinking (Clarke 1980, 138).

This model was later developed into the rational choice perspective (Clarke and Cornish 1985; Cornish and Clarke 1986), which, together with routine activity theory (Cohen and Felson 1979) and crime pattern theory (Brantingham and Brantingham 1993), comprise the three main theories of environmental criminology. The theories are complementary, not competitive, because they operate at different levels of explanation and deal with different questions, at least as far as the role of opportunity in crime is concerned. Thus, routine activity theory is a "macro" theory which deals with broad societal changes that lead to the increase or decrease of specific kinds of crime opportunities; crime pattern theory is a "meso" theory, operating at a city or neighborhood level, that deals with the ways offenders discover crime opportunities in the course of their daily lives; and the rational choice perspective is a "micro" theory that deals with the decisions that offenders must make in committing crimes (Felson and Clarke 1998). Until quite recently, these three theories provided the theoretical underpinnings for situational prevention, but Richard Wortley (2001) has used social psychological concepts to expand its rationale.

Rather than provide a detailed description of the theories supporting situational prevention, the remainder of this section identifies some of their common assumptions that have greatest relevance for situational prevention. These are as follows:

1. Crime is the result of an interaction between disposition and situation. Most traditional criminological theories try only to explain why some people become delinquent or criminal. Whether biological, psychological, or sociological in approach, these theories are "dispositional" because they are seeking to explain a general disposition or propensity to commit crime. But crime is an act, not merely a propensity, and it can only be explained in terms of the interaction between the disposition (sometimes also called "criminal motivation") and the situation that provides the opportunity and sometimes the stimulus for crime to occur.

2. Offenders choose to commit crime. As Ian R. Taylor, Paul Walton, and Jock Young (1973) pointed out many years ago, offenders are not compelled by background to commit crime. Thus, discrimination and disadvantage do not propel robbers through the doors of the bank; rather, robbers choose to rob banks because they want money. People choose to commit crimes because they believe this will bring them some benefit, which is not always financial. It can be excitement, status, acceptance by peers, sexual domination, respect, love or, in fact, anything that people might want. Whether they choose to commit crime depends on a rough calculation of the chances of obtaining the reward and the risks of failure – arrest, punishment, humiliation, etc. Their choices may be made

grandmother, they didn't muck about because it was her father's people that lived in Peabody. I was born in Peabody, I'm the third generation and we all lived in Peabodys, all the little old ladies around Peabodys were aunties and uncles and granddads to us. They were pretending uncles and we knew everybody…"

We ended both groups by giving participants a fantasy budget to create a safe and trusting community. They chose to make some investment in security features but both groups decided to allocate the largest portion of the budget to "people on the ground."

The Dynamics of Secured by Design

With so little evidence that high security and defensible space can prevent fear of crime or nurture trusting communities, how is it that this approach has become the contemporary orthodoxy? The answer may lie in the interconnected and self-perpetuating dynamics of the security, insurance, and construction industries that accompany Secured by Design policy.

Secured by Design began as a regional crime reduction initiative in the late 1980s, as British police officers were being introduced to the ideas of Oscar Newman and CPTED. Initially funded by the Home Office, it became a private company in 2000, in order, according to its director Alan McInnes, to be free from political interference. Although it is administered under the auspices of the Association of Chief Police Officers, who train the Architectural Liaison Officers, it is funded by the 480 security companies who sell products which meet Secured by Design standards.

The 480 security companies which are entitled to display the Secured by Design logo on their products are part of the private security industry. In addition, according to McInnes, the initiative is strongly backed by the insurance industry. The increasing levels of security offered by Secured by Design standards attract lower insurance premiums. In turn, developers market higher security and lower insurance as a bonus and in a virtuous circle sell properties for higher prices. American commentators describe this as the "FIRE" economy, which is an acronym for Finance, Insurance, and Real Estate, which brings developers, housebuilders, and the insurance and security industries together by offering lower insurance premiums for properties with high security.

The consequence of this dynamic is that developers become locked into the FIRE economy, even when they do not want to create high-security environments. According to a developer with the property company Argent, which is behind the new 67-acre private estate at Kings Cross in London, the company wanted to create a low-security environment in the squares and open spaces of the site, but private security was a requirement of the insurance. Housing and schools face a similar dilemma: the practitioners we talked to as part of this research frequently described struggles to avoid meeting Secured by Design requirements, which they saw as onerous and unnecessary. "We

under emotional pressure or when intoxicated. They might also be split-second, foolhardy, ill-informed, or ill-advised - but they are choices nonetheless. This is what is meant by "limited" or "bounded" rationality (Simon 1978), which is the mechanism through which the interaction is mediated between disposition and situation. If people choose to commit crime, it follows that even those who are more disposed to crime will choose to avoid it when the circumstances are unfavorable. Creating unfavorable circumstances is the objective of situational crime prevention.

3. Opportunity is an important cause of crime. Even when dispositional theorists have recognized that opportunity plays a part in crime, they have assumed that opportunity is subsidiary to motivation. In their view, motivation is the first and most important thing to explain. Environmental criminology, on the other hand, gives as much importance to opportunity as to motivation in crime causation. In fact, opportunity is an important cause of every form of crime, even a crime as important as homicide that is usually thought to be driven by strong motivation. Opportunity explains why the risk of being murdered in the United States is 6-8 times greater than in the United Kingdom and most other European countries. This is the result of the widespread availability of guns in the United States, particularly handguns - a situational variable - not because the United States is a more criminal country (Farrington, Langan, and Tonry 2004). I ascribe a more important role to opportunity by claiming that,

> "If people choose to commit crime, it follows that even those who are more disposed to crime will choose to avoid it when the circumstances are unfavorable."

    a. Criminally disposed individuals will commit a greater numbers of crimes if they encounter more criminal opportunities.

    b. Regularly encountering such opportunities could lead these individuals to seek even more opportunities.

    c. Individuals without preexisting dispositions can be drawn into criminal behavior by a proliferation of criminal opportunities.

    d. Generally law-abiding individuals can be drawn into committing specific forms of crime if they regularly encounter easy opportunities for these crimes.

    e. The more opportunities for crime that exist, the more crime there will be.

4. Situational factors can stimulate crime. The social science background to the development of situational prevention includes famous studies showing that crime and aggression can be induced or provoked in certain situations. For example Philip Zimbardo (1973) showed that a damaged, abandoned vehicle attracted further vandalism and Stanley Milgram (1974) showed that subjects in an experiment could be induced to commit apparently cruel acts. However, it is only recently that these insights have been

spend all our time fighting with them because they want to put up huge grilles everywhere. There's a lot of pressure to put in measures," said one developer.

A Peabody practitioner described how she struggled to resist demands from the Secured by Design crime prevention officer to permanently gate the entrance to Peabody Avenue. In order to avoid this Peabody had to commission a three-month study of two-story archways throughout Westminster, at a cost of £20,000. Only when this study revealed that two-story archways were not crime hot spots did the crime prevention officer relent. Secured by Design has "got some sensible things in it," she told us, "but it suffers from an unimaginative interpretation of what's going on. It's very much a tick-box."

Secured by Design creates a set of standards which, rather like Health and Safety, must be met. According to Alan McInnes, one of the initial drivers for the take-up of Secured by Design was a combination of calls from the insurance and construction industries to apply consistent standards for crime prevention. The Housing Corporation (the former social housing regulator) took up Secured by Design with great enthusiasm for this reason, said McInnes; it was more interested in nominating Secured by Design to get a standard of product, than to reduce crime. This desire for universal standards has led to Secured by Design, and the high-security environment it brings with it, becoming an entrenched part of the security, insurance, and construction industries.

In turn, these industries reinforce the principles of Secured by Design by encouraging the sale of commercial security products. While this may be good for growth in these sectors, it diverts attention from alternative solutions that are not based on security products. McInnes readily agreed that the "informal guardianship" figures of the past had created cohesion in communities that was now sorely missed, but conceded that, because of its operational model, Secured by Design would be unlikely to encourage their reintroduction.

"The increasing levels of security offered by Secured by Design standards attract lower insurance premiums. In turn, developers market higher security and lower insurance as a bonus and in a virtuous circle sell properties for higher prices."

The more worrying aspects of Secured by Design, such as the militarization of poor areas and the rollout of CCTV in schools, are almost certainly unintended consequences. McInnes claims he is shocked by the spread of CCTV in schools and says he hopes that it is not a consequence of recommendations made by Architectural Liaison Officers. The danger is that all parties are locked into a pattern of thinking which puts security first, fueled – almost invisibly – by an alliance of market forces and a standards culture, with little consideration of its social footprint.

The Wisdom of Prevention

Secured by Design standards have spread throughout the built environment. They are rooted in the history of research into defensible space and poverty, in particular the studies of deprived housing estates by Oscar Newman and Alice Coleman. This

directly incorporated into the repertoire of situational prevention techniques. On the basis of his studies of the "closed" environments of pubs and in prisons, Richard Wortley (2001) persuasively argued that situational prevention has focused too much attention on reducing situational opportunities and had neglected situational stimulants to crime. In the latest formulation of the techniques of situational prevention (see below), this omission has been remedied by the inclusion of five techniques to reduce provocations and temptations to crime.

The Methodology of Situational Prevention

These assumptions about the situational determinants of crime have helped to shape situational prevention's methodology which, like the underlying theory, is under constant refinement. Currently, the following five principles of intervention are emphasized (Clarke 2008):

1. Focus on very specific categories of crime or disorder

2. Focus on crime concentrations

3. Understand how the crime is committed

4. Use an action-research model

5. Consider a variety of solutions

Focus on Very Specific Categories of Crime

Situational prevention shows greatest success when focused on highly specific forms of crime, such as juvenile joyriding, rather than on broader categories of crime such as car thefts. This is because the situational determinants of any specific category of crime are quite different from those of another one, even one that seems similar. It may also be committed for different motives, by different offenders with quite different resources and skills.

The need for specificity can be illustrated by research on residential burglary undertaken by Barry Poyner and Barry Webb (1991) in one British city. They found that residential burglaries committed in the suburbs were quite different from those committed in the city center and that these two kinds of burglaries required different solutions. Thus, city center burglaries were committed by offenders on foot looking for cash and jewelry. Because most of the housing was built in terraces they could only get in through the front door or a front window. To prevent these burglaries, Poyner and Webb suggested improving security and surveillance at the front of the house.

Suburban burglars, on the other hand, used cars and were looking for electronic goods such as videocassette players and TVs. They were more likely to break in at the back of the house than the front. They needed cars to get to the suburbs and to transport the stolen goods. The cars had to be parked near to the house, but not so close as to attract attention. Poyner and Webb's preventive suggestions included better surveillance of parking places and improved security at the back of houses. They also suggested that the police should crack down on fencing of stolen goods, particularly electronic items - a

approach offered a "solution" to the problem of crime and fear of crime in poor places which did not have to deal with the more complex causes of poverty. Security measures would instead control behavior. In spite of scant supporting evidence, short-term, technological measures took precedence over long-term, "upstream" prevention.

The New economics foundation (nef) has argued that the focus of policy – and its interventions – should shift from dealing with "visible" problems or "what-if" scenarios to helping to build the underlying conditions that enable people to experience well-being.[26][27] It appears that we are shaping our physical environment in response to the consequences of complex social problems and in so doing are stripping away the social resources which we depend on to live well together. nef's analysis of well-being data in more than 22 countries has found the UK to have the lowest levels of trust and belonging among 16–24 year-olds in Europe.[28] Our research suggests that the physical environment we are creating is contributing to declining levels of trust and growing levels of fear.

Richard Sennett has argued against creating discrete areas with "sealed edges," claiming that "any city of isolated human islands aborts the experience of difference, rendering people less socially competent." The quality of life in a city is good, says Sennett, when its inhabitants are capable of dealing with complexity.[29]

Short-term solutions, which offer "can do" solutions to problems are often popular – both to policymakers and to communities – because they appear simple and straightforward. Long-term solutions to the prevention of fear depend on our willingness to address complex issues and relationships. This points to the need for a more thorough debate, which can begin to unpick, among much else, the underlying causes of our need to feel safer and the institutional stranglehold Secured by Design has on our lives today.

Our engagement with practitioners and residents in Peabody Avenue has revealed a substantial disconnect between the assumptions underpinning Secured by Design and the day-to-day experiences of people living among CCTV, high fences, and gates.

It was a small study, but clear conclusions have nevertheless emerged about the links between fear and trust and the removal of "guardianship" figures such as caretakers who were seen to provide the "social glue" in communities. Their loss was an indirect result of compliance with Secured by Design. Yet it appears that they were much more effective in building trust in communities than the installation of CCTV, gating, and door entry systems.

Residents and practitioners were unanimous about the need for "eyes on the ground." Arguably, the problems at Peabody Avenue, which can be found in countless estates around the country, can best be tackled by practitioners with experience of conflict resolution who understand so-called hard-to-reach young people. Often these are very talented youth and community workers – many with a chequered past themselves – who

FIGURE 5.1
Residents' reallocation of security budget

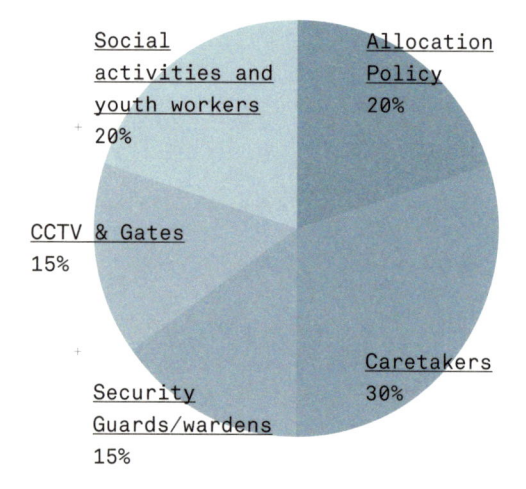

- Social activities and youth workers 20%
- Allocation Policy 20%
- CCTV & Gates 15%
- Caretakers 30%
- Security Guards/wardens 15%

FIGURE 5.2
Practitioners' reallocation of security budget

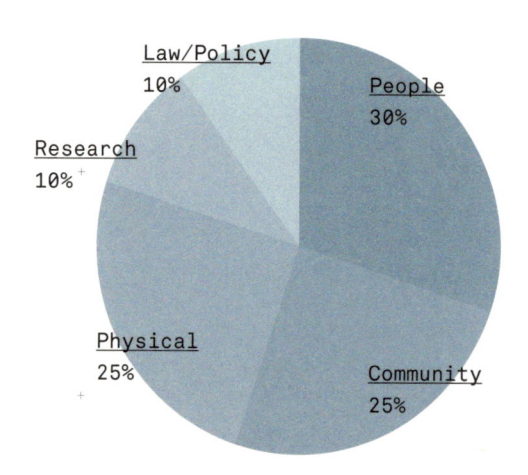

- Law/Policy 10%
- People 30%
- Research 10%
- Community 25%
- Physical 25%

tactic that would have little effect on the inner-city burglars who were primarily targeting cash and jewelry.

Focus on Crime Concentrations

It is sometimes argued that situational prevention could never be an effective means of reducing crime because opportunities for crime are infinite and everywhere and it would never be possible to reduce enough of them to make an impact on crime. At first sight this seems true, but, in fact, opportunities for crime are already severely restricted by formal and informal security. Every day, we all do such things as lock our doors, secure our valuables, counsel our children, and guard our purses and wallets to reduce the risk of crime. To this end, we also buy houses in safe neighborhoods, invest in burglar alarms, and avoid dangerous places and people. Similarly, schools, factories, offices, shops, and many other organizations and agencies routinely take a host of precautions to safeguard themselves, their employees, and their clients from crime. This does not mean that situational prevention has only a very limited role. Quite the contrary – there are still many situations in which opportunities for crime are too easy and tempting. In fact, the most tempting opportunities are highly concentrated at particular places ("hot spots"; Sherman, Gartin, and Buerger 1989), on particular people ("repeat victims"; Farrell and Pease 1993), on particular products ("hot products"; Clarke 1999), and at particular establishments, premises, and facilities ("risky facilities"; Eck, Clarke, and Guerette 2007). Focusing on these crime concentrations enables those designing situational interventions to obtain the largest preventive benefits from their actions.

Understand How the Crime is Committed

Despite its many successes, it is often claimed that situational prevention cannot work because it does not attempt to understand or change motivation. In fact, a deep understanding of motivation is rarely needed to design effective situational measures. For example, speeding in a residential street can be substantially reduced by installing speed bumps without ever understanding all the reasons why people speed there. A second example concerns an outbreak of random murders in the 1980s resulting from the deliberate contamination of painkillers with cyanide. The perpetrators were not caught and their motivation was never revealed, but the murders were brought to an end, with no documented recurrence, by the introduction of tamperproof packaging for all medicines and foods – a straightforward opportunity-blocking measure (Clarke and Newman 2005).

More important for situational prevention than understanding why offenses are committed is to understand how they are committed. Poyner and Webb (1991) could make useful preventive suggestions (see above) once they understood how the burglaries were committed and what goods were being sought. They did not spend time researching why the burglars wanted to steal goods. It was enough to know that there were some individuals out there with the motivation to steal things from other people's homes.

> "This process reveals another important fact for prevention – committing a crime is not simply of matter of snatching a bag or pocketing goods in a store. Instead, it consists of a linked series of steps, each of which involves decisions by the offender."

command the respect of young people and know how to reciprocate that respect.

There's a strong case for more work in this area, which could usefully include extended deliberative engagement; longitudinal analysis of the impacts on fear and trust; detailed examination of the patterning of social norms and behavior encouraged by high-security environments; and research into how to shape the physical and social contexts that support people to live well together.

"Our engagement with practitioners and residents in Peabody Avenue has revealed a substantial disconnect between the assumptions underpinning Secured by Design and the day-to-day experiences of people living among CCTV, high fences, and gates."

The authors would like to thank Claire Bennie, director of development at the Peabody Trust, for supporting this research.

In trying to understand how a specific form of crime is done, it is important to adopt the offender's perspective – to see the task from the offender's point of view. Sometimes interviewing offenders about their methods can be helpful (Decker 2005), but when this cannot be done, an alternative is to "think thief" (Ekblom 1995). This means putting oneself in the shoes of offenders and trying to think through in detail the decisions they must make to complete the crime.

This process reveals another important fact for prevention – committing a crime is not simply of matter of snatching a bag or pocketing goods in a store. Instead, it consists of a linked series of steps, each of which involves decisions by the offender (Cornish 1994). For example a shoplifter has to decide which store to hit, which goods to steal, how to take them without being seen, how to conceal them, how to escape from the store without being caught, how to sell them, to whom to sell them, what price to ask, and how to make sure that the goods will not be traced back to him. For some crimes, of course – for example, theft of cars for export – the process is much longer and more complicated. The important point is that understanding how a crime is committed helps in finding points of intervention to make the crime more difficult, risky, or less rewarding. And the more detailed the understanding of the process, the richer and more diverse will be the possibilities for intervention.

> "The problem-solving methodology of situational prevention is a form of 'action research.'"

Use an Action-Research Model

Unlike crime prevention through environmental design (CPTED), which tries to eliminate anticipated problems in new designs on the basis of past experience with similar designs, situational prevention seeks to eliminate existing problems. The problem-solving methodology of situational prevention is a form of "action research," which consists of a series of steps. The specific crime problem is analyzed:

1. Hypotheses about the main determinants are developed.

2. A range of solutions are identified and assessed.

3. The chosen measures are put into place.

4. The results are then evaluated.

This problem-solving methodology is very similar to the SARA model – scanning, analysis, response, and assessment – that guides problem-oriented policing, though it has probably been followed less faithfully in practice. On the other hand, most situational prevention projects have been more rigorously evaluated than problem-oriented policing ones, partly because situational prevention was developed by government researchers who were constantly challenged to demonstrate its effectiveness. Despite this, the quality should be improved of the evaluative designs used, most of which have been quasi-experimental, using before-and-after comparisons or simple time series, with or without controls. True experiments in the form of randomized controlled trials have very rarely been used in situational projects because of the practical difficulties of allocating interven-

Theme: Democracy and Security
Author: Stephen Graham

When Life Itself Is War:
The Urbanization of Military and Security Doctrine

tions randomly to places. However, this has been done routinely in other fields (Boruch et al. 2004) and could be done more often in situational prevention. Wider use should also be made of designs which permit diffusion of benefits (Bowers and Johnson 2003) and anticipatory benefits (see below) to be examined. It is also important to undertake longer follow-ups so as to learn more about possible attrition of benefits as a result of implementation "fatigue" or criminal "adaptation" (see below). Lastly, situational prevention often lends itself more easily than other interventions to cost-benefit studies, but again, there have been too few of these in the past.

Consider a Variety of Solutions

Many different solutions can be found for any specific problem of crime and disorder if it is analyzed in enough detail. To assist the process of identifying possible solutions, situational prevention researchers have classified the many different ways that exist to reduce crime opportunities. These classifications have been progressively expanded in response to developments in theory, in preventive technology, and in the practice of situational prevention. The latest classification in Table 6.1 has twenty-five opportunity-reducing techniques grouped under five main headings: (a) increase the effort, (b) increase the risks, (c) reduce the rewards, (d) remove excuses, and (e) reduce provocations (Cornish and Clarke 2003).

The potential solutions identified in any project need to be carefully assessed for their cost and benefits. In all cases, the assessment must go beyond financial considerations and must include a variety of social and ethical costs, such as intrusiveness, unfairness, inconvenience, and discrimination. Situational prevention is frequently criticized on ethical grounds (see von Hirsch, Garland, and Wakefield 2000, for an extended discussion), and even though these criticisms can be answered in general terms, they must be addressed whenever they arise in the specific context of a particular project. Because there are always many different ways to reduce opportunities, there is no necessity to adopt a particular solution if it is found unacceptable in particular respects.

Displacement and Other Offender Reactions

Many dozens of successful situational prevention studies have been reported since the concept was first described more than twenty-five years ago. In some cases, the reductions in crime achieved have been dramatic. To take two examples, a plague of robberies of bus drivers in New York and eighteen other US cities in the late 1960s/early 1970s was largely eliminated by two measures: the introduction of exact fares and the installation of bus safes into which the money was dropped (Chaiken, Lawless, and Stevenson 1974; Stanford Research Institute 1970). This meant that there was no longer any point in attempting to rob the driver. More recently, US cell phone companies largely wiped out cloning by the introduction of five new anticloning technologies; at its height, this problem had been costing the companies about $800 million per year in fraudulent phone calls.

Probably no other form of crime control can claim an equal record of evaluated successes, but the evidence is still disputed on grounds that the reductions are negated by displacement (that is, the

Introduction: The New Military Urbanism

"Political struggles are not fought on the surface of geography but through its very fabric/ation."
Pile 2000, 263

"Today, wars are fought not in trenches and fields, but in living rooms, schools and supermarkets."
Barakat 1998, 11

In an earlier article (Graham 2005), I began to explore the ways in which both the "War on Terror" and its offshoots have been conspicuously marked by overwhelmingly urban discourses, materialities, and practices. Building on this work, and drawing on research recently completed for a book project (Graham 2010), in what follows I develop an argument – deliberately transdisciplinary, synthetical and polemical in scope – which seeks to demonstrate that new ideologies of permanent and boundless war are radically intensifying the militarization of urban life in the contemporary period.

It is important to stress at the outset that such processes of urban militarization do not constitute a simple, clean break with the past. Rather, they add contemporary twists to long-standing militaristic and urban transformations – political, cultural, and economic. Together, these serve to normalize war and preparations for war as central elements of the material, political–economic, and cultural constitution of cities and urban life. Michael Geyer (1989, 79) defines the militarization process as "the contradictory and tense social process in which civil society organizes itself for the production of violence."

Militarization processes are inevitably complex, diverse and multidimensional; they link to urban sites, cultures, representations, state spaces and political economies in myriad ways (for a review, see Graham 2004). Their key constituents, however, are as old as war itself. These have invariably centered on the social construction of a powerful imagined division between the "inside" and "outside" of a nation, city, or other geographic area and the orchestrated demonization of enemies and enemy places beyond such boundaries. Practices of militarization also invariably rely on the normalization of military paradigms of thought, action, and policy; (attempts at) the aggressive disciplining of bodies, places, and identities seen not to befit the often masculinized notions of nation, citizenship, or body (and the connections between them); and the deployment of wide ranges of propagandist material which romanticizes or sanitizes violence as a

Graham

British geographer and urban researcher Stephen Graham (1965–) is a leading voice in the contemporary critical debate addressing the securitization and militarization of urban life. In this essay Graham draws upon a number of thinkers from different disciplines to unfold what he terms the new military urbanism according to five interrelated foundations: "the urbanization of military and security doctrine; the links between militarized control technologies and digitized urban life; the cultural performances of militarized media consumption; the emerging urban political economies of the 'security' industries; and the new state spaces of violence." Graham describes a range of palpable threats to our cities under such a contemporary regime.

The text was first published in the *International Journal of Urban and Regional Research* 36, no. 1 (2012).

"New ideologies of permanent and boundless war are radically intensifying the militarization of urban life in the contemporary period."

offenders shift their attention to other places, times, and targets, use different methods, or commit different crimes); that situational prevention results in escalation (that is, offenders resort to more harmful methods to gain their ends); and that even if displacement does not occur immediately, the criminal population adapts in the long run to reduced opportunities by discovering new ways to commit crime. These criticisms are addressed below under four headings: (1) displacement, (2) diffusion of benefits, (3) anticipatory benefits, and (4) adaptation.

Displacement

"Dispositional" critics of situational prevention often seem to assume that criminal motivation has the properties of a "drive" that must be expressed in criminal behavior (see Clarke 1980). This idea might be credible for some very rare crimes – some forms of arson, for example – but it is certainly not true for the great majority of crimes. For most crimes, rational choice theory offers the more realistic perspective that offenders will try to find some way of continuing to offend when they encounter blocked opportunities, but they will always evaluate the alternatives in terms of costs and benefits. For example, rational choice theory suggests that if shoppers were prevented from stealing at their local supermarket by new security measures, it is highly unlikely that they would begin to shop at some more distant store where they could continue to shoplift. Even less likely is that they would turn to mugging senior citizens because shoplifting is easier to rationalize and much less risky than mugging. In fact, almost by definition, any instance of escalation is more costly for offenders. Some of them may be prepared to make more difficult rationalizations or run additional risks, but the empirical research suggests that they will be a minority (see Ekblom 1988).

> "In fact, reviews of the evidence on displacement have found that it can occur, but it is not inevitable."

In fact, reviews of the evidence on displacement have found that it can occur, but it is not inevitable. In the most recent review, René B. P. Hesseling (1994) found no evidence of displacement in twenty-two of the fifty-five studies he examined; in the remaining thirty-three studies, he found some evidence of displacement, but in no case was there as much crime displaced as prevented. Much the same would probably be found if his review were repeated today, when many more studies of displacement have been reported. For example, little displacement seems to have occurred to "subscriber" fraud, the second-largest category of cell phone fraud, when cloning was largely eliminated in the United States. This is because they are, in fact, very different forms of crime. Subscriber fraud involves the use of a false name and address to obtain cell phone service. These crimes would be difficult to reproduce on a wide scale and would, therefore, not be attractive to organized groups. Cloned phones, on the other hand, were "mass produced" by offenders who had learned how to acquire hundreds of legitimate phone numbers and program them into stolen phones.

Diffusion of Benefits

An unexpected finding of the work on displacement was that situational prevention can result in a "diffusion of benefits." This term

means of righteous revenge or achieving some god-given purpose. Above all, militarization and war involve attempts to forge powerful new links between cultures, states, technologies, and citizenship. Invariably, these work as the means to orchestrate the rapid creative destruction of inherited geographies, political economies, technologies, and cultures, either deliberately or unintentionally.

In the discussion that follows I attempt to delineate the ways in which contemporary processes of militarization raise fundamental questions for critical urban scholarship because of the ways in which they work to permanently target everyday urban sites, circulations, and populations. Indeed, I believe that such thinking is now so dominant within contemporary state security and military thinking that is necessary to talk of a "new military urbanism." This I define as the emerging constellation of military and security doctrine and practice which posits that the key "security" challenges of our age now center on the everyday sites, spaces, and circulations of cities. As I will demonstrate below, the new military urbanism gains its power because of the ways in which such doctrine and practice increasingly fuses with the wider circuits of visual technological popular culture, political economy, and state practice. As such, it plays a crucial role in forging dynamics whereby political power centers less on sovereign, territorial, and disciplinary configurations and more on the biopolitical arrangements of life within highly urbanized, mobile, and digitally mediated societies (Foucault 2003; Foucault 2007).

"This I define as the emerging constellation of military and security doctrine and practice which posits that the key "security" challenges of our age now center on the everyday sites, spaces, and circulations of cities."

In what follows, I focus primarily on how the doctrines, cultures, and technologies sustained by the US military and security complexes are playing a central role in constituting the new military urbanism. My purpose in the current paper is twofold. First, I seek to provoke critical urban scholarship to engage with the contemporary nature of militarization and its central role in shaping contemporary cities more deeply than has thus far been the case. Second, I want to delineate precisely what is new about the new military urbanism as a way of understanding the complex linkages between contemporary cities, contemporary warfare, and the politics of security. I attempt to achieve these two goals by exploring what I argue are the new military urbanism's five interrelated foundations. These are: the urbanization of military and security doctrine; the links between militarized control technologies and digitized urban life; the cultural performances of militarized media consumption; the emerging urban political economies of the "security" industries; and the new state spaces of violence.

Battlespace: The Urbanization of Military and Security Doctrine

"The future of warfare lies in the streets, sewers, high-rise buildings, industrial parks, and the sprawl of houses, shacks,

refers to the reductions in crime that can sometimes occur beyond the immediate focus of the situational measures introduced (Clarke and Weisburd 1994). This greatly enhances the practical appeal of situational prevention, especially as the phenomenon is quite general as shown by the following examples:

1. When "red light cameras" were installed at some traffic lights in a large Scottish city, not only did fewer people "run the lights" at these locations, but also at other traffic lights nearby (Scottish Central Research Unit 1995).

2. When a New Jersey discount electronic retailer introduced a regime of daily counting of valuable merchandise in the warehouse, employee thefts of these items plummeted – but thefts also plummeted of items not repeatedly counted (Masuda 1992).

3. Newly installed CCTV cameras at the University of Surrey in England reduced car theft in the three parking lots that were given surveillance – but car theft declined by an equal amount in a fourth car park not covered by the cameras (Poyner 1991).

4. As expected, electronic tagging of books in a University of Wisconsin library resulted in reduced book thefts. However, thefts also declined of videocassettes and other materials that had not been tagged (Scherdin 1986).

5. Added security for repeatedly burgled houses in a public housing estate in England reduced burglaries for the whole of the estate, not just for the houses given additional protection (Pease 1991).

6. When street lighting was improved in a large housing estate in England, crime declined in both that estate and a nearby one where the lights were not changed (Painter and Farrington 1997).

7. The introduction of vehicle tracking systems in six large American cities led to citywide reductions in car theft, not just for car owners who purchased the devices (Ayres and Levitt 1998).

8. Widespread ownership of burglar alarms in an affluent community near Philadelphia appears to have reduced burglary rates for the community at large (Hakim, Gaffney, Rengert, and Shachmurove 1995).

> "Potential offenders often know that new prevention measures have been introduced, but they may be unsure of their precise scope."

The explanation for these results seem to be that potential offenders often know that new prevention measures have been introduced, but they may be unsure of their precise scope. They may believe the measures are more widespread than they really are and that the effort needed to commit crime, or the risks incurred, has been increased for a wider range of places, times, or targets than in fact is the case.

and shelters that form the broken cities of our world."
(Peters 1996)

The first key feature of the new military urbanism is the way it normalizes new imaginations of political violence and a whole spectrum of ambient threats to "security" which center on the everyday sites, spaces, populations, and circulations of cities. As part the defense of what Julian Reid calls "logistical societies" – societies where biopolitical threats emerge from the very central systems, flows, and networks sustaining contemporary urban life – warfare within liberal modernity increasingly centers on securitizing and targeting the prosaic architectures and circulations, of the city (see Reid 2006; Dillon and Reid 2009).

Driving the military targeting of the everyday sites, circulations, and processes of urban life across the world is a new constellation of military doctrine and theory. In this the specter of state versus state military conflict is seen to be in radical retreat. Instead, the new doctrine is centered upon the idea that a wide spectrum of global insurgencies now operates across social, technical, political, cultural, and financial networks, straddling transnational scales. These are deemed to provide existential threats to Western societies through themselves targeting or exploiting everyday urban sites, infrastructures, and control technologies that sustain contemporary cities. Such lurking threats are deemed by security and military theorists to camouflage themselves within the "clutter" of cities at home and abroad for concealment against traditional forms of military targeting. This, the argument goes, necessitates a radical ratcheting up of techniques of tracking, surveillance, and targeting centered on both the architectures of circulation and mobility – infrastructures – and the spaces of everyday urban life.

The key concept driving the current transformation in military thinking and practice is the shift from "battlefield" to "battlespace." This concept is crucial because it basically sustains what Phil Agre (2001) has called "a conception of military matters that includes absolutely everything." Nothing lies outside the multidimensional and multiscale concept of battlespace, temporally or geographically. Battlespace has no front and no back and no start or end; it is "deep, high, wide, and simultaneous: there is no longer a front or a rear" (Blackmore 2005). The concept of battlespace thus encompasses everything from the molecular scales of genetic engineering and nanotechnology through the everyday sites, spaces, and experiences of city life, to the planetary spheres of inner and outer space or the Internet's globe-straddling "cyberspace." The focus of mobilization is thus no longer focused within delimited geographical or temporal spaces of "symmetrical" state versus state warfare. Instead, it becomes increasingly unbound in time and space. Thus, state power seeks to target "asymmetric" nonstate forces and movements to the point where contemporary "warfare" becomes

"Driving the military targeting of the everyday sites, circulations, and processes of urban life across the world is a new constellation of military doctrine and theory."

Anticipatory Benefits

Just as offenders often overestimate the reach of situational prevention, they often believe that prevention measures have been brought into force before they actually have been. Crime, therefore, drops before any measures have been introduced. This is what is meant by the "anticipatory benefits" of prevention. A recent review found evidence of anticipatory benefits in perhaps as many as 40% of situational prevention projects (Smith, Clarke, and Pease 2002). Apart from using publicity, little is known about how to deliberately enhance these benefits, but they certainly provide "added value" to situational prevention.

Adaptation

The concept of criminal "adaptation" further complicates evaluation of situational prevention. It refers to the process through which offender populations discover new crime vulnerabilities after preventive measures have been in place for a while (Ekblom 1997). It is a longer-term process than displacement, which refers to the ways in which individual offenders seek to circumvent measures put in place to stop them.

> "Offender populations discover new crime vulnerabilities after preventive measures have been in place for a while."

Sabotage[F66]

A clear example of adaptation relates to baggage and passenger screening measures introduced in the early 1970s to curb hijackings of airliners between the United States and Cuba. These measures, together with an agreement between the countries to treat hijackers as criminals, quickly eliminated the hijackings (Clarke and Newman 2006; Wilkinson 1986). Other countries soon adopted the screening measures, and hijackings outside the Americas also declined. There was no real evidence of any displacement, in particular, there was no increase in sabotage bombings of airlines.

However, the screening measures introduced in the 1970s were premised on the assumption that hijackers were not intent on suicide and, in any case, the authorities became less vigilant over time. This allowed the 9/11 hijackers to find loopholes in the security and seize the airliners. Their attack is a clear example of adaptation to preventive measures. It is not displacement because the 9/11 hijackers were completely different from the offenders (those operating in the 1970s between the United States and Cuba) who made the original introduction of the screening measures necessary.

The lack of long-term evaluation makes it difficult to know how often adaptation occurs.

Apart from the hijacking example above, perhaps the best documented example of adaptation is the progressive evolution described by Michael Levi (2008) in methods of credit card fraud in response to a series of preventive measures taken by UK credit card companies in the past two decades. On the other hand, there are some documented examples of situational measures having long-term benefits. For example, Barry Webb (1994) has shown that steering column locks helped to reduce car theft over a forty-year period in Germany and over a thirty-year period in the United Kingdom and the United States, where these locks were introduced later. Further, Rachel Armitage and Hannah Smithson (2007) have shown that the burglary and fear reduction benefits of "alley-gating" (installing locked gates to close off alleys behind houses) in Liverpool were sustained for

effectively "coterminous ... with the space of civil society itself" (Dillon and Reid 2009, 128).

With wars and battle no longer declared or finished, temporalities of war threaten to extend indefinitely. "War is back and seemingly forever" (Deer 2007, 1). No wonder Pentagon gurus convinced George Bush to replace the idea of the "War on Terror" with the new "big idea" of the "long war" in 2004 (McIntyre 2004). All too easily, such a discourse slips into a world where life itself is war (Agre 2004). Indeed, many military theorists now speak of a new (fourth) generation of asymmetric warfare in which nothing is ever outside the battlespace (for a good example, see Hammes 2006). This new generation of war is based, they argue, on "unconventional" wars, "asymmetric" struggles, "global insurgencies," and "low-intensity conflicts" that pit high-tech state militaries against informal fighters or mobilized civilians. Military theorist Thomas Hammes (2006, 3), for example, argues that in the twenty-first century so-called fourth-generation warfare will dominate global security politics, rooted in the concept that "superior political will, when properly employed, can defeat greater economic and military power." Using such doctrine, US commanders in Baghdad have emphasized the need to coordinate the entire battlespace of the city based on addressing civilian infrastructure, the shattered economy, and cultural awareness, as well as "the controlled application of violence" in order to try and secure the city (Chiarelli and Michaelis 2005).

> "With wars and battle no longer declared or finished, temporalities of war threaten to extend indefinitely."

Intrinsically antiurban, such paradigms quickly transpose the prosaic social acts that together forge cosmopolitan urban life into existential, societal threats. For example, US military theorist William Lind, radically extending the US "culture wars" debates of the 1980s and 1990s, and swallowing whole Samuel Huntingdon's (1998) "clash of civilizations" binary, has even argued that acts of urban immigration must now be understood as an act of warfare. "In Fourth Generation war," Lind writes, "invasion by immigration can be at least as dangerous as invasion by a state army." Under what he calls the "poisonous ideology of multiculturalism," Lind (2004) argues that immigrants within Western nations can now launch "a homegrown variety of Fourth Generation war, which is by far the most dangerous kind."

> "Intrinsically antiurban, such paradigms quickly transpose the prosaic social acts that together forge cosmopolitan urban life into existential, societal threats."

Here we confront the realities of what the Center for Immigration Studies has called the "weaponization" of immigration (Cato 2008). Such new imaginations of warfare provide a powerful example of what happens when all aspects of human life are rendered as nothing but war; nations are imagined in narrow ethnonationalist ways and diasporic cities emerge as mere cultural pollutants (see Cowen 2007). "The road from national genius to a totalized cosmology of the sacred nation," writes Arjun

a further four years beyond the initial one-year follow-up (Bowers, Johnson, and Hirschfield 2004).

Conclusions

When first formulated, situational prevention attracted little interest from criminologists. This was partly because it diverged from the dispositional assumptions of the discipline and partly because of knee-jerk suspicion evoked by its origins in "administrative criminology." It has taken many years of sustained research effort for situational prevention to achieve the measure of acceptance that it now has. Developments in the underlying theory have removed any basis for criticizing it as a simplistic approach to crime control; its accumulating record of success has demonstrated that it can achieve very significant reductions in crime, which are not undermined by displacement; its application to a progressively broader range of crimes has shown that it is not limited to dealing only with opportunistic property crimes; and growing experience of its use has shown that many of the ethical criticisms made of it are exaggerated or one-sided. In fact, situational prevention might have fewer ethical problems than some forms of developmental crime prevention and certainly fewer than those of formal criminal justice interventions.

> "Situational prevention threatens to turn criminology from an academic discipline into a technical discourse more in tune with the police and the security industry."

None of these means that situational prevention will be adopted wholesale by criminologists. There is too much investment in dispositional theory and too much hope still invested in finding ways to modify criminal motivation. Moreover, situational prevention does not sit well with criminological ideology. Thus, it does not promote the social reformist agendas of many criminologists and it offends many of their attitudes, such as distaste for business, distrust of corporate power, and sympathy for the criminal underdog. Lastly, situational prevention threatens to turn criminology from an academic discipline into a technical discourse more in tune with the police and the security industry.

In the long run, however, criminologists will have to adapt to some wider changes, independent of situational prevention, but which are congruent with its general approach. The first of these changes is that improved data collection and processing will greatly improve the ability of criminologists to undertake crime-specific studies and studies of situational determinants of crime. These developments include more sophisticated crime mapping and geographic information systems, better capture of crime data through improved police recording practices and the increasing use of crime surveys, and more available time budget data and other indices of citizens' social and economic activities. Second, the development of proactive models of policing (for example, "broken windows" policing, COMPSTAT, problem-oriented policing, and intelligence-led policing) has required police to recruit crime analysts who can support these approaches. The criminological theories and methods that have most relevance for crime analysis are the same as those used in situational prevention. Third, advances in electronic technology, which in the form of the Breathalyzer, speed cameras, and video cameras have already

Appadurai (2006, 4), "and further to ethnic purity and cleansing, is relatively direct."

Crucially, the emerging body of urban military doctrine thus works to radically blur the traditional separation of peace and war, military and civil spheres, local and global scales, and the "inside" and "outside" of nations. On the one hand, then, a wide variety of Western military theorists now concur that that "modern urban combat operations will become one of the primary challenges of the twenty-first century" (DIRC 1997, 11). As the US military theorist of urban warfare Keith Dickson (2002, 4) puts it, the increasing perception within Western militaries is that "for Western military forces, asymmetric warfare in urban areas will be the greatest challenge of this century...The city will be the strategic high ground – whoever controls it will dictate the course of future events in the world."

> "The city will be the strategic high ground – whoever controls it will dictate the course of future events in the world."

On the other hand, the US military's search for new doctrines to deal with the perceived urbanization of war, organized violence, and security explicitly recognizes the similarities when dealing with "urbanized terrain" at home and abroad. Whilst the various warlords, gangs, militias, and insurgents operating through the burgeoning informal urban areas of the global South (see Souza 2009) are widely imagined by Western military theorists to provide the key military challenges of the twenty-first century, dense labyrinthine cities everywhere – both at home and abroad – are imagined together as key future battlespaces. "Despite the geographic differences," writes Maryann Lawlor (2007) in the military magazine *Signal*, key personnel at the US Joint Forces Command (JFCOM) in Norfolk, Virginia, have used massive war games and simulations, such as one named Urban Resolve, and in so doing "identified several key concerns common to both areas." These involve the difficulty of separating "terrorists" or "insurgents" from the urban civilian population; the high densities of infrastructure; the way cities interrupt old-style military surveillance and targeting systems; and the complex three-dimensional nature of urban battlespace.

Through such an analytical lens, the LA riots of 1992, various attempts to securitize urban cores for major sports events or political summits, the militarized responses to Hurricane Katrina in New Orleans in 2005, and the challenges of "homeland security" in US cities have all blurred together to be perceived as "urban" or "low-intensity operations" or moments of "irregular warfare," in common with episodes of counterinsurgency warfare taking place on the streets of Baghdad (see Boyle 2005). Indeed the paradigms underpinning the new military urbanism allow transnational social movements and mobilizations against state oppression or the devastating effects of market fundamentalism, ecological crises, and neoliberalization – for example, the Zapatistas or environmental and global justice campaigners – to be tackled as forms of "netwar," equivalent to the radical and murderous Islamism of Al Qaeda (see Arquilla and Ronfeldt 2001). Postoperational "lessons learned" reports drawn up after

extended the reach of situational prevention and law enforcement, will likely continue to deliver new forms of prevention. Fourth, and perhaps most importantly, crime is rapidly changing. Thus, Nick Tilley, Amanda Robinson, and John Burrows (2007) have noted that the share of all recorded crime accounted for by burglaries and car thefts declined from about 50% in the mid-1990s to just below 30% in 2005.

TABLE 6.1
Twenty-Five Techniques of Situational Prevention

Increase the effort	Increase the risks	Reduce the rewards	Reduce provocations	Remove excuses
1. TARGET HARDENING	6. EXTEND GUARDIANSHIP	11. CONCEAL TARGETS	16. REDUCE FRUSTRATIONS AND STRESS	21. SET RULES
Steering column locks and ignition immobilizers, antirobbery screens, tamperproof packaging	Go out in group at night, leave signs of occupancy, carry cell phone	Off-street parking, gender-neutral phone directories, unmarked armored trucks	Efficient lines, polite service, expanded seating, soothing music/muted lights	Rental agreements, harassment codes, hotel registration
2. CONTROL ACCESS TO FACILITIES	7. ASSIST NATURAL SURVEILLANCE	12. REMOVE TARGETS	17. AVOID DISPUTES	22. POST INSTRUCTIONS
Entry phones, electronic card access, baggage screening	Improved street lighting, defensible space design, support whistle-blowers	Removable car radio, women's shelters, prepaid cards for pay phones	Separate seating for rival soccer fans, reduce crowding in bars, fixed cab fares	"No parking," "Private property," "Extinguish camp fires"
3. SCREEN EXITS	8. REDUCE ANONYMITY	13. IDENTIFY PROPERTY	18. REDUCE TEMPTATION AND AROUSAL	23. ALERT CONSCIENCE
Ticket needed for exit, export documents, electronic merchandise tags	Taxi driver IDs, "How's my driving?" decals, school uniforms	Property marking, vehicle licensing and parts marking, cattle branding	Controls on violent pornography, enforce good behavior on soccer field, prohibit racial slurs	Roadside speed display boards, signatures for customs declarations, "Shoplifting is stealing"
4. DEFLECT OFFENDERS	9. USE PLACE MANAGERS	14. DISRUPT MARKETS	19. NEUTRALIZE PEER PRESSURE	24. ASSIST COMPLIANCE
Street closures, separate bathrooms for women, disperse pubs	CCTV for double-deck buses, two clerks for convenience stores, reward vigilance	Monitor pawn shops, controls on classified ads, license street vendors	"Idiots drink and drive," "It's OK to say No," disperse troublemakers at school	Easy library checkout, public lavatories, litter receptacles
5. CONTROL TOOLS/ WEAPONS	10. STRENGTHEN FORMAL SURVEILLANCE	15. DENY BENEFITS	20. DISCOURAGE IMITATION	25. CONTROL DRUGS AND ALCOHOL
"Smart" guns, restrict spray paint sales to juveniles, toughened beer glasses	Red light cameras, burglar alarms, security guards	Ink merchandise tags, graffiti cleaning, disabling stolen cell phones	Rapid repair of vandalism, V-chips in TVs, censor details of modus operandi	Breathalyzers in bars, server intervention programs, alcohol-free events

NOTE. From Cornish and Clarke (2003). Copyright 2003 by Criminal Justice Press (accessible at www.popcenter.org). Reprinted with permission of the author.

military deployments to contain the Los Angeles riots in 1992, credited "the 'success' of the mission to the fact that 'the enemy' – the local population – was easy to outmaneuver given their simple battle tactics and strategies" (cited in Cowen 2007, 1).

Finally, the US military's focus on military operations within the domestic urban sphere of the "homeland" has strengthened dramatically since the start of the so-called War on Terror (see Canestaro 2003). This process allows the US military to overcome traditional legal obstacles to deployment in the US itself (Canestaro 2003). It allows the tactics and lessons of planning and designing "Green Zone" urban bases in the hearts of Baghdad and other cities to be imported domestically as the basis of implanting analogous "security zones" around financial and government districts in New York and other major US cities (see Nemeth 2009). Finally, it means that high-tech targeting practices employing unmanned drones and organized satellite surveillance programs, previously limited to the permanent targeting of spaces beyond the nation's boundaries to (purportedly) make the nation safe, are also starting to colonize the domestic urban spaces of the nation (see Gorman 2008).

Significantly, the emergence of the new military urbanism works to compound long-standing trends toward punitive criminology and revanchist urban policy that have marked processes of urban neoliberalization in many Western and global South nations (see Smith 2002; Wacquant 2008). The US response to the devastation of the largely African-American city of New Orleans by Hurricane Katrina in August 2005 provides a paradigmatic example (Graham 2006). For a brief period, some US officers discussed their highly militarized responses to the Katrina disaster in New Orleans as an attempt to "take back" New Orleans from African-American "insurgencies" (Chiarelli and Michaelis 2005). In this case, rather than a massive humanitarian response treating the victims as citizens requiring immediate help, a largely military operation was (eventually) organized. Such a response merely reinforced the idea that the internal geographies of the US are the sites of state-backed wars against racialized and biopolitically disposable others as much as external actors (Giroux 2006). This operation treated those abandoned in the central city as a threat and a military objective to be contained, targeted and addressed in order to protect the property of the normalized and largely white suburban and exurban populations who had escaped in their own cars (Giroux 2006). In the process, African-American citizens of the city were rendered refugees in their own country. As Robert Stam and Ella Shohat (2007, 167) argue, "Katrina not only ripped the roofs off Gulf Coast houses but also ripped the façade off 'the national security state.'"

Together, these blurring processes thus sustain the imagination of all cities everywhere as key battlespaces requiring permanent targeting and mobilization within limitless imaginations of war.

> "It allows the tactics and lessons of planning and designing "Green Zone" urban bases in the hearts of Baghdad and other cities to be imported domestically as the basis of implanting analogous "security zones" around financial and government districts ..."

Drone[F26]

At the same time as "street crimes" like burglaries and car thefts are falling, globalization and the Internet have opened up new worlds of opportunity for electronic and transnational crimes, which are being widely exploited by organized criminals and terrorists. Rational choice and routine activity theory often provide better explanations of these crimes, and help to suggest more effective means of intervention than traditional, dispositional criminology.

If experience is any guide, situational prevention will need to be modified and extended to take account of these developments. Some already existing gaps in our knowledge about situational prevention have been noted above, the most important of which concern aspects of its effectiveness. While there is no doubt that it can be highly effective in a wide variety of specific circumstances, much less is known about the longevity and the cost-effectiveness of its interventions. More tantalizing, little is known about the overall effect of reducing opportunities for crime through the combined application of situational prevention and tightened security. If there is any validity to some recent speculation about the role of opportunity in crime (see above), it might be expected that removing some of the easiest and most tempting opportunities for crime would result in a multiplicative effect on the total volume of traditional offenses, as fewer individuals might embark upon "a life of crime." During the past twenty years, a vast amount has been done to improve security through widespread use of burglar alarms, security guards, CCTV surveillance, antifraud systems for credit cards, EAS and barcodes for merchandise in shops, electronic immobilizers for cars, better lighting, and improved building design. Indeed, the security industry has consistently been cited as one of the fastest-growing sectors of the economy and situational prevention has sometimes been described as the fastest-growing form of crime prevention. However, criminologists have rarely mentioned this vast range of activity as a possible cause of the widespread declines of crime in most industrialized nations, even though many of the common explanations for the crime drop in America (greater use of imprisonment, the waning of the crack epidemic, demographic change, improved policing, etc., Blumstein and Wallman 2000) do not hold for these other nations. This neglect has been noted by others (Farrell, Tilley, Tseloni, and Mailley 2011) and, if this stimulates the needed research, it might turn out that the value of reducing opportunities for crime could no longer be discounted by criminologists.

> "Little is known about the overall effect of reducing opportunities for crime through the combined application of situational prevention and tightened security."

In the process, they threaten to fundamentally challenge accepted notions of citizenship, law, and the distinction between a liberal "inside" of the nation, controlled through policing, separated from an illiberal "outside" where a nation's military forces are deployed (Bigo and Anastassia 2006; Cowen and Smith 2009). Instead of such (inevitably precarious and contradictory) binaries, we are rapidly moving toward a context where, as Jeremy Packer (2006, 378) puts it, "citizens and noncitizens alike are now treated as an always present threat. In this sense, all are imagined as combatants and all terrain the site of battle." The proliferation of anticipatory profiling and targeting systems, as we shall see in the next section, increasingly uses computer algorithms to define deviance, and hence threat, from the mass circulations and populations of the city, in advance of civil or criminal offenses being proven (see Amoore 2009).

> "Together, these blurring processes thus sustain the imagination of all cities everywhere as key battlespaces requiring permanent targeting and mobilization within limitless imaginations of war."

Digitality, Security and Globalized Urbanism

"Contemporary militarization runs on an economy of desire as well as an economy of fear."
Crandall and Armitage (2005, 20)

The new military urbanism's second foundation is the fusing and blurring of civilian and military applications of control, surveillance, communications, simulation, and targeting technologies. This is not surprising given that control technologies with military origins are now fundamental bases for virtually all acts of digitally mediated urban life and consumption in advanced industrial cities, and that commercial modifications of such technologies are in turn being widely reappropriated by the military.

With physical urban fortifications long forgotten or turned into tourist sites, contemporary architectures of (attempted) urban control now blend digital sensors into built space and physical infrastructure. Indeed, the new military urbanism rests on claims that contemporary cities are now, in Paul Virilio's (1991) term, "overexposed" to a wide range of ambient, mobile, and transnational security threats. These include, to name but a few, mobile pathogens, malign computer code, financial crashes, "illegal" migration, transnational terrorism, state infrastructural warfare and the environmental extremes triggered by climate change.

The permeability of contemporary cities to such malign circulations means that systems of (attempted) electronic control – stretched out to match the transnational geographies of such flows – become the new strategic architectures of city life. French philosopher Gilles Deleuze (1992) famously termed contemporary societies "societies of control." Because networked electronic control and surveillance devices are now distributed through society, Deleuze argued that everyday urban life is now modulated by a sense of ever-present tracking, scrutiny, and

Theme: National Security Strategies
Author: David Omand

Securing the State:
National Security and Secret Intelligence

electronic calculation. This builds up profiles, analyzes patterns of behavior and mobility, and increasingly – because memory is now digitized – never forgets. Thus, circulations and movements between different spaces and sites within cities or nations often entail a parallel movement of what sociologists call the "data subject" or "statistical person" – the package of electronic tracks and histories amassed on a subject or object as a means of judging their legitimacy, rights, profitability, or degree of threat.

In control societies, then, (attempted) social control increasingly works through complex technological systems stretched across both temporal and geographical zones. These work constantly in the ("calculative") background as a ubiquitous computerized matrix of (increasingly) interlinked devices: ATM cards and financial databases; GPS transponders, barcodes and chains of global satellites; radio frequency chips and biometric identifiers; mobile computers, phones and e-commerce sites; and an extending universe of sensors built into streets, homes, cars, infrastructures, and even bodies.

> "Control technologies increasingly blur into the background of urban environments, urban infrastructures, and urban life."

Such control technologies increasingly blur into the background of urban environments, urban infrastructures, and urban life. In a sense, indeed, they become the city as they are layered over and through everyday urban landscapes, bringing into being radically new styles of movement, interaction, consumption, and politics. Examples include new means of mobility (congestion charging, smart highways, budget airline travel), customized consumption (personalized Amazon.com pages) or "swarming" social movements (social networking, smart and flash mobs, etc.).

Strikingly, discussions about "homeland security" and the high-tech transformation of asymmetric war also center prominently on the purported need to use these very technologies of high-tech surveillance, data mining, and computerized algorithms to try and continually track, identify, and "target" threatening others within the mass of "clutter" provided by our rapidly urbanizing and increasingly mobile world (Amoore 2009). The technological architectures of consumption and mobility thus merge more and more into those used to organize and prosecute a full spectrum of political violence (from profiling to killing). When one looks at the links between cities and post–World War II military history, the connection is actually far from surprising. Gerfried Stocker (1998) notes that "there is no sphere of civilian life in which the saying 'war is the father of all things' has such unchallenged validity as it does in the field of digital information technology."

More than this, the new military urbanism has actually been the foundry of the new control technologies (see Virilio 1989). After World War II, military command and control strategies known as C3I – command, control, communications, and information – dominated Cold War notions of war-fighting and strategic deterrence. They also colonized the minutiae of modernizing urban life, especially in Western nations. "No part of the

> "In sum, there comes a point when the search for even greater security becomes burdensome and oppressive, and when the public will cavil at what it is being expected to give up to provide it."

Consider the artist Michaelangelo standing in front of a block of Carrera marble rough-hewn from the quarry. As he later described that moment, "I saw the angel in the marble and carved until I set him free." Sculptors need the patience to recognize that many small steps will be needed to realize their vision. The sculptor needs a strategic sixth sense that can continuously adapt the design to the conditions of the material whilst testing whether each small incision, however immediately appealing and easily achieved, will end up weakening the final structure. The sculptor needs the confidence to know that the design can be adjusted in response to the inevitable small slips and misjudgments made along the way. Call it having the ability to hold the desired ends in mind whilst being continuously aware of the ways open for achieving them and the means that are at hand. Even the most technically skilled sculptor equipped with the sharpest chisels needs to have a clear sense of the end state – to see at the outset "the figure in the marble" – that could be the final result of all the labor to come. That is the strategic cast of mind needed for planning modern counterterrorism.

In building a strategy for countering a terrorist threat there are certainly enhanced means available to government today. [...] Yet, these very reassuring strengths can lead to a pursuit of immediate gains only to find later that they may be at the expense of risking longer-term goals. Measures taken with the best of intentions to neutralize terrorist threats overseas can through collateral damage build long-term hostility and provide propaganda opportunities that help breed future threats. Local security clampdowns on minority communities can discourage the flow of information to the authorities. Providing overseas military support for combatants against today's adversaries can end up arming tomorrow's enemies. Domestic security measures (such as restrictions at airports and major events) can overtax the patience of the public. The search for preemptive intelligence on suspect individuals can lead governments into disproportionate intrusion by agents of the State into personal privacy and private life. The understandable desire to find ways of bringing terrorists to justice can strain the limits of the rule of law. In sum, there comes a point when the search for even greater security becomes burdensome and oppressive, and when the public will cavil at what it is being expected to give up to provide it. Yet the public rightly sees the provision of security as government's first responsibility: government cannot avoid these dilemmas.

Omand

David Omand (1947-) is a former director of the British security and intelligence organization Government Communication Headquarters (GCHQ) and is known for his 2010 book *Securing the State*. In this essay, Omand addresses the dilemma of the state, both in a contemporary and historical context in terms of the question, How much security is enough? The piece focuses upon terror prevention through the lens of state intelligence activity – unfolding the associated challenges in finding a necessary balance between the extremes of too much and not enough. Omand warns against the desire to entirely eliminate risk in urban settings: "The public should be invited to accept that there is no absolute security and chasing after it does more harm than good."

This text was first published in *Prism: A Journal of the Center for Complex Operations* 4, no. 3 (2013).

world went untouched by C3I," writes Ryan Bishop (2004, 61). "And it delineates the organizational, economic, technological, and spatial systems that derive from, rely on, and perpetuate military strategy."

Since the start of the Cold War, for example, it has been common for the US to devote more than 80 percent of all its expenditure to technological research and development to "defense" (Mesnard y Méndez 2002). Technologies like the Internet, virtual reality, jet travel, data mining, closed-circuit TV, rocketry, remote control, microwaves, radar, global positioning, networked computers, wireless communication, satellite surveillance, containerization, and logistics – which together now provide the basis for all aspects of everyday urban life – were thus all forged in the latter half of the twentieth century as part of the elaboration of systems of military control (see De Landa 1992).

Considered thus, "this 'insignia of the military' … manifests itself in a myriad of ways in global urban sites … The global city would not be a global city, as we have come to understand the phenomenon, without being deeply embedded in these processes" (Bishop 2004, 61). Whilst the relationship between commercial and military control and information technologies has always been a complex two-way affair, it is important to be mindful that the very technological architectures of contemporary urban life, through the crucial nexus of the new military urbanism, simultaneously bring into being the imperial geographies of empire.

The explosive recent growth of GPS applications is a salient example here (Kaplan 2006). Since the US military first deployed GPS to support the "precision" killing of the 1991 Gulf War, GPS has been partially declassified and opened up to a widening universe of commercial, governmental, and civilian applications. GPS has become the basis for civilian mobility and navigation, a ubiquitous consumer technology used in PDAs, watches, cars, and a widening array of geolocation services. GPS has been used to reorganize agriculture, transportation, navigation, logistics, municipal government, law enforcement, border security, computer gaming, and leisure activities. But few bother to consider the ways in which military and imperial power infuse through every GPS application. Every civilian use of GPS, for example, is based on atomic clocks and geostationary satellites used to continually kill as part of the permanent, distanciated "war on terror."

With a suite of surveillance and control technologies now established to try and preempt and anticipate consumption as well as risk, Anne Bottomley and Nathan Moore (2007, 181) write that "the production of knowledge [is] no longer intended to secrete and clarify what can be known, but rather to 'clarify what cannot be known.'" The city is thus increasingly "defined by the military goal of being able to know the enemy even before the enemy

> "Few bother to consider the ways in which military and imperial power infuse through every GPS application. Every civilian use of GPS, for example, is based on atomic clocks and geostationary satellites used to continually kill as part of the permanent, distanciated 'war on terror.'"

How Much Security Is Enough?

It is thus not just the choices of ways and means that can be problematic but also of the ends of counterterrorism strategy. In essence, the issue again today, as for many countries in the past, is how much security is enough. How can government best set out to exercise its primary duty to protect the public in the face of a substantial terrorist threat, and yet also intend to maintain civic harmony, uphold democratic values, and promote the rule of law at home and internationally. The initial need to combat the jihadist terrorist campaign at home and abroad justified itself; robust measures have been taken and have reduced the immediate threat. The harder policy question that is now arising is in relation to the longer-term ends of counterterrorism strategy: how much security do we think will be enough in a world of competing priorities for government attention and resources and where terrorism, however dramatic, is only one of many risks facing the public that have to be managed?

In the UK, an all-party consensus has held now for over a decade over what should be the objective of the UK national counterterrorist strategy (CONTEST, short for COuNter-TErroism STrategy).[1] When we started work on the strategy after the attacks on 9/11 we debated whether its ends should be couched in terms of defeating or eliminating terrorism but concluded such an aim was unrealizable since terrorism would be bound to remain an asymmetric tactic of choice for violent extremist groups – and no government can ever give a complete guarantee to the public that terrorists might not at some point be able to slip below the security radar however sophisticated it is. Absolute security is a chimera. Instead we focused on ways of denying the jihadist terrorists what they most seek, which is to shock and disrupt and thus erode public confidence in the ability of government to protect them. The narrative was of fortitude and resilience, setting the objective as a vigorous collective and communal effort to sustain the normality of everyday life. The formal aim of CONTEST – which is being achieved – is therefore to reduce the risk from terrorism so that people can go about their normal life freely (that is, with the rule of law upheld and without the authorities having to interfere with individual rights and liberties) and with confidence (for example, with people still traveling by air and on the underground, visitors vacationing in the UK, with financial markets stable, and so on).

The Thermodynamics of Counterterrorism

In that way, by stressing the goal of normality in a resilient society the UK strategy tries to avoid the trap that terrorists set of "the propaganda of the deed," seeking to radicalize supporters through exposing supposed fragility in Western societies and provoking overreaction from the security authorities. That is one of the eternal security lessons we should have absorbed (and learned the hard way over the years) about what could be described as the "thermodynamics" of counterterrorism.

For there is an important relationship between the necessary vigor of security measures imposed to stop terrorists, the intrusiveness of measures taken to obtain intelligence to prevent attacks, and the

> "We focused on ways of denying the jihadist terrorists what they most seek, which is to shock and disrupt and thus erode public confidence in the ability of government to protect them."

is aware of himself as such" (ibid.). The overarching feature of the new, militarized, surveillance push, regardless of whether its "targets" are located in Manhattan or Baghdad, London or Fallujah, is an attempt to build systems of technological vision in which computer code itself, along with databases of real or imagined targets, is delegated with the agency of tracking and identifying "abnormal" targets from the background "normality" or "clutter" of a homeland or war-zone city (Amoore 2009). This shift represents a process of profound militarization because the social identification of people within civilian law enforcement is complemented or even replaced by the machinic seeing of "targets." "While civilian images are embedded in processes of identification based on reflection," writes media theorist Jordan Crandall (1999), "militarized perspectives collapse identification processes into 'ID-ing' – one-way channel of identification in which a conduit, a database, and a body are aligned and calibrated."

> "The social identification of people within civilian law enforcement is complemented or even replaced by the machinic seeing of 'targets.'"

'Security' and Political Economy

As the everyday spaces and systems of urban everyday life are colonized by militarized control technologies, and notions of policing and war, domestic and foreign, peace and war blur together, so the new military urbanism's fourth pillar is constituted: a massive boom emerges in a convergent industrial complex encompassing sectors such as security, surveillance, academia, military technology, prisons, electronic entertainment and corrections. These fusing industries work to exploit the cross-fertilization and blurring between the traditional military imperatives of war external to the state, and those of policing internal to it, within the broader apparatus of James Der Derian's (2001) military–industrial–media–entertainment network.

The proliferation of wars sustaining permanent mobilization and preemptive ubiquitous surveillance within and beyond territorial borders means that the imperative of "security" now "imposes itself of the basic principle of state activity" (Agamben 2001). Georgio Agamben argues that "what used to be one among several decisive measures of public administration until the first half of the twentieth century, now becomes the sole criterion of political legitimation" (ibid.).

The result is an ever-broadening landscape of "security" blending commercial, military, and security practices with increasingly fearful cultures of civilian mobility, citizenship, and consumption. These fusions are manifest in a proliferation of digital passage-points, superimposed upon, through, and within the architectural and geographical spaces of cities and systems of cities. These continually seek to link databases of past traffic and behavior into normative judgments of rights to presence or access based on anticipations of future risk. As philosopher William Connolly (2005, 54) suggests:

> Airport surveillance, Internet filters, passport tracking devices, legal detention without criminal charges, security internment

Human Rights[F14]

level of confidence among different sections of the community in the government's commitment to protect the liberties and rights of the citizen. The right to life of the ordinary person in the face of murderous terrorism on the one hand and the right to privacy of personal and family life on the other. As with the thermodynamic relationship between the volume, pressure, and temperature of a gas, too sudden an application of force to compress it, and the temperature may rise dangerously to explosive levels; too little pressure applied, and the gas is uncontained and will expand out of control. The best approach may well be to cool things down as you gradually build up the pressure, and certainly not to do things unnecessarily that heat it up: the impact of the occupation of Iraq on domestic radicalization in the UK and elsewhere comes to mind; the impact of an Israeli attack on Iran's nuclear facilities, were one to occur, would be another.

Such an analogy to thermodynamics cannot be pushed too far – the point to be registered is the interrelationship between a nation's security effort in the face of domestic threat, the direct effect on the risks faced by the public, and the indirect effects on the rule of law, civil liberties, human rights, and thus civic harmony or "Civitas" – the public value of harmony in the community based on a shared sense of place, of belonging, regardless of ethnic roots or religious difference. The choice of security strategy is of course crucial to getting that thermodynamic judgment right. [...]

In a nutshell, the argument is that good government will always place the task of "securing the state" at the top of its priorities. With security comes confidence, economic and social progress and investment in the future. But good government also recognizes that security needs the active support of all sections of the public and thus the right relationship between justice, civic harmony, wise administration, fortitude, prudence and the other virtues to which the wise ruler and government should aspire. [...]

> "In a nutshell, the argument is that good government will always place the task of 'securing the state' at the top of its priorities."

Strategic Logic of UK Counterterrorist Strategy

The UK CONTEST counterterrorism strategy remains in force now some ten years after its initiation and is on its third major iteration under its third prime minister.[2] One of the reasons why the strategy has lasted is that it incorporates the logic of risk management. To achieve the state of normality that is its goal there are campaigns to influence each factor in the risk management equation that provides the measure of total risk: likelihood × vulnerability × initial impact × duration of disruption.

Thus the strategy aims to make attacks less likely by improving the intelligence and law-enforcement capability to uncover terrorist networks, frustrate attacks, and bring terrorists to justice (what in CONTEST was termed the Pursue campaign); it aims to reduce the incidence of radicalization in the community and overseas to stem the flow of terrorist recruits (the Prevent Campaign); to reduce the vulnerability of the critical civil infrastructure on which society depends, including aviation (the Protect Campaign); and to equip and exercise the emergency services to reduce the impact should terrorists succeed in mounting an attack (the Prepare Campaign). The value of such continuity in basic strategy in terms of maintaining

Photo Essay

WORLD TRADE CENTER, New York, NY, USA
Visited April 10, 2014

WTC, New York, NY, USA

01. Layered facade of the National September 11th Memorial

02. Surveillance tower on street in front of the National September 11th Memorial

03. Barricades and vehicle barriers outside the National September 11th Memorial

04. Temporary vehicle barriers functioning as street furniture

138 Photo Essay

5

WTC, New York, NY, USA

05. Specifically designed surveillance lamp-post on the WTC memorial site

06. Temporary vehicle barriers blocking Greenwich Street

07. Street checkpoint

camps, secret trials, "free speech zones," DNA profiles, border walls and fences, erosion of the line between internal security and external military action – these security activities resonate together, engendering a national security machine that pushes numerous issues outside the range of legitimate dissent and mobilizes the populace to support new security and surveillance practices against underspecified enemies.

It is no accident that security-industrial complexes blossom in parallel with the diffusion of market fundamentalist notions of organizing social, economic, and political life. The hyperinequalities and urban militarization and <u>securitization</u> sustained by urban neoliberalization are mutually reinforcing. In a discussion of the US government's response to the Katrina disaster, for example, Henry Giroux (2006, 172) points out that the normalization of market fundamentalism in US culture has made it much more "difficult to translate private woes into social issues and collective action or to insist on a language of the public good." He argues that "the evisceration of all notions of sociality" in this case has led to "a sense of total abandonment, resulting in fear, anxiety, and insecurity over one's future" (ibid.).

Added to this, Giroux argues that "the presence of the racialized poor, their needs and vulnerabilities – now visible – become unbearable" (ibid.). Rather than address the causes of poverty or insecurity, however, political responses now invariably "focus on shoring up a diminished sense of safety, carefully nurtured by a renewed faith in all things military." Also crucial is the effective looting of state budgets for postdisaster assistance and reconstruction by cabals of predatory lobbyists intimately linked to both governments and the burgeoning array of private military and security corporations (see Klinenberg and Frank 2005).

Given such a context, it is not surprising that, amidst a global financial crash, market growth in security services and technologies remains extremely strong. "International expenditure on homeland security now surpasses established enterprises like movie-making and the music industry in annual revenues" (*Economic Times* 2007). Homeland Security Research Corporation (2007) points out that "the worldwide 'total defense' outlay (military, intelligence community, and Homeland Security/Homeland Defense) is forecasted to grow by approximately 50%, from $1,400 billion in 2006 to $2,054 billion by 2015." By 2005, US defense expenditures alone had reached $420 billion a year – comparable to the rest of the world combined. Over a quarter of this was devoted to purchasing services from a rapidly expanding market of private military corporations. By 2010, such mercenary groups are in line to receive a staggering US $202 billion from the US government alone (Schreier and Caparini 2005).

<u>Securitization</u>[F69]

"The result is an ever-broadening landscape of 'security' blending commercial, military, and security practices with increasingly fearful cultures of civilian mobility, citizenship, and consumption."

"The hyperinequalities and urban militarization and securitization sustained by urban neoliberalization are mutually reinforcing."

effective counterterrorist effort, not least during the run-up to the recent Olympics, should not be underestimated. I judge it a success in its own terms: as the 2012 Olympics showed, the UK is a nation living in peace, despite the continuing substantial level of threat from militant jihadist extremists.

This risk-management approach has now been extended in the UK beyond countering terrorism. When the current British coalition government published its overall National Security Strategy,[3] it spelled out those major modern threats and hazards that have to be managed, from terrorism to cyberpiracy, and from instability in key regions overseas to natural disasters, as well as the continuing task of preserving the territorial independence of the United Kingdom, not least through our membership in NATO.

The National Security Strategy identifies four "top tier" risks:

1. international terrorism affecting the UK and its interests overseas;

2. hostile attacks upon UK cyberspace;

3. a major accident or natural hazard;

4. an international military crisis drawing in the UK. [...]

A Modern Approach to National Security

This modern approach to national security therefore rests on three sets of propositions.

The first step in the argument is recognition of the implications of regarding national security as a collective psychological state as well as an objective reality such as freedom from foreign invasion. People need to feel sufficiently safe to justify investment, to be prepared to travel, indeed to leave the house in the morning to get on with ordinary life and to live it to the full – even in the face of threats such as terrorism and hazards such as pandemics. Our adversaries – and the international markets – must know we have the confidence to help each other and to do what is necessary to defend ourselves.

> "We have to accept that we should be aiming for the sensible management of risk, not on attempting to eliminate risks altogether."

Looking at the type of malign threats that impact on our increasingly technologically dependent society, we have to be prepared to invest in advance to prevent attacks, to reduce our vulnerabilities, and to invest in higher levels of resilience. In a comparable way, we could tomorrow face the consequences of major natural hazards, such as the effects of "space weather" resulting from coronal ejections from the sun, or animal diseases jumping the species barrier, or those that are likely to flow from resource stress as the global climate changes. Governments need to anticipate and act now – preferably in international concert – to mitigate the consequences of such hazards. [...]

The second step in modern national security strategy builds on that recognition of the citizen-centric view of threats and hazards. We have to accept that we should be aiming for the sensible management of risk, not on attempting to eliminate risks altogether. Efforts to avoid all risk can do more harm than good, since the law

Unfortunately, very little high-quality critical urban research exists on the complex transnational political economy of what the OECD (2004) call the "new security economy" (although see Bisley 2004 for a rare example). It is clear, though, that the production and research and development aspects of the global security surge are overwhelmingly constituted within the world's key technopolitan urban centers and centered on the world's leading high-tech corporate universities. As in the Cold War, beyond the surface polish of digital utopianism that dominates the representation of places like Silicon Valley, the Washington Beltway, Tel Aviv, and Cambridge, Massachusetts, these technopolitan complexes are the foundries of global securitization and militarization. Unlike their Cold War contemporaries, however (Markusen et al. 1991), contemporary economic geographers are yet to map out these geographical political economies of the new security surge.

It is equally clear that the transnational organized coalitions between governments and corporate interests that are driving the global security surge are coalescing and operating well beyond the democratic scrutiny of national democracies. "Growth in the industry is assured by massive government contracts and generous subsidies for homeland security research and development" (Hayes and Tasse 2007). Crucial here is the argument that radical extensions in the extent and reach of national and supranational surveillance systems might be fueled by the dictates of industrial policy rather than the need to mobilize against purported security threats. Statewatch's Ben Hayes (2006, 3), for example, argues that the EU's efforts to establish a continent-wide Security Research Programme is best described as "'Big Brother' meets market fundamentalism." Its massive high-tech development and supply contracts are organized by a cabal of "EU officials and Europe's biggest arms and IT companies" (ibid.). As in the US, moreover, EU security policy as well as research is heavily influenced by massive lobbying from the main corporate security operations (many of which are recently privatized state operations). Rather than the ethics of massive securitization, the prime EU concern has been how European industries could muscle in on booming global markets. The main concern here is to allow EU corporations to take a bigger slice of booming global markets for a "myriad of local and global surveillance systems; the introduction of biometric identifiers; RFID, electronic tagging, and satellite monitoring; 'less-lethal weapons'; paramilitary equipment for public order and crisis management; and the militarization of border controls" (ibid.). Thus we face the possibility of urban securitization as a shop window for industrial policy within burgeoning "security" marketplaces. This logic operates most powerfully during the temporary urban securitization operations which surround major political summits and sporting events.

> "The EU's efforts to establish a continent-wide Security Research Programme is best described as 'Big Brother' meets market fundamentalism."

of unintended consequences often applies to the measures we take. If unreal expectations are generated, then failure will breed public cynicism and an accusatory blame culture when things do not turn out as planned. In particular, as already noted, governments in their pursuit of security can risk compromising freedom of movement and of speech, and the rule of law, thus disturbing the civic harmony that lies at the heart of successful societies. Indeed, an important ingredient in public security in a democracy is confidence in the government's ability to manage risk in ways that respect human rights and the values of society.

The third step in the argument then follows. It is to see that the key to good risk management, maintaining that delicate balance, is to have better informed decision-making by government, and thus place greater weight on the work of the intelligence community.

Now, the overall purpose of an intelligence community can be said to be to improve the quality of decision-making by reducing ignorance. Today there is more information available than ever before to help us do that. So-called secret intelligence is simply the achievement of that purpose in respect of information that other people, such as terrorists or rogue states, do not want us to have, and we normally do not want them to know we have. Obviously decisions should be based on adequate knowledge of the situation – situational awareness – plus a deep understanding of the roots of what is going on. With situational awareness plus good explanation of why the situation is as it is there is some hope that what is liable to happen next can be predicted and risks anticipated, and successfully managed, within the limits of the knowable.

With preemptive intelligence, criminal networks can be identified and individuals brought to justice without having to resort to cruder measures – the bludgeon of State power – to try to protect the public as was seen in the early 1970s in Northern Ireland, with mass arrests and internment without trial, house-to-house searches, roadblocks, and large-scale stop and search. An advantage of having adequate preemptive intelligence is that by making it possible to reduce the level of threat, political pressures are relieved that otherwise would build up on government to take more draconian measures so as reassure the majority but that may alienate the community among which the terrorist seeks sanctuary and support, feeding into the narrative of the extremist.

Thus intelligence – broadly defined – can be used to improve the odds of achieving our goals beyond what we would have managed had we simply tossed a coin to decide between courses of action, acted on hunch, or allowed events in the absence of decision to decide the outcome. But it is always a matter of odds, not certainties. Since the London bombings of 2005 there have been around a dozen jihadist terrorist plots directly affecting the UK. A few, such as the Haymarket car bombs, the plot that ended violently with the terrorists on the run attempting to crash a car loaded with gas cylinders into Glasgow Airport, failed only because of slip-ups by the terrorists. But most failed because the intelligence services and the police got onto their trail first. We had a trouble-free Olympics in 2012 in London in large part because of a great deal of preemptive work by the security authorities.

Anticipation as a component of national security strategy thus places a great responsibility on the intelligence officers and analysts who are to provide the strategic and tactical intelligence. Anticipation

Urbicidal Wars: State, Space, Violence

"The fate of empires is very often sealed by the interaction of war and debt."
(Gray 2008, 31)

Finally, and following neatly from such arguments, the new military urbanism rests fundamentally on the changing powers of states to attempt the violent reconfiguration, or even erasure, of cities and urban spaces. This operates either as a means to allay purported threats, or as way of clearing new space for the exigencies of global-city formation, neoliberal production, or as urban tabula rasa necessary for the most profitable bubbles of real estate speculation. Central here are widespread invocations of exception and emergency in justifying such violent assaults, often against a (demonized and fictionalized) urban, racial, or class enemy (Mbembe 2003, 16).

Such states of exception are called into being both to constitute the geographies of permanent violence that sustain the neoliberal economy, and to create what Achille Mbembe (2003, 16) calls "death worlds" – spaces like Palestine, where vast populations are forced to live the lives of the living dead. Both work to support broader geographies of accumulation through dispossession which, whilst as old as colonialism, have been especially central to neoliberal globalization (Banerjee 2006).

Here we confront further aspects of the complex political economies of the new military urbanism and their central integration into what Naomi Klein (2007) has diagnosed as a tendency within contemporary neoliberal capitalism to engineer, or profit from, catastrophic "natural" or political-economic shocks. In short, at issue here is the character of what, following the work of Neil Brenner (2004), we might call the new state spaces of war and violence and their relationships with political violence and geographies of dispossession in the current period.

Citing the systematic Israeli bulldozing of homes and towns in Palestine, similar erasures of hotbeds of resistance like Fallujah in Iraq, and the widespread erasure of informal settlements across the globe – as city authorities entrepreneurially reorganize urban spaces to be "global" – Kanishka Goonewardena and Stefan Kipfer (2006, 23), drawing on Frantz Fanon's (1963) classic critique of the violence intrinsic to Western colonial power, point "to an ominously normalized reality experienced by the 'damned of the earth' after the 'end of history.'" This, they argue, has summoned a new keyword in urban studies and allied disciplines: urbicide (see Graham 2004).

Defined as political violence intentionally designed to erase or "kill" cities, urbicidal violence can involve the ethnonationalist targeting of spaces of cosmopolitan mixing (as in the Balkans in the 1990s) (Coward 2009); the systematic devastation of the means of modern urban living (as with the deelectrification of

"... states of exception are called into being both to constitute the geographies of permanent violence that sustain the neoliberal economy, and to create what Achille Mbembe calls 'death worlds.'"

Urbicide[F83]

also places a huge responsibility on the shoulders of those who have to decide whether and how to act upon intelligence. As Machiavelli said, "a Prince who is himself not wise cannot be well advised."

An Effective Intelligence Community

From this line of argument flows a strong case for the increased importance for modern national security of an effective national intelligence community working with their counterparts in like-minded nations. By the term *effective* is meant an intelligence community that flexibly spans domestic and overseas interests in order to generate actionable intelligence, that works harmoniously with law enforcement and partners overseas to help disrupt threats and bring suspects to justice, and that has a well-developed analytic capability and the capacity to manage the mass of information and "big data" that modern digital technology makes available.

It is rare that raw intelligence reporting speaks for itself as an unambiguous empirical finding might. Questions of interpretation always arise, and patterns of observed evidence can have widely differing interpretations. [...]

Situational Awareness, Explanation, Prediction, and Strategic Notice: A Useful Model of Intelligence Analysis

In teaching intelligence studies in London, I offer another related way of organizing intelligence assessment. I suggest three "phenotypes" of intelligence judgment that, together with the concept of strategic notice, form a useful model of modern intelligence analysis.

The three phenotypes are:

1. the use of the best validated evidence that can be accessed to provide *situational awareness*, to answer questions of the "who, what, where and when?" type;

2. the best *explanation* of the causes of events (and the motivations of those involved) that can be devised having examined which hypotheses are most consistent with the evidence and our historical understanding, to answer questions of the "why? and what for?" type, leading in turn to the third phenotype;

3. careful *prediction* of how events might unfold in different circumstances including how all those involved might respond to the measures we and our allies might take, to answer questions of the "what next and where next?" type.

But prediction beyond a short time ahead is inherently problematic, and should be complemented by using the technique of *strategic notice*: the identification of possible future developments of interest to answer questions of the "whatever next?" type, and on which research and development can be commissioned, intelligence-gathering requirements set, and policies developed without necessarily assuming that we can know whether and when such developments will actually occur. We cannot eliminate surprise, but we can learn to live better with it by being less surprised by surprise when it happens. [...]

Iraq in 1991, the siege of Gaza in 2006–08 or the 2006 attack on Lebanon); or the simple erasure of those demonized people and places that are cast out as unmodern, barbarian, unclean, pathological, or subhuman (as with Robert Mugabe's bulldozing of hundreds of thousands of shanty dwellings on the edge of Harare in 2005) (see Graham 2003; Kipfer and Goonewardena 2007; Coward 2009).

The phenomenon is an extremely common – although often overlooked – feature in global South urban areas, where political and economic elites attempt to cast their spaces as putative "global cities" – to be the "next Shanghai" – as a legitimation of predatory planning as violent erasure (on predatory planning following the Katrina disaster in New Orleans, see Nagel and Nagel 2007). The supermodern accoutrements of highways, malls, airports, office blocks, sports stadia, and luxury condo complexes tend inevitably to be deemed more "global" than the dilapidated, self-made, and "illegal" shanty districts which house the urban poor. A recent global survey by the United Nations Habitat Programme (2007, xi) found that, between 2000 and 2002, 6.7 million people were forcibly evicted from informal settlements in 60 countries, compared to 4.2 million in the previous two years. Frantz Fanon's (1963) words are as relevant as ever here: "the business of obscuring language is a mask behind which stands the much bigger business of plunder."

To Goonewardena and Kipfer (2006, 28), the proliferation of urbicidal violence in the contemporary period reflects the shift to a world where the politics of the city, and of urban life, are inevitably absolutely central to the production and constitution of social relations; in a majority-urban world "the struggle for the city…coincides more and more with the struggle for a social order." With global urbanization intensifying (it is estimated that 75% of the global population will inhabit urban areas by 2050 – this coincidence will only crystallize further.

Architectural and urban theory thus emerge as key sites in imperial, neoliberal, corporate, or military attempts to produce or reorganize urban space (as well as in a wide spectrum of resistances to such processes). Strange appropriations are emerging here. Eyal Weizman (2007, chapter 7), for example, has shown how certain Israeli generals have appropriated the radical post-structural writings of French philosopher Gilles Deleuze to fashion new military doctrine for taking and controlling the labyrinthine spaces of Palestinian refugee camps. Here, as a result, "contemporary urban warfare," Weizman (2005, 74) writes, "plays itself out within a constructed, real, or imaginary architecture, and through the destruction, construction, reorganization, and subversion of space." Such new Israeli military doctrine, through penetrating paths through the linked walls of entire towns, seeks to "create operational 'space as if it had no borders,' neutralizing the advantages accorded by urban terrain to opponents of occupation" (Goonewardena and Kipfer 2006, 28).

"In a majority-urban world 'the struggle for the city … coincides more and more with the struggle for a social order.'"

Managing Moral Hazard

PROTINT is my term (by analogy with HUMINT and SIGINT) for the gathering of intelligence from the data-protected personal information about individuals to be found in digital databases either in public- or private-sector hands and located both on the domestic territory and overseas. What some in the CIA call the "electronic exhaust" that we all leave behind as we live our normal lives in a high-tech society becomes the spoor to be followed. It is in the nature of such databases that they will contain mostly information on the law-abiding citizen, thus information on the innocent as well as the suspect. Very recently, the explosive growth in the use of social media – Twitter, Facebook, etc. – provides another channel of access to individuals and their preferences, associations, and activities and the sentiment of the crowd. Gathering and analyzing social media to assist the authorities in providing public security, what I call SOCMINT,[4] is rapidly becoming a mainstream intelligence activity around the world.

These intrusive methods are powerful and they get results. My conclusion is that we must accept both that the modern Protecting State[5] needs preemptive intelligence in order to manage sensibly the major threats to everyday life and that gathering such secret intelligence will involve accepting the moral hazard of risking on occasions harm to others for a greater good. There is, for example, a price to be paid for obtaining intelligence on suspects moving amongst the general population, and that is some invasion of privacy, just as recruiting agents active in terrorist networks will run the risk of being accused of colluding in wrongdoing.

There is a danger of public misunderstanding of this line of argument as a call for the secret world of intelligence to be empowered to do "whatever it takes" to keep us safe.

It does not, however, follow that we have to accept those propositions as a justification for treating intelligence activity as an ethics-free zone. We do not need to accept an assumption that intelligence agencies by their hidden nature are outside the pale of moral consideration. In the end, there needs to be public trust that the intelligence and security apparatus will only be used when necessary for public protection against major dangers. The commonsense position that the citizen has a right to expect that the security authorities will use all lawful means to manage the risks from such dangers also supports the contention that public security requires the authorities to balance rights, such as the right to life – not to be blown up by a terrorist bomb – and the right to privacy and family life of the community at large, as well as the rights of those the authorities have to keep under deep surveillance. The balancing act required is within the framework of human rights, not between security on the one hand and liberty, privacy, and the rule of law on the other. [...]

In my book, *Securing the State*,[6] I argue that this approach can indeed usefully be applied to the oversight of intelligence work, when it comes to justifying the moral hazard involved, by applying a checklist of six principles:[7]

1. There must be sufficient sustainable cause.

    We need a check on any tendency for the secret world to expand into areas unjustified by the scale of potential harm to national interests.

It is startling, too, that many of the emerging urban warfare techniques of state militaries – which Goonewardena and Kipfer label "colonization without occupation" – are actually imitations of the great twentieth-century urban resistances against state militaries. "This nonlinear, poly-nucleated and antihierarchical strategy of combat in urban areas," Goonewardena and Kipfer (2006, 29) point out, "in fact plagiarizes the tactics of the defenders of the Paris Commune, Stalingrad, and the Kasbahs of Algiers, Jenin, and Nablus."

Added to this, we must also emphasize the role of techniques of the new urban militarism and urbicidal violence in disciplining or displacing dissent and resistance within the metropolitan heartlands of global capitalism, processes that reach their peaks during major urban WTO, G8, IMF, and G20 summits (Herbert 2007). We must recognize the way these discursive and material techniques erase or deligitimize those urban claims and spaces that stand in the way of increasingly "predatory" forms of urban planning (see Nagel n.d.), clearing the way for new supermodern infrastructures, production centers or urban consumption and tourist enclaves. And we must address how the new military urbanism, blurring as it does into the authoritarian turn in criminology, penology, and social policy, tries to control or incarcerate the unruly populations of the postcolonial metropolis (as in what have been termed the "internal colonies" of the French banlieues; see Dikeç 2007).

Beyond all this, though, as we have already noted, we must not forget the ways in which global processes of securitization, militarization, disinvestment, and erasure provide vital sustenance to the economies of metropolitan heartlands themselves (Keil 2007). Although it has been curiously ignored by the voluminous research on the new economic centrality of global cities, it is crucial to stress that such sites are at the very center of a world where "the military-industrial establishments of corporate capitalism, led by the US one, which produce 'life-killing commodities' as the most profitable part of global trade" (Mesnard y Méndez 2002). Global cities organize and fix financial flows, shape uneven geographic development, and draw off surpluses toward dominant corporate sectors and globalized socioeconomic elites integrated closely with national and international states. With their stock markets, technopoles, arms fairs, high-tech "clusters," and state weapons labs, such cities are literally the "brains" sustaining the highly militarized forms of globalization that have so characterized the neoliberal period. They also house the production aspects of the military-industrial-security-surveillance complex and are fringed by "garrison" cities whose economies are dominated by deployed militaries and private industrial corporations.

The new military urbanism's wars thus now operate to fuel capital accumulation through the global city system. Increasingly, this is based on new forms of "primitive accumulation"

> "Such new Israeli military doctrine, through penetrating paths through the linked walls of entire towns, seeks to 'create operational "space as if it had no borders," neutralizing the advantages accorded by urban terrain to opponents of occupation.'"

2. There must be integrity of motive.
We need integrity throughout the whole system, from collection through to the analysis, assessment, and presentation of the resulting intelligence to policymakers.

3. The methods to be used must be proportionate.
The likely impact and intrusion of the proposed intelligence-gathering operation, taking account of the methods to be used, must be in proportion to the harm that it is sought to prevent.

4. There must be right authority, including upholding of the universal ban on torture.[8]

We need sufficiently senior sign-off on sensitive operations and accountability up a recognized chain of command to permit effective oversight. Right authority too has to be lawful.

5. There must be reasonable prospect of success.
Even if the purpose is valid (guideline 1) and the methods to be used are proportionate to the issue (guideline 3) there needs to be a hardheaded assessment of risk to those involved and of collateral damage to others, and not least the risk to future operations and to institutional reputations if the operation were to go wrong.

6. Recourse to the methods of secret intelligence must be a last resort if there are open or other sources that can be used that do not run the same risk of moral hazard.

A Grand Security Bargain

To conclude, drawing on the British experience of the last decade, we can sketch out a series of propositions that can serve as the basis for an ethically defensible security strategy, representing a balance of the competing principles and interests involved.

All concerned – the executive, its agencies, legislators, and the public – have to accept that maintaining security today remains the primary duty of government and will have the necessary call on resources.

The strategic security narrative government chooses to tell about what is going on in the world should be based not just on the assessment of the threat but also the likely effects of the response, direct and indirect.

The public should be invited to accept that there is no absolute security and chasing after it does more harm than good. There is a continuing need to learn to prosper in a world of risk (opportunities as well as threats), and thus to understand – and to apply correctly – the principles of risk management. Providing security today is an exercise in risk management.

There will always be intelligence gaps and ambiguities, but overall the public must be encouraged to recognize that the work of the intelligence and security services shift the odds in the public's favor, sometimes very significantly.

Effective management of threats thus involves having preemptive intelligence to guide the work of the authorities in protecting the public. They have a duty to seek and use secret information to help manage threats to national security.

(Harvey 2003). Such a process relies on the way resource and oil wars stimulate high rates of return (especially for the petrochemical complex), rather than the use of military contracts to provide Keynesian stimulation to the economy (as in the late twentieth century) (Bichler et al. 2004). Contemporary city-building can thus be seen, at least in part, as an "accumulation strategy in a far more intense way than at any previous moment. Militarization, massive reconstructive reinvestment, and a supposed humanitarian agenda (bombs dropped alongside care packages on Kabul) all feed into this strategy of city building" (Smith 2007). Military destruction or forcible appropriation can thus act as rapid agents of creative destruction. This in turn provides major opportunities for privatization and gentrification, and the appropriation of assets through global-city stock markets.

Conclusions

In bringing together an unusually broad spread of literature and debates as a way of helping to reveal the urban dimensions of contemporary security and military doctrine, technology and practices, this article has sought to connect usually disparate debates. In the process, by means of an explicit focus on the case of the United States, it has demonstrated how new discourses and practices of war and securitization increasingly work to problematize urban life per se. Crucially, this occurs in telescopic ways which intimately link cities of metropolitan and capitalist heartlands with those on colonial frontiers and peripheries. Such two-way linkages between metropole and colony – what Michel Foucault (2003, 103) termed "boomerang effects" – whilst often obscured, play a central role in cementing the norms, discourses, imaginative geographies, and technoscientific arrangements of the new military urbanism in place (Graham 2009). In the above discussions we have explored several such linkages in detail: the ways in which contemporary discourses and practices of war and securitization center powerfully on technophiliac dreams of anticipation and omniscience; how they work to colonize fast-converging cultures of digital media; how they lead to the pervasive installation of new security technologies; and how they bring into being new political economies of state political violence.

It is clear that the challenges of excavating and exposing these linkages further should be a task to which critical urban research addresses itself. To help such a process along, our remaining job here is to consider the contribution that the current analysis makes toward identifying key challenges for future work in critical urban research on the intersections of cities, security, and militarization. Three particular challenges emerge here.

First, it is clear that the new military urbanism gains much of its power from the ways in which key exemplars of militarization and securitization emerge as mobile norms to be imitated and applied more generally, both between metropole and colony,

"Crucially, this occurs in telescopic ways which intimately link cities of metropolitan and capitalist heartlands with those on colonial frontiers and peripheries."

The ability to catch terrorists and mount successful criminal prosecutions is essential but will not by itself sufficiently protect the public, especially when the terrorist is prepared to be a suicide bomber. Using preemptive secret intelligence to help disrupt terrorist networks at home and abroad is thus essential to reducing the risk.

Secret intelligence, because it involves overcoming the efforts of others to prevent us acquiring it, inevitably involves running moral hazard.

The effectiveness of such secret intelligence rests on sources and methods that must remain hidden. The public must accept that there is no general "right to know" about security and intelligence sources and methods. Freedom of Information legislation has brought greater transparency into the work of government generally, and enabled government to be better held to account, but it cannot be at the expense of public safety.

We can nevertheless constrain our intelligence activity by an ethical approach that is based on well-understood and tested "just war" principles, and that respects human rights including the prohibition of torture. The law-enforcement, defense, security and intelligence communities thus have to accept in turn that ethics do matter: there are "red lines" that must not be crossed.

If the secrets of terrorists and serious criminals are to be uncovered and their plots disrupted there will be inevitable intrusions into privacy. These intrusive methods are powerful and they get results. In careless or malign hands they could be abused. So it is essential that the public can have confidence that the security and intelligence apparatus of the state is under democratic control, is being properly regulated and is being used lawfully for public protection against major dangers.

Democratic oversight of intelligence activity has to be by proxy. The public right to oversight of security and intelligence work has to be exercised at one remove by a trusted group of democratically elected representatives – together with judicial oversight of intrusive investigative powers with the right of redress in cases of abuse of these powers – who can on our behalf be trusted to enter the "ring of secrecy" and to give us confidence that legal and ethical standards are being maintained.

Some risks will, despite all our efforts, crystallize and thus there is value in pursuing as part of security strategy a long-term national policy of working with the private sector to build up national resilience against a range of threats and hazards, including in cyberspace.

And of course, government must never forget the importance of having an informed and supportive public that has confidence in the authorities and their methods.

The ancient Greek term *phronesis* describes the application of practical wisdom to the anticipation of risks. Phronesis was defined by the historian Edgar Wind as the application of good judgment to human conduct – consisting in a sound, practical instinct for the course of events, and an almost indefinable hunch that anticipates the future by remembering the past and thus judges the present correctly. An appropriate description for effective national security and counterterrorism strategy.

and center and periphery, and within more pervasive shifts toward securitization. Thus, for example, Israeli expertise and security technology for targeting civilian populations is increasingly being diffused globally along borders, during sporting events or political summits, or within broader attempts to securitize urban spaces and infrastructural circulations (Graham 2010, chapter 7). Meanwhile, major attempts are being made by the US Department of Homeland Security to normalize US systems for attempting to securitize ports, airports, and electronic communications and financial systems across transnational systems of circulation. Little is yet known, however, about the detailed policy processes through which certain norms emerge as mobile exemplars within and through the burgeoning transnational political economies that sustain the new military urbanism. Much more detailed comparative work is particularly required to expose how mobile events like political summits and global sports events act as particularly important moments within such processes of mobile exemplification.

> "Israeli expertise and security technology for targeting civilian populations is increasingly being diffused globally."

Second, whilst this article has specifically addressed the extremely important role of US military and security cultures, doctrines and technologies in sustaining the new military urbanism, much work needs to be done to satisfactorily understand how the contemporary trends toward the securitization of cities are refracted through different national security and military cultures and the various urban political and legal traditions. Beyond the crucial importance of mobile exemplars, transnational discourses and political economies highlighted above, care needs to be taken not to overgeneralize from US, Israeli, or any other experience within the still variegated national and urban political landscapes that constitute global neoliberal urbanism. Critical comparative work is thus urgently required to explore how the buildup of transnationally organized policing, securitization, and counterinsurgency warfare – and their norms and exemplars – intersect with persistent differences, path dependencies, and, not least, limits and resistances, in the ways in which national and local security and military organizations address urban spaces and circulations.

Finally, the perspective deployed in this article suggests that there are major conceptual and theoretical opportunities to be explored when debates about the intersections of cities and security range across questions as diverse as the urban political economies of security industries, the discursive targeting of cities within electronic visual culture, the urban "surveillance surge" and the proliferation of urbicidal violence. Such an analytical breadth helps to reveal the powerful ways in which discourses which demonize cities as intrinsically pathological and insecure spaces necessitating violent state reaction work simultaneously across multiple circuits and political economies. To further develop such work, however, there is a need to build on the latest theorizations of the biopolitics of warfare, circulation, mobility, and securitization within liberal societies (see Reid

Theme: National Security Strategies
Author: CPNI
Compiled by Haakon Rasmussen and Anders Sletten Eide

Designing Peace of Mind
Counterterrorism in Great Britain

2006; Dillon and Reid 2009). Specifically, such conceptually sophisticated but empirically disengaged political theory needs to be linked much more closely to debates in critical urban research about the specific processes whereby urban spaces, sites, infrastructures, and circulations are securitized and militarized.

Discussions about biopolitics and security need in particular to be much more fully grounded in the context of rampant urbanization, the growth of transnationally organized urban regions, the insecurities generated by neoliberal globalization, and the militarization of many civil law enforcement regimes. Necessary here is the challenge of showing how the reconstitution of urban sites and spaces, far from being mere geographic backdrops to the elaboration of biopolitical regimes of war and securitization, actually work powerfully to help constitute such highly contradictory regimes. "The city [is] not just the site," writes Eyal Weizman (2005, 53), "but the very medium of warfare – a flexible, almost liquid medium that is forever contingent and in flux."

Finally, in building up a robust and critical body of work addressing the multiple circuits which together consolidate the new military urbanism, it will also become much clearer how social and political mobilizations of various sorts and at various scales – including those from within militaries and security complexes themselves – can best jam, resist, and challenge the entrenching and diffusing norms, discourses, and technoscientific arrangements at the heart of the new military urbanism. This is a particularly pivotal challenge given the tendency across a widening series of urban sites and events to increasingly portray and imagine cities as little but key battlespaces – urban sites requiring permanent and profitable lockdown and targeting within worlds of boundless, ambient, and mobile threat.

CPNI

The Centre for the Protection of National Infrastructure (CPNI) provides advice on protective security to the British government and critical national infrastructure (CNI). The CNI includes sectors such as energy, transport (railways, airports, maritime), telecoms, finance, and so on. CPNI are also responsible for shaping and undertaking multidisciplinary research and development programs and the consequential production and dissemination of security guidance to security professionals, engineers, architects, and planners on physical, personnel, and cybersecurity threats and countermeasures. The main focus of CPNI is on providing protective security advice to the critical national infrastructure but also provides the underlying security principles, processes, and standards used in kindred fields such as the protection of crowded places and major events. CPNI operates under a mantra of "vulnerability-focused, impact-driven, and threat-informed."

CPNI is directly accountable to the Director-General of the Security Service (MI5) and is governed by the Security Service Act of 1989. Protective security has been a cornerstone of the Security Service's work since its inception in 1909.

The Policy Context

These are some of the overarching strategies and programs in the British government's security toolbox that generate a political and formal framework around the different approaches to security thinking in the UK:

> **CPNI**
> As suggested in the organization's name, the role of the UK government's Centre for the Protection of National Infrastructure (CPNI) is to protect essential infrastructure in the UK, as well as provide "the underlying security principles, processes, and standards used in kindred fields such as the protection of crowded places and major events." Hostile vehicle mitigation barriers utilized in London, for example, are either designed by CPNI or built to their standards.
>
> Due to the secured conditions of the communication and required anonymity of the contributors, this text combines edited conversations with representatives from the UK Government's Centre for the Protection of National Infrastructure (CPNI), compiled by Anders Sletten Eide and Haakon Rasmussen in 2015.

1. National Security Strategy
The UK government's National Security Strategy sets out the strategic choices on ensuring the UK's security and resilience.

   Acts of terrorism and hostile attacks in UK cyberspace are two of the highest-priority risk types identified in the strategy that need to be addressed.

2. Strategic Defense and Security Review
The Strategic Defense and Security Review sets out how the objectives of the National Security Strategy are to be pursued. These include: ensuring that key counterterrorist capabilities are maintained and in some areas enhanced, while still delivering efficiency gains, developing a transformative program for cybersecurity, which addresses threats from states, criminals, and terrorists and seizes the opportunities which cyberspace provides for our future prosperity and for advancing our security interests.

3. Counterterrorism strategy
The UK government's counterterrorism strategy (known as CONTEST) produced by the UK government's Home Office aims to reduce the risk from international terrorism so that people can go about their business freely and with confidence. Developing and delivering CONTEST involves stakeholders from across government departments, the emergency services, voluntary organizations, the

Theme: Democracy and Security
Author: David Harvey

The Right to the City

Excerpt

business sector, and partners from across the world. The strategy is divided into four principal strands: Prevent, Pursue, Protect, and Prepare. CPNI's work falls within the "Protect" strand, which is concerned with reducing the vulnerability of the UK and UK interests overseas to a terrorist attack.

4. Cybersecurity Strategy

The UK's Cybersecurity Strategy was published in November 2011. It sets out how the UK will support economic prosperity, protect national security, and safeguard the public's way of life through building a more trusted and resilient digital environment. In particular it highlights the crucial role of closer partnership between the public sector and the private sector.

To mark the second anniversary of the strategy the Cabinet Office published a list of achievements against the objectives and a forward plan.

5. National Risk Register

The most significant emergencies that the United Kingdom and its citizens could face over the next five years are monitored by the government through the National Risk Assessment (NRA). This is a confidential assessment that is conducted annually, drawing on expertise from a wide range of departments and agencies of government. The National Risk Register (NRR) is the public version and the 2010 edition reflects the latest iteration of the National Risk Assessment.

The NRA and NRR capture events which could result in significant harm to human welfare: casualties, damage to property, essential services, and disruption to everyday life. The risks cover three broad categories: natural events, major accidents, and malicious attacks.

6. Resilience of Infrastructure from Natural Hazards

The Civil Contingencies Secretariat within the Cabinet Office has developed a cross-sector Critical Infrastructure Resilience Programme (CIRP), with the aim of improving the resilience of critical infrastructure and essential services to severe disruption from natural hazards. The process, timetable, and expectations for the program are detailed in its Strategic Framework and Policy statement.

Protective Security - Preserving Freedom through Enablement?

Freedom, for those with innocent intent - the commuter, the tourist, the business owner - is to have the ability to travel to or through, or to dwell in a public space in a safe and secure way. By their very nature, such people will not have sight of the range of threats that they or the site may be vulnerable to. Freedom in such places can be seen as a blessing to the normal user but also a bonus to those people with malicious intent, including both criminals and terrorists, as the latter will have unfettered access to conduct hostile reconnaissance and criminal acts or attacks.

Protective security is providing a level of safety or assurance to people from both the occurrence and severity of malicious acts that

Civil Rights[F14]

Harvey

The renown British geographer David Harvey (1935–) is a leading voice within the field of critical and Marxist geography. He is the author of numerous influential works bridging political economics, urbanism, culture, and other fields, including: *Social Justice and the City* (1973); *The Condition of Post-Modernity* (1989); *Spaces of Hope* (2000); and *A Brief History of Neoliberalism* (2005). In this excerpt Harvey reflects upon Lefebvre's concept of the right to the city, and the freedom of citizens to affect the city, as "one of the most precious yet most neglected of our human rights." Harvey describes the increasing pressure this right is placed under within the conditions of contemporary neoliberal capitalism, and the related impact this has on the city.

This text was first published in the book *Rebel Cities* (London: Verso, 2012).

We live in an era when ideals of human rights have moved center stage both politically and ethically. A lot of political energy is put into promoting, protecting, and articulating their significance in the construction of a better world. For the most part the concepts circulating are individualistic and property-based and, as such, do nothing to challenge hegemonic liberal and neoliberal market logics, or neoliberal modes of legality and state action. We live in a world, after all, where the rights of private property and the profit rate trump all other notions of rights one can think of. But there are occasions when the ideal of human rights takes a collective turn, as when the rights of workers, women, gays, and minorities come to the fore (a legacy of the long-standing labor movement and, for example, the 1960s Civil Rights movement in the United States, which was collective and had a global resonance). Such struggles for collective rights have, on occasion, yielded important results. Here I want to explore another kind of collective right – that to the city in the context of a revival of interest in Henri Lefebvre's ideas on the topic, and the emergence of all sorts of social movements around the world that are now demanding such a right. How, then, can this right be defined?

The city, the noted urban sociologist Robert Park once wrote, is "man's most consistent and on the whole, his most successful attempt to remake the world he lives in more after his heart's desire. But, if the city is the world which man created, it is the world in which he is henceforth condemned to live. Thus, indirectly, and without any clear sense of the nature of his task, in making the city man has remade himself."[1] If Park is correct, then the question of what kind of city we want cannot be divorced from the question of what kind of people we want to be, what kinds of social relations we seek, what relations to nature we cherish, what style of life we desire, what aesthetic values we hold. The right to the city is, therefore, far more than a right of individual or group access to the resources that the city embodies: it is a right to change and reinvent the city more after our hearts' desire. It is, moreover, a collective rather than an individual right, since reinventing the city inevitably depends upon the exercise of a collective power over the processes of urbanization. The freedom to make and remake ourselves and our cities is, I want to argue, one of the most precious yet most neglected of our human rights. How best then to exercise that right?

[…] These days it is not hard to enumerate all manner of urban discontents and anxieties, as well as excitements, in the midst of

> "We live in a world, after all, where the rights of private property and the profit rate trump all other notions of rights one can think of."

Glass[F32]

"One can discuss if freedom is to maximize security so that people can get from space A to space B without being attacked, or if it is space free from security measures."

Risk Analysis[F64]

they typically have no control over themselves. This means that a wide range of threats to their welfare has to be managed down to a proportionate level.

One can discuss if freedom is to maximize security so that people can get from space A to space B without being attacked, or if it is space free from security measures. In order to create safer public space, different actors have to work together, ranging from politicians, engineers, and security advisers to designers and architects. In order to create "free space" and a space where people feel safe, there needs to be acceptance of some sort of security measures (whether physical or tactical). That being said, security does not have to be a mutually exclusive subject – it can be achieved as dual purpose with other environmental, aesthetic, safety, and design goals. A well-designed building could, for example include blast-resistant glass, which in addition to its breaking strength also would give the building a lower u-value. The challenge for those involved in security design (security R&D professionals, architects, designers, and engineers) is to anticipate the direction of the market, develop new more blast-resistant materials with the industry, and then be able to equal or better the price to be able to demonstrate "dual purpose," so that security is not the only driver to choose that system. People do adapt. For example, if a road is being relocated, the locals may protest. But in a year they will have adapted to the changes and maybe even realized that they may have benefited from it; the local stores and businesses may have had an increase in income, or there has been a reduction in traffic-related incidents which again benefits the local community and its citizens. The people didn't see it when the relocation was being approved, but they may see it later.

Just as a designer cannot ignore relevant structural codes against seismic or accidental events, a designer must recognize that not all the people who will visit or enjoy the space have totally innocent intent. For that reason the designers have a part to play minimizing the likelihood or severity of those threats manifesting themselves. Providing security does not mean they cannot create a beautiful space, but it does mean designers can provide a beautiful, safe, and secure space. Physical security if done with care and flair can enhance a public space. It can provide a level of confidence to those people visiting or owning that public space and remove or mitigate certain threat/attack vectors. Physical security measures also allow those responsible for security monitoring and tactics (including the security officers/guard force, and police) to focus their tactical measures. Such tactical measures can reduce the residual risks that are not mitigated by the physical measures, and also elucidate behaviors in those with malicious intent during their hostile reconnaissance phase, which allows monitoring and tactical measures to reconcile or disrupt.

Security as Added Value
The field of risk analysis is intricate and complex. We have to ask ourselves what risks we are willing to expose ourselves to. Unlike road safety and vehicle safety, where trends can be identified by the number of collisions and resultant casualties and easily analyzed in

even more rapid urban transformations. Yet we somehow seem to lack the stomach for systematic critique. The maelstrom of change overwhelms us even as obvious questions loom. What, for example, are we to make of the immense concentrations of wealth, privilege, and consumerism in almost all the cities of the world in the midst of what even the United Nations depicts as an exploding "planet of slums"?[2]

To claim the right to the city in the sense I mean it here is to claim some kind of shaping power over the processes of urbanization, over the ways in which our cities are made and remade, and to do so in a fundamental and radical way. From their very inception, cities have arisen through the geographical and social concentration of a surplus product. Urbanization has always been, therefore, a class phenomenon of some sort, since surpluses have been extracted from somewhere and from somebody, while control over the use of the surplus typically lies in the hands of a few (such as a religious oligarcy, or a warrior poet with imperial ambitions). This general situation persists under capitalism, of course, but in this case there is a rather different dynamic at work. Capitalism rests, as Marx tells us, upon the perpetual search for surplus value (profit). But to produce surplus value capitalists have to produce a surplus product. This means that capitalism is perpetually producing the surplus product that urbanization requires. The reverse relation also holds. Capitalism needs urbanization to absorb the surplus products it perpetually produces. In this way an inner connection emerges between the development of capitalism and urbanization. Hardly surprisingly, therefore, the logistical curves of growth of capitalist output over time are broadly paralleled by the logistical curves of urbanization of the world's population.

"From their very inception, cities have arisen through the geographical and social concentration of a surplus product."

Let us look more closely at what capitalists do. They begin the day with a certain amount of money and end the day with more of it (as profit). The next day they have to decide what to do with the surplus money they gained the day before. They face a Faustian dilemma: reinvest to get even more money or consume their surplus away in pleasures. The coercive laws of competition force them to reinvest, because if one does not reinvest then another surely will. For a capitalist to remain a capitalist, some surplus must be reinvested to make even more surplus. Successful capitalists usually make more than enough both to reinvest in expansion and satisfy their lust for pleasure. But the result of perpetual reinvestment is the expansion of surplus production. Even more important, it entails expansion at a compound rate — hence all the logistical growth curves (money, capital, output, and population) that attach to the history of capital accumulation.

The politics of capitalism are affected by the perpetual need to find profitable terrains for capital surplus production and absorption. In this the capitalist faces a number of obstacles to continuous and trouble-free expansion. If there is a scarcity of labor and wages are too high, then either existing labor has to

order to create safer junctions and cars, terrorism is normally not statistically summarized. The number and irregular occurrence of serious injury and fatal terrorist incidents is (thankfully) simply too small to justify on a similar cost-benefit basis (widespread) security measures based on the previous attack. The responsibility of the analysts and consultants is to predict how future attacks may materialize, and always be one step ahead in terms of developing measures to counter or mitigate them. The goal is always to create measures that not only have a sole security purpose, but maybe a dual, triple and even quadruple purpose that can bring good qualities to a public space. If that goal is achieved, people seem more willing to accept these security measures being implemented in their surroundings.

The security industry aims to meet the demand of the customers, that being private or public clients. Security in design and building or space operation is not always imposed; it is often expected by employees, occupants, and citizens alike. Cultural differences between countries and their citizens develop naturally as threats morph. The UK citizen has been exposed to terrorist threats in various forms for a long time and has a certain expectation of safety. Safety is often delivered through security measures, be it technical or operational, covert or overt. Public- and private-sector bodies have duties of care and will always consider tailored and proportionate security measures (hard and soft) to reduce the risk of an attack or to mitigate the consequences. A failure to deliver safety and security may manifest itself in a lack of trust, particularly in the event that an attack takes place or significant national security vulnerabilities are exposed, both of which can lead to a lack of confidence in the government both on the national and international stage.

"Just as a designer cannot ignore relevant structural codes against seismic or accidental events, a designer must recognize that not all the people who will visit or enjoy the space have totally innocent intent."

DOC[F22]

The Royal Institute of British Architects (RIBA), has developed a guide on designing out crime.[1] This was made to make clients aware of the advantages of crime prevention at an early stage in all design processes. If a design does not include security professionals at the very beginning then any necessary security apparatus included later in the design process will undoubtedly not be as blended-in as it could otherwise have been. CPNI and other stakeholders have also put out tailored guidance and training for the various parties who design, build, and operate infrastructure and they have sponsored public (British, European, and International) standards in order that successfully tested materials can be specified appropriately.

Security measures like bollards disguised as benches, planters, lampposts, or art has been one of the focal points for the British security industry. Depending on what kind of vehicle attack a site is trying to avoid, both antiram and regular street furniture could have substantial effect. Regular furniture correctly spaced (1.2 m air gap) combined with a holistic perimeter protection at a good standoff distance from an asset, can provide mitigation from parked and encroachment styles of vehicle-borne attack. If protection from penetrative impact is also required then standard street furniture is not robust enough. The UK has worked with the industry to develop architectural street furniture with antiram qualities. In the last twelve

Standoff Distance[F73]

be disciplined (technologically induced unemployment or an assault on organized working-class power – such as that set in motion by Thatcher and Reagan in the 1980s – are two prime methods) or fresh labor forces must be found (by immigration, export of capital, or proletarianization of hitherto independent elements in the population). New means of production in general and new natural resources in particular must be found. This puts increasing pressure on the natural environment to yield up the necessary raw materials and absorb the inevitable wastes. The coercive laws of competition also force new technologies and organizational forms to come on line all the time, since capitalists with higher productivity can out-compete those using inferior methods. Innovations define new wants and needs and reduce the turnover time of capital and the friction of distance. This extends the geographical range over which the capitalist is free to search for expanded labor supplies, raw materials, and so on. If there is not enough purchasing power in an existing market, then new markets must be found by expanding foreign trade, promoting new products and lifestyles, creating new credit instruments and debt-financed state expenditures. If, finally, the profit rate is too low, then state regulation of "ruinous competition"; monopolization (mergers and acquisitions), and capital exports to fresh pastures provide ways out.

If any one of the above barriers to continuous capital circulation and expansion becomes impossible to circumvent, then capital accumulation is blocked and capitalists face a crisis. Capital cannot be profitably reinvested, accumulation stagnates or ceases, and capital is devalued (lost) and in some instances even physically destroyed. Devaluation can take a number of forms. Surplus commodities can be devalued or destroyed, productive capacity and assets can be written down in value and left unemployed, or money itself can be devalued through inflation. And in a crisis, of course, labor stands to be devalued through massive unemployment. In what ways, then, has capitalist urbanization been driven by the need to circumvent these barriers and to expand the terrain of profitable capitalist activity? I argue here that it plays a particularly active role (along with other phenomena such as military expenditures) in absorbing the surplus product that capitalists are perpetually producing in their search for surplus value.[3]

[...] As in all the preceding phases, this most recent radical expansion of the urban process has brought with it incredible transformations in lifestyles. Quality of urban life has become a commodity for those with money, as has the city itself in a world where consumerism, tourism, cultural and knowledge-based industries, as well as perpetual resort to the economy of the spectacle, have become major aspects of urban political economy, even in India and China. The postmodernist penchant for encouraging the formation of market niches, both in urban lifestyle choices and in consumer habits, and cultural forms, surrounds the contemporary urban experience with an aura of freedom of choice in the market, provided you have the money and can protect yourself from the privatization of wealth redistribution through burgeoning criminal activity and predatory fraudulent

years they have adjusted their approach, going from the architects prettifying the equipment to holistic approaches where architects would develop the vision for the site (whilst abiding by the maximum air gap and minimum height rules) and the industry and consultants have advised what hard measures can go inside that vision to achieve everyone's goal.

There is a tendency for the focus of security to be limited to physical attributes. The importance of staff and public awareness, increased vigilance, and security messaging should not be underestimated and are all examples of "soft security" measures, which play a significant role in a layered protective security scheme and which can deter and disrupt terrorist attack planning, particularly during the hostile reconnaissance phase.

Economic Incentives for Flexible Security

Physical security stays as long as the building material, the concrete and metal it is designed of, holds together. Like other architecture the world moves forward while the built remains. How can physical security adapt to the change, reduction, or disappearance of threat or the change of tenants? Manpower, as in security guards and police, would be the first layer of security to be affected. Tactical security like guard force taskings would be modified and adjusted to the new situation. Employees are expensive. In a city center with pedestrianized areas secured by planters and benches, the measures would typically not be removed. People adapt to their surroundings, and the public would generally benefit from car-free city centers. If the cost of removal exceeds the maintenance cost in the foreseeable future, the security actors would see it as a beneficial arrangement to let security remain.

In the UK the user pays principle is usually normal. This means that clients of building projects would have to consider what kind of tenants and probable risk factors are at play. Security is just one factor in an organization's mandate, and would normally only be prioritized if the risk assessment shows potential vulnerabilities. But money is not always a factor when it comes to security: it does not have to be expensive. Operational instructions for security personnel could be as important as physical or technological measures. Staff awareness, attitude, uniforms, education, and training do not cost much to implement, but can often be the glue that strengthens the security schemes that organizations use.

In the end the clients always hold the finances. They have competing priorities besides security, and ultimately the decision is theirs – based on their risk appetite. If they are committed to security and follow a good operational requirement process, they will end up with a proportionate purpose scheme. Again it is important to remember the holistic approach that blends the physical, cyber, and personnel security initiatives together. If security equipment salesmen steer the design, then there could be mission creep or poorly tailored engineering or tactical solutions. This is why the industry advocates the inclusion of security from the very first line on the drawing board. There have been many examples where additional security measures have not been considered proportionate to the threats that an organization has

> "Security measures like bollards disguised as benches, planters, lampposts, or art has been one of the focal points for the British security industry."

practices (which have everywhere escalated). Shopping malls, multiplexes, and box stores proliferate (the production of each has become big business), as do fast-food and artisanal marketplaces, boutique cultures, and, as Sharon Zukin slyly notes, "pacification by cappuccino." Even the incoherent, bland, and monotonous suburban tract development that continues to dominate in many areas, now gets its antidote in a "new urbanism" movement that touts the sale of community and a boutique lifestyle as a developer product to fulfill urban dreams. This is a world in which the neoliberal ethic of intense possessive individualism can become the template for human personality socialization. The impact is increasing individualistic isolation, anxiety, and neurosis in the midst of one of the greatest social achievements (at least judging by its enormous scale and all-embracing character) ever constructed in human history for the realization of our hearts' desire.

> "Quality of urban life has become a commodity for those with money."

But the fissures within the system are also all too evident. We increasingly live in divided, fragmented, and conflict-prone cities. How we view the world and define possibilities depends on which side of the tracks we are on and on what kinds of consumerism we have access to. In the past decades, the neoliberal turn has restored class power to rich elites.[4] In a single year several hedge fund managers in New York raked in $3 billion in personal remuneration, and Wall Street bonuses have soared for individuals over the last few years from around $5 million toward the $50 million mark for top players (putting real estate prices in Manhattan out of sight). Fourteen billionaires have emerged in Mexico since the neoliberal turn in the late 1980s, and Mexico now boasts the richest man on earth, Carlos Slim, at the same time as the incomes of the poor in that country have either stagnated or diminished. As of the end of 2009 (after the worst of the crash was over), there were 115 billionaires in China, 101 in Russia, 55 in India, 52 in Germany, 32 in Britain, and 30 in Brazil, in addition to the 413 in the United States.[5] The results of this increasing polarization in the distribution of wealth and power are indelibly etched into the spatial forms of our cities, which increasingly become cities of fortified fragments, of gated communities and privatized public spaces kept under constant surveillance. The neoliberal protection of private property rights and their values becomes a hegemonic form of politics, even for the lower middle class. In the developing world in particular, the city is splitting into different separated parts, with the apparent formation of many "microstates." Wealthy neighborhoods provided with all kinds of services, such as exclusive schools, golf courses, tennis courts, and private police patrolling the area around the clock intertwine with illegal settlements where water is available only at public fountains, no sanitation system exists, electricity is pirated by a privileged few, the roads become mud streams whenever it rains, and where house-sharing is the norm. Each fragment appears to live and function autonomously, sticking firmly to what it has been able to grab in the daily fight for survival.[6]

faced. A clear understanding of a CNI asset, its redundancy and dependencies, is critical to developing a security strategy. It is often the case that security is achieved by increased redundancy, separation, and improved business continuity planning rather than deploying hard security measures.

Within the discussion on situational crime and terror prevention strategies there is an inherent criticism of displacement, both an internal criticism from the theorist themselves (for example, Ronald V. Clarke and Graeme Newman, *Outsmarting the Terrorists*, 2005), and an external criticism from the advocates against securitization. One of the effects of displacement drawn up by the internal criticism is that by securing one target you make other targets more attractive and therefore more vulnerable. An external criticism regarding displacement claims that by securing parts of the city you make the unwanted elements from that part of the city move to other neighborhoods. Good protective security can deter (primary goal) and can help to identify hostile reconnaissance (which also helps investigations to disrupt the threat). But there is always the possibility of geographical displacement of the threat or in terms of modus operandi (hopefully to a less injurious attack vector). That being said, managing the overall risk downward is what drives security professionals.

Risk Assesments – Tailored Security

To understand the necessity of security, we need to understand what the security is protecting. In the context of protection of critical national infrastructure (CNI), an asset is any element, service, function, or event that the UK citizen is reliant on or that the UK is dependent on for economic, political, or security reasons. It can comprise both physical entities such as people or equipment, and nonphysical entities such as networks and systems. To a private company its most valuable assets will be those critical to their business success, competitive advantage, and continuing operation. Targets are anticipated recipients of an attack, whether it's physical, personnel-oriented or cyber.

One of the most common pitfalls in executing and implementing security measures is poor or nonexistent operational requirements. CPNI advice is always to write a thorough operational requirement from which concept, initial, and detailed designs and performance specifications for equipment can be derived and a good scheme targeting the original concerns is developed and delivered. This should always be underpinned by a thorough risk assessment which will have identified the need for any changes. It is crucial for clients to carry out a thorough risk assessment that will help identify the full spectrum of threats, and also prioritize which ones need to be addressed by overt or covert measures. This will provide the client with the basis for further action which, coupled with a good operational requirement that clearly defines the problem to be solved and the appropriate and proportionate security measures to implement, will help to address your specific problems. If some of those problems are synonymous with those of other nations and they have already developed a successful and palatable solution, then adopt it. If for example a problem requires a

"In the end the clients always hold the finances. They have competing priorities besides security, and ultimately the decision is theirs – based on their risk appetite."

Under these conditions, ideals of urban identity, citizenship, and belonging, of a coherent urban politics, already threatened by the spreading malaise of the individualistic neoliberal ethic, become much harder to sustain. Even the idea that the city might function as a collective body politic, a site within and from which progressive social movements might emanate, appears, at least on the surface, increasingly implausible. Yet there are in fact all manner of urban social movements in evidence seeking to overcome the isolations and to reshape the city in a different social image from that given by the powers of developers backed by finance, corporate capital, and an increasingly entrepreneurially minded local state apparatus. Even relatively conservative urban administrations are seeking ways to use their powers to experiment with new ways of both producing the urban and of democratizing governance. Is there an urban alternative and, if so, from where might it come? Surplus absorption through urban transformation has, however, an even darker aspect. It has entailed repeated bouts of urban restructuring through "creative destruction." This nearly always has a class dimension, since it is usually the poor, the underprivileged, and those marginalized from political power that suffer first and foremost from this process. Violence is required to achieve the new urban world on the wreckage of the old. Haussmann tore through the old Parisian impoverished quarters, using powers of expropriation for supposedly public benefit, and did so in the name of civic improvement, environmental restoration, and urban renovation. He deliberately engineered the removal of much of the working class and other unruly elements, along with insalubrious industries, from Paris's city center, where they constituted a threat to public order, public health, and, of course, political power. He created an urban form where it was believed (incorrectly, as it turned out, in 1871) sufficient levels of surveillance and military control were possible so as to ensure that revolutionary movements could easily be controlled by military power. But, as Engels pointed out in 1872, in reality, the bourgeoisie has only one method of solving the housing question after its fashion – that is to say, of solving it in such a way that the solution perpetually renews the question anew. This method is called "Haussmann" [by which] I mean the practice that has now become general of making breaches in the working-class quarters of our big towns, and particularly in areas which are centrally situated, quite apart from whether this is done from considerations of public health or for beautifying the town, or owing to the demand for big centrally situated business premises, or, owing to traffic requirements, such as the laying down of railways, streets (which sometimes seem to have the aim of making barricade fighting more difficult)...No matter how different the reasons may be, the result is always the same; the scandalous alleys disappear to the accompaniment of lavish

> "Increasing polarization in the distribution of wealth and power are indelibly etched into the spatial forms of our cities, which increasingly become cities of fortified fragments, of gated communities and privatized public spaces kept under constant surveillance."

"By securing one target, you make other targets more attractive and therefore more vulnerable."

unique Norwegian solution, then pioneer and measure it and sell its success.

During 2014 a project called Servator was conducted with great success. The project was designed to deter and detect any criminal or terrorist activity. Some of the most important factors in the project were special training of officers and CCTV operators qualifying them to better detect suspicious behavior. Public awareness campaigns and requesting tips from the public has also been key in the Servator project. As the project has proven successful, it is now carried out in the whole of the City of London district and was used during the 2014 Commonwealth Games in Scotland. Education and pioneering methodology is crucial to tackle current, potential, and future criminals.

Working With Private Security Actors

The context for the private security sector is different in the UK and Norway. In the UK there are some forty-five different police forces operating on different levels and expertise, while in Norway there is a centralized police. The UK also has a long history of attacks and threats of terror, hence collaboration between the police, private security, and the public has been crucial in order to create a resilient and crime-free society. The private security guards are to some extent trained by the police, and to a much greater extent utilized as projections of the police. The importance of the security officer in the overall security system should not be ignored. In addition to the UK requirement for security officers that have a public-facing role to be licensed, it is vital that the role of the security officer in an organization is clearly defined with meaningful key performance indicators that will enhance overall security.

Security officers should be motivated and properly trained so that they can effectively respond to the threats and risks that they have been contracted in to mitigate. Like physical security there should be an operational requirement written (that would form the basis of the procurement process) that clearly identifies what roles and tasks the security officers are to fulfill, what threat they are responding to, and how they are helping to manage the risk. The right posture, profile, and presence of the security officer can send a powerful deterrence message to hostiles.

A survey by the British Security Industry Authority from 2013 estimated the total number of CCTV cameras in Britain to approximately 5 million, 1 for every 14 citizens.[2] In Oslo the corresponding relation is 1:634. Although some of the cameras are operated by the police, most of them are run by private security companies. The exchange of knowledge and information between the industry and the police is therefore crucial for the police to conduct its service the best way possible. The deterrence effect of CCTV covers wider crime prevention issues and any associated public reassurance. In terms of counterterrorism, the ability to pick up, investigate, and reconcile acts of hostile reconnaissance should not be underestimated. CCTV can also provide a good forensic capability after an event, whether an isolated incident or large-scale events such as widespread disturbances. When a new set of cameras is installed, the role of the CCTV

self-praise by the bourgeoisie on account of this tremendous success, but they appear again immediately somewhere else... The breeding places of disease, the infamous holes and cellars in which the capitalist mode of production confines our workers night after night, are not abolished; they are merely shifted elsewhere! The same economic necessity that produced them in the first place, produces them in the next place.[7]

[…] Urbanization, we may conclude, has played a crucial role in the absorption of capital surpluses and has done so at ever-increasing geographical scales, but at the price of burgeoning processes of creative destruction that entail the dispossession of the urban masses of any right to the city whatsoever. Periodically this ends in revolt, as in Paris in 1871, when the dispossessed rose up seeking to reclaim the city they had lost. The urban social movements of 1968, from Paris and Bangkok to Mexico City and Chicago, likewise sought to define a different way of urban living from that which was being imposed upon them by capitalist developers and the state. If, as seems likely, the fiscal difficulties in the current conjuncture mount and the hitherto successful neoliberal, postmodernist, and consumerist phase of capitalist absorption of the surplus through urbanization is at an end, and if a broader crisis ensues, then the question arises: Where is our '68 or, even more dramatically, our version of the Commune?

By analogy with transformations in the fiscal system, the political answer is bound to be much more complex in our times precisely because the urban process is now global in scope and wracked with all manner of fissures, insecurities, and uneven geographical developments. But cracks in the system are, as Leonard Cohen once sang, "what lets the light in." Signs of revolt are everywhere (the unrest in China and India is chronic, civil wars rage in Africa, Latin America is in ferment, autonomy movements are emerging all over the place, and even in the US the political signs suggest that most of the population is saying "enough is enough" with respect to rabid inequalities). Any of these revolts could suddenly become contagious. Unlike the fiscal system, however, the urban and peri-urban social movements of opposition, of which there are many around the world, are not tightly coupled at all. Indeed, many have no connection to each other. It is unlikely, therefore, that a single spark will, as the Weather Underground once dreamed, spark a prairie fire. It will take something far more systematic than that. But if these various oppositional movements did somehow come together – coalesce, for example, around the slogan of the right to the city – then what should they demand?

The answer to the last question is simple enough: greater democratic control over the production and use of the surplus. Since the urban process is a major channel of use, then the right to the city is constituted by establishing democratic control over the deployment of the surpluses through urbanization. To have a surplus product is not a bad thing: indeed, in many situations

"The whole neoliberal project over the last thirty years has been oriented toward privatization of control over the surplus."

system should be clearly defined. It is important for the operators to know what kind of information they are looking for when browsing through thousands of cameras. Proactively monitoring or recording evidence could be two very different objectives when it comes to the operational instructions for the security staff. Operators need to be trained to effectively seek the information they want, and the increasing technology that can be found in control rooms needs to assist them in making any decisions.

The Dilemma of Secrecy

Security experts and advisers are not allowed to share all information with the public. While terrorism usually is partially motivated by media coverage and exposure of the cause, many covert or planned attack plans are stopped before ever materializing. But a zero/low frequency of attacks does not mean the threats are nonexistent or that people are not aware of the prevailing threats. According to the Home Secretary, UK security services has foiled forty attacks since the 7/7 bombings in 2005.[3] The secrecy of the business creates a void between the public and security personnel, because the only incidents and implications that the public notice and see are the ones that go badly. The work being conducted on a daily basis in order to prevent incidents from happening is seldom expressed to the public.

Governments and the security and intelligence agencies and police forces cannot tackle terrorism alone – the public have an important role to play too as a force multiplier, hence the need for regular campaigns to help maintain public vigilance and awareness, keeping threats in the public mind without scaremongering. The importance of community engagement in working together to drive the risk down and ultimately making it more difficult for any one area to be targeted should never be underestimated. In the summer of 2014 the Norwegian Police Security Service publically proclaimed an attack on Norwegian soil by international terrorists in the near future. This is the first time since the 1970s that this strategy has been used in Norway.[4] Whether or not it was correct of the government to inform the public about the increased threat is open for discussion. There is a fine line between providing important information to make people feel safe and spreading of unnecessary fear. From the point of the industry, this particular (and many alike) incident can be viewed as a jigsaw puzzle; imagine you have a 500-piece puzzle where 300 pieces are in place, but 200 missing. You can clearly see what the picture is showing, but you are lacking the finer details. Comparing that to the work security personnel are conducting, you could usually say that of the 500 pieces, they almost always only have 50 of them. So in order to be able to see the whole image they appreciate the help of the public. In this case, the public becomes the extended eyes and ears of the Police Security Service. The number of reports on suspicious behavior was higher than normal in the same period, and the majority of the public (85%) felt that the openness of the threat was a wise decision by the police.[5] For the security advisors this type of knowledge sharing is unusual and rarely seen. Often

"The deterrence effect of CCTV covers wider crime prevention issues, and any associated public reassurance. [...] CCTV can also provide a good forensic capability after an event, whether an isolated incident, or large-scale events such as widespread disturbances."

a surplus is crucial to adequate survival. Throughout capitalist history, some of the surplus value created has been taxed away by the state, and in social-democratic phases that proportion rose significantly, putting much of the surplus under state control. The whole neoliberal project over the last thirty years has been oriented toward privatization of control over the surplus. The data for all OECD countries show, however, that the share of gross output taken by the state has been roughly constant since the 1970s. The main achievement of the neoliberal assault, then, has been to prevent the state share expanding in the way it did in the 1960s. One further response has been to create new systems of governance that integrate state and corporate interests and, through the application of money power, assure that control over the disbursement of the surplus through the state apparatus favors corporate capital and the upper classes in the shaping of the urban process. Increasing the share of the surplus under state control will only work if the state itself is both reformed and brought back under popular democratic control.

Increasingly, we see the right to the city falling into the hands of private or quasi-private interests. In New York City, for example, we have a billionaire mayor, Michael Bloomberg, who is reshaping the city along lines favorable to the developers, to Wall Street and transnational capitalist class elements, while continuing to sell the city as an optimal location for high-value businesses and a fantastic destination for tourists, thus turning Manhattan in effect into one vast gated community for the rich.

[...] One step, though by no means final, toward unification of these struggles is to focus sharply on those moments of creative destruction where the economy of wealth accumulation piggybacks violently on the economy of dispossession, and there proclaim on behalf of the dispossessed their right to the city – their right to change the world, to change life, and to reinvent the city more after their hearts' desire. That collective right, as both a working slogan and a political ideal, brings us back to the age-old question of who it is that commands the inner connection between urbanization and surplus production and use. Perhaps, after all, Lefebvre was right, more than forty years ago, to insist that the revolution in our times has to be urban – or nothing.

> "Perhaps, after all, Lefebvre was right, more than forty years ago, to insist that the revolution in our times has to be urban – or nothing."

"The public becomes the extended eyes and ears of the Police Security Service."

the ruling bodies of a country will be criticized both if they in fact share information, and also if they don't, and incidents occur.

Whether or not upscaling security measures is the correct thing to do, society should not have to wait for new incidents to happen. The question is not *when* or *if* to implement security measures, but *how*. In essence you can compare the security advisors and heritage bodies by their ultimate objective: preservation of our physical surroundings.

172 Photo Essay

ISRAEL/PALESTINE
Visited October 7–13, 2013

1

2

Israel/Palestine

01. Construction work taking place in East Jerusalem behind the separation barrier

02. Ras al-Amud checkpoint in East Jerusalem

03. House in East Jerusalem divided in two halves. One side occupied by Jewish settlers, the other side by an elderly Palestinian woman and her family.

04. Heavily surveilled settlement in the East Jerusalem neighborhood of Silwan

Photo Essay

5

05. 06. The separation barrier,
East Jerusalem

07. Jewish children overlooking the valley
to Silwan, a large Palestinian neighborhood
in East Jerusalem

Israel/Palestine

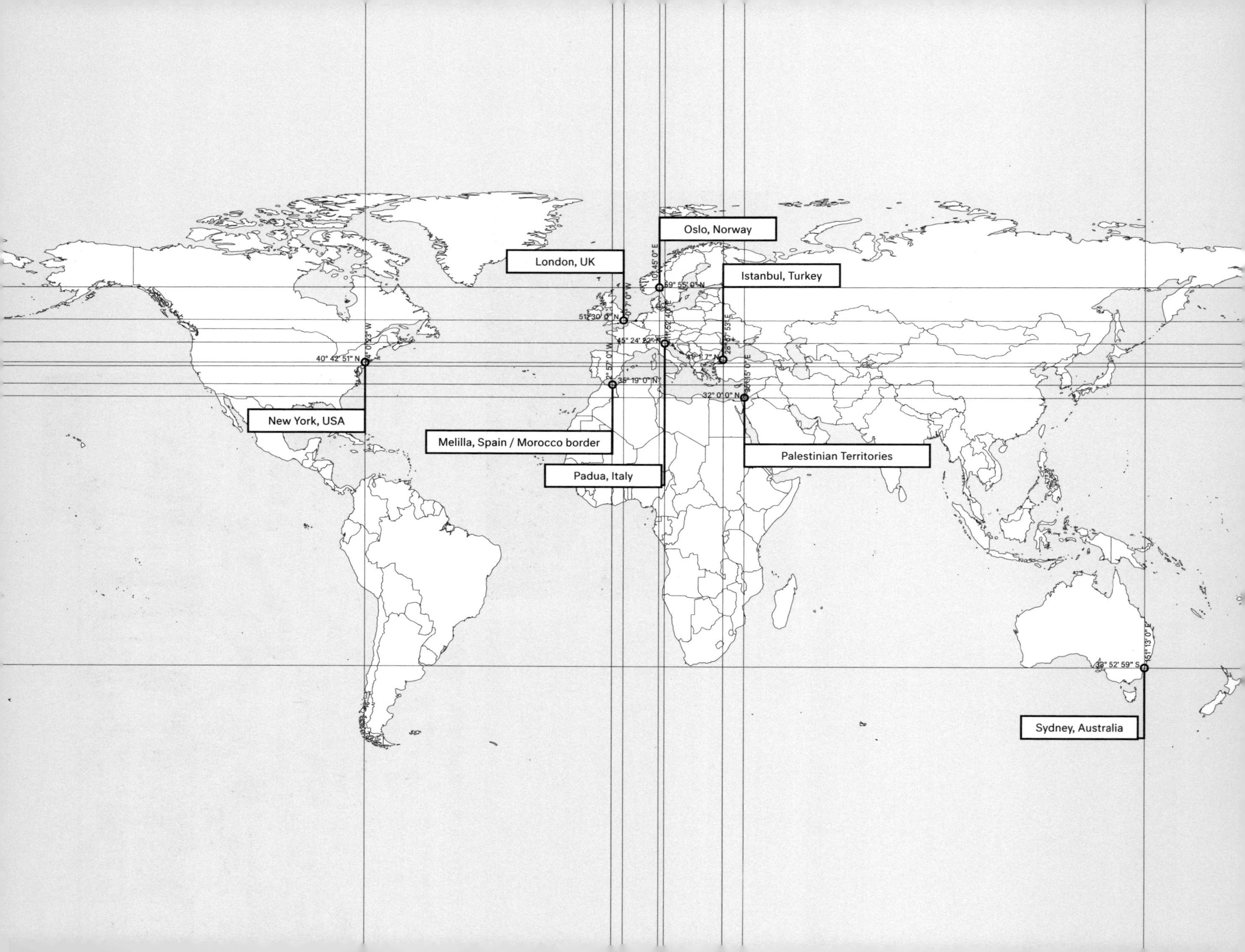

Oslo, Norway
10° 45' 0" E
59° 55' 0" N
London, UK
0° 7' 0" W
51° 30' 0" N
Istanbul, Turkey
28° 57' 53" E
41° 1' 7" N
New York, USA
40° 42' 51" N
4° 0' 23" W
Melilla, Spain / Morocco border
2° 57' 0" W
35° 19' 0" N
Padua, Italy
11° 52' 40" E
45° 24' 22" N
Palestinian Territories
35° 15' 0" E
32° 0' 0" N
Sydney, Australia
151° 13' 0" E
33° 52' 59" S

Contested Sites

The following documents describe selected instances of security architecture – in which space is instrumentalized in the name of security.[1] The existence of this species of space is commonly justified according to a series of threats – whether actual or constructed – ranging from: terror, crime, and uncontrolled migration to contraband, urban disorder, political extremism, and dissent. Spaces securitized according to a declared threat of terror include: political spaces such as parliaments and embassies; major financial districts; global sports events; and political summits. Borderlines and border checkpoints represent an additional category of securitized sites presented here – typically justified according to the threats of uncontrolled migration and contraband and in some cases the threat of terror. Privately owned public spaces are a further category of sites securitized in reaction to supposed threats of crime or urban disorder, while securitized responses to demonstrations and protests in public space, justified according to threats of urban disorder and political extremism or dissent, represent an additional category of sites and situations.

Collectively, these cases contribute to an inventory of spatial instruments and techniques – deployed by supranational, state, municipal, corporate, or other organizations or individuals – that unfold aspects of the militarized character of contemporary urban space. Such an inventory would include: electric fences, walls, barbed wire fencing, Jersey barriers, barricades, retractable vehicle barriers, moats, bunds, berms, chicanes, bollards, antitire spikes, energy-absorbing planters, antitunnel barriers, laminated glass films, checkpoints, guard booths, watch towers, gates, floodlights, tunnels, panic rooms, remote-controlled pepper sprayers, movement-activated CCTV surveillance, and so forth. These instruments are supplemented by a range of equipment and technologies, including: CCTV with automatic number plate recognition, metal detectors, X-ray scanners, heat sensors, explosive sniffers, heartbeat-detecting radar, night-vision goggles, surveillance drones, infrared cameras, lie detectors, signal jammers, electronic surveillance, water cannons, tear gas, assault weapons with plastic bullets, sniper rifles, assault ships, surface-to-air missiles, etc.

The presentation of sites is ordered according to longitude: beginning in London (0° west), heading westward through New York, Sydney, Istanbul, the West Bank and Gaza, and ending in Oslo. Isometric drawings, maps, analytical diagrams, and timelines are used to describe the composition, organization, and disposition, as well as the consequences, of the securitization of space in different settings.

WORLD TERRORISM INDEX AND EVENTS

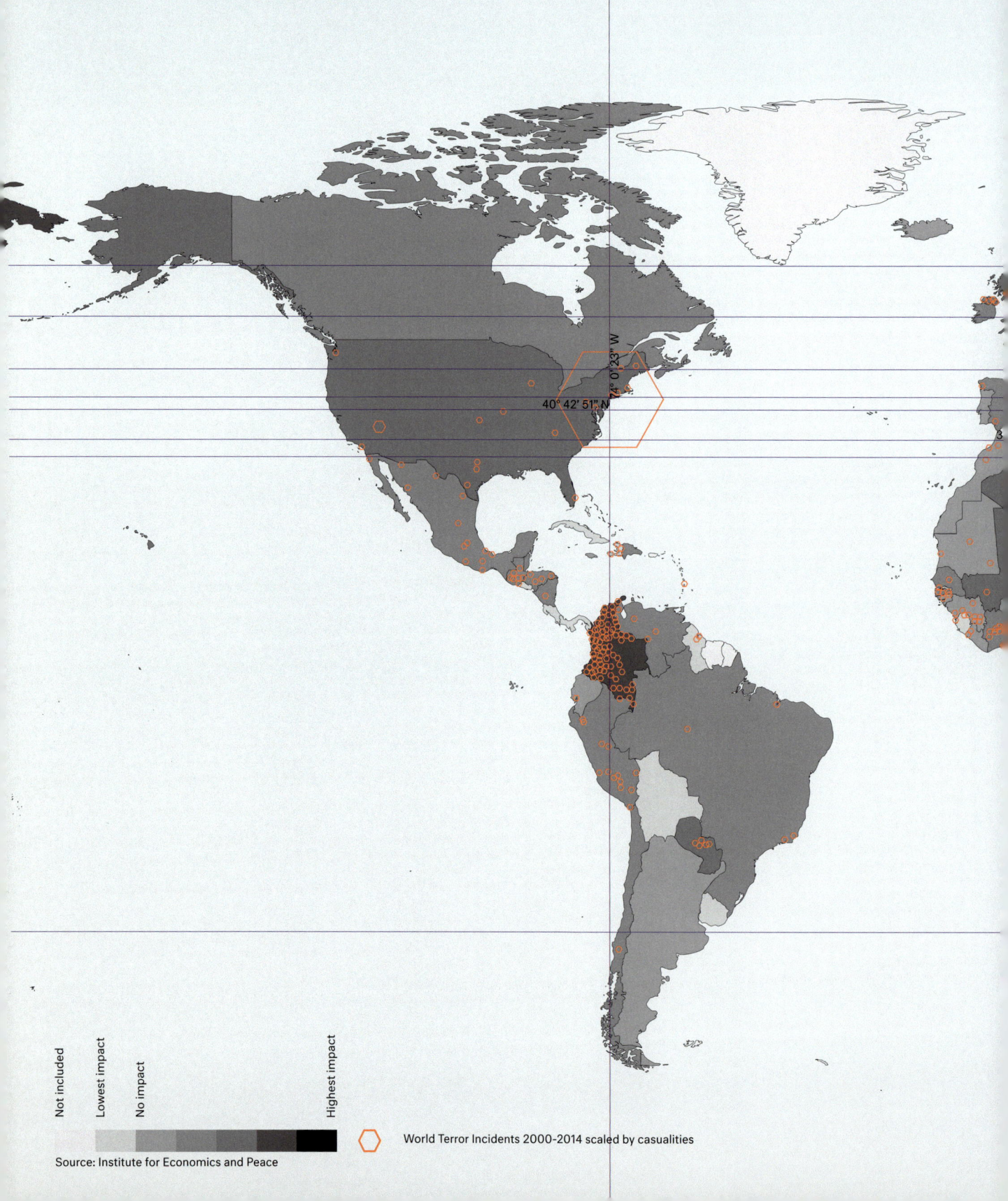

40° 42' 51" N
74° 0' 23" W

Not included
Lowest impact
No impact
Highest impact

○ World Terror Incidents 2000-2014 scaled by casualities

Source: Institute for Economics and Peace

World Maps

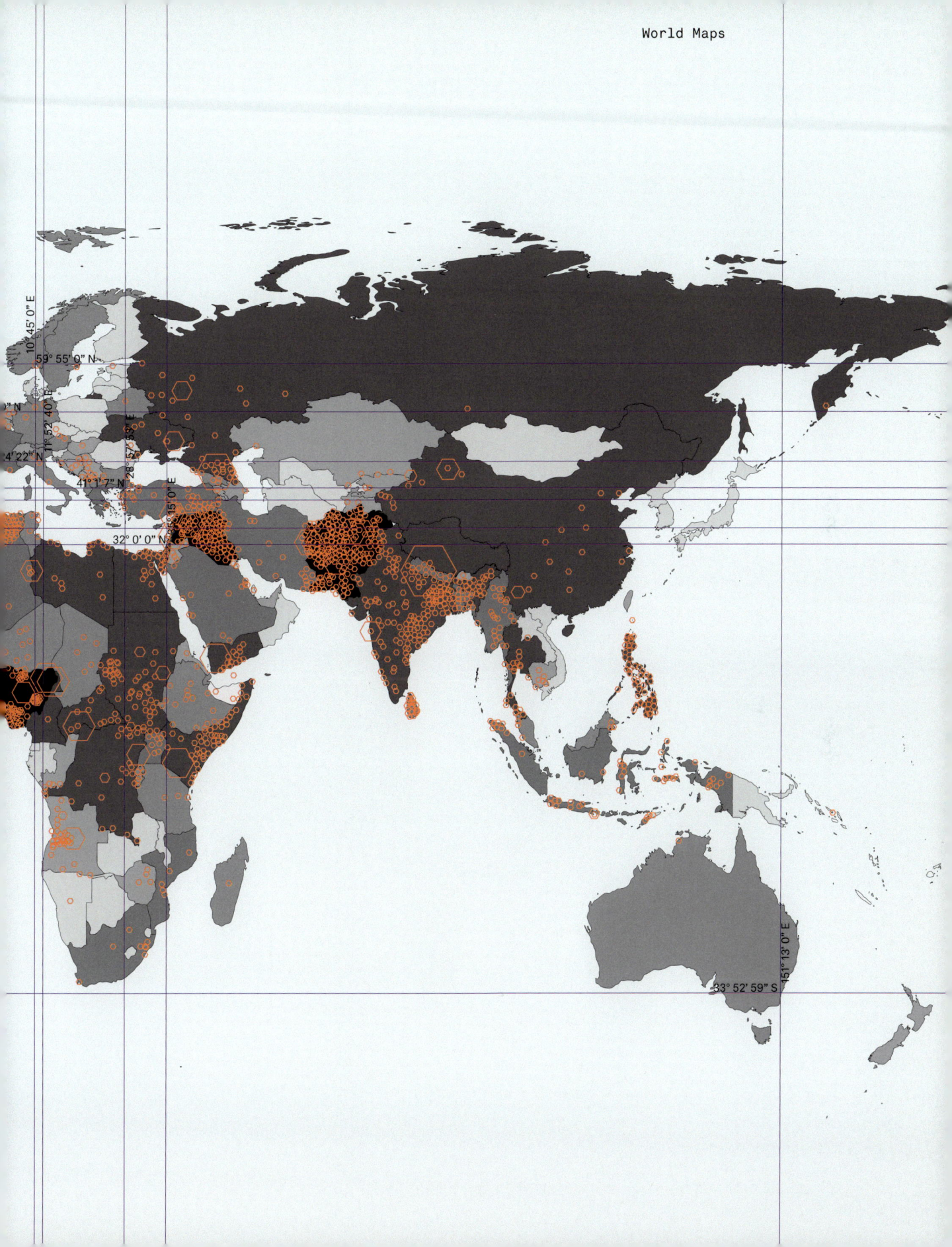

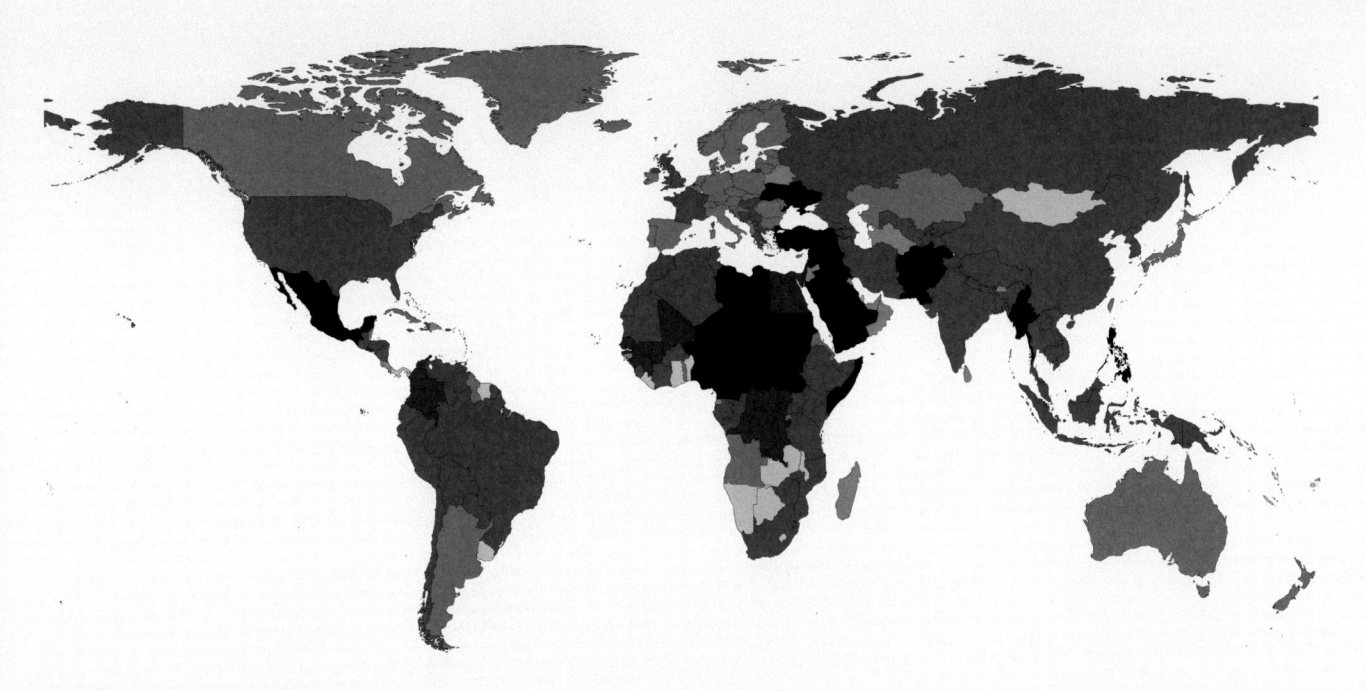

WORLD CONFLICT INDEX (Source: Heidelberg Institute for International Conflict Research[I])

- War
- Limited war
- Violent Crisis
- Nonviolent Crisis
- Dispute
- No Conflict

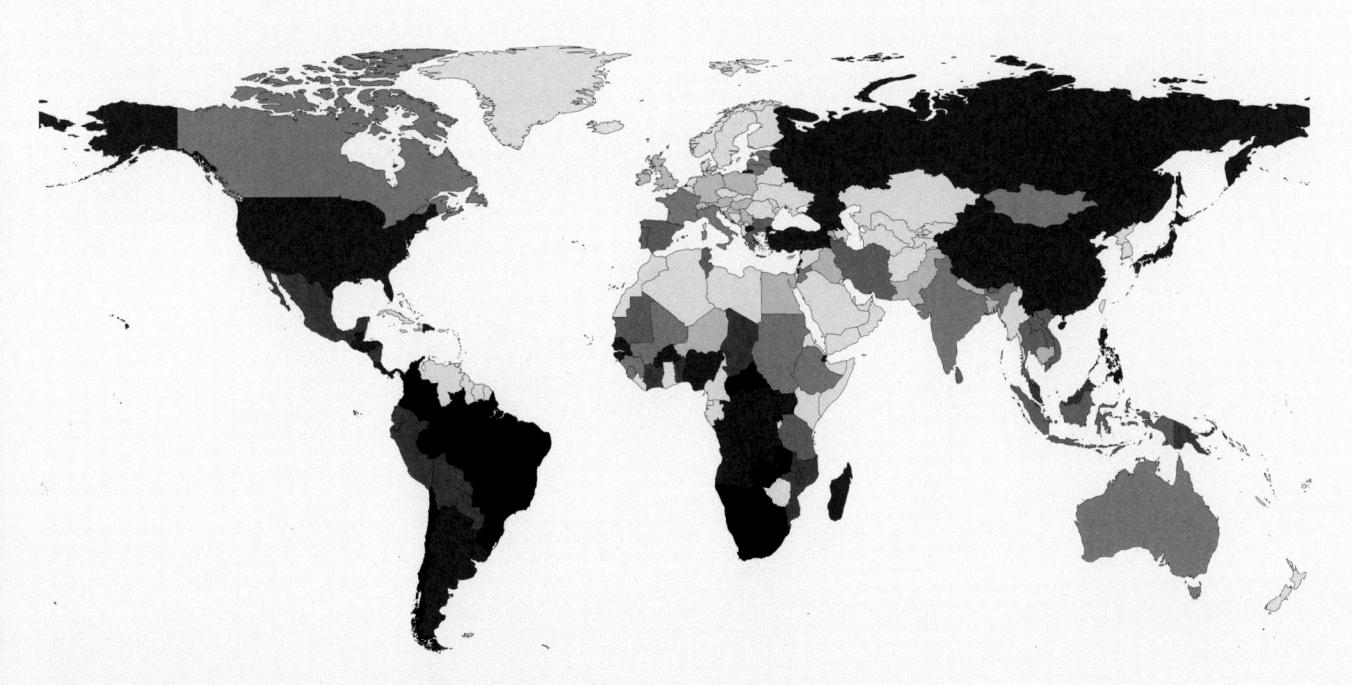

WORLD INEQUALITY INDEX, GINI SCORE 2013 (Source: World Economic Forum[II])

63.38 High Inequality

29.08 Low Inequality

World Maps

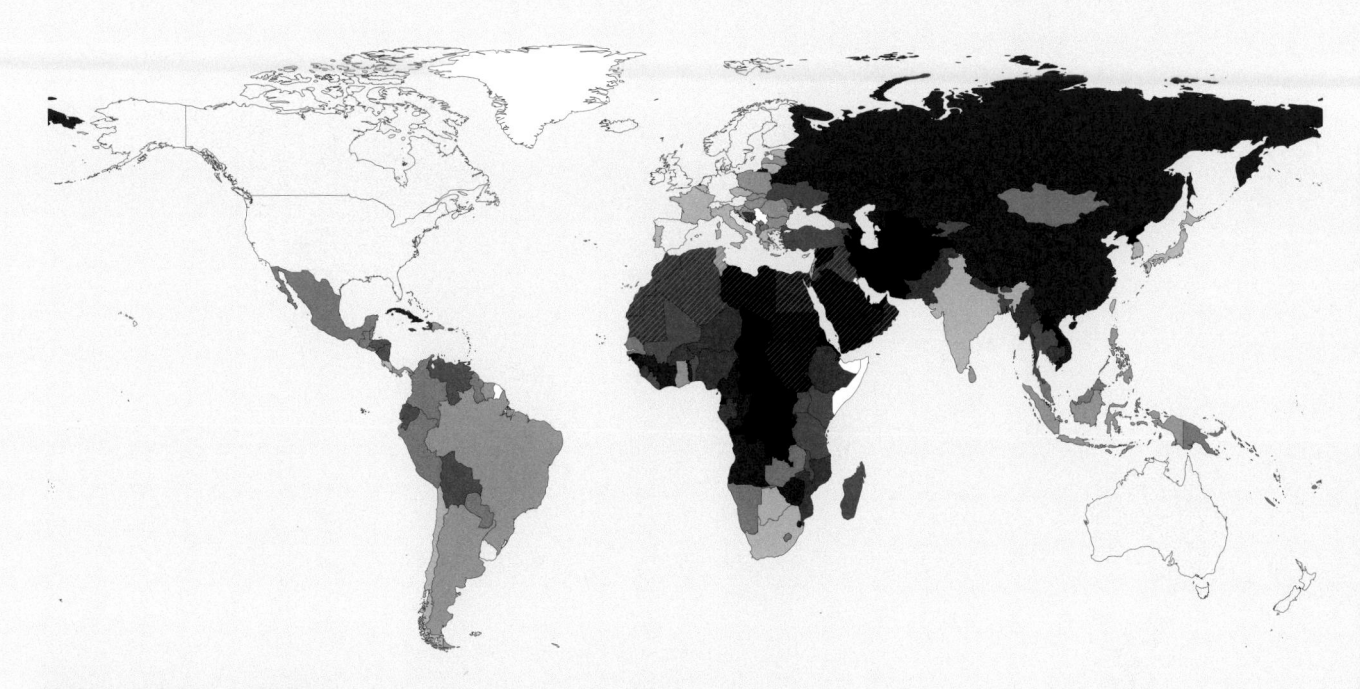

WORLD DEMOCRACY INDEX 10=Perfect (Source: Economist Intelligence Unit[III])

- < 2.79
- 2.79 – 3.71
- 3.71 – 4.85
- 4.85 – 5.88
- 5.88 – 6.67
- 6.67 – 7.45
- 7.45 – 8.05
- > 8.05
- Countries involved in the Arab Spring[IV]

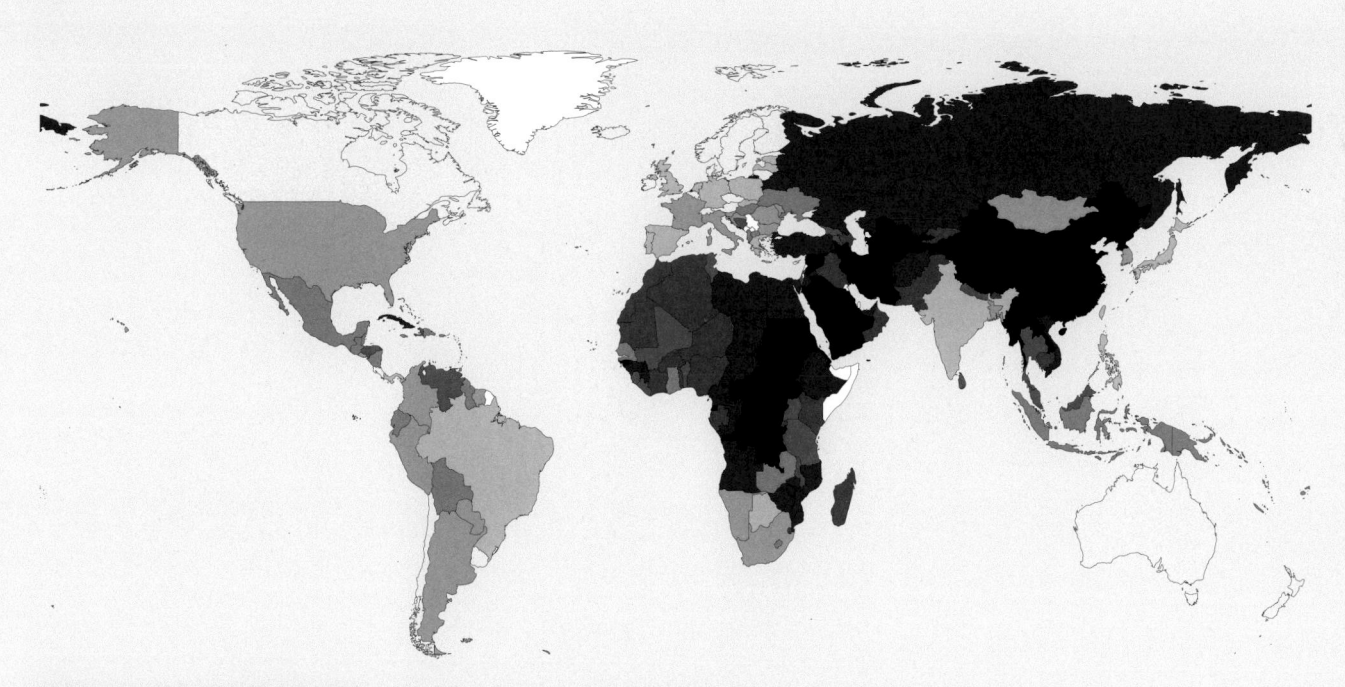

WORLD CIVIL LIBERTIES INDEX 10=Perfect (Source: Economist Intelligence Unit[V])

- < 2.65
- 2.65 – 3.82
- 3.82 – 5.29
- 5.29 – 6.76
- 6.76 – 7.94
- 7.94 – 8.82
- 8.82 – 9.41
- > 9.41

Statistical Comparison of Selected Nations and Cities

	GDP	INCOME SHARE HIGHEST AND LOWEST 10%[1]	MILITARY BUDGET[II]
NORWAY Population: 5,051,275 Population density: 15.5/km²		21.9 / 3.3	
OSLO Population: 634,463 Population density: 1,400/km²	512,580 bill. USD		% of GDP: 1.4 7,176 bill. USD
UNITED KINGDOM Population: 64,097,085 Population density: 265/km²		28.8 / 1.9	
LONDON REGION Population: 8,615,246 Population density: 5,354/km²	2,678,454 bill. USD		% of GDP: 2.2 58,925 bill. USD
USA Population: 318,892,103 Population density: 35/km²		29.6 / 1.4	
NEW YORK CITY Population: 8,405,837 Population density: 10,725/km²	16,768,100 bill. USD		% of GDP: 3.8 637,187 bill. USD
ISRAEL Population: 8,157,300 Population density: 377/km²		31.3 / 1.7	
JERUSALEM Population: 890,426 Population density: 6,400/km²	290,550 bill. USD		% of GDP: 5.6 16,270 bill. USD

Highest 10%
Lowest 10%

1. Measures the impact of terrorism in 162 countries. Each country is given a score that represents a five-year weighted average.

183   C

ACTIVE/PASSIVE MILITARY[III]	MILITARY PERSONNEL PER 1,000 INHABITANTS[III]	POLICE PERSONNEL PER 1,000 INHABITANTS[IV]	GLOBAL TERROR INDEX[1,V]	DEMOCRACY INDEX[2,VI]	FREEDOM OF PRESS[3,VII]
Total: 69,700 Active: 24,450 Passive: 45,250	Total 15 Active 5.5	2.22	44 / 3.57	1 / 88.3	3 / 6.52
Total: 191,410 Active: 45,110 Passive: 73,970	Total 3.7 Active 3	2.37	27 / 5.17	14 / 79.9	33 / 19.93
Total: 2,231,447 Active: 1,369,532 Passive: 843,750	Total 7.1 Active 4.4	2.48	30 / 4.71	15 / 78.8	46 / 23.49
Total: 749,500 Active: 176,500 Passive: 465,000	Total 94.4 Active 23.4	3.39	32 / 4.66	21 / 73.7	96 / 31.19

Total / Active / Passive

Total / Active

Rank / Score   Rank / Score   Rank / Score

2. Based on 60 indicators grouped in five different categories: electoral process and pluralism, civil liberties, functioning of government, political participation, and political culture.

3. Countries are given a score of between 0 and 100 for each of the six overall criteria, with 0 being the best possible score and 100 the worst.

184   Contested Sites

EUROPE

The contemporary European approach to the theme of security is informed to a certain extent by its recent past. In the aftermath of World War II, the project of a collective Europe would be consolidated with the establishment of institutions such as NATO in 1949, the European Economic Community in 1958, and what would become the European Union in 1993. These developments would represent a concerted attempt to further reconstruct the economies of Europe and to ensure lasting peace (in the context of Europe's several-hundred-year history of war). This project was furthered with the end of the Cold War, the collapse of the Soviet Union, and the expansion of the European project to the east. The 1995 Schengen Area Agreement would further interweave European nations through the ambition of a borderless Europe containing more than 400 million inhabitants within an integrated work market with common migratory terms. The agreement would be predicated on a more protected outer Schengen perimeter – operated by Frontex[2] – charged with limiting "illegal immigration and terrorist infiltration." Elevated political attention directed toward migration throughout Europe during the last two decades, together with a heightened public perception of the threat of terror, has led to new challenges in the performance of the Schengen treaty – a situation intensified by the presence of heightened conflict and poverty near the outer borders of the Schengen Area.

LEGENDS

- XX / XX Country / Percentage of immigrants 1990/2013[1]
- EU member Schengen countries
- Non-EU Schengen countries
- Non-Schengen EU countries
- NATO countries and applicants
- Borders Frontex operated

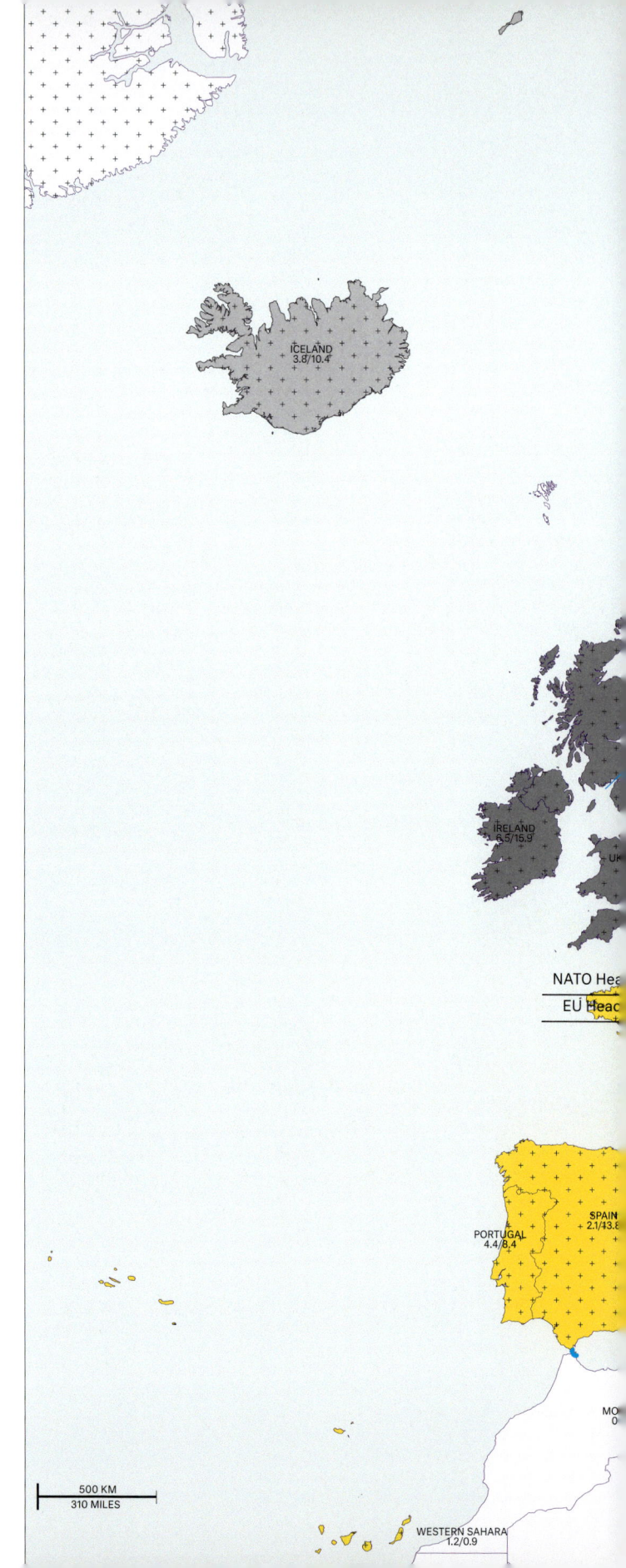

NORWAY	4.6/13.8
SWEDEN	9.2/15.9
FINLAND	1.3/5.4
RUSSIAN FEDERATION	7.8/7.7
ESTONIA	24.4/16.2
LATVIA	24.2/13.8
LITHUANIA	9.4/4.9
DENMARK	4.6/9.9
BELARUS	12.2/11.6
NETHERLANDS	8.0/11.7
POLAND	3.0/1.7
GERMANY	7.4/11.9
BELGIUM	8.9/10.4
LUXEMBOURG	29.8/43.3
CZECH REPUBLIC	1.1/4.0
SLOVAKIA	2.5/9.4
UKRAINE	13.3/11.4
KAZAKHSTAN	22.4/21.1
AUSTRIA	10.3/15.7
LIECHTENSTEIN	37.9/33.1
SWITZERLAND	20.9/28.9
HUNGARY	3.3/4.7
ROMANIA	0.6/0.9
REPUBLIC OF MOLDOVA	13.3/11.2
SLOVENIA	8.9/11.3
CROATIA	9.9/17.6
ITALY	2.5/9.4
SAN MARINO	13.7/15.4
BOSNIA AND HERZEGOVINA	1.2/0.6
SERBIA	1.0/5.6
BULGARIA	0.2/1.2
GEORGIA	6.2/4.4
UZBEKISTAN	8.0/4.4
MONTENEGRO	NA/8.2
ALBANIA	1.9/3.1
F.Y.R. MACEDONIA	4.7/6.8
ARMENIA	18.6/10.6
AZERBAIJAN	5.0/3.4
TURKMENISTAN	8.4/4.3
ANDORRA	4.0/56.9
GREECE	4.9/8.1
TURKEY	NA/NA
MALTA	4.0/8.0
CYPRUS	5.7/18.2
SYRIA	5.7/6.4
IRAN	7.6/3.4
ALGERIA	1.0/0.7
TUNISIA	0.5/0.3
LEBANON	19.4/17.6
ISRAEL	36.3/26.5
PALESTINE	13.9/5.9
JORDAN	34.1/40.2
KUWAIT	77.0/60.2
LIBYA	10.7/12.2
EGYPT	0.3/0.4
SAUDI ARABIA	30.8/31.4

Headquarters, Brussels
Headquarters, Brussels
Headquarters, Geneva

LONDON, ENGLAND

London holds a long-standing position in the discourse on security in general, and terrorism in particular. The militarized British reaction to the Northern Ireland conflict in the twentieth century is a classic example of Foucault's "boomerang effect," whereby security measures and techniques tested in foreign or colonial settings would be reintroduced locally in the UK. The measures first built to separate territories within the city of Belfast, for instance, were developed and extended by the UK military, and applied later to the Ring of Steel defense in the City of London.[3] CCTV would became a central element in the Northern Ireland strategy, which was further applied to the securitization of British cities in the 1980s and 1990s in response to IRA bombings. Police realized the potential of using cameras installed for traffic observation to observe public order incidents and demonstrations. In a contemporary context, London has one of the highest CCTV per capita rates in the world.[4] Securitization, driven by a vigorous private-security industry in the UK, has expanded its reach to incorporate the full gamut of the environment, with the support of organizations such as Security by Design.

In the post-9/11 era, with the UK's involvement in conflicts in Afghanistan and Iraq, elevated concerns over terror have emerged from the intelligence community and the media. The July, 7, 2005, transit bombings would further impact the UK situation, giving rise in a way not dissimilar to the US to antiterrorism regulations that assign controversial powers to the police including detention without charge, stop and search without suspicion, and restrictions on public space use that effectively limit citizens' rights to the city.

187   C   London 0°W

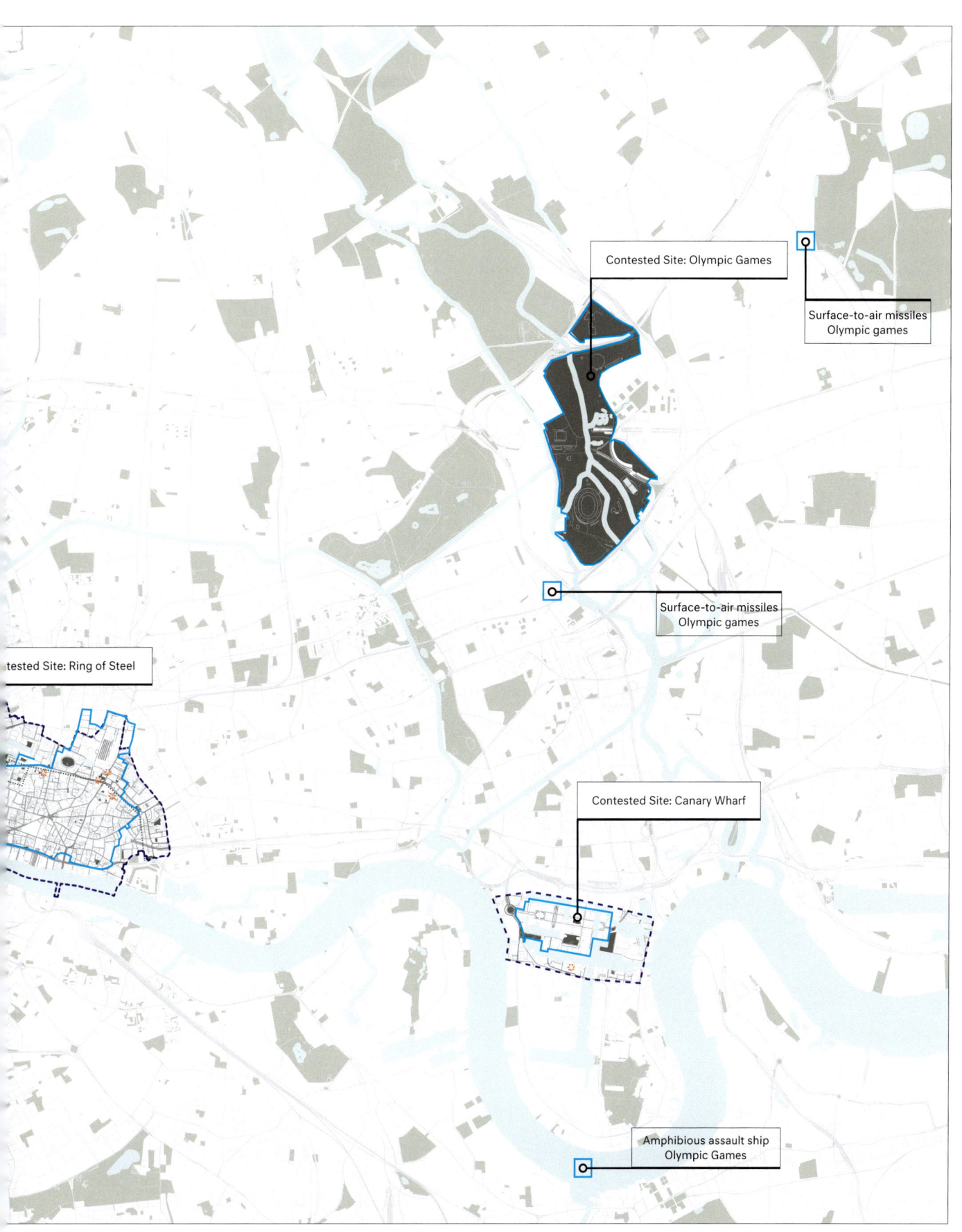

Contested Site: Olympic Games

Surface-to-air missiles
Olympic games

Surface-to-air missiles
Olympic games

Contested Site: Ring of Steel

Contested Site: Canary Wharf

Amphibious assault ship
Olympic Games

188 Contested Sites

500 M
1000 FEET

QUEEN ELIZABETH OLYMPIC PARK

- Queen Elizabeth Olympic Park
- Militarized outposts
- 01 Detail at Lexington Gardens
- 02 Detail at security fences
- 03 Detail at canal checkpoint

SUMMARY OLYMPICS, 2012

The goal of Olympism is to place sport at the service of the harmonious development of humankind, with a view to promoting a peaceful society concerned with the preservation of human dignity.
   The Olympic Charter, Fundamental Principles of Olympism(1)

As a global event that has been exposed to previous terror incidents (for example, Munich 1972, Atlanta 1996), the effort to secure the Summer Olympics in London in 2012 would become the largest peacetime military operation in Britain's history, with a total of US$1.6B spent on security.[5] In the context of considerable cuts in social welfare and housing subsidies in London, along with rising unemployment, the magnitude of expenditure on the security apparatus and the games in general was highly controversial[6] – triggering numerous protests and demonstrations during the period leading up to the games.[7]

Related concerns would emerge in relation to temporary laws passed prior to the games, including the London Olympic Games Act[8] of 2006, which was challenged by many critics as authoritarian based on a range of measures that would include unprecedented bail limitations. ASBOs (Anti-Social Behaviour Orders) allowed police to impose restraining orders on individuals to exclude them from Olympic venues. This was first applied in the period leading up to the games to activist Simon Moore,[9] who had protested against the construction of the Olympic basketball stadium at Leyton Marsh; and most infamously during the games, when 182 cyclists on a Critical Mass bicycle ride were arrested for public order offenses related to not complying to a police restraining order on their usual path.[10]

The building up of security personnel for the games attracted further controversy. British multinational G4S – the world's largest private-security firm – was awarded the £284M[11] security contract, by committing to supply more than 10,000 guards to the games. As the opening of the event approached, the total force had reached only 6,000 guards, of whom most were poorly trained according to several reports.[12] As a result, the prime minister and UK cabinet were forced to call in 3,500 Royal Navy soldiers to meet the shortage.[13] Over the course of the games, the total number of soldiers appointed to Olympic security would reach more than double the total number of British soldiers deployed in Afghanistan.

Rapier missiles
Barn Hill, Netherhouse Farm

Rapier missiles
William Girling Reservoir, Lea Valley Reservoir Chain

High-velocity missiles
Fred Wigg Tower, Montague Road Estate

Queen Elizabeth Olympic Park

High-velocity missiles
Lexington Gardens, Fairfield Road

River Thames

Canary Wharf

Amphibious assault ship
HMS Ocean

Rapier missiles
Blackheath Common, Blackheath

Rapier missiles
Oxleas Meadows, Shooters Hill

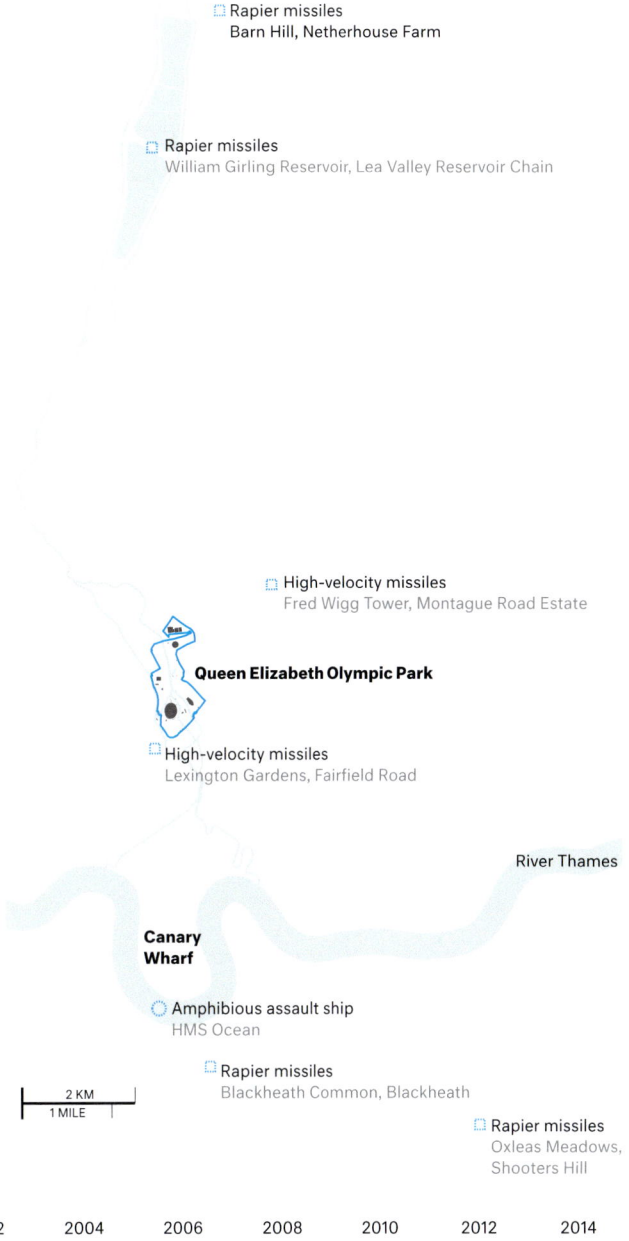

Olympic Games security costs

	1988	1992	1994	1998	2000	2002	2004	2006	2008	2010	2012	2014
	Seoul	Barcelona	Lillehammer	Nagano	Sydney	Salt Lake C.	Athens	Turin	Beijing	Vancouver	London	Sochi
Total	US$ 7.82B[I]	US$ 15.6B[I]	US$ 2.97B[I]	US$ 17.59B[I]	US$ 6.67B[I]	US$ 2.68B[I]	US$ 18.53B[I]	US$ 2.63B[I]	US$ 43.5B[I]	US$ 8.1B[I]	US$ 14.2B[I]	US$ 50.8B[I]
Security	US$ 224M[VI]	US$ 113M[V]	US$ 18M[VII]	US$ 266M[VIII]	US$ 252M[IX]	US$ 669M[IX]	US$ 1.91B[IX]	US$ 131M[IX]	US$ 7.27B[IX]	US$ 1.1B[IX]	US$ 1.67B[IX]	US$ 3.05B[X]

Contested Sites

Lexington Gardens, Tower Hamlets

As part of the securitization process that took place during the London Olympic Games, the Royal Artillery established six sites with Rapier and Starstreak high-velocity missile systems around the city. Antiaircraft missiles were deployed on open meadows surrounding the city and on top of Lexington Gardens and the Fred Wigg Tower, causing particular alarm, and protests, among residents concerned that the missile installations would make their buildings potential terrorist targets. Army administrators denied the claim, and legal action by residents against the military was rejected by the High Court. Colonel Jon Campbell would give the perplexing explanation: "We're trying to demilitarize this (games) and let the sport do the talking. The Lexington building is the best available location away from the Olympic Park."[14]

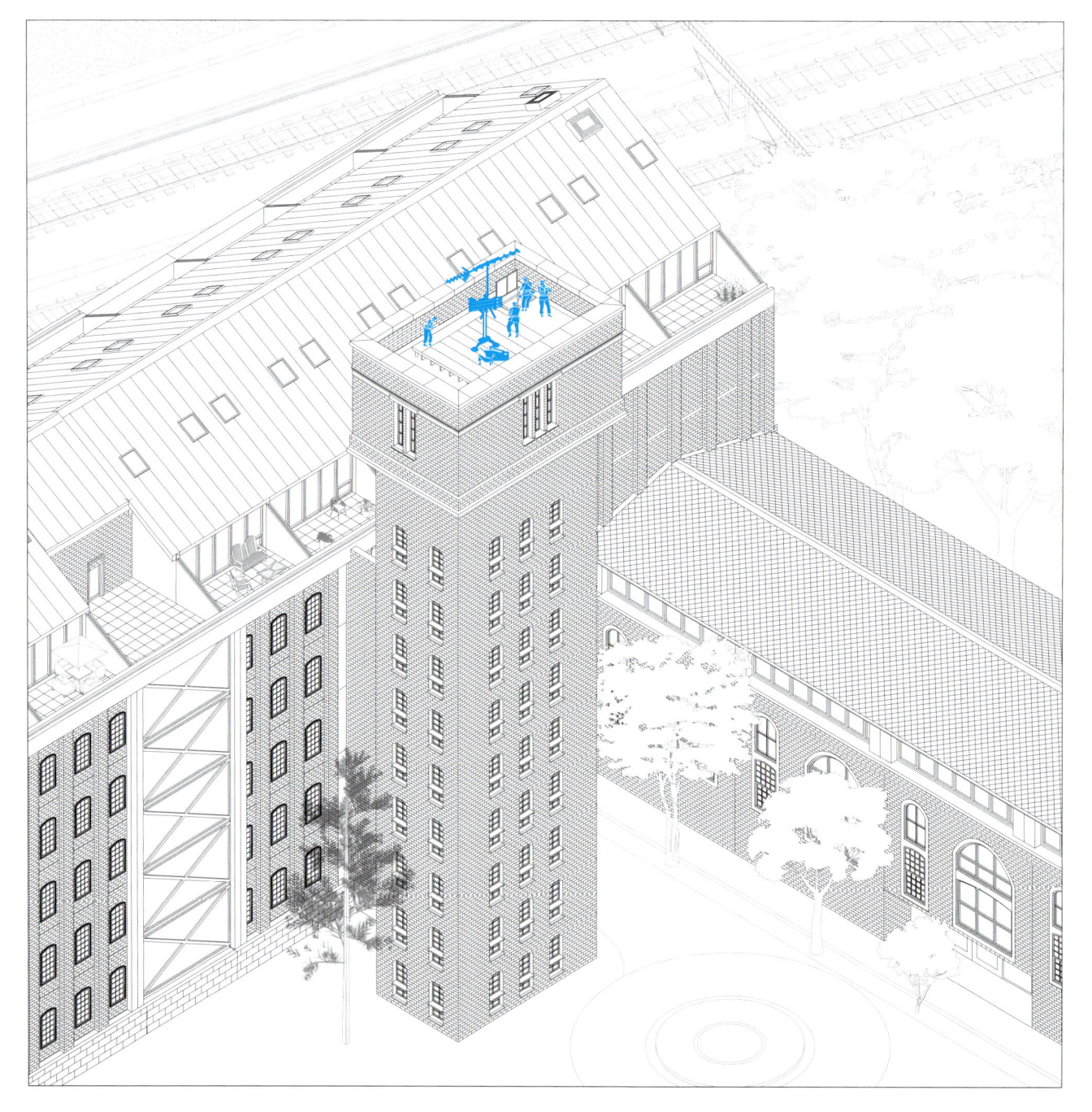

— Security Measures

Queen Elizabeth Olympic Park

One of the most evident physical manifestations of what many described as exaggerated security measures during the London Olympics was an 11-mile-long, 5,000-volt electrified fence topped with razor wire around the Olympic Park. Approximately 900 surveillance cameras monitored this outer perimeter,[15] while the adjoining water bodies were sealed off with manned gates and boat patrols. The UK's largest assault ship, HMS Ocean, was stationed a few miles south, near Canary Wharf, as a logistical hub and a deployment base for Royal Navy Lynx helicopters and sniper teams.[16]

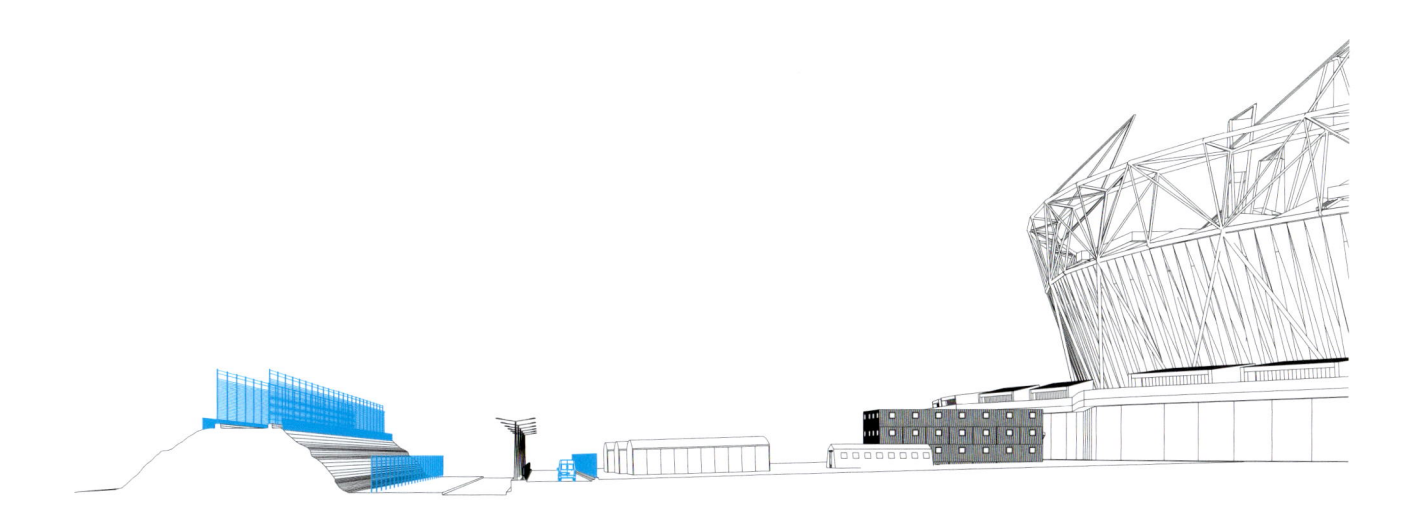

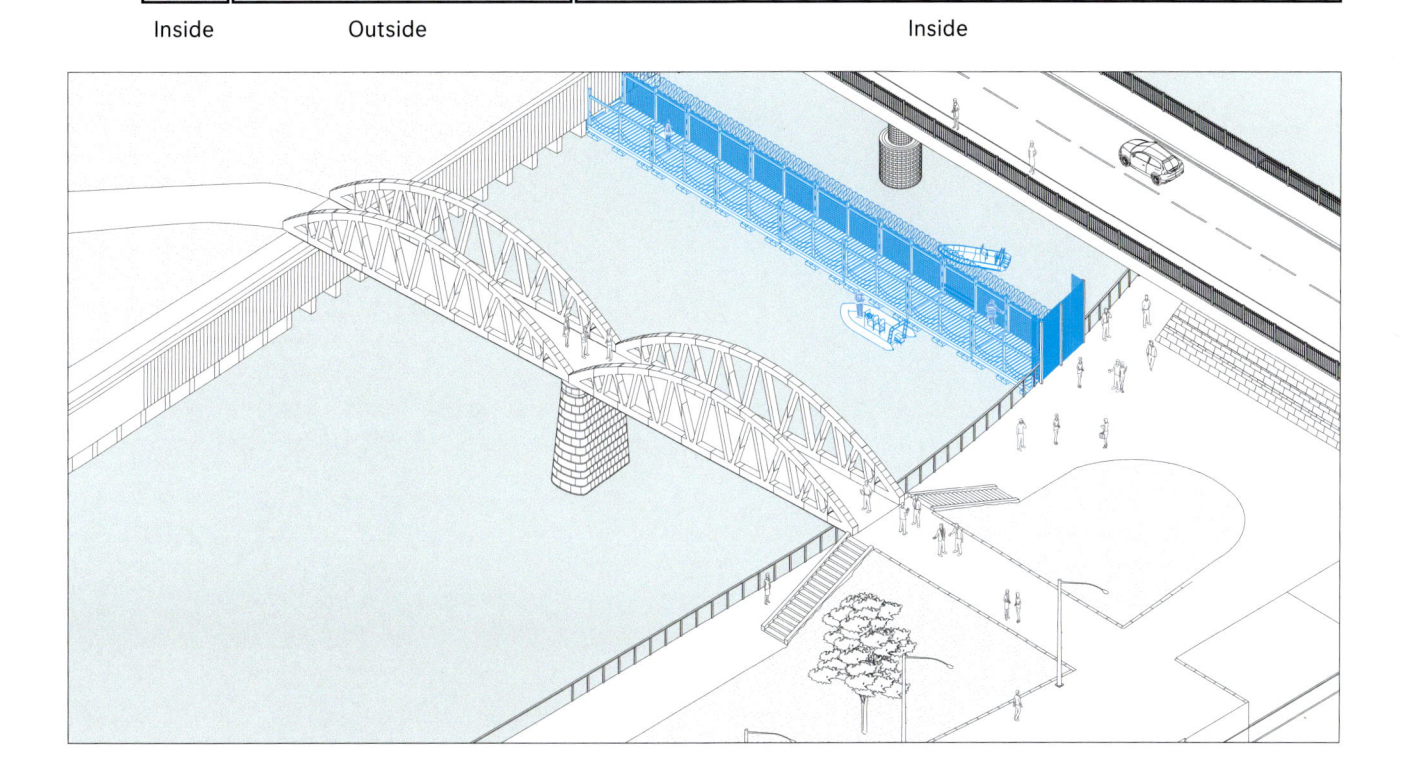

Contested Sites

RING OF STEEL[I, II]

City of London and the Ring of Steel	--- Old roman city wall	△ Road blocks
① Detail at Moor Lane	▪▪▪▪ Ring of Steel	◌ IRA bombing sites
② Detail at Vandy Street	☐ Entry points	○ Financial assets
--- City of London borough border	■ Exit points	

RING OF STEEL

51° 30′ 48.6108″ N
0° 5′ 20.3640″ W

The "Ring of Steel" is the popular name for the security and surveillance cordon established around the City of London after the IRA bombings at the Baltic Exchange (1992) and Bishopsgate (1993).[17] Covering 1.12 square miles, or less than 0.2 percent of the wider metropolitan area, the City of London is an onshore tax haven and the center of the UK's financial industry – home to institutions such as The London Stock Exchange, the Bank of England, and the international insurance market Lloyd's of London. The area's unusual status is underlined by the disparity between an almost nonexistent resident population (approx. 7,000) and a considerably larger commuting working population (more than 300,000).[18] The City's position as a world financial center made it a target of attacks during the IRA's bombing campaign in the 1980s and 1990s, and a site of security concern in more recent years.[19]

Despite its name, the Ring of Steel is perceived largely as an inconspicuous barrier along the City border, following in part the line of the ancient London Wall. As a form of "fortress urbanism"[20] first tested in military conflict zones prior to its return to a civilian context, the Ring of Steel is focused upon limiting, monitoring, and controlling entry and exit points to and from the City of London. This is evident in two-thirds of the streets that used to lead into the area being closed off to vehicle traffic – while the remaining nineteen are heavily controlled.[21] The system is composed of CCTV cameras, vehicle checkpoints with ANPR, chicanes, sentry boxes, closed streets, one-way systems, bollards, vehicle barriers, and oversized planters and flower pots.

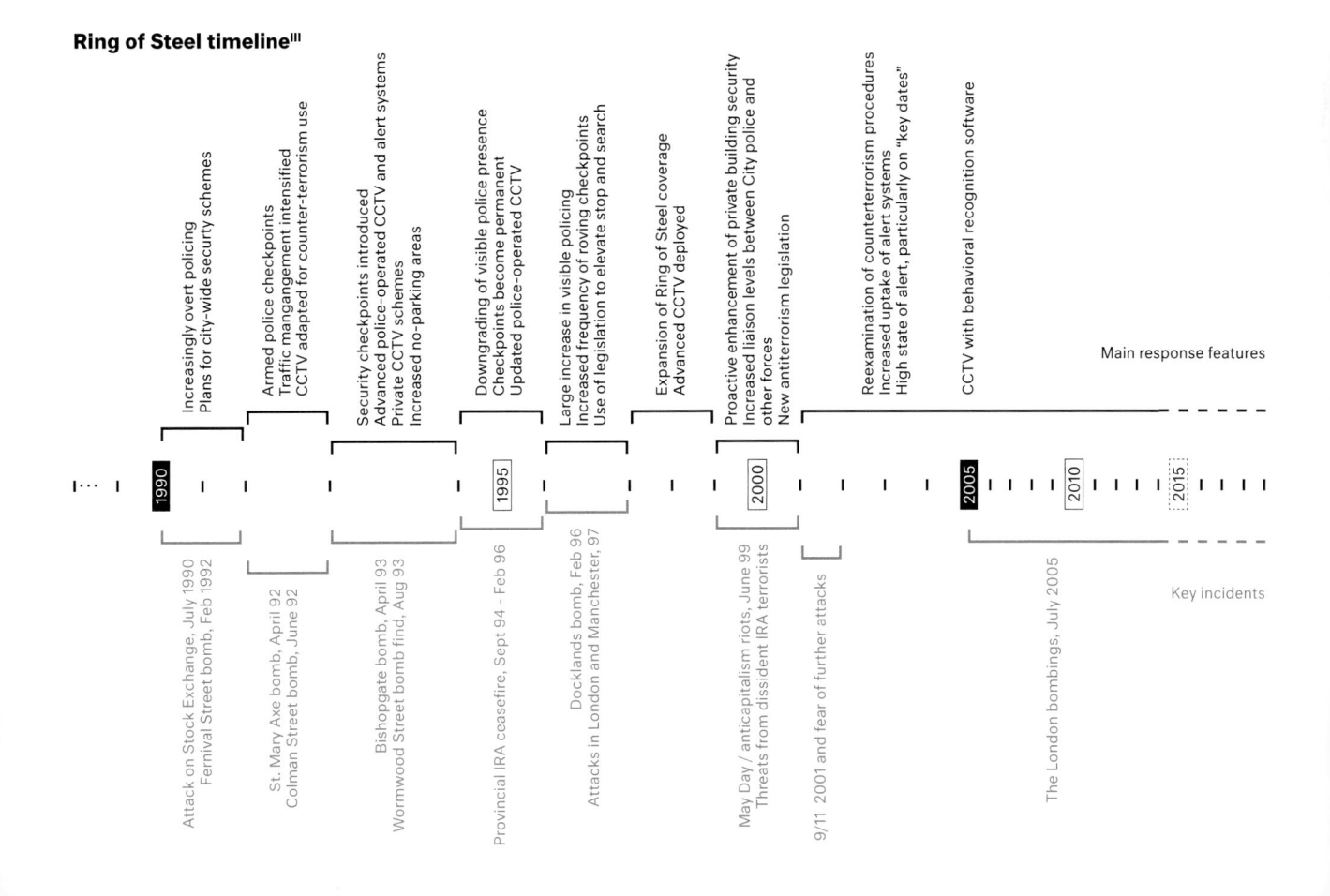

Ring of Steel timeline[III]

Contested Sites

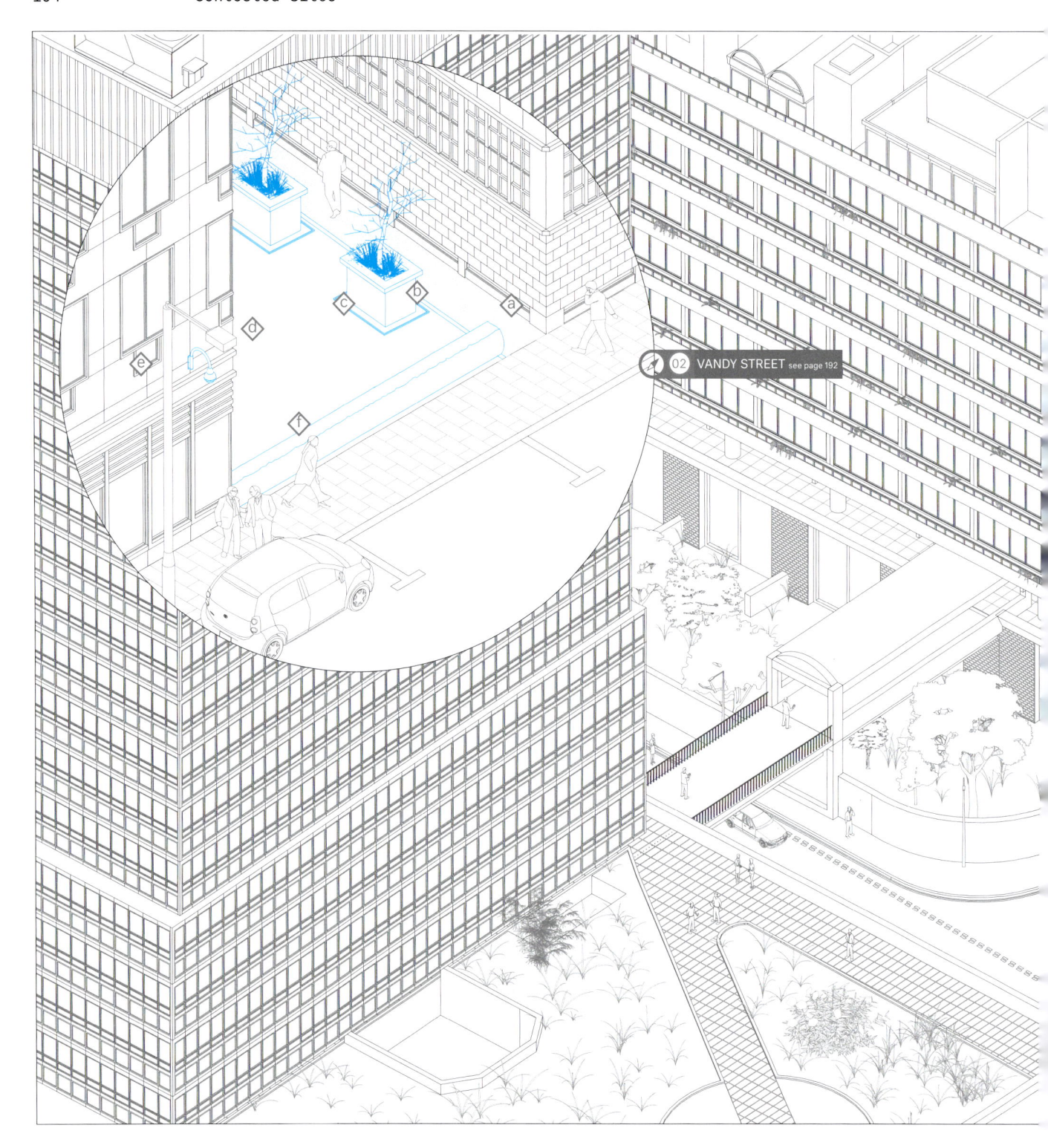

THE BARBICAN, MOOR LANE

A	Vehicle checkpoint	01	Zoom-in checkpoint at Moor Lane	d	Vehicle barrier
	Security Measures	a	Automatic numberplate recognition (ANPR)	02	Detail at Vandy Street
		b	Bollards	a	Pathway for pedestrians 1.2m wide
		c	Guarded security booth	b	Layer of fine-grained pebblestones

195 C Ring of Steel 0°W

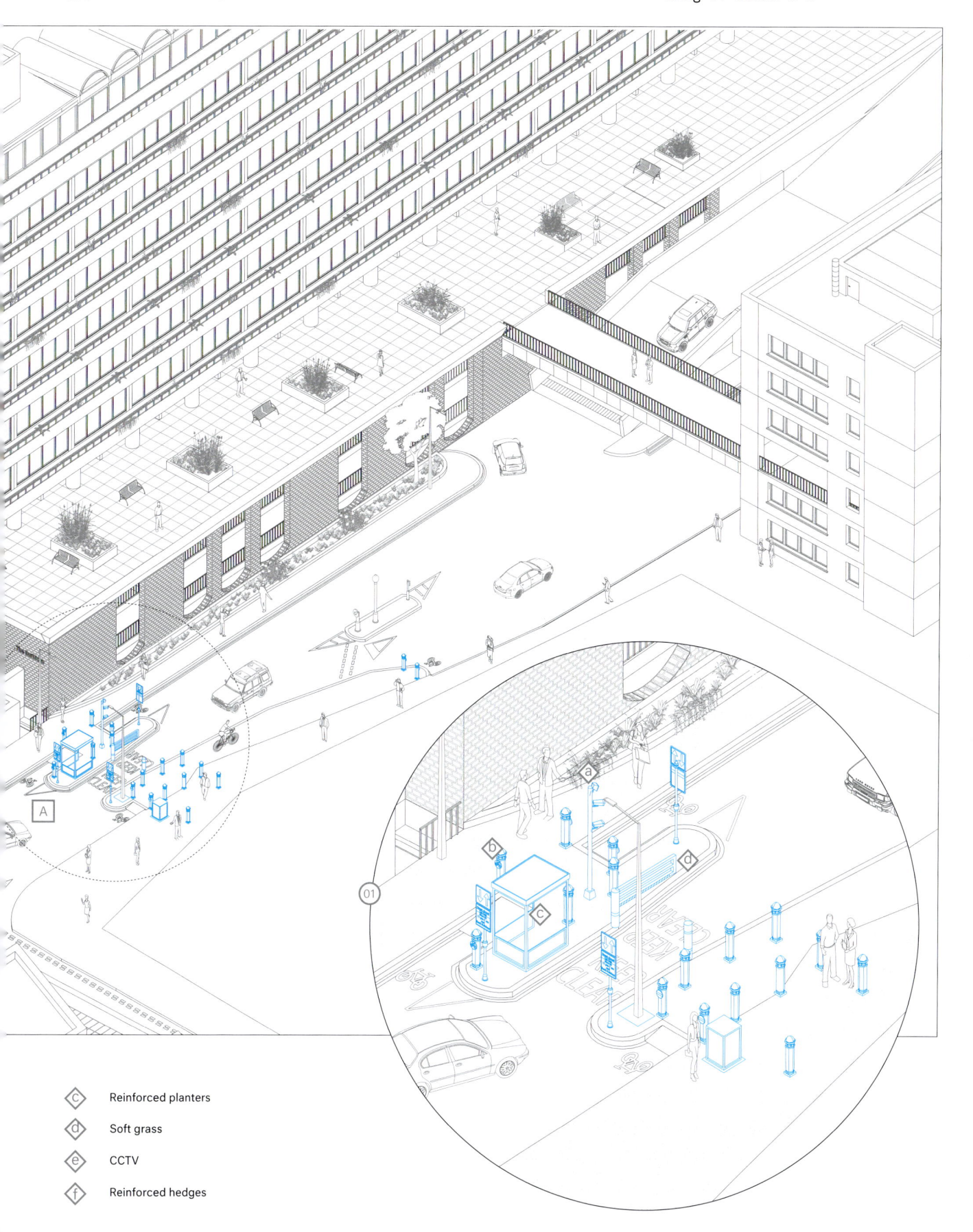

◇ c Reinforced planters
◇ d Soft grass
◇ e CCTV
◇ f Reinforced hedges

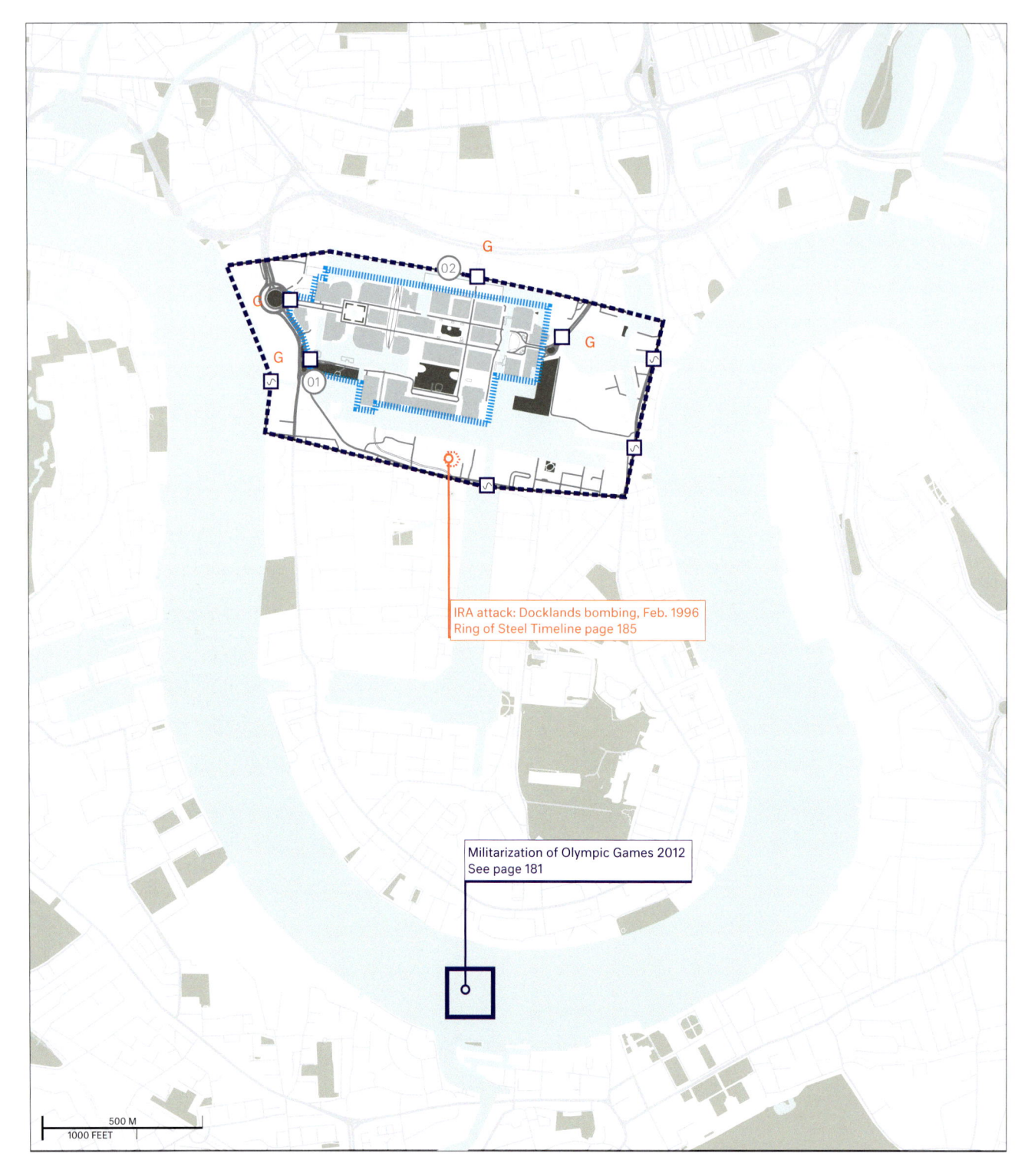

IRA attack: Docklands bombing, Feb. 1996
Ring of Steel Timeline page 185

Militarization of Olympic Games 2012
See page 181

ISLE OF DOGS AND CANARY WHARF

- 01 Detail at Heron Quays
- 02 Detail at Bank Street
- Canary Wharf inner security perimeter
- Canary Wharf outer security perimeter
- Vehicle checkpoints
- Canal checkpoints
- G Google streetview limitations

CANARY WHARF

51° 30' 17.2404" N
0° 1' 5.0808" W

As London's second financial district, Canary Wharf's 97 acres of office and retail space is home to more than 100,000 workers and headquarters of many of Europe's and the world's major banks, professional services firms, and media organizations.[22]

The district emerged in the 1980s in response to growth in the financial services sector and corresponding expanded demand from major businesses and corporations for up-to-date accommodation in the center of London. With limitations preventing large new developments within the City of London and escalating terror attacks by the IRA leading to expanded demand for heightened security, a site on the Isle of Dogs was selected as an appropriate home for London's new financial district. In 1982 land was leased to commercial investors and developers with favorable exemptions from development land tax, business taxes; and relaxed planning controls, along with 100 percent tax allowances for building construction costs.[23] The first tenants moved into Canary Wharf in 1991.[24] As a privately owned development, the open space of Canary Wharf does not function as public space in the proper sense. The area is closely guarded by private security guards rather than police, with the behavior of members of the public stringently controlled and monitored.

Socio-economic asymmetry

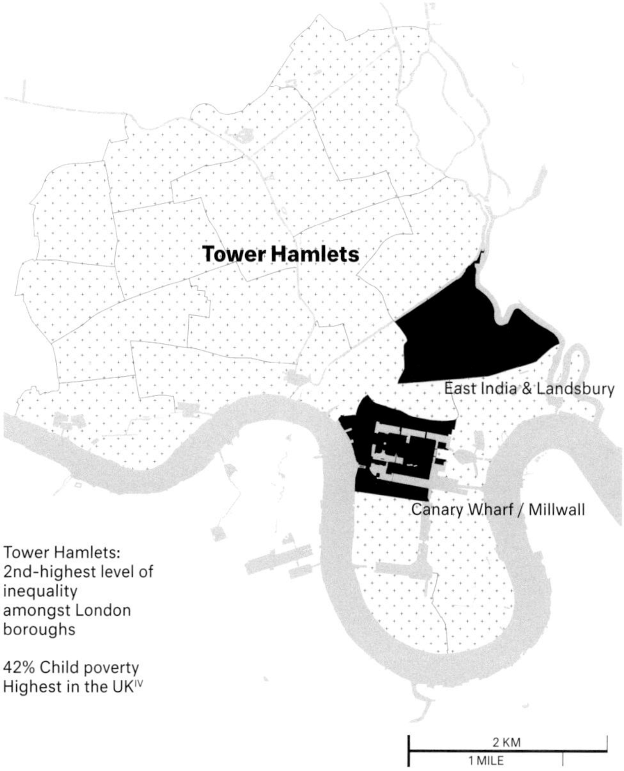

Tower Hamlets: 2nd-highest level of inequality amongst London boroughs

42% Child poverty Highest in the UK[IV]

	London	The City	Tower Hamlets	Canary Wharf / Millwall	East India & Landsbury
Median household income[I]	36,886	46,788	37,073	61,030	25,871
Median housing prices[II]	400,000	595,000	320,000	430,000	275,000
Unemployment rate[III]	9.2	3.8	13.5 2nd-highest in London	5.1	15
Index of deprivation[III] (rank where 1=most deprived)	N/A	551 / 627	7 / 326	326 / 627	2 / 627

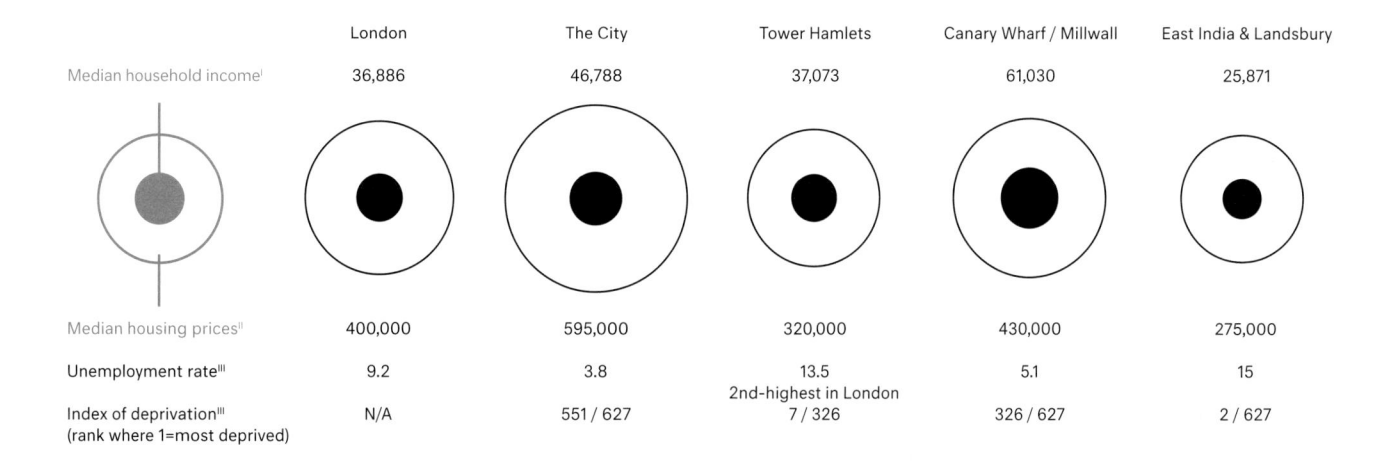

198   Contested Sites

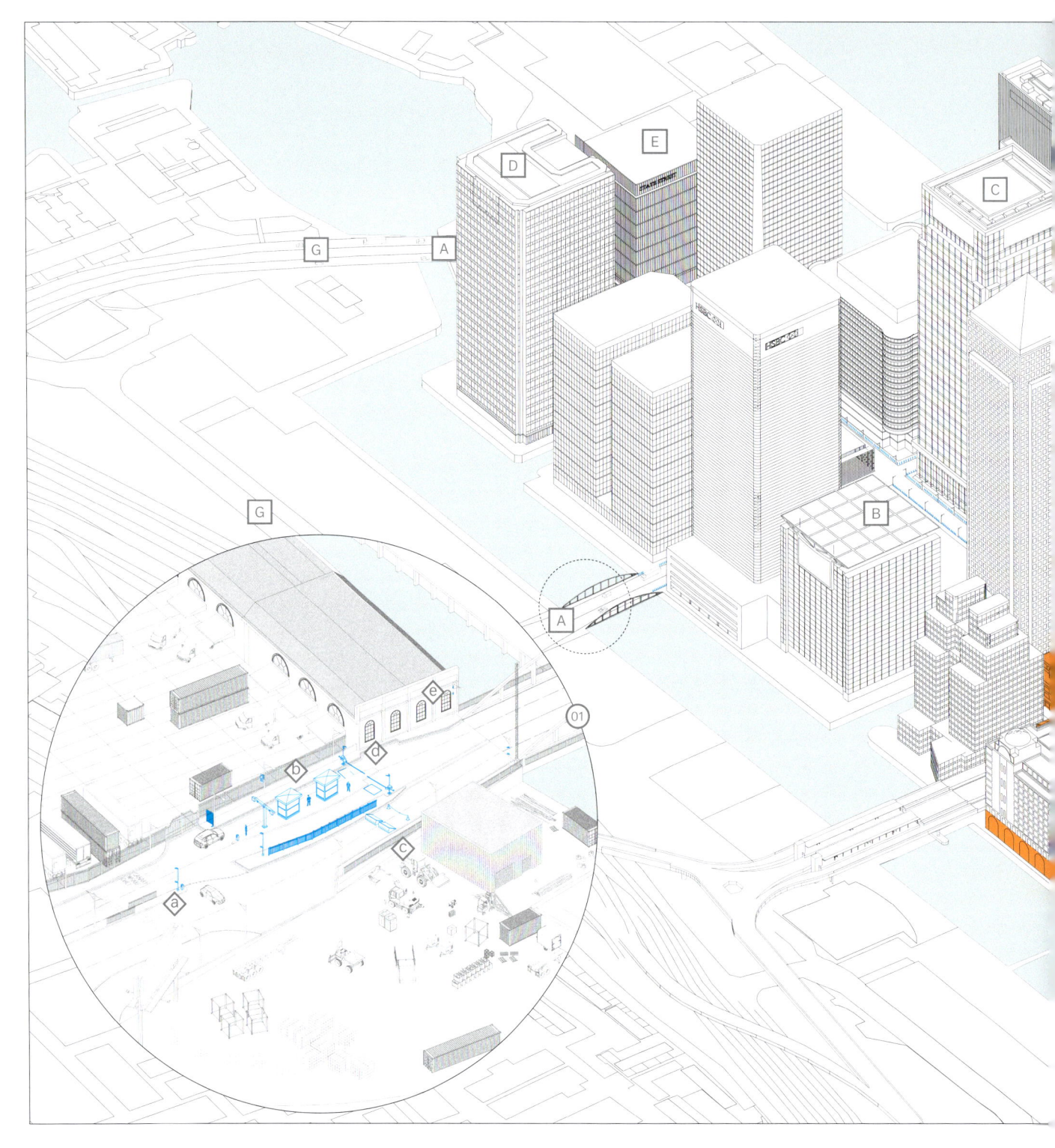

CANARY WHARF

- ■ Security measures
- ■ Public accessible program
- [A] Checkpoints
- [B] Asset spread: Credit Suisse
- [C] Asset spread: Morgan Stanley
- [D] Asset spread: Barclay and Barclays Capital
- [E] Asset spread: JP Morgan
- [F] Boat checkpoint
- [G] Extent of Google Street View access

199 C Canary Wharf 0°W

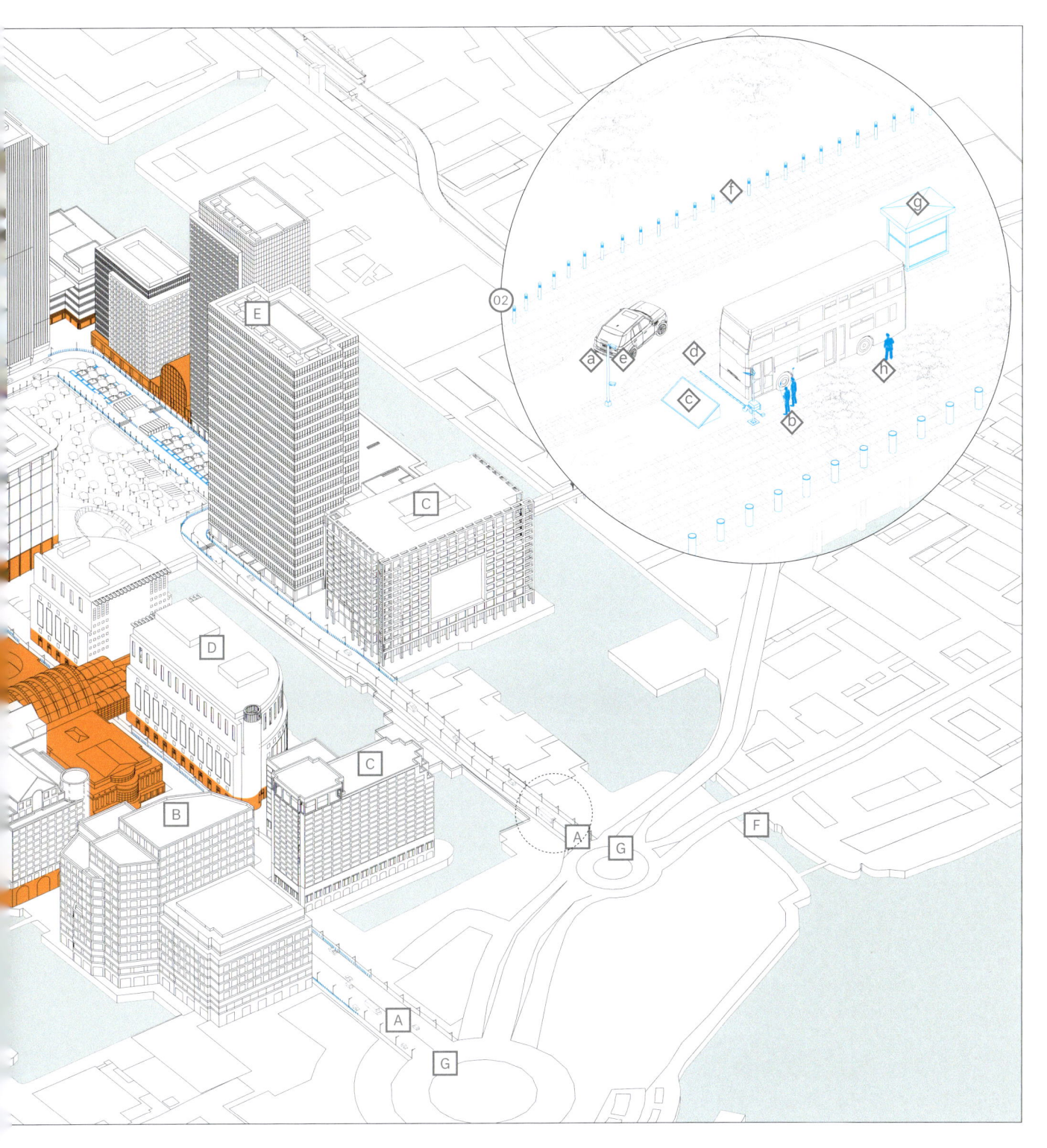

01 02 Detail of Heron Quay/Bank Street
a Automatic numberplate recognition (ANPR)
b Guarded security checkpoint
c Retractable vehicle barriers
d Security gate
e CCTV
f Bollards
g Security booth
h Vehicle bomb search

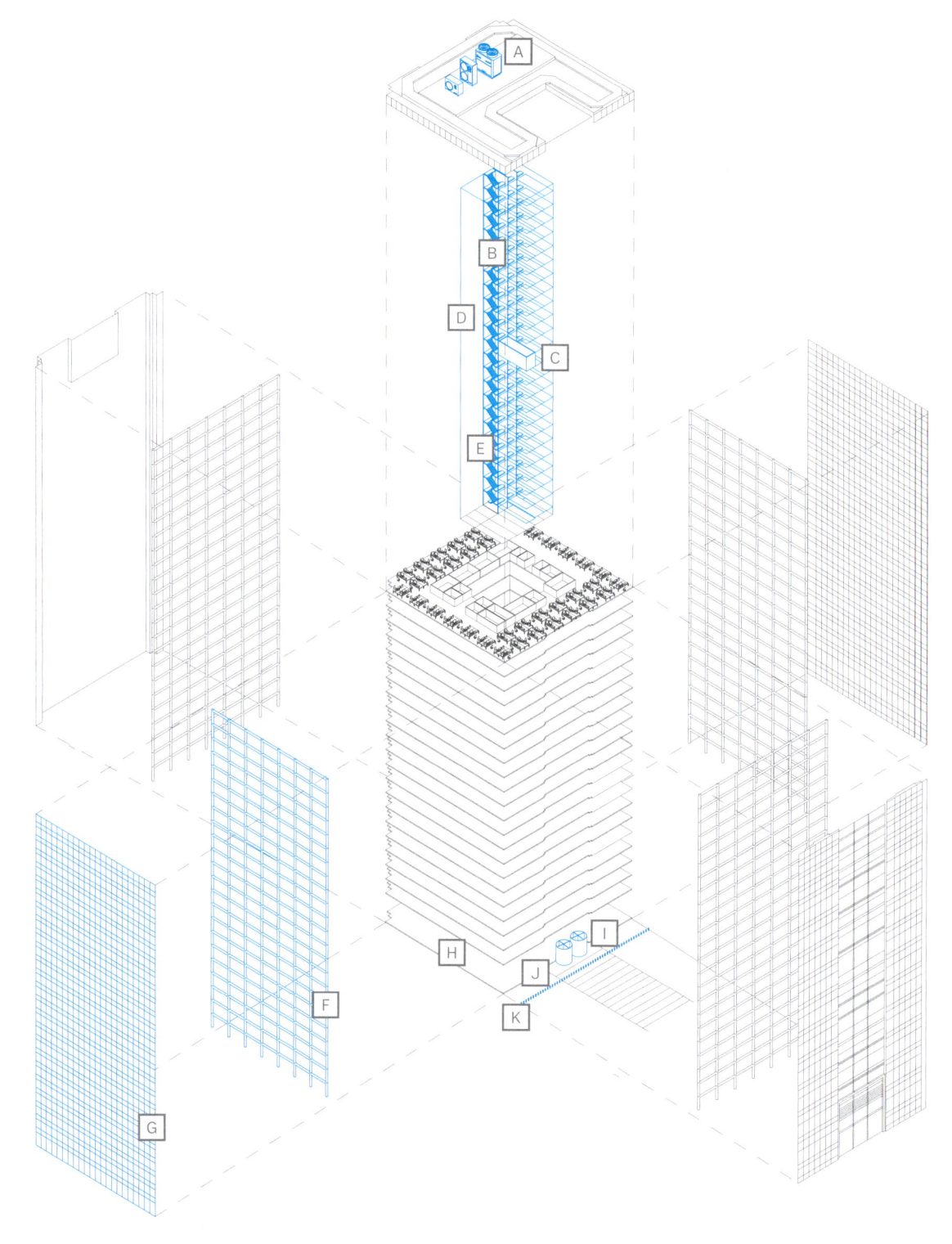

BARCLAYS HEADQUARTERS

Exploded isometric of so-called terror-proof building

- A Ventilation on rooftop
- B Evacuation stairs
- C Panic rooms
- D 40 cm reinforced concrete inner core
- E Tannoy PA system
- F Fireproofed steel framework
- G Laminated glass
- H Interior access control with CCTV surveillance
- I Turnstile doors
- J Private security desk
- K Bollards

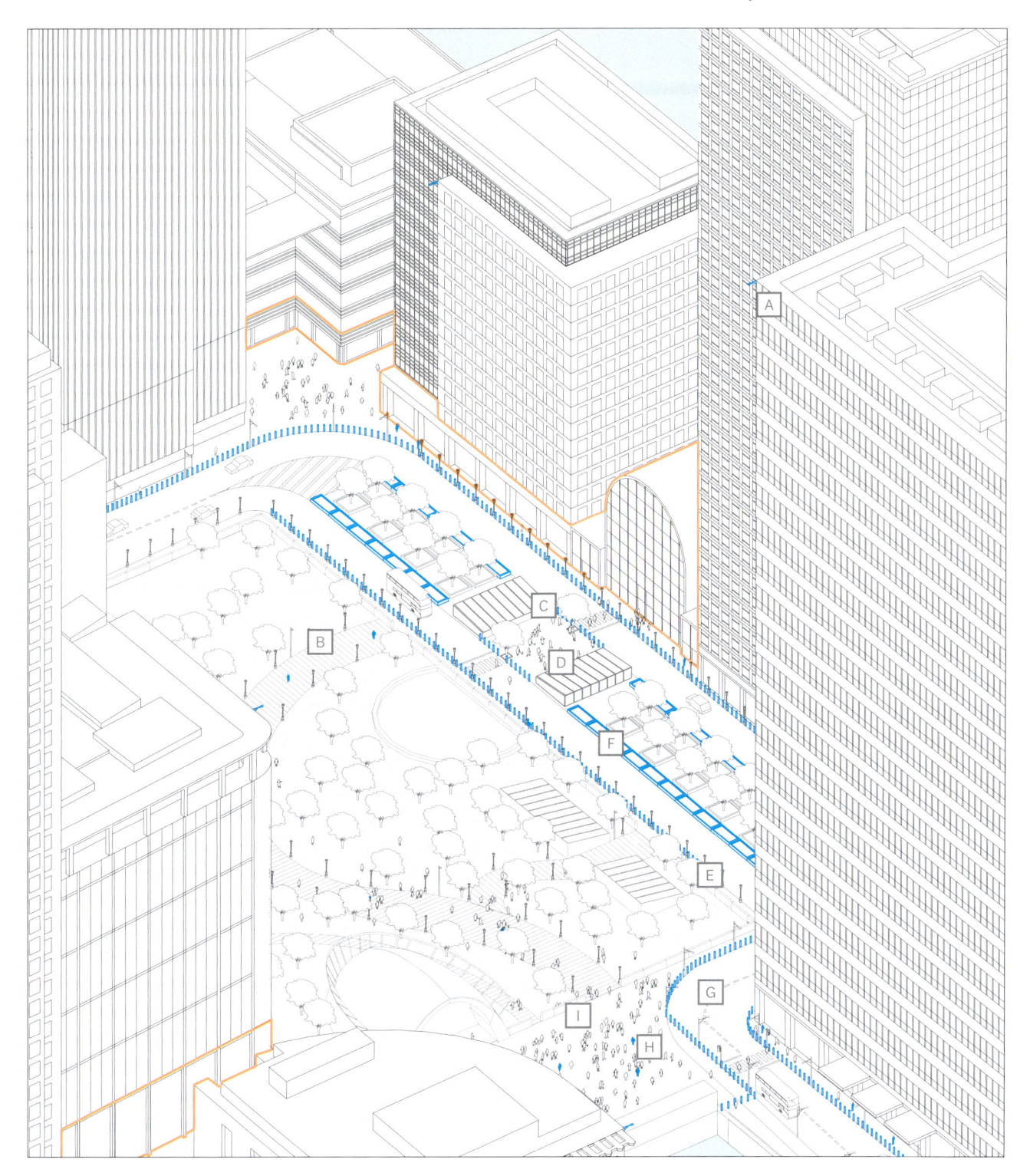

JUBILEE PARK

Security measures to "public" space

A	Overhead CCTV surveillance
B	Lamppost-mounted CCTV
C	Trees perform as bollards
D	Bollard layering
E	Streetlamps as bollards
F	Energy-absorbing planters
G	Chicane
H	Canary Wharf security force
I	Intended participatory surveillance

202   Contested Sites

SPAIN-MOROCCO BORDER

■ 12 km long neutral zone

□ Checkpoint

A Centro de Estancia Temporal de Inmigrantes
Reception center for immigrants built for
400 persons, but commonly holding over
2,000 immigrants awaiting case verdicts.

B Gourougou Mountains
Well-known temporary camp typically
inhabited by African immigrants awaiting
attempts to pass border.

MELILLA ENCLAVE
Spain/Morocco Border

Spain - Morocco Border 2°56'W

35° 17' 32.1972" N
2° 56' 17.1492" W

Melilla is one of two Spanish enclaves located on the North African coast serving as a key entry and exit port for persons and goods traveling in and out of Morocco. Historically, the cities of Melilla and Ceuta were centers of trade and commerce, connecting North and West Africa with Europe via the Saharan trade routes.[25]

Both cities remain part of the Spanish Eurozone and enjoy a relatively low tax rate, making the prices of goods lower than the rest of Europe. Spanish and European tourists arrive from mainland Spain by ferry and by air, making the cities important points of entry for visitors to North Africa. A number of Moroccans also live in these cities or cross their borders daily to work or shop. Melilla and Ceuta are sites of ongoing claims by Morocco – meanwhile, Spain argues that its historical presence in these locations predates the existence of the modern nation state of Morocco, and therefore refuses to turn over the cities.

African and Middle Eastern migrants have used the enclaves (both legally and illegally) as starting points to reach mainland Europe. The flow of illegal immigrants through the area into southern Spain reached its peak between 2005 to 2007, when tens of thousands of illegal immigrants were estimated to have crossed the Strait of Gibraltar per year. As a result, the borders at Ceuta and Melilla were reinforced to the extent that by 2015, they were considered to be the most heavily guarded borders of the EU.[26] According to Frontex, which oversees the border, the flow of illegal immigrants across the Cueta and Melilla borders dropped considerably.[27] For example, border agents intercepted 500 illegal immigrants during the first three months of 2014, down 82 percent from the total of 2,780 intercepted during the same period the year before.

Refugee and external border funds, Spain 2007–2013[I]

External Borders Fund
€289,394,768.35

Refugee Fund
€9,342,834.50

Illegal border crossings Ceuta and Melilla 2008–2013 Western Mediterranean Route[II]

No:	6,500	6,650	5,000	8,450	6,400	6,800	6,200
Year:	2008	2009	2010	2011	2012	2013	2014[Jan-Aug]

Human Development Index 2014[III]

A composite index measuring average achievement in three basic parameters of human development; longevity and healthy life, education, standard of living. Spain and Morocco represent the largest gap found between neighboring states.

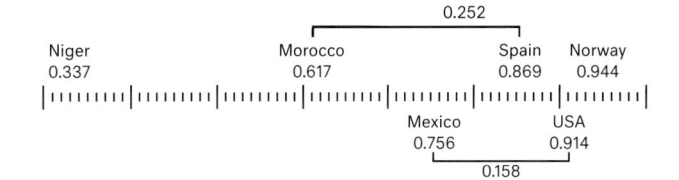

0.252

Niger	Morocco	Spain	Norway
0.337	0.617	0.869	0.944

Mexico 0.756
USA 0.914
0.158

Illegal border crossings Europe 2014[IV]

Eastern Border Route	Western Balkan Route	Eastern Medit. Route	Central Medit. Route	Western African Route
Origin: Russia, Georgia, Afghanistan	Origin: Syria, Afghanistan, Kosovo	Origin: Syria, Afghanistan, Somalia	Origin: Syria, Eritrea, Sub-Sahara	Origin: Morocco, Mali, Guinea
Transit country: Ukraine	Transit country: Hungary	Transit country: Turkey, Greece, Cyprus	Transit country: Libya	Transit country: Senegal, Mauritania
Number of crossings: 1,000	Number of crossings: 17,000	Number of crossings: 43,000	Number of crossings: 153,000	Number of crossings: 190

Total crossings: 220,390

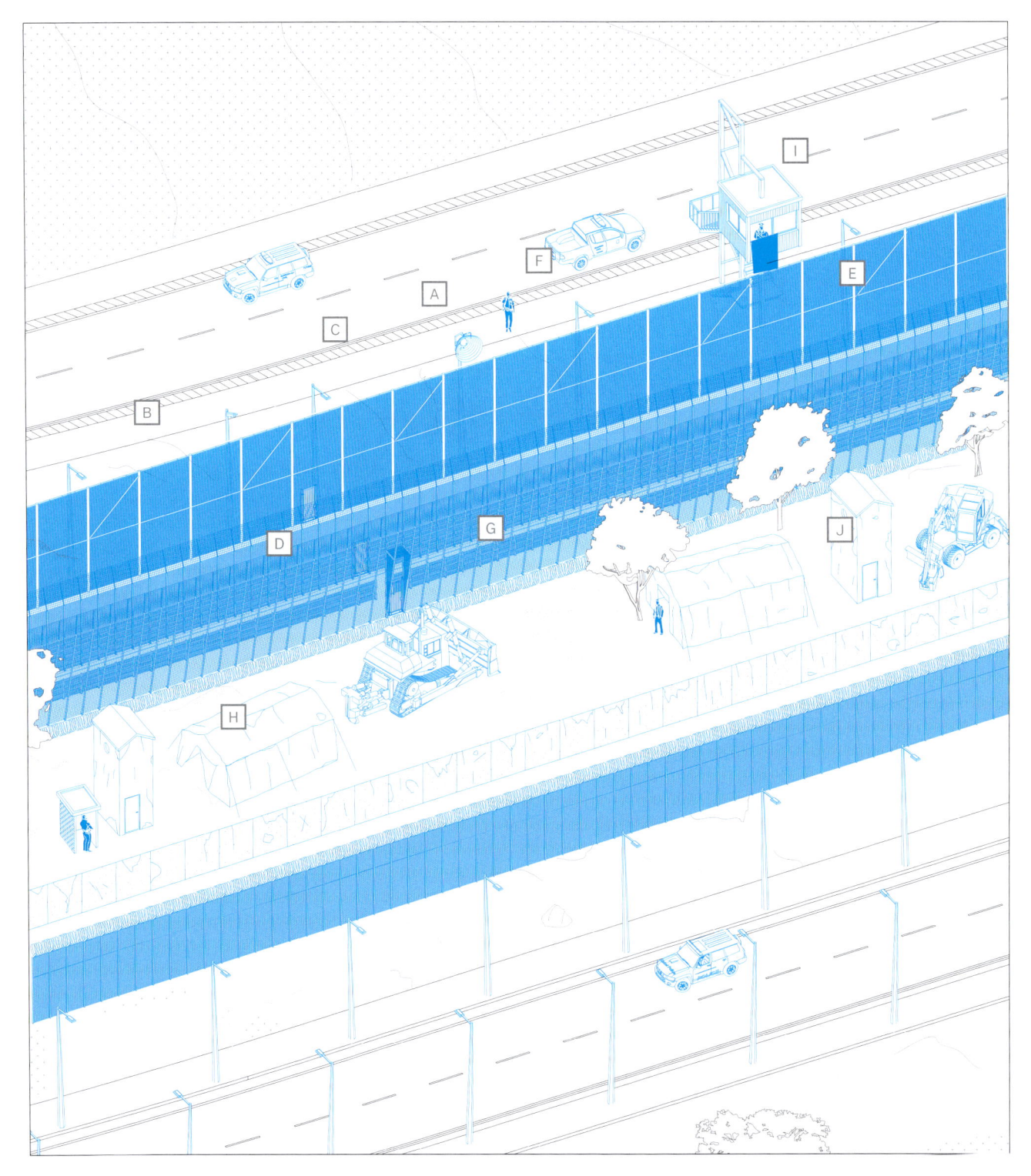

SPAIN-MOROCCO BORDER

- ▨ Moroccan Gendarmerie/ Spanish Guardia Civil
- A Heartbeat-detection radar system
- B Floodlights
- C Movement-activated CCTV
- D Remote-controlled pepperspray
- E Warning lights & Sirene
- F Guardia Civil with thermal night vision goggles
- G Three dimensional flexible towline
- H Moroccan guard tent
- I Spanish guard booth
- J Moroccan guard booth

BORDER EVOLUTION

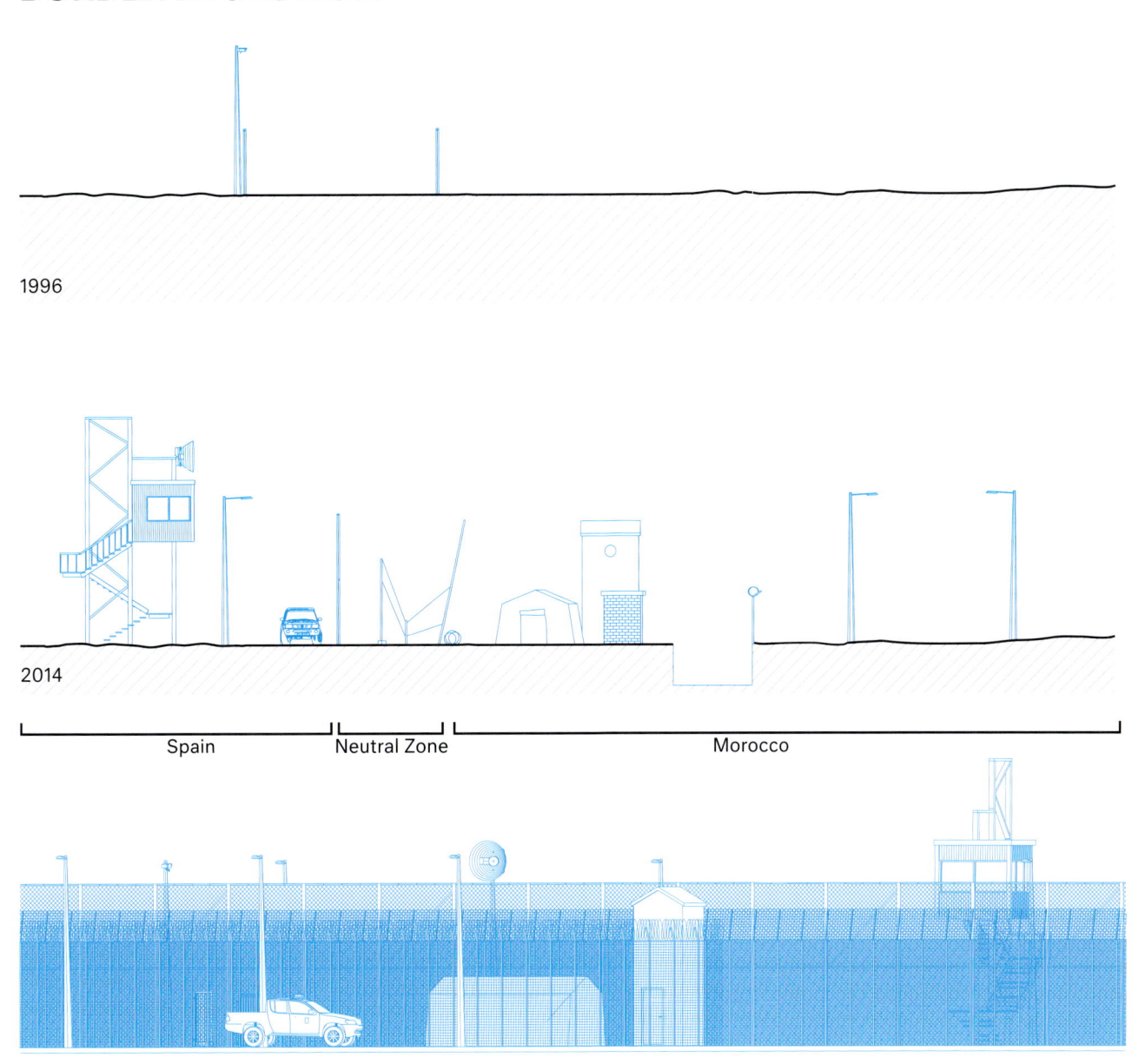

1996

2014

Spain | Neutral Zone | Morocco

Melilla has functioned as a laboratory for the production of extreme spatial separation barriers. The current Melilla fence cost Spain €33M to construct and consists of two parallel 6-meter-high fences topped with barbed wire.[28] Between the tall fences lies a lower fence with a system of flexible steel wire stretched from one fence to the other, making placement of ladders nearly impossible. Tall surveillance towers are positioned on the Spanish side of the fence along with a road accommodating police patrols. Underground cables connect spotlights, noise and movement sensors and video cameras to a central control booth. The Moroccan side of the border includes a moat, an extra layer of razor wire, and guard booths positioned every 50 meters.[29]

In spite of the heavy fortification, migrants still attempt to cross the border. Several incidents, reported both in international and Spanish media, have involved deaths or injuries to African migrants – the most extreme involving an incident when hundreds of migrants approached the fence. Caught between Spanish rubber bullets and Moroccan gunfire, 18 died and more than 50 were wounded.[30]

NEW YORK

Terror attacks on the US, on September 11, 2001, with greatest impact on New York City, would have considerable effect on the American security landscape, on the urban spaces of the American city, and on the right to the city – particularly in New York City. This impact was felt considerably more so then than as a result of the 1993 bombing of the World Trade Center. In parallel to the reduction of civil liberties in the name of increased security – through legislation such as the USA PATRIOT Act[31] and the founding of the Department of Homeland Security – the city itself would undergo a process of militarization, as would its police force. These transformations would take place within the context of an ongoing gentrification of inner-city neighborhoods and the privatization of plazas and parks – which would make demonstrations and expressions of political dissent increasingly difficult. This was clearly evident in the treatment of the Occupy Movement in New York City in 2011 – a domestic protest movement which was erroneously monitored by the Department of Homeland Security and the FBI's Terrorism Task Force, and exposed to several instances of excessive policing.

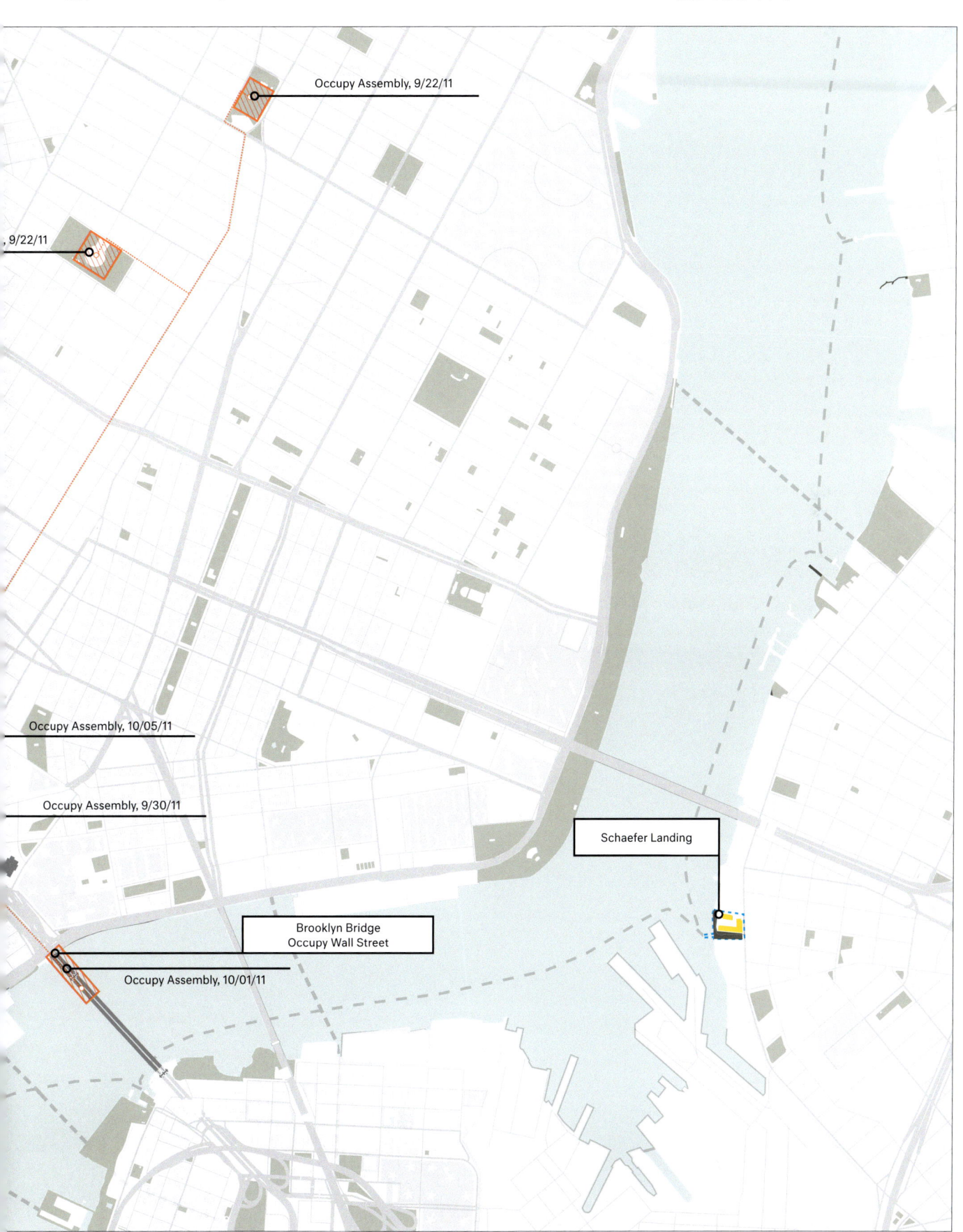

New York 74°W

- Occupy Assembly, 9/22/11
- 9/22/11
- Occupy Assembly, 10/05/11
- Occupy Assembly, 9/30/11
- Schaefer Landing
- Brooklyn Bridge Occupy Wall Street
- Occupy Assembly, 10/01/11

208   Contested Sites

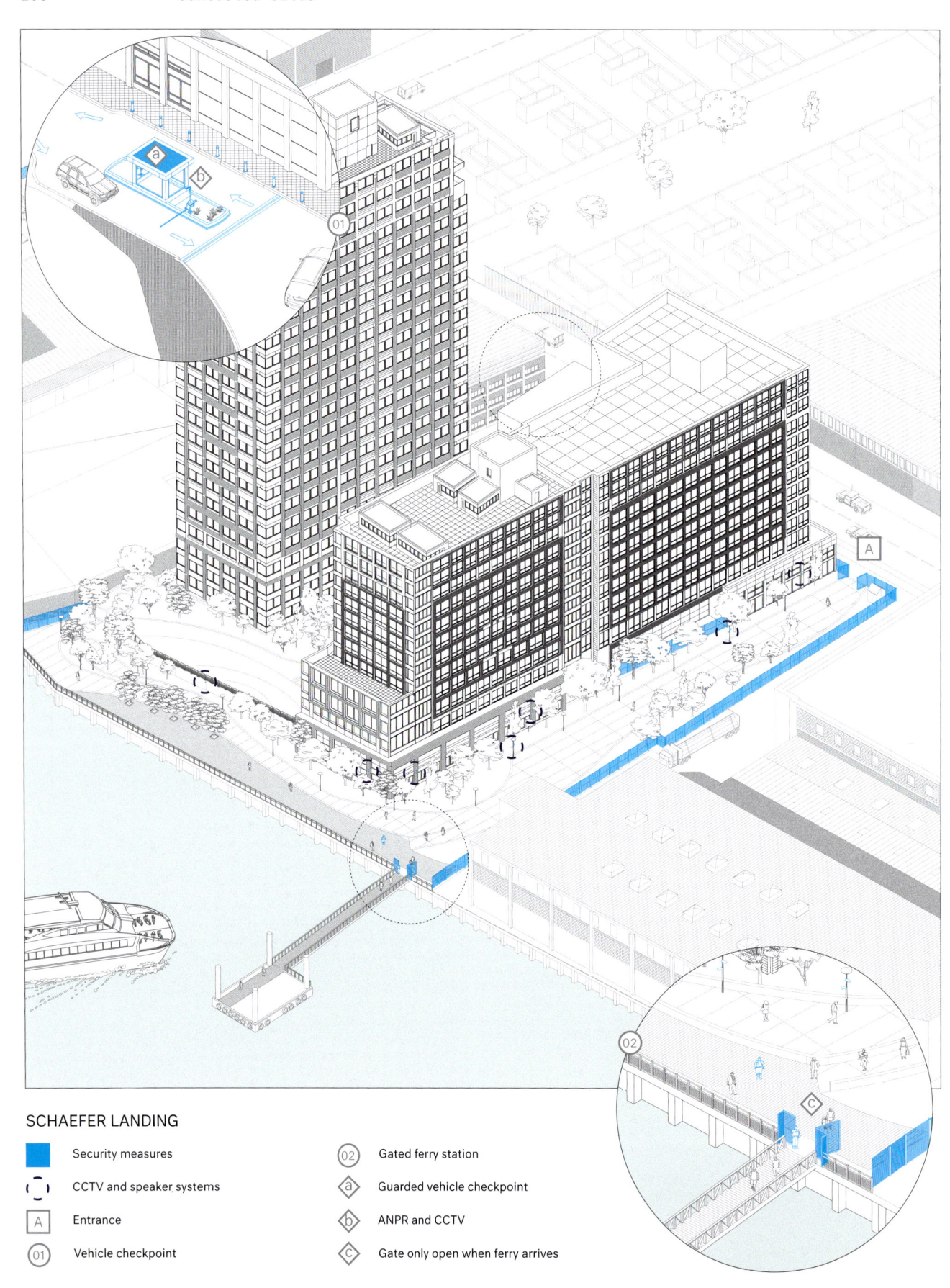

SCHAEFER LANDING

- ▮ Security measures
- ⌀ CCTV and speaker systems
- Ⓐ Entrance
- ① Vehicle checkpoint
- ② Gated ferry station
- ⓐ Guarded vehicle checkpoint
- ⓑ ANPR and CCTV
- ⓒ Gate only open when ferry arrives

SCHAEFER LANDING
Williamsburg, Brooklyn

40° 42′ 32.1768″ N
73° 58′ 8.8644″ W

"Privately Owned Public Spaces, abbreviated as 'POPS,' are an amenity provided and maintained by a developer for public use, in exchange for additional floor area."
— New York City Department of City Planning

Schaefer Landing – a two-building 350-unit residential development completed in 2006 in Williamsburg, Brooklyn – occupies a plot where Schaefer Beer was brewed between 1916 and 1976.[32] The project is among the first to have taken advantage of a 2005 zoning law change allowing new residential buildings in former industrial waterfront areas – with Schaefer Landing exemplifying the ongoing process of gentrification in the neighborhood.[33] The majority of the units are luxury apartments, with amenities including a doorman, gym, and guarded parking garage. An East River Ferry stop at Schaefer Landing provides public transport to and from Wall Street during rush hour.

An esplanade park was established to "give back" amenities to the community as compensation for the new tall building constructed on the site. The park results from the Map and Zoning Regulation of 1961 – which offers incentives to developers to provide public space within their projects in exchange for added building height.[34] The park is surrounded by security fences and is locked at dusk. The pier is classified as MARSEC Level 1 and fenced off from the Esplanade.[35] It has numerous controls on behavior, including CCTV cameras and a speaker system used by guards to instruct people to abide by park rules, which include no skating, no bicycles, no drinking, no BBQing, no swimming, no fishing, no ball playing, etc.

Value of Land
Tax assessment of land, per square foot

● Privately owned public space
5,000 dollars* / sqft
200 dollars* / sqft
35 dollars* / sqft
0 dollars* / sqft

*Assessed value is not market value. Also assessed value for this data set seems low.
The total value of Manhattan is $88b, whereas published total tax assessment for FY2004 is actually $169b.

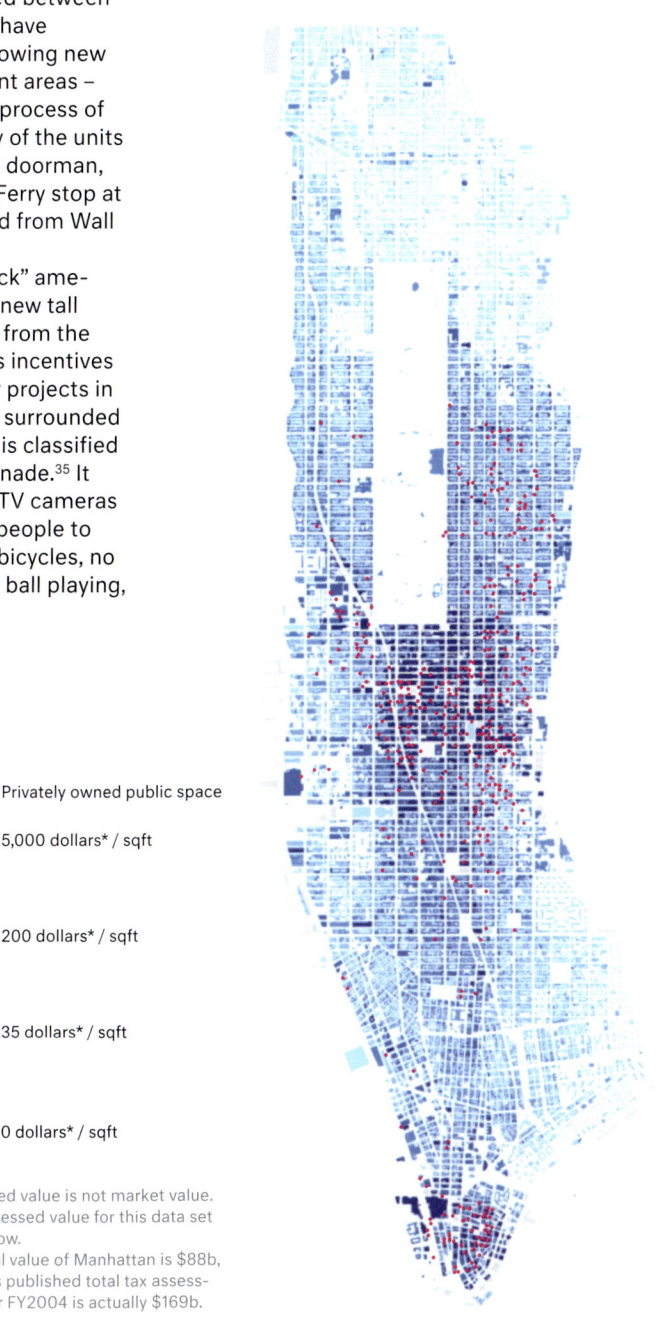

LAND VALUE[I]
www.radicalcartography.net
According to Bill Rankin; "Tax assessments are a tricky data source, since they do not measure market value — indeed, there are even tax-assessed 'values' on public buildings and parks. (Here Central Park is 'valued' at $1.9 billion.) But they do give a rough sense of relative values within the city: the pocket of wealth up near the cloisters, and the relative sparseness of the Lower East Side.

Note: even though this map shows building footprints, the land value shown for each building is per square foot of lot size."

The original artwork is overlaid with data from NYC´s privately-owned public space (POPS) inventory.[II] The coherency between higher land value and density of privately owned public space is self-evident.

Contested Sites

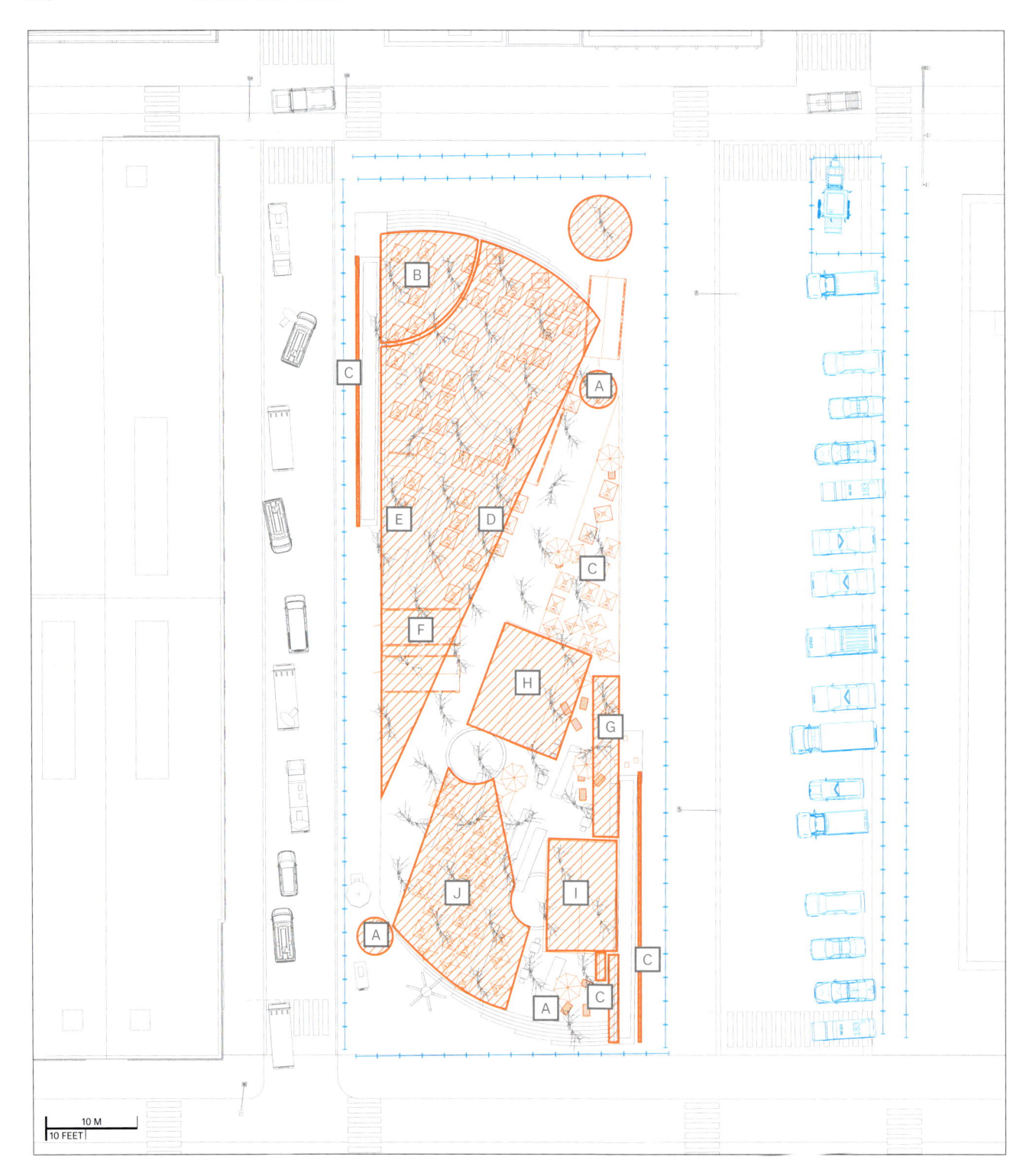

ZUCOTTI PARK

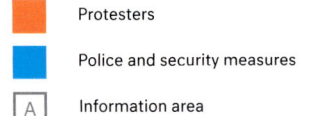

- ▬ Protesters
- ▬ Police and security measures
- A Information area
- B Social area
- C Art / Library
- D Comfort
- E Medical
- F Sleeping
- G Sanitation
- H Kitchen
- I Media Outreach
- J Assembly

OCCUPY WALL STREET, 2011

40° 42′ 33.3540″ N
74° 0′ 40.5432″ W

The protest movement Occupy Wall Street (OWS) is best known for its occupation of Zuccotti Park in New York City's Wall Street financial district beginning on September 17, 2011 – an encampment initiated by advertisements in the Canadian anti-consumerist magazine Adbusters. Inspired by the Arab Spring and Spanish anti-austerity demonstrations, OWS would receive global attention, sparking an international protest movement against social and economic inequality. Operating under the slogan "We are the 99%," Occupy protests took place in more than 951 cities across 82 countries in the following years.[36]

In New York City, OWS renamed Zuccotti Park "Liberty Square," laying out an encampment consisting of a range of communal functions. These would include a common kitchen with recycling bins; a tent camp with comfort station, supplies, and medical help; a library with donated books; information stations, and working groups, media, and sign creation areas. As amplified sound was only allowed with a permit, meetings took place by relayed voice – referred to as the "human mic."[37]

As a privately owned property, Zuccotti Park's status determined that police could not legally force protesters to leave without the request of the property owner.[38] The occupation lasted for nearly two months before protesters were evicted by the NYPD, based largely on claims of unsanitary conditions from the property owner and the city.

Conflict between OWS protesters, police, and security broke out in different settings: a protest walk across the Brooklyn Bridge on October 1, 2011, resulted in 700 arrests. Protesters claimed the violation of their constitutional rights, while the NYPD argued that protesters were given multiple warnings and were arrested for blocking the street.[39]

TIMELINE OCCUPY MOVEMENT NEW YORK[I]

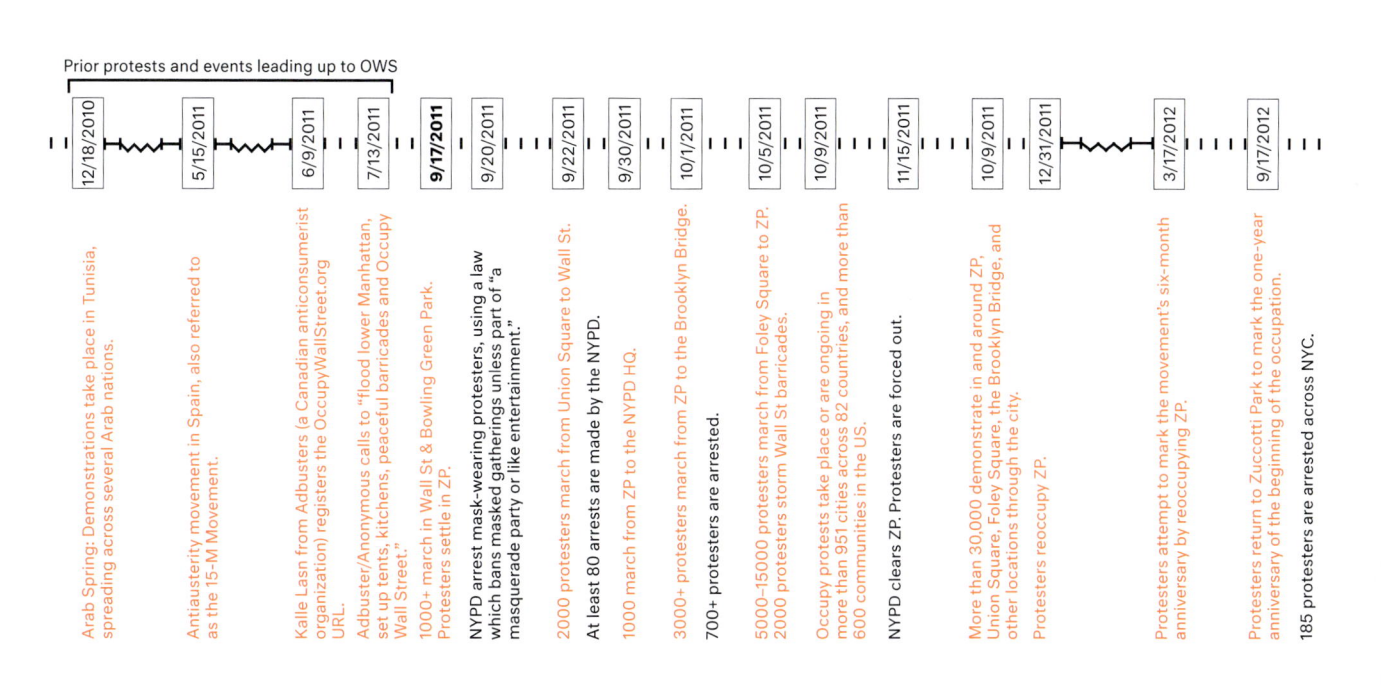

Prior protests and events leading up to OWS

- **12/18/2010** — Arab Spring: Demonstrations take place in Tunisia, spreading across several Arab nations.
- **5/15/2011** — Antiausterity movement in Spain, also referred to as the 15-M Movement.
- **6/9/2011** — Kalle Lasn from Adbusters (a Canadian anticonsumerist organization) registers the OccupyWallStreet.org URL.
- **7/13/2011** — Adbuster/Anonymous calls to "flood lower Manhattan, set up tents, kitchens, peaceful barricades and Occupy Wall Street."
- **9/17/2011** — 1000+ march in Wall St & Bowling Green Park. Protesters settle in ZP.
- **9/20/2011** — NYPD arrest mask-wearing protesters, using a law which bans masked gatherings unless part of "a masquerade party or like entertainment."
- **9/22/2011** — 2000 protesters march from Union Square to Wall St.
- **9/30/2011** — At least 80 arrests are made by the NYPD.
- **10/1/2011** — 1000 march from ZP to the NYPD HQ.
- **10/5/2011** — 3000+ protesters march from ZP to the Brooklyn Bridge. 700+ protesters are arrested.
- **10/9/2011** — 5000–15000 protesters march from Foley Square to ZP. 2000 protesters storm Wall St barricades.
- **11/15/2011** — Occupy protests take place or are ongoing in more than 951 cities across 82 countries, and more than 600 communities in the US.
- **10/9/2011** — NYPD clears ZP. Protesters are forced out.
- **12/31/2011** — More than 30,000 demonstrate in and around ZP, Union Square, Foley Square, the Brooklyn Bridge, and other locations through the city. Protesters reoccupy ZP.
- **3/17/2012** — Protesters attempt to mark the movement's six-month anniversary by reoccupying ZP.
- **9/17/2012** — Protesters return to Zuccotti Park to mark the one-year anniversary of the beginning of the occupation. 185 protesters are arrested across NYC.

Contested Sites

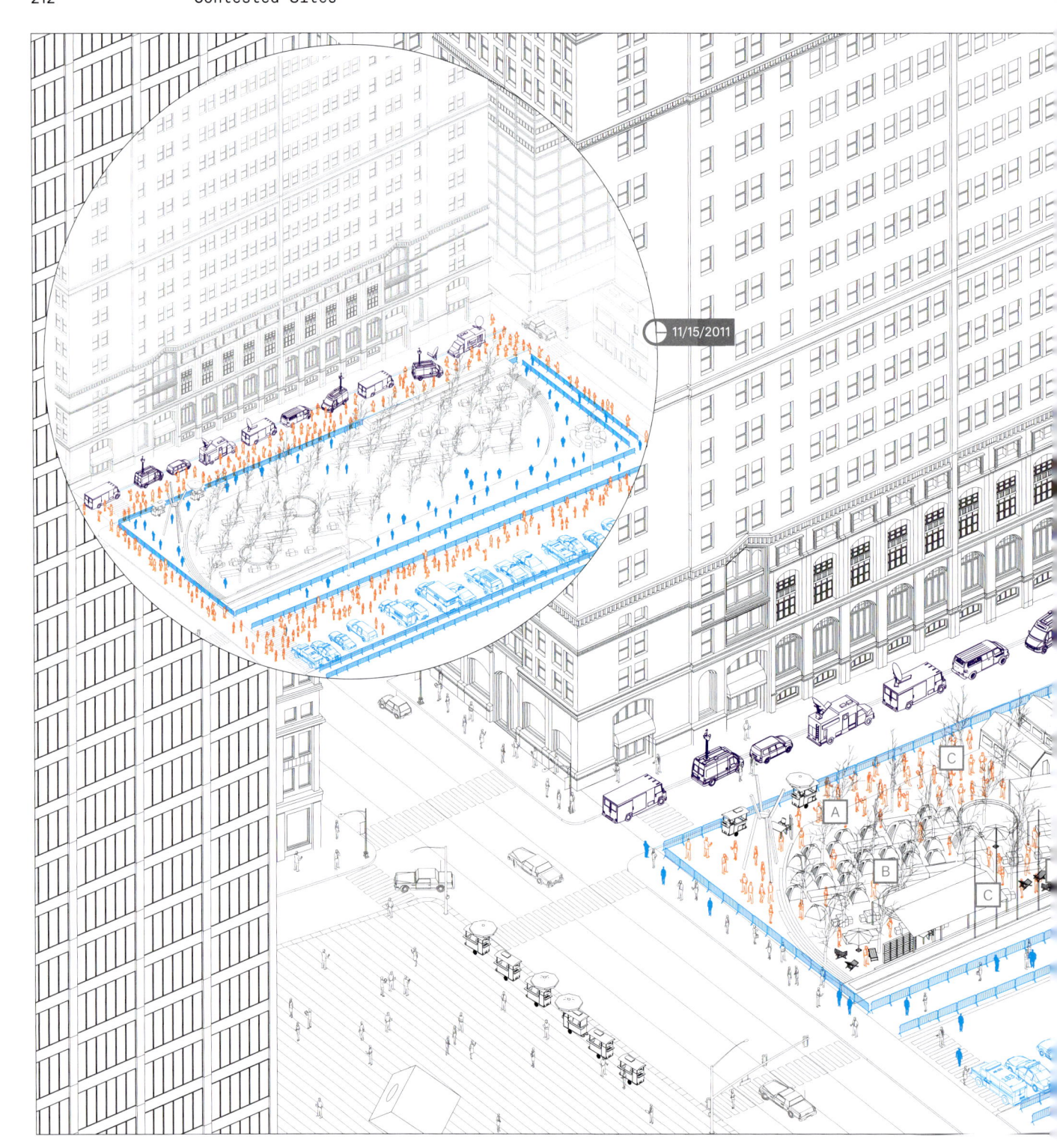

OCCUPY WALL STREET, ZUCOTTI PARK

- Security measures
- Protesters
- Media
- A Information area
- B Social area
- C Art / Library
- D Comfort
- E Medical
- F Assembly
- G Sanitation
- H Kitchen
- I Media Outreach

213   C   Occupy Wall Street 74°W

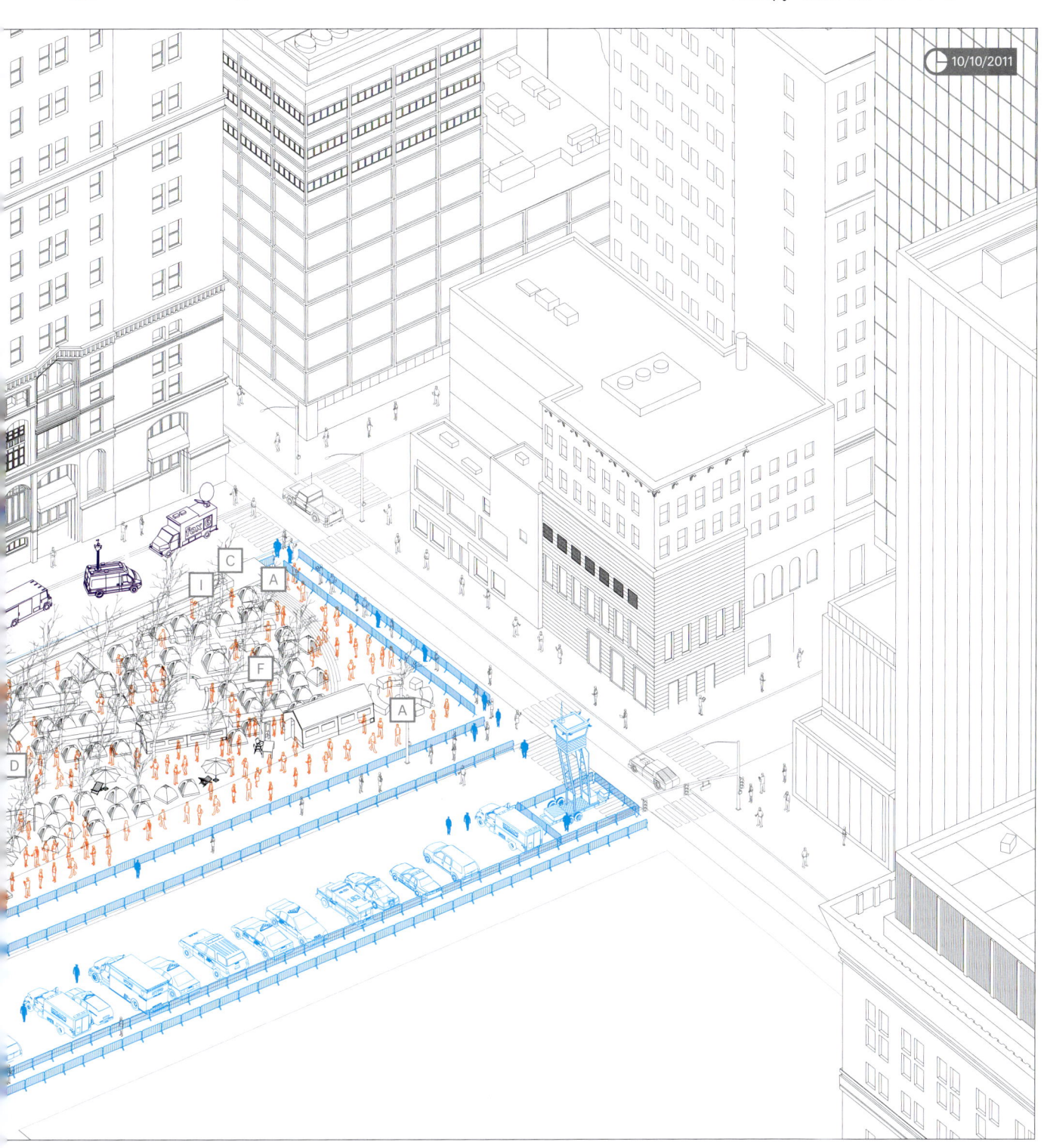

10/10/2011

NUMBER OF OCCUPY PROTESTERS WORLDWIDE[ii]

*organized before Occupy as 15-M

CANADA

Protesters in total
16,742

Major cities:
Vancouver: 4,000
Montreal: 3,000
Toronto: 2,500

USA

Protesters in total
85,581

Major cities:
New York: 30,000
Portland: 10,000
Boston: 10,000

EUROPE

Protesters in total
2,385,435

Major cities:
Madrid*: 500,000
Barcelona*: 400,000
Rome: 200,000

LATIN AMERICA

Protesters in total
15,420

Major cities:
Santiago: 10,000
Porto Alegre: 8,000

ASIA

Protesters in total
3,800

Major cities:
Tel Aviv: 1,500
Seoul: 1,000

OCENANIA

Protesters in total
11,130

Major cities:
Melbourne: 4,000
Sydney: 3,000
Aukland: 3,000

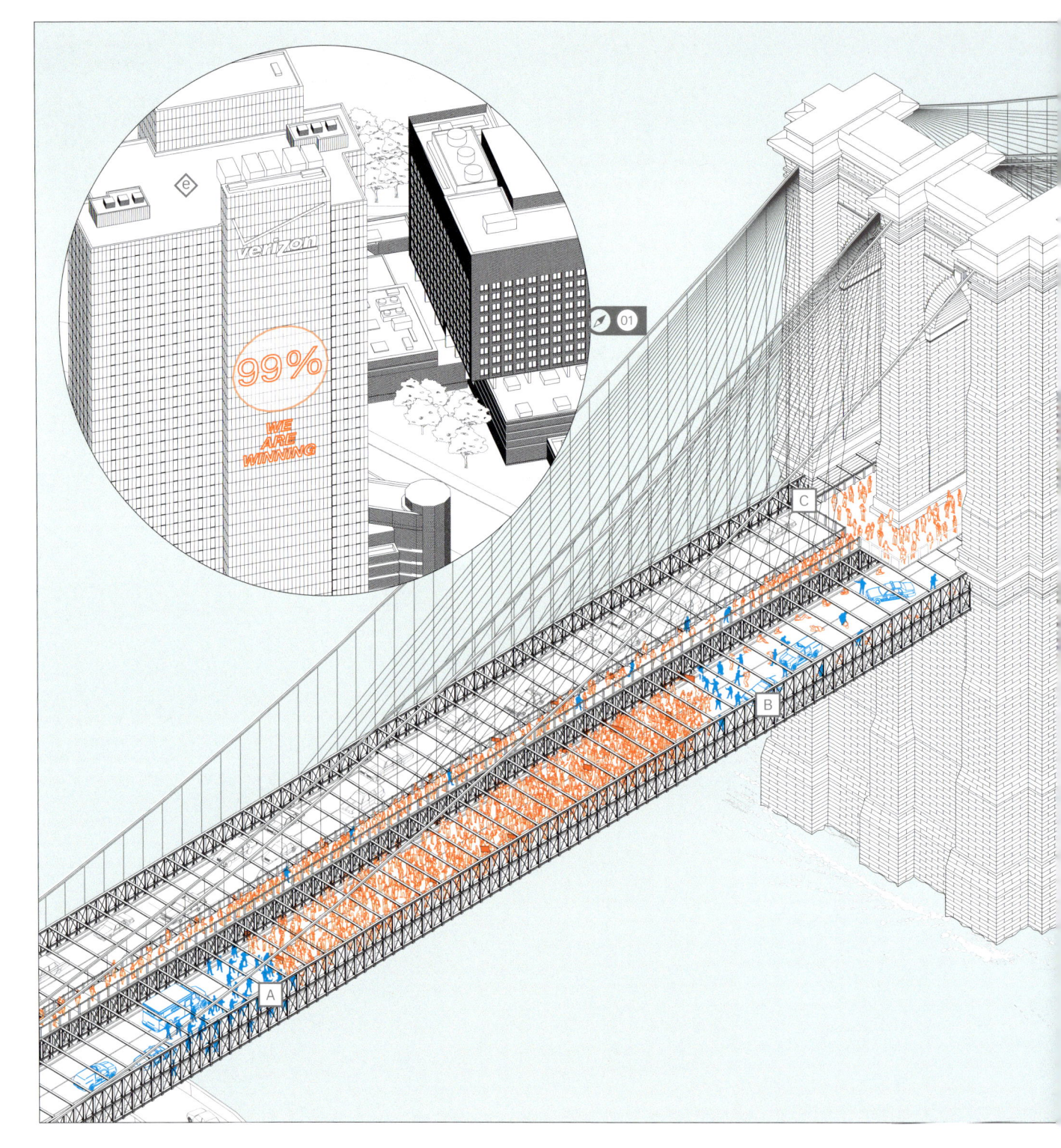

214   Contested Sites

BROOKLYN BRIDGE, OCCUPY WALL STREET

- 🟦 Approximately 300 New York police
- 🟧 More than 1000 Occupy Wall Street protesters
- A Police positioned to stop and hold protesters.
- B Police kettle protesters on the bridge.
- C Protesters on the pedestrian walkway are not subject to arrest.
- 01 "99%" projected on building walls
- 02 Police arrest protesters.
- a Incidents of police brutality are documented during the demonstrations.
- b Protesters are placed along the bridge.
- c Approximately 700 people are arrested.

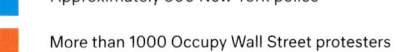

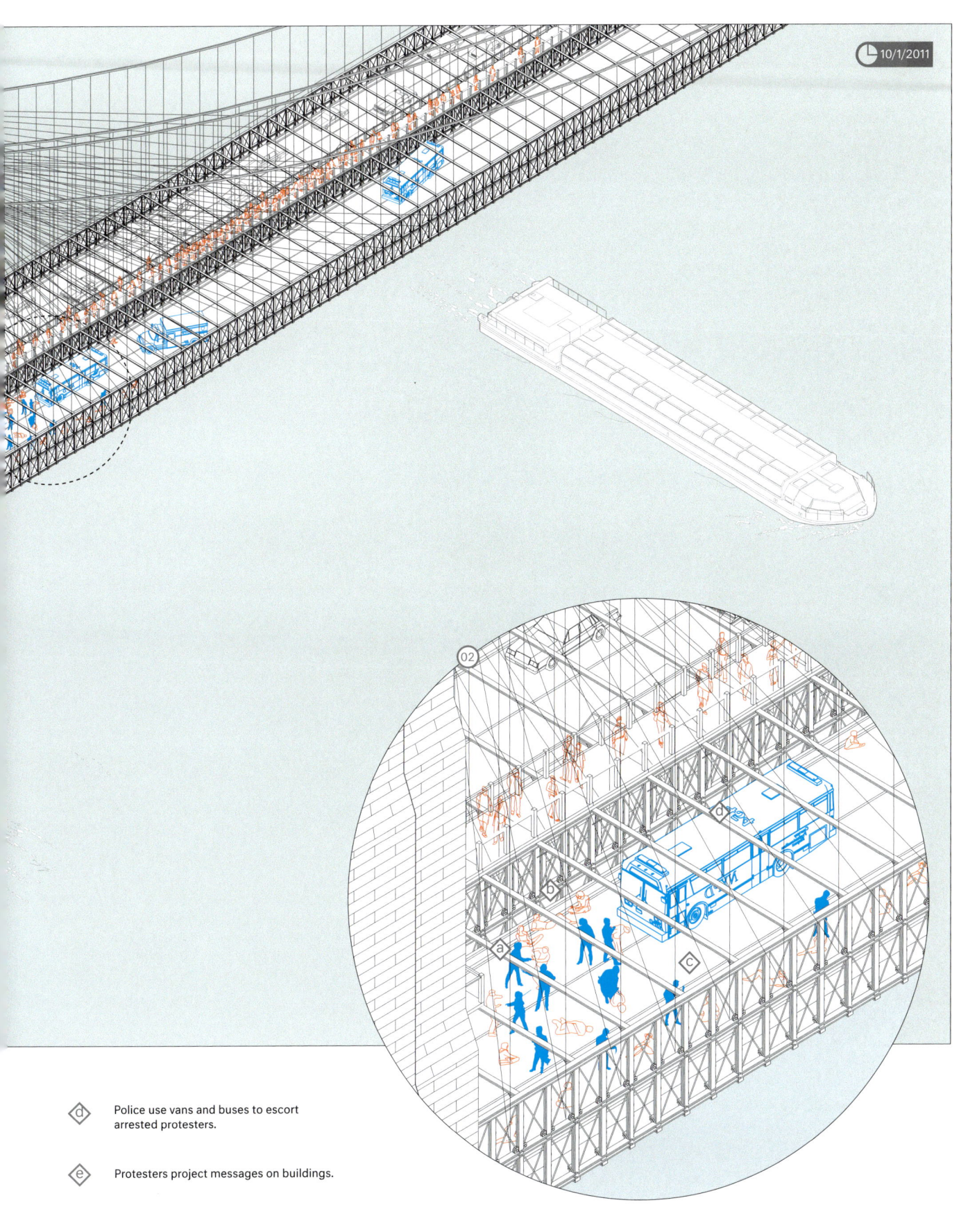

215   C   Occupy Wall Street 74°W

10/1/2011

ⓓ Police use vans and buses to escort arrested protesters.

ⓔ Protesters project messages on buildings.

216 Contested Sites

Zucotti Park

New York Stock Exchange

100 M
100 FEET

WALL STREET

- - - Security perimeter, Wall Street

▨ NYC Stock Exchange

A Triangular roadblocks w/guard booths

B Submerged roadblocks

C Fence on wheels., guards, tents, roadblocks

D Bollards, guards, security booth and "rocks"

E Security tent

F Fence and bollards around NYSE

WALL STREET

Wall Street 74°W

40° 42′ 21.6288″ N
74° 0′ 31.7340″ W

"It may well be the case that democracy and capitalism, which at moments in their youth were allies, cannot live together once both have come of age."
– Richard H. Tawney, 1938

Located in Lower Manhattan, Wall Street is the home of the New York Stock Exchange (NYSE), the world's largest stock exchange, with a market capitalization of US$19.60 trillion (2015). Due to its scale and emblematic character – as a symbol of the American financial sector as a whole – it is widely considered as one of the most important elements of the US economy. As a result, the security of the NYSE has been considered of great significance. The September 11, 2001, attacks that destroyed the nearby World Trade Center would have a considerable effect on the Wall Street area. As a result of the disruptions caused by the attacks and the increased fear of Manhattan's perceived vulnerability to future attacks, a number of companies moved their offices out of Lower Manhattan, in many cases out of state. Physical security measures around the NYSE, Wall Street, and the downtown financial district as a whole were significantly increased following the attacks – leading to protests from citizens and residents over the evident militarization of the neighborhood and the considerable reduction of public space in the area. Wall Street and the surrounding area has attracted further attention in recent years, particularly in the context of the 2011 Occupy Wall Street Movement, in which demonstrators addressing systemic problems of socioeconomic inequality protested in parks and plazas around Wall Street – a series of events and occupations taking place over several months that tested the limits of such militarized urbanisms to accommodate or support dissent.

Growth in financial jobs post-9/11[I]

- 4% NYC
- 20% Other states on average
- 21.6% Connecticut
- 56.5% Texas

Office space rented in New Jersey for former Wall Street firms post-9/11[II]

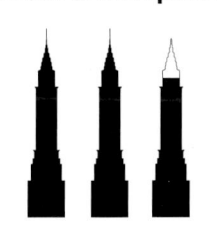

316,000m²
Equals roughly the Chrysler Building x 3.

Financial jobs relocated from Lower Manhattan post-9/11[III]

- Midtown 33,000
- New Jersey 7,500
- Lower Manhattan 4,500
- Other locations 5,000

Timeline NY Stock Exchange[IV, V, VI,]

1772 – The beginning: 24 brokers sign the Buttonwood Agreement outside 68 Wall Street to begin trading securities.

1817 – Formally constituted as the New York Stock & Exchange Board, in rooms rented at 40 Wall Street.

1863 – Name changed to New York Stock Exchange (NYSE).

1868 – Membership: The only means of obtaining membership is by purchasing seat from an existing member.

1903 – NYSE moves into 18 Broad Street.

1918 – New Technology: Pneumatic tubes allow floor brokers to more quickly send orders.

1920 – September 16: A bomb explodes on busiest corner of the financial district, killing 38 and seriously injuring 143 people.

1929 – Black Tuesday: October 29, 1929, Wall Street crash, Great Depression begins – the Dow Jones Industrial Average plummets, wiping out $14 billion of stock-market wealth in a trading frenzy of more than 16 million shares. The trading-volume record stands for nearly 40 years.

1953 – The exchange is controlled by members—limited to 1,366.

1981 – Technological transformation: Renovation updates the NYSE trading floor. Large metal frame is added to hold up the weight of floor and support the new wiring and technology that comes with upgrade.

1995 – Technological transformation: Large-scale installations of flat-screen panels, hand-held terminals and fiber optic cabling transforms the NYSE into a technology-powered commerce hub with the fastest operations available.

2002 – End of seat-holders: NYSE begins trading as a public company.

Stock market and corporate finance boom

2006 / **2007** – Globalization: NYSE merges with Euronext, a large European exchange.

2008 – Acquisitions: NYSE Euronext acquires the American Stock Exchange for $260 million. The U.S. stock exchange owned by the NYSE trades a total of 802 billion shares in 2008, the highest-volume year ever.

2013 – Acquisitions: Nov. 13, electronic commodities- and derivatives-exchange operator Intercontinental Exchange completes its $8.2 billion acquisition of NYSE Euronext.

218   Contested Sites

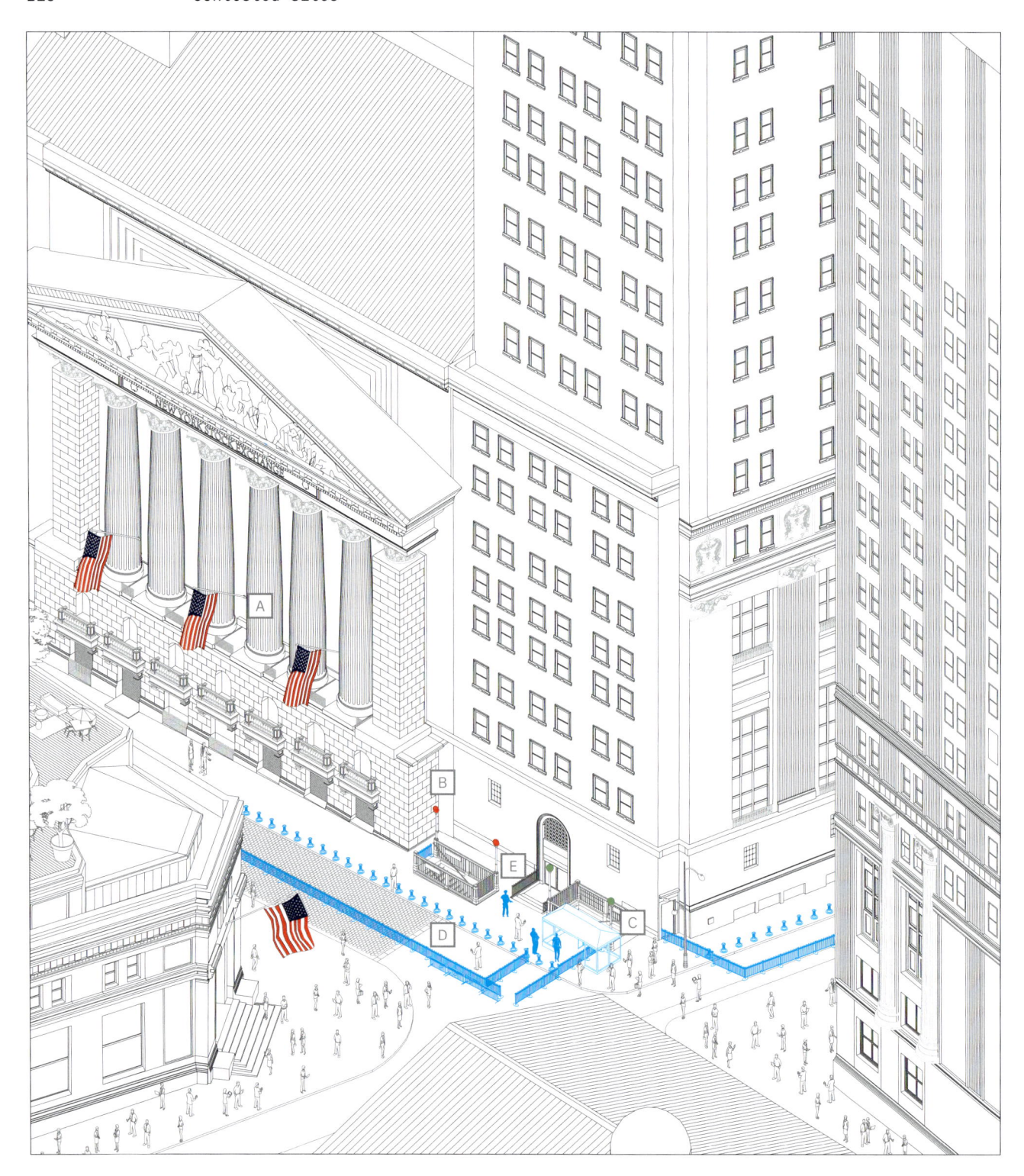

WALL STREET

- ▮ Security measures
- A New York Stock Exchange
- B Gated subway entrance
- C ID checkpoints
- D Mobile fences
- E Police armed with machine guns are distributed at key points around the building.

In the extended period after the 2001 attacks efforts were made to improve the design of physical security measures. New York architects Rogers Marvel, for example, were granted the commission to redesign physical security measures around the Wall Street area. Their proposal involved replacing generic retractable bollards with a sculptural system of bronze-clad road-blocking elements. Bollards positioned on two separate turntables would rotate to allow vehicles to be held and checked by security guards between the turntables.[40] Due to unforeseen challenges the turntables failed to function – leading to a compromised solution involving Jersey barriers, barricades, and a double set of buried vehicle barriers.[41]

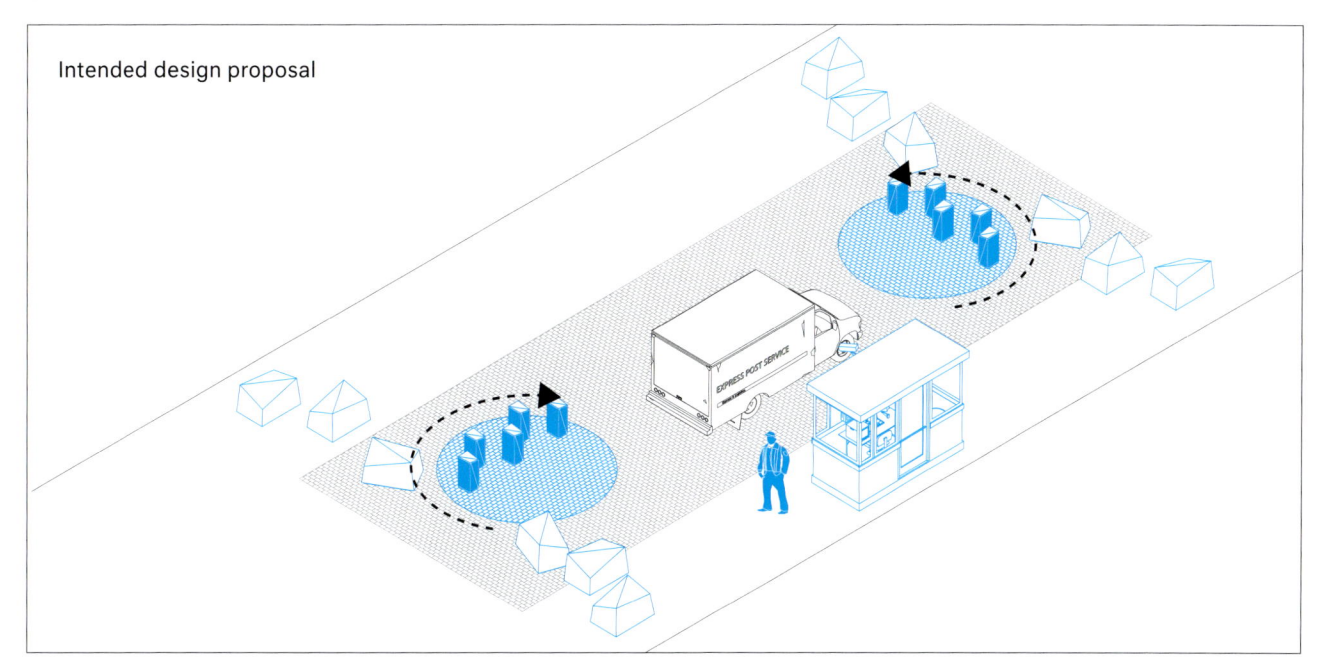

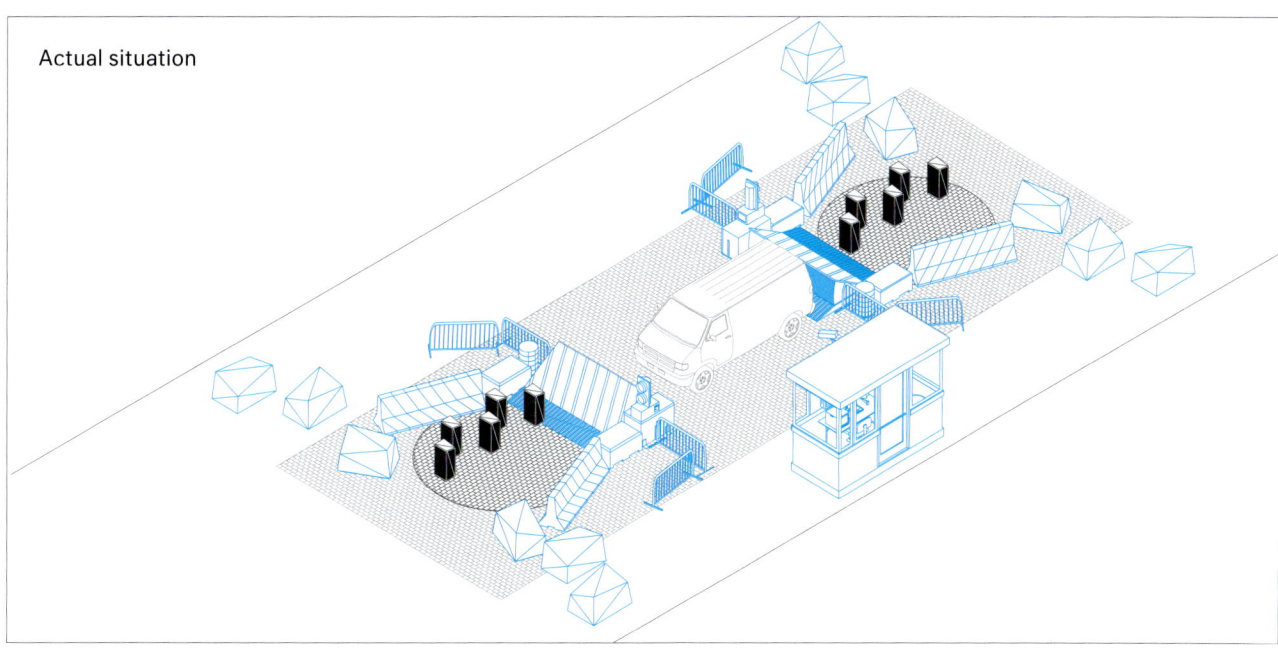

Intended design proposal

Actual situation

OUTER PERIMETER CHECKPOINTS

■ Security measures

220 Contested Sites

Eric J. Tilford, September 17, 2001, US NAVY

WORLD TRADE CENTER

40° 42′ 41.4288″ N
74° 0′ 45.7920″ W

Located on the west side of Lower Manhattan and designed by Yamasaki and Associates in 1964, the World Trade Center (WTC) would consist of 12 million square feet of space. WTC's two highest towers, known as the Twin Towers, were the tallest buildings in the world when completed in 1973.[42]

The targeting by terrorist attacks has been attributed to the complex's symbolic association with America's economic might. The first attack on the WTC occurred on February 26, 1993, when a truck bomb was detonated in the complex's underground garage, killing 6 persons. While security measures would be significantly increased in response to the 1993 attack, a second attack occurred on September 11, 2001, when two hijacked airliners were flown into the Twin Towers, leading to the collapse of both towers, much of the rest of the complex, and the death of 2,753 persons.

The redesign of the heavily damaged area, based on a master plan by architect Daniel Libeskind, would respond to the logic of the contemporary real estate market, memorialize the 1993 and 2001 events, and necessarily include extensive new security requirements and measures. WTC1, or the Freedom Tower, for example, designed by SOM architect David Childs, was forced to be redesigned due to security concerns from the NYPD and the NY State Governor.[43] This would necessitate a new setback from West Street, while the tower's base was required to be transformed into a blast-resistant 200-foot-high cube with 3-foot-thick concrete walls housing a windowless lobby. Office windows were required to be upgraded to tempered, laminated, and multilayered glass to provide additional protection.[44] Other mandatory security features would include: enhanced fireproofing, structural redundancy, biological and chemical air filters, widened pressurized staircases, interconnected redundant exits, encased safety systems, a dedicated firefighter staircase, and special "areas of refuge" on each floor. Further security requirements would play out in the public spaces of the redesigned complex – that would meet similar concerns and protests from local residents as was the case with the securitization of Wall Street.

Timeline World Trade Center

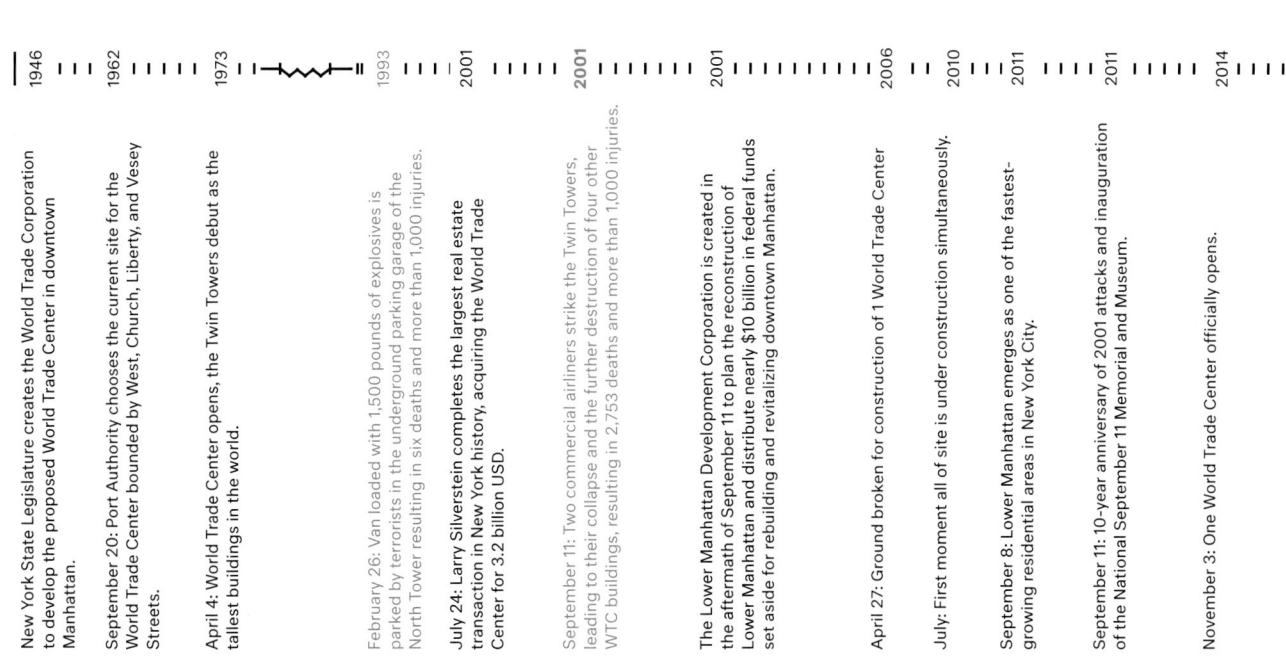

1946: New York State Legislature creates the World Trade Corporation to develop the proposed World Trade Center in downtown Manhattan.

1962 September 20: Port Authority chooses the current site for the World Trade Center bounded by West, Church, Liberty, and Vesey Streets.

1973 April 4: World Trade Center opens, the Twin Towers debut as the tallest buildings in the world.

1993 February 26: Van loaded with 1,500 pounds of explosives is parked by terrorists in the underground parking garage of the North Tower resulting in six deaths and more than 1,000 injuries.

2001 July 24: Larry Silverstein completes the largest real estate transaction in New York history, acquiring the World Trade Center for 3.2 billion USD.

2001 September 11: Two commercial airliners strike the Twin Towers, leading to their collapse and the further destruction of four other WTC buildings, resulting in 2,753 deaths and more than 1,000 injuries.

2001: The Lower Manhattan Development Corporation is created in the aftermath of September 11 to plan the reconstruction of Lower Manhattan and distribute nearly $10 billion in federal funds set aside for rebuilding and revitalizing downtown Manhattan.

2006 April 27: Ground broken for construction of 1 World Trade Center.

2010 July: First moment all of site is under construction simultaneously.

2011 September 8: Lower Manhattan emerges as one of the fastest-growing residential areas in New York City.

2011 September 11: 10-year anniversary of 2001 attacks and inauguration of the National September 11 Memorial and Museum.

2014 November 3: One World Trade Center officially opens.

222 Contested Sites

DECORATIVE COVER
56 m / 185 ft tall windowless concrete-and-steel base designed to withstand vehicle bomb.

WORLD TRADE CENTER

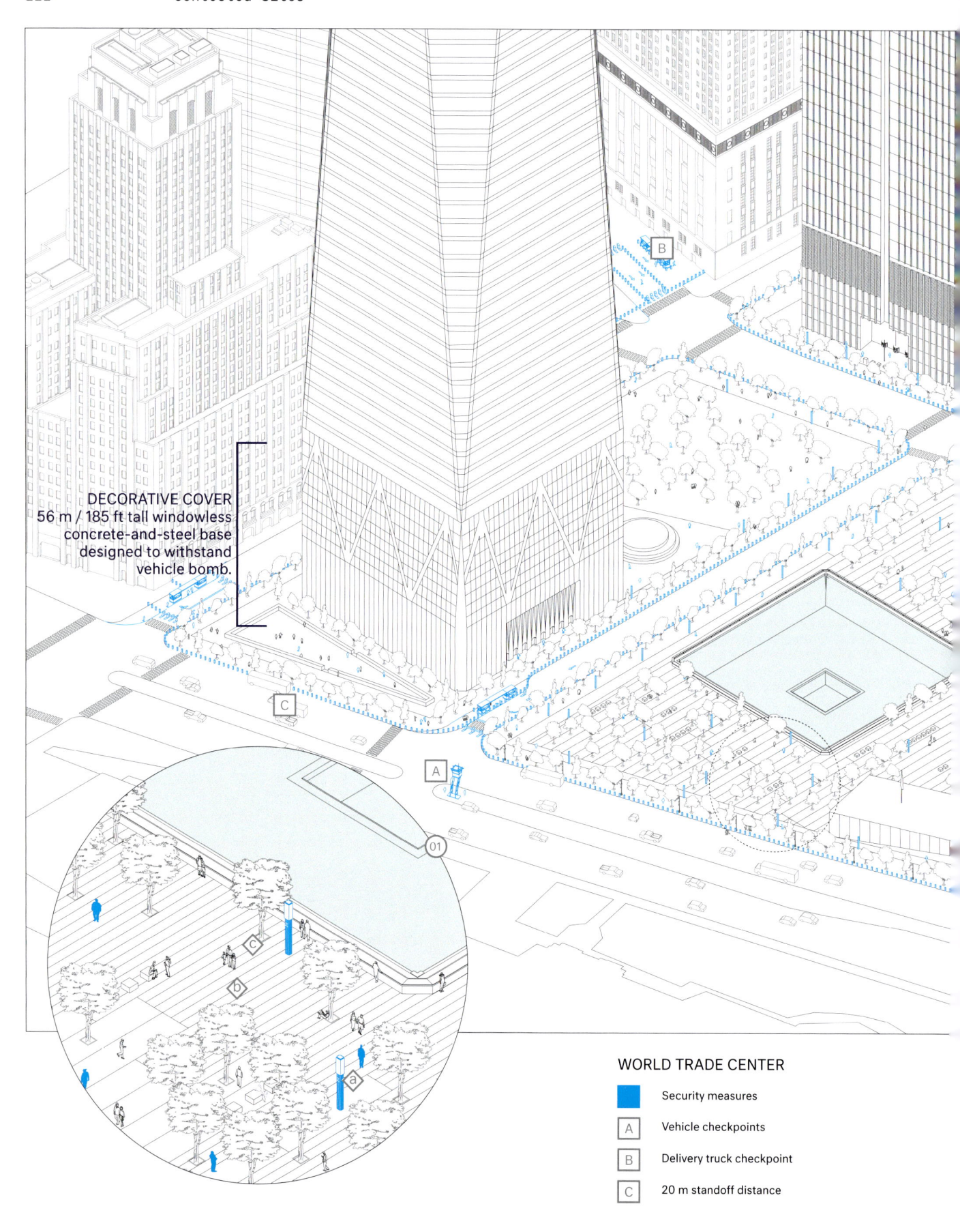

▪ Security measures
A Vehicle checkpoints
B Delivery truck checkpoint
C 20 m standoff distance

223   C   World Trade Center 74°W

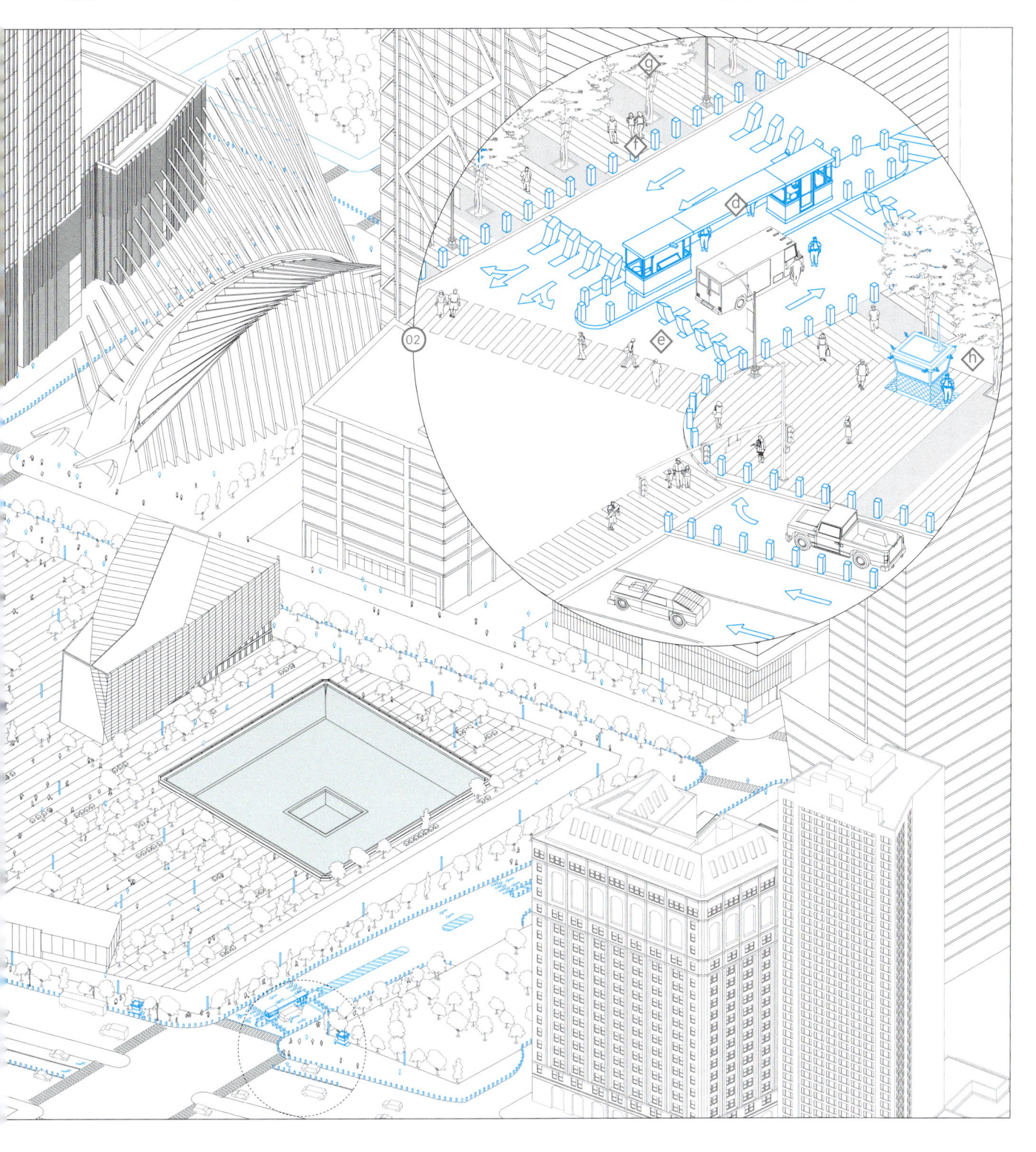

① National September 11 memorial	⟨c⟩ Designed lampposts with integrated CCTV	⟨g⟩ Trees as bollards
② Liberty St. vehicle checkpoint	⟨d⟩ Guarded vehicle checkpoints	⟨h⟩ Portable police towers
⟨a⟩ 200 Port Authority policemen	⟨e⟩ Retractable vehicle barriers	
⟨b⟩ Intended participatory surveillance	⟨f⟩ Bollards	

224 Contested Sites

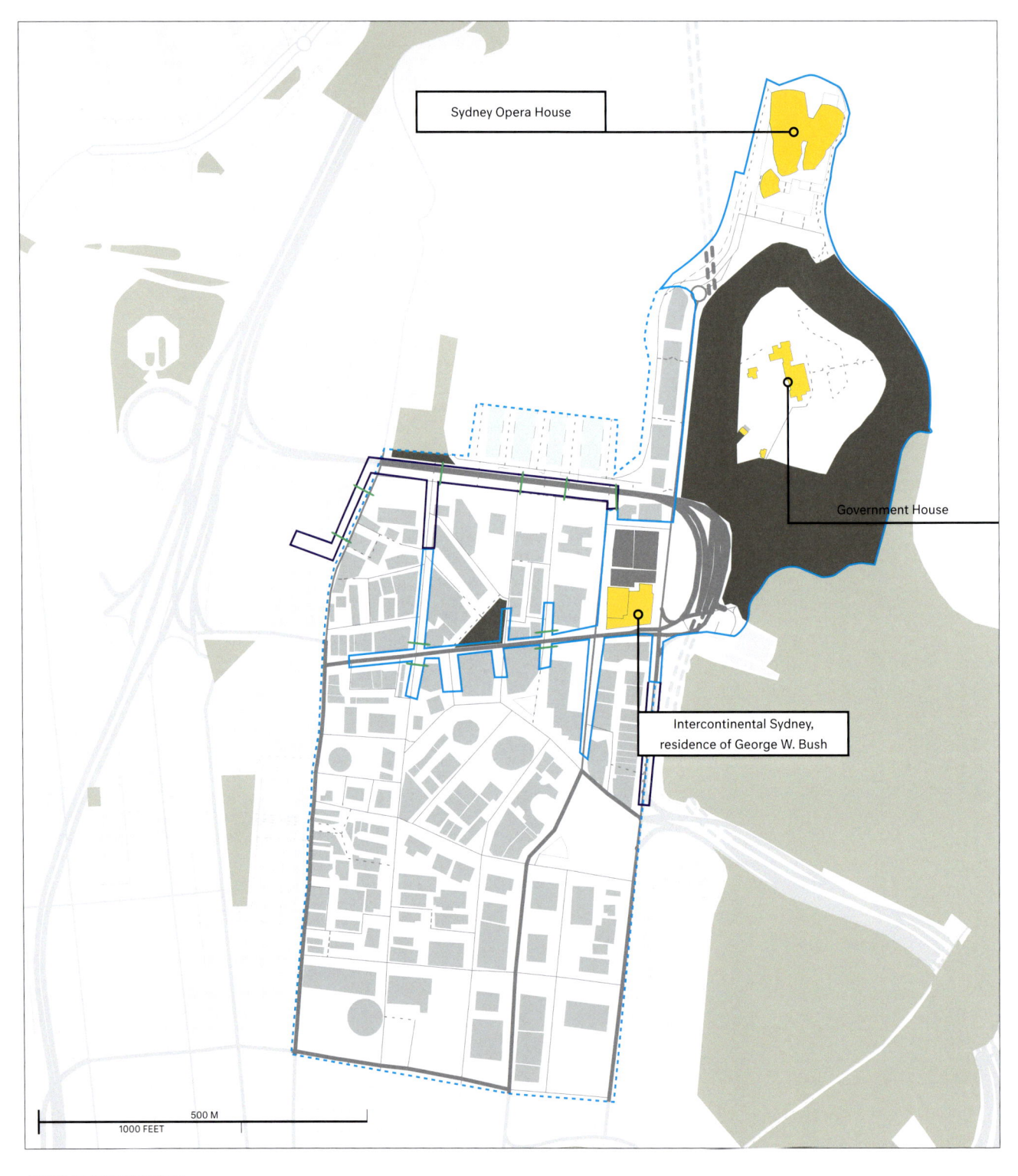

Sydney Opera House

Government House

Intercontinental Sydney, residence of George W. Bush

500 M
1000 FEET

APEC SUMMIT 2007

— Red zone, bounded by 2.5 m. high steel fence
▪▪▪ Declared area, outer security zone
— Intermittently closed roads
— Police-controlled pedestrian crossing

■ Heavily guarded buildings

SYDNEY, AUSTRALIA
Apec Summit, 2007

33° 51′ 25.9092″ S
151° 12′ 54.5040″ E

APEC MEMBER COUNTRIES:

Chinese Taipei	Brunei	People's Republic of China	Republic of Korea	Mexico	Papua New Guinea
Australia	Japan	Canada	The Republic of the Philippines	Peru	New Zealand
Indonesia	Vietnam	Malaysia	Chile	Hong Kong	Singapore
The Russian Federation				Thailand	United States

Founded in 1989, the Asia-Pacific Economic Cooperation (APEC) consists of twenty-one nations, focused on promoting free trade between member states. Attended by heads of state, APEC's yearly summit meetings have become events dominated by heavy security measures. At the 2007 APEC Summit, held in Sydney, Australia, more money was reportedly spent on security over two days than during the entire duration of the 2000 Sydney Olympics, leading to protests from politicians, mainstream media, and the general public over the infringement of civil liberties and access to the city.[45] A large area of the central business district was fenced off from the public to prevent protesters from approaching the venues, while an outer perimeter, described as a "declared zone," was set up in which temporary legislation allowed heightened police powers, random bag searches, etc. In addition, a public holiday in central Sydney was imposed during the period of the summit, so that most of the areas nearby the summit venues would be as uninhabited as possible.[46] Leading up to the event, and in anticipation of protests, police converted thirty buses to "mobile holding cells" and publicly presented their newest riot-control weapon, an AUD 700,000 water cannon. Although this was said to be coincidental and not APEC-related, the New South Wales premier said that it could cause "serious injury" and that people considering "riotous behavior" should take notice.[47]

Following the summit, the Sydney security operation was heavily criticized for its disproportionate scale, particularly as no major incidents were reported and the entire city was affected by the confining spatial strategies and the no-go zone.[48]

ESTIMATED SECURITY EXPENDITURE

$170,000,000[I]

APEC Summit 2007

Participants:	≈4,000 delegates[II]
Largest rally:	5,000[III]
Security personell:	≈5,000[III]
Duration:	7 days

$ 157,000,000[IV]

G8 2005 Gleneagles Summit, United Kingdom

Participants:	2,375[V] delegates
Largest rally:	10,000[VI]
Security Personell	9,000[VII]
Duration:	2 days

TIMELINE APEC[VIII]/G8[IX] SUMMITS

Nov. 2001 — APEC: Shanghai, China / G8: Genoa, Italy
Nov. 2002 — APEC: Los Cabos, Mexico / G8: Kananaskis, Canada
Nov. 2003 — APEC: Bangkok, Thailand / G8: Évian-les-Bains, France
Nov. 2004 — APEC: Santiago, Chile / G8: Sea Island, Georgia, USA
Nov. 2005 — APEC: Busan, Korea / G8: Gleneagles, UK
Nov. 2006 — APEC: Hanoi, Vietnam / G8: Strelna, St. Petersburg, Russia
Nov. 2007 — APEC: Sydney, Australia / G8: Heiligendamm, Germany
Nov. 2008 — APEC: Lima, Peru / G8: Toyako (Lake Toya), Japan
Nov. 2009 — APEC: Singapore / G8: L'Aquila, Italy
Nov. 2010 — APEC: Yokohama, Japan / G8: Huntsville, Canada
Nov. 2011 — APEC: Honolulu, Hawaii, USA / G8: Deauville, France
Sept. 2012 — APEC: Vladivostok, Russia / G8: Camp David, USA
Oct. 2013 — APEC: Bali, Indonesia / G8: Loch Erne, UK
Nov. 2014 — APEC: Beijing, China[VIII] / G8: Brussels, Belgium[IX]

226   Contested Sites

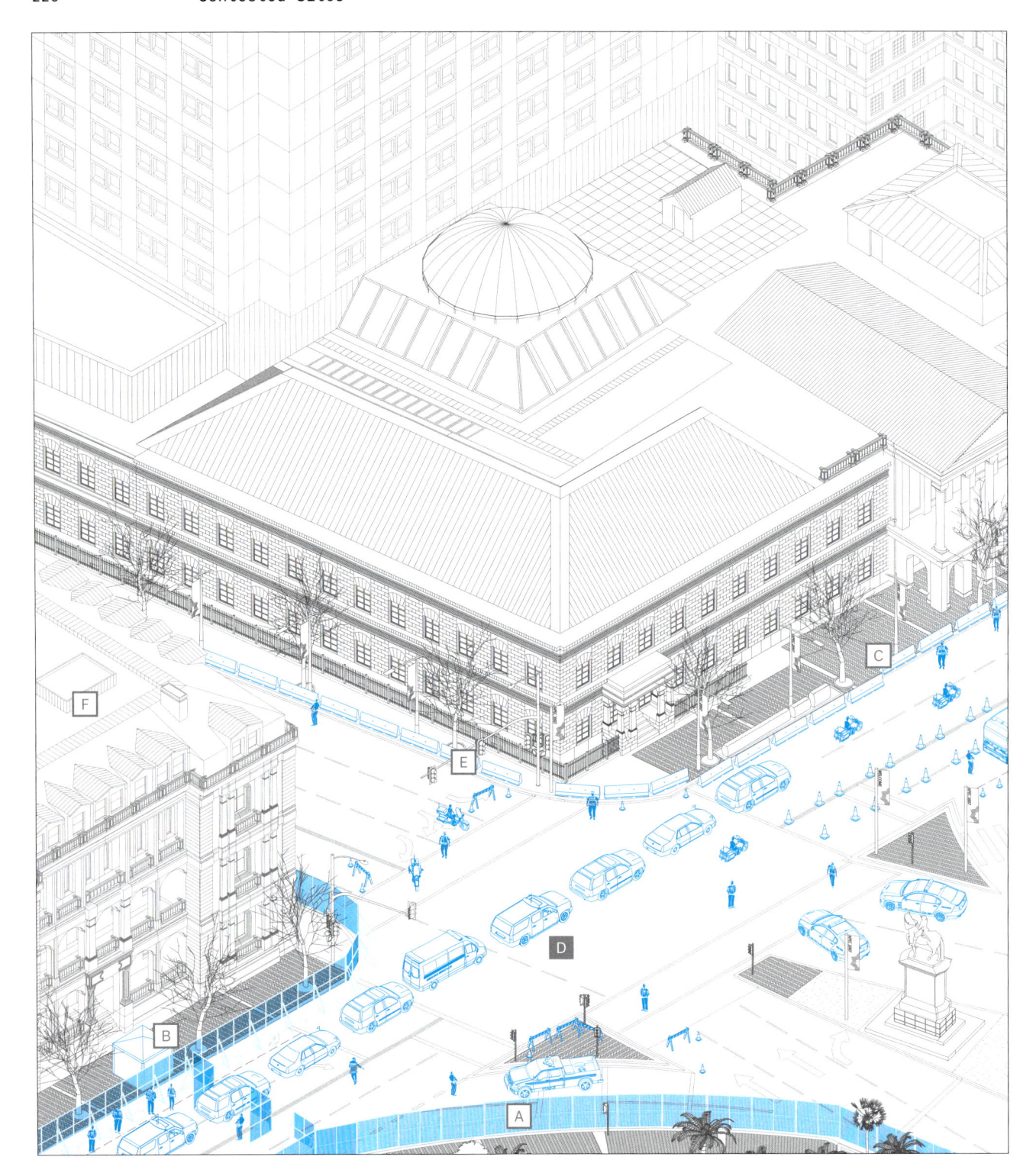

SECURITY MEASURES INSIDE RED ZONE

- ▇ Security measures
- A 2 m. fence separating street
- B Temporary police outpost
- C Jersey barriers
- D George W. Bush motorcade
- E Welded manholes
- F Secret Service snipers

Apec Summit 2007 151°E

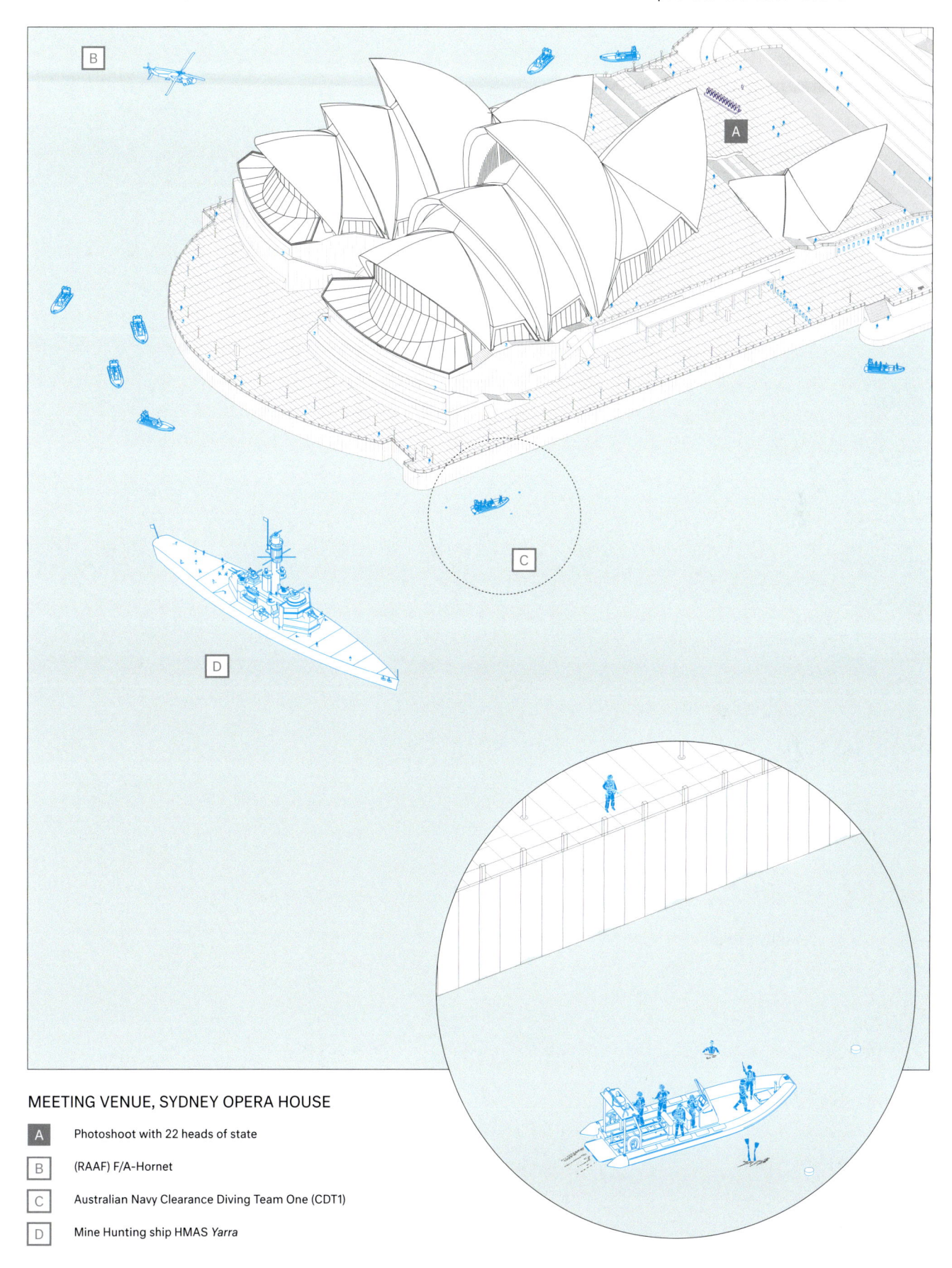

MEETING VENUE, SYDNEY OPERA HOUSE

- A Photoshoot with 22 heads of state
- B (RAAF) F/A-Hornet
- C Australian Navy Clearance Diving Team One (CDT1)
- D Mine Hunting ship HMAS *Yarra*

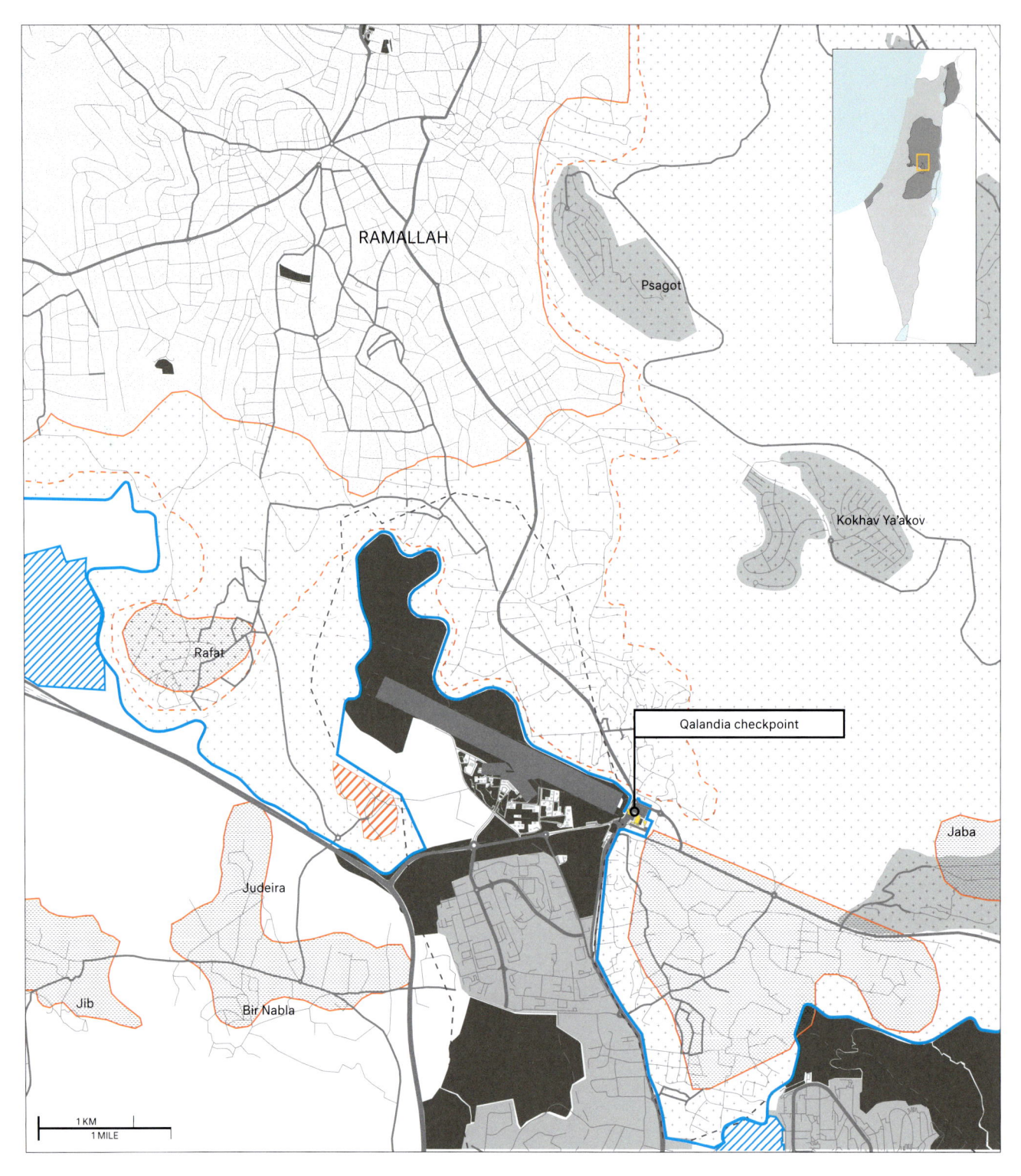

QALANDIA CHECKPOINT

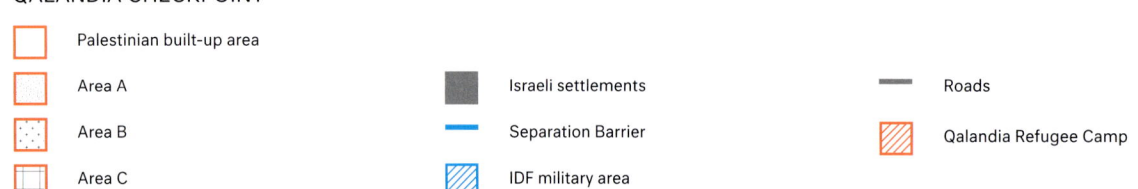

- Palestinian built-up area
- Area A
- Area B
- Area C
- Israeli settlements
- Separation Barrier
- IDF military area
- Roads
- Qalandia Refugee Camp

RAMALLAH, WEST BANK
Qalandia Checkpoint

Qalandia Checkpoint 34°E

31° 14′ 53.1708″ N
34° 15′ 25.6320″ E

The Israeli–West Bank Separation Barrier, "Security Fence," or "Apartheid Wall" as it is variously known, was approved by the Israeli cabinet in 2002. While the declared objective of the permanent physical barrier was to prevent the entry of Palestinian suicide bombers, critics have addressed other agendas. According to B'Tselem, rather than being based solely on the security of Israeli citizens, "A major aim in planning the route [of the Barrier] was de facto annexation of part of the West Bank: when the Barrier is completed, 9.5 percent of the West Bank, containing 60 settlements, will be situated on its western, 'Israeli' side."[49]

Palestinians are required to hold valid resident permits and identification cards in order to cross the dozens of checkpoints and gates, which are often congested and unpredictable. Apart from being universally condemned for its extensive violation of human rights, the restrictions on Palestinians' freedom of movement caused by the barrier obstruct the flow of everyday life, further contributing to the deterioration of the Palestinian economy and unemployment and poverty among its citizens.[50] Palestinians needing to pass for work, education, or medical care are hindered, while family ties and social connections are also adversely affected.

The busiest and most notorious of the military checkpoints (or "crossings" as they are referred to by the IDF) along the separation barrier is Qalandia, located between Jerusalem and Ramallah and the central West Bank. Qalandia transformed over several years into a large and technologically sophisticated instrument of control. According to the IDF, an average of 15,000 people pass through Qalandia daily.[51]

Statistics

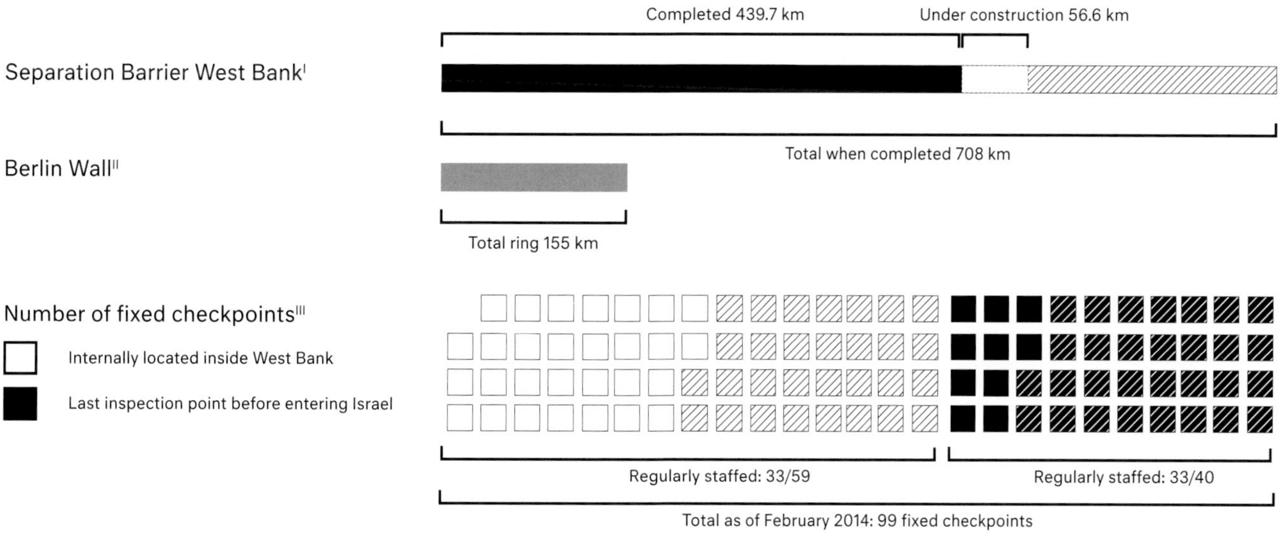

Separation Barrier West Bank[I]

Completed 439.7 km   Under construction 56.6 km

Total when completed 708 km

Berlin Wall[II]

Total ring 155 km

Number of fixed checkpoints[III]

☐ Internally located inside West Bank
■ Last inspection point before entering Israel

Regularly staffed: 33/59   Regularly staffed: 33/40

Total as of February 2014: 99 fixed checkpoints

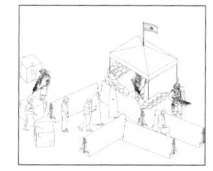

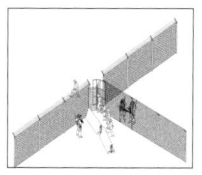

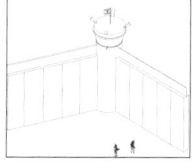

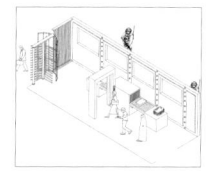

Timeline Qalandia checkpoint

------ 2001 ------ 2002 ------ 2003 ------ 2004 ------ 2005 ------ 2006 ------

230 Contested Sites

QALANDIA CHECKPOINT

■ Israeli Defense Force measures

■ Civilians and vehicles, predominantly Palestinian

A IDF area only

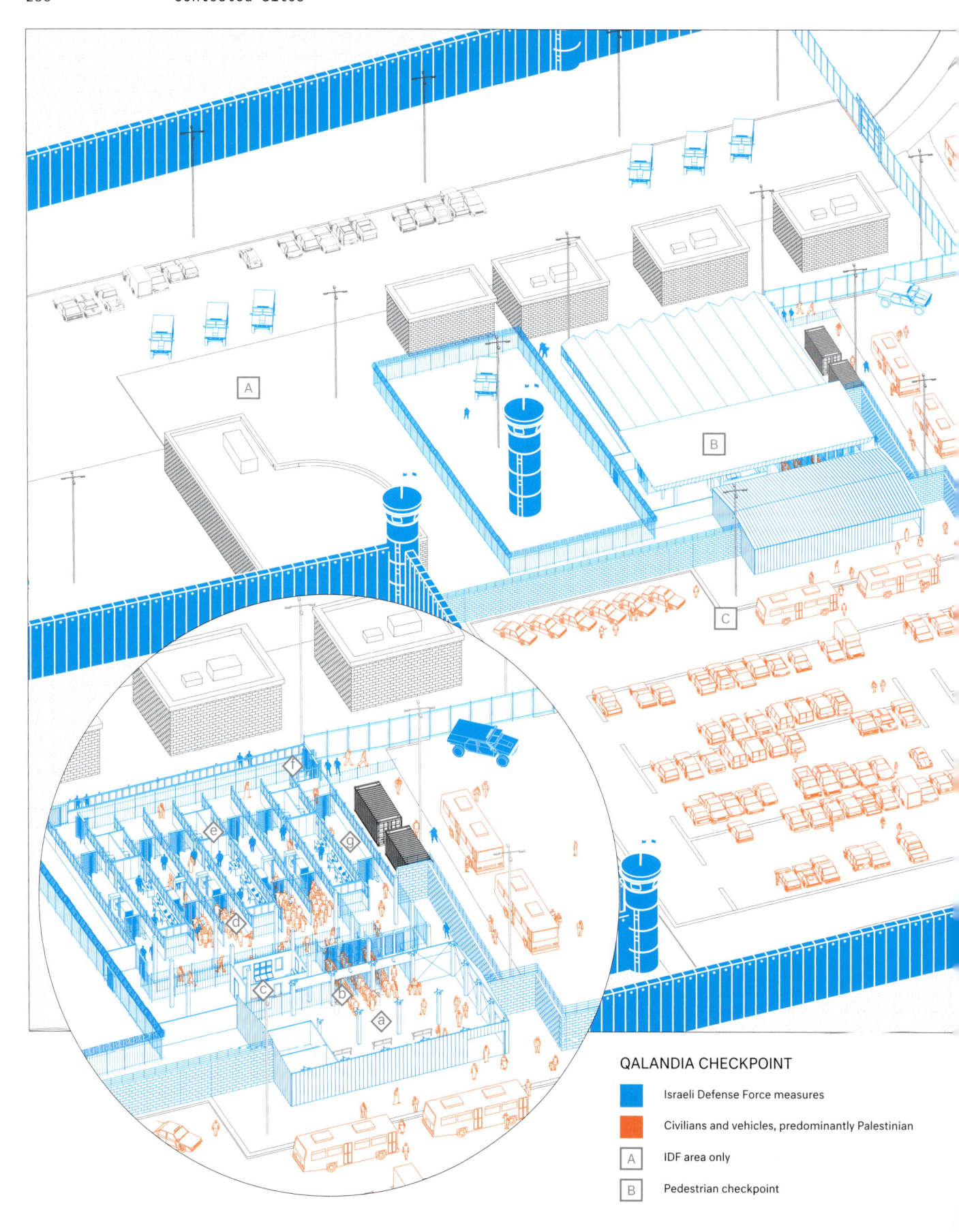

B Pedestrian checkpoint

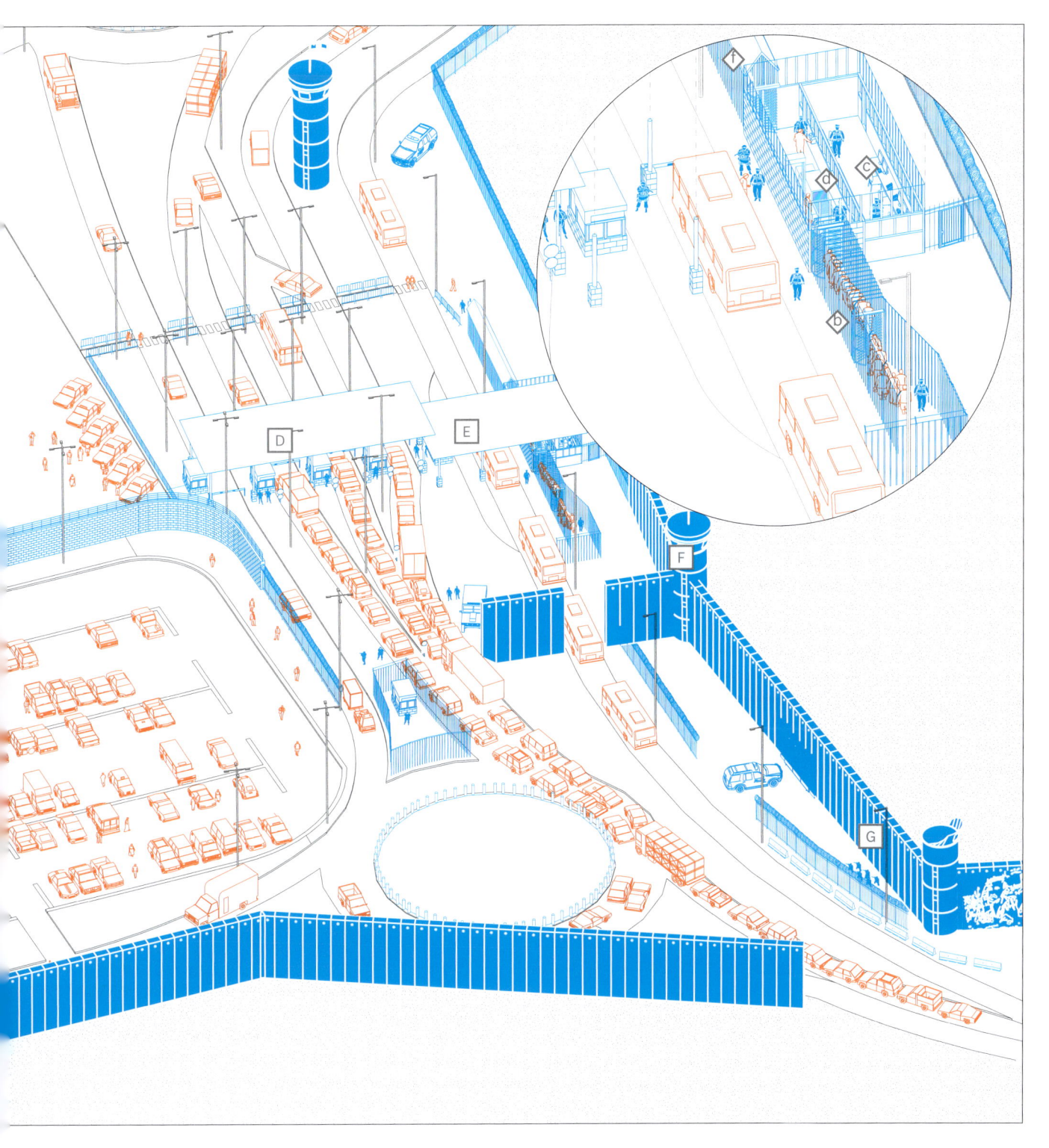

231 C Qalandia Checkpoint 34°E

C	Drop-off / pickup for bus and taxi	G	Separation Barrier	d	Security check
D	Vehicle checkpoint	a	Waiting area	e	Interrogation room
E	Bus checkpoint	b	50 cm wide metal chutes	f	Exit to Israel
F	IDF watchtower	c	Control room	g	Security check Israel to West Bank

232 Contested Sites

20 NAUTICAL MILE LIMIT, GAZA - JERICO AGREEMENT, 1994

International sea border

12 NAUTICAL MILE LIMIT, BERLIN AGREEMENT, OCT 2002

10 NAUTICAL MILE LIMIT, IDF, APRIL 2006

6 NAUTICAL MILE LIMIT, IDF, OCTOBER 2006

3 NAUTICAL MILE LIMIT, IDF, JANUARY 2009 TO PRESENT DAY

Jabalaia

City of Gaza

Khan Yunis

Rafah

Rafah border crossing

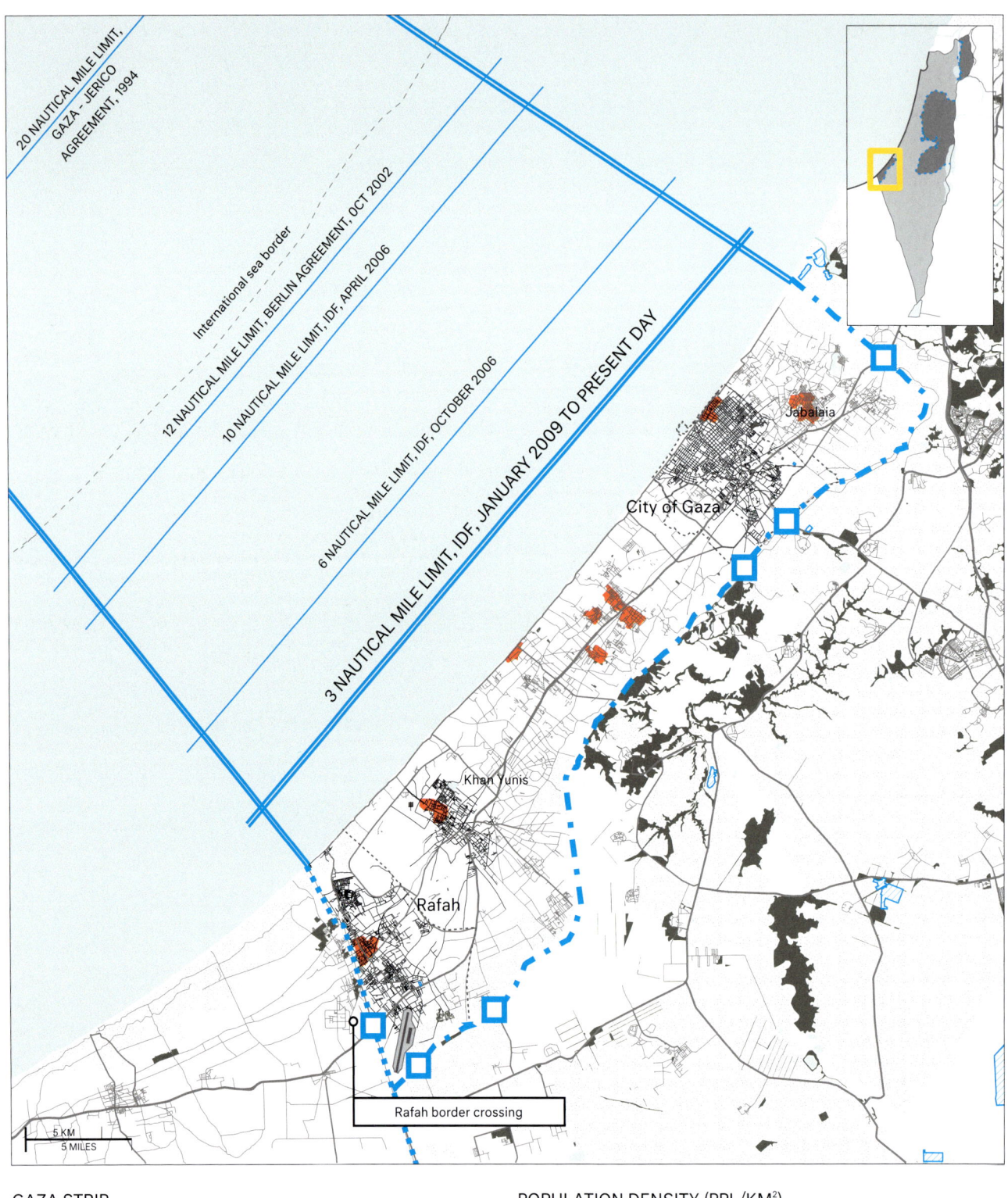

5 KM
5 MILES

GAZA STRIP

- Checkpoints
- Gaza–Israel border
- Gaza–Egypt border
- Naval blockade
- Roads
- Refugee camps
- Military areas

POPULATION DENSITY (PPL/KM²)

Dhaka	Jabalia, Gaza	City of Gaza	New York	London	Oslo
114,000/km²	78,571/km²	13,067/km²	10,725/km²	5,354/km²	1,400/km²

GAZA, PALESTINE
Egypt–Gaza Border

31° 14′ 53.1708″ N
34° 15′ 25.6320″ E

As a result of decades of occupation, war, and conflict, the borders between the Palestinian territory of Gaza, Egypt, and Israel, have become heavily militarized, with crossings taking place through only five highly controlled checkpoints. When Hamas came to power in Gaza in 2007, Egypt and Israel closed their borders, preventing Palestinians traveling to or from Gaza. Both countries imposed land-, sea- and air-blockades on Gaza, leaving millions of civilians isolated and in poverty in one of the world's most densely populated territories.

Currently, Israel controls the Gaza Strip's 52-kilometer-long northern and eastern borders, as well as its territorial waters and airspace, while in agreement with Israel, Egypt controls the Gaza Strip's 12-kilometer-long southern border. The Palestinian Authority and the European Union have been attempting to negotiate control of the border crossings and lifting of blockades with little success. The constant blockade of the Gaza Strip has resulted in the digging of an unknown number of tunnels underneath the borders. This network of tunnels is a vital lifeline for Gaza, bringing in an estimated 30 percent of total goods into the territory. This underground infrastructure consists of smuggling tunnels between Gaza and Egypt, defensive tunnels inside Gaza used for command centers and weapons storage, and tunnels used for offensive cross-border attacks on Israel.[52] Hamas describes the tunnels as an exercise of Gaza's "right to protect itself" while according to the Israel Ministry of Foreign Affairs, the tunnels under the Israel – Gaza border have been constructed by the military wing of Hamas for the purpose of "terrorist attacks" on Israel.[53]

The border consists of wire fencing with posts, sensors, cameras, and buffer zones on lands bordering Israel, and concrete and steel walls on lands bordering Egypt. Both Egyptian border control and IDF use multiple tactics in order to destroy the tunnels and prevent new tunnels from being created, including: flooding with water or gas, underground barriers, bombing and detection systems with sensors, and special transmitters to locate underground tunnels.

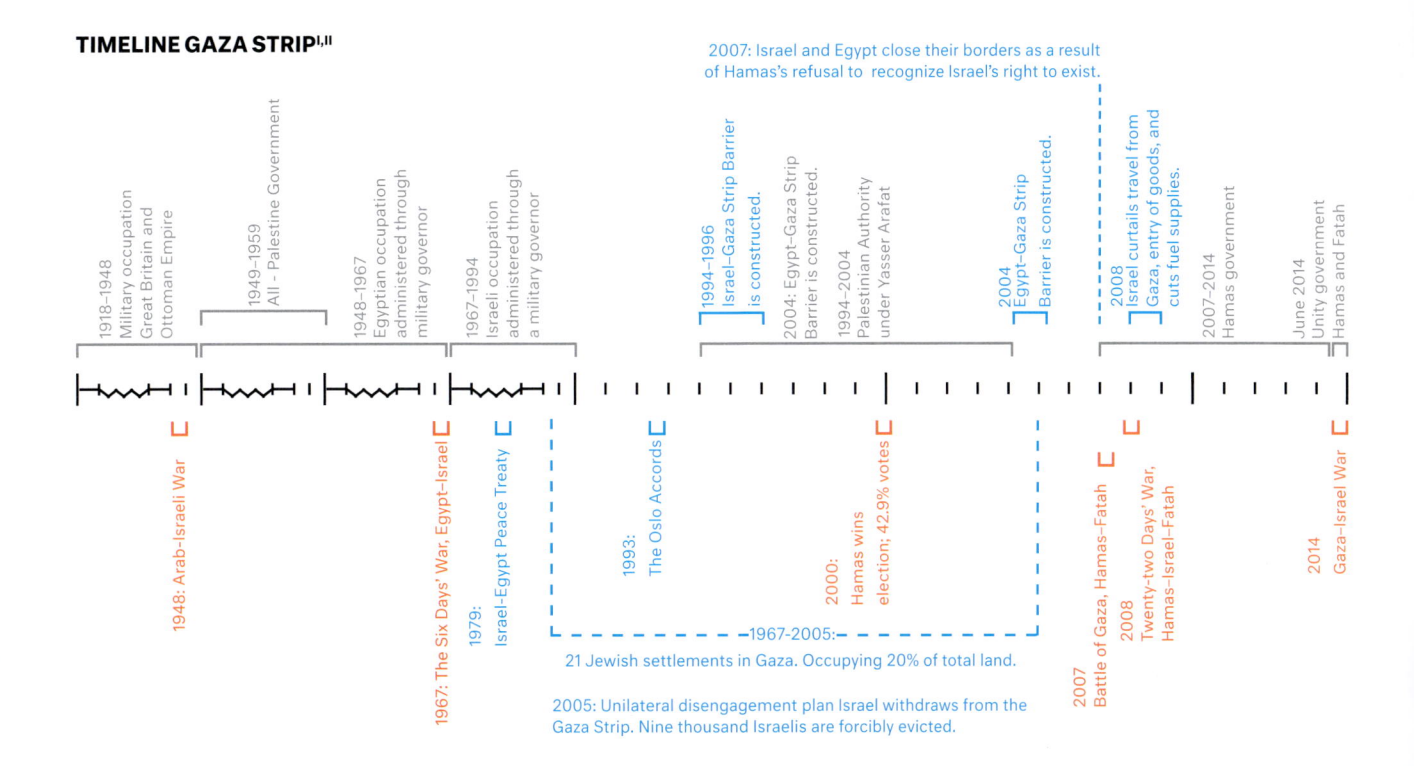

TIMELINE GAZA STRIP[I,II]

1918–1948: Military occupation Great Britain and Ottoman Empire
1948: Arab-Israeli War
1949–1959: All – Palestine Government
1948–1967: Egyptian occupation administered through military governor
1967: The Six Days' War, Egypt-Israel
1967–1994: Israeli occupation administered through a military governor
1979: Israel-Egypt Peace Treaty
1993: The Oslo Accords
1994–1996: Israel-Gaza Strip Barrier is constructed.
1994–2004: Palestinian Authority under Yasser Arafat
2000: Hamas wins election; 42.9% votes
2004: Egypt-Gaza Strip Barrier is constructed.
2004: Egypt-Gaza Strip Barrier is constructed.
1967-2005: 21 Jewish settlements in Gaza. Occupying 20% of total land.
2005: Unilateral disengagement plan Israel withdraws from the Gaza Strip. Nine thousand Israelis are forcibly evicted.
2007: Israel and Egypt close their borders as a result of Hamas's refusal to recognize Israel's right to exist.
2007: Battle of Gaza, Hamas-Fatah
2007–2014: Hamas government
2008: Israel curtails travel from Gaza, entry of goods, and cuts fuel supplies.
2008: Twenty-two Days' War, Hamas-Israel-Fatah
June 2014: Unity government Hamas and Fatah
2014: Gaza-Israel War

234 Contested Sites

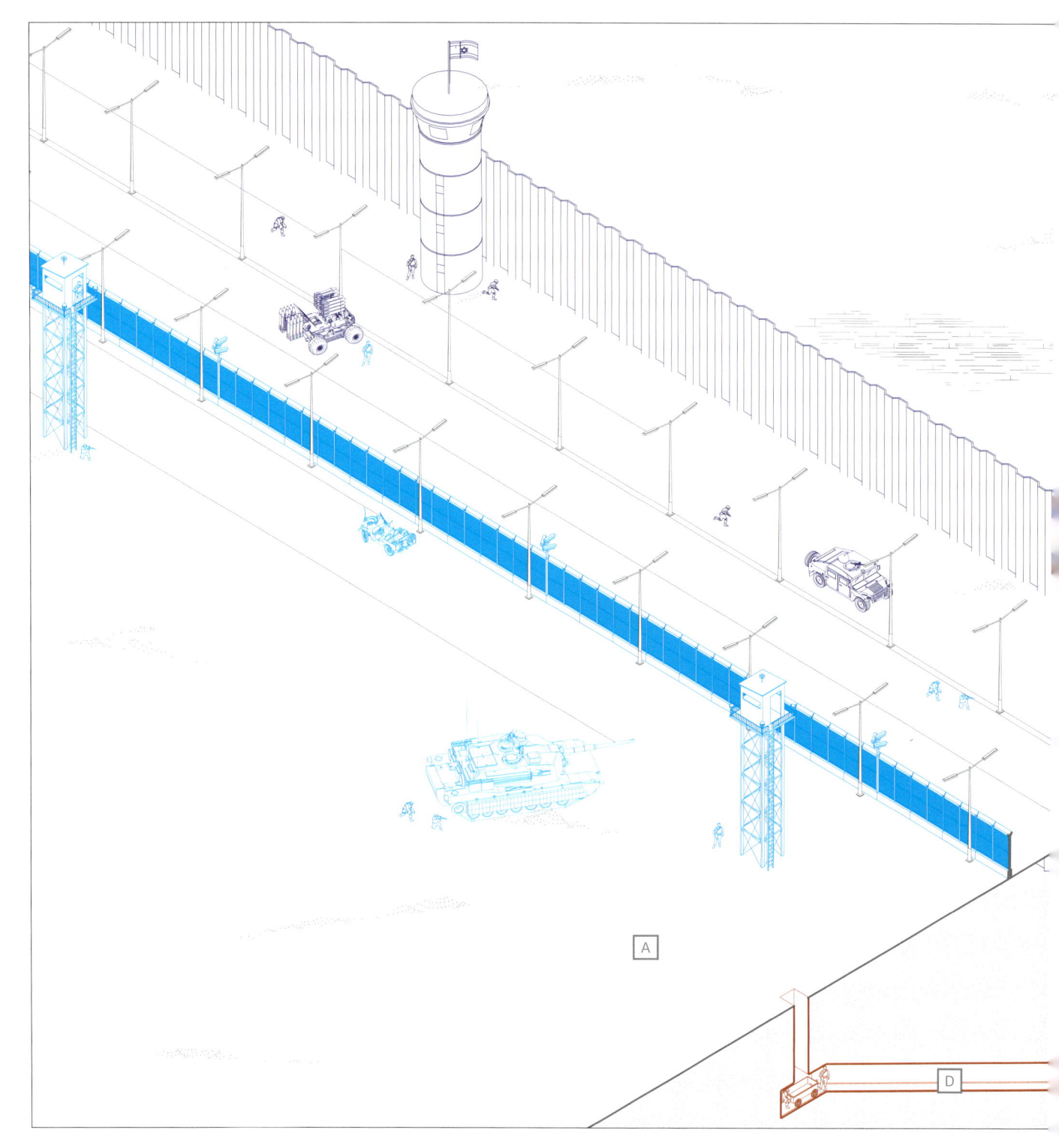

EGYPT–GAZA BORDER

- ■ Israeli Defense Force
- ■ Palestinian tunnelers
- ■ Egyptian border control measures

A	Rafah, Egypt
B	Philadelphi Road / Israeli - Egypt control
C	Rafah, Gaza
D	Smuggling tunnels
E	Underground 20 m metal barrier
F	Ventilation shafts
G	Palestinian militants Rafah, Gaza IDF demolishes all buildings within 300 m of the steel fence
H	Hamas reportedly works from basements in houses.

235　　　C　　　　　　　　　　　　　　　　　　　　　　　　　　　　　　　　　　Gaza Border 34°E

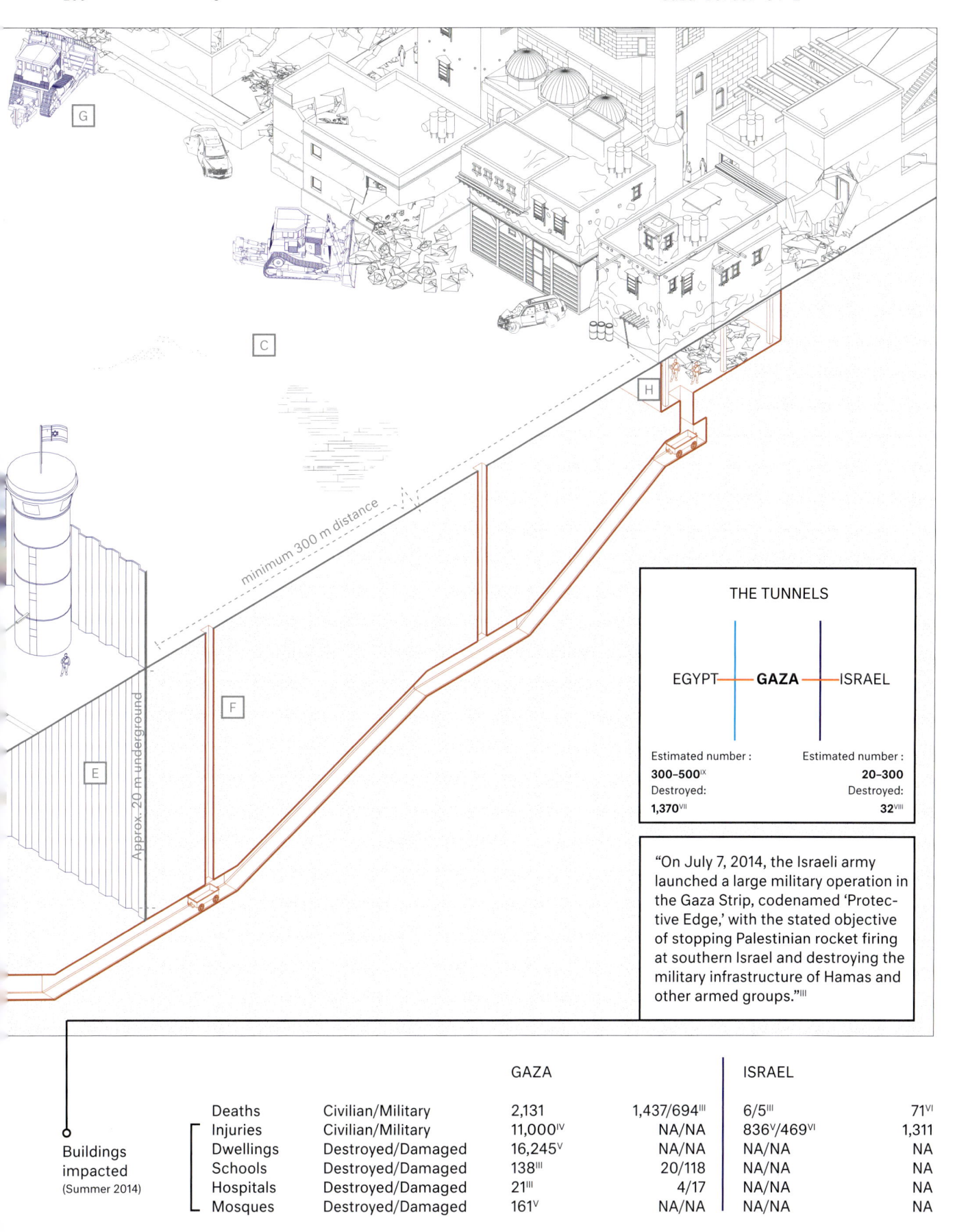

THE TUNNELS

EGYPT —— **GAZA** —— ISRAEL

Estimated number: **300–500**[IX]
Destroyed: **1,370**[VII]

Estimated number: **20–300**
Destroyed: **32**[VIII]

"On July 7, 2014, the Israeli army launched a large military operation in the Gaza Strip, codenamed 'Protective Edge,' with the stated objective of stopping Palestinian rocket firing at southern Israel and destroying the military infrastructure of Hamas and other armed groups."[III]

minimum 300 m distance

Approx. 20 m underground

Buildings impacted (Summer 2014)

		GAZA		ISRAEL	
Deaths	Civilian/Military	2,131	1,437/694[III]	6/5[III]	71[VI]
Injuries	Civilian/Military	11,000[IV]	NA/NA	836[V]/469[VI]	1,311
Dwellings	Destroyed/Damaged	16,245[V]	NA/NA	NA/NA	NA
Schools	Destroyed/Damaged	138[III]	20/118	NA/NA	NA
Hospitals	Destroyed/Damaged	21[III]	4/17	NA/NA	NA
Mosques	Destroyed/Damaged	161[V]	NA/NA	NA/NA	NA

GAZA FLOTILLA, 2010

32° 23′ 54.6576″ N
33° 40′ 3.3708″ E

21.00-00.41 ○ First encounter

04.28 ○ Boarding of M.M.

Naval Blockade Zone
International waters
GAZA

On May 31, 2010, a flotilla of six vessels rendezvoused outside of Cyprus, planning to break the naval blockade of Gaza. Seventy-two nautical miles from land they were boarded by the IDF, resulting in 9 casualties and several injured. The vessels were carrying people and humanitarian supplies.

As a result of the almost complete blockade by the Israeli and Egyptian governments since 2007, Gaza suffers shortages of supplies, particularly medicine, but also food, construction materials, etc. According to the Fourth Geneva Convention of 1949, an occupying state (in this case Israel, despite its so-called Unilateral Disengagement Plan of 2005) is obliged to allow humanitarian personnel and aid across the border. Blanket restrictions imposed on a whole population justified by incidents performed by a government or armed group, are considered a breach of international law. According to a 2014 report by the Human Rights Watch, 70 percent of Gaza inhabitants are now dependent on aid for survival, and while several aid organizations are working inside of Gaza (for example, UNRWA, MECA, PCRF), and the blockade has been somewhat downscaled, the import of necessary goods is still substantially lower than prior to 2007.[54]

In response to this crisis, a flotilla of six civilian vessels carrying humanitarian workers, supplies, and construction materials, rendezvoused outside Cyprus on May 31, 2010, with the intention of breaking Israel's naval blockade of Gaza.[55] The flotilla was organized by the Free Gaza Movement, and the Turkish NGO IHH, and staffed by a combination of journalists, volunteers, academics, and religious leaders. IHH stated that besides providing humanitarian aid, their objective was to create global awareness of the situation in Gaza.[56] As the vessels approached Gaza, they received several warnings from the Israeli navy to turn back. The vessels were eventually boarded by the IDF seventy-two nautical miles from the coast. Formal reviews of the event by the UN and Turkey were highly critical of the actions of the IDF, particularly the excessive, disproportionate use of force by the Israelis, which resulted in nine deaths and thirty-eight injuries. These actions were condemned by the UN Security Council, the EU, and more than sixty nations worldwide. Included in the inquiries into the incident was a questioning of the nature of the intent of around forty of the flotilla passengers who had stored and used makeshift weapons on the *Mavi Marmara*.[57]

Main events during takeover (Based on IDF videos)[1]

21.00-00.41 / 30.05.2011 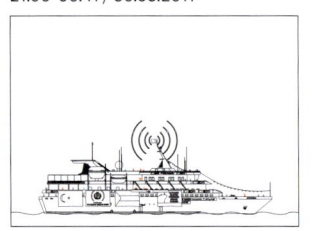
IDF Navy issues radio warnings to turn vessel around.

04.20 / 31.05.2011 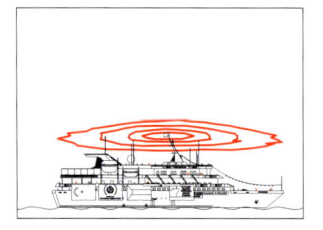
IDF Navy conducts electronic signal jamming to avoid outgoing traffic from *Mavi Marmara*.

04.28 / 31.05.2011 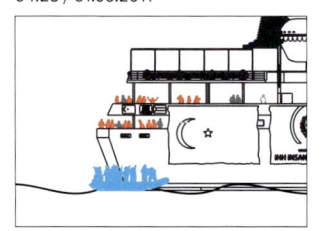
Two RIBs with special forces S13 soldiers attempt to board the ship, but are met with waterhoses and artifacts thrown from the stern of the ship.

04.30 / 31.05.2011 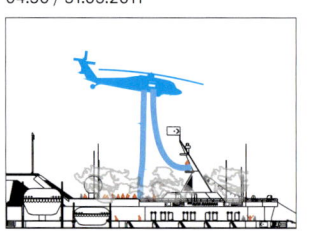
Black Hawk helicopter hovers over ship. Stun grenades are thrown to disperse activists on upper deck. Rappelling rope is thrown from helicopter, but tied to the mast by three of the activists.

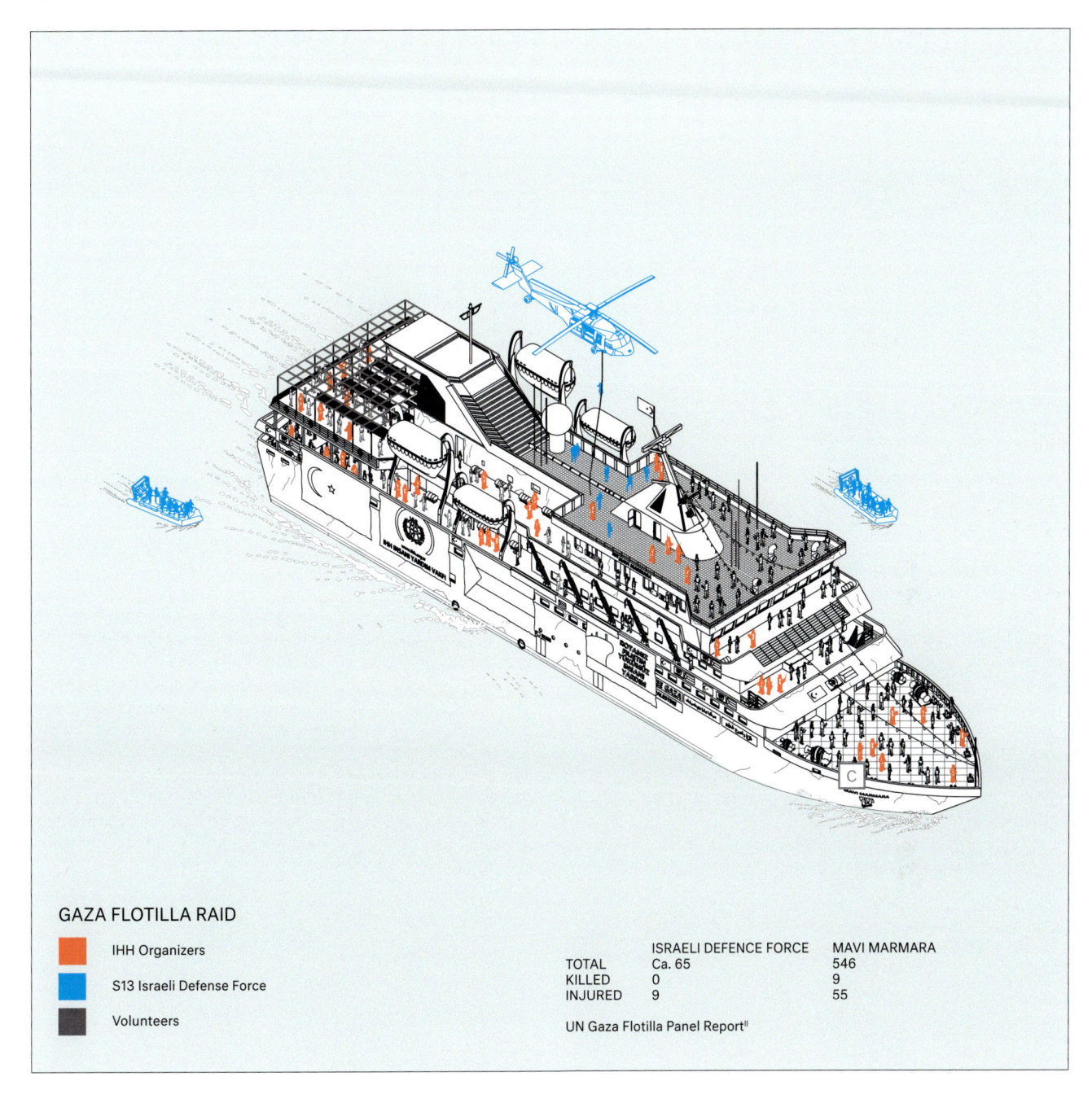

237   C   Gaza Flotilla 33°E

GAZA FLOTILLA RAID

- IHH Organizers
- S13 Israeli Defense Force
- Volunteers

	ISRAELI DEFENCE FORCE	MAVI MARMARA
TOTAL	Ca. 65	546
KILLED	0	9
INJURED	9	55

UN Gaza Flotilla Panel Report[II]

04.35 / 31.05.2011 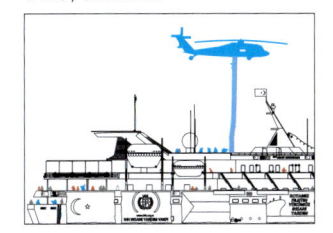
Second Black Hawk arrives. Twelve soldiers hoisted down to the *Mavi Marmara*. At same time, RIBs successfully returns and boards the ship.

04.46 / 31.05.2011 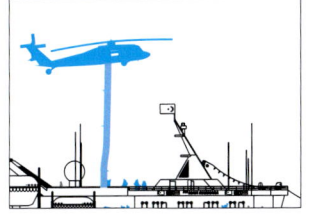
A third helicopter carrying 14 soldiers arrives. By this point several shots have been fired as the soldiers are met by greater resistance than anticipated.

05.04 / 31.05.2011 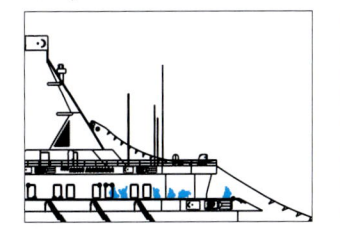
Soldiers take control over the ship's bridge. Within 10 minutes all soldiers are accounted for and the operation is concluded.

Morning after / 31.05.2011 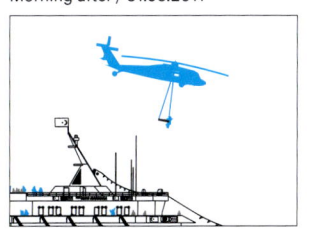
IDF evacuates the ship, including 38 wounded, before entering the Ashdod Port, where crew and guests are detained.

238 Contested Sites

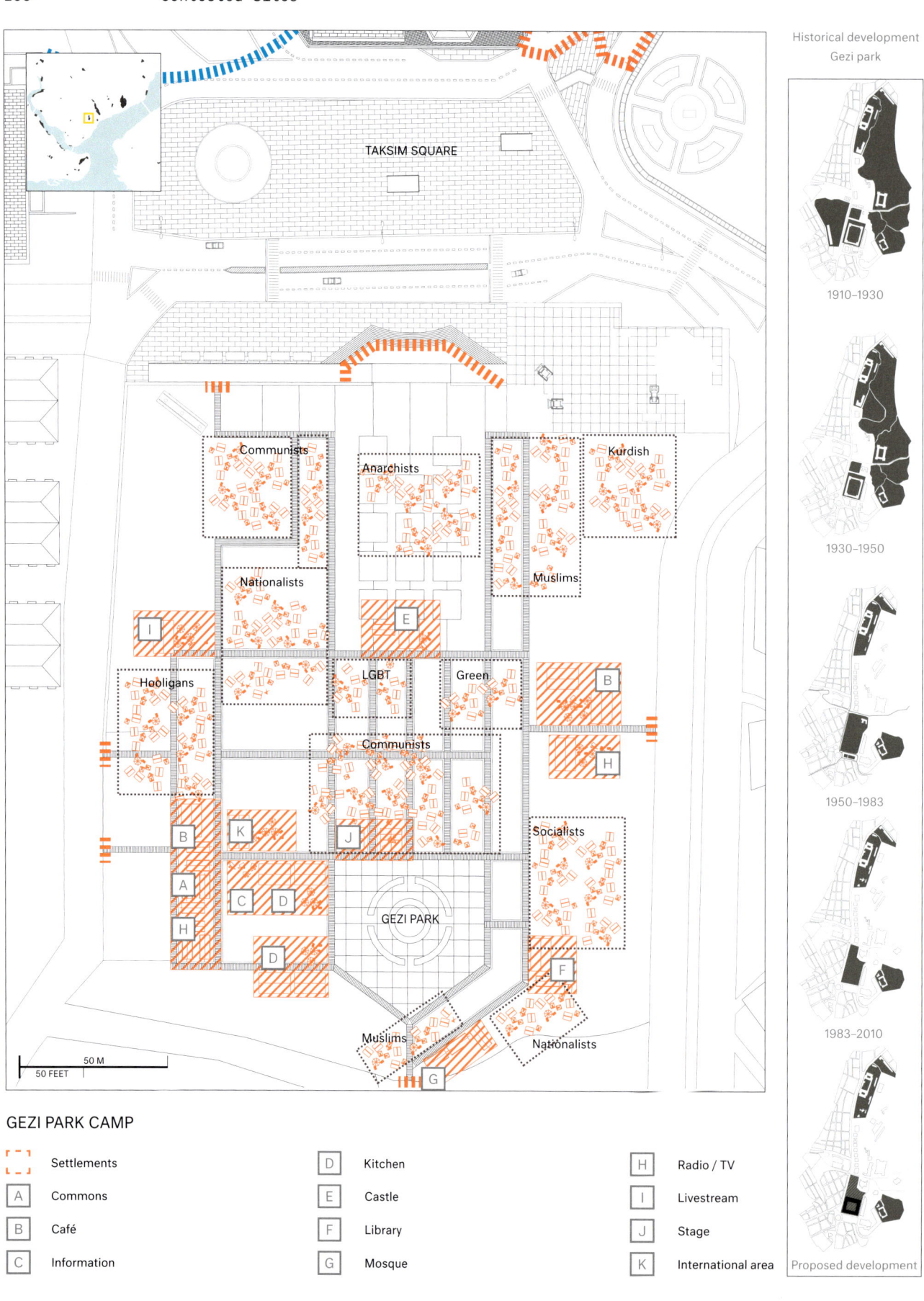

Historical development Gezi park

1910–1930

1930–1950

1950–1983

1983–2010

Proposed development

GEZI PARK CAMP

- ⌐ ⌐ Settlements
- A Commons
- B Café
- C Information
- D Kitchen
- E Castle
- F Library
- G Mosque
- H Radio / TV
- I Livestream
- J Stage
- K International area

ISTANBUL, TURKEY
Gezi Park, 2013

41° 2′ 16.3752″ N
28° 59′ 11.9184″ E

Gezi Park, a public park adjacent to Taksim Square, is one of the last remaining green spaces of the inner core of the European side of Istanbul. Government sponsored development plans to demolish the park and replace it with a shopping mall sparked massive public protests in 2013. The first clash took place on May 28, 2013, when police attacked a group of environmental protesters who were occupying the park to prevent existing trees being destroyed. The reported use by police of disproportionate force, including the indiscriminant use of tear gas and pepper spray; and its resulting publicity on social media, led to an escalation in the protests. Police carried out further raids on protesters and the encampment on May 30 and 31, with water cannons, tear gas, pepper spray, tent burnings, and beatings, along with the barricading of parts of the square to limit possible reoccupation.[58] Police temporarily abandoned attempts to clear the Gezi Park encampment on June 1, with the site developing into an Occupy-like setting made up of a conglomeration of diverse groups.

As demonstrations multiplied in other Turkish cities, their focus expanded from the Gezi Park demolition to a nationwide demonstration against the policies and "creeping authoritarianism" of Turkish prime minister Tayyip Erdogan and his Justice and Development Party, AKP, along with public concerns addressing police brutality, corruption, lack of public consultation, and media censorship and disinformation.[59] After a range of police interventions in the following days, many of which involved the use of plastic bullets by police, Taksim Square and the Gezi Park encampment were cleared on June 15. Soon after, the suspension of the shopping mall project was announced, with the promise by Erdogan of a referendum should the courts support its reactivation.

An estimated 3.5 million Turkish citizens were active in approximately 5,000 demonstrations related to the Gezi Park protests across Turkey – with more than 3,000 arrests, more than 8,000 injured, and 11 deaths.[60]

Statistics[I, II]

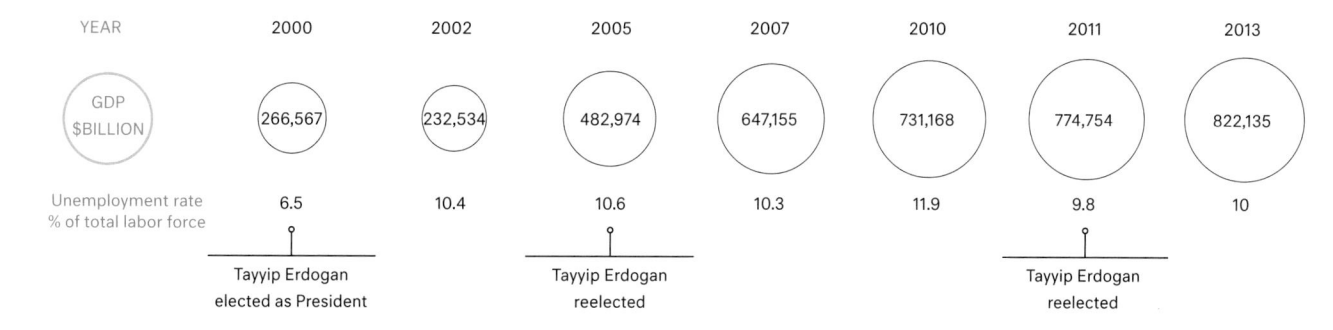

YEAR	2000	2002	2005	2007	2010	2011	2013
GDP $BILLION	266,567	232,534	482,974	647,155	731,168	774,754	822,135
Unemployment rate % of total labor force	6.5	10.4	10.6	10.3	11.9	9.8	10

Tayyip Erdogan elected as President (2002)
Tayyip Erdogan reelected (2007)
Tayyip Erdogan reelected (2011)

Timeline Taksim and Gezi[III]

5/27/2013: Small group of the "Right to the city" association assembles in Gezi Park to protest against shopping mall planned on site. Bulldozers are forced to stop work, as some protesters stay in tents overnight. Police use tear gas to clear the park.

5/28/2013: Police wake protesters up at 5:00 in morning with tear gas while setting fire to tents. Bulldozers return, and police resume use of tear gas to disperse protesters. Two members of Parliament position themselves in front of bulldozers, leading to a further stop in work.

5/29/2013: Several hundred people assemble, creating small festival with music and calm atmosphere. Official announcement: "Whatever you do, we have decided, and we will go on as planned."

5/31/2013: Between 5,000 and 10,000 people gather in park during day. Police make second attempt to raid park by waking protesters at 5:00 with tear gas and setting fire to tents. During approx. 40-hour fight between police and protesters, police exhaust their tear gas supplies, forcing them to order in more from neighboring counties. "We will build artillery barracks, it can either be a shopping mall or a museum." "No matter what you do, we have made our decision and we will execute it." Approx. 40,000 people gather in Istanbul neighborhoods and walk toward Gezi Park. Police barricade park and close down all routes toward Taksim Square.

6/11/2013: Police carry out an violent intervention in Taksim Square, ending a 11 day nonviolent occupation. Clashes between the police and demonstrators throughout the day. In the evening the police enter Gezi Park with tear gas, plastic bullets and water cannons.

6/23/2013: Almost 2.5 million people have taken part in demonstrations in 79 of Turkey's 81 provinces the Ministry of the Interior reports.

240 Contested Sites

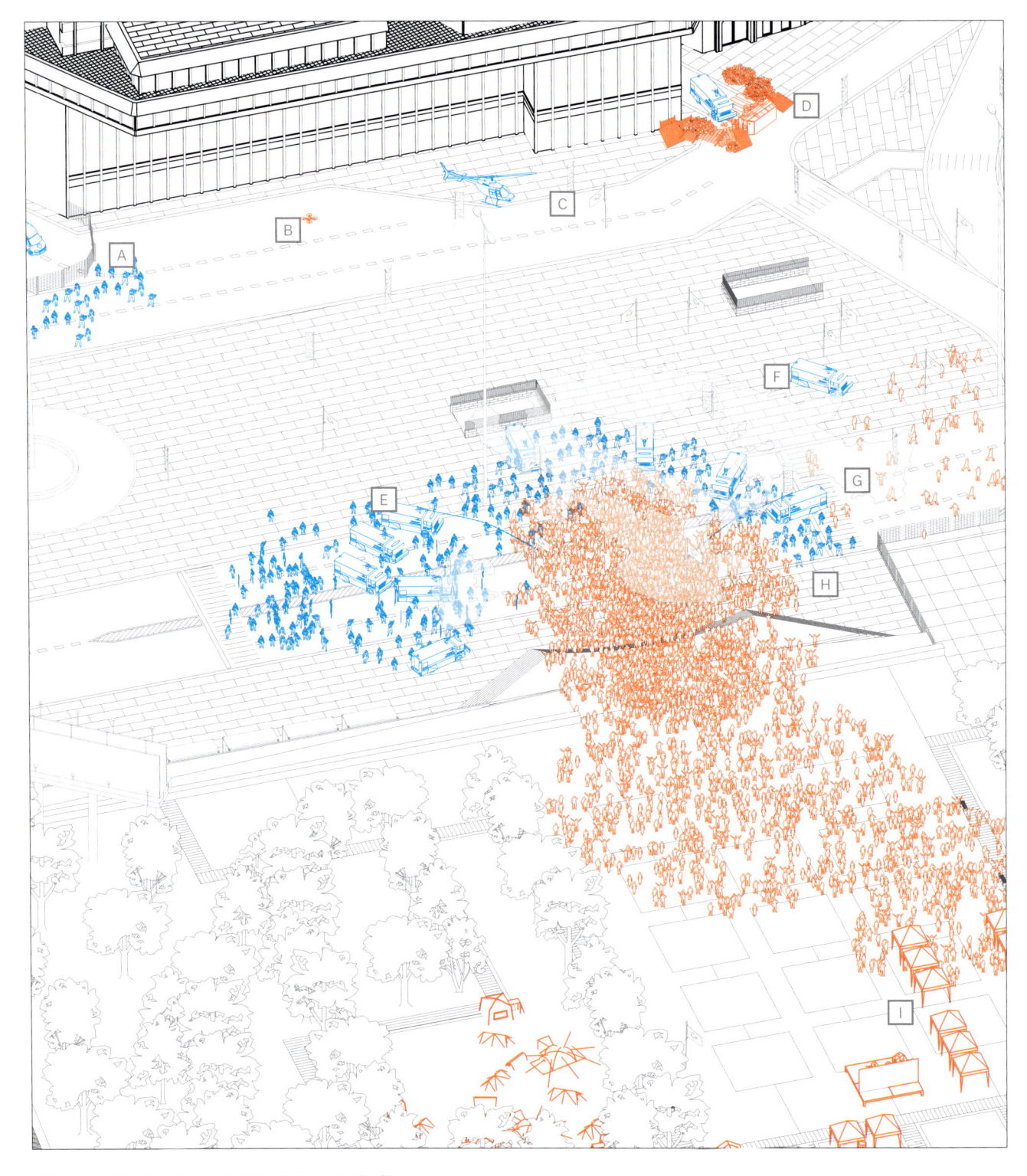

THE POLICE RECLAIM TAKSIM SQUARE, 6/11/2013

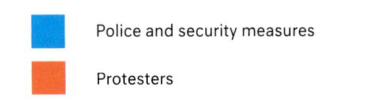

- ■ Police and security measures
- ■ Protesters
- A Police blocking ambulance from entering
- B Protesters use drones for documentation.
- C Tear gas dropped from helicopters
- D TOMA (Toplumsal Olaylara Müdahale Aracı/ Intervention Vehicle to Social Incidents) with plow to ram barricades
- E Water with CS (tear) gas solution
- F TOMA riot-contol vehicle
- G Tear gas
- H Police equipped with shields and softguns
- I Protesters camp inside Gezi Park

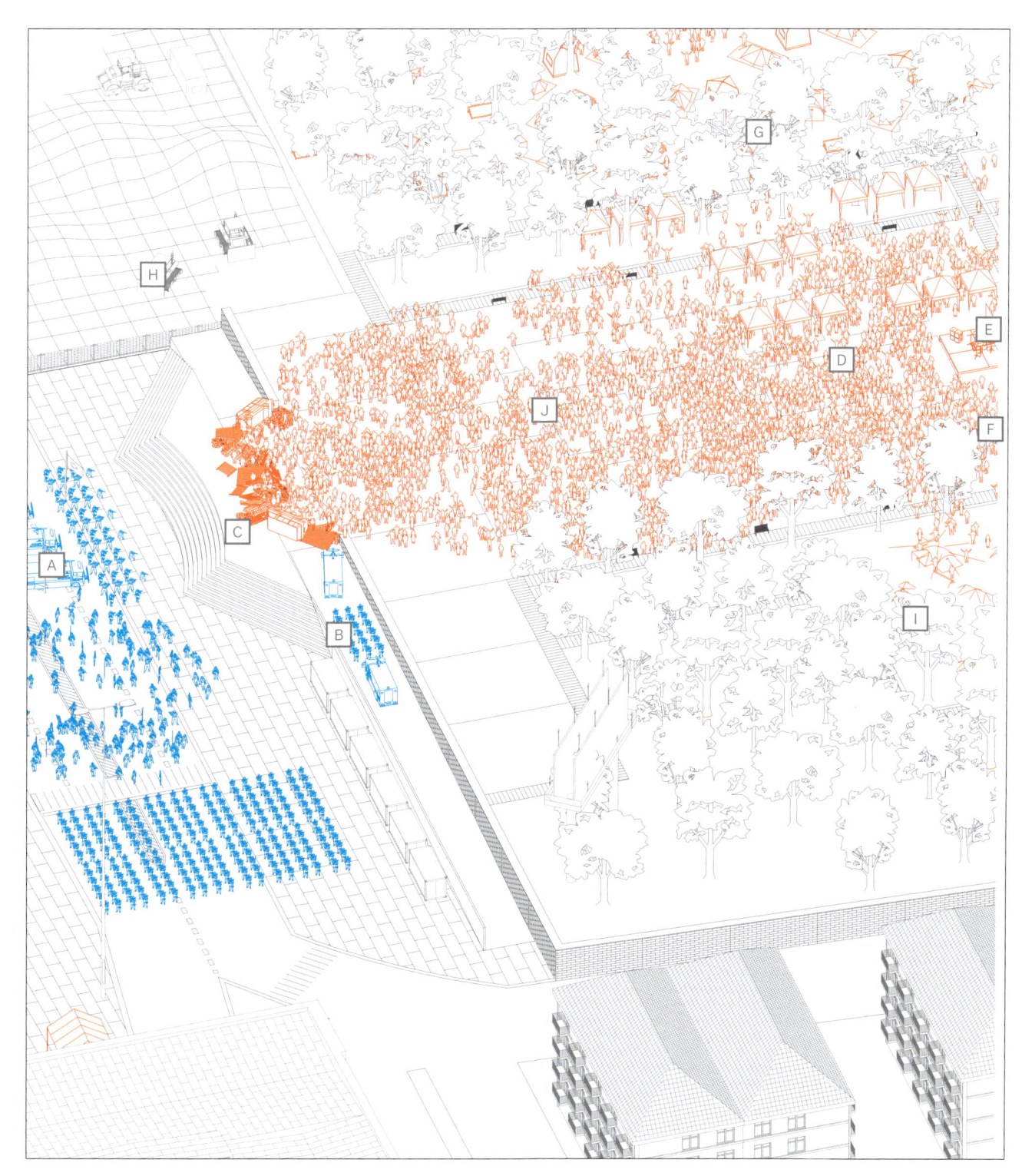

PROTESTERS BARRICADE THEMSELVES INSIDE GEZI PARK, 6/11/2013

A	Police advancing	E	Social media tent	I	Police setting fire to protesters tents
B	TOMA	F	Stage	J	Broadcast blackouts of Turkish mainstream media and suspected blocking of social media sites by the government
C	Barricade	G	Camp		
D	Medical center	H	Construction site of proposed shopping mall		

**CONFRONTATIONS
MOVE TO THE STREETS**

■ Police and security measures

■ Protesters

IFTAR MEAL
August 6, 2013

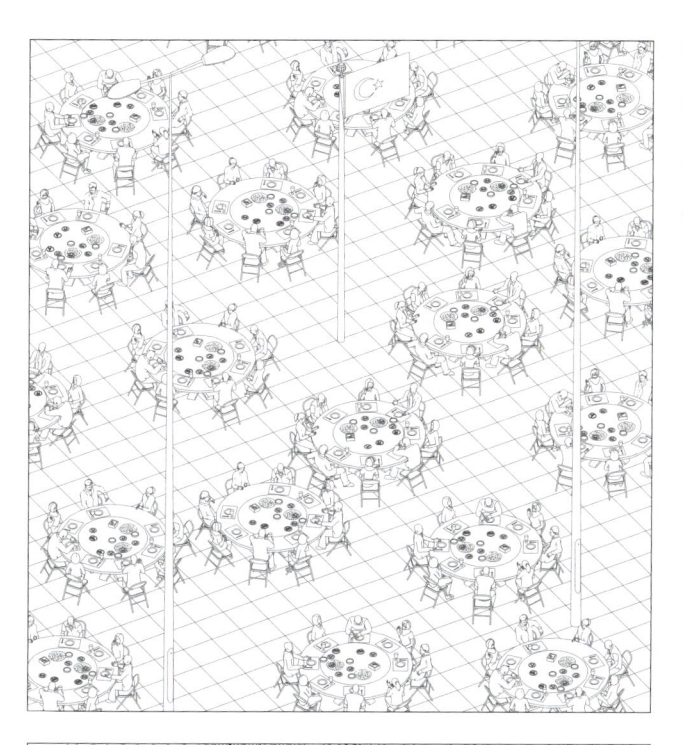

On August 6, 2013, as a three-week closure of Gezi Park was soon to be relaxed, rumors circulated concerning the protester groups' plans to arrange an Iftar meal – the evening meal during the Ramadan daytime fasting period – in Gezi Park. In response, the government closed down the park again, arranging their own meal in the adjacent Taksim Square – largely for members and associates of the ruling AKP party.

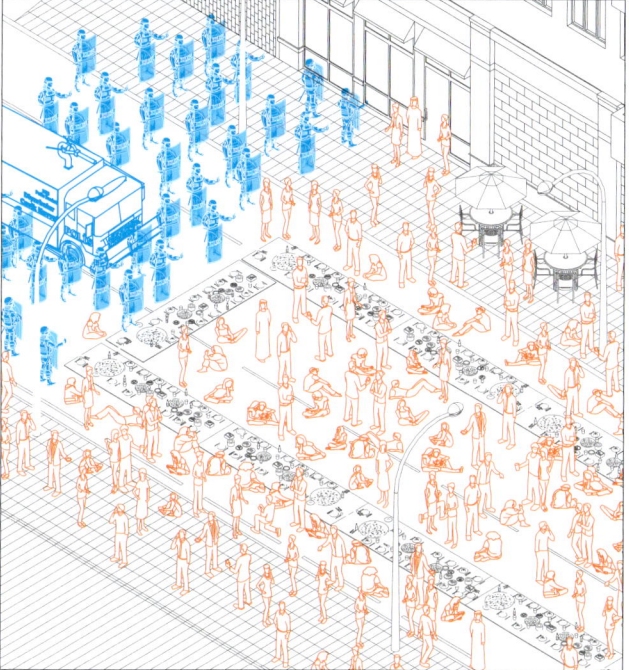

Approximately 300 meters away, surrounded by police with TOMAs (crowd control vehicles with water cannons), former Gezi Park protesters set up their own one-kilometer-long dinner service in the streets.[61]

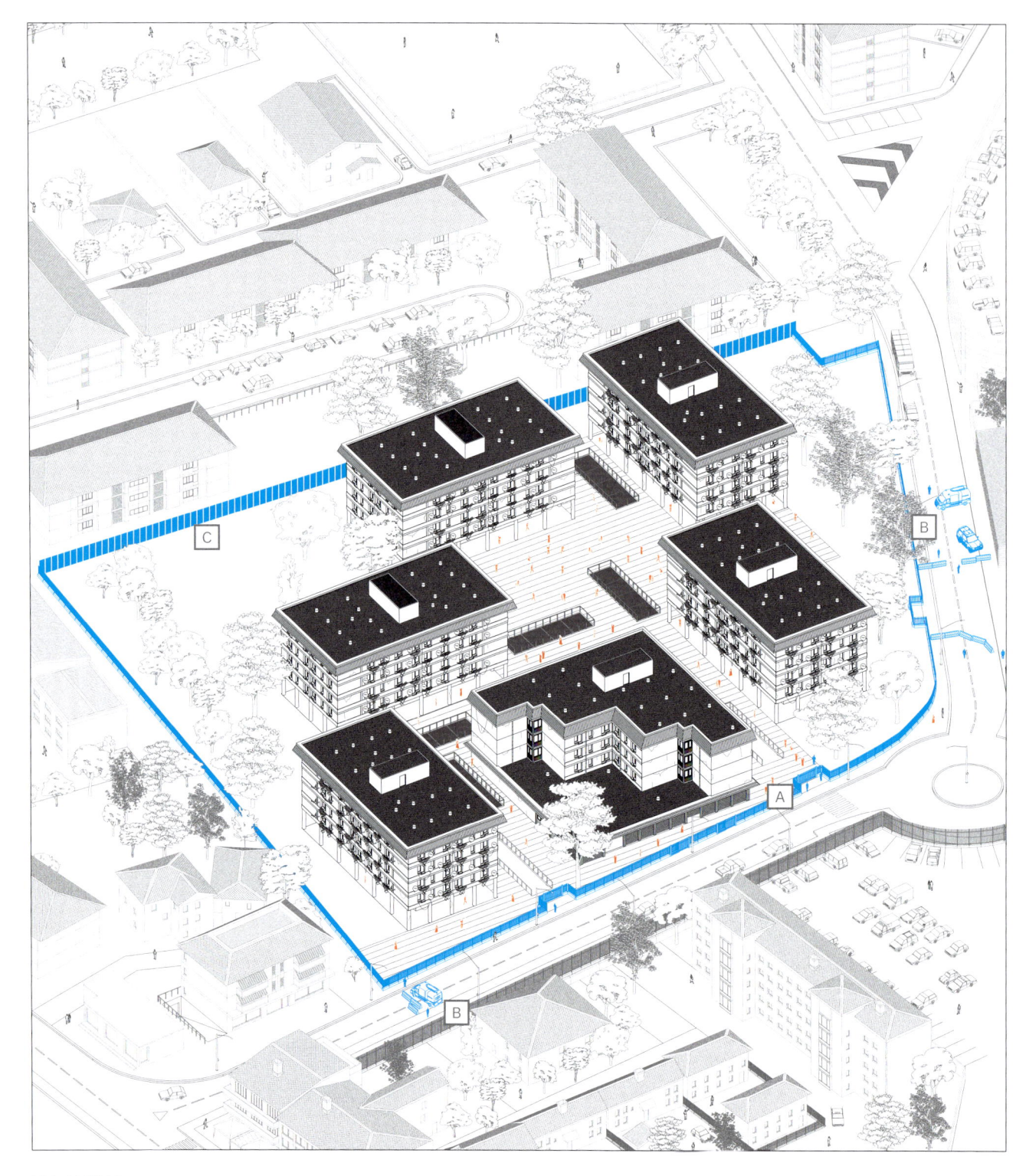

VIA ANELLI

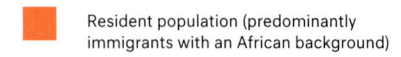

- Resident population (predominantly immigrants with an African background)
- Security measures

A 3–4 carabinieri searching in- and outgoing inhabitants of the compound.
B Jersey barriers block Via Anelli.
C Steel wall, 3 meters high × 85 meters long

PADUA, ITALY
Via Anelli Wall, 2006

45° 24′ 38.9052″ N
11° 54′ 13.7448″ E

The Serenissima housing estate in the suburbs of Padua consists of 273 apartments units within a six-block housing complex. It was constructed as future student housing by the University of Padua in the 1970s – a time when the university planned to relocate to the area. With a change in the university's plans however, the apartments were sold on the private market. In the 1990s, as original owners vacated the property, a predominantly migrant population began renting apartments in the complex. Complaints addressing overcrowding, drug dealing, and prostitution later emerged, lodged by residents of the surrounding middle-class neighborhood. According to Guardian journalist Barbara McMahon, "Six, seven or eight immigrants shared each space and slept in shifts to reduce the rent even further. Unable to work legally, and with little money, the new arrivals hung around with nothing to do. Petty crime flourished and prostitutes and drug dealers targeted the area. Italians who couldn't afford to move out became too scared to open their doors at night."[62] Following a violent clash between rival Moroccan and Nigerian gangs in July 2006, which was broken up with police tear gas, the municipality erected a 3-meter-high steel wall around the estate with a police checkpoint screening incoming and outgoing persons. Flavio Zanonato, the mayor who commissioned the wall, would go on to argue: "It's not an instrument of segregation, we just want to limit the activity of the drug pushers here. This isn't a wall in Palestine. It's just something that's harder for drug dealers to jump over."[63] Critics, in contrast, referred to it as "obscene and racist," and as a form of "segregation, like the concentration camps or the Jewish ghettos."[64]

By July 2007 all residents of Via Anelli had been relocated and geographically dispersed around the city to avoid formation of a new ghetto. The complex was to be demolished and replaced with luxury condominiums; however, these plans remain on hold due to the economic situation. The wall remains.[65]

Location

Venice
PADUA - Via Anelli
Veneto Region

Inhabitants

1,500 inhabitants
25 police officers

6 blocks
45 apartments/block
273 apartments in total
5.3 inhabitants/apt

Immigration statistics

	Immigrants	Total residents	Ratio Immigrants / total
PADUA[II]	30,933	214,198	14%
VENETO[I]	481,000	4,938,000	9.7%
ITALY[I]	4,235,000	60,636,000	6.9%
SPAIN[IV]	5,598,691	46,600,000	12%

[III]
Morocco	13.6%
Romania	13.4%
Albania	10.4%
Serbia and Montenegro	6.7%
China	5.1%
Macedonia	4.3%
Other countries	46.5%

246 Contested Sites

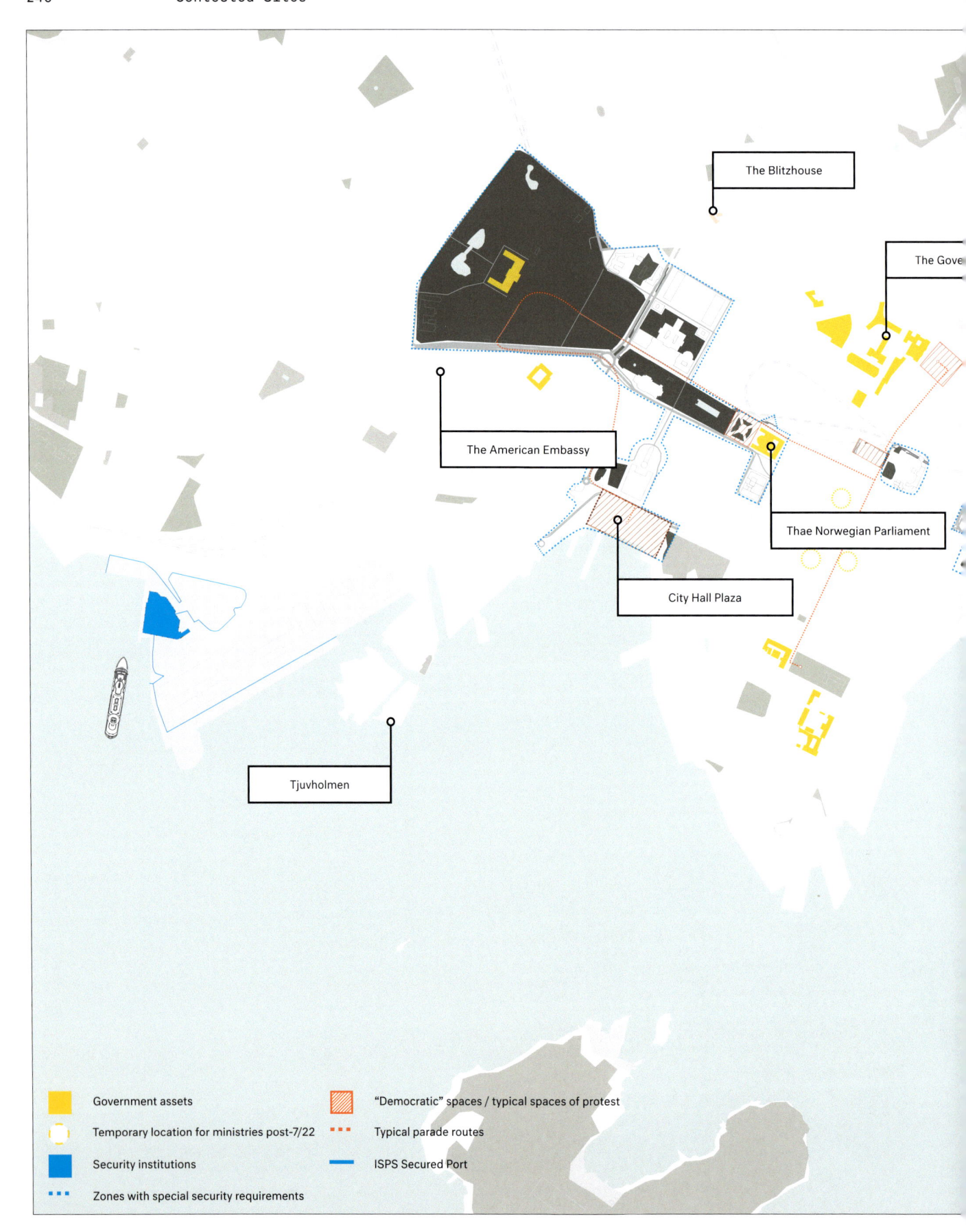

The Blitzhouse

The Gove[rnment]

The American Embassy

Thae Norwegian Parliament

City Hall Plaza

Tjuvholmen

- Government assets
- Temporary location for ministries post-7/22
- Security institutions
- Zones with special security requirements
- "Democratic" spaces / typical spaces of protest
- Typical parade routes
- ISPS Secured Port

OSLO, NORWAY

Ruled first by the Danish and then the Swedish thrones, Norway passed its constitution in 1814 but did not gain full independence until 1905. Inspired by the US Constitution (1789) and France's Declaration of the Rights of Man (1789), the Constitution of Norway was at the time considered to be one of the most liberal or radically democratic constitutions in the world granting separation of executive, legislative, and judicial power; freedom of speech and protection against unreasonable searches and seizures.

Today Norway is a part of the Schengen Area and NATO but it is still outside the European Union. The state-owned oil industry fuels the Norwegian economy and the government pension fund Global supports the delivery of public services and the maintenance of a welfare state.[66] The nation prides itself on its reputation as an international peacemaker.

Oslo, the capital and most populous city of Norway, has a municipal population of 658,000, and a wider urban population of 942,000. As one of the fastest-growing cities in Europe, it has an increasingly diverse citizenry with approximately 30 percent of Oslo's population being immigrants, or born to immigrants.

Tjuvholmen Residential Area

59° 54′ 22.7808″ N
10° 43′ 11.2872″ E

Tjuvholmen is a former prisoner execution islet dating back to the 1600s. In 2003 the 51-acre site was sold by the Port of Oslo to private developers as part of the Fjord City urban renewal program.[67] Completed in 2014, the new area consists largely of privately owned high-end apartments, commercial space, and the Renzo Piano–designed Astrup Fearnley Museum of Modern Art. In July 2014 conflicts emerged between residents of the area and members of the public attempting to enjoy an evening swim. Tjuvholmen Drift AS, the private company responsible for safety and technical operations in the area, posted restrictions prohibiting swimming and leisure activities at the outer pier after 8 p.m.[68] Security guards were hired and cordons were set up to prevent the public from using the beach.[69] Although the area is privately owned, there are no official regulations for timed closures, as a number of streets, squares, leisure, and recreation areas are zoned for public use, including part of the larger public harbor esplanade.

— Security measures

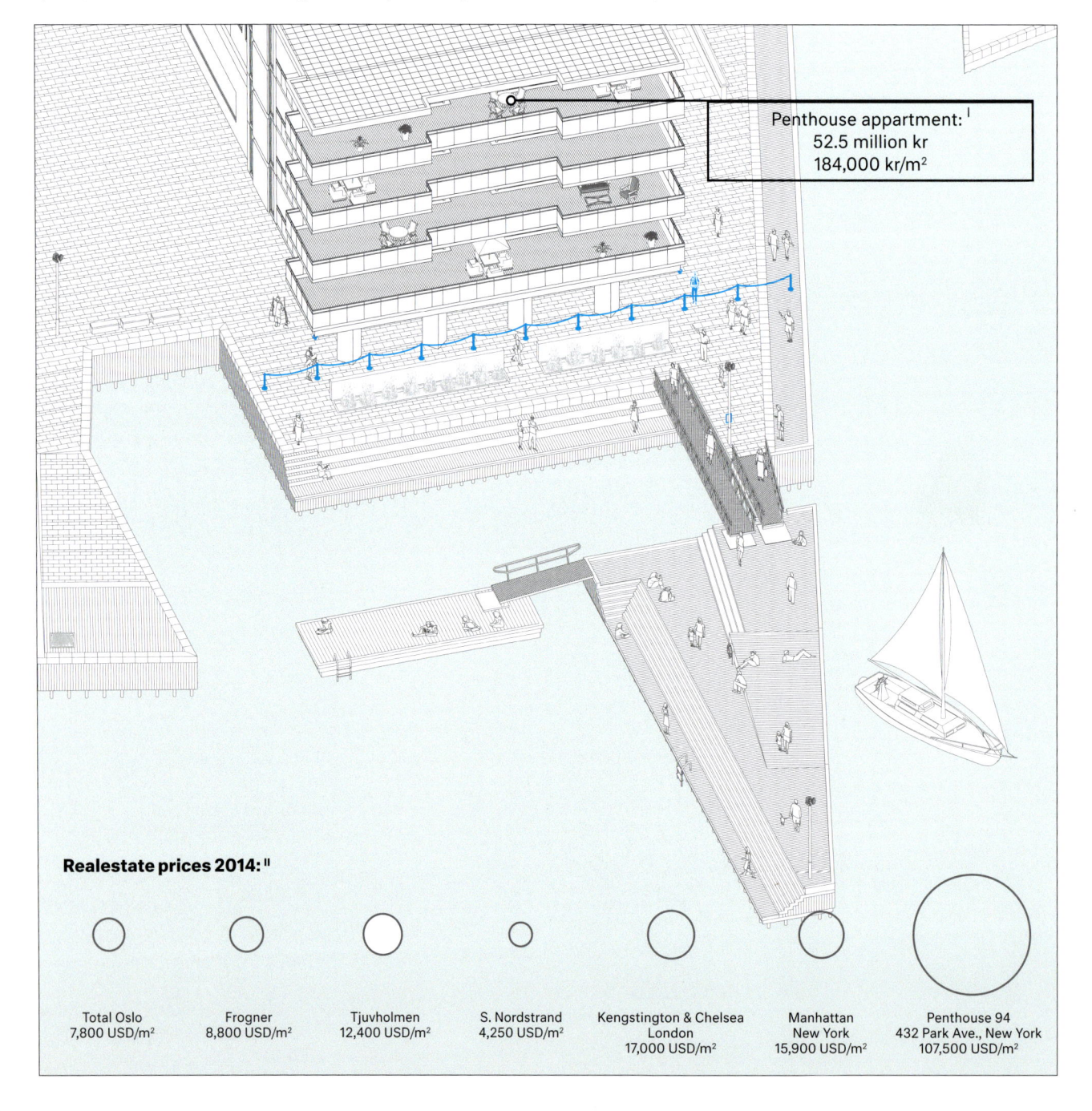

Penthouse appartment: [I]
52.5 million kr
184,000 kr/m²

Realestate prices 2014: [II]

Total Oslo	Frogner	Tjuvholmen	S. Nordstrand	Kengstington & Chelsea London	Manhattan New York	Penthouse 94 432 Park Ave., New York
7,800 USD/m²	8,800 USD/m²	12,400 USD/m²	4,250 USD/m²	17,000 USD/m²	15,900 USD/m²	107,500 USD/m²

Blitz and the Blitzhouse

59° 55′ 6.5820″ N
10° 44′ 14.9784″ E

Blitz is a youth community that emerged in 1982 from a group of mostly left-wing activists, punks, anarchists, socialists, and communists.[70] Based in the so-called Blitz House in central Oslo, the group became known for its political demonstrations during the 1980s and 1990s which occasionally developed into street battles with police, leading in some cases to injuries on both sides and a number of arrests.[71] The building itself would become increasingly fort-like over this time. Proposals for the group's eviction from the building and for the demolition of the Blitz House would lead to further actions by Blitz and their supporters. After lengthy negotiations however, an agreement between the City Council and the Church City Mission was made in 2004, allowing Blitz to remain in the building. Today it contains a café, information shop with political reading material and music, a local radio station, rehearsal rooms for bands, a women's cultural center, and a rock club.[72]

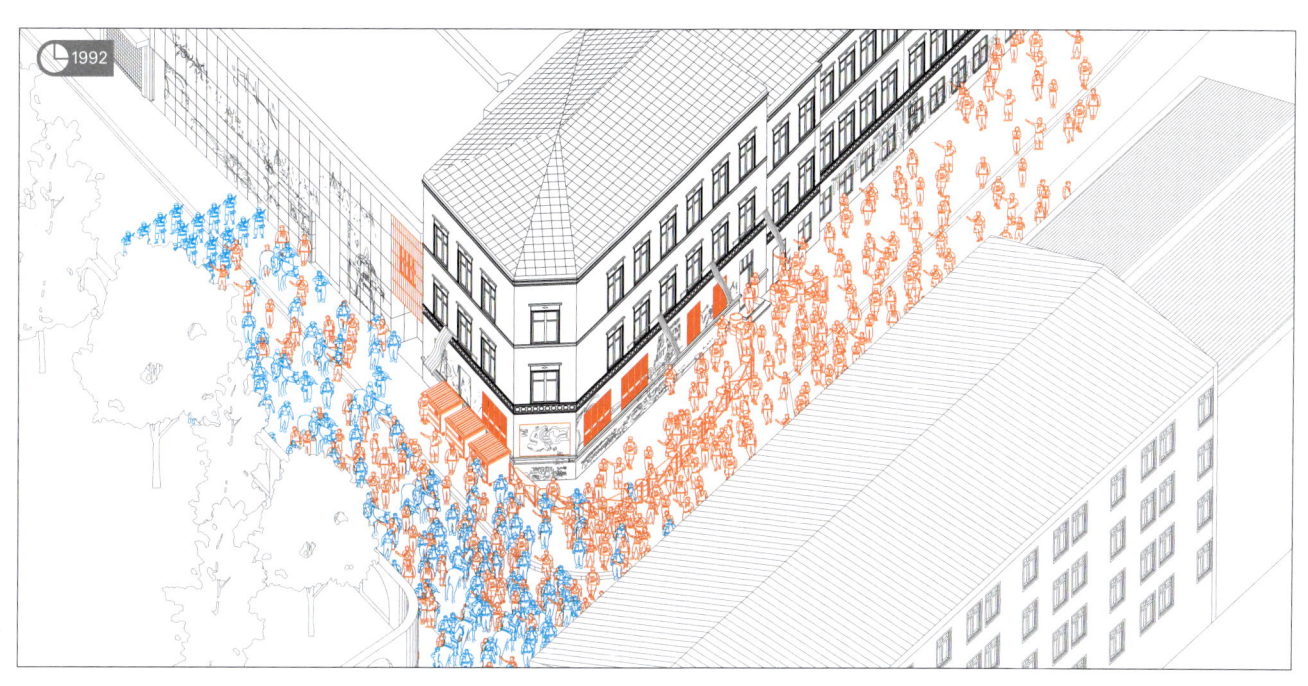

— Police
— Protesters

The American Embassy

59° 54′ 54.5400″ N
10° 43′ 27.1632″ E

The American Embassy in Oslo has been located on the edge of the Royal Palace Park since 1959, in an attractive location in the center of Oslo. The embassy building was originally designed to function as both a cultural center and an embassy, but increased threat levels led to new security measures and demands, altering the appearance and use of the building.[73]

The location of the current embassy contributes to congestion in the city center and no longer meets current American security requirements. As with many other American embassies worldwide, the security operations around these complexes produces a form of "security theater" which can be disruptive of everyday life in the surrounding neighborhoods. In 2012 for example, a suspected bomb at the Oslo embassy resulted in the evacuation of central city spaces and transport hubs and froze much of city life in central Oslo for half a day.

The embassy is in the process of being relocated to a suburban area outside the city center,[74] where a range of security measures are intended to be disguised within a so-called traditional Norwegian building design.[75]

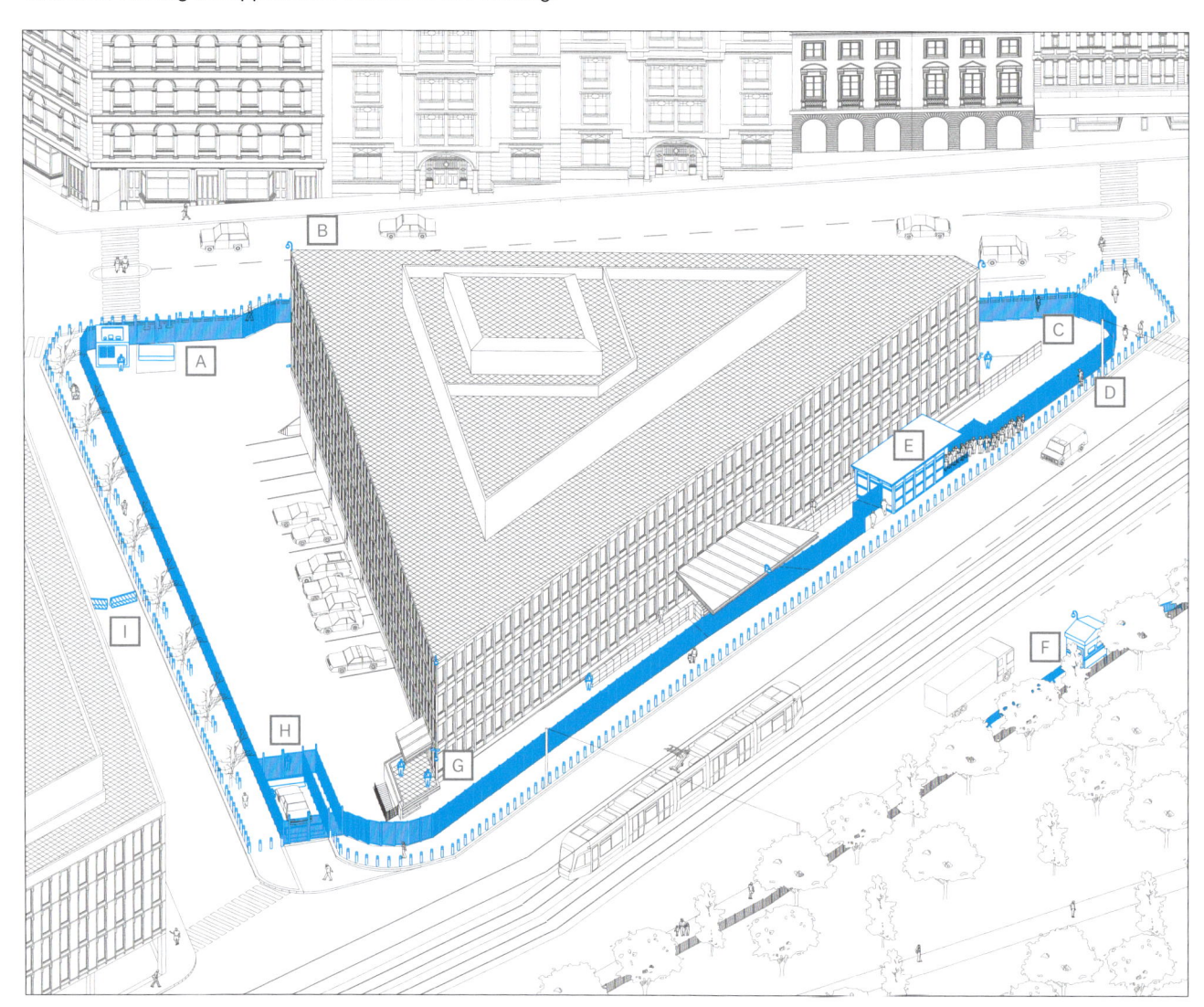

THE AMERICAN EMBASSY

- Security measures
- A Guarded vehicle checkpoint
- B CCTV on all roof corners
- C 2.5m high steel fence
- D Bollards
- E Visitors security checkpoint
- F 24h police watchtower
- G 24h private securty force
- H Vehicle checkpoint
- I Jersey barricades

The Norwegian Parliament

59° 54′ 46.9476″ N
10° 44′ 24.2088″ E

The Norwegian Parliament has historically been a building completely open to the public and without significant security measures. Following the July 22, 2011, attack however, politicians and security experts requested a hardening of both the outer perimeter and access control to the building. Since 2013 a movable barrier has sealed off the street behind the Parliament, while a standoff distance from the facade facing Karl Johan Street has been introduced through the installation of a series of large, metal flower planters.[76]

The square in front of the Parliament, considered one of the most important spaces for public demonstration, is the site of numerous events each year. An example depicted here is an Israeli-Palestinian demonstration that took place in 2013 in which police were concerned about a possible confrontation between the pro-Israel demonstrators inside a line of barricades with pro-Palestinian protesters outside.[77] On a day-to-day basis there are no fences or parked police cars surrounding the park, which is open to the general public.

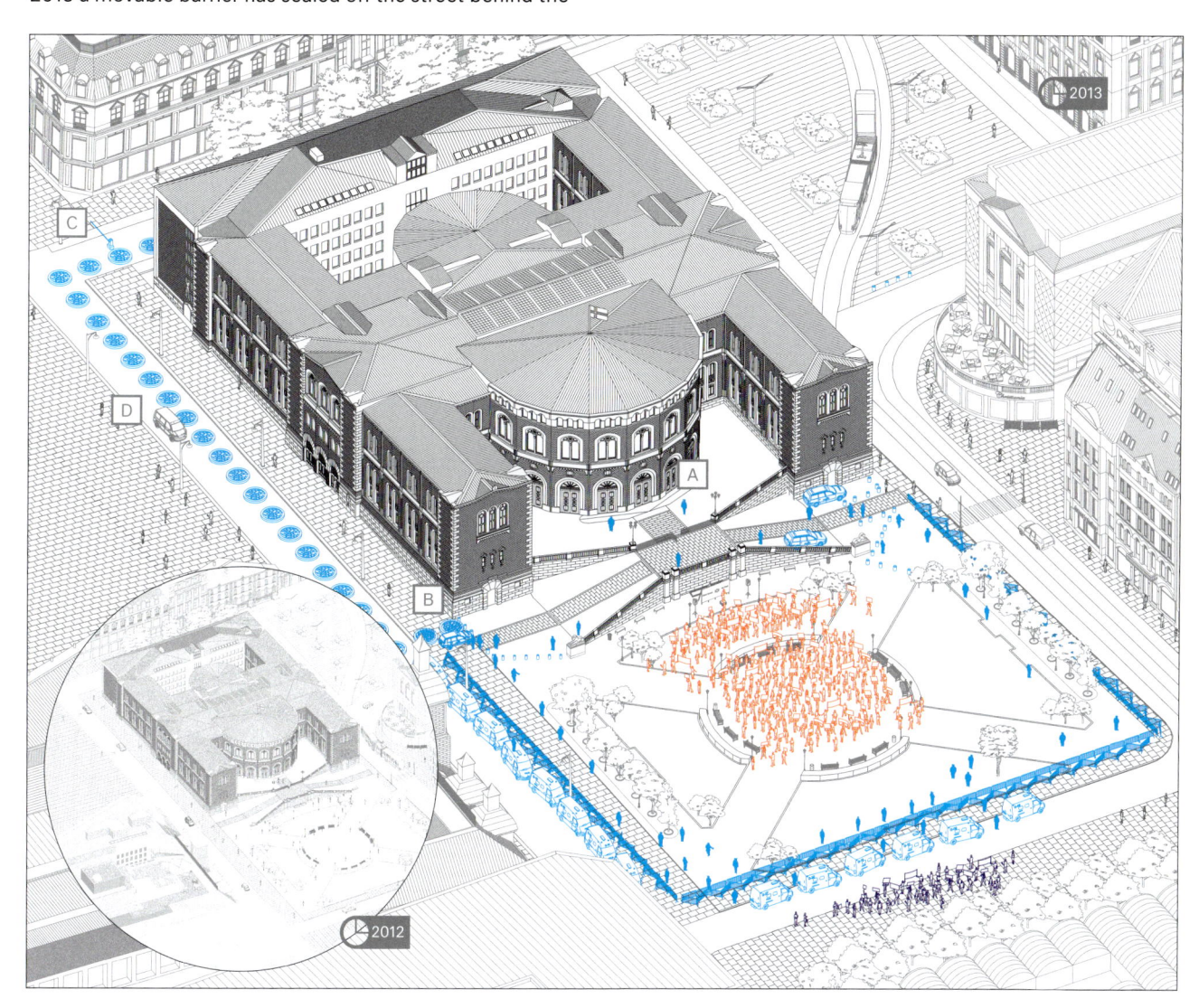

PRO-ISRAEL DEMONSTRATION 11.08.2013

- Security measures
- Pro-Israel Protesters
- Pro-Palestine protesters

A Main entrance
B Controlled vehicle barrier
C Retractable bollards
D Mobile flower pot vehicle barrier

252　　　　　　　Contested Sites

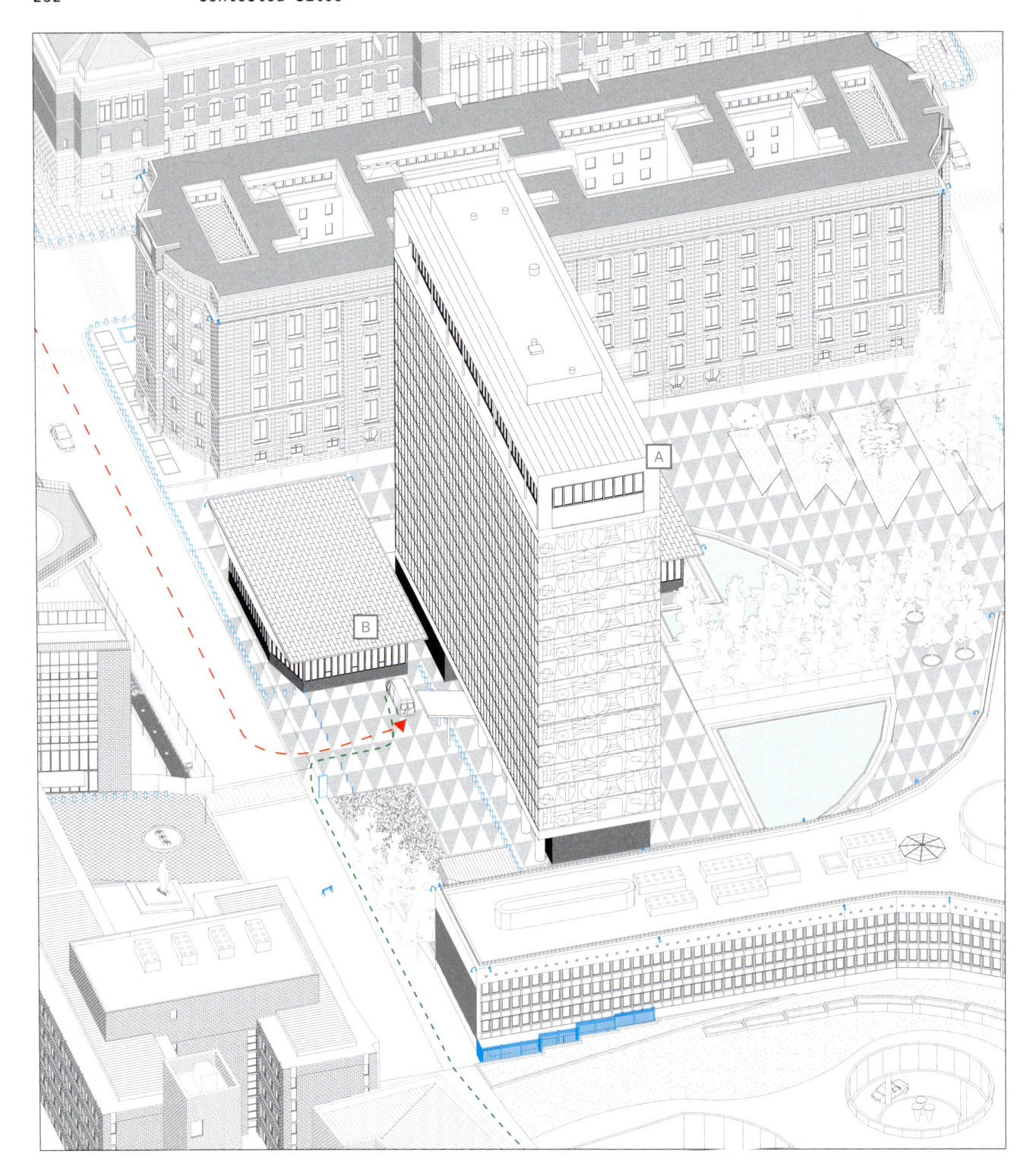

GOVERNMENT QUARTER, OSLO

- A　Høyblokken, the Prime Minister's Office
- B　Volkswagen Crafter carrying improvised bomb
- ▰ ▰ ▰　Van path
- ▰ ▰ ▰　Terrorist on foot

Government Quarter

59° 54' 55.0800" N
10° 44' 45.5676" E

A 2004 report by the National Police Directorate identified 197 points of security concern in the Oslo Government Quarter, including one concern addressing the possibility for a vehicle to park directly in front of the H-Block building containing the prime minister's office.[78] According to the Ministry of Local Government and Modernization, most of these issues had been addressed before July 22, 2011, with the exception of one major task: the control of vehicle access in the streets of the quarter.[79]

On July 22, 2011, Norwegian right-wing extremist Anders Breivik parked a white van with a home-made fertilizer bomb in front of the main entrance of the H-Block. Minutes later the bomb exploded, killing 8 and injuring 209 people and severely damaging several government office buildings.[80] Breivik would go on to murder 68 and injure 110 persons on the island of Utøya. In the aftermath of the Government Quarter bombing, several reports criticized the government for not preventing the attack.

Blast radius

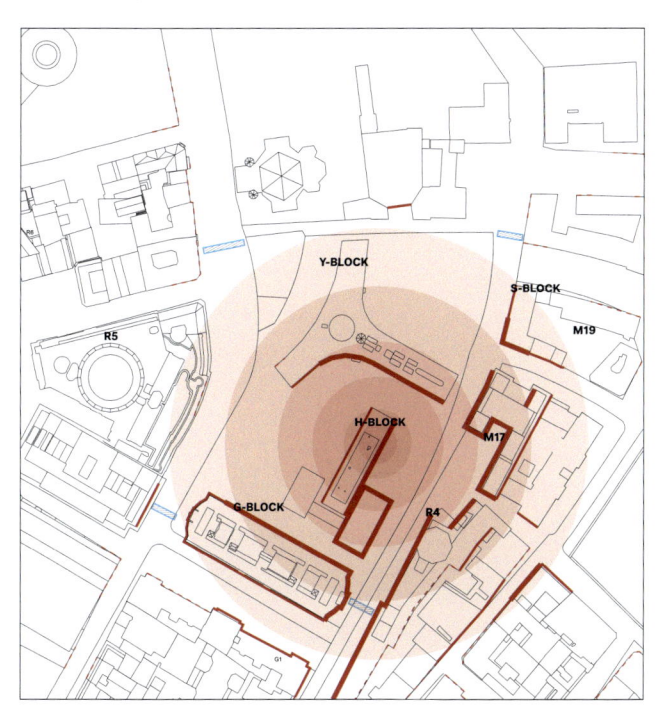

Damage assessment

Y-Block
Built:	1970
Load-bearing:	Cast in situ concrete
Structural damage:	NO
Facade:	Natural concrete, teak frames
Damage:	Windows, internal walls and ceilings

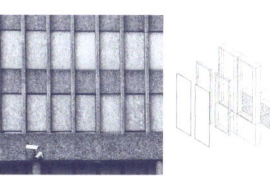

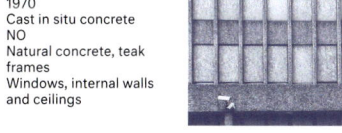

G1
Built:	1940
Load-bearing:	Cast in situ concrete
Structural damage:	NO
Facade:	Stone facade panels
Damage:	Windows

R6
Built:	2011
Load-bearing:	Cast in situ concrete
Structural damage:	NO
Facade:	Aluminum
Damage:	NO

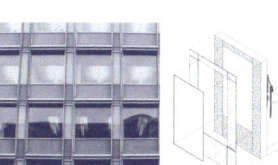

R5
Built:	1996
Load-bearing:	Cast in situ concrete
Structural damage:	NO
Facade:	Granite, marble, zinc, aluminum
Damage:	Minor

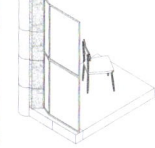

S-Block
Built:	1978
Load-bearing:	Cast in situ concrete
Structural damage:	NO
Facade:	Brick
Damage:	Windows, internal walls and ceilings

R4+M17
Built:	1988
Load-bearing:	Prefab concrete, reinforced core
Structural damage:	NO
Facade:	Brick, aluminum panels
Damage:	Windows, internal walls and ceilings

M19
Built:	1866
Load-bearing:	Bricks
Structural damage:	NO
Facade:	Plastered bricks
Damage:	Windows, roof

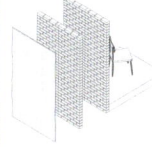

G-Block
Built:	1904/1978
Load-bearing:	Bricks
Structural damage:	YES
Facade:	Granite
Damage:	Newer steel columns were skewed

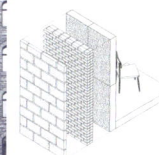

H-Block
Built:	1958/1990
Load-bearing:	Cast in situ concrete
Structural damage:	NO
Facade:	Natural concrete, teak frames
Damage:	Windows, internal walls and ceilings

254   Contested Sites

SATELLITE MINISTRIES AND SECURITY ZONES

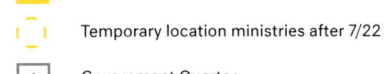

- 🟨 Government assets
- ⬚ Temporary location ministries after 7/22
- A Government Quarter
- B Ministry of Forreign Affairs
- C Ministry of Defense
- D Ministry of Justice
- E American Embassy
- — Zones with permanent security measures
- ▨ Zones with temporary security measures
- ⋯ Zones with special security requirements
- ■ Security institutions

1 KM / 1 MILE

Temporary Security Measures

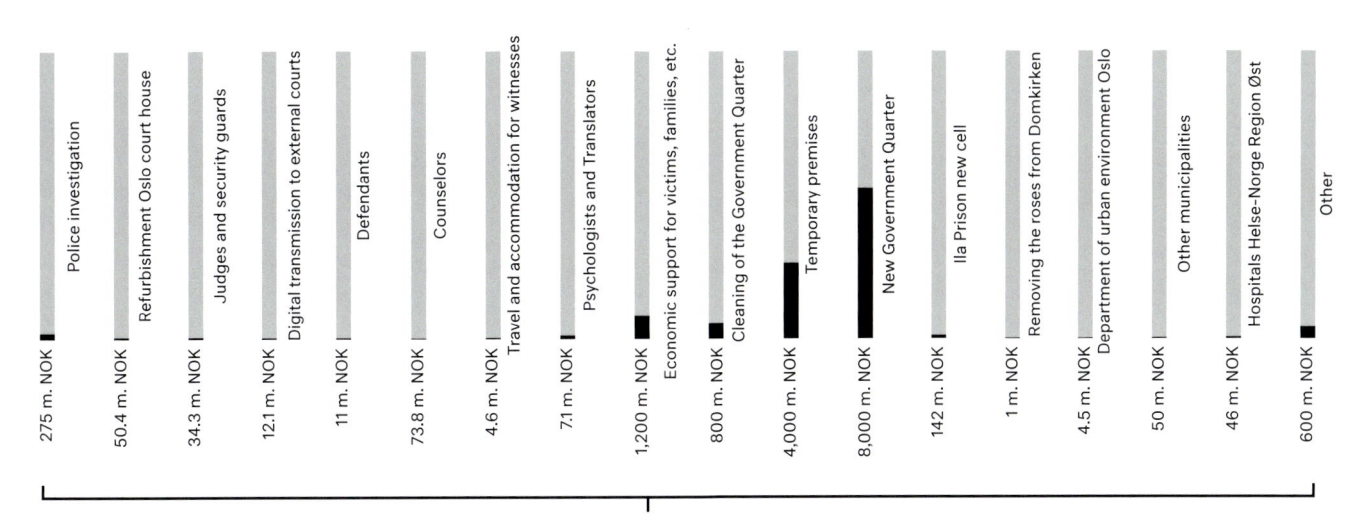

Police investigation	275 m. NOK
Refurbishment Oslo court house	50.4 m. NOK
Judges and security guards	34.3 m. NOK
Digital transmission to external courts	12.1 m. NOK
Defendants	11 m. NOK
Counselors	73.8 m. NOK
Travel and accommodation for witnesses	4.6 m. NOK
Psychologists and Translators	7.1 m. NOK
Economic support for victims, families, etc.	1,200 m. NOK
Cleaning of the Government Quarter	800 m. NOK
Temporary premises	4,000 m. NOK
New Government Quarter	8,000 m. NOK
Ila Prison new cell	142 m. NOK
Removing the roses from Domkirken	1 m. NOK
Department of urban environment Oslo	4.5 m. NOK
Other municipalities	50 m. NOK
Hospitals Helse-Norge Region Øst	46 m. NOK
Other	600 m. NOK

15,312,100,000 NOK (2013 CURRENCY)[i]

ESTIMATED TOTAL COST OF 7/22/2011

With a significant number of government buildings from the Government Quarter either destroyed or severely damaged from the terror attack, the government was forced to relocate many of its offices. Buildings relocated to are mostly existing nongovernmental buildings with insufficient security measures in place. These buildings have been retrofitted to new security standards inside and out with bomb-resistant laminated glass. The most visible transformations are in the form of temporary concrete barriers and roadblocks spread around the city. While obviously unsightly and problematic, according to one security advisor: "Temporary is good, because you can remove it. It's when these temporary measures become permanent we have a problem."

In the project description for the new Government Quarter, one of five key focus points will be security – opening up questions as to how security will be addressed in the new setting.[81]

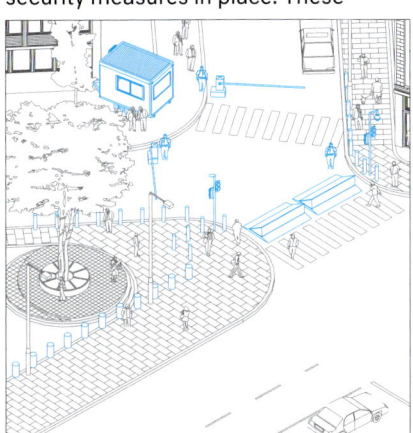

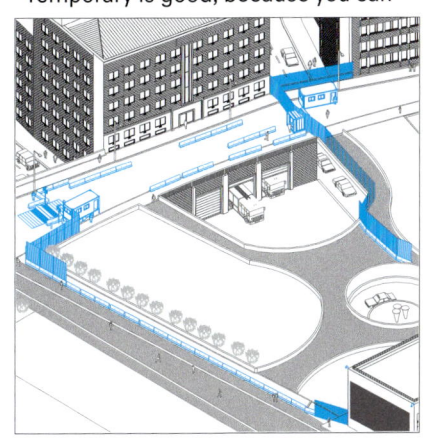

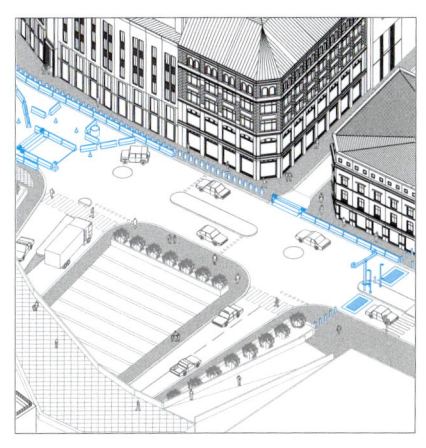

Contested Sites

City Hall Plaza

59° 54′ 40.3452″ N
10° 43′ 58.6236″ E

Communal memorial in aftermath of Utøya shooting and Government Quarter bombing

A flower march event was held three days after the Oslo attacks with an estimated 100,000 people gathered outside Oslo City Hall.[82] The then prime minister, Jens Stoltenberg, said in his speech that the country would "stand firm in defending our values" of an "open, tolerant and inclusive society." "The Norwegian response to violence is more democracy, more openness and greater political participation." "We will not let fear break us! [...] The strongest weapon in the world – that is freedom of expression and democracy." He called the gathering a "march for democracy, a march for tolerance, a march for unity."[83]

OSLO, NORWAY
Visited November 12, 2014, and October 14, 2013

1. Contested bathing area, Tjuvholmen

2. Blitz House exterior

3. Retractable vehicle barrier at the Tjuvholmen residential area

4. Facade with security elements as reminder of Blitz's more conflictual past

Oslo, Norway

Photo Essay

5. Layered outer perimeter of Government Quarter, with Jersey barriers outside pre-2011 bollards

6. 2011 bomb blast area repaired, and under discussion for redevelopment

7. Checkpoint entry to damaged Government Quarter

8. Temporary vehicle barriers during the redevelopment of the Government Quarter

Oslo, Norway

Interview:
Léopold Lambert

Léopold Lambert is the editor in chief of *The Funambulist Magazine* and blog, and its podcast *Archipelago* (http://thefunambulist.net/). His work addressing space and the body traverses different fields, such as history, philosophy, and political theory while maintaining the spatial focus of an architect and urbanist. Lambert has been writing extensively about the militarization of architecture and cities and its political and spatial consequences.

This interview was conducted by Skype between the editors, situated in New York and Bergen, and Lambert in Paris.

Editors: One of the main discussions in this book concerns how public space and the right to the city is related to the freedom of expression, civil rights, and democracy. In the twenty-first century democratic movements have emerged in a number of nations, and cities and public space have been the arenas where democratic processes have taken place. If you were to briefly define the word *freedom*, how would you describe it? And how does that definition encompass people, buildings, and territories?

LL: I have a suspicion to the notion of freedom – I guess because it was placed on too many ideological flags throughout history with consequences that we are all aware of. I would prefer to think of a term that is less charged with positive value. Freedom is almost like an undiscussable value, so instead I would introduce the term of *power*, which is less immediately positive or negative. The term is less individualized than the question of freedom, and it implies a relation between bodies. And this relation is precisely what I am very interested in, relations of power and the way people form a society through these relations, and how buildings and territories are emerging from these relations of power. I am not inventing anything here, the last decades of political philosophy have been built on that, so when we design buildings, when we design spaces or intervene in territories, we are very much triggering or modifying new forms of power relationships. My intuition is that the less we think about it, the more we tend to reinforce the dominant relationship of power, and the more we think about it, the more we will have maybe a little chance to influence it toward our own political agenda.

Editors: Another central discussion in the book revolves around physical security – how security architecture affects space and how spaces of securitization operate. Security has emerged as a huge industry, which has, according to some, tended to address the concerns of particular segments of society. It is in some cases directed toward securing those groups from actual or imagined threats from those with more limited access to resources, or those otherwise critical of the status quo: radicals, eccentrics, extremists, terrorists, etc. Architecture can be used as one such instrument in the securing of buildings, people, or economic assets. If you were to briefly define the word *security* how would you describe it? And how does that definition encompass people, buildings, and territories from your perspective?

LL: I am OK to consider the word *security* because security is primarily a form of negotiation, and therefore it is very much involved in the relation I was describing. It necessarily involves a form of otherness. It is interesting because through this otherness we can put an entire imaginary. In the times we are in right now in Europe, or in the Western world in general, we can see that there is a very fearful imaginary of the image of otherness. There is always a form of us and something else. In the discourse of security there always seems to be an absolute schism between this us and this other thing. Most of the time it is not about natural disasters, but about the foreigner, migrants, everything about otherness that feels like a differentiation from oneself. The consequences in terms of architecture are for example what we see very often, what I recently saw in Latin America: All these gated communities and all those securitarian apparatuses that constitute a sort of self-imprisonment by a part of the population – the higher social classes, or even the middle classes. There is a very clear architectural language that corresponds to this securitarian desire that is based on all those fantasies. I use the term *fantasy* in a way that doesn't mean that it does not respond to any forms of real, it is just that it involves an entire production of imaginary, so there are these architectural consequences which are based on fear. It is interesting to see it as a negotiation once again because the more fear, the more you build around you, and the more you imprison yourself. Obviously you can see some very, very comfortable prisons, as an entire class of the people imprison themselves by the fear of the otherness.

Editors: For you as an architect, why is it important to discuss the law and the judicial system?

LL: I keep thinking of the law as diagrammatic lines that organize the body within space, as I was saying about architecture, and architecture as the materiality of these lines enforcing the diagram of the law upon bodies in the material world. Which is not to say that the law and architecture are the same thing, I think it is much more interesting than that. Architecture would be a sort of translation of the law into the material world. Again, I realize it is a little bit problematic to think of the law as a nonmaterial thing; maybe that's my own definition of it in relation to architecture. The way architects relate to it, what architects do when they draw a plan, it is not so much about drawing architecture but drawing the law almost, in the sense that the only thing architects do is draw lines and those lines are absolute especially since the profession of architecture has been shifting its means of representation from ink and pencil to the computer. I'm being overly abstract here, but it is quite interesting to think of an architectural drawing, a plan in ink, and the ink having a sort of thickness (we will return to the thickness of the line later), whereas when you draw a line in AutoCAD this line is a mathematical one in a sense that it is an absolute line, it is a line as the mathematicians define a line, which is a relationship between two points without any thickness involved. To me this whole process is a realm of the law; its translation into materiality is a realm of architecture. What's interesting is what is lost and what is being produced in this translation. I think there are some really interesting things that are being produced that we will discuss later.

Editors: In your work you are often referring back to what you call "the thickness of a line" as a concept. Could you explain the phrase and perhaps offer an example of it?

LL: The major differentiations that I see between the diagrammatic of these lines and their translation to architecture is the fact that those lines are acquiring a thickness, which is paradoxical in a geometrical, mathematical point of view. The line is defined by its absence of thickness, but architecture cannot do lines without thickness. What's very interesting about that is that nothing has been thought for the thickness of the line. By definition you cannot think of it when you are thinking of lines. You can only observe it when these lines have become materialized in architecture. Once again I am being a little bit abstract. Some very down-to-earth materialization of these lines is some of the most dreadful. It's not about liberation, it's not about that the law did not think about the thickness of the line, let's all go to the thickness of the line and we will be liberated. It is much more complex.

Editors: Some of the security personnel we have talked to during this project understand fences/walls/ditches not as security measures but rather as different ways of making jurisdictional lines visible (on this side of the fence/wall/barrier one law is present, on the other it is not) — this applies to the architecture of borders both within cities and between nations. These lines vary from being as thin as a fence or a wall, up to a 100-meter-wide no-man's-land that creates an ambiguity as to what jurisdiction one is present in. Is it possible that architectures of security, like fences, could be thought of as lines that demark jurisdictional changes? If so, what takes place when the bodies cross the line in, for example, Melilla or Israel, versus those bodies occupying the space within the thickness of the line?

LL: A very good example is something that happened in 2011 when you had this group of twenty-one Eritrean refugees who tried to migrate to Israel and managed to cross Egypt, and to exit Egypt from the border but never managed to enter Israel. They were de facto trapped in the thickness of the line that separates Egypt from Israel. For a week they were denied food and given a minimal amount of water; one of the women, who was pregnant, miscarried because of that. After that they finally got arrested and deported by Israel. For a week those bodies that were caught within the thickness of the line, a space that was not thought of by the law — that could not have been thought of by the law — were very simply stripped of any form of rights. That is what I am saying. I also thought of the thickness of the line as being William Burroughs's

"I keep thinking of the law as diagrammatic lines that organize the body within space, as I was saying about architecture, and architecture as the materiality of these lines enforcing the diagram of the law upon bodies in the material world."

interzone, a zone of chaos where the law doesn't seem to be very active except maybe by its absence. It is always interesting how the absence of the law produces maybe even more things than the presence of the law. What I mean by this example is that it is not about saying that the thickness of the line is an emancipatory space, it is just a space where the rights have been stripped from the bodies. We should not think of it as a moralistic way, but more look at what those spaces are and we can think of the concept of bare life to describe those bodies. I think this is really the space to look for the relation of law and architecture because there are faults of translation, and I would say that it is why I am interested in the figure of the funambulist, because the funambulist is not liberated from the line — he walks on the line. This figure is very much determined by the line, but you don't find his body on one side or the other of the line that has been organized for him or her but rather subvert this dichotomy of space that the line creates by simply walking on it.

Editors: In a way, it could be the funambulist who has power over the line, in contrast to the Eritrean refugees who are powerless because they are inside the line. There are two ways of relating to the line.

LL: I don't think of the funambulist as a liberated figure. I only think of it as a figure that experiences the line in another way than the line has been created for. Another example I also always give: On November 9, 1989, Berliners did not just cross the wall that had become obsolete — they stood on it. They stood on the thickness of the line that was the wall, and by doing so proved the obsolescence of the wall.

Editors: *Standing on the barricades* is another expression.

LL: The barricade is another interesting figure that I like to look at as well. The barricade is obviously a line as well. It would be ridiculous to say it would escape from what a line is. But it might be a sort of aggregate of a sort of broken line to some degree. I wrote an entire article about how the barricade is a materialization of abject, of the abject and the abjection, what the anthropologist Mary Douglas defines as "the matter out of space." The matter that you cannot reintroduce to the system of production; it has been taken away from it. I thought of this notion of abject because of the way US mayors have been coordinating their action against the Occupy movement as systematically justifying the eviction of the squares using a hygienistic terminology, saying that the camps could develop disease and how everything was dirty. Honestly I don't know if anyone believed that, but I don't think it is only hypocrisy. I think the mayors truly — at a certain unconscious level — rejected all those bodies, tents, sleeping bags, all this matter that was occupying squares, they thought it was disgusting. This matter was not taking part within the production system they want to live in. The barricade is architecture of this abject matter.

Editors: The police barricade is different?

LL: The police barricade is different. I was surprised when I came to the US that they were called barricades; in French they are not called barricades. The police barricade enters entirely within a system of production. There is this interesting text by J. J.

Moreno and Ernesto Audial that talks about how the cardboard box is adapted to the container that is adapted to the ship that is adapted to the truck that is adapted to the width of the highway – that everything is built on the same unit; and the police barricade is very much within that system. Trucks with barricades that fit perfectly on their back. Everything works within the same unit system: that is what totally differentiates the police barricade from the insurgent one. The insurgent barricade fundamentally disrupts this order. The insurgent barricade is a mess. Put an engineer to it and he or she will tell you how badly constructed it is and how it would work better in another way. This whole disruption from this rationalized system is inevitably what makes it an abject architecture and therefore an object of interest.

Editors: Following the concept of lines dividing space into zones or jurisdictions, we think it could be interesting to discuss not only the lines on the ground but also the vertical lines that Eyal Weizman, for example, describes in his work. Here one can see the space as different jurisdictional zones stacked upon one another. Some are very easy to define, like the difference between ground and underground, or ground and air, while others are more gradual. We see other tendencies that could contribute to this vertical framework, such as the democratization of access to aerial space in certain parts of the world as drones become increasingly inexpensive. Could we be seeing the thickening of vertical lines as well?

LL: Rather than vertical lines I would like to look at something that has to do with the atmosphere. The atmosphere is something I am increasingly interested in. It is difficult to talk about atmospheres without talking about Peter Sloterdijk and his work on *atmoterror*. He places this new paradigm starting with chemical war during World War I. Without necessarily historicizing the shift of paradigm, everything we are breathing and maybe bathing in could not possibly be politically neutral. So I am not sure about the part of the question about drones in the air and Eyal Weizman's political verticality. But what is for sure is that we cannot think of politics as a two-dimensional thing but rather much more volumetric and atmospheric. That is the essence of biopolitics, we are breathable bodies – and again, when I say *breathable* I don't just mean air going through our lungs; I mean we evolved within atmospheres rather than on a surface.

Editors: In the Funambulist pamphlet *Legal Theory* you print the text "Power, Violence, Law" by Costas Douzinas, which, among other things, discusses the violence that is inscribed in the law because of the violence in the revolutions that created it in France and the US. You, on the other hand, write about the violence inscribed in architecture. We are not only discussing the architecture of securitization and control, but also protest and revolt in the book. Do you think there is a difference between the violence that is inscribed in architecture and the violence inscribed in the law itself? If so, how do you think it differs?

"If I just look above my computer I see laws that make it hard for anyone but my family to penetrate inside these walls. Private property is very much a legal regime that finds its implementation through the wall."

Perhaps this relates also to capitalism. There are laws, and there are laws of different countries, and the laws are there to insure some kind of influence from citizens on the law and on society, and there is this economical system that goes another way. How do you see this? Are the laws corresponding to capitalism or is there a resistance or a friction there? How are people's reactions to public space, or how are people changing or influencing laws?

LL: I will answer something different and you can bounce back to what I am saying. It is related to what I was mentioning earlier. It is very hard to find a law in our society that is not actively materialized by architecture. If I just look above my computer I see laws that make it hard for anyone but my family to penetrate inside these walls. Private property is very much a legal regime that finds its implementation through the wall. What I am interested in is how basically when you invent the wall you invent the prison; you don't necessarily want a prison, so what you come to invent as well is the door. The operative is for bodies to go on one side of the wall to the other, but the door does not come by itself: the door comes with a lock. A lock allows some exclusive bodies to be able to have this power on matter and therefore to have an agency to space that will allow them to not be subjected to the violence of architecture, to the violence of the wall. The law has some reservations. I have a very simple example: You build a house in such a way that no one else can enter: thick walls, windows that lock, doors that lock. You have this house, you are very happy and protected; this goes back to the idea of security. The law allows you to have this house, and the law produces this house in the sense that it guarantees your private property. However, come the situation of martial law, a state of exception or something like that, a quarantine or a curfew is being imposed – all of a sudden the walls that were protecting you are now preventing you from going outside. Nothing of architecture changes, only the legal regime changes. But because of the violence of the wall already integrated in the original law, because it was preventing bodies to enter from outside, it was also preventing bodies going from the inside to the outside. While pacification of the key and the lock would allow the body to go outside and allow the body to go inside. The violence of the law has been instrumentalized in a way, I would like to argue, that was within the architecture from the beginning even though the law was not implemented.

Editors: We see the tendency for public space to become increasingly privatized, restricted, and exclusive, and this is to some extent supported by the process of legal change. This is of considerable concern in the Western world. What you say is very absolute. If every wall at all times and in every situation is violent, it sounds very black and white in a sense. Are you only interested in talking about it on this fundamental level?

LL: Let's go back to the black and white later. The very fact of talking about public space involves the fact that there is a private space. The very notion of retroactively legitimizing private property in the sense that if there is a public space there is also a private space is what we have to accept. I am not necessarily saying that my agenda is for every space not to be private, it is just that when we talk about one we have to talk about both of them together in a system. What I came to realize is we came to think of private space as a sort of inside and public space as the remaining space. I don't think this is true; when we create a private space as an interior, we create a second interior that is a public space. What I mean by that is, if every human was homeless, we obviously would not call them *homeless*. It is only because there are people who are not homeless that we call the people who do not have a home homeless. We create a social position which is a precarious one by creating a position that is not precarious, so I think it is there the entire balance always plays out. I think we always need to keep that in mind when we talk about public space. Referring back to that walls are necessarily violent is a black and white discourse, I realize I should do something about my language because that is obviously not what I mean to say. I think when we say that things are a little bit more

"What I came to realize is we came to think of private space as a sort of inside and public space as the remaining space. I don't think this is true; when we create a private space as an interior, we create a second interior that is a public space."

complex – not every wall is violent – we think of violence in a very moralistic way and we think that violence is something we should escape from. My intuition is that we will never escape from it. And I go back to the idea that when we create a shelter, we create people who have access to the shelter and people who don't, and the primary violence of the wall is as simple as the basic materiality, the physical law that says the way a wall is being built contributes a material density that the human body cannot cross. I always say if you try to cross a wall that is in front of you I am pretty sure you are going to hurt yourself because this wall was built in such a way that you cannot do that. And so that is what I call the intrinsic violence of architecture, that cannot be instrumentalized apolitically. I think you cannot escape that. What you can do is to have your own political agenda, political manifestos, and you can use this violence for different agendas. I don't find any better word than *violence*. It seems to evoke an imaginary of a lot of pain and something like that. I see things as you say very absolute, I think there is always violence, but it doesn't mean that the violence is always the same: obviously a small fence between my neighbor's garden and my garden doesn't carry the same violence as the wall between Mexico and the US. Nonetheless they both contain their own violence. If we want to live under the legal regime of private property, so be it, and that is one way of instrumentalizing the violence of the wall. At least we should be aware of it and embrace it.

Editors: Architecture is not only the building of walls but also the organization of space. Do you see any positive ways in which architecture can support spaces where people can organize, or be brought together, instead of being separated or excluded?

LL: This is the most important question in my life, and I don't have a strict answer. I don't believe there is any emancipatory (liberating) architecture – only practices are emancipatory. You might need to destroy rather than to construct, there might be ways of creating architecture that allows pockets within this environment in which this kind of organization can be facilitated. In a very simplified reading of twentieth-century architecture, we went from the modernist belief that architecture could cure people and cure society, to the observation that this might not be possible and the embracing of architecture's avert quality. I think that architecture does not cure, that architecture is violent, that it hurts bodies, but through this understanding of it we might be able to serve people's agenda. The example I can think of is from my book, *Weaponized Architecture*, it is a Palestinian project in an area of the West Bank, implementing disobedience to the colonial legislation. So what's important to me is not to think of architecture as a solution, because solution is "end of history" (capitalism wants us to think that capitalism is the solution); talking about solutions after the Holocaust, which was called "the final solution," makes the term *solution* highly problematic. I advocate both for a humble architecture and for an architecture that agrees that it carries a certain violence within society, but maybe through this understanding it can contribute to distributing this violence throughout society, and not focus on the same set of bodies always.

Addendum February 2016

Editors: In the light of the terror events in Paris in November 2015, would you comment on the subsequent state of exception/security response and how it plays out in the streets?

LL: As I write these lines, the state of emergency is still ongoing. This exceptional suspension of rights was promulgated by President François Hollande on November 13, 2015, immediately after the attacks; it was then adopted by vote in a quasi-unanimous manner by the French Parlement on November 20 for a length of three months. In all likelihood, the Parlement will approve its extension for another three-month duration. People who live in Paris or France's most populous cities get a sense of what this means through the presence of armed police officers – before the January 2015 attacks, patrolling police officers would never have more than a handgun; they are now holding rifles and machine guns – and, even more intimidating, armed patrolling soldiers. Parisians were used to seeing soldiers in train stations since the wave of attacks in 1995, but never in the streets or in the subway. In the month that followed the November attacks, some streets were closed to vehicles, and guarded by police officers. I temporarily lived in the neighborhood of the prime minister's residence, and had to pass a police checkpoint each time I went home.

These are manifestations of the state of emergency to middle and upper classes living in Paris who do not suffer from any racist characterization by the police. The real violence of the state of emergency is being deployed through more than 3,000 administrative perquisitions of homes, workplaces, and religious sites since its promulgation, leading, in their overwhelming majority, to nothing incriminating. People who are subjected to such violence are members of the French Muslim community (4.5 million people), who are sometimes awakened in the middle of the night by shouting and insulting police officers who undertake to search their homes. When inhabitants are not at home, they find their doors broken and their apartments turned upside down. Many of these perquisitions occur in the numerous banlieues (suburbs) of French cities, where a population, whose families often come from France's former colonial empire, lives in economic precariousness.

I am convinced that these administrative perquisitions are used not only as an intimidation method against persons and communities considered as practicing a radical interpretation of Islam but also as a means to construct a police cartography of the banlieues' semiprivate and private spaces, which is an opportunity that only rises during the application of a state of exception. This is something on which I reflected right after the 2013 police manhunt after the Boston Marathon attacks. The state of emergency is a great opportunity for a police state to produce knowledge; it does not care to be proven wrong in court because this knowledge, and the fear that it succeeded in creating, cannot be erased.

Interview:
Ludovica Rogers

Ludovica Rogers is an architect who is focused on the public realm in both her practice and research. Rogers has worked on projects of different scales, from large-scale master plans to small interventions in public space. Her interest is in how the design of such spaces can influence users' behavior within them. Rogers has been involved in Occupy since October 2011 and with other groups that have formed from it, or around it, such as the movement of the Commons, the #NoTTIP campaign, and DebtResistanceUK. Within these groups she takes on different roles, from maintaining and strengthening international networks to organizing actions and protests. Rogers also facilitates horizontal discussions in small and large groups and sets up online platforms for collaboration and participation.

This interview was conducted by e-mail during the autumn of 2014.

Editors: One of the main discussions in this book concerns how public space and the right to the city is related to the freedom of expression, civil rights, and democracy. In the twenty-first century democratic movements have emerged in a number of nations, and cities and public space have been the arenas where democratic processes have taken place. If you were to briefly define the word *freedom*, how would you describe it? And how does that definition encompass people, buildings, and territories?

LR: Freedom is the condition in which one can speak and act according to one's own will.

The freedom I strive for is one that is limited only by respect for the rights and needs of other people and of our natural world. This is a relational freedom that acknowledges that we are not isolated individuals, but that our actions have effects on other people and the environment in which we live.

Buildings and territories are inherently limitations of freedom as they are determined by boundaries, which bring with them concepts of right of access and governance. In the modern world these elements tend to be associated with ownership. Who owns a building or a territory tends to have more right of access to it and governance over it. This perspective ignores the extreme wealth imbalance of our current social and economical system, and accepts that privilege, be it of a person or a corporation, determines who controls and has access to what. It follows that property rights often take priority over human rights (the right to evict versus the right to shelter, the right to profit versus the right to protest, etc.). In addition, ownership rights bring with them rights to exchange assets freely. As a result, many resources to which access should be a human right (water, homes, etc.) become speculative commodities, allowing the freedom of the market to prevail over the rights of people.

If instead we take the perspective that human rights should be given priority over property rights, our attitude toward access and governance changes drastically. I look forward to a world where there is no ownership of common resources, but only rights of access to them and democratic governance over them. One where resources when abundant are shared openly, and when they are scarce, are collectively managed. This in short is what the movement for the Commons suggests. It is based on the idea that we are all temporary residents of this beautiful planet, and so we have no more or less rights than others to live and enjoy it. But also we have a duty to make sure that other people both in the present day and in the future have the same access to these resources as us. Thus freedom of use and access to buildings and territories should be limited by the sustainability and good function of those resources, in relation to the needs and rights of the present and future communities and of the natural world.

Editors: Another central discussion in the book revolves around physical security — how security architecture affects space and how spaces of securitization operate. The globalization of the world economy, technological advancements, general improvements in the standard of living — these tendencies have developed as we have experienced an increasingly uneven distribution of resources, growing tensions between rich and poor worldwide, and the emergence of asymmetrical warfare. Security has emerged as a huge industry, which has, according to some, tended to address the concerns of particular segments of society. It is in some cases directed toward securing those groups from actual or imagined threats from those with more limited access to resources, or those otherwise critical of the status quo: radicals, "eccentrics," extremists, terrorists, etc. Architecture can be used as one such instrument in the securing of buildings, people, or economical assets. If you were to briefly define the word *security* how would you describe it? And how does that definition encompass people, buildings, and territories from your perspective?

"More and more laws are being passed that give increased power to police and government to monitor and arrest people simply based on suspicion. By building a culture of fear, laws are introduced that clearly reduce our civil liberties and are reversing the fundamental concept that someone is innocent until proven guilty."

LR: Security is the state of being free from danger or threat.

Everyone should be granted a secure life for themselves, their family, and their community. But just as for freedom, the guarantee of their security should be balanced against the security and freedom of others.

Security in relation to buildings and territories varies depending on what danger or threat needs to be addressed. It can be related to physical aspects (structural stability, health and safety, etc.) or to protecting a space from other people or animals. Unfortunately what we are experiencing increasingly today is a tendency to abuse otherwise legitimate security measures. For example, Health and Safety regulations are being used to displace people from their homes, to evict people from occupations, or to refuse people the use of communal spaces "for their own safety," while often the real motive is to remove obstacles to the private market.

Of relevance to our time is also the great importance given to national security in face of terrorist threats. More and more laws are being passed that give increased power to police and government to monitor and arrest people simply based on suspicion. By building a culture of fear, laws are introduced that clearly reduce our civil liberties and are reversing the fundamental concept that someone is innocent until proven guilty. What concerns us is that these laws are being extended to nonviolent political organizations and individuals that have no links to terrorism whatsoever. For example in the first months of Occupy we were labeled "domestic terrorists" as Kevin Rawlinson wrote in the *Independent* on May 12, 2011, giving immense powers to the police to act against us. More recently a fellow activist was interrogated at the airport, where site-specific antiterrorist laws apply, and refused entry to the UK for the simple reason that he was a blogger and had interviewed Julian Assange.

Furthermore in the UK security is being increasingly handed over to private companies like G4S and Serco, that not only provide poor and unreliable services (G4S for example stepped out of their contract a few weeks before the Olympics, forcing the government to deploy military forces instead) but also have been associated with scandalous activities such as abuse of detainees both in the UK and abroad that you could read about in the *Guardian* on May 17 and June 4, 2014. The handing over of security to private firms and the progressive cuts that police forces are facing are the cause of great concern, as such an important sector is removed from public control and developed as a profit-driven industry.

Editors: What do you see as the threats today to free democratic expression in public space?

LR: One of the inhibitors to protest is the fact that one must ask permission to do so. This involves providing personal details of the organizers to the police, negotiating with them the conditions, like time and route, and in some cases, such as in Parliament Square, having to take out a Public Liability Insurance. Apart from the inherent contradiction of having to ask permission to protest, this fact acts as a deterrent by putting the organizers in the spotlight and exposing them not only to possible present and future surveillance, but also to liability should anything undesirable happen during the event.

Another aspect is related to the large amount of public space privately owned in London whose owners are entitled to apply injunctions so to prohibit protest on their premises. This can not only cut off entire sections of the city from democratic expression, but also limit the access of citizens to the object of their protest, as the same premises may host at the same time private businesses and important public services, like for example the City Hall of London that Jeevan Vasagar wrote about in the *Guardian* on June 11, 2012.

Another threat we are facing is the demonization of protest achieved as a result of often unjustified violent repression by the police, and accompanied by wide exposure of footage of clashes by the mass media, while images of people enjoying a peaceful protest rarely make the headlines. Of great importance in counteracting both aspects are the production and use of our own media.

Besides video and photographic documentation, live-streaming has become a powerful tool for this. Not only does it enable us to share live the peaceful and meaningful parts of our protests, like talks, performances, or creative actions, but it also allows us to document how this may then be repressed by the police. We use footage not only to inform the general public, but also as evidence in court cases, as, fortunately, it cannot be destroyed should a live-streamer be arrested, as while filming it is simultaneously uploaded online. Another form of self-defense is what we call Legal Observers, people who decide voluntarily not to take part in a protest, but take on the specific role of monitoring it and the police. They usually wear high-visibility vests to identify themselves, take notes at regular intervals describing what they observe, and take photos. Not only have their contributions proven valuable in the court cases, but simply their presence makes police more aware of their actions and protesters feel more secure.

Another deterrent is that protesters are conscious that they are constantly surveilled. Not only is there on average one CCTV camera every eleven people in the UK, but police actively film people on protest. Furthermore once you get involved in activism you start to live with the suspicion (many of us actually have proof) that someone is monitoring all your online and offline activities, a fact the *Guardian* acknowledged on October 30, 2011, and October 18, 2013. Personally, I feel that every move I make could be controlled, and that this could be

"It has also been proven that police infiltrate nonviolent activist groups, some even having children with members of the group."

used against me at any moment, even if I am a law-abiding citizen. A recent example of this was when in the USA the military turned up at a couple's home to arrest them on the suspicion that they were building a bomb, simply because they had simultaneously been searching online for a backpack and a pressure cooker, also written about in the *Guardian* August 1, 2013. Finally, it has also been proven that police infiltrate nonviolent activist groups, some even having children with members of the group. This has definitely had psychological effects on activists some of whom feel they can't even trust their friends, therapists, or even partners, as they might be undercover intelligence-gathering agents working either for the government or the corporations.

Editors: How do you think physical security can improve public space?

LR: Physical security in the urban space is supposed to protect the rights and safety of citizens.

The kind of interventions made to improve it depend on which threats and dangers one is trying to address. In the UK there seems to be a belief that the biggest threat to normal citizens is terrorism, ignoring the fact that we face daily forms of dangers that are statistically more likely to affect our lives. An obvious example is the situation for cyclists in London, where on average there is more than one fatal accident a month, but little is being done to improve the safety of our roads for cyclists.

It is also questionable if the forms of control currently being used actually make us feel safer. An extreme case of physical security for the public good was during the Olympics where some residents in East London were forced to accept the installation of missiles on the roofs of their homes in defense of a possible attack from the sky. Imagine how secure that made them feel – transforming a residence into a potential military target. Surely transforming cities into war zones can't be the best way to protect citizens.

In more common situations, security for a building or a territory is obtained by regulating access to it and controlling what happens within it. In London, boundaries and fences strongly define the urban landscape, signs tell you obsessively what you can or cannot do, while cameras remind you constantly to abide as you are being watched. It's questionable if these elements are actually being used to protect normal citizens, and not rather the interests of private property, businesses, and elites.

If we were really to put citizens at the center when designing safe and secure places, we would probably use a different approach. We might focus on the use of appropriate lighting, bright enough to allow good visibility, soft enough to make a space feel welcoming without creating dark contrasting spaces. We would take into account which communities would be using the space and cater for them all, so that social friction would not be exasperated but rather respect and interaction fostered. We would create the conditions for a sense of belonging and community so that if something happens to us we feel there is someone close to call on. Basically the opposite of what happens now, where the use of surveillance cameras, large fences, and signs remind us that we are in constant danger and that we should distrust everyone around us.

Editors: From your perspective as part of the Occupy movement in London, and as an architect, could you briefly take us through the story of the Occupy movement and the coinciding anti-Olympic movement, and their use of public space for protest? What were the main events, and when did they start? Where did the protests take place? Did they have a clear ending or are they still continuing? What is the status of the Occupy movement today?

LR: Occupy London was one of the hundreds of occupations set up on October 15, 2011, following a call to action by the Spanish 15M movement. It is part of the so-called Squares movement, which started early that year with the Arab Spring and continues to propagate across the globe through occupations of common spaces, the most recent one being Occupy Hong Kong.

The first Occupy London camp, OccupyLSX, was meant to be set up in front of the London Stock Exchange to protest the role of the financial sector in causing the economic crisis. But the private company, owner of the square, issued an injunction that prohibited access to it. As a result, having found the area fenced off and surrounded by police, the protesters occupied the closest open space, which happened to be in front of St. Paul's Cathedral. Thanks to the intervention of the Cathedral's Canon, and because it was unclear to whom the land belonged, the police were not able to clear the new occupation.

Having taken the space, the occupation developed into a self-sufficient camp, with a kitchen, toilets, a university, a library, a first aid and welfare tent, and a meditation space. The camp grew rapidly and soon could not accommodate more people, so further occupations were set up, one in a public square (Finsbury Square) and three in buildings in the surrounding areas. These were evicted after just a few weeks, while the camps, LSX and Finsbury Square, were evicted in February and June of 2012 respectively.

> "Since then, Occupy has developed in various ways. Some activists have joined issue-specific groups, the anti-Olympics campaign being one of them; others continue to be actively involved in Occupy, organizing direct actions, protests, events, teach-ins, skill-shares, etc."

OCCUPY WALL STREET, NEW YORK, NY, USA
Visited October 23, 2011, and November 14, 2011

1. To enforce "passive recreation" certain behavior is prohibited in Zuccotti Park.

2. Protesters using "human microphones" to relay messages during the demonstration.

3. Police barriers separate Zuccotti Park from the adjacent street.

OWS, New York, NY, USA

Photo Essay

4. 7. Mobile police surveillance towers

5. 6. Extensive NYPD presence.

275

OWS, New York, NY, USA

7

Since then, Occupy has developed in various ways. Some activists have joined issue-specific groups, the anti-Olympics campaign being one of them; others continue to be actively involved in Occupy, organizing direct actions, protests, events, teach-ins, skill-shares, etc.

Recently, Occupy has attracted the attention of the media again as it was violently repressed by the police when it attempted to occupy Parliament Square in mid-October 2014. This new form of Occupy, called #OccupyDemocracy (see http://occupydemocracy.org.uk/), has stated that to highlight the capture of our democracy by corporate power, it intends to reoccupy Parliament Square for a weekend every month until the elections in May 2015. As a result, Parliament Square is now policed daily and surrounded by high fences "to protect the grass," making it inaccessible to any member of the public.

"To get round this, a knowledgeable activist decided to organize a tourist tour instead. Holding up an umbrella in his hand, just like many tour guides, he took a large group of interested citizens around Canary Wharf, highlighting all the terrible things the corporations situated in those skyscrapers were up to. No one was arrested, and Occupy London Tours continues to this day!"

for the future control of any form of protest in the area, by prohibiting the use of amplification and structures without previous permission. At the same time, in the run-up to these events, we saw an increase of arrests during protests that subsequently resulted in dropped charges. Some of those arrested were given bail conditions that lasted months and that prevented them from entering or crossing entire boroughs of the city, in particular those where these spectacular events were going to take place.

Another unusual use of law was the case of Critical Mass. The London version of this global bike movement has been holding their rides regularly for twenty years on the last Friday of every month starting on the South Bank of the Thames. In June 2012 the ride happened to be on the same night as the Olympics opening ceremony. To everyone's surprise, that night the police banned people from cycling north of the river. Cyclists decided anyway to cross the bridges in small groups, some to go home, some to join up later to continue the ride together. As there is no way to tell if someone is or not part of Critical Mass, potentially anyone riding a bicycle north of the river could be arrested. According to a BBC reporter, 182 cyclists were arrested that night, ironically to protect an event whose aim was to celebrate sport!

Editors: When you described your experiences from the Occupy movement during our meeting September 2013 you explained that the UK government and police issued permanent or semipermanent conditions on protest within geographically defined zones of the city. These conditions give the police the jurisdiction to detain and register unwanted users of zones like the area around the Olympic Village and the privately owned public space of Canary Wharf. Can you describe how these conditions work and their implications on the use of public space?

LR: We experienced a strong increase in the limitations on the right to protest during 2012, the year in which London became the center stage of two major events, the Queen's Diamond Jubilee and the Olympic Games. For example – as you could read in the Telegraph on January 17, 2012 – the change of laws regulating the use of Parliament Square, which gave authority to the police to forcefully remove a famous peace camp that had been there for at least ten years, while preparing the ground

Editors: Have these conditions affected how people use public space? Have they influenced, for example, the Occupy movement, in its current form, and its strategies for carrying out protest and events in public space? Occupy London Tours works around one of the conditions at Canary Wharf. Can you explain how they do it?

LR: The use of the above forms of control have not changed our strategies. On the contrary, since we have won most of our legal battles, we are even more conscious of how legal and justified our forms of protest are. But we are also more prepared, knowing which are the boundaries within which we can act lawfully, and when overstepping them can play against us. Occupy London Tours is an emblematic example. In the early days of Occupy London the privately owned business quarter of Canary Wharf issued an injunction that prohibited protest on their premises. To get round this, a knowledgeable activist decided to organize a tourist tour instead. Holding up an umbrella in his hand, just like many tour guides, he took a large group of interested citizens around Canary Wharf, highlighting all the terrible things the corporations situated in those skyscrapers were up to. No one was arrested, and Occupy London Tours continues to this day!

But even if we can be strategic about the way we protest, we cannot underestimate the intimidating impact the abuse of the law has on activist groups and the personal lives of their members. Of great concern is the increasing tendency to arrest people with no serious grounds. We have won most of our cases, but this cannot cancel the effects of what it means for a law-abiding citizen to face arrest, bail conditions, and court proceedings. The effects on protest groups are immediate. The activists put under bail conditions are often not allowed to protest, or if they are they will tend to restrain themselves until the date of their court hearing so not to risk worsening their case. Even more worryingly, once the court case is over, many still face depression and burnout due to the stress that they had to go through and do not come back to action for long periods of time. As this appears to be a clear tactic to try to deactivate crucial campaigners and destabilize protest groups, a few activists will be now taking legal action against the police.

Editors: How do you see the 99 percent movement playing out? What future do you see for social grassroots movements in general in the current security climate?

LR: Unfortunately I am very worried for social grassroots movements in the current security climate, as the powers we are fighting against are creating new ways to control us ever more. On one side they are becoming conscious of the widening gap between the superrich and the rest of society and are preparing solutions to protect themselves against social unrest. On the other side, they know they must find ways to control resistance as they attempt to extract wealth from places that have up to now been considered common (natural resources, public services, etc.). Security and freedom should first and foremost concern the rights of people and the well-being of the planet, not the corporations. People and planet before profit. This in short is what grassroots movements are fighting for today.

Interview:
Sunniva F. Meyer

Sunniva F. Meyer is a research officer at the Institute of Transport Economics (TØI) in Norway, specializing in situational measures against crime, including terrorism. TØI is a national institution for transport research and development. The Institute was set up in 1958, first as a government secretariat and later as a separate research institution. In 1986 the Institute became a private, independent research foundation. The main objectives of the Institute are to carry out applied research on issues connected with transport and to promote the application of research results by advising authorities, the transport industry, and the public at large. Special emphasis is placed on the practical application of research results, and most of the studies and projects carried out here are commissioned. In Norway most of the clients are central government bodies and local authorities, with some commissions from the private sector.

This interview was conducted by e-mail during the autumn of 2014.

Editors: If you were to briefly define the word *freedom*, how would you describe it? And how does that definition encompass people, buildings, and territories?
  SM: Freedom is the absence of necessity, coercion, or constraint in choice or action. Lately, I have been focusing on the right for all people to move within city areas at all hours and still both be secure and feel safe.
Editors: If you were to briefly define the word *security*, how would you describe it? And how does that definition encompass people, buildings, and territories?
  SM: Security is both the state of being protected or safe from harm and the process of obtaining this protection. People, buildings, and territories can be at risk and in need of protection, and/or contribute to security by being part of the protection of other person/objects at risk.
Editors: What do you see as the threats today to free democratic expression in public space?
  SM: Surveillance of public spaces is a measure sometimes used to increase security. Such surveillance could also be used to monitor people's general political activities without these political activities being in any way connected to illegal

activities. To ensure that such surveillance is not misused in this sense, we need to ensure that we have satisfactory control mechanisms that both prevent such misuse and ensure that Norwegian citizens feel safe that they can voice their opinions in public space without being persecuted.

Editors: How do you think physical security can improve public space?

SM: I believe well-designed physical security can improve our security (and reduce risk) without compromising other essential values, including urban and democratic values.

Editors: As one of the experts on situational crime prevention in Norway we would like to discuss how security based on situational crime prevention can protect our cities and how it might influence our city spaces. Can you first briefly explain what situational crime prevention is?

SM: Situational crime prevention focuses, quoting Ronald Clarke, "on specific crime types, seeking to change the immediate environment such that potential offenders either are physically prevented from committing the crime or perceive the opportunities as limited and the risk as high, and thus might choose against committing the crime."

By focusing on the environment rather than the offenders, situational crime prevention theory can assist us in finding security measures that do not incur unreasonable costs on minority groups. Situational crime prevention measures can, of course, also have negative externalities, but most of such externalities hit indiscriminately, which I think is more just; and if we choose our measures wisely, we hopefully can improve security while minimizing negative externalities.

Editors: Situational crime prevention and situational terror prevention are based on the same twenty-five strategies. Do you think it represents good practice to use the same strategies for crime and terror? How would you argue for using the same/different strategies?

SM: The twenty-five techniques of situational prevention were developed to deal with traditional crimes such as burglary and various kinds of theft. They have, however, also been successfully employed to a broader range of crimes, such as identity theft and sexual abuse as Ronald Clarke and Graeme Newman acknowledged in the book *Outsmarting the Terrorists* (2006). The principal value of these twenty-five techniques is to broaden the consideration of possible responses when dealing with specific forms of crime, including terrorism. Some of the techniques are of course better suited to terrorism prevention than others, such as target hardening versus assist compliance, and the list of twenty-five techniques is not exhaustive. I therefore use the twenty-five techniques as a useful starting point when analyzing how to prevent any type of crime, and supplement them with other methods and tools to increase creativity when suggesting measures.

Editors: In the essay you published in *Crime Science* in 2013 you analyzed the July 22 attack in Oslo by using what you call *crime scripts*. Can you briefly explain how a crime script works?

SM: Crime scripts describe the practical procedure a criminal goes through when committing a specific type of crime. By spelling out the actions (and their goals) necessary to complete the crime, the script can, and here I quote Derek Cornish, "enhance situational crime prevention policies by drawing attention to a fuller range of possible intervention points."

Editors: From what we understand from your lectures about how you use crime scripts, many of the scripts describe specific spatial conditions as a part of the script. Can you give an example of how the crime script relates to space?

SM: A prerequisite for successfully executing many crimes is movement. Often the offender needs to move close to a target, whether it is in public space, inside a building, or a building is the target. Frequently, the offender also needs to transport a tool or a weapon to the site of the offense. In addition, the offender usually wants to escape the site without being hurt, identified, or captured. Such movements should be included as actions/steps in the crime scripts to illuminate that if we change the spatial conditions and make it impossible to complete these movement steps, we also prevent the successful completion of the crime.

Editors: Several of the different steps in the crime script seem to be influenced by conventions that define the city as a space with inherent rules. Not rules of law but of physics and sociology. Some writers today, such as Geoff Manaugh, are looking at how, for example, criminals use the city in ways that move outside these rules, say by using the air or underground networks or by looking at buildings not as walls and floor slabs but as spaces of ducts, vertical connections, and airspaces. Could security measures based on situational crime prevention and the building of crime scripts limit city development to the conventions these scripts are based on? And as a citizen, do you think it is for the good if we assume these conventions and make security measures according to them?

SM: The challenge you are adhering to is important, but it is caused by how security analysts use the methods rather than the methods per se. People innovate when using public and private space in the city, whether for criminal or other purposes. Security is a continuous process which must always consider such innovations. Old security analyses and crime scripts should, therefore, be regularly updated and extended to encompass these changes. If the people in charge of security only use old situational crime prevention measures and crime scripts without updating the threats, they may overlook changes in the risk picture and thus forget to protect against new types of attacks. This challenge will arise regardless of the method/tool used in the original analysis.

Editors: Another aspect of situational crime and terror prevention that we would like to discuss is related to the previous question. In a city, there are many people who do not follow the conventions

"My impression is that in other countries, maybe especially in the US, their tolerance for implementing security at the expense of other values is higher than in Norway."

of society but still are not criminals or terrorists. Some people take pictures in strange places, some walk in places not made for walking, and so forth. Looking at situational crime and terror prevention, these people can easily become suspects because they do not behave according to the rules of conduct or according to a script. Is there a way around this, and is it right to limit the free use of space to ensure security for others?

SM: This challenge is difficult, and I do not think there is a general answer. I am of the opinion that if a target is so sensitive that it cannot allow people to spend time in nearby public spaces, the target should be moved to rural areas where it is possible to lay claim to enough private land to keep people at bay. I also think that what we call normal behavior should always be allowed in public space. However, we do already put limits on how people can behave in public areas. For example, by law, we are not allowed to drink in public space and there are limits to the amount of noise we are allowed to make. These rules are not always enforced, but were introduced to protect public order. So I think it is legitimate to put some limits on behavior in public space. I am also open to putting some extra limitations on behavior around especially sensitive targets, but in each case the benefit of the ban must be weighed against the disadvantage for the people being limited by it.

Editors: In the book we are discussing if there might be a Norwegian way of securing its public spaces – and what that could look like in comparison to, for example, the British culture of security or the American. Norway is still in the early stages of implementing new standards and regulations for the physical security of buildings. At the same time there are discussions addressing whether the country should maintain some security measures that may be seen as specific to Norway and Norwegian culture, such as the police not wearing weapons normally, or should Norway adapt to what is taking place in the rest of the world? Do you think there is a potential for developing a Norwegian culture of security? And if you were to speculate, what do you think that way would look like?

SM: Implemented security measures affect the surroundings. Sometimes positively, such as when a ban on vehicles reduces pollution from traffic, but unfortunately also negatively, such as barriers' contributing to ugly and uninviting public areas. My impression is that in other countries, maybe especially in the US, their tolerance for implementing security at the expense of other values is higher than in Norway. Norwegian society seems willing to invest more resources in developing solutions that increase security without compromising other important values, such as openness and accessibility. I am not sure that I would term this a "Norwegian way," but I do believe we in Norway can contribute to the security field by demonstrating that it is possible to achieve security while also preserving other important values.

Interview:
Susannah C. Drake

Susannah C. Drake is the principal of Dlandstudio Architecture and Landscape Architecture, and a professor at Cooper Union. Before founding Dlandstudio, Drake designed the streetscape and security master plan for Battery Park City as an associate at Rogers Marvel Architects. More recently in her own practice Drake designed the security environment for the New York City Police Department headquarters in lower Manhattan.

This interview was conducted by e-mail during the autumn of 2014.

Editors: If you were to briefly define the word *freedom*, how would you describe it? And how does that definition encompass people, buildings, and territories?

SD: In an urban setting there are many controls designed for public safety. Stoplights may inhibit vehicular freedom, but enable movement of pedestrians. Guardrails on a waterfront may keep people from falling into the water but they also prohibit boaters from getting out of the water. These are not antiterrorist security measures, nor are they storm-resilience security measures, but they affect our freedom of movement.

Transparency of the systems that organize circulation through the urban environment can help to define types of movement. The challenge with so many of the barriers and checks, surveillance systems, and patrols is that they reduce the efficiency of how the city operates. The definition of territory is a dangerous phenomenon that can lead to more rather than less violence.

Editors: If you were to briefly define the word *security*, how would you describe it? And how does that definition encompass people, buildings, and territories?

SD: There are different theories about how to provide security. Some experts feel that there should be a very visible presence to make a site feel secure. Others suggest that maintaining openness but with less visible but similarly strong security measures add more amenities to the city. Operation within the city at the building level can be frustrating, particularly if one is profiled as unacceptable for admittance.

Editors: What do you see as the threats today to free democratic expression in public space?

SD: All activities cannot be allowed in public space. For instance, Mount Auburn Cemetery outside of Boston, Massachusetts, became a popular pleasure ground in the nineteenth century and its management had to set rules to prohibit picnicking and the discharge of firearms on the burial ground. Freedom of expression does not mean that everyone can do everything everywhere all the time. While restrictions on the use of open space to maintain public safety and help preserve the capital assets are often necessary, such restrictions can be problematic if they exclude a particular demographic segment of society. Accessibility is very important in cities but there are sensitive areas that require pedestrian and vehicular interdiction zones because of threats to national economies. If space is taken away, it should be balanced with additions in other places.

Editors: How do you think physical security can improve public space?

SD: Creating an automotive interdiction zones could create new pedestrian opportunities. Streetscape furniture and amenity can be incorporated with security design.

Editors: This book is partly triggered by the terror attack that took place in Norway in 2011. As an architect practicing in New York both before and after 9/11, have you experienced any major changes in how architects relate to the question of security in the US?

SD: Before 9/11 I was hired to design the streetscape of the North neighborhood of Battery Park City. It was an urban design and landscape architecture project. After 9/11 security was added to the project. Security is now required for federal buildings. The post-9/11 hysteria has died down somewhat, but there are still concerns among clients who feel they are potential targets of terrorist attack. When we did the security for the New York City Police Department the client wanted it not only to be secure but to look secure.

Editors: In your practice you have integrated security design for both private- and public- sector clients into public and private spaces. Looking back at your work at Dlandstudio and at Rogers Marvel, what would you say are the major issues when integrating security measures in design?

SD: The work at RMA [Rogers Marvel Architects] on BPCA [Battery Park City Authority] actually really helped us make the pedestrian environment more friendly and livable. We were also able to add a lot of planting in the new security project. It's a challenge to not have security elements impede pedestrian circulation. Fire Department access also requires some finesse. In some areas new security measures have created ugly security screening zones, marring the beauty of historic landmarks.

> "In some areas new security measures have created ugly security screening zones, marring the beauty of historic landmarks."

Editors: It is striking how you combine security measures with pedestrian-friendly cityscapes. During the Master studio and the work with this book we have been told many times by security advisors that "If you solve hostile vehicle mitigation you have solved a lot of the security issues." From your perspective how can strategies for hostile vehicle mitigation be used to create good cityscapes?

SD: There are two big issues related to hostile vehicles: speed, and how close they can get to their target. Changing the street geometry to slow vehicle speeds can reduce the effective size of barriers. It also makes cars go slower in the area around the buildings, which is good for pedestrians. Increasing setback distance, that is, creating public space that keeps vehicles that could be loaded with explosives away from target buildings, is important.

Editors: When we began our conversation with the Norwegian Police Security Service, there was an immediate discussion from their side as to how to make security measures appear aesthetically pleasing. In London there are differently designed bollards in different parts of the city (the Centre for the Protection of National Infrastructure is funding the design of new bollards), while on Wall Street in New York we see the characteristic diamond-shaped bollards. What is your take on this issue? Should security measures be present, and made to look attractive, or should they be hidden (camouflaged as flower beds, benches, etc.) and/or made completely invisible?

SD: I like a hybrid. If a bollard is encased in granite to make it "look nice" and that means that it's much bigger, it's a no-go for me. I want the streetscape to be organized, logical, fluid, and comfortable.

Editors: Do you think there are urban sites or situations that require or justify strict security measures, and on the other hand sites or situations where security measures should be toned down or phased out?

SD: Yes. Perceived threat usually follows disaster and then fades. Security is a serious issue that should be carefully assessed to determine the level of threat. This is not a job for a designer, but for trained security advisors.

Editors: In Norway a new legal framework for physical security brings up sites of symbolic value as possible locations requiring protection. One might say this introduces a highly cultural aspect to security – that culture should be secured. In the US, security measures are already implemented around symbolic places and monuments. How do you think this affects how we perceive these sites?

SD: At the Statue of Liberty the security experience has an extremely detrimental impact on the experience. From the ferry screening to checks along the way, it is unpleasant and unsightly. This is but one example of similar landmarks.

Editors: Lastly we would like to ask you about fear. Do you think security measures are inducing or reducing fear?

SD: I think it actually increases fear if you aren't used to seeing it. After a while it just becomes background. For visitors, I don't think it sends a good message if it's too fortress-like.

Interview: Yuval Yasky

Yuval Yasky is the head of the Department of Architecture at the Bezalel Academy of Art and Design, Jerusalem. Yasky's research and teaching address the conditions of spatial organization in an Israeli context. In addition to publishing extensively internationally, he has curated several exhibitions, among them the Israeli Pavilion at the Venice Architecture Biennale in 2010. The critical approach of the Bezalel Academy faculty, which Yasky leads, to local spatial politics plays an important role in the complex debate over security and freedom in Israel.

This interview was conducted by e-mail during the autumn of 2014.

Editors: If you were to briefly define the word *freedom*, how would you describe it? And how does that definition encompass people, buildings, and territories?

YY: It is quite hard to define *freedom* briefly, but nonetheless, if I have to try and do that I will resort to the definitions of liberal thinkers like John Stuart Mill and John Rawls, who have influenced my own thoughts on this topic as a young philosophy student some twenty years ago. In their thinking, freedom can be defined as a set of basic liberties that are the birthright of every human being. These liberties are based on the idea that each individual has the right to advance himself and his own personal agendas as long as it does not come at the expense of another person's rights. If I need to break this idea into the specific liberties I would say the more important rights are: the liberty of speech; the liberty of occupation; the liberty of mobility; the liberty of religious practice; and so on and so forth. The role of the government in this kind of thinking is the role of a regulator and defender of these rights as well as (as Rawls argued) to act for the advancement of the general good and to minimize injustice within society.

The territorial aspects of the liberal definition of *freedom* are quite self-evident. The basic liberty of people to live wherever they choose and their right for maximum, uninterfered mobility has territorial and urban implications on the role of the government as the provider of infrastructure which is accessible to everyone, and as the responsible institution for the safety and well-being of every user of the public realm, be it public buildings, roads, or any other public amenity.

Editors: If you were to briefly define the word *security* how would you describe it? And how does that definition encompass people, buildings, and territories?

YY: Under my preliminary definition of *freedom*, I will define *security* as the basic condition that allows everyone to practice his or her liberties without the risk of experiencing any sort of violence. In that sense, granting personal security is one of the most basic tasks of the government.

The way it relates to people, buildings, and territories is through the understanding that individual liberties are practiced within the framework of social interaction that is, almost by definition, located in the public realm, both the open public spaces of the city and other public institutions.

Editors: What do you see as the threats today to free democratic expression in public space?

YY: Two main threats that I recognize worry me the most – the first of them is the way security acts as a means, or an excuse, to deny, or at least severely limit, people's access to the public space on the basis of ethnicity, religion, gender, etc. The second threat is the privatization of public space. Handing over the responsibility over public space to private bodies, such as private police forces or homeowner associations in the US, poses a great threat to democratic expression; it narrows the space and opportunity of social interaction in such a way that eliminates some people's capacity to relate to other people who are not from his own group and the understanding of civil society as a diverse, dynamic body composed from individuals sharing the space and negotiating it with others. The new model that arises from this kind of thinking gets us closer by the day to a new era of fascism, a phenomena that is very clearly happening in Israel, and especially in Jerusalem.

Editors: How do you think physical security can improve public space?

YY: As long as physical security is granted to each and every one on an equal basis, I see it as a necessary tool that enables everyone to get engaged in the everyday practices without the fear of random violence.

Editors: The situation in Israel is very different from the situation in Europe. In Europe, especially outside the UK, terror attacks are a fairly new phenomena. One of the discussions in this book concerns how and to what extent nations, cities, and other entities should secure themselves against these rare but extreme events. In Israel there is a constant threat of war, and security is partly directed toward a potential war situation and partly against terror. How do you think this affects security architecture in Israel? Within the discussion of securitization, how do you think having a more tangible threat (in relation to an abstract terror threat) pushes the debate?

YY: I think it is very interesting to note the fact that the normal (or routine) situation in Israel is such that it makes security measures somewhat more transparent to many people, especially those who are less used to living here. Unlike in the US, police presence is not very strong, and there aren't so many security barriers in Israeli towns. This is due to the very strict and efficient manner that Israeli security forces deal with the situation in the territories of origin. The way Israel governs the occupied territories, makes life in Israel itself very comfortable and relatively calm in terms of personal safety. This of course comes at the expense of the Palestinian population in the West Bank and Gaza, whose life is conducted under constant scrutiny, and an imminent feeling that at any given moment a burst of arbitrary, institutionalized violence can occur.

This kind of transparency of the security measures taken by Israeli authorities to protect the Israeli (Jewish) population was clearly demonstrated by a new antirocket weapon, the Iron Cap, that made the war in Gaza this summer acceptable by many Israelis. This approach uncovers the internal map of interests and priorities of the Israeli government, for example, in relation to the Bedouin population in the South of Israel, who have no shelters. And the government refuses to build any since they are living in informal, unauthorized, and unrecognized villages.

Editors: In Israel, the militarization of security architecture extends far beyond the architecture of fences, bollards, walls, and hardened buildings. As Eyal Weizman (*Hollow Land*, 2007) and Malkit Shoshan (*Atlas of the Conflict*, 2010) have shown, it influences all infrastructural systems, such as water, roads, tunnels, and so on. From your point of view would you say that this is visible to the common Israeli or Palestinian, and how do you think it affects the way they understand city planning?

YY: I accept both Weizman's and Shoshan's observations about the way infrastructure in Israel is fully recruited to the war against terror. I would say that while every Palestinian experiences the way his life is totally manipulated and controlled by layers of different security measures disguised as many other things, usually justified in legal terms, Israelis at the same time will not experience any such measures unless he lives in the territories, and then he sees it only as something that is happening to "the other."

As far as the Jewish Israeli population is concerned, I think the general view is of city planning as a necessary task in order to get things organized and functioning. On the other hand, Palestinians and Israeli Arabs have to feel quite the opposite.

For many years Israel has neglected the planning of Arab towns and villages, leaving them in a state of spatial chaos and forcing them to build informally, taking the risk of demolition, which in many cases indeed happened. At the same time, planning was used as a tool of land confiscation and as a control-and-containment mechanism as planning of Israeli towns and settlements thrives at the expense of 20 percent of the population.

Editors: In the works referenced above both Weizman and Shoshan show how architecture can work as an occupational device. Do you think there is a distinction between architecture built solely for security reasons and architecture that also works as occupational devices?

YY: I think that one of the more sophisticated elements in the Israeli architecture that acts as an occupational device is the lack of any distinct feature apart from the usual bomb protection room that every apartment in Israel has to have. It is usually totally disguised and assimilated into very banal architecture that resembles some kind of routine Israeli architecture. This does not apply to architecture that is built solely for security reasons.

Editors: If a two-state solution to the Israeli-Palestine conflict was realized, how do you think this would alter the border checkpoints and separation walls, and the amount of security architecture in general?

YY: If I had to guess I would assume that for many years Israel will invest a lot of resources to build up more barriers between the Palestinian state and Israel. After many years of brainwashing and cultivating fear and hatred it will have to take its time to get rid of it. There is a saying in Hebrew that says Tall fences make good neighbors. This sentence will probably be the motto for the period soon after a peace agreement was signed.

Editors: Have you ever felt provoked or prejudged by security measures? Do you experience, in your everyday life, moving through more or less secure venues, areas, or surroundings? Where do you feel less or more safe? Why? What role does the focus on security and the footprint of security have in your university as a subject of investigation for students and researchers?

YY: I must admit I have never really felt prejudged or provoked by security measures. It is not that I have never been questioned in airports (outside of Israel), but I assume that as an Israeli, such inquiries are seen as quite normal to me and I find myself indifferent to it. Thus, my own personal experience is of relative security, and maximum accessibility to wherever I need. I have experienced the opposite while traveling with others whose profile is different than mine, and that experience made the "transparency" of security measures very much present. This issue was most evident when I traveled (more than once) with a Palestinian member of my faculty; in those instances I have witnessed, firsthand, the gap between my perception of relative security and his perception of security as a means of control, humiliation, and arbitrariness, which made me fully understand the privileged position that I have due solely to my ethnic and religious background.

In my department the issues of security, whether as a specific and focused issue or as a secondary research topic, are very present in the discussions we have with our students. In general my department is very much involved in research and criticism of the politics of Israeli space. The venues of our research into these issues are mostly through studio work within the framework of what we call the advanced design research unit that occur in the fourth and fifth years of study. Among the eight units, three are focused on these issues directly; two of those are focused on Jerusalem itself – one on social issues within the discourse of the right to the city, and one that deals directly with the social and spatial implication of the segregation caused by the separation wall in East Jerusalem. The third unit deals with these issues from the perspective of the Palestinian population; it is led by a Palestinian Israeli professor and concentrates on the informal mechanisms of space production in Arab settlements in Israel that emerge out of the lack of formal public planning in those places. This unit dealt for many years with the situation in East Jerusalem and shifted its focus to Jaffa just recently.

Editors: In our discussion in October 2013, you started to explain the biopolitics of Israeli securitization, where you as a Jew with the right social status and the right language and dialect are treated differently both from other Jews but especially from Palestinians or foreigners. Can you shortly explain how you think the Israeli security personnel use this differentiation and how that kind of profiling works?

YY: As I said in my lecture, Israeli security is very much based on categorization and classification of people into distinct groups that have identifiable characteristics, be it physical or other. It is very much evident in the way that security personnel uses profiling in order to recognize the person in front of them and assign him to the categories of risk they use – the best example of that kind of filtering and profiling is the vehicular entrance gate to Ben Gurion International Airport; at the gate, armed security officers always engage the passenger in a brief conversation – saying hello and asking where the passenger is going to and on what flight, using the person's look and his accent as indicators in the process of risk evaluation. From there on the passengers go through a series of interviews with trained security personnel who identify and classify them into distinct risk groups. It is interesting to note that conventional security measures, meaning screening etc., seems quite minor to Israeli security authorities, definitely in comparison to other airports.

I can't say I have a full understanding of the way Israeli security works with the information gathered through the profiling, how this information is integrated from different sources and the risk profile is constructed, but I assume it is based on clear criteria and parameters, along with educated intuition of the security personnel themselves.

Editors: In a January 19, 2014, op-ed piece in the *New York Times* ("Fifty States of Fear"), Peter Ludlow looks at securitization through the lenses of the philosophers Thomas Hobbes and Lars Svendsen. He argues that as much as it is a response to the threat from terrorist attacks, securitization is a way for the state to put the focus on certain fears rather than other problems with the state. The state, Svendsen writes, "has to convince the people that certain things should be feared rather than others, since the people will not, just like that, fear what is appropriate from the point of view of the state. Hobbes points out that this can necessitate a certain amount of staging by the state, which magnifies certain phenomena and diminishes others." Security theater, like airport security, is one of the examples mentioned as a fear-inducing mechanism. Would you say that one can see indications of this in Israel and if so, in what direction is the state directing the fear?

YY: There is no doubt in my mind that government induces fear as a self-survival mechanism. This, I think, is more typical to right-wing administrations then to left-wing ones, but nevertheless it is a strong mechanism used by most governments. In Israel we can see this very clearly in the way the Israeli government, and mostly the Israeli PM, uses the rhetoric of fear almost continuously, shifting his focus from Iran to the Hamas, to ISIS, to the Palestinian Authority. This is done in order to justify the Israeli government's lack of political will to attempt to negotiate with the Palestinians, and more so to justify the obscene amount of resources going into the military, which makes any civilian investment in education, welfare, infrastructure, health, etc., almost impossible. The lack of hope has always been a good tactic for nationalist regimes, and the way hope for a better future in our region has diminished in the last two decades since the assassination of PM Yitshak Rabin is one very good example of that. In the last few years Israel is moving, fast, downward to an almost fascist condition. It is not there yet, the justice system is still holding ground, and it is still a democratic state, but the legislators, fueled by fear from terror, which was deepened lately with the rise of ISIS and the instability in Arab countries, along with lack of hope for a better future, is doing the best it can to narrow the influence of the justice system, mainly the Supreme Court, so it can pass legislation that limits basic human rights. These tendencies put a great stress on the Israeli tradition of liberal democracy which has managed to hold its ground for more than forty years with the inconsistency that the occupation of the West Bank and Gaza have created, and the two justice systems that were installed to deal with the situation. It is no surprise that the situation is deteriorating fast in the last decade since the Second Intifada that has put Israeli society in a posttraumatic state; the surprise is probably the fact that for many years the two systems coexisted in relative separation and managed to ignore the inherent contradiction of the situation.

Editors: What approach to security measures, if any, would you propose Norway should consider adopting in the context of the Breivik attacks in 2011 and the recent IS threats?

YY: I do not see myself as an expert in security issues, or in the threats Norway is facing, so I can't really give any advice. I definitely see the risk to many European countries today in the light of the war against terror, both from within and from external organizations, and I think what is really at stake, and what is threatened in such situations, is the way fear from arbitrary terror and violence can easily push liberal societies, such as the Norwegian society, toward solutions that compromise individual liberties and civil rights based on ethnic and religious profiling.

Interview: Ivor Terret

Ivor Terret is director of training and consulting at the Israel office of AS Solution – a company with headquarters in North America. Among other responsibilities, Terret is responsible for high-level risk, threat, and vulnerability assessments and resulting security master plans on fixed sites from the building design phase through to completion.

This interview was conducted by e-mail during the autumn of 2014.

Editors: One of the main discussions in this book concerns how public space and the right to the city is related to the freedom of expression, civil rights, and democracy. In the twenty-first century democratic movements have emerged in a number of nations, and cities and public space have been the arenas where democratic processes have taken place. If you were to briefly define the word *freedom*, how would you describe it? And how does that definition encompass people, buildings, and territories?

IT: In this context, freedom of movement between authorized spaces to conduct permitted activities.

Editors: Another central discussion in the book revolves around physical security – how security architecture affects space and how spaces of securitization operate. If you were to briefly define the word *security* how would you describe it? And how does that definition encompass people, buildings, and territories?

IT: Effective, practical security consists of two parts, the first being preventative measures to safeguard assets under the security person's responsibility from intentional harm or damage by another individual or organization. The second part of the definition is the reaction to confirmed threats and minimizing the damage caused. As such the key points are: prevention from intentional harm and reaction to confirmed threats.

Editors: What do you see as the threats today to free democratic expression in public space?

IT: I don't see any threat to free democratic expression through security measures, so long as no laws are broken.

Security does not limit democracy in any way. It may limit freedom of movement by controlling access etc., but only as a filter while the visitor's true motives are assessed. I would liken this to a red traffic light; movement is controlled in order to prevent tragic consequences. Another example is passport control/immigration at any port of entry to a country. I do not see much difference when examining access control or physical security to both private and public spaces.

If the correct procedures are in place and the correct staff trained in the procedures working, it should not pose a problem for the innocent visitor.

Editors: How do you think physical security can improve public space?

IT: There are several aspects to this. Firstly the principal of effective security is to stop the attack as early as possible and as far as possible from the protected asset. As such, physical security is a very effective tool to control the environment and the people within. The more control the security apparatus has, the more effective the prevention of intentional damage or harm by keeping an attacker from getting close to the target/asset. In broad terms this is achieved by designing where unauthorized and authorized people can enter and move in the area and also by designing buildings that are resistant to harm, as per each location, risks, and threats.

Editors: The situation in Israel is very different from the situation in Europe. In most of Europe, apart from in the UK, terror attacks are a fairly new phenomena and one of the discussions in this book concerns to what extent, and how one should secure for these rare but extreme events. In Israel there is a constant threat of war, and security is partly directed toward a potential war situation, and partly against terror. How do you think this affects security architecture in Israel? Within the discussion of securitization, how do you think having a more tangible threat (in relation to an abstract terror threat) pushes the debate?

IT: Regarding the threat of war: since the 1991 Gulf War, where Iraq launched thirty-nine Scud missiles at population centers in Israel, all residential properties must have a reinforced concrete safe room. This safe room's primary purpose is to protect the inhabitants from shrapnel as the result of a missile attack and is built as an extra room in each home, regardless of whether it is a house or apartment. Offices and hotels are required to have one safe room per floor. Buildings built prior to 1991, however, are not required by law to have this safe room; but most have a bomb shelter either in the basement or a municipal public bomb shelter nearby. With the increased threat of nonconventional weapons, some safe rooms and bomb shelters have been fitted with air filtration systems, but this is not a requirement, rather it is privately added at the residents' expense.

With regards to the threat of terrorism, there has not been a major change in architecture and design. This includes residential, commercial, and industrial design and complex protection methods such as blast analysis are generally not conducted on the majority of buildings.

Editors: Norway is currently experiencing calls for greater security in the aftermath of the July 22, 2011, terror attack, and the terror threat posed to the country in the summer of 2014 by IS sympathizers. If you were to point to one incident in Israel that has changed the way of thinking about security, which would it be?

IT: The single most influential incident would be the first suicide bomber within Israel. This took place at the town of Afula, where a bus was blown up by a suicide bomber on April 6, 1994, and marked the era of the suicide bomber.

Editors: Would you say there are risks attached to allowing singular incidents to affect security policy, or is this a natural learning curve, in your mind?

IT: This is an excellent question. Strategically, security policy should be examined holistically over time but tactically, vulnerabilities and mistakes that enabled a successful attack need to be examined and lessons learned and implemented immediately.

Editors: To what extent is security profiling productive, and to what extent does it suffer limitations? Could effective profiling soften the necessary security level required at a location or reduce the need for physical security measures?

IT: Effective site security has five pillars: physical security, technological means, manpower, and procedures. The fifth pillar is that all the previous four are designed to complement one another and work together. Profiling would fall into the procedures category, and without a doubt is an effective means of determining if the visitor's intentions of entering the site are innocent or sinister. Profiling would reduce the need for physical security measures, if the profiling is conducted far enough from the facility and other access to the facility is limited.

Editors: Do you think that some people change their behavior due to concerns about how it would affect their "profile"?

IT: Yes, however humans' behavior is either voluntary or involuntary. A person aware of the severity of a major attack they are about to carry out may be able to control voluntary behavior; however, involuntary, stress-related behavior would be impossible to control in the vast majority of cases.

Editors: Is there a risk that people can be mistakenly perceived as a threat, or that some kind of security prejudice exists or develops?

IT: Unfortunately this is a natural phenomenon, especially when persons of a particular race or creed are the primary perpetrators in a particular environment. As such, clear procedures to limit cognitive bias must be defined and all security staff must be aware of these procedures. In addition, procedures must be defined to provide the visitor with every opportunity to prove that they are indeed innocent

> "This took place at the town of Afula where a bus was blown up by a suicide bomber on April 6, 1994, and marked the era of the suicide bomber."

290 Photo Essay

TAHRIR SQUARE, CAIRO, EGYPT
Visited March 1–17, 2012

Tahrir Square, Cairo, Egypt

1. Streets leading to the Parliament blocked in 2012, with inhabitants inside separated from the rest of the city. The only possible exit or entry points are through barbed wire checkpoints.

2. Billboard of plans for Tahrir Square and reconstruction of adjacent hotel

3. Barricades frequently painted by street artists

Photo Essay

4. Protest outside the Egyptian Museum, Tahrir Square

5. Tent structures and rallies at the Square

6. Tents organized for small protest groups while individuals continue to stay at the square

7. Protest with mannequins in the square

Tahrir Square, Cairo, Egypt

of harmful intentions so as to provide a safeguard to both the visitor and security staff and avoid mistaken escalation.

Editors: Do you think there are situations where security measures become obsolete? How do you think that would play out? Would the obsolete security measures be removed, and is it possible as a security consultant to say that the measures a nation/enterprise/person once needed are not necessary anymore?

IT: Yes, a good example is the hotel industry in Israel. As a result of the barrage of suicide bombings of the mid-1990s, hotels (and other publically accessible locations) were required by police order to have armed security present. Due to a reduced threat, this requirement was removed in 2013, and some hotels ceased to employ security guards.

Editors: Do you think government use security measures, in part, as a way of establishing trust? If so, how is that trust built?

IT: Please see a recent academic paper titled "A Critical Account of the Explanations for the Increasing Fragmentation of Policing and the Rise of the Private Security Industry in Israel" that I wrote in 2015 on another topic, but this excerpt is relevant to your book:

"Achieving independence in 1948, Israel has faced an ongoing challenge of defending its citizens and properties against terrorism on the home front as well as protecting its citizens abroad (Samy 2010). During the Second Intifada, or Second Palestinian Uprising between the years 2000 to 2005, there was a dramatic increase in terrorist attacks within Israel proper (Brym and Araj 2006). Many of these attacks took place in heavily populated civilian areas and resulted not only in multiple casualties, but also in a great demoralization of the public and high levels of related depression, stress, and increased incidence of Posttraumatic Stress Disorder (Morag 2005). The frequency of these attacks, combined with the loss of life and limb, financial damage, detrimental effect on morale, and clear strategic victory by terror groups, resulted in several tactical steps taken by the Israeli security apparatus. These actions, of which the private security industry played a small tactical part, collectively resulted in a significant reduction of casualties by acts of terror. Between July 2003 and July 2004 there were 25 casualties from acts of terror compared to 400 casualties between September 2001 and September 2002, at the height of the Uprising (Morag 2005). From a social aspect, and to understand the effect, if any, that the private security industry had on the public's feeling of safety, as well as to gain insight regarding the support or encouragement of the Israel Police in fragmenting aspects of policing, a comprehensive approach is required and as such a basic understanding of relevant Israeli law is necessary. At the licensing level, since 1968, private business, regardless of industry, has been somewhat dependent on the Israel Police. The Business Licensing Law of 1968 (Ministry of Finance 2015), states that businesses, regardless of size or function, require approval from the police force. This law includes terrorist-specific security requirements for businesses, but it is mostly concerned with safety and with businesses where crowds may gather, such as movie theaters, sports stadiums, and shopping malls. In an attempt to provide more guidance to private sector security, in 2001 a new position — the Police Security Liaison Officer — was created within the Israeli Police Force. This police officer was responsible for liaison between the police and municipalities, inspectors, and security officers of guarded sites including public institutions, movie theaters, hotels, hospitals, private security guards, and parking attendants, but did not provide an effective solution for regulating the private security industry in practice. Regardless of the 1968 law concerned primarily with larger businesses, as a result of the attack on a restaurant in Haifa in March 2002, the police officially ordered (Sehayak 2003) that small businesses have security measures in place and be guarded by armed private security, but did not provide precise guidelines on what procedures these guards should adhere to. The level of security was to be decided by the business itself, based on perceived or actual risk and as the entire expense was incurred by the business, it was always influenced by cost (Sehayak 2003). This recommendation can be considered a milestone event in the private security industry in Israel and in the fragmentation of policing as it resulted in responsibilities traditionally conducted by the police, such as ensuring public safety, to be shared by private security companies. This knee-jerk reaction not only provided a very quick, visible response to an economy that was losing money (Frey, Luechinger, and Stutzer 2007) but also helped to restore the feeling of public safety. This is evident in the results of a study conducted by the Jaffa Center for Strategic Studies, Tel Aviv University, which states that in 2003, 83 percent of those interviewed felt that someone close to them would be harmed in a terror attack; this was significantly less than the 92 percent in 2002 (Arian 2003), which is the same year casualties were highest and the same year

"The starting point would always need to be a deep understanding of what we are protecting against."

the police recommended having armed security at all publicly accessible sites. Of course, there are several factors that influence this feeling of safety, but having a visible security presence contributes to this. For the purpose of comparison, another survey examining Israelis' feeling of safety in 2013 presented results that 76 percent of Israeli citizens, both Arabs and Jews, felt that their personal safety level was high; however, there is a significant fear of criminally motivated violence after dark, specifically around the participants' neighborhoods. The biggest sources of fear amongst the Jewish population was 60 percent of participants fearing property crime, 57 percent fearing acts of terror, and 55 percent expressing fear from organized crime. Within the Arab population, the biggest fear was from vandalism at 45 percent, extortion at 37 percent, and acts of terror at 36 percent. Comparing statistics representing feelings of safety and the offenses that were feared from 2002, 2003, and 2013 indicates a trend of reduction in fear from terror attacks (Ministry of Public Security 2014). This positive change in feeling cannot be directly mapped to the Israeli private security industry growth nor should private industry be seen as the sole source of the trend. It should, however, be noted that in 2002 the private security industry comprised 1.8 percent of the entire workforce and grew by 10.8 percent in 2003 with 56.6 thousand people, totaling 2 percent of the workforce that were employed in the private security industry (Hendeles 2004). Furthermore, this trend continued and in 2011, 124.5 thousand people were employed by the private security industry, which now comprised 2.5 percent of the workforce (Israel Central Bureau of Statistics 2012). The trend of the increased feeling of public safety with the increased growth of the private security industry somewhat negates the theory that commodification is taking place. In this case a higher security presence resulted in reducing the feeling of insecurity and did not increase the feeling of public insecurity as is suggested with commodification."

Editors: Norway is beginning to implement international standards and regulations to physically secure urban infrastructure and buildings. Discussions are taking place concerning whether there should be some uniquely Norwegian security strategies, such as the police not normally carrying weapons. Do you think there is a potential for developing a more liberal Norwegian way of securing buildings, events, and cities in comparison to, for example, the British or the American approach? If you, as a security specialist from another context, both culturally and with regards to the level of threat, would give Norway some advice – what would it be?

IT: My advice would be to base the standards on what has been proven to work, but without a doubt to consider the local nuances and culture. In addition, heavy importance should be given to the risk and threat, as well as to the means and capabilities of the adversary. As such, if the threat, risk, means, and capabilities of the adversary allow for a more liberal approach, then it may be implemented. In other words, the starting point would always need to be a deep understanding of what we are protecting against.

Interview:
Jack Fischer Eriksen

Jack Fischer Eriksen is the managing director of the Norwegian Business and Industry Security Council (NSR). Eriksen has had a diverse career in the Norwegian security environment. He has policed the streets of Oslo, protected VIPs, and he has worked in the private sector as a security consultant. Before joining NSR he was an officer in the Norwegian Police Security Service (PST). As a representative of the PST he was one of the collaborators in the studio preceding this book.

This interview, exploring Eriksen's different roles in the Norwegian security sector, was conducted in Oslo in the autumn of 2014.

Editors: How can the Norwegian security mind-set be understood compared to national security mind-sets elsewhere, exemplified by the US and the UK?

JFE: I am of the opinion that there are huge differences, and there are many reasons for this — historical as well as cultural. Since World War II, Norway has been a nonviolent country. Hostilities and offensive actions against populations, buildings, and communities are things we read about in the news. I think the fact that Norway has been so peaceful has contributed to a culture of, I don't want to use the word *naïveté*, but we are rather open. Interaction and communication and finding peaceful solutions have become ingrained in our culture throughout history. But then the environment changes and external threats are drawing closer, as they already have done in the UK for a while. This has affected their culture, their mind-set, and what people do to protect themselves. It is a rather complex issue, but I think this part of culture is about to change in Norway, too.

Our credulousness, if that is the right word to use, will probably diminish over time. We are probably not as naive today as we used to be, and we focus more on security because we feel that threats are more imminent. From an international perspective, Norway is exposed to such threats through what we see happening in the Middle East, for instance. This affects us politically and it has an influence on the police, the government, and the general public. A new kind of mind-set is arising where the focus on security is strong, and I think this has influenced the debate about police armament in Norway as well as the debate about how we should protect public buildings, installations, and parks. Ultimately, it will affect how we see our society. One result is that private institutions, those who have the opportunity and the financial muscle to introduce a higher level of security to protect themselves, are the ones who will step ahead and take measures that we have not seen before. In the US, there is a long-standing culture for self-preservation, resistance, and the right to bear arms. In Norway, the mind-set has been the complete opposite: we have kept a strict gun policy to ensure our freedom.

Editors: Are there other examples of unique aspects of law enforcement in Norway?

JFE: Yes. If we compare Norway and other countries, it is rather unique that the police force is also involved in disaster relief and handling major crises. In Norway, the military is kept out until the last minute. I think this is an important discussion and an important principle. In many other countries, the military is mobilized in times of crises. In Norway, the military comes in to the aid of the inhabitants, while they are more likely to take control and demonstrate power in other countries. When should the military go in and what kind of resources should they use? It is a political debate, and also a debate within the military organization as well as within the police organization as to where the resources should be distributed and who should do what. It comes down to a fight for resources.

Editors: Substantial legal measures have been taken to lower the threshold for military intervention and assistance. This might be seen as a step in the same direction as the international community – and this would in turn represent a threat to Norway's specific approach. What are your thoughts about this, and of the possibility of arming the police?

JFE: In fact, I have yet to make up my mind about that. Previously, when I was in the police, I was of course positive because it was something I felt was right, so that was my personal opinion. Now, I am not so sure anymore, but I still think that more officers should be armed in the field. I do not think that everyone in the police should carry guns, but I am of the opinion that some special units should have arms more easily available than just in their cars. There is also a debate whether guards should be armed, private guards hired by private companies, like the ones we see in the UK. This is a dangerous path to set out on, I think. However, with the elevated threat level we currently have, we cannot avoid having more armed police officers for a period of time. It would be naive to think that we can solve situations by keeping guns locked inside the cars. They need to have them available. Especially when we look at the development in other countries, where there have been attacks on large groups of people. In such a situation it would be unfortunate if the police officers would have to run to their car before they took action.

Editors: What do you see as the impact of the Norwegian mentality we talked about earlier? Does it make actual police work better or worse?

JFE: Coming across as a fellow human being is extremely important to build trust. It is crucial that the police force reflects the rest of the society, that they focus on being protective and not someone that the general public should fear. When someone approaches a police officer, they should feel that there is openness, that they want contact – not that they approach a suspicious, armed officer who wants nothing to do with them. That is the way it has been with the Norwegian police, and it still is like that. They depend on the public's trust. However, I do not think they will lose that trust if they are armed. Investigations into July 2014's event showed the same – that the police still enjoyed the public's confidence. Furthermore, in that particular situation the police being armed was in fact positive, because there was a security aspect to it. The general public felt the police could make a difference when it came to the threat that was rising. Given that particular situation, when it was already communicated that there was a serious threat and that the police would be armed, it turned to something assuring. If we balance it and do it right, it adds to the trust. But if the police would have kept their weapons in everyday situations after this, I am not so sure that the same level of confidence would have remained.

Editors: The fact that they raised the bar in that situation was conceived as some kind of –

JFE: That the police take things seriously, that they show the lengths they will go to to protect the public. People expect that, I think, that they adapt to the situation and the level of threat. As Hadia Tajik said, this doesn't mean that we should have an armed police force, it means that it was necessary in this particular situation – and I think it was important to build trust. And then we need a debate in the wake of this; whether the police carrying weapons or not should depend on the situation. We need to consider thoroughly why we do it, so the decision is not made haphazardly. Over time, I think people would get used to seeing the police armed.

Editors: Will the requirements for securing buildings be affected by international standards and expectations? if so, could it be possible to work around those international laws and expectations to implement an equivalent local Norwegian approach to the way we secure buildings? It seems to me that you consider Norwegianness as something positive. Do you think it would be possible to keep the positive aspects of this in the local approach to physical security measures?

JFE: One good example of this is dock areas, where the regulations are international and we cannot choose not to follow them. But in other areas, it is possible to adapt the measures to the local culture and avoid copying everything other countries do. This is where education is important, architectural and engineering as well as security education programs, to be able to make conscious choices about how we should react to these requirements in our country. For example in the finance sector, requirements could arise as to how businesses in the financial services industry should protect themselves. Are we then bound to follow international models, or is it possible to find a Norwegian method? In my opinion, we need to strike a balance between openness and security – exactly the research you have conducted. We need to find a Norwegian model for how we should protect ourselves, but it must be robust and of a high standard. Maybe there are better ways than we see in other countries. It is extremely important that we are conscious in the process of developing these processes. The studies at Bergen School of Architecture is an important part of this, and we must pursue these lines of thought to avoid copying the requirements from other countries. Of course, some aspects should be similar, but we must develop a Norwegian model. To do that, we need a set of tools, and we need to develop our own methods that will still be approved by the international community. If not, we will be forced to have fences of a certain height surrounding the docks and so on. We need alternatives.

Editors: In July 2014, when PST announced publicly that there was a terror threat in Norway, many thought this was a sign of a different kind of openness than we have seen previously in Norway or in the rest of the world. Publicly announcing "We are not sure what is going on, but we are quite worried about it" is definitely another kind of openness than we see on CNN. Do you think it was a conscious choice by PST to respond in this way, or do you think it happened because PST is not used to eliminating this kind of threat?

JFE: In PST, they handle threats on a regular basis, and they have broad experience with many different kinds. I believe PST has moved in that direction on purpose, and we have seen this tendency for quite some time. They tell the public a bit more now, because the public has the right to know. Personally, I think it was sensible to say something about the situation, because we do not have armed police. When PST chose to take action and arm the police, the public would of course ask why they did that. Ultimately, they were forced to give out some information because our police are normally unarmed, and people would react if they suddenly were.

Editors: PST spoke openly about not having the situation under control, but wanting to take some measures. Is this a typical of a local Norwegian approach or modus operandi, or do we see this in other countries as well?

JFE: We see this in other countries too. For instance in London, they let the public know when there is a terror threat, and the same thing happens in Australia and the US, but traditionally, the level of openness has not been this high. I believe they made a situational judgment under unusual circumstances, and they saw that this openness was required.

Editors: In many countries with an elevated state of readiness, that level has remained high for extended periods of time. In the US there are sometimes discussions about what is perceived as a permanently raised threat level. The fact that in this situation, PST was specific as to when the level was raised and when it was lowered may have given the public the impression that they were in control and knew what they were doing. Can it be difficult to lower the state of readiness and the terror threat after raising it?

JFE: This is definitely a complex task that requires strong leadership and a sense of responsibility. I am glad I do not have to make that decision. Having the stomach to communicate it to the public and take the responsibility is difficult, but also extremely important to be considered reliable. At the same time, PST indicated that the threat could be prolonged. I believe the hardest part is lowering it, as with everything else in the security industry. It is not an option to start having open cockpits after we first started locking them. Another example is seat belts in cars. When you start having them as standard equipment in cars, you do not stop. You see that it works, and no one wants less safe cars in the future. When you raise the security level and reduce the risk, there is good reason to keep on doing the same thing. But everything is different when it comes to the threat only. When you take other measures to reduce the risk, there is no reason to go back. Here, we are only talking about the threat, not the entire risk triangle.

Editors: After the recent shootings in the Canadian parliament in October 2014, PST chose to issue a warning that there is a threat to uniformed personnel and military personnel. Do you believe it is difficult to find the right balance as to which information you should make public? Inevitably, it causes fear. Is it relevant to ask if this is information that everyone needs to have?

JFE: From a business perspective I want to ask: "How do you know only the police, the military and the politicians are under threat? If we make sure they are safe, what does it do to me as a member of society? What does it do to businesses nearby?" I have been asked these kinds of questions many times. I have been in countless meetings lately, and the questions are always the same: "What does this threat mean to us?" "What should we protect ourselves against?" "Do we need to take any measures at all, are we even under threat?" The question of how it affects us is an extremely difficult one. Should the business community consider the possibility that they could be under threat too? They may need more time to take the appropriate measures. And it is not as if banks or shopping centers or insurance companies can get police protection without a concrete threat. So, they use the resources they have available, namely security guards. And then the question arises: Can security guards protect them from this kind of threat? How can we find the right measures to take? We cannot accept it if there is a risk that a vehicle enters a shopping center or bank, and these are issues that can be solved. But when it comes to knife attacks or attacks with bombs taped to a body, it is another story. How can we protect ourselves from that kind of scenario? The debate about this particular topic is obviously a difficult one for the business community to handle.

Editors: The reported cost of the terror threat announced during the summer of 2014 was NOK 77.5M. Do you consider this sum to be sizable, given the circumstances, or is this kind of money used for other scenarios that we never hear about? Will expanded budget allocations be necessary to give room for increased terror preparedness in the future?

JFE: For the business community, it is important that we focus not only on security and preparedness, but also on the day-to-day police work. There has been a hot debate about police investigations and the investigation competence the police possesses, and the fact that cases are not investigated because the police have no capacity. It is important to be able to hold two thoughts in mind at the same time. When resources are drained from a police district due to terrorism preparedness measures, we should be able to consider how both issues could be solved with a satisfactory result. It is important to the man in the street as well as to the business community that normal cases are investigated.

Editors: Post–July 22, 2011, there has been a tendency to introduce temporary physical security measures outside buildings in Oslo. The current political environment paired with the catastrophe appears to make this a necessary requirement. There are also a number of permanent security installations in Oslo. Do you think that it is possible to argue for the removal of some of these in the future, because they will no longer be considered necessary, or is the increased security level irreversible?

JFE: In general, I believe it is difficult to reverse security measures, which is why we need to change the way we think about this issue. If you introduce basic protective measures, they will be permanent. If you change your windows to a type that can withstand an explosives attack, you will not change them back. The same is valid for fences or drive-through prevention barriers around a facility. This is why I believe we should think about the different stages of protection. In the larger zone there could be situational measures that could be removed, or they could remain but made less visible. Let us say there are drive-through prevention barriers in a shopping street – it should be possible to remove them for the national day parade or if there is a concert and a lot of people there. Physical security measures do not have to be permanent, but they could be applied when necessary.

Editors: What you say here is in accordance with the guidelines issued by PST and NSM [Nasjonal Sikkerhetsmyndighet, Norway's National Security Authority] about different levels of security in an area based on a risk assessment and a threat evaluation. But who makes the decision as to which measures are necessary? A substantial effort and competency is required to exploit the flexibility, and there may be certain thresholds that make this difficult in practice.

JFE: Absolutely. The reason for increasing the security measures may be unknown, and not all threats can be measured. This makes it hard to remove the protective measure – because what happens if you remove a security measure and something actually happens – which forces will be against you for leaving the gates open because there was no threat at that particular moment? This is part of the reason why such measures often become permanent.

Editors: Someone actually needs to take the risk and downsize the security setup. It would appear to take some courage to take responsibility for this.

JFE: This is where we start thinking about cause and effect. If you are good at impact assessment, such a downsizing should not have any negative effect. It is crucial that the protective measures you choose to introduce, especially outside buildings, are so good that they can be permanent. That you will not be annoyed by what you did for the next ten years, for instance because the city died around you or people started avoiding the place. The security measures we take now ought to be so efficient that they also have an added value. We are not aware of the threat level at all times, so we need to assess the situation based on what we know and consider if it is an acceptable risk or not. Looking at crime it is possibly easier to take measures. Like lighting: We know that a large proportion of crime happens between 11:00 p.m. and 4:00 a.m., and as a consequence of this, we may choose to light up an area between those hours. However, there is also a risk that something happens after 4 o'clock, but we cannot keep the lights on all night. In this case, it is possible to be a bit more dynamic – dealing with terror and sabotage is more difficult.

Editors: Do you think there is a risk that foreign companies coming from cultures where greater physical security measures are required, who are seeking to establish themselves in Norway, expect or demand the same kind of security measures they are already used to – in conflict with the less aggressive Norwegian approach we discussed earlier?

JFE: I haven't heard about this being an issue yet, but I assume we will get there. We cooperate with British oil and gas companies, and they are used to armed protection around their facilities. Here, we have fences to lock out sheep and wild animals. I believe Norwegian companies will be forced to consider this in a longer perspective. Companies trading with other countries where they depend on our production will probably be the first to introduce more security measures, because there could be enormous economic losses as a consequence. A strong security plan is an economic asset, because clients know that deliveries can be made even in times of crisis – this is a normal way of thinking for many businesses today.

Editors: In comparing Canary Wharf in with DNB's headquarters in the Barcode in Oslo, there is a huge difference in the level of security. Do you think the Barcode area will remain as open as it is today, or would you anticipate stronger security measures being introduced for this area in the future?

JFE: That is a difficult question. I cannot tell if PST has given them any advice, but it is an area that has our attention. In my opinion, it is surprisingly open, and it seems that they to a certain degree have failed to take the terror incidents in Norway and abroad into account in their security strategy. It could be a form of risk acceptance and a conscious choice, but there is a potential in the architecture for an entirely different solution. One example is bike stands that are lit at night – I am surprised that they haven't introduced well-known measures that can double as security measures and a way to highlight the architecture in the area. It is also an interesting question, seen in relation to the previous question if we should adopt methods from other countries or if the situation in Norway requires other measures. The fact that we build a new business area with such a degree of openness is a reflection of the Norwegian culture. I am not sure if it is a conscious choice or not, but in my opinion it is strikingly vulnerable.

Editors: In the mid-1980s the political landscape in Norway was more polarized, with stronger left- and right-wing factions. An example from the left was the Blitz community, which started out as a group occupying buildings in Oslo as a political statement against speculation taking place in the private property market, and continued as an anarchist youth community and activist center. The group questioned who owned the right to the city. Do you think this kind of occupation can be justified?

JFE: The challenge at the time was that I failed to grasp what they wanted to communicate. It took some time to understand why they resorted to occupation. At the time, the general public saw it more as a rebellion or just vandalism, and they were considered a mix between a mob and political activists. Their political message was overshadowed by violent demonstrations and vandalism, and I think that is a shame. I saw only the violent side of it, and there was a polarization – the police against the Blitz activists. I knew little about what they stood for, and couldn't tell if I agreed with them or not. They had a hostile image, and it was easy to justify the police crackdown on the Blitz demonstrators without reflecting over why they protested. In the early phase there was little understanding between the groups and why we were fighting each other. Now we understand more and the police have a milder attitude, where they do not necessarily use gas and stun grenades or cut through roofs to evict occupants from houses. It took years before the police and the politicians began to understand the reasons why they were fighting each other. I cannot remember that we had any lengthy discussions about the underlying causes for the existence of Blitz, their idealism or their political agenda. I think the same pattern repeats itself today for other groups, that a hostile image is created.

Editors: Would you rather that all of this had not happened, or did anything good come out of it?

JFE: I believe especially the police learned a lot from these incidents. Today, they have another approach when dealing with demonstrations, a softer approach. The police enter the discussion early; they are proactive and more accommodating and try to start a dialogue instead of contributing to the escalation of riots.

Editors: We spent some time with representatives of Occupy London, and got the impression that the situation between police and demonstrators is constantly escalating. Is it possible that the Blitz situation contributed to the particular local, or Norwegian, policing culture of today that we talked about earlier?

JFE: Yes, I think you have a point there. Someone must take responsibility and change the situation, and in my opinion that ought to be the government's concern. Of course, sometimes there is a need to fight fire with fire, but if there are methods available to solve conflict peacefully, these ought to be used. In many cases, this is not an option. As for the Blitz situation, the way the police used their power can be justified, and house occupants are still met with force. They are taking other people's property into possession, and the owners have the right to make decisions about their property. The police must and should intervene, but it is important that they start a dialogue before they resort to physical methods of eviction. The distance between demonstrators and police response units has grown, and they are not used in an early phase when they may escalate the situation. I think the Norwegian police force has learned a lot from dealing with Blitz.

Editors: Were there ever discussions about how the violence could be reduced at the time?

JFE: Yes. The administration and the operational police officers had opposing views. The administration stopped the operations and let them do what they did, to be able to go in and catch them later. They realized that the situation would escalate if they tried to stop it. That was frustrating for us, we wanted to go out there and catch the enemy. We did not understand how they could let it pass. In my experience there are different cultures within the police. The operational officers often want to make an effort and stop the action, while officers higher up in the system have a more holistic approach. What does it bring about, what are the long-term synergistic effects? I did not have that perspective at the time. If that was the administration's responsibility or my own, I do not know.

Editors: Maybe it could be said that what happened here in Norway contributed to a better police, but perhaps it can happen in other international contexts, that fronts mobilize in response to a situation arising, and as a result, it can lead to a permanent condition where police are more aggressive and confrontational.

JFE: Gathering information about the opponent makes you better prepared and creates a relationship of trust that may move toward cooperation as time passes. Norway's police force has been visiting the other Nordic countries on a number of occasions to talk about our methods. They have been interested in learning how we handle these types of conflicts, for instance in Copenhagen and Malmö, where there are often riots. There are many ways to achieve a goal.

Editors: The Blitz community is still protecting their house with their own security measures even though public law protects the house, and they are under police protection. Why do you think they do that?

JFE: That is an interesting point that I haven't thought about. I think it has become symbolic. It is part of the narrative of the house and the community. If they were to remove their own security measures, the house would change and become an ordinary youth club. The window bars and the graffiti is kept, while the barricades on the sidewalk have been removed – it shows that the measures change when the threat level changes.

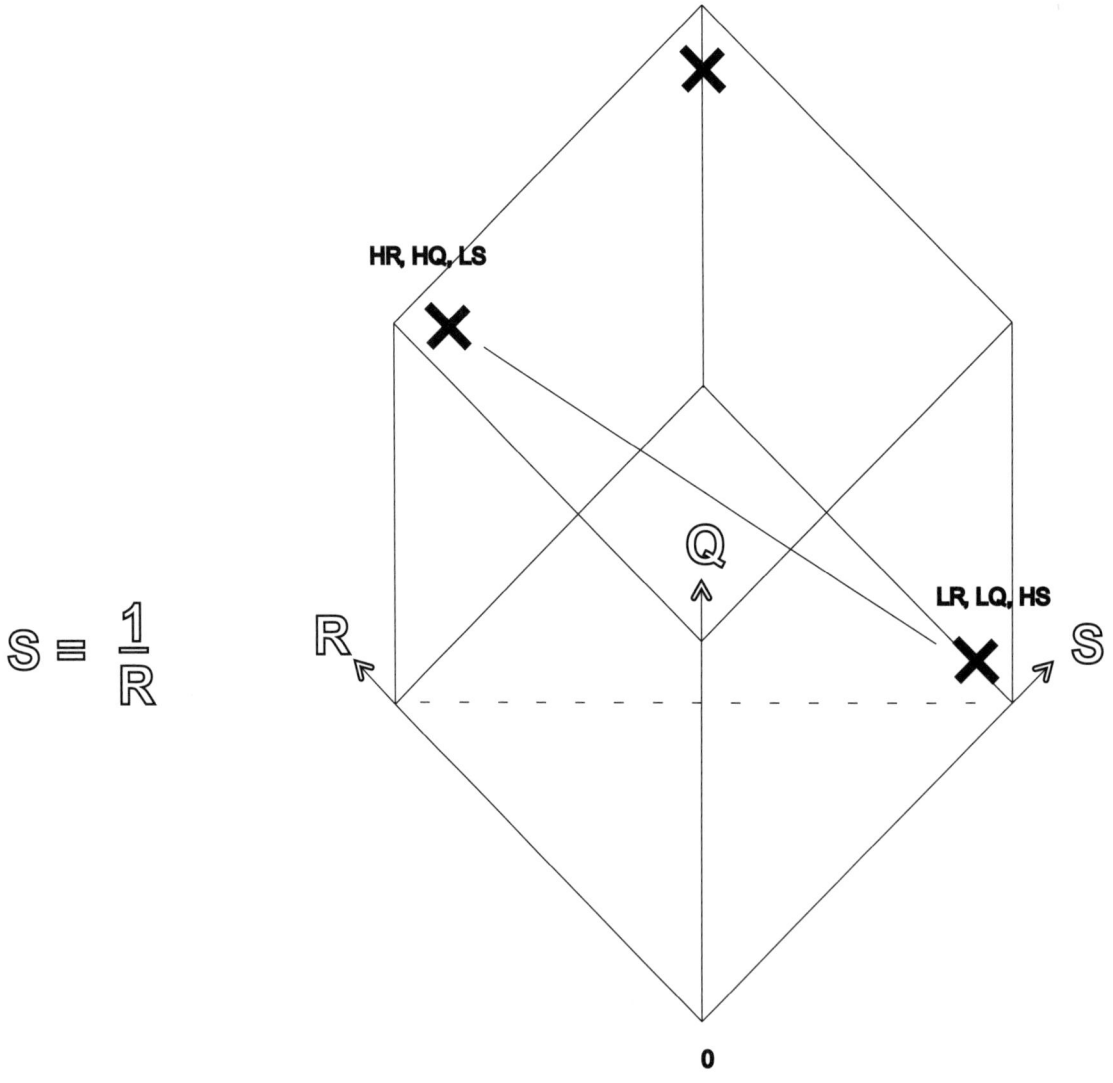

HR, HQ, HS

HR, HQ, LS

$$S = \frac{1}{R}$$

R **Q** **LR, LQ, HS** **S**

0

The 3-D diagram visualizes possible relationships between high and low levels of urban quality (Q), security (S), and the right to the city (R) used to discuss the projects.

HQ = HIGH QUALITY
LQ = LOW QUALITY
HS = HIGH SECURITY
LS = LOW SECURITY
HR = HIGH RIGHT TO THE CITY
LR = LOW RIGHT TO THE CITY

DISCURSIVE DESIGN PROPOSALS

The projects presented on the following pages explore possible scenarios for the reconstruction of the Oslo Government Quarter affected by the July 22 bombing. Developed by students within the masters program of the Bergen School of Architecture, the proposals investigate a range of responses to the pressures for securitized urban space, from the prioritization of the design of security measures to a negotiated balance between security measures on the one hand and architectural/urban quality and the right to the city – to outright resistance to the securitization of urban space – on the other.

In building up a theoretical foundation for the projects, the group explored competing discourses addressing the theme of security and the city on the one hand and of the city as a site of liberty, freedom, and democracy on the other. The relationship between the interests these discourses articulate is most commonly represented in terms of a zero-sum game – an "inescapable trade-off between security and liberty."[1] The students were asked to explore these relations, asking could they be reframed or reconciled in other ways? This would in turn trigger a series of related questions:

– To what extent do the pressures of security-centric thinking, for example, security by design, impose adverse effects on: (a) the quality of architecture and urban design; and (b) the performance of those spatial regimes in supporting the public's accessibility and right to the city?

– To what extent can the assumptions and orthodoxies of security by design and broader security-centric thinking, be challenged? Is there the possibility for security strategies to be hijacked or exploited for the purpose of generating more productive, positive, and novel architectural and urban qualities, atmospheres, or social potentials – new forms of sociospatial liberation? In these terms, are there possibilities for the architecture of securitization to support rather than limit exchange, conflict, negotiation, protest, diversity, coexistence, transparency, engagement, empowerment, and participation? Could there be any viability to ambitions such as these?

– Is it even possible to comprehensively secure public spaces through design – particularly as the methods of carrying out crime or terror attacks responds so quickly and dynamically to existing security measures? Is there the danger of giving up more in freedom than what is gained in security in the unattainable desire to eliminate all risk from our cities?

Rather than providing definitive answers to these questions, the projects of the studio attempted to collectively map a range of possible responses to this broad set of challenges.

OSLO GOVERNMENT QUARTER

DYSTOPIAN SCENARIO FOR EXTREME SECURITY

LINE MYHRE

- **01** 1.5 m thick × 15 m high shock-absorbing concrete wall
- **02** Electric fences with cameras on alternate lamp posts
- **03** Manipulated landscape
- **04** Watchtowers with automated snipers
- **05** Sniper drones
- **06** Decoy road in front of VIP entrance
- **07** Automated snipers moving back and forth on top of the wall
- **08** 360 degrees surveillance camera towers
- **09** Vehicle checkpiont #1, with guard, barriers, AMPR, access panel with print, face, and eye recognition
- **10** Reinforced bollards
- **11** Personnel checkpoint #1. Access panel with print, face, and eye recognintion. Only people going to H-, Y-, S-block, R4, M17, and M19 can pass beyond this point.
- **12** X-ray, gamma-, heat-detection cameras
- **13** Entrance for prime minister, ministers and other VIP guests. Laser gate
- **14** Persons denied access are escorted from premises by security guards.
- **15** 12 m high electric fence
- **16** Quicksand between the wall and the electric fence
- **17** X-ray, gamma-, heat- and bomb-detection control point. Person entry only possible through control point they have been granted access to.

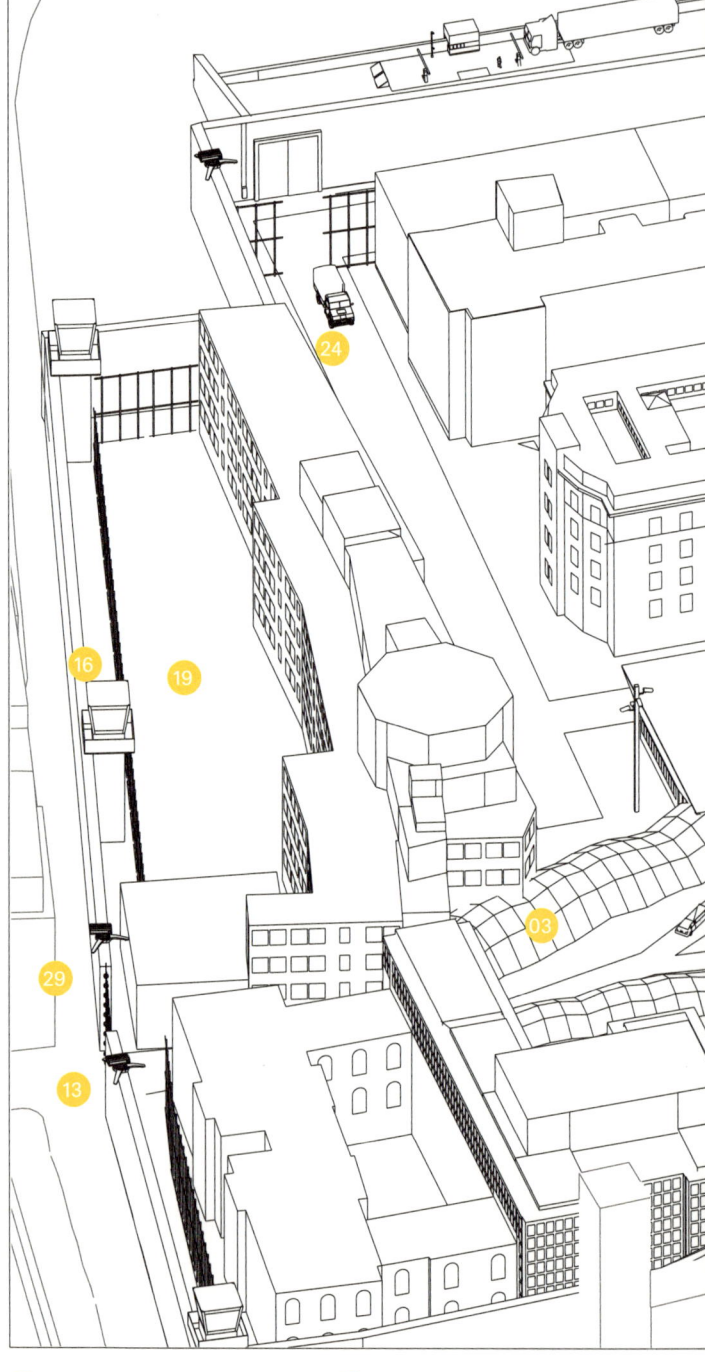

E — Dystopian Scenario for Extreme Security

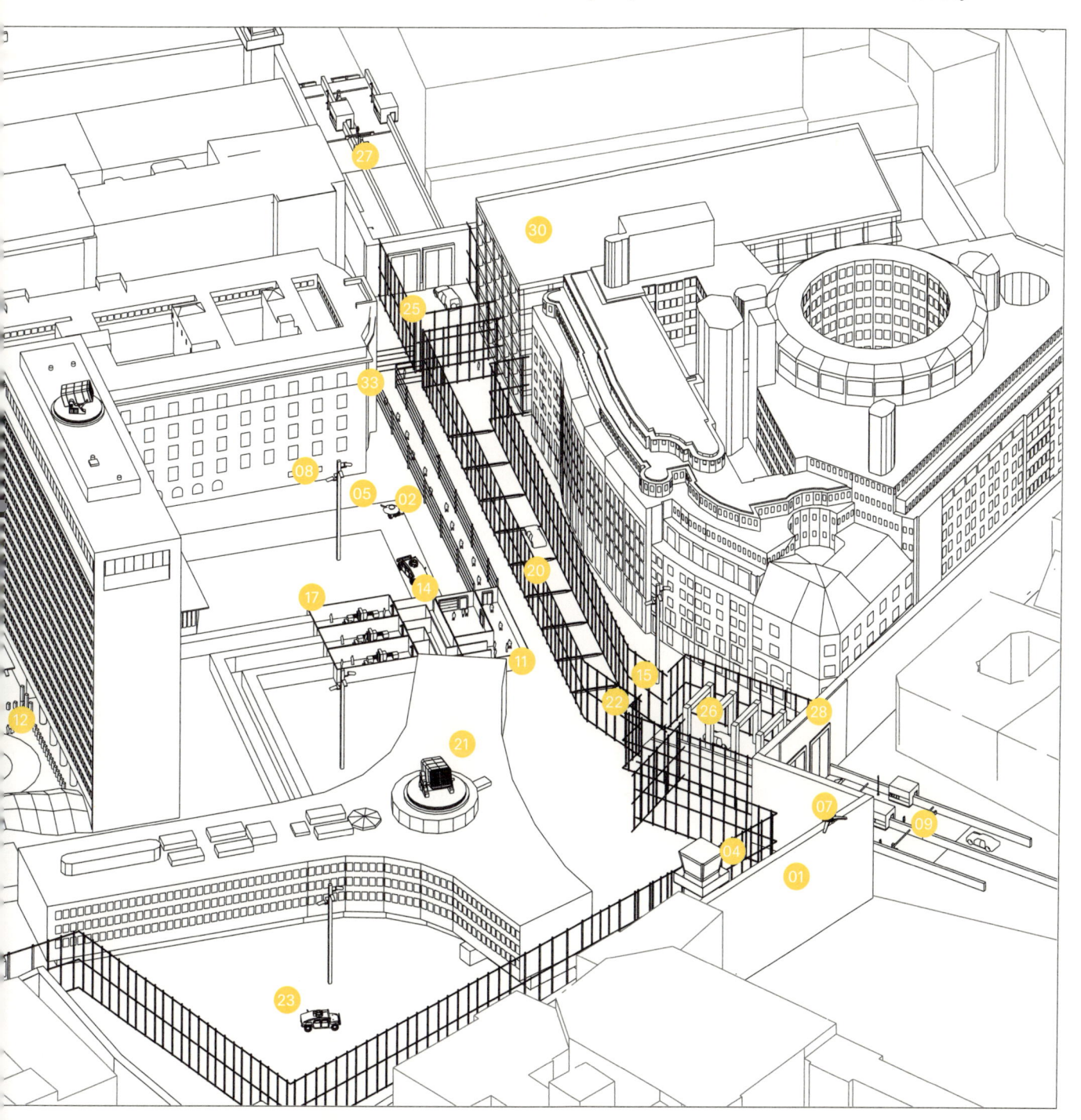

18	Delivery truck checkpoints with guard, barriers, AMPR, X-ray, gamma, heat- and bomb-detection devices	22	Narrowing of road	27	Exit vehicle checkpoint with guard, barriers, AMPR, X-ray, gamma-, and heat-detection devices	31	Personnel checkpoint #2. Only personnel with access to S-block, R4, M17 and M19 can pass beyond this point.
19	Buildings too close to governmental buildings demolished	23	Armored vehicles patrolling area	28	Steel gate	32	Demolishing and relocating of nearby buildings. New building replacing R6 is built.
20	Tire stoppers	24	Internal delivery trucks	29	All surrounding streets become pedestrianized.	33	Personnel are directed towards buildings they are working in through narrow protected pathways.
21	Missile detection and defense weapons	25	Exit vehicle checkpoint	30	Old buildings demolished, new common parking complex built		
		26	Vehicle checkpoint #2. X-ray, gamma-, heat- and bomb-detection devices				

POSITIVE-SUM GAME

Government Quarter

ANDERS SLETTEN EIDE

	Main Interventions	**Security Effect**	**Urban Effect**
01	Dense, low, noniconic buildings	Resilience Technical surveillance Escape routes	Readability Recognizable scale
02	Mixed program Flexible governmental program	Passive surveillance Dispersed assets Redundancy, reduced target aquisition	Transparency Activity, offers
03	Pedestrianization Lighting	Standoff, Situational crime prevention	Safety, usability Universal access
04	Benches, stairs, moat, water, landscaping	Hostile vehicle mitigation Vehicle barrier	Urban furniture Multiple-use space
05	Plaza	Surveillance	Public space

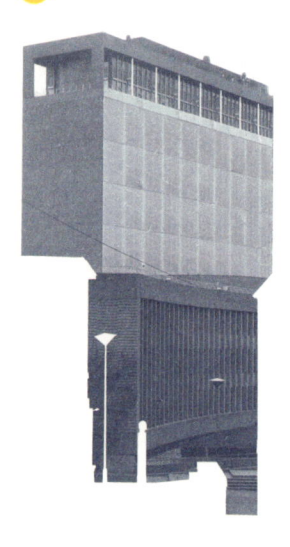

Present urban profile/Power typology

Future urban profile/Power typology

This project explores the question: is there the possibility of a positive-sum outcome between architectural and urban qualities on the one hand, and public security on the other? Could such an approach challenge the conventional securitization impulses and protocols that tend toward monofunctionality, separation, and walling in an urban context?

The proposal pedestrianizes the government quarter. Its outer perimeter is articulated with benches, moats, steps, and planters excluding vehicles (and potential vehicle bombs). New architectural interventions are tactile and modest in scale, with mixed nongovernmental programs and public activities on their ground floors. The scale of architecture is intended to facilitate an accessible and human interaction with the state. Within the new city block structure, the most vulnerable government offices are organized around internal courtyards, while the outer street side accommodates guests and visitors. Improved lighting, the elimination of blind spots, and an increase in daytime and evening programs invite citizens to spend time in the transformed quarter that is now reconnected with Oslo in the east-to-west direction. In contrast to what was formerly a relatively unpopulated (and at night, desolate) monofunctional area, the vision involves a vibrant urban quarter with improved natural and passive surveillance.

Positive-Sum Game

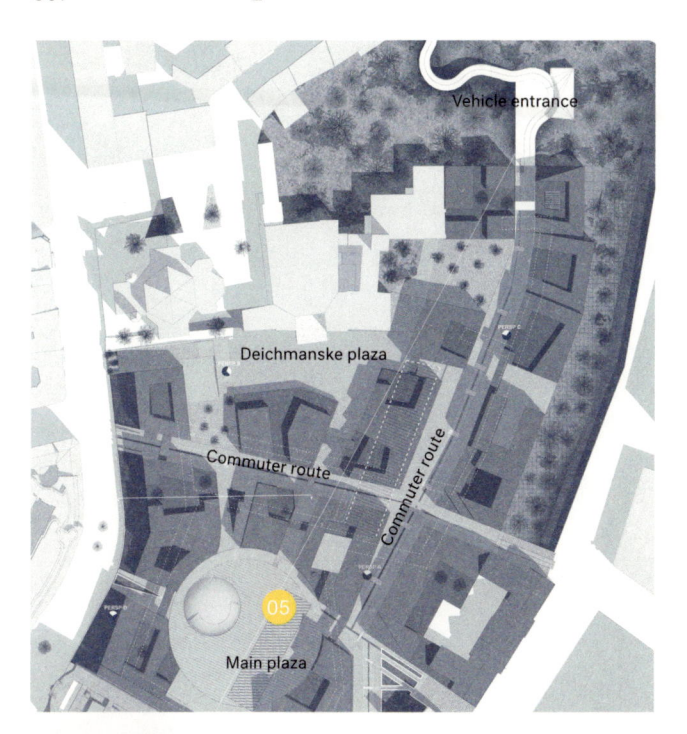

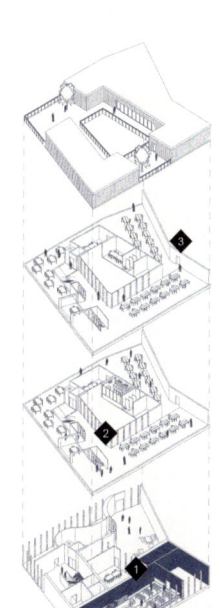

- 1 Typical mixed program block: external meeting room
- 2 Server room placed toward the inner courtyard
- 3 Work stations spaced from windows
- 4 Present (left) and future (right) public space scenario
- 5 Standoff distance supports urban qualities
- 6 Ram-proof flower planters
- 7 Flowerbeds tilt from 120–20 cm, creating seating.

MUTUAL CONCESSIONS

LINE MYHRE

Government Quarter

	Main Interventions	Security Effect	Urban Effect
01	Centralized program Iconic building	Target hardening Espionage protection	Monoprogrammatic Rational programming
02	Single entrance Connection to square	Technical surveillance Escape routes Access control Secure zone	Power / government / public relation Transparency Readability
03	Park	Passive surveillance Standoff distance Mixing zone	Public space Universal access
04	Cordoning, separation, security-landscaping	Hostile vehicle mitigation	Urban, landscape qualities

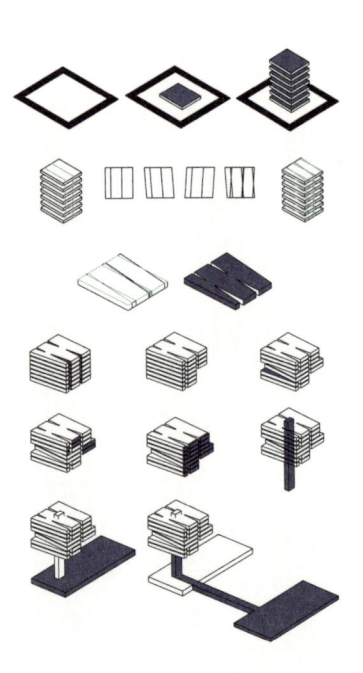

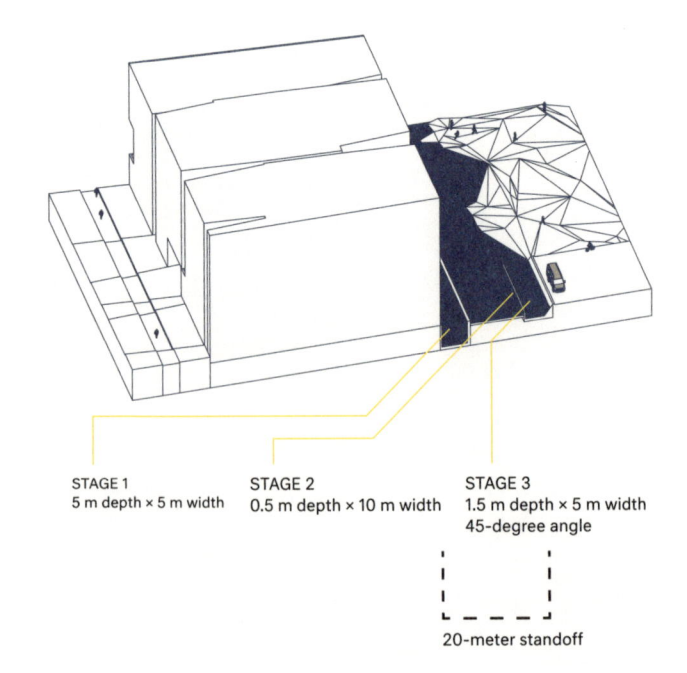

STAGE 1
5 m depth × 5 m width

STAGE 2
0.5 m depth × 10 m width

STAGE 3
1.5 m depth × 5 m width
45-degree angle

20-meter standoff

If, according to the requirements of the government, it is necessary to secure ministerial office buildings, could the footprint of the secured ministry be reduced to a minimum so as to maximize the remainder of the government quarter as a public park for the citizens of Oslo?

The park, intended as a new venue for political protest, is linked by a public passage underneath the new building to the existing square used most for protest in Oslo: Youngstorget. The outer perimeter of the government offices, defined by a moat, offers access via one main entrance. The offices are conceived of as open-plan spaces with connection to their own outdoor area adjacent to the moat.

The majority of workspaces and meeting rooms overlook the park, which has platforms and spaces providing visual interaction between government workers and citizens.

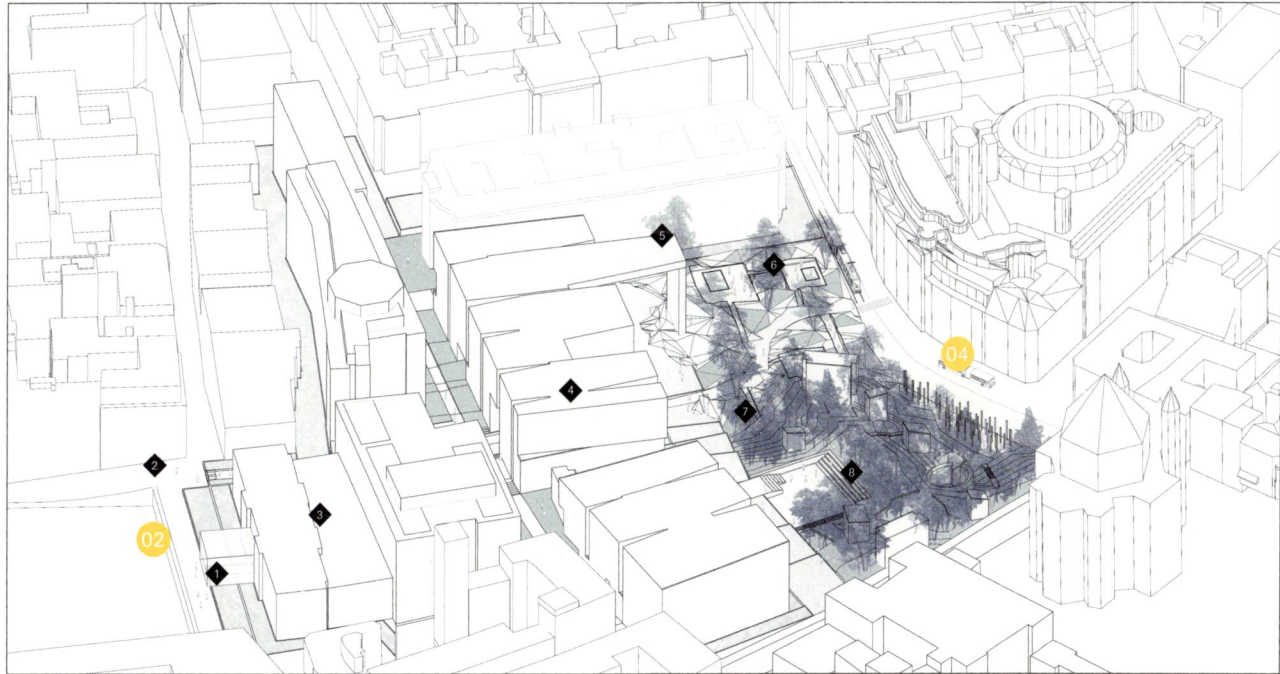

① Ministerial building main entrance	⑤ Public climbing wall	⑧ Clearing in the woods overlooks the secure governmental park on the other side of the moat.
② Pedestrian underground passage leading from Youngstorget to the new public park	⑥ Rocky landscape functions as a vehicles barrier.	
③ Main reception area for guests / visitors; security checkpoint for employees	⑦ Moat. Parts in contact with the park are open for public use.	
④ New ministerial buildings		

GRAFTING THE POLITICAL TO THE PROCESSIONAL

PAVEL WADDLING

	Main Interventions	Security Effect	Urban Effect
01	Uniform pedestrian surface	Reduced target acquisition	Public space Universal access
02	Information and service booths	Hostile vehicle mitigation Access control	Power / government / public relations Transparency
03	Cultural programs in the government quarter	Passive surveillance	Activity, offers Multiple-use space
04	New connections between significant buildings	Escape routes Dispersed assets Resilience	Transparency Readability

Representational political space
- 1 King's Castle
- 2 Oslo University/National Theatre
- 3 City Hall
- 4 Parliament
- 5 Government Quarter
- 6 Youngstorget
- 7 Oslo Cathedral
- 8 Stock Exchange
- 1 Supreme Court
- 2 Court of Appeal
- --- Parade routes

This proposal challenges conventional securitization strategies that attempt to reduce risk through zoned separation of the quarter to be secured – a strategy that typically results in the disconnection of that quarter from the rest of the city. Instead, the project attempts to graft the government quarter and its public spaces – conceived as a political and cultural hub – onto the existing network of processional, representational, and ceremonial spaces in Oslo. Collectively, this significant sequence of spaces is pedestrianized and given a clear identity through a continuous uniform ground surface – defining a series of formal and informal political spaces in the city. An infrastructure of vehicle-blocking architectural objects with public programs define the edges of this new pedestrian zone. The public services this architecture supplies include public toilets, charging stations, drinking fountains, benches, electronic billboards for political expression, and walls for posters and graffiti. Incorporated into the architectural installations is a system of mobile elements that can transform to accommodate changing public needs and circumstances in everyday life during protests or celebrations. Overall, the project's ambition is to provide a better infrastructure to engage citizens in the participatory democratic system, and to support openness and accessibility rather than restricting citizens' field of action.

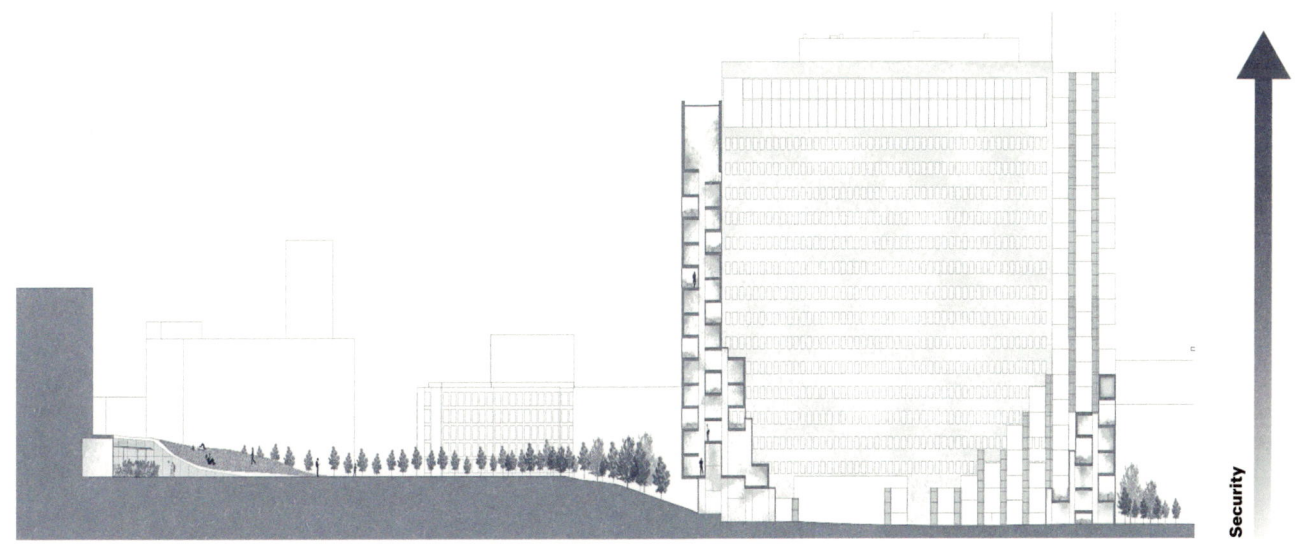

E — Grafting the Political to the Processional

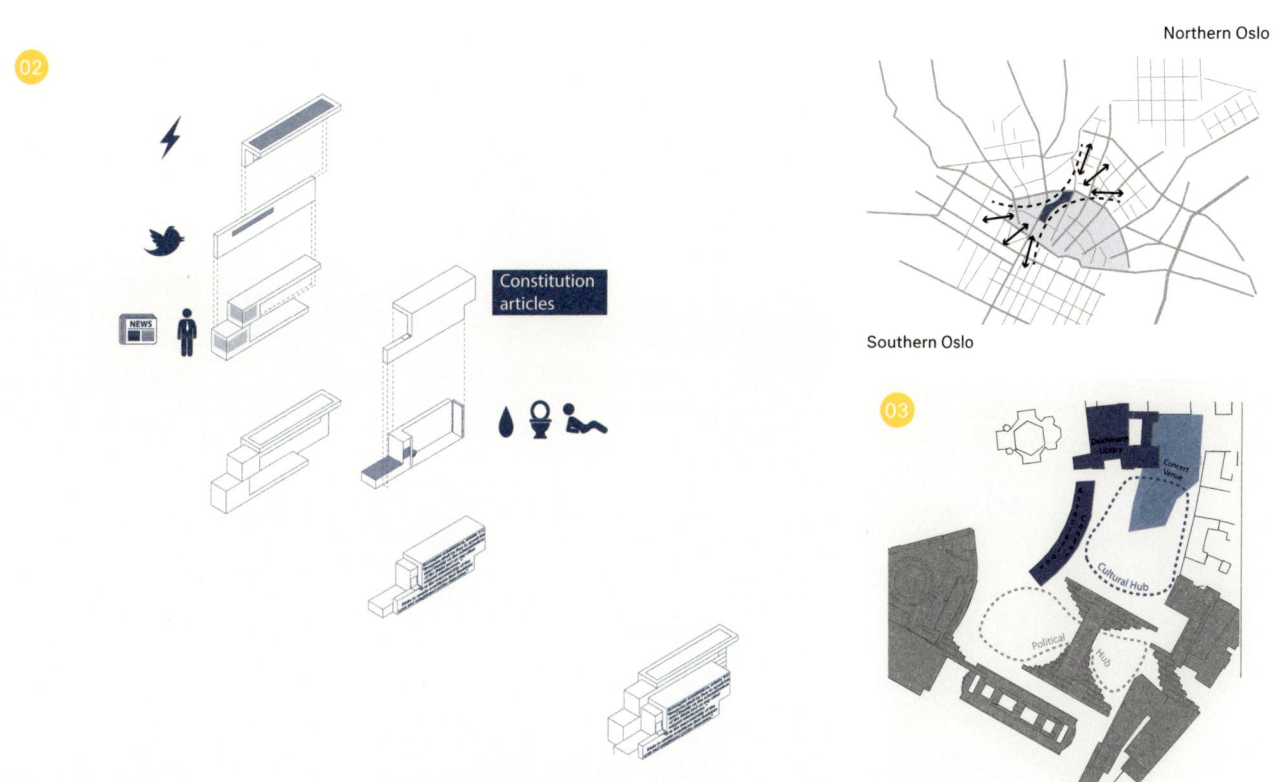

Security

Northern Oslo

Southern Oslo

Constitution articles

PARTICIPATORY ADAPTATION

Government Quarter

SHREYA NAGRATH

Main Interventions	Security Effect	Urban Effect
01 New program in existing buildings	Resilience De-iconization	Reuse Accessability
02 Urban farming, closed streets	Territoriality Social control Hostile vehicle mitigation Passive surveillance	Green city Food production Ownership Public-private space
03 Rebuild on existing structure		Preservation Integration of old, temporary, and new programs

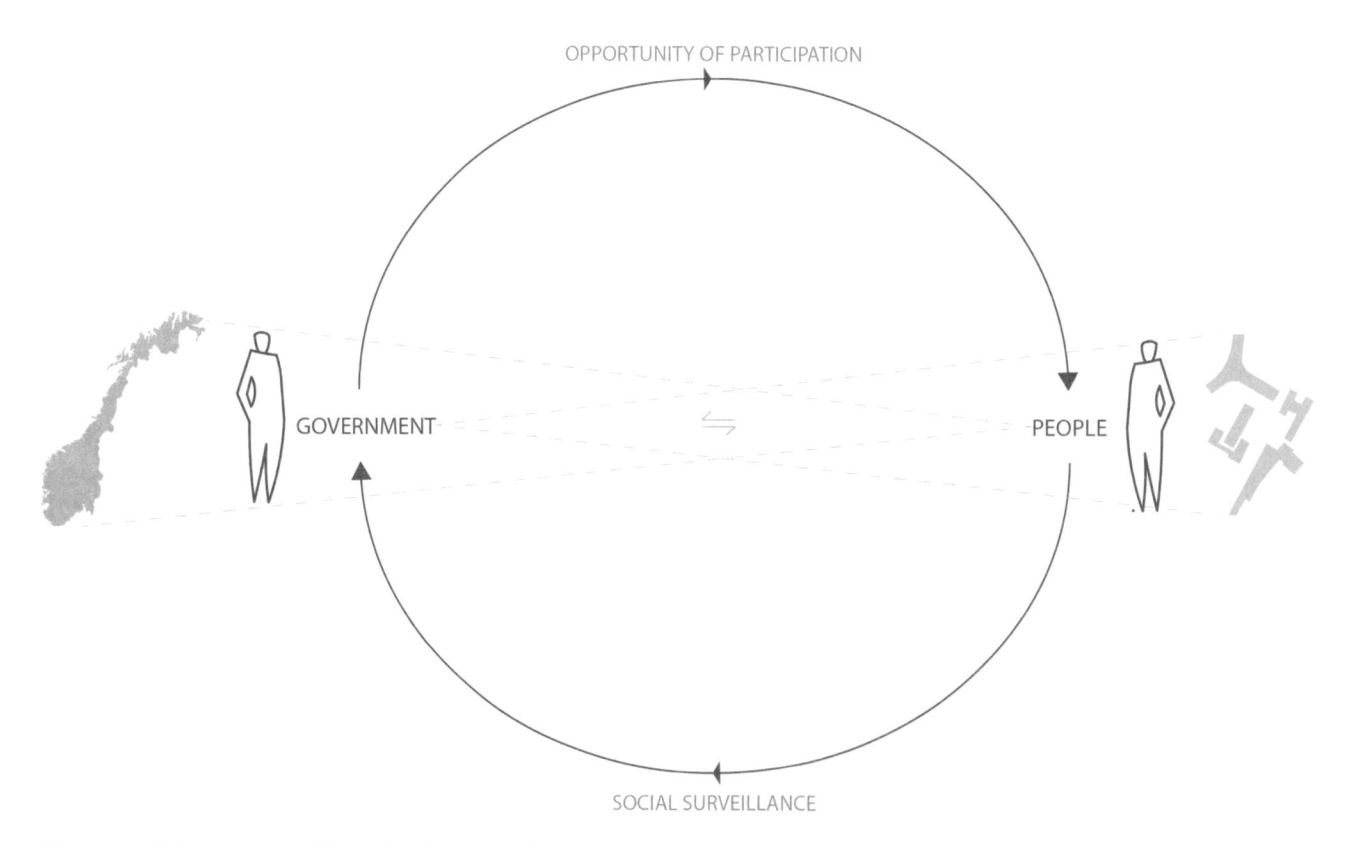

OPPORTUNITY OF PARTICIPATION

GOVERNMENT ⇌ PEOPLE

SOCIAL SURVEILLANCE

The point of departure for this project is an organic process whereby the barricades and roadblocks, the wrapped facades and boarded windows of the government quarter slowly transform by being opened up for public access and reappropriation through participatory actions such as collective urban farming.

Deterioration and mutation are embraced as continuous processes of adaptation and change. The spaces between the buildings slowly transform into transitional spaces. One hundred 10 × 10-meter plots are offered for collective farming, while public spaces of different scales accommodate and include different groups and activities. The existing building structures become the foundations and framework for new structures such as storage facilities offered to collectives engaged in farming, educational workshops, and bee-keeping. Over time, the site becomes less and less a power symbol or a frozen witness/monument to an act of terror. Ministries find their way back to the transformed site and develop open and accessible government offices that support direct interaction with citizens.

2013
Unwrapping the buildings
Retrieved temporary objects

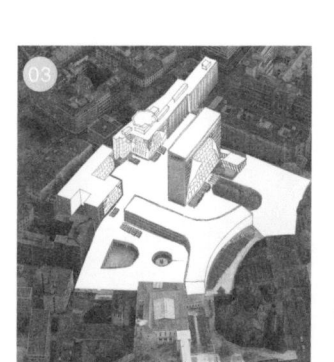

2014
Urban farming
Tools and techniques
Active participants

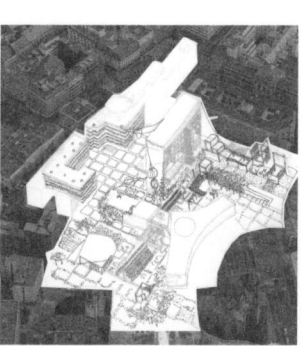

2020
Preparations for additions
Public space review
Exploring concrete and steel modules

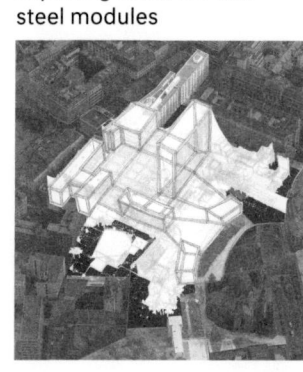

2020
Growth, evolution, morphosis

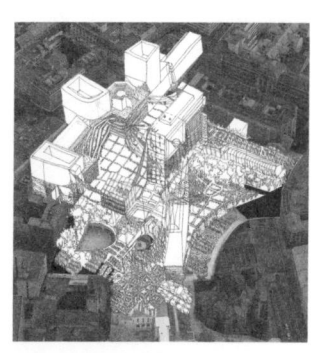

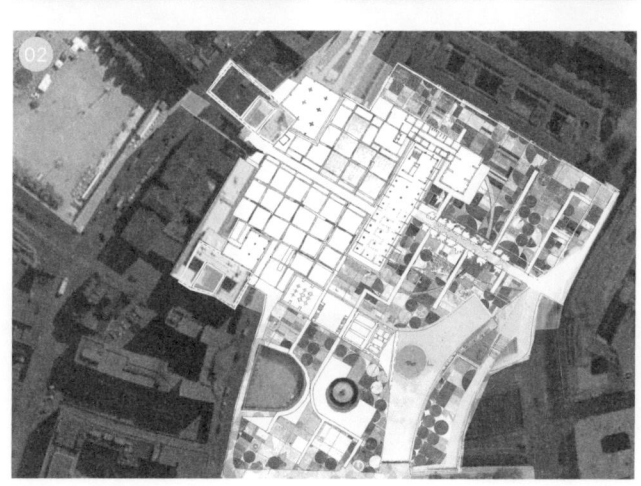

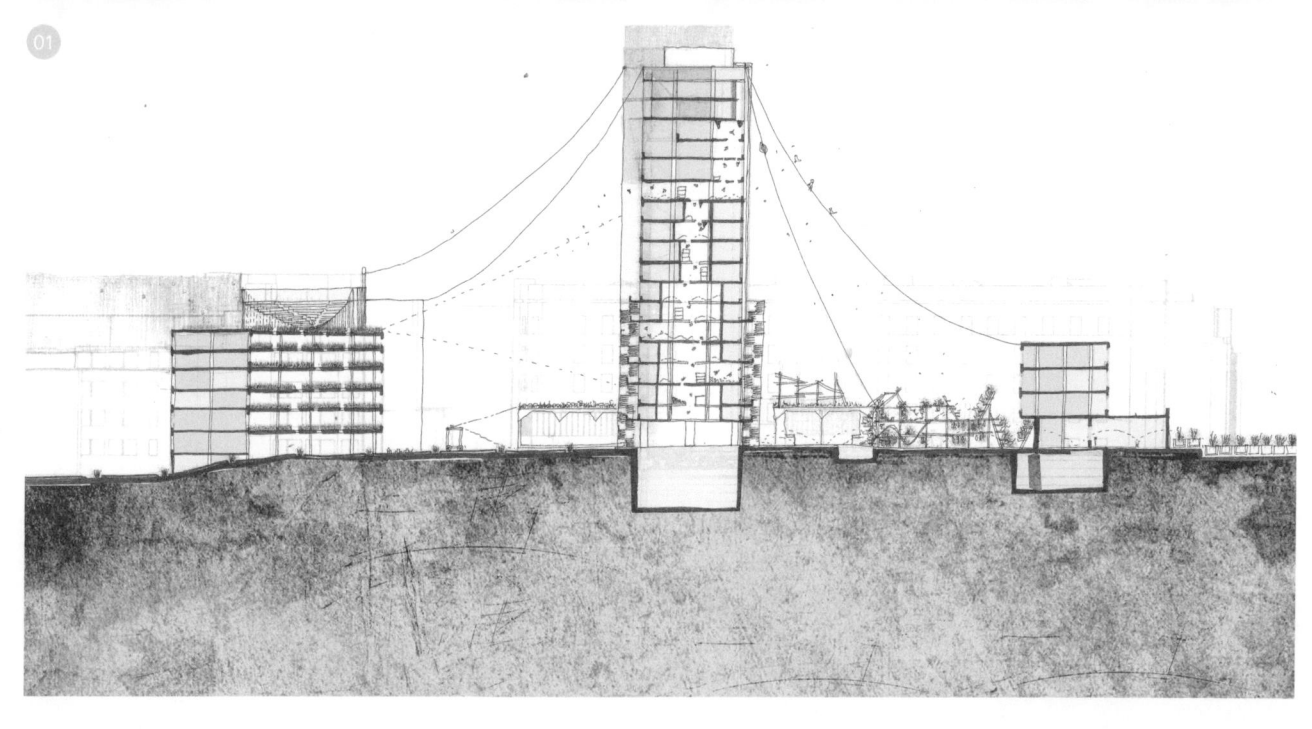

IN(TRO)VERTED SECURITY

Government Quarter

MATHILDE RØNNING

	Main Interventions	**Security Effect**	**Urban Effect**
01	Raised structure on columns	Standoff Passive surveillance Separated assets	Public space Layered infrastructure New experience of the city
02	Water landscape	Standoff Hostile vehicle mitigation Security layering	Attraction Air quality Water-sensitive urban design
03	Tower	Target hardening Reduced target acquisition	Government and public meeting point New urban landscape
04	Preservation of selected building components		Preservation Reuse

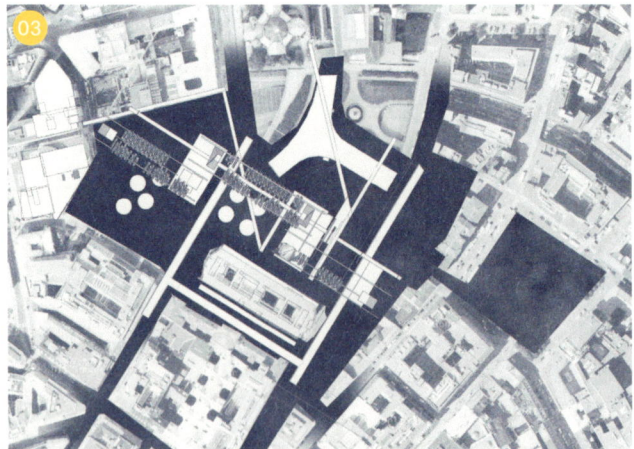

**The hungry alligator/crocodile watchdog.
Feed it, don't befriend it.**

The project takes up the key points of the official KVU Report – addressing security requirements for future buildings in the government quarter – to explore an imaginary architecture based on those specific design criteria. Starting with the most dystopian scenario – in which the interests of security override those of openness and access, the project would be developed further to incorporate public and cultural spaces, art, and environment, but without compromising security requirements. Rather than compromising these physical and symbolic borders, the project explores how security and free access may coexist, or in fact hold highly conflictual relations.

One example is the use of shark-filled ponds and aquariums that protect the columns bearing the elevated structure from bombs, while also providing aesthetic and calming qualities. Rather than solving the problem of the security-democracy relation, this project attempts to problematize the foundational role security plays in such settings.

Creatures cunningly trained for watching.

DECENTRALIZED SECURITY

WENZEL MIELKE

	Main Interventions	**Security Effect**	**Urban Effect**
01	Decentralizing government offices	Reduced target acquisition Redundancy Dispersed assets	Inclusion Spread development Regional development
02	Repeatable building format	Technical surveillance	Readability Flexibility Rational programming
03	Open ground floor	Technical surveillance Passive surveillance Mixed zones	Activity, service Universal access Public space Transparency
04	Secure second floor	Access control Secure zone Hostile vehicle mitigation Standoff	Transparency Readability Efficiency

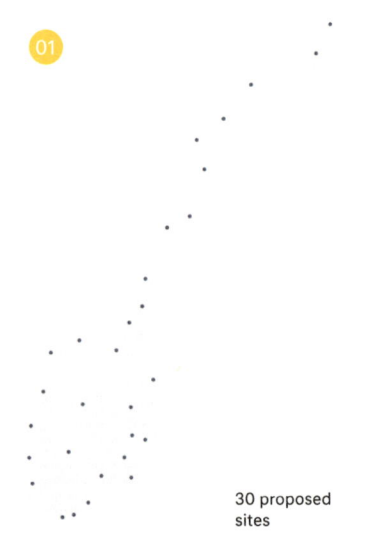

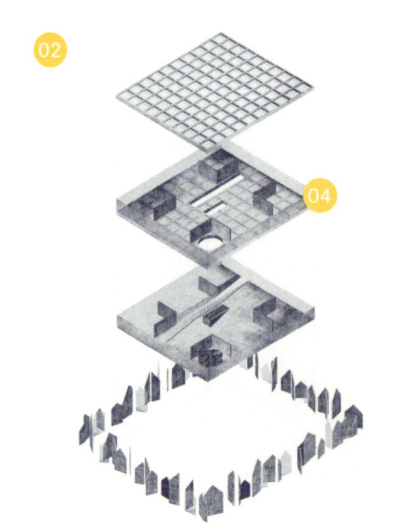

30 proposed sites

Rather than concentrating government offices in a single, potentially vulnerable location, would a decentralized approach to offices spread throughout the country both distribute the risk of possible attack and offer a closer, more democratic and transparent relationship between citizens and the government? Thirty locations are proposed nationally, based on existing population density and the transport infrastructure. The same recognizable and familiar building typology is repeated at each location, while the exterior envelope of the building is clad with local materials and building techniques. The protective skin defines the perimeter of a plaza for public debate, while the offices of local politicians are situated on a floor above. The open plan, flexible facade, dual transparency, and lines of sight support both passive and active surveillance.

SECURITY THROUGH URBAN MIXTURES

BJARTE SANDAL

	Main Interventions	**Security Effect**	**Urban Effect**
01	Mixed programs Dense low buildings Noniconic buiding	Passive surveillance Dispersed assets Mixed zones Access control Reduced target acquisition	Multiprogrammatic Activity Offers
02	New pedestrian and bike network	Hostile vehicle mitigation Standoff	Pedestrianization Universal access Efficiency Public space

01

Blue=Dwelling
White=Offices

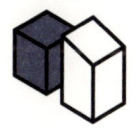

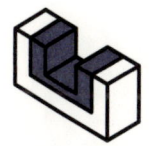

In contrast to the ideals of the ancient Greek agora, modern government quarters have tended to be large, monofunctional structures separated from the city and displaced from civic life. This proposal challenges that tendency through a comprehensive approach to programmatic mixing – with dwellings mixed with offices on upper floors and nongovernmental programming on the lower ground floors – enabling closer interaction and encounters caused by this mix.
As a security measure, spaces for residents and government workers are strategically separated back to back within the same building so that assets and dwellers do not face each other directly. Standoff distance from streets with vehicle access is implemented, while paths for pedestrians and cyclists connect streets and green courtyards. Escape routes and security zones are provided for, while an active public nightlife enhances natural security.

Glossary

Term
Origin
Description

01 Agora

Greek, meaning "open place of assembly"; from *ageirein*, meaning "to assemble"

Designated area in ancient Greek cities, serving as a marketplace and space of public debate and assembly for (free-born, land-owning male) citizens.

02 ASIS

Founded in 1955 as the American Society for Industrial Security, ASIS was renamed ASIS International in 2002. According to its own promotional material, it is "the leading organization for security professionals, with more than 38,000 members worldwide. [...] ASIS is dedicated to increasing the effectiveness and productivity of security professionals by developing educational programs and materials that address broad security interests, such as the ASIS Annual Seminar and Exhibits, as well as specific security topics. ASIS also advocates the role and value of the security management profession to business, the media, government entities, and the public."[1]

03 Asset

"Mid-sixteenth century: from an Anglo-Norman legal term, from Old French *asez*, meaning 'enough,' based on Latin *ad* 'to' + *satis* 'enough.'"[2]

The word *asset* is most commonly employed as an economical term: referring to "an item of property owned by a person or company, regarded as having value and available to meet debts, commitments, or legacies."[3] Within the security industry however, the term is commonly used to describe objects or information worthy of protection. The UK's Centre for the Protection of National Infrastructure (CPNI), for example, uses the term *assets* in the following context: "Not everything within a national infrastructure sector is 'critical.' Within the sectors there are certain 'critical' elements of infrastructure, the loss or compromise of which would have a major detrimental impact on the availability or integrity of essential services, leading to severe economic or social consequences or to loss of life. These 'critical' assets make up the nation's critical national infrastructure (CNI) and are referred to individually as 'infrastructure assets.' Infrastructure assets may be physical (e.g., sites, installations, pieces of equipment) or logical (e.g., information networks, systems)."[4]

04 Asset Evaluation

Specifically refers to the value assessment of assets, whether data, information, personnel, or produced goods, etc.

05 Atmoterrorism

A partial collapse of terms *atmospheric* and *terrorism*

A term introduced by Peter Sloterdijk in his book *Terror from the Air*, atmoterrorism refers to the shift from the body as the target of warfare to where the environment, the atmosphere itself, becomes a weapon, either intentionally or unintentionally. Sloterdijk locates its origins in the first use of chlorine gas on enemy troops during World War I.

06 Balanced Protection

A term employed within the security industry to describe an optimized relationship, or balance, between physical security, detection, action, and reaction.

07 Barricade

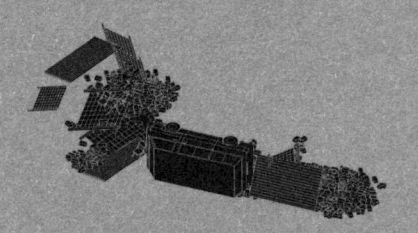

French, from *barrique*, meaning "cask"; from Spanish *barrica*; related to *barrel* (barrels often being used to build barricades).

"An improvised barrier erected across a street or other thoroughfare to prevent or delay the movement of opposing forces."[5] Often constructed of accessible materials, it is aggregated by piling up matter like tires, furniture, garbage, or construction materials and reinforced to withstand force. Some of its more notable deployments are associated with Paris in 1830, 1848, and 1968.

In the US, portable fences used by the police for crowd control and to direct vehicular traffic are also referred to as barricades.

08 Blast Zone

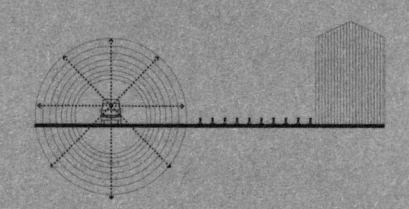

A region or area affected by an explosive blast. The extent of the blast zone is largely a function of the quantity of explosives, but is influenced by additional factors including obstructions, terrain, and so forth. The constant force of an explosion expands spherically from its center. As this occurs, the surface of the sphere increases exponentially with its radius, and its force decreases exponentially with its distance from the origin of the explosion.

09 Bollard

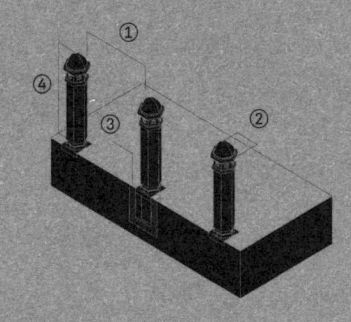

1. maximum distance between bollards 1200 mm
2. diameter depending on amount of force to be resisted
3. underground base cast in concrete
4. height between 500 and 1200 mm

Old Norse *bolr*, meaning "trunk" or "tree"

Historically, a bollard is a short vertical post in the form of a partially buried cannon barrel, at a dock or harbor, to which ships' ropes are attached.

The term is increasingly used to refer to vertical posts used to direct traffic and avert vehicles from a particular area. Bollards are used commonly as security devices in hostile vehicle mitigation (HVM). Bollards can be deployed in tandem with other techniques, such as traffic calming using horizontal deflections (for example, chicanes); or with vehicle restraint using gravity (for example, bunds or berms).

Bollard technology has advanced in recent years with the use of cast manganese steel, which is capable of withstanding the impact of large vehicles traveling at considerable speed.

10 Border

Whether geographically or abstractly defined spatial boundaries between nation states or other administrative entities, borders are often sites of concerted security efforts. In the US for example, the US-Mexico border in particular has been presented as a strategic location in the "war on terror," the "war on drugs," and the "war on illegal immigration" – with increasing resources dedicated to the deployment of military technologies such as drones and thermal sensing equipment. According to the US Department of Homeland Security: "Protecting our borders from the illegal movement of weapons, drugs, contraband, and people, while promoting lawful entry and exit, is essential to homeland security, economic prosperity, and national sovereignty."[6] Despite the European Schengen Area agreement, which since 1995 has facilitated open borders between member countries, changes in the political climate and perceived threats to the EU in the mid-2010s have placed this openness under increasing pressure.

11 Capable Guardians

In Marcus Felson and Lawrence Cohen's routine activity theory, a component of the broader crime opportunity theory, the absence of a capable guardian is one of three necessary components of a crime – the others being a likely offender and a possible target.[7] The capable guardian may be either a person with social ties to the offender or the target, but the role could similarly be performed by a CCTV camera. The theory is controversial in its denial of sociological causes of crime – just as the concept of capable guardians becomes problematic in a discussion of the escalating weaponization of criminals.

12 Closed-Circuit Television (CCTV)

Video surveillance deployed in public or private space, often for the purpose of crime prevention. Other common uses include traffic monitoring, home security, and industrial applications.

From being used in the public transport and retail sectors in the UK in the 1970s, CCTV would go on to play a larger role in cities like London in the 1980s, as police realized the potential of using the cameras installed for traffic observation to observe public order incidents and demonstrations. The first permanent surveillance system in public space was introduced in Bournemouth in 1985. With an estimated 4.2 million CCTV cameras, the UK has reportedly the highest CCTV-to-capita rate in the world.[8]

13 Checkpoint

Checkpoints can be divided into two categories: the border checkpoint, where people try to move between two countries or regions and at which they and their belongings and/or vehicle are checked before they can move on; and the checkpoint placed within a geographic region, where people are stopped and their personal information, vehicles, or belongings are checked before they can continue. A security checkpoint can be static, located at the entrance to a secured building, airport, or similar. Or it can be a flying checkpoint, which is not fixed to a constant place – emerging unexpectedly at a location. In Israel and in Israeli-controlled locations in the West Bank, checkpoints are built as imposing architectural objects, surrounded by concrete walls and equipped with an array of monitoring and control apparatuses. Using devices ranging from electronic turnstiles to security cameras and biometric identification, soldiers control the operation of the checkpoints from remote locations.

14 Civil Rights / Human Rights

In the US, the Constitution of 1789, the Bill of Rights of 1791, and the Civil Rights Act of 1871 offer specific protections of individual liberty and justice and place restrictions on the powers of government. Together they define individual civil rights and an itemized social contract of democratic philosophy. The First Amendment avows the freedom of religion, freedom of speech, freedom of the press, and the rights to assembly and to petition the government. The Fourth Amendment protects against unreasonable search and seizure of self or property by government officials. The UK has a longer history of civil rights. Though in reality it gave only limited rights to the entire population, the Magna Carta, written in 1215, is considered to be the first modern constitution giving rights to those other than the king and nobles, by defining cities as free zones. The legacy of the Magna Carta is still embedded in current UK law.

Whereas civil rights are typically associated with laws or constitutions developed within nation-states, human rights are typically understood as more universal in nature. The United Nations Universal Declaration of Human Rights signed in 1948 includes:

"Article 1: All human beings are born free and equal in dignity and rights. They are endowed with reason and conscience and should act towards one another in a spirit of brotherhood.

"Article 2: Everyone is entitled to all the rights and freedoms set forth in this Declaration, without distinction of any kind, such as race, color, sex, language, religion, political or other opinion, national or social origin, property, birth or other status. Furthermore, no distinction shall be made on the basis of the political, jurisdictional or international status of the country or territory to which a person belongs, whether it be independent, trust, non-self-governing or under any other limitation of sovereignty.

"Article 3: Everyone has the right to life, liberty, and security of person.

"Article 12: No one shall be subjected to arbitrary interference with his privacy, family, home or correspondence, nor to attacks upon his honor and reputation. Everyone has the right to the protection of the law against such interference or attacks.

"Article 13: (1) Everyone has the right to freedom of movement and residence within the borders of each state. (2) Everyone has the right to leave any country, including his own, and to return to his country.

"Article 20: (1) Everyone has the right to freedom of peaceful assembly and association. (2) No one may be compelled to belong to an association."

In the aftermath of World War II and inspired by the Universal Declaration of Human Rights, the European Convention of Human Rights (1949–1953) was established – giving further rights to the European population since.

[See also Norwegian Constitution]

15 Commons

"Originally a medieval term, the common has in recent times been redeveloped and expanded to become an important theoretical and operational tool for a variety of disciplines in a wide field ranging from activist groups to academic scholars. Generally defined as the shared rights of the use of resources, the commons represents an alternative to the conventional dichotomy public-private...."[9]

In the context of the city and conflicting interests between the securitized city on the one hand and the open city on the other, urban common space is of relevance in a discussion of the struggle to maintain common access and use. This is particularly the case with privately owned public space – a discussion relating to Henri Lefebvre's concept of the right to the city as the possibility to create the city collectively as a commons, and David Harvey's later elaboration of this notion.[10] [See also Right to the City]

16 Copenhagen School of Security Studies

[See Securitization]

17 Counter-Terrorism Act, UK

A parliamentary act ratified in 2008 building upon the previous antiterrorism laws that were put in place in 2001 (in the aftermath of the September 11, 2001, attacks in New York City and Washington, DC), 2003, 2005, and 2006 (in the aftermath of the July 7, 2005, attacks in London). Collectively, these acts grant extended powers and new procedures to the UK police in addressing terrorism. The 2008 act for example allows for enhanced gathering and sharing information for counterterrorism purposes. It extends the period possible to detain suspects without charge (up to forty-two days), and provides expanded powers in obtaining fingerprints and DNA samples from individuals subject to a control order. It also allows for postcharge questioning. As it allows for authorities to charge a person on the basis of reasonable suspicion rather than the conventional realistic prospect of conviction it has been heavily criticized by a range of organizations and figures. Amnesty International, for example, claims that the act undermines the presumption of innocence and the right to silence.

18 CPTED (Crime prevention through environmental design)

The term was introduced by C. Ray Jeffery in his 1971 book, *Crime Prevention Through Environmental Design*. An important related work from 1972 is Oscar Newman's *Defensible Space: Crime Prevention through Urban Design*. The premise of Crime Prevention Through Environmental Design (CPTED) is that informed design and effective use of the built environment can reduce the incidence and fear of crime. Four principles of CPTED are: natural surveillance, natural access control, territorial reinforcement; maintenance; and management.

19 Decoy

"A person or thing used to mislead or lure an animal or person into a trap."[11]

20 Deer of Šumava

A publication in Czech by zoologist Pavel Šustr, leader of a research team, describing the results of the monitoring of the spatial behavioral patterns of red deer.

During the Cold War period, the Iron Curtain separating West Germany from Czechoslovakia was manifested by an electric fence that split the forest in two, separating people, but also the area's rich fauna. This led to herds of red deer's being separated in different territories, slowly going through the stages of the path-dependent process. By trial and error they learned the hard way that the fence should not be approached, and this was then taught through generations from does to fawns. Consequently, when the fence was removed after the collapse of the Soviet bloc, the deer instinctively kept to their learned territories. During a five-year research project, German and Czech zoologists monitored the behavioral patterns of the deer, and concluded that in 2011, twenty-two years after the removal of the fence, the deer still rarely crossed the former barrier.[12] This example suggests the relevance of addressing both the immediate as well as the long-term effects of the ongoing and increasing securitization and militarization of our cities.

21 Democracy

From Greek *dēmokratia*, from *dēmos* "the people" + *-kratia* "power, rule"

"A system of government by the whole population or all the eligible members of a state, typically through elected representatives."[13]

22 Designing Out Crime (DOC)

A design approach coined in the UK informed by principles of CPTED, working with concepts such as "reducing anonymity of the offender, territoriality – the relationship between private space and public space, environmental design and physical security measures. Offenders feel more vulnerable in private space and adjoining public spaces can feed off this reaction making it appear that potential crime targets in the public area are under the control of residents. This empowerment of residents is sometimes called defensible space."[14]

23 Dispersement

Within the security industry, this term refers to the dispersal of assets and the production of redundancy as a security measure. In the event of one asset's being affected, the remainder of dispersed assets are intended to continue operating as a functional system.

24 Displacement

Mid-sixteenth century, from Old French *desplacer*, meaning "to cause (something) to move from its proper or usual place"

A term commonly used within situational crime/terror prevention theory to describe the risk of an attack moving geographically from an asset that is highly secured to a less secured target nearby. Displacement is central to both the internal and external critique of situational crime/terror prevention theory – in other words, some argue that situational crime prevention will only displace crime rather than eliminate it.

25 Ditch / Trench

Within the security industry, ditches or trenches may be used as an alternative to bollards in hostile vehicle mitigation (HVM). The dimensions and angles of the walls of ditches or trenches however are quite specific, to ensure that vehicles of varying sizes, weights, and speeds are unable to pass.

26 Drone

A popular term for unmanned aerial vehicles (UAV). Drones have been employed in security applications for surveillance by police and other state entities as well as by private individuals and enterprises.

27 Espionage

In addition to securing against sabotage and terrorism, securing against espionage is the third charge of national security organizations such as the Norwegian Police Security Service (Politets sikkerhetstjeneste, PST) or the Norwegian National Security Authority (Nasjonal Sikkerhetsmyndighet, NSM).[15]

28 Fence / Wall

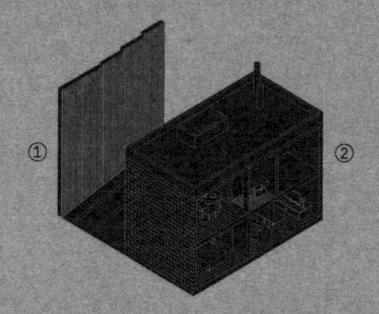

1. Separation wall
2. House wall

"A barrier, railing, or other upright structure, typically of wood or wire, enclosing an area of ground to mark a boundary, control access, or prevent escape."[16]

As Reinier de Graaf has commented, "The fastest growing communities are those of people [...] in search of a fence. And this happens in a historical moment when the world has demolished its most important fence, the wall between East and West. Fences have never been more popular."[17] Such a position is reiterated by Jon Henley, who argues that since the fall of the Iron Curtain: "...the world has been busy building separation barriers at a rate perhaps unequalled in history: at least 6,000 miles of wire, concrete, steel, sand, stone, mesh; anything to keep peoples out – or in."[18]

29 Foucault's Boomerang

According to Michel Foucault, "While colonization, with its techniques and its political and juridical weapons, obviously transported European models to other continents, it also had a considerable boomerang effect on the mechanisms of power in the West, and on the apparatuses, institutions, and techniques of power. A whole series of colonial models was brought back to the West, and the result was that the West could practice something resembling colonization, or an internal colonialism, on itself."[19] Stephen Graham has described these specifically with respect to the problem of securitization: "Israeli drones designed to vertically subjugate and target Palestinians are now routinely deployed by police forces in North America, Europe, and East Asia. Private operators of US 'supermax' prisons are heavily involved in running the global archipelago organizing incarceration and torture that has burgeoned since the start of the war on terror. Private military corporations heavily colonize reconstruction contracts in both Iraq and New Orleans. Israeli expertise in population control is regularly sought by those planning security operations for major summits and sporting events. Guided missiles and private armies work to securitize key events, from Olympics or World Cups to G20 summits and political summits."[20]

30 Frontex

Founded in 2004, the European Agency for the Management of Operational Cooperation at the External Borders of the Member States of the European Union (Frontex) is responsible for controlling and surveilling the borders of the Schengen Area on behalf of the European Union. It emerged as the need for coordinated border control became evident with the introduction of the Schengen cooperation in 1995, and its incorporation within the EU framework in 1999. Today it is responsible for joint border operations, risk analysis, information sharing, technological research, and in assisting in return operations of immigrants, among other tasks.

31 G4S

World's largest private security company, operating in more than 125 countries with over 620,000 employees. Infamous for its failed performance as the main security contractor during the 2012 London Olympics.

32 Glass

According to the security industry, 95 percent of explosive blast casualties from terror blasts are a result of flying fragments; and 95 percent of those are from glass. There are considerable differences in loss of life when nearby glass buildings are glazed with laminated glass as opposed to those with nonlaminated glass.

33 Home Office, "Protecting Crowded Spaces"

Design and technical guidelines produced by the UK Home Office in 2014. According to the guide, crowded spaces include: "shopping centers, sports stadia, bars, pubs and clubs which are easily accessible to the public and attractive to terrorists."[21] In addition to offering guidelines for protecting spaces with various types of measures, the guide also notes the difficulty in protecting against all possible attacks, particularly as "...terrorists are innovative and their methodology can be expected to change over time."[22]

34 Homeland Security

The United States Department of Homeland Security (DHS) was formed in 2002 as a merger of several existing governmental organs – as a reaction to the September 11, 2001, terror attacks. In addition to securing the US against terrorism, the DHS is charged with preventing and responding to man-made accidents and natural disasters. DHS states on their website: "The missions of the Department of Homeland Security are to prevent and disrupt terrorist attacks; protect the American people, our critical infrastructure, and key resources; and respond to and recover from incidents that do occur. [...] The agency also promotes preparedness and emergency prevention among citizens. Policy is coordinated by the Homeland Security Council at the White House, in cooperation with other defense and intelligence agencies, and led by the Assistant to the President for Homeland Security." The Department has been criticized for several aspects of its organization and performance, for example, its secrecy and wasting of resources. The size of the organization is unclear but some figures indicate that every day across the United States, 854,000 civil servants, military personnel, and private contractors with top-secret security clearances are scanned into 1,300 facilities protected by electromagnetic locks, retinal cameras, and fortified walls.

35 Hostile Architecture

Also referred to as defensive or disciplinary architecture. The purpose of hostile architecture is to reduce the usability or functionality of an architectural space or object for a particular set of citizens. This is commonly achieved by applying spikes or other protruding objects to the surfaces of benches, parts of the ground or other surfaces to make it uncomfortable to sit, lie down, skate, etc.

36 Hostile Vehicle Mitigation (HVM)

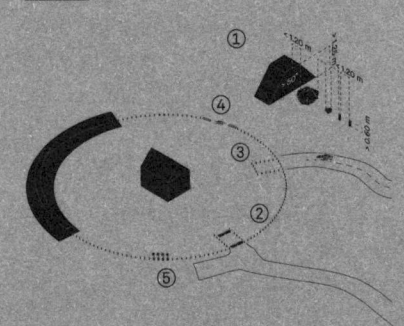

1. Dimensioning, HVM
2. Multiple entrances/exits
3. Layered entrance with retractable bollards to hold and search vehicles
4. Reinforced furniture
5. Reinforced planters

Hostile vehicle mitigation (HVM) is a collective term addressing different protective security strategies to prevent hostile vehicles' penetrating the perimeter of a building or critical area. According to the UK Centre for the Protection of National Infrastructure (CPNI), "Vehicle-borne threats range from vandalism to sophisticated or aggressive attacks by determined criminals or terrorists. The mobility and payload capacity of a vehicle offers a convenient delivery mechanism for a large explosive device."[23] The development of measures used in HVM is supported by research and design carried out by organizations such as the CPNI – which provides many of the European standards used in HVM.

37 Human Chain

A formation sometimes employed during protests, in which people hold hands to create a chain of bodies protecting what is behind or within the chain line.

38 Insider Threat

Typically, a current or former employee, contractor, or business partner who has, or had, authorized access to a building, area, infrastructure, network, or data set, and who intentionally misused or plans to misuse that access for purposes of committing sabotage, fraud, espionage, or to stage an attack. Insiders do not always act alone and may not be aware they are aiding a threat actor (that is, an unintentional insider threat).

39 Iron Dome

Common term for Israel's missile defense system designed to intercept and destroy short-range missiles and grenades. Operational since 2011, the system consists of three components: control center (Battle Management and Weapon Control), movable missile firing units, and movable detection and tracking radar units.

40 Linear Defense

Defense conceived of as a linear system. Within such a system it is common for strongpoints to exist along the line.

41 Lock

"A mechanism for keeping a door, window, lid, or container fastened, typically operated by a key.
"A facility on a computer or mobile phone that requires a user to verify their identity with a passcode or other form of authentication in order to access the full functionality of the device."[24]

42 Medieval Modernity

Nezar AlSayyad and Ananya Roy frame our contemporary urban moment as one of "medieval modernity," in which the logics of "modern nationalism, medieval enclaves, and imperial brutality [...] coexist in nonlinear fashion."[25]

43 Moat

"A deep, wide ditch surrounding a castle, fort, or town, typically filled with water and intended as a defense against attack."[26] Originally a popular ancient fortification strategy, it is still employed as an effective Hostile Vehicle Mitigation measure, for example in the newly built US embassy in Beijing, or the planned US embassy in London.

44 Molotov Cocktail

A bottle-based improvised incendiary weapon containing a flammable substance such as petrol or napalm, lit with an ignition wick. Named by Finnish troops during World War II. Also known as the "poor man's bomb," it is still used today. Notable recent uses include the Arab Spring in Cairo in 2011 and the Ukrainian Revolution in Kiev in 2014.

45 National Defense Authorization Act (NDAA)

Yearly US legal act specifying the allocation of funds to US national defense. The 2012 NDAA legitimized the containment of suspected terrorists without trial, therefore implicitly legitimizing the Guantanamo Bay detention camp. This situation has been heavily criticized by a range of actors and organizations.

46 National Security Act [Norwegian]

The Norwegian National Security Act (2001) regulates the Norwegian authority's preemptive obligations for national security. Until 2011 these were limited to information security and security clearances for personnel. In 2008 the law of object (asset) security was ratified and it was incorporated within the national laws in 2011. The laws of object security determine which assets/objects the government should protect and how to do so. The law does not define persons as objects to protect, only buildings and vital infrastructure.

47 Natural (or Passive) Surveillance

A recurring concept within secured-by-design and crime-prevention-through-environmental-design approaches. "Natural surveillance limits the opportunity for crime by taking steps to increase the perception that people can be seen. Natural surveillance occurs by designing the placement of physical features, activities, and people in such a way as to maximize visibility and foster positive social interaction. Potential offenders feel increased scrutiny and limitations on their escape routes."[27]

This thinking can be traced back to American urbanist Jane Jacobs and theories of the social control of spaces; and later to Oscar Newman's work on defensible space. According to Jacobs: "A city street equipped to handle strangers, and to make a safety asset, in itself, out of the presence of strangers, as the streets of successful city neighborhoods always do, must have three main qualities:

"First, there must be a clear demarcation between what is public space and what is private space. Public and private spaces cannot ooze into each other as they do typically in suburban settings or in projects.

"Second, there must be eyes upon the street, eyes belonging to those we might call the natural proprietors of the street. The buildings on a street equipped to handle strangers and to insure the safety of both residents and strangers, must be oriented to the street. They cannot turn their backs or blank sides on it and leave it blind.

"And third, the sidewalk must have users on it fairly continuously, both to add to the number of effective eyes on the street and to induce the people in buildings along the street to watch the sidewalks in sufficient numbers. Nobody enjoys sitting on a stoop or looking out a window at an empty street. Almost nobody does such a thing. Large numbers of people entertain themselves, off and on, by watching street activity."[28]

48 Network Defense

Also called *in-depth defense*, characterized by points of strength scattered along two axes. It is more flexible than a linear defense, and adaptable to change if one strongpoint is overtaken.

49 Norwegian Constitution

Inspired by the US Constitution (1789) and France's Declaration of the Rights of Man (1789), the Constitution of Norway (1814) was considered to be one of the most liberal or radically democratic constitutions in the world granting separation of executive, legislative, and judicial powers; freedom of speech; and guarding against unreasonable searches and seizures. It is today the second-oldest single-document national constitution in the world still in continuous force. The constitution was followed by social reforms including worker protection laws, and the right of women to vote (1913). During May 2014 the Norwegian parliament passed the most substantial changes since 1814, incorporating additional provisions on human rights.

[See also Civil Rights / Human Rights]

50 Occupy Movement

Protest movement most known for its occupations, first in New York's Wall Street district, followed by occupations in public spaces both in the US and internationally in 2011 and 2012. According to Occupy, "Occupy Wall Street is a people-powered movement that began on September 17, 2011, in Liberty Square in Manhattan's Financial District, and has spread to over 100 cities in the United States and actions in over 1,500 cities globally. #OWS is fighting back against the corrosive power of major banks and multinational corporations over the democratic process, and the role of Wall Street in creating an economic collapse that has caused the greatest recession in generations. The movement is inspired by popular uprisings in Egypt and Tunisia, and aims to fight back against the richest 1 percent of people that are writing the rules of an unfair global economy that is foreclosing on our future."[29]

51 Onion Principle

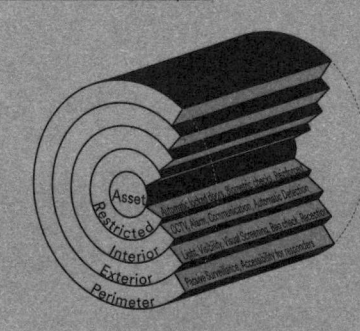

The onion stands as an emblem for layered security or layered defense strategies – a type of general strategy also referred to as *defense in depth*. Originally emerging from IT security, the term is increasingly used within the general security industry to describe the layering of physical security measures. One of the main advantages of the common concept of a layered security is to extend the time it takes to attack, allowing for the possibility to mount countermeasures before the attack penetrates the innermost layer of the onion.

52 Open City

Framed by Dutch architect and planner Kees Christiaanse, and informed by thinkers such as Jane Jacobs, Richard Sennett, and Albert Pope, the "'Open city' is a somewhat utopian term: it refers to efforts by architects and urban designers to translate the ideals of an 'open society' – a society with a tolerant and inclusive government, where diverse groups develop flexible mechanisms for resolving inevitable differences – into physical spaces. It refers to places where people of different backgrounds can coexist, where interaction leads to cultural enrichment and innovation, and where the market flourishes."[30] This is a reaction to the observation that "cities were becoming increasingly closed. Monofunctional residential neighborhoods with limited car-access entry, covered shopping malls, gated communities, guarded campuses, landscapes compartmentalized by traffic infrastructure: these are the physical symptoms of increasing social fragmentation."[31]

53 Panopticon

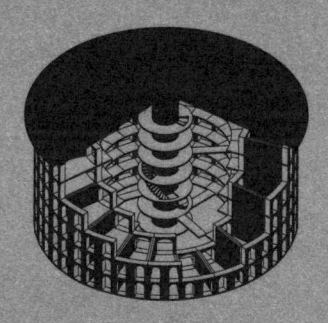

Developed by English philosopher and social theorist Jeremy Bentham in the latter part of the eighteenth century, the panoptical penitentiary was later described by Michel Foucault in *Discipline and Punish* as analogous to the workings of the disciplinary state, and its associated forms of surveillance and control.[32]

A panoptical prison is commonly circular in plan, with cells organized around the outer wall and oriented inward toward a single central core manned by a single guard. As inmates are unable to tell if they are being watched due to the relative darkness inside the observation tower, they lead daily lives effectively controlling their own behavior as if they were being watched at all times.

54 Paranoia

"A mental condition characterized by delusions of persecution, unwarranted jealousy, or exaggerated self-importance, typically worked into an organized system. It may be an aspect of chronic personality disorder, of drug abuse, or of a serious condition such as schizophrenia in which the person loses touch with reality."[33]

For many critics, such as Michael Sorkin, Setha Low, or Stephen Graham, our post–September 11, 2001, period is one characterized increasingly by a form of societal fear and paranoia.

55 Participatory Surveillance

Surveillance provided actively by participating citizens in response to a call from authorities. For example, the New York Police Department's campaign "If you see something, say something" is a call for participatory surveillance. Another type of participatory surveillance occurs in the use of electronic social media. For example, as the publishing of social media user information makes that information easily retrievable by the authorities or others, users contribute to a participatory form of surveillance of themselves and others.

56 Pedestrianization

Derived from *pedestrianize,* "Close (a street or area) to traffic, making it accessible only to pedestrians."[34]

The urban strategy of inner-city pedestrianization – popularized in the late twentieth and early twenty-first centuries in the international urban consultancy work of Danish architect and urbanist Jan Gehl, for example – represents a particular case in which widely accepted strategies toward enhancing the spatial and life quality in cities coincide with strategies for heightening the security of a public space from the risk of car bombs or truck bombs.

57 PMSC (Private and Military Security Company)

The increased outsourcing of military and security operations over the last decades to private and military security companies is leading to an increasingly blurred condition between civilian security and military operations, and between state and private ones. The explosion of this industry has been connected to the repurposing of weapons and personnel immediately after the end of the Cold War, and in the wake of September 11, 2001, a considerable expansion of demand for security products worldwide and domestically in the US. This security would extend to the protection of demarcated territories, such as the Green Zone in Baghdad, or the protection of governmental representatives or NGOs working in areas such as Afghanistan. While arguments exist for the advantages of outsourcing security, there are a number of challenges and concerns that problematize the roles of these organizations. Some of the greatest concerns for critics of PMSCs are the risk and potential for misconduct in the industry – as was unfolded in the Blackwater (now renamed Academi) massacre in Nisour Square, Baghdad, Iraq, in September 2007.[35]

58 Pool Re (Pool Reinsurance Company Limited)

A public-private partnership to allow for commercial property insurance against terror attacks in the United Kingdom. According to the organization's website: "The Pool Re scheme was set up in 1993 by the insurance industry in cooperation with the UK Government in the wake of the IRA bombing campaign on the UK Mainland. Pool Re is a mutual reinsurer whose Members comprise the vast majority of insurers and Lloyd's Syndicates which offer commercial property insurance in the UK, with membership of the scheme affording them a guarantee which ensures that they can provide cover for losses resulting from acts of terrorism, regardless of the scale of the claims."[36] The cost of repairing extensive damage resulting from the IRA bombings "caused insurers and reinsurers to focus on the difficulties of providing terrorism cover for commercial properties, in particular the high potential cost of losses and the lack of any reliable method of estimating what the future loss experience might be. Insurers depended on reinsurers for financial protection should very large claims occur and, accordingly, both insurers and reinsurers decided they could no longer provide terrorism cover using traditional methods."[37]

The cost of insurance is related to two factors: location and security. With higher security one is able to pay lower premiums. This is one of the aspects that supported the concentration and fortification of specific business areas in the City of London and at Canary Wharf.

59 *The Protest Handbook*

From a review of the publication from the legal department of Occupy: "Designed for lawyers with activists in mind, the Handbook takes the reader through the powers of police at protests, our rights and the procedures that we should expect in the police station, criminal court procedures, common offenses and defenses, occupations and how to hold the police to account. It is an important tool in the fight back against overzealous use of police power and aims to redress the balance ensuring our rights as protected in law are realized."[38]

60 Public Space

Stéphane Tonnelat argues that "In urban planning, public space has historically been described as 'open space,' meaning the streets, parks, and recreation areas, plazas, and other publicly owned and managed outdoor spaces, as opposed to the private domain of housing and work. However, the recent evolutions of the forms of urban settlement and the growing number and variety of semipublic spaces managed by private-public or entirely private partnerships questions this notion inherited from a legal perspective. Somehow today, public space needs to be understood as different from the public domain of the state and its subdivisions, but rather as a space accessible to the public."[39]

A more political definition of the term can be traced to Jürgen Habermas and Hannah Arendt. For both Arendt, with her term *public realm,* and Habermas, with his *public sphere,* the public space is a space for participation and action. The space is important if not essential for participatory political action and democracy. Others, like Judith Butler, describes this participatory action as a way of creating a public space that was not public or was not public enough. In his work, Stephen Graham foregrounds the problem of the "Increasing securitization, fragmentation and privatization of public space."[40]

61 Razor Wire / Barbed Wire

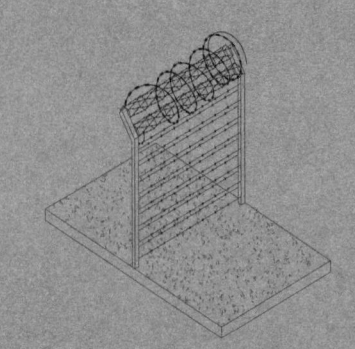

Barbed wire was an invention from the mid-nineteenth century designed to contain cattle. As early as the 1880s barbed wire saw its first deployment in wartime. This application escalated in the context of World War I, when barbed wire became an important defense weapon. Razor wire was developed during World War I, as a wire more difficult to negotiate than barbed wire. Both formats of wire are still in use today for the purpose of separation, both to keep bodies in (for example, in prisons) and to keep bodies out (for example, to fortify borders against migrants or asylum seekers).

62 Resilience

Resilience, for Stephen Graham, is a term "increasingly common in debates about climate change, sustainability, 'peak oil,' water, food and energy crises, economic collapse, social polarization, urban infrastructure, etc. [It was] originally a physical sciences term: 'the power or ability to return to the original form, position, etc., after being bent, compressed, or stretched.' Also used to describe [the] ability of ecological communities to withstand crises and shocks. Now 'migrating' to dominate debates about cities, risk, vulnerability and security."[41] In security terms it both describes the ability to withstand an attack and the theory that one cannot entirely protect oneself but can make the system – the infrastructure, neighborhood, building, city – so robust that it won't collapse if parts of it are rendered useless by an attack or a natural disaster. Resilience makes a system resistant and robust by material measures, social measures, and routines.

63 Right to the City

According to Stephen Graham, "Instead of legal or human rights based on universal citizenship, [...] the emerging security politics of cities are founded on the privatization of public spaces, combined with the profiling of individuals, places, behaviors, associations and groups in advance of any alleged misdemeanor or crime. This in turn is creating the biggest shift in our ideas of citizenship and national boundaries since the mid-seventeenth century."[42]

The concept of the right to the city was developed by the French sociologist and philosopher Henri Lefebvre and first appeared in his *Le Droit à la Ville* (1968). Later interpreted by David Harvey: "The right to the city is far more than the individual liberty to access urban resources: it is a right to change ourselves by changing the city. [...] The freedom to make and remake our cities and ourselves is, I want to argue, one of the most precious yet most neglected of our human rights."[43] In her short definition Anna Plyushteva argues that "the Right to the City defends two elements of citizenship: the ability of all groups and individuals to live in the city, being present and enjoying in all its parts; and partaking in the control over the decisions that shape the city, using its spaces to exercise their citizenship."[44]

The term is referred to within various social and political struggles in its clear opposition to the orthodoxies of neoliberal urban development. At the same time, it has become a platform for codifying legal terms of citizen rights.

64 Risk Analysis

Evaluation of the threats and vulnerabilities from a risk assessment against criteria like the cost of protecting an asset versus the cost of that asset's being compromised. Risk analysis can be "broadly defined to include risk assessment, risk characterization, risk communication, risk management, and policy relating to risk, in the context of risks of concern to individuals, to public- and private-sector organizations, and to society at a local, regional, national, or global level."[45]

65 Risk Assessment

Evaluates potential threats faced and their likelihood to determine a qualitative and quantitative assessment of risk. Assessments typically include an identification of vulnerabilities and the potential impact of exploitation. A risk assessment can be divided into three steps:
1. Identify all assets – human and physical – and their importance.
2. Identify threats to these assets.
3. Identify vulnerabilities in the organization that could affect the assets. The assessment becomes the foundation for a risk management plan and possibly a plan for physical security.

66 Sabotage

"Deliberately destroy, damage, or obstruct (something), especially for political or military advantage."[46]

67 Schengen Agreement / Area

The Schengen Agreement (1985) is a part of the European international law regulating free movement within Europe. When it took effect in 1995, it abolished checks at internal borders of the signatory states and created a single external border where immigration checks for the Schengen Area are carried out in accordance with identical procedures. Common rules regarding visas, right of asylum and checks at external borders were adopted to allow the free movement of persons within the signatory states without disrupting law and order. It also includes an information system (SIS) where member states can retrieve information about people and objects.

68 Secured by Design

"The official UK Police flagship initiative combining the principles of 'designing out crime' with physical security."[47] Established in 1989, Secured by Design (SBD) is a not-for-profit company formed by the Association of Chief Police Officers (ACPO) and is the corporate title for a group of national police projects focused on the design and security for new and refurbished homes, commercial premises, and car parks as well as the acknowledgment of quality security products and crime prevention projects. It runs as a not-for-profit. Its approaches are based on crime prevention theories.

69 Securitization / Security

Security:
"1 The state of being free from danger or threat
  "1.1 The safety of a state or organization against criminal activity such as terrorism, theft, or espionage
  "1.2 Procedures followed or measures taken to ensure the security of a state or organization
  "1.3 The state of feeling safe, stable, and free from fear or anxiety."[48]

Stephen Graham argues for the profoundly political nature of security, risk and threat by foregrounding different and conflicting notions such as national security; urban security, or human security, etc. – foregrounding the question "Who's security from what in the city?"[49] "Some threats to cities (terrorism) become a political obsession; others (2 million annual deaths through traffic accidents) are largely ignored. Securitization is the process through which elites call attention to certain alleged risks as a focus of government action."[50] Graham's work expands upon the influential article "Securitization and Desecuritization" by Ole Wæver of the Copenhagen School of Security Studies which challenged the existing impasse in 1990s securitization discourse.[51] Rather than engaging in the debate concerning the objective or subjective nature of security threats, Wæver would argue that security should rather be understood as a "speech act" made by a securitizing actor. This would represent a shift in focus toward the ways in which particular issues such as migration, environmental degradation, or terrorism are socially constructed as grave existential security threats requiring extraordinary responses – ones that may require the suspension of existing laws, public debate, and democratic processes. According to the Copenhagen School: "A securitizing speech act needs to follow a specific rhetorical structure, derived from war and its historical connotations of survival, urgency, threat, and defense. [...S]ecuritization as a speech act [...] has to fulfill three rhetorical criteria. It is a discursive process by means of which an actor (1) claims that a referent object is existentially threatened, (2) demands the right to take extraordinary countermeasures to deal with the threat, and (3) convinces an audience that rule-breaking behavior to counter the threat is justified."[52]

70 Security-Industrial Complex

According to James Risen, "The Homeland Security Industrial Complex operates differently than the traditional Military Industrial Complex. Instead of spending on ships, airplanes, and other big weapons systems, much of the money goes to secretive intelligence contractors who perform secret counterterrorism work for the CIA, the FBI, the Pentagon and other agencies. Because it is all classified, there is no public debate about the massive amounts of money being poured into these contractors. And with little oversight, there is no way to determine whether these contractors have performed well or poorly. Four trillion dollars is the best estimate for the total price tag of the War on Terror, including the wars in Iraq and Afghanistan, and much of it has gone to shadowy contractors. It is one of the largest transfers of wealth in American history, and yet it has gone largely unnoticed."[53]

71 Situational Crime (or Terror) Prevention (SCP)

Popularized in the 1980s by the criminologists Ronald Clarke and Oscar Newman, SCP is an "approach that seeks to prevent criminal behavior by either implementing strategies to manipulate specific situations to make it impossible for the crime to be committed, or by reducing cues that increase a person's motivation to commit a crime during specific types of events."[54] SCP was originally based upon twenty-five strategies, many of which have spatial consequences such as (1) target hardening or (4) deflect offenders. SCP would be later adapted to become situational terror prevention.

72 Sousveilance

Participant-based video surveillance recording made possible by handheld or body-mounted devices. Increasingly used both by protesters to document police activity during demonstrations, and by police forces during protests or everyday duties.

73 Standoff Distance

A security measure intended to prevent unscreened persons or vehicles from approaching within a certain distance of a location where a bomb is believed to be positioned, or where other threats may be present.

74 Stoltenberg, Jens

Secretary General of NATO and former prime minister of Norway. Sitting prime minister at the time of the terror attack on July 22, 2011. In the aftermath of the events, Stoltenberg repeatedly stated: "Our answer [to the terror attacks] is more democracy, more openness, and more humanity. But never naivety"[55] – suggesting a potentially different response to security than that evident in the US or UK. After the attacks in Canada and France in 2014 and 2015, Norway was cited as an example of how to answer to terror.

75 Surveillance

Early nineteenth century, from French, from *sur-* meaning "over" + *veiller* meaning "watch" (from Latin *vigilare,* "keep watch")

Developing technologies, the perception of new threats, and the restructuring of society have transformed the nature of surveillance in recent decades. Stephen Graham describes a post-9/11 "Surveillance Surge" – which has four features:
"Ubiquitous antiterror discourse undermines criticism and democratic debate: 'chilling effect'; Surveillance 'creep' as antiterrorism rationale added to others, for example, London Road Pricing; 'Security' mantra overwhelms civil, social and urban policy domains; Huge supply push, as military-industrial companies colonize civil markets with military technologies."[56]

76 Target Acquisition

The detection, identification, and location of a target in sufficient detail to permit the effective employment of weapons.[57]

77 Target Hardening

"Security measures that make committing a crime [or a terror attack] more difficult and reduce the opportunities for criminals to achieve their goal."[58]

78 Tear Gas

"Gas that causes severe irritation to the eyes, chiefly used in riot control to force crowds to disperse."[59]
According to tear gas researchers, "Governments and manufacturers justify the use of tear gas and other less lethals by making claims to their safety. Yet medical associations around the world say more studies must be done. Canister strikes to the head, grenades launched into enclosed spaces and smoke inhalation continue to leave people dead, disfigured, and with chronic health conditions."[60]

The 1997 Chemical Weapons Convention prohibits the use of chemical weapons in war, while permitting the use of tear gases for "law enforcement including domestic riot control purposes."[61] This exception has led to many questions around how we define the difference between a chemical agent and a chemical weapon.

79 Territoriality

"An area of land under the jurisdiction of a ruler or state
"Zoology: an area defended by an animal or group of animals against others of the same sex or species
"An area defended by a team or player in a game or sport
"An area in which one has certain rights or for which one has responsibility with regard to a particular type of activity
"[with modifier] land with a specified characteristic."[62]

The contemporary world is territorialized, from the territories of the nation-state to the myriad of smaller territories in cities, buildings, and landscapes. The space occupied or claimed by someone, or a group of persons, is a common interpretation of territory. Traditionally, the discussion of this term has been led by biologists, anthropologists, and psychologists describing territoriality as a part of human nature. Conversely later theorists such as Erving Goffman or Ed Soja have argued for an understanding of space in terms of spheres of influence forming identity and social life – a discourse on territoriality that may be linked to a discussion of defensible space.

80 Terror Porn

A video genre among security professionals consisting largely of low-resolution CCTV footage of well-known and lesser-known terror events. The genre is characterized by a lack of soundtrack and the inevitable impacts, explosions, shock waves, and, in several cases, silently collapsing bodies. This genre is closely related to another: counterterrorism porn, consisting of the documentation of tests, such as those with loaded trucks driving into barriers, ditches, or chicanes; or those staged in mocked-up office buildings with human-scale dolls sitting at desks while being buffeted by various forms (tempered, laminated, etc.) of flying glass.

81 Terrorism

Definitions of Terrorism in the U.S. Code:

"18 U.S.C. § 2331 defines 'international terrorism' and 'domestic terrorism' for purposes of Chapter 113B of the Code, entitled 'Terrorism':

"[…]'terrorism' means activities with the following […] characteristics:

– Involve violent acts or acts dangerous to human life that violate federal or state law;

– Appear to be intended (i) to intimidate or coerce a civilian population; (ii) to influence the policy of a government by intimidation or coercion; or (iii) to affect the conduct of a government by mass destruction, assassination, or kidnapping. […]"[63]

82 USA PATRIOT Act of 2001

Hastily assembled and signed into law by US President George W. Bush approximately six weeks after the attacks of September 11, 2001, the 132-page-long USA PATRIOT Act (an acronym for "Uniting and Strengthening America by Providing Appropriate Tools Required to Intercept and Obstruct Terrorism" Act of 2001) was intended to expand the powers of the state, counterterrorism forces, and police in the "War on Terror."

It is a highly controversial piece of legislation, as has played out in discussions over whether the temporary provisions should be extended or expired. According to Susan Herman, president of the American Civil Liberties Union, the act "needlessly jeopardize[s] our fundamental constitutional values, including freedom of speech, association and religion, privacy and due process."[64] Or law professor Jeffrey Rosen, "Fears of [the PATRIOT Act's] extraordinary surveillance powers to investigate political dissent or low-level offenses have been vindicated."[65]

83 Urbicide

From Latin *urbs*, meaning "city" + *occido*, meaning "to massacre"

"The destruction of a city or its character."[66]

Science fiction author Michael Moorcock is credited with the first use of the term *urbicide*, introduced in the novella *Dead God's Homecoming* (*Science Fantasy*, no. 59 [June 1963]). The term would subsequently be applied to various contexts over recent decades, from Sarajevo, Palestine, and The Bronx, to New Orleans, and Baghdad. Stephen Graham introduces *urbicide* in the following terms "Both the informal ('terrorist') and the formal (state) violence, war, and terror that characterize the post–Cold War and post-9/11 periods, largely entail systematic and planned targeting of cities and urban places. In an urbanizing world, cities provide much more than just the backdrop and environment for war and terror. Rather, their buildings, assets, institutions, industries and infrastructures; their cultural diversities and symbolic meanings have long actually themselves been the explicit targets for a wide range of deliberate, orchestrated, attacks."[67] Graham describes seven key points of discussion around the theme of urbicide: (1) Urbicide often requires purposive urban/technoscientific planning; (2) Urbicide often involves dialectics of construction and erasure; (3) Urbicide can also involve "civilian" planning; (4) Urbicide requires a casting out; (5) These days, urbicide is often "asymmetric"; (6) Urbicide increasingly involves everyday technics and forced disconnection; (7) Urbicide is legitimized through a militarized popular culture.[68]

84 Vehicle Ramming

According to a Department of Homeland Security/FBI Roll Call Release, "Terrorists overseas have suggested conducting vehicle ramming attacks—using modified or unmodified vehicles—against crowds, buildings, and other vehicles. Such attacks could be used to target locations where large numbers of people congregate, including sporting events, entertainment venues, or shopping centers. Vehicle ramming offers terrorists with limited access to explosives or weapons an opportunity to conduct a Homeland attack with minimal prior training or experience."[69] One of the most well-known examples is the so-called Jerusalem Bulldozer Attack of 2008, in which four were killed and forty-five wounded.

85 White Van Syndrome

An irrational fear of parked white cargo vans among Oslo-based governmental workers – a syndrome related to a direct awareness of the delivery method of the Government Quarter bomb on July 22, 2011. According to security officials working with government departments in Oslo, there are dozens of concerned telephone calls received when a white cargo van parks near a ministry, but not in the case of other colored vans parking in similar positions.

Notes and Referencess

Jack Fischer Eriksen, Thomas Haneborg, Håvard Walla
Foreword : PST/NSM

1 Nasjonal Sikkerhetsmyndighet (NSM)
2 Politiets Sikkerhetstjeneste (PST)
3 Bergen Arkitekthøgskole (BAS)
4 Kriminalpolitisentralen (KRIPOS)
5 Departementenes sikkerhets- og serviceorganisasjon (DSS)

Deane Simpson, Vibeke Jensen, Anders Rubing
Introduction: On urban indefensibility: friction lines in the production of the open city

1 See Stephen Graham, *Cities under Siege: The New Military Urbanism* (London: Verso, 2010), for example.
2 Stephen Graham, "Cities and the 'War on Terror,'" in *Indefensible Space, ed.* Michael Sorkin (New York: Routledge, 2007), 6.
3 Another distinguishing feature of the Oslo attack from others listed above is the fact that the instigator acted as a lone individual, and that it came from extreme right-wing leanings as a statement against the perceived "Islamification" of Europe.
4 There was obvious hesitancy over the prospect of engaging in a dialogue with agencies of this kind based on what they represented from the perspective of late twentieth- and early twenty-first-century critical academic discourse - particularly in the context of what was coming to light (from Edward Snowden and others) regarding the expanded and intrusive nature of the electronic state security apparatus in general.
5 See for example, publications such as Sigmund Diamond, *The Compromised Campus: The Collaboration of Universities with the Intelligence Community, 1945-1965* (New York: Oxford University Press, 1992); or Noam Chomsky and Ira Katznelson, *The Cold War and the University: Towards an Intellectual History of the Postwar Years* (New York: The New Press, 1997).
6 Graham, *Cities under Siege*, 10 (see note 1).
7 Ibid., xxix.
8 Ibid.
9 David Harvey, "The Right to the City," *New Left Review*, no. 53 (September-October 2008): 23-40.
10 It is worth mentioning that these moments of political dynamism and dissent have been essential in recent history in establishing basic and accepted human rights: for example, the American civil rights movement, enabled in part by riots in Selma, Alabama, in 1965; and the LGBT rights movement that began with the Stonewall riots in New York in 1969, to use two American examples. These forms of protest have become increasing difficult in the contemporary climate with respect to examples such as the Occupy Wall Street movement.
11 See, for example, "Major Causes of Death v. Threat Budget Allocations," *Think by Numbers*, accessed June 1, 2016, http://i1.wp.com/thinkbynumbers.org/wp-content/uploads/2008/03/death-and-dollars.jpg; and Julia Jones and Eve Bower, "American Deaths in Terrorism vs. Gun Violence in One Graph," http://edition.cnn.com/2015/10/02/us/oregon-shooting-terrorism-gun-violence/.
12 Dag Bjarne Astor, Head of Section, Departementenes sikkerhets- og serviceorganisasjon (DSS), lecture given August 27, 2013, at BAS.

Deane Simpson, Vibeke Jensen, Anders Rubing
The City Between Security and Freedom: Project Journal

1 Kjell Hole and Lars-Helge Netland, "Toward Risk Assessment of Large-Impact and Rare Events," *IEEE Security and Privacy* 8, no. 3 (2010): 21-27.

Jon Coaffee
Protecting Vulnerable Cities from Terrorism:
Enhancing the Resilience of Everyday Urban Infrastructure

1 Jon Coaffee, "Rings of Steel, Rings of Concrete and Rings of Confidence: Designing Out Terrorism in Central London Pre- and Post-9/11," *International Journal of Urban and Regional Research* 28, no. 1 (2004): 201-11.
2 Jon Coaffee et al., "The Visibility of (In)security: The Aesthetics of Planning Urban Defences Against Terrorism," *Security Dialogue* 40, no. 4/5 (2009): 489-511, here, 500.
3 Ibid., 500.
4 See for example, Trevor Boddy, "Architecture Emblematic: Hardened Sites and Softened Symbols," in *Indefensible Space*, ed. Michael Sorkin (Abingdon: Routledge, 2007), 277-304.
5 The other option that was readily considered for embassies after 9/11 was relocation to out-of-city sites.
6 Robert Booth, "Ambassador, You Are Spoiling Our View of the Thames with This Boring Glass Cube," *The Guardian*, February, 24, 2010, 13.
7 Jon Coaffee, *Terrorism, Risk and the City: The Making of a Contemporary Urban Landscape* (Aldershot: Ashgate, 2003).
8 See for example, Stephen Brown, "Central Belfast's Security Segment: An Urban Phenomenon," *Area* 17, no. 1 (1985): 1-8.
9 Large explosive devices exploded in the city of London in April 1992 and April 1993 and in 1996 in the London Docklands. A number of further attacks were thwarted. See Jon Coaffee, "Rings of Steel" (note 1) for a detailed account.
10 See for example, Arnon Soffer and Julian. V. Minghi, "Israel's Security Landscapes: The Impact of Military Considerations on Land-Use," *Political Geographer* 38, no. 1 (1986): 28-41.
11 See for example, Eve E. Hinman and David. J. Hammond, *Lessons from the Oklahoma City Bombing: Defensive Design Techniques* (Reston: American Society of Civil Engineers, 1997).
12 Jon Coaffee and Paul O'Hare, "Urban Resilience and National Security: The Role for Planning," *Proceedings of the Institution of Civil Engineers Urban Design and Planning*, 161, no. 4 (2008): 173-82.
13 Martha Baer, Katrina Heron, Oliver Morton, and Evan Ratliff, *Safe: The Race to Protect Ourselves in a Newly Dangerous World* (New York: Harper Collins, 2005).
14 See for example Stephen Graham, "Special Collection: Reflections on Cities: September 11th and the 'War on Terrorism' - One Year On," *International Journal of Urban and Regional Research* 26, no. 3 (2002): 589-90.
15 Jon Coaffee et al., "Resilient Design for Community Safety and Terror-Resistant Cities," *Proceeding of the Institute of Civil Engineers: Municipal Engineer 161, no. 2 (2008):* 103-10.
16 See for example, Andrew Silke, ed., *Research on Terrorism: Trends, Achievements, Failures* (London: Frank Cass, 2004).
17 Coaffee et al., "Resilient Design" (see note 15). Moreover, others have charted this shift from "hard" government targets toward "soft" targets with the assertion that paying taxes legitimizes the targeting of citizens in the minds of terrorists: see for example, Adam Dolink, "Assessing the Terrorist Threat to Singapore's Land Transportation Infrastructure," *Journal of Homeland and Emergency Management* 4, no. 2 (2007): 1-22.
18 Home Office, *Working Together to Protect Crowded Places* (London: Home Office, 2009), 11.
19 *Countering International Terrorism: The United Kingdom's Strategy* (London: TSO, 2006). See also the third updated version of CONTEST published in 2011.
20 CPNI, accessed November 30, 2007, http://www.cpni.gov.uk/About/whatWeDo.aspx.
21 CPNI provides integrated security advice to the businesses and organizations which comprise the national infrastructure so as to reduce the vulnerability of the national infrastructure to terrorism and other threats. It is an interdepartmental governmental organization comprising the Security Services and other departments with responsibility for infrastructure.
22 CPNI, accessed November 30, 2007, http://www.cpni.gov.uk/About/cpniContext.aspx.
23 Coaffee, "Rings of Steel" (see note 1).
24 These security devices had been specifically designed to provide maximum protection and are intended to be used by designers, planners, architects, security managers, and facilities managers within the public and private sectors. These security barriers and bollards have Publically Available Specifications awarded by the British Standards Institute (PAS 69:2006, PAS 68 2007).
25 Jon Coaffee, "Urban Renaissance in the Age of Terrorism - Revanchism, Social Control or the End of Reflection?" *International Journal of Urban and Regional Research* 29, no. 2 (2005): 447-54, here, 453.
26 Trevor Boddy, in "Architecture Emblematic" (see note 4) for instance, refers to this as an architecture of reassurance.
27 Coaffee et al., "The Visibility of (In)security" (see note 2).
28 Jon Coaffee, "Protecting the Urban: The Dangers of Planning for Terrorism," *Theory, Culture & Society* 26, no. 7/8 (2009): 343-55.
29 On March 11, 2004, commuter trains in Madrid were attacked a by series of coordinated bombings, killing 191 people and wounding 1,800.
30 "London Terror Attack Inevitable," BBC News, http://news.bbc.co.uk/1/hi/uk_politics/3515312.stm, last updated March 16, 2004.
31 "City a Target, Police Chief Fears," BBC News, http://news.bbc.co.uk/2/hi/business/4137068.stm, last updated August 10, 2005.
32 See "New Security Challenges," *ESRC Society Today*, http://webarchive.nationalarchives.gov.uk/20100210151716/http://esrcsocietytoday.ac.uk/esrcinfocentre/research/research_programmes/security.aspx, last updated March 26, 2009.
33 See http://www.globaluncertainties.org.uk, accessed March 12, 2010.
34 One such project, the research for which forms the basis of this chapter, was the "Resilient Design (RE-Design) for Counter-Terrorism: Decision Support for Designing Effective and Acceptable Resilient Places" project supported by an Engineering and Physical Sciences Research Council grant (EP/F008635/1).
35 Coaffee et al., "Resilient Design," 108 (see note 15).
36 On June 29 two car bombs were left strategically outside a well-known central London nightclub. A day later Glasgow International Airport was attacked when a jeep loaded with gas canisters was driven into the doors of the airport terminal and set ablaze.
37 See "Statement on Security," accessed May 4, 2008, http://www.number10.gov.uk/output/Page12675.asp.
38 This was undertaken by Counter-Terrorist Security Advisors - security specialists trained by the National Counter-Terrorist Security Office and working across the UK - see http://www.nactso.gov.uk/ctsa.php, accessed March 12, 2010.
39 Jacqui Smith, "Protective Security," House of Commons Debate, Written Statements, November 14, 2007, Col. 45WS.
40 Gordon Brown, "National Security," House of Commons Debate, Debates and Oral Answers, November 14, 2007, Col. 667.
41 See "Statement on Security," accessed May 4, 2008, http://www.number10.gov.uk/output/Page13763.asp.
42 This focus upon crowded places was backed up by further government reports such as *National Security Strategy: Security in an Interdependent World* (London: Cabinet Office, 2008) and *National Risk Register* (London: Cabinet Office, 2008).
43 Home Office, *Working Together*, 4 (see note 18).
44 Ibid., 5.
45 Gordon Brown, House of Commons Debate, quoted in Jon Coaffee and Paul O'Hare, "Urban Resilience and National Security" (see note 12).
46 Lee Bosher, *Hazards and the Built Environment: Attaining Built-in Resilience* (London: Taylor and Francis, 2008), 13.
47 Jon Coaffee and Lee Bosher, "Integrating Counter-Terrorist Resilience into Sustainability," *Proceedings of the Institution of Civil Engineers Urban Design and Planning* 161, no, 2 (2008): 75-83, here, 75.
48 Stephen Bayley, "From Car Bombs to Carbuncles," *The Observer*, accessed November 18, 2007, http://observer.guardian.co.uk/review/story/0,,2212697,00.html.
49 Coaffee et al., "The Visibility of (In)security," 498-99 (see note 2).
50 For example, see Rachel Briggs, "Invisible Security: The Impact of Counter-Terrorism on the Built Environment," in *Joining Forces: From National Security to Networked Security* (London: Demos, 2005), 68-90.
51 Boddy, "Architecture Emblematic," 291 (see note 4).
52 Department for Communities and Local Government, *National Indicators for Local Authorities and Local Authority Partnerships: Handbook of Definitions, Draft for Consultation* (London: DCLG, 2007).
53 See http://www.nactso.gov.uk/argusprofessional.php, accessed March 12, 2010.
54 These are called Architectural Liaison Officers or Crime Prevention Design Advisors.
55 *The United Kingdom's Strategy for Countering International Terrorism* (London: Home Office, 2009). See also See also CPNI's 2011 *Integrated Security A Public Realm Design Guide for Hostile Vehicle Mitigation*, http://www.cpni.gov.uk/documents/publications/2011/2011mar01-integrated_security_v1.0.pdf.
56 Ibid., 7. See also CONTEST III, published in 2011.
57 A senior police detective cited in David Leppard, "Police Expect Mumbai-style Attack on the City of London," *The Times* (London), December 20, 2009, http://www.timesonline.co.uk/tol/nwes/uk/crime/article6962867.ece.
58 Coaffee, "Protecting the Urban" (see note 28).
59 *The United Kingdom's Strategy*, 117 (see note 55).
60 See in particular the Civil Contingences Act 2004, accessed March 12, 2010, http://www.opsi.gov.uk/acts/acts2004/ukpga_20040036_en_1.

61 Richard Little, "Holistic Strategy for Urban Security," *Journal of Infrastructure Systems* 10, no. 2 (2004): 52–59, here, 57.

62 See for example, "The United Kingdom Security and Counter-Terrorism Science and Innovation Strategy" (London: Home Office, 2007); and "The United Kingdom's Science and Technology Strategy for Countering International Terrorism" (London: Home Office, 2009).

63 See for example Peter Adey, "May I Have Your Attention: Airport Geographies of Spectatorship, Position, and (Im) mobility," *Environment and Planning D* 25 (2007): 515–36.

64 "Countering the Terrorist Threat: Social and Behavioural Science – How Academia and Industry Can Play Their Part" (London: Home Office, 2010).

65 Ibid., 12.

66 Ibid.

67 This is potentially an important development given the clear indication that traditional surveillance is no deterrent against the new breed of urban ("suicide") terrorist.

68 The implementation of this system followed extensive trials, which initially had little to do with terrorism and predated 9/11. The original intention was to develop a crowd flow monitoring system that morphed into something more as its potential to spot those waiting on station platforms to commit suicide was realized.

69 See Jon Coaffee, *Terrorism, Risk and the Global City: Towards Urban Resilience* (Farnham: Ashgate, 2009) for a full description.

70 Home Office, *Working Together (see note 18).*

71 *Crowded Places: The Planning System and Counter-Terrorism* (London: Home Office, 2010); and *Protecting Crowded Places: Design and Technical Issues* (London: Home Office, 2010). These documents were revised and rereleased in 2014.

72 "Russia: Shared Scourge, Different Causes," *The Guardian*, March 29, 2010, 30.

Oscar Newman
Architectural Design for Crime Prevention:
Chapter 1. Defensible Space as a Crime Preventive Measure

1 Lee Rainwater, "Fear and the House-as-Haven in the Lower Class," *Journal of the American Institute of Planning* 32, no. 1 (January 1966).

2 The President's Commission on Law Enforcement and Administration of Justice, *The Challenge of Crime in a Free Society* (New York: E. P. Dutton, 1968), 40.

3 Ibid., 66–67.

4 Ibid., 130–32.

5 *The Challenge of Crime in a Free Society* was also published by Superintendent of Documents, U.S. Government Printing Office, Washington, DC 20402.

6 Lee Rainwater, *Behind Ghetto Walls: Black Families in a Federal Slum* (Chicago: Aldine, 1970), 370.

Anna Minton and Jody Aked
"Fortress Britain": High Security, Insecurity and the Challenge of Preventing Harm

1 Bobby Duffy, Rhonda Wake, Tamara Burrows, and Pamela Bremner. "Closing the Gaps: Crime and Public Perceptions," *International Review of Law, Computers and Technology* 22, no. 1/2 (2008): 17–44.

2 Secured by Design, www.securedbydesign.com.

3 Clifford D. Shearing and Philip C. Stenning, "Modern Private Security: Its Growth and Implications," *Crime and Justice* 3 (1981): 193–245.

4 Jon Coaffee, "Protecting Vulnerable Cities," *International Affairs* 86, no. 4 (2010): 939–54.

5 Ibid.

6 Lucia Zedner, *Security* (London: Routledge, 2009).

7 G4S had a £284m contract to provide 10,400 staff for the London 2012 Olympics but could not supply enough personnel, leaving some 4,700 members of the armed forces to stand in.

8 Oscar Newman, *Defensible Space: People and Design in the Violent City* (London: Architectural Press, 1972).

9 Jane Jacobs and Loretta Lees, "Defensible Space on the Move: Revisiting the Urban Geography of Alice Coleman," *International Journal of Urban and Regional Research* 37, no. 5 (September 2013): 1559–83.

10 Ibid.

11 Ibid.

12 Ibid.

13 Margaret Thatcher, *The Downing Street Years* (New York: Harper Collins, 1993), mentioned in Jacobs and Lees, "Defensible Space on the Move" (see note 9).

14 "Schools," www.securedbydesign.com/pdfs/schools.pdf.

15 Ibid.

16 Nick Pickles and Stephanie Benbow, "Is the Use of CCTV Cameras in Schools out of Hand?" *The Guardian*, September 12, 2012.

17 "Schools" (see note 14).

18 Jason Ditton, "Crime and the City, Public Attitudes to Open Street CCTV in Glasgow," *British Journal of Criminology* 40, no. 4 (2000): 692–709.

19 Adam Crawford, Stuart Lister, Sarah Blackburn, and Jonathan Burnett, *Plural Policing: The Mixed Economy of Visible Patrols in England and Wales* (Bristol: Policy Press, 2005).

20 Coaffee, "Protecting Vulnerable Cities" (see note 4).

21 Lynne Friedli, *Mental Health, Resilience and Inequalities* (Copenhagen: WHO Regional Office for Europe, 2009).

22 Kevin Lynch, "The Openness of Open Space," in *City Sense and City Design: Writings and Projects of Kevin Lynch*, ed. Tridib Bannerjee and Michael Southworth (Cambridge, MA: MIT Press, 1995).

23 Margaret Wheatley, "When Change Is out of Our Control," in *Human Resources for the 21st Century*, ed. Marc Effron, Robert Gandossy, and Marshall Goldsmith (Hoboken, NJ: Wiley, 2003).

24 Anna Minton, *Ground Control: Fear and Happiness in the 21st-Century City*, 2nd. ed. (New York: Penguin, 2012).

25 Juliet Michaelson, Saamah Abdallah, Nicola Steuer, Sam Thompson, and Nic Marks, *National Accounts of Well-Being: Bringing Real Wealth onto the Balance Sheet* (London: New Economics Foundation, 2009).

26 Jody Aked, Nicola Steuer, Ellis Lawlor, and Stephen Spratt, *Backing the Future: Why Investing in Children Is Good for Us All* (London: New Economics Foundation, 2009).

27 Anna Coote and Jane Franklin, *Green Well Fair* (London: New Economics Foundation, 2009).

28 Michaelson et al., *National Accounts of Well-Being* (see note 25).

29 Richard Sennett, "Why Complexity Improves the Quality of Life," *Hong Kong: Cities, Health and Well-Being*, https://lsecities.net/media/objects/articles/why-complexity-improves-the-quality-of-city-life/en-gb/, published November 2011.

Ronald V. Clarke
Situational Crime Prevention: Theoretical Background and Current Practice

Armitage, Rachel, and Hannah Smithson. 2007. "Alley-gating Revisited: The Sustainability of Residents' Satisfaction." *Internet Journal of Criminology*: 1–38.

Ayres, Ian, and Steven D. Levitt. 1998. "Measuring Positive Externalities from Unobservable Victim Precaution: An Empirical Analysis," *The Quarterly Journal of Economics* (February): 43–77.

Bandura, Albert. 1976. "Social Learning Analysis of Aggression." In *Analysis of Delinquency and Aggression*, edited by Emilio Ribes-Inesta and Albert Bandura, 203–32. Oxford: Lawrence Erlbaum.

Blais, Etienne, and Jean-Luc Bacher. 2007. "Situational Deterrence and Claim Padding: Results from a Randomized Field Experiment," *Journal of Experimental Criminology* 3, no. 4: 337–52.

Blumstein, Alfred, and Joel Wallman. 2000. *The Crime Drop in America*. New York: Cambridge University Press.

Boruch, Robert, et al. 2004. "Estimating the Effects of Interventions That Are Deployed in Many Places: Place-randomized Trials," *American Behavioral Scientist* 47, no. 5: 608–33.

Bowers, Kate J., and Shane D. Johnson. 2003. "Measuring the Geographical Displacement and Diffusion of Benefit Effects of Crime Prevention Activity," *Journal of Quantitative Criminology* 19, no. 3: 275–301.

Bowers, Kate J., Shane D. Johnson, and Alex F. G. Hirschfield. 2004. "Closing Off Opportunities for Crime: An Evaluation of Alley-Gating," *European Journal on Criminal Policy and Research* 10, no. 4: 285–308.

Brantingham, Patricia L., and Paul J. Brantingham. 1993. "Environment, Routine and Situation: Toward a Pattern Theory of Crime." In *Routine Activity and Rational Choice*, edited by R. V. Clarke and Marcus Felson, 259–94. New Brunswick: Transaction Press.

Chaiken, Jan M., Michael W. Lawless, and Keith A. Stevenson. 1974. *The Impact of Police Activity on Crime: Robberies on the New York City Subway System* (Report No. R-1424-N.Y.C.). New York: Rand Institute.

Clarke, Ronald V. 1980. "Situational Crime Prevention: Theory and Practice," *British Journal of Criminology* 20: 136–47.

——. 1999. "Hot Products: Understanding, Anticipating and Reducing the Demand for Stolen Goods" (Police Research Series, Paper 98). London: Home Office.

——. 2008. "Situational Prevention." In *Environmental Criminology and Crime Analysis*, edited by Richard Wortley and Lorraine Green Mazerolle. Cullompton: Willan Publishing.

Clarke, Ronald V., and Derek B. Cornish. 1982. *Crime Control in Britain*. Albany, NY: State University of New York Press.

——. 1985. "Modeling Offenders' Decisions: A Framework for Research and Policy." In *Crime and Justice* 6: 147–85.

Clarke, Ronald V., Rick Kemper, and Laura Wyckoff. 2001. "Controlling Cell Phone Fraud in the US: Lessons for the UK 'Foresight' Prevention Initiative," *Security Journal* 14, no. 1: 7–22.

Clarke, Ronald V., and Graeme R. Newman. 2005. "Modifying Criminogenic Products: What Role for Government?" In *Designing Out Crime from Products and Systems*, edited by Ronald V. Clarke and Graeme R. Newman, 7–84. Crime Prevention Studies 18. New York: Criminal Justice Press.

——. 2006. *Outsmarting the Terrorists*. Westport: Praeger Security International.

Clarke, Ronald V., and David Weisburd. 1994. "Diffusion of Crime Control Benefits: Observations on the Reverse of Displacement." In *Crime Prevention Studies*, edited by Ronald V. Clarke, 165–83. Crime Prevention Studies 2. Monsey: Criminal Justice Press.

Cohen, Lawrence E., and Marcus Felson. 1979. "Social Change and Crime Rate Trends: A Routine Activity Approach," *American Sociological Review* 44, no. 4: 588–608.

Cornish, Derek B. 1994. "The Procedural Analysis of Offending, and Its Relevance for Situational Prevention." In *Crime Prevention Studies*, edited by R. V. Clarke, 151–96. Crime Prevention Studes 3. Monsey: Criminal Justice Press.

Cornish, Derek B., and Ronald V. Clarke, eds. 1986. *The Reasoning Criminal: Rational Choice Perspectives on Offending*. New York: Springer-Verlag.

——. 2003. "Opportunities, Precipitators and Criminal Decisions." In *Theory for Practice in Situational Crime Prevention*, edited by Martha J. Smith and Derek B. Cornish, 41–96. Crime Prevention Studies 16. Monsey: Criminal Justice Press.

Decker, Scott H. 2005. *Using Offender Interviews to Inform Police Problem Solving*. Problem-Oriented Guides for Police (Problem Solving Tools Series, No. 3). Office of Community Oriented Policing Services. Washington, DC: US Dept. of Justice.

Eck, John, Ronald V. Clarke, and Rob T. Guerette. 2007. "Risky Facilities: Crime Concentrations in Homogeneous Sets of Establishments and Facilities." In *Imagination for Crime Prevention*, edited by Graham Farrell et al., 225–64. Crime Prevention Studies 21. Monsey: Criminal Justice Press.

Ekblom, Paul. 1988. "Preventing Post Office Robberies in London: Effects and Side Effects." *Journal of Security Administration* 11, no. 2: 36–43.

——. 1995. "Less Crime, by Design," *Annals of the American Academy of Political and Social Science* 539: 114–29.

——. 1997. "Gearing Up against Crime: A Dynamic Framework to Help Designers Keep Up with the Adaptive Criminal in a Changing World," *International Journal of Risk, Security and Crime Prevention* 2, no. 4: 249–65.

Ekblom, Paul, and Nick Tilley. 2000. "Going Equipped: Criminology, Situational Crime Prevention and the Resourceful Offender," *British Journal of Criminology* 40, no. 3: 376–98.

Farrell, Graham, and Ken Pease. 1993. "Once Bitten, Twice Bitten: Repeat Victimisation and Its Implications for Crime Prevention." Crime Prevention Unit Series Paper 46, Police Research Group). London: Home Office.

Farrell, Graham, Nick Tilley, Andromachi Tseloni, and Jen Mailley. 2011. "The Crime Drop and the Security Hypothesis." *British Society of Criminology Newsletter* 62: 17–21.

Farrington, David P., Patrick A. Langan, and Michael H. Tonry, eds. 2004. *Cross National Studies in Crime and Justice*. Washington, DC: US Department of Justice, Office of Justice Programs, Bureau of Justice Statistics.

Felson, Marcus. 2002. *Crime and Everyday Life*, 3rd ed. Thousand Oaks: Sage Publications.

Felson, Marcus, and Ronald V. Clarke. 1998. *Opportunity Makes the Thief: Practical Theory for Crime Prevention*. Police Research Series, paper 98. London: Home Office.

Hakim, Simon, Mary Ann Gaffney, George Rengert, and Johannan Shachmurove. 1995. "Costs and Benefits of Alarms to the Community: Burglary Patterns and Security Measures in Tredyffrin Township, Pennsylvania," *Security Journal* 6, no. 3: 197–204.

Hesseling, Rene B. P. 1994. "Displacement: A Review of the Empirical Literature." In *Crime Prevention Studies*, edited by Ronald V. Clarke, 197–230. Crime Prevention Studies 3. Monsey: Criminal Justice Press.

Jeffery, C. Ray. 1971. *Crime Prevention through Environmental Design*. Beverly Hills: Sage.

Levi, Michael. 2008. "Combating Identity and Other Forms of Payment Fraud in the UK: An Analytical History." In *Perspectives on Identity Theft*, edited by Megan M. McNally and Graeme R. Newman, 111–32. Crime Prevention Studies 23. Monsey: Criminal Justice Press.

Martinson, Robert. 1974. "What Works? Questions and Answers about Prison Reform," *The Public Interest* 35 (Spring): 22-54.

Masuda, Barry. 1992. "Displacement vs. Diffusion of Benefits and the Reduction of Inventory Losses in a Retail Environment," *Security Journal* 3: 131-36.

Mayhew, Patricia M., Ronald V. Clarke, A. Sturman, and J. M. Hough. 1976. "Crime as Opportunity." Home Office Research Studies no. 34. London: Home Office.

McNally, Megan M., and Graeme R. Newman, eds. 2008. *Perspectives on Identity Theft*. Crime Prevention Studies 23. Monsey: Criminal Justice Press.

Milgram, Stanley. 1974. *Obedience to Authority: An Experimental View*. New York: Harper & Row.

Mischel, Walter. 1968. *Personality and Assessment*. New York: Wiley.

Morgan, Russell, and Ronald V. Clarke. 2006. "Legislation and Unintended Consequences for Crime," *European Journal on Criminal Policy and Research* 12: 189-211.

Newman, Graeme R., and Ronald V. Clarke. 2003. *Superhighway Robbery: Preventing E-commerce Crime*. Cullompton: Willan Publishing.

Newman, Oscar. 1972. *Defensible Space: Crime Prevention through Urban Design*. New York: MacMillan.

Painter, Kate, and David P. Farrington. 1997. "The Crime-Reducing Effect of Improved Street Lighting: The Dudley Project." In *Situational Crime Prevention: Successful Case Studies*, 2nd ed., edited by Ronald V Clarke, 209-26. Albany: Harrow and Heston.

Pease, Ken. 1991. "The Kirkholt Project: Preventing Burglary on a British Public Housing Estate," *Security Journal* 2: 73-77.

Poyner, Barry. 1991. "Situational Prevention in Two Parking Facilities," *Security Journal* 2: 96-101.

Poyner, Barry, and Barry Webb. 1991. *Crime-Free Housing*. Oxford: Butterworth Architect.

Scherdin, Mary Jane. 1986. "The Halo Effect: Psychological Deterrence of Electronic Security Systems," *Information Technology and Libraries* (September): 232-35.

Scottish Central Research Unit. 1995. *Running the Red: An Evaluation of the Strathclyde Police Red Light Camera Initiative*. Edinburgh: The Scottish Office.

Sherman, Lawrence W., Patrick R. Gartin, and Michael E. Buerger. 1989. "Hot Spots of Predatory Crime: Routine Activities and the Criminology of Place," *Criminology* 27: 27-55.

Simon, Herbert A. 1978. "Rationality as Process and Product of Thought," *American Economic Review* 8, no. 21: 1-11.

Sinclair, Ian, and Ronald V. Clarke. 1982. "Predicting, Treating and Explaining Delinquency: The Lessons from Research on Institutions." In *The Prevention and Control of Offending*, edited by Maurice Philip Feldman, 51-78. Developments in the Study of Criminal Behavior 1. New York: Wiley.

Smith, Martha J., Ronald V. Clarke, and Ken Pease. 2002. "Anticipatory Benefits in Crime Prevention." In *Analysis for Crime Prevention*, edited by Nick Tilley, 71-88. Crime Prevention Studies 13. Monsey: Criminal Justice Press.

Stanford Research Institute. 1970. *Reduction of Robbery and Assault of Bus Drivers*, vol. 3, *Technological and Operational Methods*. Stanford, CA: Stanford Research Institute.

Sykes, Gresham M., and David Matza. 1957. "Techniques of Neutralization: A Theory of Delinquency," *American Sociological Review* 22, no. 6: 664-70.

Taylor, Ian R., Paul Walton, and Jock Young. 1973. *The New Criminology*. London: Routledge & Kegan Paul.

Tilley, Nick. 2005. "Crime Prevention and System Design." In *Handbook of Crime Prevention and Community Safety*, edited by Nick Tilley, 266-93. Cullompton: Willan Publishing.

Tilley, Nick, Amanda Robinson, and John Burrows. 2007. "The Investigation of High-Volume Crime." In *Handbook of Criminal Investigation*, edited by Tim Newburn, Tom Williamson, and Alan Wright, 226-54. Cullompton: Willan Publishing.

Van de Bunt, H. G., and Cathelijne van der Schoot. 2003. *Prevention of Organised Crime: A Situational Approach*. WODC Report 215. The Hague: Dutch Ministry of Justice.

Von Hirsch, Andrew, David Garland, and Alison Wakefield, eds. 2000. *Ethical and Social Issues in Situational Crime Prevention*. Studies in Penal Theory and Penal Ethics. Oxford: Hart Publishing.

Webb, Barry. 1994. "Steering Column Locks and Motor Vehicle Theft: Evaluations from Three Countries." In *Crime Prevention Studies*, edited by Ronald V. Clarke, 71-90. Crime Prevention Studies 2. Monsey: Criminal Justice Press.

Wilkinson, Paul. 1986. *Terrorism and the Liberal State*, 2nd ed. New York: New York University Press.

Wortley, Richard. 2001. "A Classification of Techniques for Controlling Situational Precipitators of Crime," *Security Journal* 14: 63-82.

——. 2002. *Situational Prison Control: Crime Prevention in Correctional Institutions*. Cambridge: Cambridge University Press.

Wortley, Richard, and Stephen Smallbone, eds. 2006. *Situational Prevention of Child Sexual Abuse*. Crime Prevention Studies 19. Monsey: Criminal Justice Press.

Zimbardo, Philip G. 1973. "A Field Experiment in Auto Shaping." In *Vandalism*, edited by Colin Ward, 85-90. London: Architectural Press.

Stephen Graham
When Life Itself Is War: The Urbanization of Military and Security Doctrine

Agamben, Giorgio. 2001. "Security and Terror," Theory and Event 5, no. 4: 1-2.

Agre, Philip E. 2001. "Imagining the Next War: Infrastructural Warfare and the Conditions of Democracy," Radical Urban Theory (September 14), http://polaris.gseis.ucla.edu/pagre/war.html.

Amoore, Louise. 2009. "Algorithmic War: Everyday Geographies of the War on Terror," Antipode 41, no. 1 (January): 49-69.

Appadurai, Arjun. 2006. Fear of Small Numbers: An Essay on the Geography of Anger. Durham: Duke University Press.

Arquilla, John, and David F. Ronfeldt. 2001. Networks and Netwars: The Future of Terror, Crime, and Militancy. Santa Monica: Rand.

Banerjee, Subhabrata Bobby. 2006. "Live and Let Die: Colonial Sovereignties and the Death Worlds of Necrocapitalism," Borderlands 5, no. 1, accessed September 7, 2016, http://www.borderlands.net.au/vol5no1_2006/banerjee_live.htm.

Barakat, Sultan. 1998. "City War Zones," Urban Age (Spring): 11-19.

Bichler, Shimshon, and Jonathan Nitzan. 2004. "Dominant Capital and the New Wars," Journal of World-Systems Research 10, no. 2 (August): 254-327.

Bigo, Didier, and Anastassia Tsoukala, eds. 2006. Illiberal Practices of Liberal Regimes: The (In)security Games. Paris: L'Harmattan.

Bishop, Ryan. 2004. "'The Vertical Order Has Come to an End': The Insignia of the Military C3I and Urbanism in Global Networks." In Beyond Description: Singapore Space Historicity, edited by Ryan Bishop, John Phillips, and Wei-Wei Yeo. London: Routledge.

Bislev, Sven. 2004. "Globalization, State Transformation, and Public Security," International Political Science Review 25, no. 3 (July): 281-96.

Blackmore, Tim. 2005. War X: Human Extensions in Battlespace. Toronto: University of Toronto Press.

Boal, Ian, T. J. Clark, Joseph Matthews, and Michael Watts. 2005. Afflicted Powers: Capital and Spectacle in a New Age of War. London: Verso.

Bottomley, Anne, and Nathan Moore. 2007. "From Walls to Membranes: Fortress Polis and the Governance of Urban Public Space in 21st-Century Britain," Law and Critique 18, no. 2 (July): 171-206.

Boyle, Phil. 2005. "Olympian Security Systems: Guarding the Games or Guarding Consumerism?" Journal for the Arts, Sciences, and Technology 3, no. 2: 12-17.

Bratton, Benjamin H. 2009. "On Geoscapes and the Google Caliphate: Reflections on the Mumbai Attacks," Theory, Culture and Society 26, no. 7/8 (December): 329-42.

Brenner, Neil. 2004. New State Spaces: Urban Governance and the Rescaling of Statehood. Oxford: Oxford University Press.

Burston, Jonathan. 2003. "War and the Entertainment Industries: New Research Priorities in an Era of Cyber-Patriotism." In War and the Media: Reporting Conflict 24/7, edited by Daya Kishan Thussu and Des Freedman. London: Routledge.

Canestaro, Nathan. 2003. "Homeland Defense: Another Nail in the Coffin for Posse Comitatus," Washington Journal of Law & Policy 12: 99-144.

Cato. 2008. "The Weaponization of Immigration," Center for Immigration Studies, accessed September 7, 2016, http://www.cis.org/weaponization_of_immigration.html.

Chiarelli, Peter W., and Patrick R. Michaelis. 2005. "Winning the Peace: The Requirement for Full-Spectrum Operation," Military Review (July-August), http://www.au.af.mil/au/awc/awcgate/milreview/chiarelli.pdf.

Connolly, William E. 2005. Pluralism. Durham: Duke University Press.

Coward, Martin. 2009. Urbicide: The Politics of Urban Destruction. London: Routledge.

Cowen, Deborah. 2007. "National Soldiers and the War on Cities," Theory and Event 10, no. 2: (no page numbers).

Cowen, Deborah, and Neil Smith. 2009. "After Geopolitics? From the Geopolitical Social to Geoeconomics," Antipode 41, no. 1: 22-48.

Crandall, Jordan. 1999. "Anything That Moves: Armed Vision," C Theory, accessed September 7, 2016, http://ctheory.net/ctheory_wp/anything-that-moves-armed-vision/.

——, ed. 2004. Under Fire: The Organization and Representation of Violence. Rotterdam: Witte de Witte.

Crandall, Jordan, and John Armitage. 2005. "Envisioning the Homefront: Militarization, Tracking and Security Culture," Journal of Visual Culture 4, no. 1: 17-38.

Davis, Mike. 2002. Dead Cities: And Other Tales. New York: New Press.

De Landa, Manuel. 1992. War in the Age of Intelligent Machines. New York: Zone Books.

Deer, P. 2007. "Introduction: The Ends of War and the Limits of War Culture," Social Text 25, no. 2: 1-15.

DIRC (Defense Intelligence Reference Document). 1997. The Urban Century: Developing World Urban Trends and Possible Factors Affecting Military Operations. Quantico: US Marine Corps Intelligence Agency.

Deleuze, Gilles. 1992. "Postscript on the Societies of Control," October 59 (Winter), http://www.n5m.org/n5m2/media/texts/deleuze.htm.

Der Derian, James. 2001. Virtuous War: Mapping the Military-Industrial-Media-Entertainment Complex. Boulder: Westview.

——. 2002. "The Rise and Fall of the Office of Strategic Influence," INFOinterventions, http://www.watsoninstitute.org/infopeace/911/index.cfm?id=9.

——. 2003. "Who's Embedding Whom?" INFOinterventions, http://www.watsoninstitute.org/infopeace/911/index.cfm?id=13.

Dickson, Keith. 2002. "The War on Terror: Cities as the Strategic High Ground." Unpublished paper.

Dikeç, Mustafa. 2007. Badlands of the Republic: Space, Politics and Urban Policy. Oxford: Blackwell.

Dillon, Michael, and Julian Reid. 2009. The Liberal Way of War: Killing to Make Life Live. London: Routledge.

Economic Times. 2007. "Spending on Internal Security to Reach $178 BN by 2015," http://economictimes.indiatimes.com/articleshow/msid-2655871,prtpage-1.cms.

Fanon, Frantz. 1963. The Wretched of the Earth. New York: Grove.

Feldman, Allen. 2004. "Securocratic Wars of Public Safety," Interventions: International Journal of Postcolonial Studies 6, no. 3: 330-50.

Finoki, Bryan. 2007. "The Military Planks of Capital Accumulation: An Interview with Neil Smith," Subtopia: A Field Guide to Military Urbanism, July 10, 2007, http://subtopia.blogspot.com/2007/07/military-planks-of-capital-accumulation.html.

Foucault, Michel. 2003. "Society Must Be Defended": Lectures at the Collège de France, 1975-1976. London: Allen Lane.

——. 2007. Security, Territory, Population: Lectures at the Collège de France, 1977-1978. Basingstoke: Palgrave Macmillan.

Geyer, Michael. 1989. "The Militarization of Europe, 1914-1945." In The Militarization of the Western World, edited by John Gillis. New Brunswick: Rutgers University Press.

Giroux, Henry A. 2006. "Reading Hurricane Katrina: Race, Class, and the Biopolitics of Disposability," College Literature 33, no. 3: 171-96.

Goonewardena, Kanishka, and Stefan Kipfer. 2006. "Postcolonial Urbicide: New Imperialism, Global Cities and the Damned of the Earth," New Formations, no. 59: 23-33.

Gorman, Siobhan. 2008. "Satellite-Surveillance Program to Begin Despite Privacy Concerns," Wall Street Journal, October 1, http://online.wsj.com/article/SB122282336428992785.html?mod=googlenews_wsj.

Graham, Stephen. 2003. "Lessons in Urbicide," New Left Review (January/February): 63-78.

——. 2005. "Cities and the 'War on Terror,'" International Journal of Urban and Regional Research 30, no. 2: 255-76.

——. 2006. "'Homeland' Insecurities? Katrina and the Politics of 'Security' in Metropolitan America," Space and Culture 9, no. 1: 63-67.

——. 2009. "Cities as Battlespace: The New Military Urbanism," City 13, no. 4: 383-402.

——. 2010. Cities under Siege: The New Military Urbanism. London: Verso.

Graham, Stephen, ed. 2004. Cities, War, and Terrorism: Towards an Urban Geopolitics. Oxford: Blackwell.

Gray, Chris Hables. 1997. Postmodern War: The New Politics of Conflict. London: Routledge.

Gray, John. 2008. "A Shattering Moment in America's Fall from Power," The Observer, October 28, 31.

Hammes, Thomas X. 2006. The Sling and the Stone: On War in the 21st Century. New York: Zenith.

Harvey, David. 2003. The New Imperialism. Oxford: Oxford University Press.

Hayes, Ben. 2006. "Arming Big Brother: The EU's Security Research Programme," Statewatch, http://www.statewatch.org/analyses/bigbrother.pdf.

Hayes, Ben, and Roch Tassé. 2007. "Control Freaks: 'Homeland Security' and 'Interoperability,'" Different Takes, no. 45 (Spring): 1-4.

Hedges, Chris. 2003. War Is a Force That Gives Us Meaning. New York: Anchor.

Homeland Security Research Corporation. 2007. www.photonicsleadership.org.uk/files/MarketResearch_DefenceSecurity.doc.

Houlgate, Kelly P. 2004. "Urban Warfare Transforms the Corps," Naval Institute Proceedings (November), http://www.military.com/NewContent/0,13190,NI_1104_Urban-P1,00.html.
Huntingdon, Samuel P. 1998. The Clash of Civilizations and the Remaking of World Order. New York: Simon & Schuster.
Johnson, Bruce K. 2007. "Dawn of the Cognetic Age: Fighting Ideological War by Putting Thought in Motion with Impact," Air & Space Power Journal (Winter), http://www.au.af.mil/au/afri/aspj/airchronicles/apj/apj07/win07/johnson.html.
Jordan, John W. 2007. "Disciplining the Virtual Home Front: Mainstream News and the Web during the War in Iraq," Communication and Critical/Cultural Studies 4, no. 3: 276–302.
Kaplan, Caren. 2006. "Precision Targets: GPS and the Militarization of US Consumer Identity," American Quarterly 58, no. 3: 693–714.
Keil, Roger. 2007. "Empire and the Global City: Perspectives of Urbanism after 9/11," Studies in Political Economy 79 (Spring): 167–92.
Kipfer, Stefan, and Kanishka Goonewardena. 2007. "Colonization and the New Imperialism: On the Meaning of Urbicide Today," Theory and Event 10, no. 2: (no page numbers).
Klein, Naomi. 2007. The Shock Doctrine: The Rise of Disaster Capitalism. London: Allen Lane.
Klinenberg, Eric, and Thomas Frank. 2005. "Looting Homeland Security," Rolling Stone (December 15).
Lawlor, Maryann. 2007. "Military Changes Tactical Thinking," Signal Magazine (October), http://www.afcea.org/content/?q=military-changes-tactical-thinking.
Lind, Wiliiam S. 2004. "Understanding Fourth Generation War," Military Review (September/October), http://www.au.af.mil/au/awc/awcgate/milreview/lind.pdf.
McIntyre, David H. 2004. "Strategies for a New Long War: Analysis and Evaluation," Statement to the House of Representatives Committee on Government Reform, Subcommittee on National Security, Emerging Threats, and International Relations, http://www.iwar.org.uk/homesec/resources/counterterrorism/McIntyre.pdf.
Markusen, Ann, Peter Hall, Scott Campbell, and Sabina Deitrick. 1991. The Rise of the Gunbelt: The Military Remapping of Industrial America. New York: Oxford University Press.
Mbembe, Achille. 2003. "Necropolitics," Public Culture 15, no. 1: 11–40.
Mesnard y Méndez, Pierre. 2002. "Capitalism Means/Needs War," Socialism and Democracy Online 16, no. 2 (Summer-Fall), http://sdonline.org/32/capitalism-meansneeds-war/.
Nagel, Kiara. n.d. "Predatory Planning," Design Studio for Social Intervention, http://ds4si.org/predatoryplanning.
Nagel, Kiara, and Eva J. Nagel. 2007. "Losing Our Commons: Predatory Planning in New Orleans," Multicultural Review 16, no. 1: 28–33.
Nemeth, Jeremy, and Justin Hollander. 2009. "Security Zones and New York City's Shrinking Public Space," International Journal of Urban and Regional Research 34, no. 1: 20–34.
OECD (Organisation for Economic Cooperation and Development). 2004. The Security Economy. Paris: OECD.
Packer, Jeremy. 2006. "Becoming Bombs: Mobilizing Mobility in the War of Terror," Cultural Studies 20, no. 4/5: 378–99.
Page, Max. 2008. The City's End: Two Centuries of Fantasies, Fears, and Premonitions of New York's Destruction. New Haven: Yale University Press.
Parks, Lisa. 2007. "Insecure Airwaves: US Bombings of Aljazeera," Communication and Critical/Cultural Studies 4, no. 2: 226–31.
Peters, R. 1996. "Our Soldiers, Their Cities," Parameters (Spring) http://www.carlisle.army.mil/usawc/Parameters/96spring/peters.htm
Pile, Steve. 2000. "The Troubled Spaces of Frantz Fanon." In Thinking Space: Critical Geographies, edited by Mike Crang and Nigel Thrift, 260–77. London: Routledge.
Reid, Julian. 2006. The Biopolitics of the War on Terror: Life Struggles, Liberal Modernity, and the Defence of Logistical Societies. Manchester: Manchester University Press.
Robb, David L. 2004. Operation Hollywood: How the Pentagon Shapes and Censors the Movies. New York: Prometheus Books.
Schreier, Fred, and Caparini, Marina. 2005. Privatising Security: Law, Practice and Governance of Private Military and Security Companies. Occasional Paper 6. Geneva: Centre for the Democratic Control of Armed Forces (DCAF), http://dcaf.ch/content/download/34919/525055/file/op06_privatising-security.pdf.
Smith, Neil. 2002. "New Globalism, New Urbanism: Gentrification as Global Urban Strategy," Antipode 34, no. 3: 427–50.
Souza, Marcelo Lopes de. 2009. "Social Movements in the Face of Criminal Power: The Socio-Political Fragmentation of Space and 'Micro-level Warlords' as Challenges for Emancipative Urban Struggles," City 13, no. 1: 27–52.
Stam, Robert, and Ella Shohat. 2007. Flagging Patriotism: Crises of Narcissism and Anti-Americanism. New York: Routledge.
Stocker, Gerfried. 1998. "InfoWar: The Re-ordering of Things." In Ars electronica 98: InfoWar, edited by Gerfried Stocker and Christine Schöpf, 18–23. Vienna: Springer-Verlag.
Thussu, Daya Kishan. 2003. "Live TV and Bloodless Deaths: War, Infotainment and 24/7 News." In War and the Media: Reporting Conflict 24/7, edited by Daya Kishan Thussu and Des Freedman, 117–32. London: Routledge.
UN Habitat. 2007. State of the World Cities 2006/7. Nairobi: United Nations.
Virilio, Paul. 1989. War and Cinema: The Logistics of Perception. London: Verso.
——. 1991. Lost Dimension. San Francisco: Semiotext(e).
Wacquant, Loïc. 2008. "The Militarization of Urban Marginality: Lessons from the Brazilian Metropolis," International Political Sociology 2, no. 1: 56–74.
Weizman, Eyal. 2005. "Lethal Theory," LOG Magazine (April): 74.
——. 2007. Hollow Land: Israel's Architecture of Occupation. London: Verso.

Professor Sir David Omand
Securing the State: National Security and Secret Intelligence

1 HM Government, *CONTEST: The UK's Strategy for Countering International Terrorism* (London: HMSO Cm 8123, July 2011), available on line at http://www.homeoffice.gov.uk/counter-terrorism.
2 Earlier versions of the UK counter-terrorism strategy can be found in: *HM Government, CONTEST: The UK's Strategy for Countering International Terrorism* (London: HMSO Cm 8123, July 2011), available on line at http://www.homeoffice.gov.uk/counter-terrorismHM Government, *The UK's Strategy for Countering International Terrorism* (London: HMSO Cm 7547, March 2009) available online at http://www. official-documents.gov.uk/document/cm75/7547/7547.pdfHM Government, *Countering International Terrorism: The UK's Strategy*, (London: HMSO Cm 6888, July 2006) available online at http://www.official-documents.gov.uk/document/cm68/6888/6888.pdf.
3 *A Strong Britain in an Age of Uncertainty: The UK National Security Strategy* (London: HMSO Cm 7953, October 2010), available online at http://www.number10.gov.uk/news/national-security-strategy/.
4 See David Omand, Jamie Bartlett, and Carl Miller, *#Intelligence* (London: Demos, 2012) and idem, "Introduction to Social Media Intelligence," *Intelligence and National Security* 27, no. 6 (December 2012).
5 See Peter Hennessy, ed., *The New Protective State* (London: Continuum Books, 2007).
6 David Omand, *Securing the State* (Oxford: Oxford University Press, 2010).
7 Alan Rusbridger, the editor of *The Guardian* newspaper, has also suggested in his blog that these principles could also be applied to govern the use of intrusive investigative methods by newspapers and other media in the wake of the current allegations of phone hacking by News Corporation papers. See http://www.guardian.co.uk/commentisfree/2011/jul/07/phone-hacking-alan-rusbridger
8 Convention against Torture and Other Cruel, Inhuman or Degrading Treatment or Punishment, Dec 10, 1984, 1465 U.N.T.S 85. This position is reflected in the offense in the UK Criminal Justice Act 1988, s. 134, which is committed by any public official or person acting in an official capacity in the UK or elsewhere who "intentionally inflicts severe pain or suffering on another in the performance or purported performance of his official duties."

CPNI, compiled by Haakon Rasmussen and Anders Sletten Eide
Designing Peace of Mind: Counterterrorism in Great Britain

1 Ian Colquhoun, *Design Out Crime: Creating Safe and Sustainable Communities* (Amsterdam: Architectural Press, 2004).
2 Steven Ranford, "The Picture Is Not Clear: How Many CCTV Cameras in the UK?" (Worcester: British Security Industry Association, 2013).
3 Alexandra Topping, "Theresa May Claims 40 Terror Plots Have Been Foiled Since 7/7 Attacks," *The Guardian*, November 24, 2014, http://www.theguardian.com/politics/2014/nov/24/theresa-may-london-attacks-40-terror-plots-foiled.
4 Stian Fyen, "Tar trusselen svært alvorlig," *Dagsavisen*, July 25, 2014, http://www.dagsavisen.no/innenriks/tar-trusselen-svÊrt-alvorlig-1.287216.
5 "Befolkningen positive til åpenhet om terrortrusselen," *Politiet*, August 19, 2014, https://www.politi.no/politidirektoratet/aktuelt/nyhetsarkiv/2014_08/nyhet_14118.xml.

David Harvey
The Right to the City

1 Robert Park, *On Social Control and Collective Behavior* (Chicago: University of Chicago Press, 1967), 3.
2 See Friedrich Engels, *The Condition of the Working-Class in England in 1844* (London: Penguin Classics, 2009); and Georg Simmel, "The Metropolis and Mental Life," in *On Individualism and Social Forms*, ed. David Levine (Chicago: University of Chicago Press, 1971).
3 For a fuller account of these ideas see David Harvey, *The Enigma of Capital and the Crises of Capitalism* (London: Profile Books, 2010).
4 See David Harvey, *A Brief History of Neoliberalism (Oxford: Oxford University Press, 2005)*; and Thomas Edsall, *The New Politics of Inequality* (New York: Norton, 1985).
5 Jim Yardley and Vikas Bajaj, "Billionaires' Ascent Helps India, and Vice Versa," *New York Times, July 27*, 2011.
6 Marcello Balbo, "Urban Planning and the Fragmented City of Developing Countries," *Third World Planning Review* 15, no. 1 (1993): 23–25.
7 Friedrich Engels, *The Housing Question* (New York: International Publishers, 1935): 74–77.

Contested Sites

1 This material was first produced by students of the BAS masters course in 2013/14. It has been subsequently developed by the book's research and design team.
2 Christian On, "European Agency for the Management of Operational Cooperation at the External Borders (Frontex)," *AALEP*, July 24, 2015, http://www.aalep.eu/european-agency-management-operational-cooperation-external-borders-frontex.
3 Nick Garbutt, "Defensive Planning: How the Military Shaped Belfast," *Scope*, January 8, 2015, http://scopeni.nicva.org/article/if-peace-walls-had-ears.
4 Clive Norris, Mike McCahill, and David Wood, "The Growth of CCTV: A Global Perspective on the International Diffusion of Video Surveillance in Publicly Accessible Space," *Surveillance & Society* 2, nos. 2/3 (2004): 110–35, http://www.surveillance-and-society.org/cctv.htm.
5 "London Olympics by the Numbers," *CNN*, July 27, 2012, http://edition.cnn.com/2012/07/27/world/olympics-numbers/.
6 Stephen Graham, "Olympic 2012 Security: Welcome to Lockdown London," The *Guardian*, March 12, 2012, http://www.theguardian.com/sport/2012/mar/12/london-olympics-security-lockdown-london.
7 Daniel Bernhard and Aaron K. Martin, "Rethinking Security at the Olympics," in *Security Games*, 20–35, ed. Colin Bennett and Kevin Haggarty (Oxon: Routledge, 2011); manuscript at http://personal.lse.ac.uk/martinak/Olympics/Rethinking_security.pdf.
8 "London Olympic Games and Paralympic Games Act 2006," *Legislation.gov.uk*, n.d., http://www.legislation.gov.uk/ukpga/2006/12/crossheading/advertising.
9 Peter Walker, "Protester Receives Olympics ASBO," The *Guardian*, April 17, 2012, http://www.theguardian.com/society/2012/apr/17/protester-receives-olympic-asbo.
10 "Mass Arrests at Monthly Cycling Event in London on Olympic Ceremony Night," *Russia Today*, July 27, 2012, http://www.rt.com/news/london-police-olympics-arrests-269/.
11 Ryan Kisiel, "I Signed Up for Olympics Security Course in 90 Seconds! Mail Reporter Experiences the Shambolic G4S Training Centre First Hand," *Daily Mail*, July 13, 2012, http://www.dailymail.co.uk/news/article-2173338/London-2012-Olympics-Mail-reporter-experiences-shambolic-G4S-training-centre.html.
12 Nick Hopkins and Owen Gibson, "Olympic Security: Army Reinforcements Called in to Fill G4S Shortfall," The *Guardian*, July 12, 2012, http://www.theguardian.com/sport/2012/jul/11/army-reinforcements-olympics.
13 CATSA Annual Report 2014, http://www.catsa.gc.ca/sites/default/files/imce/AnnualReport2014.pdf.
14 Anthony Bond and Ian Drury, "Armed and Ready: For the First Time since the Second World War, London's Green Space Is Transformed by Anti-Aircraft Guns for Olympic Ring of Steel," *Daily Mail*, July 12, 2012, http://www.dailymail.co.uk/news/article-2172909/Olympic-security-Londons-green-space-transformed-anti-aircraft-guns-Olympic-ring-steel.html.
15 Philip Comerford, "The Olympic Security Fence Is a Modern-Day Form of Enclosure," *Open Democracy UK*, July 27, 2012, https://www.opendemocracy.net/ourkingdom/philip-comerford/olympic-security-fence-is-modern-day-form-of-enclosure.
16 Bond and Drury, "Armed and Ready" (see note 14).

17 "Ring of Steel," *Wikipedia*, n.d., https://en.wikipedia.org/wiki/Ring_of_steel_%28London%29.
18 Henrietta Williams and George Gingell, "Ring of Steel," *MAS Context*, n.d., http://www.mascontext.com/issues/22-surveillance-summer-14/ring-of-steel/.
19 "City of London," *Wikipedia*, n.d., https://en.wikipedia.org/wiki/City_of_London.
20 Stephen Graham, *Cities under Siege: The New Military Urbanism* (London: Verso, 2010), 278.
21 Jon Coaffee, *Terrorism, Risk and the Global City: Towards Urban Resilience* ((Farnham: Ashgate, 2009), 302–3; see also idem., "Rings of Steel, Rings of Concrete and Rings of Confidence: Designing Out Terrorism in Central London Pre and Post September 11th," *International Journal of Urban and Regional Research* 28, no. 1 (2004): 201–11.
22 "About Us," *Canary Wharf Group PLC*, n.d., http://group.canarywharf.com/about-us/.
23 Caroline Herling and Caroline Liljedahl, "Canary Wharf: An Establishment of a Major Business District," master's thesis (Stockholm: KTH Stockholm 2005), https://www.kth.se/polopoly_fs/1.176793!/Menu/general/column-content/attachment/284.pdf.
24 Anna Minton, "We Are Returning to an Undemocratic Model of Land Ownership," The *Guardian*, June 11, 2012, http://www.theguardian.com/commentisfree/2012/jun/11/public-spaces-undemocratic-land-ownership.
25 Brian Baskerville, "The Spanish Enclaves of North Africa," *About.com*, December 4, 2014, http://geography.about.com/od/spainmaps/a/The-Spanish-Enclaves-Of-North-Africa.htm.
26 Sahid Saddiki, "Border Fences as an Anti-Immigration Device," in *Borders, Fences and Walls: State of Insecurity?*, 181, ed. Elisabeth Vallet (London: Routledge, 2016; originally published in 2014 by Ashgate).
27 *FRAN Quarterly Q1* (January–March 2014), http://frontex.europa.eu/assets/Publications/Risk_Analysis/FRAN_Q1_2014.pdf.
28 "Melilla Border Fence: What Were the Consequences?: *Historiana*, n.d., http://historiana.eu/case-study/post-colonial-migration-europe/melilla-border-fence.
29 Markel Redondo Ibarrondo, "The Borders of Human Rights 2013–14," master's thesis (Amsterdam: Universiteit van Amsterdam, 2014), *Academia.edu*, https://www.academia.edu/9634270/The_Borders_of_Human_Rights_Protection_of_Migrants_and_Refugees_at_the_Spanish_Enclaves_in_North_Africa.
30 Elie Goldschmidt, "Storming the Fences: Morocco and Europe's Anti-Migration Policy," *Middle East Report* 36 (Summer 2006), http://www.merip.org/mer/mer239/storming-fences.
31 "Highlights of the USA PATRIOT Act," n.d., *US Department of Justice*, https://www.justice.gov/archive/ll/highlights.htm.
32 "Building: Schaefer Landing North," *StreetEasy*, n.d., http://streeteasy.com/building/schaefer-landing-north.
33 "Greenpoint–Williamsburg Land Use and Waterfront Plan," (New York: Department of City Planning, New York City, 2004).
34 "City Planning Commission Department of City Planning Map and Zoning Regulation of 1961" (New York: Department of City Planning, New York City, 1961).
35 "U.S. Coast Guard Maritime Security (MARSEC) Levels," *United States Coast Guard*, n.d., https://www.uscg.mil/safetylevels/whatismarsec.asp.
36 *Occupy Wall Street*, occupywallst.org
37 *The Occupied Wall Street Journal*, http://occupiedmedia.us/.
38 Ben Fractenberg, "Zuccotti Park Can't Be Closed to Wall Street Protesters, NYPD Says," *dna info*, September 28, 2011, https://www.dnainfo.com/new-york/20110928/downtown/zuccotti-park-cant-be-closed-wall-street-protesters-nypd-says.
39 "By what right do mayors, police chiefs, military officers and state officials tell we, the people, that they have the right to determine what is public about 'our' public space, and who may occupy that space, and when? When did they presume to evict us, the people, from any space we, the people, decide collectively and peacefully to occupy?" David Harvey, "The Party of Wall Street Meets Its Nemesis," *Verso Books*, October 28, 2011, http://www.versobooks.com/blogs/777-david-harvey-the-party-of-wall-street-meets-its-nemesis.
40 Blair Kamin, "How Wall Street Became Secure, and Welcoming," *Chicago Tribune*, September 9, 2006, http://www.chicagotribune.com/chi-090806wallstreet-story-story.html.
41 James Russell, "World Trade Center Bosses Turn Site into Grim Fortress," *Bloomberg*, July 25, 2013, http://www.bloomberg.com/news/articles/2013-07-25/world-trade-center-bosses-turn-site-into-grim-fortress.
42 "The WTC History," and "FAQ about 9/11," *9/11 Memorial*, n.d., https://www.911memorial.org/world-trade-center-history; and https://www.911memorial.org/faq-about-911.
43 Michelle Jahn, "WTC Timeline," *Atlantisonline*, n.d., http://atlantisonline.smfforfree2.com/index.php?topic=30299.0;wap2.
44 Phil Hirschkorn, "New WTC Tower Design Made Public," *CNN International*, June 29, 2005, http://edition.cnn.com/2005/US/06/29/wtc.tower.redesign/index.html?iref=mpstoryview.
45 "APEC Security to Cost $24m a Day," *News.com.au*, June 3, 2007, http://www.news.com.au/national/apec-security-to-cost-24m-a-day/story-e6frfkvr-1111113665331.
46 APEC Public Holiday Act 2007, *Australian Government Federal Register of Legislation*, http://www.comlaw.gov.au/Details/C2007A00139.
47 Andrew Clennell, "Wet v Wild: Riot Squad Shows Off Its $700.000 Weapon," *Sydney Morning Herald*, August 21, 2007, http://www.smh.com.au/news/national/wet-v-wild-riot-squad-shows-off-its-700000-weapon/2007/08/20/1187462176707.html.
48 Manfred B. Steger and Anne McNevin, *Global Ideologies and Urban Landscapes* (Oxon, England: Routledge, 2011).
49 "The Separation Barrier," *B'Tselem*, January 1, 2011, http://www.btselem.org/separation_barrier.
50 Amer Aruri, "Qalandia Checkpoint, March 2014: An Obstacle to Normal Life," *B'Tselem*, 2014, http://www.btselem.org/photoblog/201404_qalandiya_checkpoint.
51 "What's the Truth Behind Checkpoints and Crossings in Judea and Samaria?" *Israel Defence Forces* May 6, 2013, https://www.idfblog.com/blog/2013/05/06/reality-check-the-truth-behind-crossings-in-judea-and-samaria/.
52 Nidal Al-Mughrabi, "Egyptian Flooding Drowns Gaza's Tunnel Business," *Reuters*, November 4, 2015, http://www.reuters.com/article/us-palestinians-egypt-tunnels-idUSKCN0ST1N620151104.
53 "Behind the Headlines: Hamas' Terror Tunnels," *Israel Ministry of Foreign Affairs*, July 22, 2014, http://mfa.gov.il/MFA/ForeignPolicy/Issues/Pages/Hamas-terror-tunnels.aspx.
54 "World Report 2014: Israel and Palestine," *Human Rights Watch*, 2014, https://www.hrw.org/world-report/2014/country-chapters/israel/Palestine.
55 *Report of the Secretary-General's Panel of Inquiry on the 31 May 2010 Flotilla Incident* (New York: United Nations, 2011), 3, http://www.un.org/News/dh/infocus/middle_east/Gaza_Flotilla_Panel_Report.pdf.
56 Ibid., 46.
57 "IDF Forces Met with Pre-Planned Violence when Attempting to Board Flotilla," *Israel Ministry of Foreign Affairs*, May 31, 2010, http://mfa.gov.il/MFA/PressRoom/2010/Pages/Israel_Navy_warns_flotilla_31-May-2010.aspx.
58 Amnesty International, *Gezi Park Protests* (London: Amnesty International, 2013), https://www.amnestyusa.org/sites/default/files/eur440222013en.pdf.
59 Ibid.
60 Christopher de Bellaigue, "Turkey: Surreal, Menacing, Pompous," *New York Review of Books*, December 19, 2013.
61 "Police Seal Off Gezi Park ahead of Alternative Iftar Event," *Hurriyet Daily News*, July 28, 2013, http://www.hurriyetdailynews.com/police-seal-off-gezi-park-ahead-of-alternative-iftar-event.aspx?pageID=238&nID=51592&NewsCatID=341.
62 Barbara McMahon, "Out of Sight, Out of Mind," *The Guardian*, August 14, 2006, http://www.theguardian.com/world/2006/aug/14/italy.worlddispatch.
63 Christian Fraser, "Ring of Steel Divides Padua," BBC News, September 29, 2006, http://news.bbc.co.uk/2/hi/europe/5385752.stm.
64 McMahon, "Out of Sight, Out of Mind" (see note 62).
65 "Cinque anni dopo Via Anelli cade a pezzi tra topi e melma," *Il Mattino Di Padova*, March 4, 2013, http://mattinopadova.gelocal.it/padova/cronaca/2013/03/03/news/via-anelli-tra-topi-e-melma-1.6631110.
66 "Norway: The rich cousin," *The Economist*, February 2, 2013, http://www.economist.com/news/special-report/21570842-oil-makes-norway-different-rest-region-only-up-point-rich.
67 "Tjuvholmen," *Oslo Kommune*, n.d., https://www.oslo.kommune.no/politikk-og-administrasjon/prosjekter/fjordbyen/tjuvholmen.
68 "Tjuvholmen," *Osloby*, July 25, 2014, http://www.osloby.no/nyheter/--Er-ikke-klokken-atte-litt-tidlig-7648592.html.
69 Tommy H. S. Brakstad, "Her nekter rikinger folk å bade," *Nettavisen*, 2014, http://www.nettavisen.no/na24/her-nekter-rikinger-folk-a-bade/8468465.html.
70 "Blitz: 25 år på barrikadene," NRK, April 28, 2007, http://www.nrk.no/skole/klippdetalj?topic=nrk:klipp/274862
71 "Blitz," *Store Norske Leksikon*, December 3, 2012, https://snl.no/Blitz.
72 "Om Blitz," *Blitz*, n.d., http://www.blitz.no/om-blitz.
73 "Embassy Building," *Embassy of the United States, Oslo, Norway*, n.d., http://norway.usembassy.gov/chancery.html.
74 "New Embassy at Huseby," *Embassy of the United States, Oslo, Norway*, n.d., http://norway.usembassy.gov/naehuseby.html.
75 "Moving towards Huseby," *Embassy of the United States, Oslo, Norway*, January 28, 2011, http://norway.usembassy.gov/jan_28_2011.html.
76 "Stortinget blir skuddsikkert," *Teknisk Ukeblad*, August 1, 2012, http://www.tu.no/artikler/stortinget-blir-skuddsikkert/244928.
77 Paal Wergeland and Anne Linn Kumano-Ensby, "Motdemonstrantene ¯dela ikke st¯ttemarkering for Israel," NRK, August 10, 2014, http://www.nrk.no/norge/stottemarkering-for-israel-i-oslo-1.11872097.
78 Mona Strande, "22. Juli kommisjonens rapport: Sju år gamle planer hadde holdt," *Teknisk Ukeblad*, August 13, 2012, http://www.tu.no/bygg/2012/08/13/sju-ar-gamle-planer-hadde-holdt.
79 "Krever å få se terrorrapport," *Dagens Perspektiv*. November 8, 2011, http://www.ledelse.as/nyheter/krever-a-fa-se-terrorrapport.
80 Gunn Evy Auestad, Vilde Helljesen, Martin Herman, Camilla Wernersen, "Alle navn offentliggjort etter terrorangrepene," NRK, July 30, 2011, http://www.nrk.no/norge/alle-navn-pa-drepte-offentliggjort-1.7727791.
81 Metier AS, OPAK AS og LPO arkitekter AS, Konseptvalgutredning for fremtidig regjeringskvartal, Kommunal- og moderniseringsdepartementet, Regjeringen, Oslo, 2013 https://www.regjeringen.no/globalassets/upload/fad/vedlegg/bst/konseptvalgsutredningen_rkv.pdf
82 Sam Jones and Ben Quinn, "Norway Attack Aftermath: Monday 25 July" *The Guardian*, July 25, 2011, http://www.theguardian.com/world/2011/jul/25/norway-attack-live-coverage-anders-breivik.
83 Helen Pidd and James Meikle, "Norway Will Not Be Intimidated by Terror Attacks, Vows Prime Minister," *The Guardian*, July 27, 2011, http://www.theguardian.com/world/2011/jul/27/norway-terror-attacks-prime-minister.

Contested Sites, Drawing and Map Sources

Page 178–179, World Maps

I *Global Terrorism Index 2015* (Sydney: Institute for Economics and Peace, 2015), http://economicsandpeace.org/wp-content/uploads/2015/11/2015-Global-Terrorism-Index-Report.pdf.
II *Global Terrorism Index 2014* (Sydney: Institute for Economics and Peace, 2014), http://economicsandpeace.org/wp-content/uploads/2015/06/Global-Terrorism-Index-Report-2014.pdf.

Page 180–181, World Maps

I Heidelberg Institute for International Conflict Research, *Conflict Index 2015* (Heidelberg: University of Heidelberg, 2015), http://www.hiik.de/en/konfliktbarometer/pdf/ConflictBarometer_2015.pdf.
II Joe Myers, "5 Maps on the State of Global Inequality," *World Economic Forum*, November 25, 2015, https://www.weforum.org/agenda/2015/11/5-maps-on-the-state-of-global-inequality/.
III Economist Intelligence Unit, "Democracy Index," *Actualitix*, updated January 16, 2016, http://en.actualitix.com/country/wld/democracy-index.php.
IV "The Arab Spring Country by Country," *The National*, June 17, 2011, http://www.thenational.ae/world/middle-east/the-arab-spring-country-by-country.
V Economist Intelligence Unit, "civil Liberties," *Actualitix*, updated January 16, 2016, http://en.actualitix.com/country/wld/civil-liberties.php.

Page 182–183 Statistical Comparison of Selected Nations and Cities

I "Income Share Held by Highest/Lowest 10%," *The World Bank*, accessed December 2, 2014, http://data.worldbank.org/indicator/SI.DST.FRST.10?view=map; and http://data.worldbank.org/indicator/SI.DST.10TH.10?view=map.
II "Military Expenditure (% of GDP)," *The World Bank*, accessed December 2, 2014, http://data.worldbank.org/indicator/MS.MIL.XPND.GD.ZS.
III "List of Countries by Number of Military and Paramilitary Personnel," *Wikipedia*, accessed December 2, 2014, https://en.wikipedia.org/wiki/List_of_countries_by_number_of_military_and_paramilitary_personnel.
IV "List of Countries and Dependencies by Number of Police Officers," *Wikipedia*, accessed December 2, 2014, https://en.wikipedia.org/wiki/List_of_countries_and_dependencies_number_of_police_officers.

V   Institute of Economics and Peace, "Global Terrorism Index," *Vision of Humanity*, accessed December 2, 2014, http://www.visionofhumanity.org/#/page/indexes/terrorism-index.

VI "The Democracy Ranking of the Quality of Democracy 2013," *Global Democracy Ranking*, accessed December 2, 2014, http://democracyranking.org/wordpress/rank/democracy-ranking-2013/.

VII "The Freedom of the Press," *Freedom House*, accessed December 2, 2014, www.freedomhouse.org.

Page 184–185 Europe

I   United Nations, "Trends in International Migrant Stock: The 2013 Revision," accessed September 10, 2013, esa.un.org/unmigration/TIMSA2013/Data/subsheets/UN_MigrantStock_2013T6.xls.

Page 188–189 Summer Olympics

I   Adam Taylor, "Why Sochi Is by Far the Most Expensive Olympics Ever," *Business Insider*, January 17, 2014, http://www.businessinsider.com/why-sochi-is-by-far-the-most-expensive-olympics-ever-2014-1.

II Matthew Knight, "Sochi 2014: Winter Olympics Lessons from Lillehammer," CNN, November 5, 2013, http://www.cnn.com/2013/11/05/sport/sochi-2014-lillehammer-winter-olympics/.

III Peter Berlin and International Herald Tribune *"What did Olympics bring Sydney?" The New York Times*, December, 24, 2003, http://www.nytimes.com/2003/12/24/news/what-did-olympics-bring-sydney.html#whats-next

IV Selena Roberts, "Olympics Notebook; I.O.C.'s Rogge Steps into the Cold," *The New York Times*, February 4, 2002, http://www.nytimes.com/2002/02/04/sports/olympics-notebook-ioc-s-rogge-steps-into-the-cold.html?_r=0.

V   Christopher A. Shaw, *Five Ring Circus: Myths and Realities of the Olympic Games* (Gabriola Island: New Society Publishers, 2008), 185.

VI "Securing the Olympic Games," Mindfully.org, August 22, 2004, http://www.mindfully.org/Reform/2004/Olympic-Games-Security22aug04.htm.

VII Helge Mjelde, Organising Committee for the Olympic Winter Games in Lillehammer in 1994, Official Report of the XVII Olympic Winter Games in Lillehammer in 1994 (Lillehammer: LOOC AS, 1995), accessed December 9, 2014, http://library.la84.org/6oic/OfficialReports/1994/E_BOOK1.PDF.

VIII Shaw, *Five Ring Circus*, 185 (see note V).

IX Matthew Black, "Winner's Curse? The Economics of Hosting the Olympic Games," CBC News, July 30, 2012, http://www.cbc.ca/news/canada/winner-s-curse-the-economics-of-hosting-the-olympic-games-1.1186962.

X   Mikhail Bushuev, "Security at All Costs in Sochi," *Deutsche Welle*, January 7, 2014, http://dw.com/p/1Aluf.

Page 193–195 Ring of Steel

I   George Gingell, Henrietta Williams, "Ring of Steel", *MAS Context Issue 22, Surveillance*, Summer 2014, http://mascontext.com/pdf/MAS_Context_Issue22_SURVEILLANCE.pdf

II Henritta Williams, "Ring of Steel: Entering the Panopticon", www.henriettawilliams.com August 22, 2012, http://henriwilliams.blogspot.no/2010/08/entering-panopticon-study-of-ring-of.html

III Jon Coaffee, "Terrorism, Risk and the Global City, Towards Urban Resilience" (Farnham: Ashgate, 2009) 93-133

Page 196–197 Canary Wharf

I   Trust for London and New Policy Institute, "Income Inequalities by Wards within London Boroughs," *London's Poverty Profile*, last updated October 14, 2013, http://www.londonspovertyprofile.org.uk/indicators/topics/inequality/income-inequalities-within-london-boroughs/.

II Land Registry, "Average House Prices, Ward, LSOA, MSOA, *London Datastore*, February 12, 2014, http://data.london.gov.uk/dataset/average-house-prices-ward-lsoa-msoa.

III "Borough Profiles 2014," *London Datastore*, accessed September 12, 2014, http://londondatastore-upload.s3.amazonaws.com/instant-atlas/borough-profiles/atlas.html.

Page 202–203 Melilla Enclave

I   "Fortress Spain Causing Misery for Migrants," *The Local*, July 9, 2014, http://www.thelocal.es/20140709/fortress-spain-slammed-for-immmigration-policies.

II "Western Mediterranean Route," *Frontex*, accessed January 5, 2015, http://frontex.europa.eu/trends-and-routes/western-mediterranean-route/.

III "Human Development Reports," *United Nations Development Programme*, accessed January 6, 2015, http://hdr.undp.org/en/content/table-1-human-development-index-and-its-components.

IV "Migratory Routes Map," *Frontex*, accessed January 6, 2015, http://frontex.europa.eu/trends-and-routes/migratory-routes-map/.

Page 208–209 Schaefer Landing

I   Bill Rankin, "Value of Land (2006)" *Radical Cartography*, accessed February 14, 2015, http://www.radicalcartography.net/manhattan-value.gif.

II Department of City Planning, City of New York, "Privately Owned Public Spaces," nyc.gov, accessed February 14, 2015, http://www1.nyc.gov/assets/planning/download/pdf/plans/pops-inventory/pops-inventory.pdf.

Page 210–213 Occupy Wall Street

I   "Timeline of Occupy Wall Street," *Wikipedia*, accessed February 3, 2015, http://en.wikipedia.org/wiki/Timeline_of_Occupy_Wall_Street.

II "List of Occupy Movement Protest Locations," *Wikipedia*, accessed February 2, 2015, http://en.wikipedia.org/wiki/List_of_Occupy_movement_protest_locations.

Page 216–217 Wall Street

I   24/7 Wall Street, "Where Wall Street Went after 9/11," NBC News, updated September 8, 2011, http://www.nbcnews.com/id/44428288/ns/business-us_business/t/where-wallstreet-went-after/#.VSTlELqSPRW.

II Saskia Sassen, "Global Financial Centers after 9/11," Working Paper # 474, Wharton, University of Pennsylvania, http://realestate.wharton.upenn.edu/research/papers.php?paper=474.

III Nicole Pohl, "Where Is Wall Street? Financial Geography after 09/11," *The Industrial Geographer* 2, no. 1 (2004): 72-93, http://igeographer.lib.indstate.edu/pohl.pdf.

IV "New York Stock Exchange," *Encyclopædia Britannica*, accessed October 21, 2014, http://global.britannica.com/EBchecked/topic/412514/New-York-Stock-Exchange-NYSE.

V   Andrew Beattie, "The Birth of Stock Exchanges," *Investopedia*, updated September 8, 2014, http://www.investopedia.com/articles/07/stock-exchange-history.asp.

IV Tynan DeBold, Bradley Hope, Daniel Huang, and Mike Sudal, "The NYSE's 222-Year Evolution," *Wall Street Journal*, September 1, 2014, http://graphics.wsj.com/the-nyse-evolution/.

Page 220–221 World Trade Center

I   Eric J. Tilford, September 17, 2001, US NAVY, accessed October 8, 2014, https://commons.wikimedia.org/wiki/File:September_17_2001.jpg.

Page 224–225 Apec Summit

I   Jim Dickins, "APEC Security to Cost $24m a Day," News.com.au, June 3, 2007, http://www.news.com.au/national/apec-security-to-cost-24m-a-day/story-e6frfkvr-1111113665331.

II "George Bush Arrives in Sydney for APEC," *The Daily Telegraph* (Sydney), September 4, 2007, http://www.dailytelegraph.com.au/news/nsw/bush-arrives-in-sydney-for-apec/story-e6freuzi-1111114345038.

III Tim Prenzler, *Policing and Security in Practice: Challenges and Achievements* London: Palgrave Macmillan, 2012.

IV John Kirton, Jenilee Guebert, and Shamir Tanna, "G8 and G20 Summit Costs," G8 and G20 Research Groups, Munk School for Global Affairs, University of Toronto, July 5, 2010, www.g8.utoronto.ca/evaluations/factsheet/factsheet_costs.pdf.

V   Amory Starr, Luis Fernandes, and Christian Scholl, *Shutting Down the Streets: Political Violence and Social Control in the Global Era* (New York: New York University Press).

VI Alex Bainbridge, "Scotland: G8 Protesters," *Global Policy Forum*, July 13, 2005, https://www.globalpolicy.org/component/content/article/174/30932.html.

VII "The G8 Gleneagles Summit: The Gleneagles Hotel," *Corporate Watch*, accessed October 30, 2014, https://corporatewatch.org/content/corporate-watch-g8-report-g8-gleneagles-summit-gleneagles-hotel.

VIII "APEC CEO Summit," *APEC*, accessed October 16, 2014, http://www.apec.org/About-Us/About-APEC/Business-Resources/APEC-CEO-Summit.aspx.

IX "Previous G8 Leaders' Summits," *Understanding the G8*, accessed October 16, 2014, http://www.g8.co.uk/previous-g8-leaders-summits/..

Page 229 Qualandia Checkpoint

I   "Separation Barrier," *B'Tselem*, accessed October 16, 2014, http://www.btselem.org/separation_barrier/statistics

II "Berlinmuren (hhd10-6)," *Norsk Utenrikspolitisk Institutt*, accessed October 16, 2014, http://www.nupi.no/Publikasjoner/Innsikt-og-kommentar/Hvor-hender-det/HHD-fakta/Berlinmuren-hhd10-6

III "Restriction of movement," *B'Tselem*, accessed October 16, 2014, http://www.btselem.org/freedom_of_movement/checkpoints_and_forbidden_roads

Page 232–235 Egypt–Gaza Border

I   Jennifer Jenkins, Hiroko Masuike, Nathan Ashby-Kuhlman, and Rogene Fisher, "Timeline: Israel, the Gaza Strip and Hamas," *New York Times*, January 4, 2009, http://www.nytimes.com/interactive/2009/01/04/world/20090104_ISRAEL-HAMAS_TIMELINE.html?_r=0.

II Alessandria Masi, "Timeline of Events in Gaza and Israel Shows Sudden, Rapid Escalation," *International Business Times*, July 23, 2014, http://www.ibtimes.com/timeline-events-gaza-israel-shows-sudden-rapid-escalation-1636264.

III United Nations Office for the Coordination of Humanitarian Affairs (OCHA), "Occupied Palestinian Territory: Gaza Emergency Situation Report," September 4, 2014, http://www.ochaopt.org/documents/ocha_opt_sitrep_04_09_2014.pdf.

IV Lizzie Dearden, "Israel-Gaza Conflict: 50-Day War by Numbers," *Independent*, August 27, 2014, http://www.independent.co.uk/news/world/middle-east/israel-gaza-conflict-50-day-war-by-numbers-9693310.html.

V   Amnesty International, *Unlawful and Deadly: Rocket and Mortar Attacks by Palestinian Armed Groups during the 2014 Gaza/Israel Conflict* (London: Amnesty International, 2015), https://www.amnesty.com/download/Documents/MDE2111782015ENGLISH.PDF.

VI Ben Hartman, "50 Days of Israel's Gaza Operation, Protective Edge - By the Numbers," *The Jerusalem Post*, August 28, 2014, http://www.jpost.com/Operation-Protective-Edge/50-days-of-Israels-Gaza-operation-Protective-Edge-by-the-numbers-372574.

VII "Egypt 'Destroys 1370 Gaza Smuggling Tunnels' Says Army," Ma'an News Agency, updated March 13, 2014, http://www.maannews.com/Content.aspx?id=680987.

VIII ISRAEL DEFENCE FORCE. (2014) Operation Protective Edge by the numbers[Online] Available from: http://www.idfblog.com/blog/2014/08/05/operation-protective-edge-numbers/ [Accessed: 4th Nov 2014].

IX Avi Issacharoff, "Gazans Hope Egypt Will Ease Clampdown on Smuggling Tunnels," *Haaretz*, August 14, 2012, http://www.haaretz.com/middle-east-news/gazans-hope-egypt-will-ease-clampdown-on-smuggling-tunnels-1.458034.

Page 236–237 Gaza Flotilla

I   Israel Defense Forces, "Timeline of the *Mavi Marmara* Incident," YouTube, uploaded May 22, 2011, https://www.youtube.com/watch?v=z31GesVrBjc.

II *Report of the Secretary-General's Panel of Inquiry on the 31 May 2010 Flotilla Incident*, 32, accessed February 22, 2016, http://www.un.org/News/dh/infocus/middle_east/Gaza_Flotilla_Panel_Report.pdf.

Page 238–239 Gezi Park

I   "GDP (current US$)" *The World Bank*, accessed December 2, 2014, http://data.worldbank.org/indicator/NY.GDP.MKTP.CD?locations=TR

II "Unemployment, total (% of total labor force) (modeled ILO estimate)", *The World Bank*, accessed December 2, 2014, http://data.worldbank.org/indicator/SL.UEM.TOTL.ZS?locations=TR

III "Gezi Park Protests: Brutal Denial of the Right to Peaceful Assembly in Turkey." *Amnesty International*, 2013, pp.54-58 https://www.amnestyusa.org/sites/default/files/eur440222013en.pdf

IV "Timeline of Gezi Park protests," *Hürriyet Daily News*, June 2013, accessed December 2, 2014, http://www.hurriyetdailynews.com/timeline-of-gezi-park-protests-.aspx?pageID=238&nID=48321&NewsCatID=341

V "Turkish PM shelves mall plan on Gezi Park, wants end to protests," *Hürriyet Daily News*, June 07, 2013, accessed December 2, 2014, http://www.hurriyetdailynews.com/turkish-pm-shelves-mall-plan-on-gezi-park-wants-end-to-protests.aspx?pageID=238&nID=48418&NewsCatID=338

Page 244-245 Via Anelli

I "Chapter 7: Listening to the Population to Keep Up with Change," in *Statistical Report 2011* (Veneto, 2011), http://statistica.regione.veneto.it/ENG/Pubblicazioni/Rapporto-Statistico2011/I_numeri_del_Veneto.html.

II "The City of Padua: A Global-Local Approach to Discrimination," accessed December 11, 2014, http://di-ci.cittalia.com/dici_images/Annex%2017_CASE%20STUDY%20Padua_EN_Final.pdf.

III Andrea Del Mercato, "Managing Migration and Integration at Local Level: The Experience of the City of Venice and the Veneto Region," accessed December 12, 2014, http://ec.europa.eu/regional_policy/opendays/od2007/doc/presentations/d/PPT_Andrea%20DEL%20MERCATO_10D15_SHORT.ppt.

IV "Avance del Padrón municipal a 1 de enero de 2009. Datos provisionales," Instituto Nacional de Estadistica, June 3, 2009, http://www.ine.es/prensa/np551.pdf.

Page 248 Tjuvholmen

I Bente Bjørndal, "Markedets dyreste leilighet: Vil ha 184.000 kroner per kvadratmeter," *Dagens Nærlingsliv*, updated February 11, 2014, http://www.dn.no/privat/eien dom/2013/09/27/markedets-dyreste-leilighet-vil-ha-184000-kroner-per-kvadratmeter.

II "Boligprisstatistikk for Oslo Oktober 2013," *Krogsveen*, accessed January 13, 2015, http://krogsveen.no/Boligprisstatistikk/Historikk/2013/Oktober/Boligprisstatistikk-for-Oslo-oktober-2013.

Page 253 Government Quarter

I Metier, Opak, and LPO, *Dagens tilstand: Bygninger og Departementer*, accessed November 24, 2013, https://www.regjeringen.no/globalassets/upload/kmd/bst/rkv/dagens_tilstand_bygninger_og_departementeroffent ligversjon.pdf.

Page 255 Temporary Security Measures

I Hans Jørn Næss, Sigurd E. Roll, and Roar Valderhaug. "Terrorens pris: Hele 22. juli-regnskapen. *Kapital* 42, no. 17 (2012): 50-59.

Interview: Ivor Terret

Brym, Robert J., and Bader Araj. 2006. "Suicide Bombing as Strategy and Interaction: The Case of the Second Intifada," *Social Forces* 84, no. 4: 1969-86, doi: 10.1353/sof.2006.0081.

Central Bureau of Statistics. 2012. "Chapter A: Main Findings Civilian Labour Force Characteristics 2011," accessed December 29, 2014, http://www1.cbs.gov.il/publications 13/1504/pdf/intro01_e.pdf.

Danby Grahame, and Fiona Poole. 2001. "The Private Security Industry Bill (HL), Bill 67 of 2000/01." House of Commons Library Research Paper 01/34.

Davis, Robert C., Christopher Ortiz, Robert Rowe, et al. 2006. *An Assessment of the Preparedness of Large Retail Malls to Prevent and Respond to Terrorist Attack*, research report submitted to the US Department of Justice, January 1, 2006, accessed January 1, 2015, https://www.ncjrs.gov/pdffiles1/nij/grants/216641.pdf.

Department of Criminology. 2010. "Law, Procedures and Security Management." Leicester, UK: University of Leicester.

Falk, Ophir, and Henry Morgenstern. 2009. *Suicide Terror: Understanding and Confronting the Threat*. Hoboken: John Wiley & Sons.

Frey, Bruno S., Simon Luechinger, and Alois Stutzer. 2007. "Calculating Tragedy: Assessing the Costs of Terrorism," *Journal of Economic Surveys* 21, no. 1: 1-24, doi: 10.1111/j.1467-6419.2007.00505.x.

Gold, John R., and George Revill. 2014. *Landscapes of Defence*. Hoboken: Routledge.

Grieve, John, Clive Harfield, and Allyson MacVean. 2007. *Policing*. London: SAGE Publications Ltd.

Israel Police. 2014. *The Center for Police Studies*, http://www.police.gov.il/contentPage.aspx?pid=323&mid=11, accessed December 30, 2014.

Knesset. 2005. Authority Law for Providing Guarding to the Public, accessed December 28, 2014, http://www.knesset.gov.il/privatelaw/data/16/3/3118_3_1.rtf.

Ministry of Economy. 2004. Protocol 323 from the Internal and Environmental Committee, accessed December 30, 2014, http://www.moital.gov.il/NR/exeres/E89D2F17-D2AE-44AD-8FC0-FF0EBE05B60A.htm.

Weisburd, David, Thomas E. Feucht, Idit Hakimi, et al., eds. 2009. *To Protect and Serve: Policing in an Age of Terrorism*. New York: Springer-Verlag.

Discursive Design Proposals

1 See, for example, Eric Posner, "There's Still a Need for the PATRIOT Act," *New York Times*, updated June 7, 2013, http://www.nytimes.com/roomfordebate/2011/09/07/do-we-still-need-the-patriot-act/theres-still-a-need-for-the-patriot-act.

Glossary

1 "About ASIS," *ASIS International*, accessed March 2, 2016, https://www.asisonline.org.
2 "Asset," *Oxford Dictionaries*, accessed March 2, 2016, http://www.oxforddictionaries.com/definition/english/asset.
3 Ibid.
4 "The National Infrastructure," *The Centre for the Protection of National Infrastructure*, accessed March 2, 2016, http://www.cpni.gov.uk/about/cni/.
5 "Barricade," *Oxford Dictionaries*, accessed March 2, 2016, http://www.oxforddictionaries.com/definition/english/barricade.
6 "Border Security Overview," *Department of Homeland Security*, accessed March 5, 2016, https://www.dhs.gov/border-security-overview.
7 Marcus Felson and Lawrence E. Cohen. "Social Change and Crime Rate Trends: A Routine Activity Approach," *American Sociological Review* 44, no. 4 (August 1979): 588-608.
8 Michael McCahill and Clive Norris, "CCTV in London," Working Paper No. 6. RTD-Project 2002, http://www.urbaneye.net/results/ue_wp6.pdf.
9 Anne Romme, "Aspirations for an Architecture Commons" (PhD dissertation, Det Kongelige Danske Kunstakademis Skoler for Arkitektur, Design og Konservering, 2014), 17.
10 Henri Lefebvre, *Le Droit à la ville* (Paris: Anthropos, 1968); David Harvey, "The Right to the City" *New Left Review* 53 (September-October 2008): 23-40.
11 "Decoy," *Oxford Dictionaries*, accessed March 2, 2016, http://www.oxforddictionaries.com/definition/english/decoy.
12 Pavel Šustr, *Jelenoviti na Šumavě* (Deer of Šumava) (Vimperk: Správa Národního parku a Chráněné krajinné oblasti Šumava, 2013). See also "Zoology," Šumavě National Park, accessed March 6, 2016, http://www.npsumava.cz/cz/3501/4659/clanek/; and Associated Press in Prague, "Czech Deer Still Wary of Iron Curtain Boundary," *The Guardian*, April 23, 2014, accessed March 6, 2016, https://www.theguardian.com/science/2014/apr/23/czech-deer-iron-curtain-fences.
13 "Democracy," *Oxford Dictionaries*, accessed March 2, 2016, http://www.oxforddictionaries.com/definition/english/democracy.
14 "FAQ," *Secured by Design*, accessed March 2, 2016, http://www.securedbydesign.com/faq/.
15 Håvard Walla, NSM, meeting with authors, May 22, 2013.
16 "Fence," *Oxford Dictionaries*, accessed March 2, 2016, http://www.oxforddictionaries.com/definition/english/fence.
17 In Joseph Grima et al., eds., *The State of the Art of Architecture* (Zurich: Lars Müller, 2016).
18 Jon Henley, "Walls: An Illusion of Security from Berlin to the West Bank," *The Guardian*, November 19, 2013, http://www.theguardian.com/uk-news/2013/nov/19/walls-barrier-belfast-west-bank.
19 Michel Foucault, *"Society Must Be Defended": Lectures at the Collège de France, 1975-1976* (New York: Picador, 2003), 103.
20 Stephen Graham, "Foucault's Boomerang: The New Military Urbanism," *openDemocracy*, February 14, 2013, https://www.opendemocracy.net/opensecurity/stephen-graham/foucault's-boomerang-new-military-urbanism.
21 *Protecting Crowded Places: Design and Technical Issues* (London: Home Office, 2014), 5, https://www.gov.uk/government/uploads/system/uploads/attachment_data/file/302016/DesignTechnicalIssues2014.pdf.
22 Ibid., 6.
23 "Hostile Vehicle Mitigation (HVM)," *Centre for the Protection of National Infrastructure*, accessed March 2, 2016, http://www.cpni.gov.uk/advice/Physical-security/Vehicle-borne/.
24 "Lock," *Oxford Dictionaries*, accessed March 2, 2016, http://www.oxforddictionaries.com/definition/english/lock.
25 Nezar AlSayyad and Ananya Roy, "Medieval Modernity: On Citizenship and Urbanism in a Global Era," *Space and Polity* 10, no. 1 (April 2006): 1-20.
26 "Moat," *Oxford Dictionaries*, accessed March 2, 2016, http://www.oxforddictionaries.com/definition/english/moat.
27 "Crime Prevention," Secure Options Consulting, accessed March 2, 2016, http://www.secureoptionsconsulting.com/Crime_Prevention.html; "Crime Prevention Through Environmental Design," *Connect Our Future*, accessed March 2, 2016, http://www.connectourfuture.org/tools/crime-prevention-through-environmental-design-cpted/.
28 Jane Jacobs, *The Death and Life of Great American Cities* (New York: Random House, 1961), 35.
29 "About," *Occupy Wall Street*, accessed March 2, 2016, http://occupywallst.org/about/.
30 Kees Christiaanse and Nancy Levinson, "Curating the Open City: An Interview with Kees Christiaanse," *Places Journal* (September 2009), https://placesjournal.org/article/curating-the-open-city/.
31 Ibid.
32 See Michel Foucault, *Discipline and Punish*, 2nd ed. (New York: Vintage, 1995), 195-228.
33 "Paranoia," *Oxford Dictionaries*, accessed March 5, 2016, http://www.oxforddictionaries.com/definition/english/paranoia.
34 "Pedestrianize," *Oxford Dictionaries*, accessed March 2, 2016, http://www.oxforddictionaries.com/definition/english/pedestrianize?q=pedestrianization#pedestrianize__13.
35 See "PMSCs: Risk and Misconduct," *Global Policy Forum*, accessed March 2, 2016, https://www.globalpolicy.org/pmscs/50208-contractor-misconduct-and-abuse.html.
36 "About Pool Re," accessed March 2, 2016, http://www.poolre.co.uk.
37 "History of the Pool Re Scheme," accessed March 2, 2016, http://www.poolre.co.uk.
38 Occupy Legal, review of *The Protest Handbook*, September 2012, accessed March 2, 2016, http://www.theprotesthandbook.com/reviews/.
39 Stéphane Tonnelat, "The Sociology of Urban Public Spaces," in *Territorial Evolution and Planning Solution: Experiences from China and France*, edited by Hongyang Wang, Michel Savy, and Guofang Zhai (Paris: Atlantis Press, 2010), 84.
40 Stephen Graham, "Public Space and Security," uploaded February 24, 2014, http://www.slideshare.net/sdng1/public-space-and-security.
41 Stephen Graham, "Secure Cities," uploaded February 24, 2014, http://www.slideshare.net/sdng1/secure-city.
42 "Studying Surveillance in Our Cities," accessed March 2, 2016, http://www.ncl.ac.uk/research/impact/areasofresearchimpact/studying-surveillance/#discovermore.
43 Harvey, "The Right to the City," 23 (see note 10).
44 Anna Plyushteva, "The Right to the City and the Struggles over Public Citizenship: Exploring the Links," *The Urban Reinventors*, no. 3 (November 2009), http://urbanreinven tors.net/paper.php?issue=3&author=plyushteva.
45 "About the Society for Risk Analysis," accessed March 2, 2016, http://www.sra.org/about-society-risk-analysis/.
46 "Sabotage," *Oxford Dictionaries*, accessed March 2, 2016, http://www.oxforddictionaries.com/definition/english/sabotage.
47 Home page, *Secured by Design*, accessed March 2, 2016, http://www.securedbydesign.com.
48 "Security," *Oxford Dictionaries*, accessed March 2, 2016, http://www.oxforddictionaries.com/definition/english/security.
49 See Stephen Graham, *Cities under Siege* (London: Verso, 2011), and Graham, "Secure Cities" (see note 41).
50 Ibid.
51 Ole Wæver, "Securitization and Desecuritization," in *On Security*, edited by Ronnie Lipschutz (New York: Columbia University Press, 1995), 46-86.
52 Rens van Munster, "Securitization," *Oxford Bibliographies*, last modified June 26, 2012, accessed March 2, 2016, http://www.oxfordbibliographies.com/view/document/obo-9780199743292/obo-9780199743292-0091.xml#obo-9780199743292-0091-bibItem-0007.
53 Mark Karlin, "Interview: James Risen: The Post-9/11 Homeland Security Industrial Complex Profiteers and Endless War," *Truthout*, November 16, 2014, accessed March 2, 2016, http://www.truth-out.org/progressivepicks/item/27425-james-risen-the-post-9-11-homeland-security-industrial-complex-profiteers-and-endless-war.